# FROM ROMAN

# TO MEROVINGIAN GAUL

READINGS IN MEDIEVAL CIVILIZA
series editor: Paul Edward Dutton

D0905592

# FROM ROMAN

# TO MEROVINGIAN GAUL

## A READER

edited and translated by

ALEXANDER CALLANDER MURRAY

broadview press

**Canadian Cataloguing in Publication Data**

Main entry under title:

From Roman to Merovingian Gaul : a reader

(Readings in medieval civilizations and cultures ; 5)
ISBN 1-55111-102-0

1. Gaul – History – 58 B.C.–511 A.D. – Sources.   2. France – History – To 987 – Sources.
3. Romans – France – History – Sources.   4. Merovingians – France – History – Sources.
I. Murray, Alexander C., 1946-   .   II. Series.

DC60.F76 1999          944'.01          C99-930709-6

Broadview Press Ltd., is an independent, international publishing house, incorporated in 1985.

North America:
P.O. Box 1243, Peterborough, Ontario, Canada K9J 7H5
3576 California Road, Orchard Park, NY 14127
TEL: (705) 743-8990; FAX: (705) 743-8353;
E-MAIL: customerservice@broadviewpress.com

United Kingdom: Turpin Distribution Services Ltd.,
Blackhorse Rd., Letchworth, Hertfordshire SG6 1HN
TEL: (1462) 672555; FAX (1462) 480947; E-MAIL: turpin@rsc.org

Australia: St. Clair Press, P.O. Box 287, Rozelle, NSW 2039
TEL: (02) 818-1942; FAX: (02) 418-1923

www.broadviewpress.com

Cover illustration: An ivory in the Rheinisches Landesmuseum Trier.

Book design and composition by George Kirkpatrick.
PRINTED IN CANADA

DIS MANIBUS PARENTUM

# CONTENTS

## CHAPTER EIGHT: THE WORLD OF SIDONIUS APOLLINARIS: FROM ROMAN TO VISIGOTHIC GAUL • 193

## CHAPTER NINE: CLOVIS, KING OF THE FRANKS, A. 481/2-511 • 259

# LIST OF ILLUSTRATIONS AND MAPS

# ABBREVIATIONS

| | |
|---|---|
| a. | *anno*, the year(s) |
| ca. | *circa*, around (the year) |
| CCSL | Corpus Christianorum, Series Latina |
| MGH | Monumenta Germaniae Historica |
| AA | Auctores Antiquissimi |
| LL | Leges |
| SRM | Scriptores Rerum Merovingicarum |
| s.a. | *sub anno*, under the year |

# PREFACE

Those likely to consult the preface to this Reader are probably in little need of guidance on the strengths and weaknesses of the genre, but a few remarks might be helpful about the selection of the material it contains. This book, like others of its kind I suspect, began with a general idea but grew in unexpected ways — the undertaking would hardly have been so interesting had it been otherwise. The final form of the book is a subject of both regret and satisfaction. The regret springs largely from the need to call a halt to its growth and to admit that the constraints of time and space have determined that now is the time to put the volume before whatever interested readership it might attract. I began with the hope that it might be possible to fashion a useful handbook of Gallic history from the late fourth to the early eighth century. Narrative sources of various kinds are consequently a prominent feature of the compilation. I have tried to supply enough material for readers to piece the general history of the period together on their own, or, if relying on modern surveys, to use the Reader as a resource for sources that are often referred to but rarely quoted at length. I never believed completeness was possible of course and I will leave it to the experience of individual readers to decide if I have reasonably achieved the utility I was aiming for.

Not everyone will agree with the compromises that selection imposes on the compiler. I am aware that there could be more attention paid to Byzantine sources. Institutional history, rarely a pleasure to read, should at least be adequately served; but if there seems to be too much of *Lex Salica*, I hope that any misconceptions that emphasis on this particular codification might create are offset by a better understanding of its law, which has received inadequate treatment in modern scholarship, and of Frankish procedure, which had an important role to play in the law of the kingdom as a whole. Cultural and religious history have not fared as well as they might have and, where they do appear, will often be found doing multiple duty as sources of political, social, and institutional history. This circumstance is a consequence of the purpose of the present work, but readers are entitled to suspect that it converges with a particular type of historical approach to the period.

Sections covering the fourth and fifth centuries have obviously been written with knowledge that political authority in Roman Gaul would in the course of time largely become the prerogative of Frankish kings. I have tried not to let this anchronism determine the selection process too much, but it is of course the reason why the book begins with the early Franks and why I have taken pains to gather together basic texts on the Franks prior to the time their impact on Gallic history became paramount. Readers with a special interest in the Alamanni, for example, or the Goths in their pre-Gallic phase, will have to look elsewhere.

There is a saying that the playwright does not put a shotgun over the mantel in the first act if it is not to be used in the third. Neither history nor historiography can (or should) achieve the dramatic interconnectedness of the fictional narrator. I do hope, however, that readers will notice in the selections the recurrence of themes and subject matter. These regularities are due not just to concious and subconcious processes of selection but also to regularities in the nature of the source material itself and continuities in the cultural and institutional structures of the region from which it comes. For example, one of the pleasant surprises in compiling Merovingian historical legends and romance was realizing the extent to which the end of the Reader (really the penultimate chapter) recalls in its topsy turvy way the course of the previous chapters and, incidentally, helps make this a book about history not just as we see it but as the people of the time saw it. I hope that readers will look for connections among the chapters and will find the selections, taken as a whole, as self-contained and as inter-connected as I believe them to be.

Thanks are due to a number of people, for reading and commenting on the manuscript in whole or in part, for supplying me with books or articles that have eased the process of selection and translation, and sometimes for doing both: Paul Dutton, Walter Goffart, Steve Muhlberger, Joan Murray, and Barbara Rosenwein. Walter Goffart and my wife Joan, being close at hand, have also had to endure far too much single-minded chatter about Latinity and Gallic politics. My sons, interested in neither of these subjects, have borne with good grace a father who, while present in the flesh, seemed to be off in his own incomprehensible world. Special thanks are due to Paul Dutton for asking me to undertake what turned out to a be a rewarding enterprise and for his patience and reassuring composure in the face of repeated optimistic (and erroneous) predictions of a completion date.

Much of the translation in this Reader is original, but little of it is new. As a mere historian I am aware of owing a special debt of gratitude to translators — English, French, and German, medievalists and classicists — who have gone before me, many of whom have long since departed. My choosing not always to follow them, even when it would have been convenient to do so, is not intended to be a reflection on the quality of their translations, but arose from the growing conviction on my part that a modern and consistent voice should shape the sound of the present work. I have tried, no doubt not always successfully, to eschew an English that reads like a gloss of the Latin, heavy with cognates and sticking to the (in English) unwieldy periods of Latin syntax; those who may still prefer their Sidonius that way should try that approach on Fredegar. I have had modest aims as far as style is concerned, striving simply for accuracy, clarity, and readable English expressed in a contemporary idiom.

Alexander Callander Murray
Orton, Ontario

# CHAPTER ONE

# THE EARLY FRANKS

*Roman sources of the late Empire apply the name Franks (*Franci*) to various peoples living on the right bank of the lower and middle Rhine. It is not clear if the currency of the term was due mainly to the Romans or the Rhineland peoples themselves. The etymology of* Franci *is uncertain ('the fierce ones' is the favorite explanation), but the name is undoubtedly of Germanic origin. Many scholars have supposed from this fact that it originated as a term for a confederation or association of distinct Rhineland peoples; but what might have constituted the common link among these peoples is disputed. A similar explanation is used to explain the origin of the Alamanni of the upper Rhine. In the sources the generic term Franks long co-existed with individual ethnic names; exactly which peoples were considered by the sources to be Franks is not always clear, a circumstance that should hardly occasion surprise. In the fourth century, the Chamavi, Salii, and Bructeri are regularly identified as Franks, though there are other candidates.*

*The following selections are grouped in two sections: (1) the earliest references to the Franks in historical sources; (2) from the relatively well-documented period 354-58, references to Franks not only as raiders and unwelcome intruders, but also as valuable and successful recruits to Roman service.*

## A. THE EARLIEST SOURCES

## 1. AURELIUS VICTOR, FROM THE *EMPERORS* (*DE CAESARIBUS*)

*The earliest reference to the Franks is commonly said to appear in Aurelius Victor's De Caesaribus, describing barbarian invasions during the dark days of the mid-third century in the reign of Gallienus (Caesar, a. 253; Augustus, a. 260-267). The reference is unlikely to be contemporary, however. The De Caesaribus, written about 361, dates from a century after the events it recounts. Its author, Aurelius Victor, was born in Africa ca. 320 and at an early age began a very successful career in imperial service at Rome, holding positions under Constantius, Julian, and Theodosius the Great; his last post was that of urban prefect of Rome in 388/89. His history, which is not immune to anachronism, made extensive use of a now lost contemporary work, known to scholarship as KG ('Kaisergeschichte'). The history of Eutropius, written a few years after Victor's, contains an equally hostile and not always accurate account of Gallienus's rule paralleling the passage below, and also based on KG. Like Victor, Eutropius refers to the Goths and the Alamanni, but applies the even more generic term 'Germani' to Victor's 'Frankish' invaders of Spain. As Caesar, Gallienus campaigned on the Rhine; coins of 258 give him the title Germanicus.*

*The excerpt below gives only a partial list of Gallienus's failings according to Victor. Gallienus's reign as Augustus coincided with the so-called 'Gallic Empire,' under the usurper Postumus.*

Source: F.R. Pichlmayr and R. Gruendel, *Sexti Aurelii Victoris Liber de Caesaribus* (Leipzig, 1966), 33, pp. 108-09. Translation by A.C. Murray.

At the same time [ca. 260], Licinius Gallienus, though vigorously attempting to keep the Germans out of Gaul, lost no time in descending on Illyricum. There at Mursa he defeated first the governor of Pannonia Ingebus, who had been seized by a passion to rule the empire...and then Regalianus...

Their demise being lucky and beyond what Gallienus had prayed for, he became quite unhinged by favorable circumstances, as humans tend to do. He and his son Salonius, on whom he had conferred the rank of Caesar, virtually wrecked the Roman state, to the point that the Goths readily penetrated Thrace and seized Macedonia, Achaea, and regions bordering on Asia; the Parthians seized Mesopotamia, and bandits, or rather a woman [Zenobia], controlled the east. At that time, the violence of the Alamanni also afflicted Italy. Frankish peoples (*gentes Francorum*) despoiled Gaul and occupied Spain, where they laid waste and almost plundered the town of Tarragona. Some of them, after conveniently obtaining ships, got as far as Africa. Even the territories across the Danube, which Trajan had secured, were lost.

And so over the whole world the mightiest things were mixed up with the small, the lowest with the highest, as if by winds raging from all sides. And at the same time, Rome was afflicted by the plague, which often breaks out amid grave anxieties and despair.

## 2. FROM THE *LATIN PANEGYRICS (PANEGYRICI LATINI)*

*Contemporary references to the Franks first appear in the late third century in the so-called* Panegyrici Latini, *where the name seems already well-established.*

*The* Panegyrici Latini *is a collection of twelve panegyrics, eleven of which were delivered between 289 and 389 to various emperors by Gallic rhetors, mainly at Trier, the principal imperial residence in the north-west; a twelfth specimen is a highly respected model piece by Pliny, delivered before Trajan two centuries earlier.*

*The panegyric in its imperial dress was a formal eulogy made before the emperor, praising his achievements with exaggerated flattery, passing over his setbacks, and deni-grating, sometimes heaping vituperation on, his enemies. The relation of panegyric to truth is often incidental but the genre, for all its tendentiousness, can still cast valuable light, not only on what happened, but also on the ideological face of power, political culture, and public fidelity.*

*Most of the pieces in the collection were delivered to the tetrarchs, Maximian (a. 286-305), Constantius I (a. 293-306), and Constantine (a. 306-337), roughly in the decades around 300. These emperors, and the senior colleague in the east, Diocletian (a. 284-305), were responsible for stabilizing imperial fortunes after the troubles of the third century.*

Source: *In Praise of Later Roman Emperors: The Panegyrici Latini*, trans. C.E.V. Nixon and Barbara Saylor Rodgers (Berkeley/Los Angeles/Oxford, 1994), Pan. VI, VIII, X, XI, XII.

### a. Panegyrics X and XI on Maximian

*The Franks first appear as a group in Pan. XI, delivered at Trier in 291: typical of barbarians in a panegyric, they are pictured surrendering to the emperor. The events alluded to in this panegyric are related to references in a slightly earlier one (no. X, delivered ca. 289), which mentions a king, almost certainly Frankish, called Gen-nobaudes. The events took place in 285-286 when Maximian was fighting Gallic rebels (Bacaudae) and barbarians (Chaibones and Heruli) as well as attempting to suppress a usurper from Britain by the name of Carausius, who had allied himself with the Franks of the lower Rhine.*

*The mention of pirates refers to Carausius and his allies. Maximian had taken the title 'Herculius' to parallel the title 'Jovius' of Diocletian.*

(X 10.2-5)...Yet you see, Emperor, that I cannot find anything with which to compare you in all antiquity unless it be the example of the race of Hercules. For even Alexander the Great now seems insignificant to me for restoring his realm to the Indian king when so many kings, O Emperor, are your clients, when Gennobaudes recovered his kingdom, thanks to you, indeed received it from you as a gift. For what else did he seek by coming to your presence with all his people other than that he should reign at last with unimpaired authority, now that he had appeased you? He displayed you repeatedly, I hear, to his people, and ordered them to rest their gaze upon you for a long time and to learn submissiveness, since he himself was subject to you.

(XI 7.1-2)...I ignore even those things which were done by the fear of your arms as if accomplished by arms: the Franks coming with their kings to seek peace and the Parthian soliciting your favor with wonderful gifts.

...Those laurels from the conquered nations inhabiting Syria and from Raetia and Sarmatia made you, Maximian, celebrate a triumph in pious joy; and by the same token the destruction here of the Chaibones and Eruli and the victories across the Rhine and the wars with the pirates who were suppressed when the Franks were subdued made Diocletian share in your vows.

## b. Panegyric VIII on Constantius

*This piece was a thanksgiving, delivered probably at Trier in the spring of 297, on behalf of the city of Autun on the occasion of the restoration of Britain to the empire in 296. The emperor responsible for the defeat of the British rebels under Carausius and his successor Allectus was Maximian's colleague, the Caesar Constantius I. An important stage in the defeat of the rebels was Constantius's capture of the Gallic port of Boulogne. Then, before proceeding to Britain, Constantius had to build a fleet and deal with the Franks who were occupying Batavia and the land around the Scheldt river. This excerpt illustrates the problems of campaigning in the region and the fate of barbarian captives. Soon after these events a unit of the Chamavi is attested serving in Egypt.*

(VIII 7.4-9.4) During the whole of this period [after the siege], however, you never ceased to destroy those enemies whom terra firma permitted you to approach, although that region which was liberated and purged of the enemy by your divine campaigns, Caesar, through which the Scaldis [Scheldt] flows with its meandering channels and which the Rhine embraces with its two arms is hardly land at all, if I may hazard the expression. It is so thoroughly soaked and drenched with waters that not only where it is obviously marshy does it yield to pressure and engulf the foot which treads it, but even where it seems a little firmer it shakes when subjected to the tramp of feet and attests by its movement that it feels the weight from afar. Thus the fact is that this land swims on what underlies it and, suspended there, trembles so extensively that one might claim with justification that such terrain existed to give soldiers practice in naval warfare. But neither the treacherous nature of this region nor the very many refuges which were to be found in its forests could protect the barbarians from being compelled to give themselves up en masse to the control of your divinity, and with their wives and children and the rest of their swarm of relatives and chattels they crossed over to lands long since deserted in order to restore to cultivation through their servitude what they themselves, perhaps, had once devastated by their plundering.

What god could have persuaded us, before you became our rulers, that what we have seen and are now seeing would ever come to pass, even if he had been willing to address us in person? In all the porticoes of our cities sit captive bands of barbarians, the men quaking, their savagery utterly confounded, old men and wives contemplating the listlessness of their sons and husbands, youths and girls fettered together whispering soothing endearments, and all these parceled out to the inhabitants of your provinces for service, until they might be led out to the desolate lands assigned to be cultivated by them. It is a pleasure, by Hercules, to exult in the name of all the Gauls together, and — I say this by your leave — to attribute the triumph to the provinces themselves. And so it is for me now that the Chamavian and Frisian plows, and that vagabond, that pillager, toils at the cultivation of the neglected countryside and frequents my markets with beasts for sale, and the barbarian farmer lowers the price of food. Furthermore, if he is summoned to the levy, he comes running and is crushed by discipline; he submits to the lash and congratulates himself upon his servitude by calling it soldiering...

*The plague of rebellion causes the panegyrist to recall a previous exploit of Frankish captives.*

(VIII 18.3) Indeed it recalled to mind that incredible audacity and undeserved good fortune of a few Frankish captives in the time of the deified Probus [a. 276-82], who seizing some ships, plundered their way from the Black Sea right to Greece and Asia and, driven not without causing damage from very many parts of the Libyan shore, finally took Syracuse itself, once renowned for its naval victories, and, after traveling on an immense journey, entered the Ocean where it breaches the lands, and thus showed by the outcome of their boldness that nothing is closed to a pirate's desperation where a path lies open to navigation...

*The concluding observations are addressed to Diocletian, Maximian, and Constantius (only Constantius would have been present) and cover a number of campaigns. This excerpt contains the earliest mention of 'laeti.' Laeti were not an ethnic group but barbarian settlers of various origins planted in the empire with a distinct and hereditary status. They are distinguished here from recently captured Franks. Postliminium is a term for the full restoration of rights following a person's return from captivity.*

(VIII 21) And so as formerly on your orders, Diocletian Augustus, Asia filled the deserts of Thrace by the transfer of its inhabitants, and as later, at your bidding, Maximian Augustus, the Laeti, restored by right of *postliminium*, and the Franks, admitted to our laws, have cultivated the empty fields of the Arvii [Armorica] and the Treveri, so now through your victories, Constantius, invincible Caesar, whatever land remained abandoned in the territory of the Ambiani [Amiens], Bellovaci [Beauvais], Tricasses [Troyes], and Lingones [Langres] turns green again under cultivation by barbarians.

Indeed, in addition, that city of the Aedui, which is most devoted to you, and in the name of which I must render special thanks to you, has received by virtue of the victory in Britain very many artisans, which those provinces have in abundance, and now rises up with the reconstruction of old houses and the repair of public buildings, and the restoration of temples. Now it considers that it has had restored to it that ancient appellation "brothers of Rome," since it has in you a second founder.

### c. Panegyric VI on Constantine

*This was delivered ca. 310 at Trier, on the anniversary of the city's founding, by a rhetor from Autun. The emperor in question, Constantine, is one of the great figures of western history, largely because of his acceptance of Christianity. He was the son of Constantius I and was proclaimed his father's successor in 306 at York in Britain. Crossing to Gaul, he waged several campaigns against the Franks between then and the date of the oration; the Bructeri were located opposite Cologne.*

(VI 10-13.1) You have visited with punishment for their rashness, I believe, some contemptible band of barbarians who tested the very beginnings of your reign with a sudden attack and unexpected brigandage. You did not hesitate to punish with the ultimate penalty the kings of Francia themselves, who took the opportunity of your father's absence to violate the peace, and were not at all afraid of the perpetual hatred of that race and their implacable fury. For why should an emperor who can secure what he has done think twice about any hatred arising from a severity that is just?...

You have renewed, O Emperor, that old confidence of the Roman Empire which exacted capital punishment from captured enemy chiefs. For then captive kings graced triumphal chariots from the gates right up to the Forum, and as soon as the commander began to turn his chariot toward the Capitol they were cast into prison and killed...

Hence this peace, Emperor, which we now enjoy. For we are protected now not by the boiling waters of the Rhine, but by the terror aroused by your name. Let this river dry up with the heat of summer or freeze with the cold as it will, the enemy will dare to exploit neither opportunity to cross. For Nature shuts off nothing with such an insuperable rampart that audacity may not penetrate, if one is left some hope in trying. But it is an impenetrable wall which the reputation for courage erects. The Franks know that they can cross the Rhine, and you would freely admit them to their death, but they can hope for neither victory nor pardon. What remains for them they judge from the execution of their own kings, and so far are they from endeavoring to cross that river that they are rather in despair at the bridge you have begun. Where now is that famed ferocity of yours, that ever untrustworthy fickleness? Now you do not even dare to live at a distance from the Rhine, and can scarcely drink in safety from the rivers of the interior. On the other hand the forts placed at intervals on our side are more an ornament for the frontier than protection. The farmer cultivates that once terrible bank unarmed, and our flocks immerse themselves all along both branches of that river. O Constantine, this is your everyday and eternal victory from your punishment of Ascaric and Merogaisus, one to be ranked above all former successful battles: defeated once in battle, they have become an example for ever. For the common herd does not comprehend its own defeat, however many have perished; the swiftest way to conquer the enemy completely is to have removed its leader.

However, so that the monstrous power of the barbarians might be broken in every way, and so that the enemy should not merely grieve over the punishment of their kings, you have made in addition, invincible Emperor, a devastating raid on the Bructeri. In this the first aim of your strategy was to attack them when they were off guard by suddenly throwing your army across, not that you, who would have preferred to attack openly, doubted the outcome of an open battle, but that this nation, which is accustomed to frustrate warfare by taking refuge in forests and marshes, should lose the opportunity for flight. And so countless numbers were slaughtered, and very many were captured. Whatever herds there were were seized or slaughtered; all the villages were put to the flame; the adults who were captured, whose untrustworthiness made them unfit for military service and whose ferocity for slavery, were given over to the amphitheater for punishment, and their great numbers wore out the raging beasts. This is to be reliant on one's courage and good fortune, Emperor; this is not to buy peace by sparing the foe, but to procure victory by inciting him.

In addition, by also building a bridge at Cologne you lord it over the remnants of a shattered nation, so that it may never put aside its fear, but must always quake, always stretch out suppliant hands. But you do this more to add glory to your command and an ornament to the frontier than to give yourself an opportunity, as often as you wish, of crossing into enemy territory, since the whole Rhine is furnished with armed ships, and soldiers are posted, poised for action, on every bank right down to the Ocean.

## d. Panegyric XII on Constantine Augustus

*The following oration was delivered at Trier, probably in 313 when Constantine was celebrating games in which Frankish captives were again used in the spectacle. The emperor had concluded his campaign against Maxentius in Italy the year before. The Calendar of Philocalus lists Frankish games (ludi Francici) under July 15 and 20.*

(XII 21.5-24.2) Worn out by battles and sated with victories you did not, as Nature demands, give yourself up to leisure and rest, but on the same march on which you returned to your Gauls you continued to the borders of Lower Germany. Of course, after such a great interval of time and such a short distance between locations — after a campaign of a year's duration — you immediately began operations from the Tiber to the Rhine, or rather (as the omen and similarity of names as well as your greatness of spirit, Emperor, promise) you will extend the Empire from Tuscan Albula [Tiber] to German Alba [Elbe].

Now what is this constant impatience of yours? What is this divinity thriving on perpetual motion? All things have interruptions: the earth rests in fallow lands, rivers are said to stand still now and then, the sun itself reposes at night. You alone, Constantine, tirelessly follow one war with another, heap one victory upon another. As if the past is blotted out if you cease, you think you have not conquered unless you are conquering. The fickle and flighty nation of savages broke its promise, and having chosen leaders of the invasion for their strength and daring, was reported to be threatening the Rhine. You were instantly there to meet them and by your presence you frightened them from daring the crossing. And then you appeared to have achieved the opposite of what you prayed for, because if the invasion were prevented there would be no source of victory; but you employed the unexpected plan of departing with a pretended announcement of a greater disturbance on the border of Upper Germany, you offered their dull and savage intellects an opportunity to come into our territory, and left behind in concealment generals who would attack them when they least expected it. When they had crossed over, Fortune attended your plan. With the whole bed of the Rhine filled with ships you descended and devastated their lands and mourning and sorrowful homes, and you inflicted destruction and desolation so extensive on the perjured nation that in time to come it will possess scarcely any name.

Go now, if it please you, all barbarian nations, and set in motion enterprises fatal to yourselves: you have an example. For although our Emperor accepts the submission of friendly kings and the very fact of his being feared and cultivated by the noblest kings counts the same as praise for victory, yet he is glad that the fame of his valor is increased as often as it is challenged. What is lovelier than this triumphal celebration in which he employs the slaughter of enemies for the pleasure of us all, and enlarges the procession of the games out of the survivors of the massacre of the barbarians? He threw so great a multitude of captives to the beasts that the ungrateful and faithless men experienced no less suffering from the sport made of them than from death itself.

This is the reason why, although they might defer their end, they rush to their ruin and offer themselves to lethal wounds and to death. It is apparent from this very fact how great a thing it is to have conquered men so wasteful of themselves.

It is easy to conquer timid creatures unfit for war, such as the pleasant regions of Greece and the charms of the Orient produce, who can barely tolerate a light cloak and silken garments to keep off the sun, and who if they ever get into danger forget freedom and beg to be slaves. But a Roman soldier, whom training disposes and the sanctity of his oath confirms to be who and what he is, or the grim Frank filled only by the flesh of wild beasts, who despises life because of the meanness of his sustenance, how much trouble it is to overcome or capture these! And you, Emperor, have done this both lately in Italy and not long ago in the very sight of barbarian lands.

# B. RAIDERS, INVADERS,
# AND ROMAN SOLDIERS, a. 354-360

*The following events fall in the period 354-60, during the reign of Constantius, the son of Constantine, and are drawn principally from the history of Ammianus Marcellinus. Ammianus is the author of one of the major works of Roman historiography. Written around 390, his history was conceived as a continuation of Tacitus and ends with the famous battle of Adrianople in 378. Only books 14-31, covering the final twenty-five year period from 354, survive. Ammianus was of Greek origin, though he wrote his work in Latin, and served for a period as an army officer under Constantius and Julian. His history was shaped by his antipathy to Christianity and Christian emperors. He hated the court surrounding the emperor Constantius II, whom he compared unfavorably to his pagan hero Julian, called the Apostate by Christians.*

## I SILVANUS THE USURPER

## 3. THE HISTORY OF AMMIANUS
## MARCELLINUS, XV 5

*Silvanus was a high ranking general (*magister peditum*) of Frankish extraction in the service of the emperor Constantius. According to Aurelius Victor (*De Caesaribus, 42), he was "born in Gaul of barbarian parents and came from the military caste." Ammianus gives the circumstance surrounding Silvanus's usurpation of the imperial title in great detail and directly participated in bringing about the usurper's downfall.*

*The plot against Silvanus and his fall took place in 354-55. At the time the court under the emperor Constantius was stationed at Milan, within reach of the Rhine and Danube frontiers. The regiments mentioned in the extract, the* Gentiles *and* Armaturae, *were units of the imperial body-guard (*Scholae Palatinae*).*

Source: *Ammianus Marcellinus: Römische Geschichte*, ed. W. Seyfarth (Leipzig, 1978). Translation by A.C. Murray.

Gaul, through long neglect, had been suffering bitter slaughters, depredation, and burning, with barbarians rampaging at will and no one offering any help. And so, at the command of the prince, Silvanus the commander of the infantry arrived there as someone capable of correcting the situation. Arbitio [master of the cavalry] hurried this course along by any means he could, because he wanted his rival, whose survival still irked him, absent from the court and carrying out a dangerous mission.

*Silvanus's enemies, leading court officials, contrived his undoing by forging over his signature letters that seemed to indicate Silvanus had designs on the imperial title. The letters were then presented to the emperor.*

The letters were read before the consistory, and the tribunes whose names were mentioned in the letters were ordered placed under guard and the private persons brought from the provinces. Immediately Malarich, commander of the Foreign Guards (*Gentiles*), aroused by the injustice of the affair, called together his colleagues and, complaining ferociously, declared that men devoted to the empire should not be undone by factions and deception. Malarich tried to get himself dispatched quickly to bring back Silvanus, who had attempted no such undertaking as the bitter plotters had concocted, and offered to leave his own family as hostages, with Mallobaudes, tribune of the heavy brigade of guards (*Armaturae*), acting as surety for his return; he begged, alternatively, to be allowed to be surety for Mallobaudes, who in turn would expeditiously fulfill the promise he himself had made. For Malarich swore that he knew without a doubt that if a stranger were to be sent, Silvanus, who was quite cautious by nature even when there was no threat, would end up overthrowing the arrangements.

And although Malarich's warnings were useful and required by the situation, he was talking vainly to the winds. For at Arbitio's doing, Apodemius, a persistent and dangerous enemy of all good men, was sent with a letter to recall Silvanus...

*Arriving in Gaul, Apodemius treated Silvanus' property in a high-handed fashion, as if Silvanus was already proscribed, but never came in contact with the general himself. Another letter was forged, this time implicating Malarich, but the letter by mistake fell into Malarich's hands.*

Malarich received the letter at a time when he was still troubled and depressed, and groaning loudly over his own lot and that of his countryman Silvanus. He called together the Franks, a large number of whom were at the time doing well for themselves in the palace, and he spoke even more boldly, raising an uproar now that the plot was revealed and the deception that evidently was threatening their safety disclosed. The emperor, when he learned of this, decided that the officials of his consistory and the army together should investigate and look into the matter carefully...

*The letter was shown to be a forgery and high officials were interrogated without much result.*

While these events were taking place, Silvanus was serving at Cologne and heard by continuous reports from his friends how Apodemius was ruining his fortune. Knowing the pliant disposition of the fickle emperor, he feared that he would be cut down far from the court without a hearing; placed as he was in the worst kind of position, he considered entrusting himself to the good graces of the barbarians. But Laniogaisus, who was a tribune at the time,...stopped him from doing so, telling him that the Franks, from whom he derived his origin, would kill him or turn him over for a price. Silvanus figured there was no safety as matters stood and so he was driven to extreme measures. He gradually spoke more boldly to the chief officers and, inciting them with the promise of great reward, tore the purple decorations as a temporary measure from the standards of the cohorts and companies and assumed the imperial title.

*When news of the usurpation reached Milan, the general Ursicinus, also under suspicion, was sent to Gaul to ingratiate himself with Silvanus and betray him. Accompanying Ursicinus as a member of his staff was Ammianus himself. Troops bribed for the purpose caught Silvanus unaware, "on his way to a service of the Christian religion," dragged him from the chapel where he fled for refuge and killed him.*

# II JULIAN IN GAUL: SALIANS AND CHAMAVI, a. 357-58

*Following the fall of Silvanus, Constantius appointed his cousin Julian as Caesar and sent him to Gaul in December 355; at the same time news reached Italy that Cologne had fallen to barbarian attack. Julian was an inexperienced student and, for the first year, was closely supervised by Constantius's officials; during this time Cologne was recovered from the Franks. In the second campaign year of 357, the young Caesar was given more authority and took an active part in military affairs; that year he defeated the Alamanni at the battle of Strasbourg. Eventually, at Paris in 360, Julian usurped the imperial title of Augustus and, marching east, became sole emperor when Constantius died. Julian himself was killed in 363 leading a failed expedition against the Persians.*

*The following excerpts concern Julian's campaigns in Gaul, and especially his dealings with the Franks in 357-58.*

## 4. THE EMPEROR JULIAN, FROM HIS *LETTER TO THE ATHENIANS*

*When Julian decided to march against Constantius in 360, he sent letters to a number of important cities justifying his actions. Only the letter to Athens survives. In it Julian offers his own evaluation of his achievements in Gaul. The letter contains the first reference to the Salian Franks.*

*Julian begins his account at the point when he was granted active command in the spring of 357, but he covers events of the previous year as well. Three hundred stades (stadia) measured about 35 miles.*

Source: *The Works of the Emperor Julian*, trans. Wilmer Cave Wright (Cambridge, MA./London, 1913), vol. 2, Letter to the Athenians 279-280.

And when the grain was ripe I took the field; for a great number of Germans had settled themselves with impunity near the towns they had sacked in Gaul.

Now the number of towns whose walls had been dismantled was about forty-five, without counting citadels and smaller forts. And the barbarians then controlled on our side of the Rhine the whole country that extends from its source to the Ocean. Moreover those who were settled nearest us were as much as three-hundred stades from the banks of the Rhine, and a district three times as wide as that had been left a desert by their raids; so that the Gauls could not even pasture their cattle there. Then too there were certain cities deserted by their inhabitants, near which the barbarians were not yet encamped. This then was the condition of Gaul when I took it over.

I recovered the city of Agrippina [Cologne] on the Rhine which had been taken about ten months earlier and also the neighboring fort of Argentoratum [Strasbourg], and there I engaged the enemy not ingloriously. It may be that the fame of that battle has reached even your ears. There though the gods gave into my hands as prisoner of war the king of the enemy [Chnodomar of the Alamanni], I did not begrudge Constantius the glory of that success. And yet though I was not allowed to triumph for it, I had it in my power to slay my enemy, and moreover I could have led him through the whole of Gaul and exhibited him to the cities, and thus have luxuriated as it were in the misfortunes of Chnodomar. I thought it my duty to do none of these things, but sent him at once to Constantius who was returning from the country of the Quadi and the Sarmatians. So it came about that, though I had done all the fighting and he had only traveled in those parts and held friendly intercourse with the tribes who dwell on the borders of the Danube, it was not I but he who triumphed.

Then followed the second and third years of that campaign, and by that time all the barbarians had been driven out of Gaul, most of the towns had been recovered, and a whole fleet of many ships had arrived from Britain. I had collected a fleet of six hundred ships, four hundred of which I had built in less than ten months, and I brought them all into the Rhine, no slight achievement, on account of the neighboring barbarians who kept attacking me. At least it seemed so impossible to Florentius [the praetorian prefect] that he had promised to pay the barbarians a fee of two thousand pounds weight of silver in return for a passage. Constantius when he learned of this — for Florentius had informed him about the proposed payment — wrote to me to carry out the agreement, unless I thought it absolutely disgraceful. But how could it fail to be disgraceful when it seemed so even to Constantius, who was only too much in the habit of trying to conciliate the barbarians? However no payment was made to them. Instead I marched against them, and since the gods protected me and were present to aid, I received the submission of part of the Salian tribe, and drove out the Chamavi and took many cattle and women and children. And I so terrified them all, and made them tremble at my approach that I immediately received hostages from them and secured a safe passage for my food supplies.

It would take too long to enumerate everything and to write down every detail of the task that I accomplished within four years. But to sum it all up: three times while I was Caesar, I crossed the Rhine; one thousand persons who were held as captives on the further side of the Rhine I demanded and received back; in two battles and one siege I took captive ten thousand prisoners, and those not of unserviceable age but men in the prime of life; I sent to Constantius four levies of excellent infantry, three more of infantry not so good, and two very distinguished squadrons of cavalry. I have now with the help of the gods recovered all the towns, and by that time I had already recovered almost forty.

## 5. THE HISTORY OF AMMIANUS MARCELLINUS, XVII 2, 8

*The excerpts below begin after Julian's victory over the Alamanni at Strasbourg.*

*Severus's encounter with Frankish raiders seems to have taken place along the so-called* limes Belgicus, *the modern term for a fortified road running between Cologne and Bavai. The subsequent campaign against the Salian Franks was to the north of that road. It is commonly supposed that Julian conceded Toxandria to the Salians after he received their surrender.*

Source: *Ammianus Marcellinus: Römische Geschichte*, ed. W. Seyfarth (Leipzig, 1978). Translation by A.C. Murray.

Returning to winter quarters, Julian found there was still work left to do. As the commander of the cavalry Severus was on his way to Rheims by way of Cologne and Juliers, he ran into very strong bands (*cunei*) of Franks, numbering, as was later revealed, six hundred lightly armed skirmishers. They were plundering districts emptied of their garrisons. This bold crime arose because of their belief that, while Caesar was busy in the haunts of the Alamanni, there would be no one to prevent them from glutting themselves on a rich haul of plunder. But now in fear of the army which had returned, they took over two forts that had been evacuated some time ago and defended themselves as best they could.

Julian was shocked by this novelty, and aware of where it would all lead if he passed on leaving them unharmed, he halted the army and made arrangements to invest the strongholds, which were on the bank of the river Meuse. For fifty-four days, that is for the months of December and January, a protracted siege dragged on, the barbarians stout-heartedly resisting with unbelievable stubbornness.

Then Caesar, being very shrewd and fearing that the barbarians might wait for a moonless night and cross the frozen river, had troops coast up and down the river in patrol craft every day from dusk to dawn, breaking up the ice surface and giving no one a chance of easily breaking out. Because of this device, they willingly surrendered, worn out by starvation, lack of sleep, and utter despair. Immediately they were sent to the court of the Augustus.

A host of Franks had set out to free them from danger, but when they found out they had been captured and carried off, they returned home without daring anything else. With these successes, Caesar returned to Paris to spend the winter...

The Caesar Julian, spending the winter at Paris, was very anxious to forestall the Alamanni, who had not yet assembled into one force but as a whole were bold and savage to the point of madness after the battle of Strasbourg. He was apprehensive for some time as he awaited the month of July, the beginning of the campaign season in Gaul. For he could not leave until the cold and frost were gone and provisions were brought up from Aquitaine with the return of summer.

But as careful planning overcomes almost all difficulties, he considered a number of different possibilities and at last hit upon just this one, of attacking the barbarians unexpectedly without waiting for the right time of the year. Once this plan was devised, he had a twenty-day supply of grain taken from the provisions of the camps and baked, so it would keep, and loaded this biscuit, as it is commonly called, on the backs of willing soldiers. Relying on this supply, he set out with favorable auspices, as before, thinking that two pressing and necessary campaigns could be completed by the fifth or sixth month.

With these preparations, he first of all set out after the Franks, specifically those customarily called Salians. They had the audacity some time ago of boldly establishing settlements for themselves on Roman soil in the district of Toxandria. When he reached Tongres, a delegation of theirs met him, imagining that the emperor was even then still in winter quarters. They offered peace as if they were on their own land on condition that no one harm or harry them as long as they refrained from causing trouble. He went over the matter fully, presented the emissaries in turn with some complicated proposals and sent them away with gifts, as if he were intending to remain in the same district. Quick as a flash he set out behind them, sent his general Severus along the river bank, and suddenly attacked them all, striking like a thunder-bolt. Now that they were offering entreaties rather than resistance, he used his victory as a timely opportunity to show mercy and received their surrender along with their property and children.

He also attacked the Chamavi, who had dared to do the same as the Salians, quickly killing a number of them; some who fought back fiercely and were taken alive he put in chains. Others retreating in headlong flight home-ward he allowed for the moment to get away unharmed in case he tire out his soldiers with a long chase. They sent emissaries a little later to make entreaties and to look after their interests. The emissaries prostrated them-selves on the ground before him and he granted them peace with the under-standing that they could return safely to their homes.

## 6. LIBANIOS OF ANTIOCH, FROM HIS FUNERAL ORATION OVER JULIAN

*Julian's exploits lost nothing in their retelling by Libanios, a famous sophist of the city of Antioch, who wrote a eulogy on Julian after the emperor's death in Persia in 363. Libanios, like Eunapius (below, 7) and even Ammianus, was a great admirer of the philosophical and religious ideals of Julian and hoped that Julian would fulfill the ideal of the pagan philosopher-soldier-emperor.*

*This selection corresponds to the events of 357-58; it differs in detail from that of Ammianus. References to Sphacteria and the Ten Thousand are allusions to well-known events in the works of Thucydides and Xenophon, respectively.*

Source: *Libanius: Selected Works*, ed. and trans. A. F. Norman (Cambridge, MA./London, 1969), vol. I, Oration XVIII 70-79.

[I]n midwinter he had to deal with a thousand of the Franks, to whose taste snows and blossoms come alike. They were engaged in ravaging some villages in the center of which was a deserted fort. Here he surrounded them and kept them penned up until he forced them to surrender from starvation. Then he sent them in chains to his superior — an event without precedent, for it was their way to conquer or die. For all that they were put in chains, just like the Spartans at Sphacteria. The emperor who received them described them as a gift and drafted them into his own regiments, confident that he was enrolling pillars of strength for himself, since every one was the match for many ordinary men.

This then was one of his major exploits that winter, but there was another no less remarkable. When a whole enemy tribe suddenly overran part of the province, he hastened to dislodge them in concert with the forces garrisoning the threatened area, but on the news of the raid, anticipating his coming they themselves ejected the enemy, inflicting heavy losses. So the emperor, both upon his arrival and before it, was alike victorious. And this feat he performed as he just then arose from the midst of his books — or rather as he went against the foe, he went with his books for company.

For he always had in his hands either books or arms, for he considered warfare to be greatly helped by philosophy, and that in an emperor ability to use his wits was more effective than belligerency. For instance, the two following devices were certainly beneficial to the community and indications of his superior intellect, first that he increased the eagerness of good men by the honors that he sponsored for them from the distributor of such things, and secondly, that in the harrying of the enemy territory, he allowed them possession of whatever they got their hands on, for this is obviously on a par with his [earlier] proclamation that anyone who brought in the head of an enemy should receive a gold piece for his courage...

[A]s soon as the season called for the raising of the standard he went on campaign. He made a lightning appearance on the Rhine, and so terrified a whole enemy tribe that they asked permission to migrate and form part of his empire, judging it better to dwell beneath his sway than in their own country. They asked for land and got it. And against barbarians he employed barbarians who thought it more honorable to pursue in his company than to flee in theirs.

This much was achieved without a fight; but he resolved to cross the river again, and through lack of boats he set his infantry and cavalry to swim across. Then he advanced, ravaging and collecting booty, with none to say him nay. The wretched inhabitants at last offered a tardy submission, as they had to do or else be burned out. But he felt that the day had come that should cure all the ills of Gaul, and so he at first sent them off contemptuously, but they came back again with their chieftains in person as suppliants, and the wielders of the sceptre abased themselves to the ground.

Then he reminded them of their reign of terror and the incalculable damage they had wrought, and he told them to buy peace at the cost of healing the harm they had done, by rebuilding the towns and restoring the inhabitants. They agreed to this and were true to their word. Timber and iron were brought to rebuild houses, and every [Roman] captive set at liberty to return and, so that he would not bear malice, was cosseted by the man who had earlier flogged him. The captives whom they did not restore, they proved were dead, and the truth in this matter was decided by those released. In the army of the Ten Thousand, after their long toils and endless mountains, the first sight of the sea evoked shouts and tears of joy, and those who shared those dangers embraced one another. These folk now did the same at the sight not of the sea but of each other, as they saw their kinsfolk restored from slavery or as they recovered homes and kindred. Everyone else, who though not connected by family ties yet saw their embraces, began to weep also, and tears flowed, tears far sweeter than those once shed at parting, for now they were tears of joy at their reunion.

# 7. EUNAPIUS OF SARDIS, FRAGMENT 18.6

*The campaign against the Chamavi figures in the history of another pagan supporter of Julian, Eunapius of Sardis, author of a universal history in Greek that ended in 404; it was published in parts before that date, and its account of Julian may first have been written around the time Ammianus was composing his history. Eunapius claimed he used in part a memoir written by Julian's personal physician. His history survives only in excerpts in later works. The following is from the* Excerpta de legationibus, *a collection of historical extracts made in the tenth century dealing with embassies and delegations. A confused, but possibly more circumstantial version appears in the* New History *of the early sixth-century Greek historian Zosimos.*

*Though one or two details of the following account seem reliable, the Chamavi serve principally as a source of pathos and as a foil for the high-minded didacticism of the Caesar. The dating of the campaign to the autumn is incorrect.*

Source: *The Fragmentary Classicising Historians of the Later Roman Empire: Eunapius, Olympiodorus, Priscus and Malchus*, trans. R.C. Blockley (Liverpool, 1983), vol. 2, Eunapius, Frag. 18.6, pp. 25-29.

When Julian entered the enemy's territory, the Chamavi begged him to treat this land, too, as if it were his own. Julian agreed and ordered their king to come to him. When the king came and saw him standing on the bank, the Caesar embarked in a boat and, keeping the boat out of arrow range, spoke to the barbarians through an interpreter. They were willing to do all he demanded, and since he saw that peace was obviously desirable, indeed necessary for him (for without the acquiescence of the Chamavi it is impossible to transport the supplies of grain from the island of Britain to the Roman garrisons), guided by his own advantage, he granted peace, demanding hostages as a pledge. When they said that those whom the Romans captured were sufficient, Julian replied that he held them as a result of the fighting, not by agreement; now he was seeking their best men, lest they use deceit in respect of the peace agreement. They agreed and begged him to name whom he wished. In reply he demanded the king's son, whom he held as a prisoner, pretending that he did not have him. Thereupon the barbarians and their king threw themselves on their faces and with plentiful groans and lamentations besought Julian not to enjoin what they could not carry out; they were unable to raise up the fallen and deliver the dead as hostages.

When silence was restored, the barbarian king declared at the top of his voice, "Would that my son were alive so that, as a hostage with you, Caesar, he might enjoy a bondage more blessed than my kingly power."

*The king continued his speech, lamenting his own loss and the danger that would ensue for his people if Julian refused to believe his son was dead.*

When the Emperor heard this, his heart was saddened and he readily wept tears at the words. Just as when, in a play, the complications of the plot come to an inextricable impasse, the so-called *deus ex machina* is adventitiously dragged onto the stage, bringing everything around to a clear and satisfactory conclusion, so, too, Julian...brought forward the young man whom he had treated as befits royalty, and showed him to them all. Then having told him to say whatever he wished to his father, Julian returned to consider the business in hand.

What followed this was a fitting sequel. Those present would never be able to witness and describe a day like this. The Chamavi, turned from groaning and lamentation to stunned amazement and consternation, were struck motionless, as if Julian had showed them not the young man, but his ghost. When a silence had fallen, more profound than at all the Mysteries, the Emperor addressed them all in a deep voice: "This boy, whom your aggression had destroyed, as you thought, God, allied with the philanthropy of the Romans, has saved. I shall keep him as a hostage, not handed over by you under agreement, but taken in war; for I am satisfied with my victory. He will lack nothing but the best while he is with me, but you, if you attempt to break the treaty, shall suffer everything. I do not say that then I shall punish the hostage, whom I have not received from you as a pledge of peace, but whom I hold as proof of our bravery against you. Besides, it is unfair and ungodly to rend and tear to pieces those who are innocent in the place of those who do harm, as wild beasts do to those in their path when they are being pursued by others. But I do say that you shall be the first to raise hands to injustice, the most self-destructive act that men can perform, even if in the short term it brings apparent gain. And secondly I remind you that you will have to reckon with the Romans, and me, their ruler, whom you have never bested either in war or when seeking peace."

At this all the Chamavi threw themselves down and blessed him thinking him a god for these words. So Julian made peace, demanding only the mother of Nebisgastes, and the barbarians straightway ratified the peace and handed her over. When these things had been accomplished, the emperor broke camp, since it was now late autumn and the cold of winter was already beginning.

# III JULIAN PROCLAIMED AUGUSTUS, a. 360

## 8. THE HISTORY OF AMMIANUS MARCELLINUS, XX 4

*According to Ammianus Marcellinus, who was not an impartial commentator, Julian was forced to take up the purple by his troops angry at having to leave their homelands to fight in the east against the Persians. Ammianus's description of the consequences of Constantius's decision to call on the crack regiments of Gaul is revealing about the recruitment practices of the Roman army.*

Source: *Ammianus Marcellinus: Römische Geschichte*, ed. W. Seyfarth (Leipzig, 1978). Translation by A.C. Murray

[Constantius] sent Decentius, tribune and secretary, to take immediately from Julian his auxiliaries, the Heruli and Batavi, as well as the Celts and Petulantes, and three-hundred picked men from each of the other units. They were ordered to hurry along on the pretext that they might join up with the forces being mustered to attack the Parthians in early spring. Lupicinus alone was called upon to expedite the departure of the auxiliaries and the three-hundred-man detachments..., but Sintula, the Caesar's tribune of the stables at the time, was ordered to select the best of the Scutarii and the Foreign Guard (*Gentiles*) and to lead them personally.

Julian said nothing and acquiesced to these measures, yielding completely to the will of one more powerful. On one matter, however, he could not pretend indifference or keep silent: those men, he said, who had left their homes across the Rhine and had enlisted on condition that they would never be transferred across the Alps should not be affected. For he expressed the fear that barbarian volunteers accustomed to coming over to our forces under this form of agreement might after this stay away when they heard of the transfer. But he spoke in vain.

*The departing troops were all routed through Paris, where Julian was in residence. Led by the Petulantes, they mutinied, and proclaimed Julian Augustus.*

# CHAPTER TWO

# OROSIUS ON EMPIRE, BARBARIANS, AND USURPERS IN THE LATE FOURTH AND FIFTH CENTURIES

*Orosius was a priest of the church of Braga, in what is modern-day Portugal. Passionately interested in the theological disputes of the day, he left Spain ca. 414 — a time when barbarian invasions had disrupted Gaul and the Iberian peninsula — to visit Saint Augustine in North Africa and Saint Jerome in Palestine. He is known for three works: a treatise against Priscillianism, a defense of his own religious views, and a history in seven books.*

*His fame rests on the* Histories, *written shortly after 417. The work was intended to supplement the historical arguments of Augustine's* City of God *and, in particular, to counter the complaint that the current troubles, especially the recent sack of Rome by Alaric and the Goths in 410, had happened because Romans had abandoned traditional religion and accepted Christianity. Though occasioned by Augustine's* City of God, *the arguments are Orosius's own, and do not necessarily conform to Augustine's historical perspective. Orosius's* Histories *were a survey of history from Adam to the present, with a special emphasis on the history of Rome. It soon became very influential in the west.*

*The following selections concern Orosius's view of the Roman Empire in the scheme of divine providence and especially the events of Orosius's own lifetime, drawn from the final book. On the four kingdoms or empires, cf. Daniel 2.*

*To facilitate reading and reference, I have added subheadings at the point where Orosius numbers the reign of the senior Augustus. Note that emperors may have assumed the imperial title before that date.*

Source: Book II translated by A.C. Murray, based on the Budé edition of Marie-Pierre Arnaud-Lindet (Paris, 1990); Book VII translated by Irving Woodworth Raymond, *Seven Books of History against the Pagans* (New York, 1936), with minor revisions

## 9. FROM THE *HISTORIES AGAINST THE PAGANS*

### BOOK II

1...But if powers come from God, all the more so do kingdoms (*regna*) from which the remaining powers proceed. And if there are various kingdoms, all the more reasonable is it that one of the kingdoms be supreme, to which the power of the other kingdoms is entirely subject. In the beginning this was the case with the Babylonian kingdom, then the Macedonian, then the African [Carthaginian], and finally the Roman, which endures to the present time. By the same inexplicable plan, the four kingdoms achieved pre-eminence at different rates at the four cardinal points of the world: the Babylonian kingdom in the East, the Carthaginian in the South, the Macedonian in the North, and the Roman in the West. Between the first and the most recent of these kingdoms (that is between the Babylonian and the Roman), as between an aged father and a small son, the African and Macedonian kingdoms came briefly in the middle, like a guardian and a trustee who take charge because of force of circumstance not by right of inheritance...

2...Babylon was dishonored under the prefect Arbatus in the very year when, to speak accurately, the seeds of Rome were sown during the reign of Procas [grandfather of Rhea Silvia, the mother of Romulus]. Babylon was finally overthrown by Cyrus just at the time when Rome was freed from the despotism of the Tarquin kings. Indeed it was as if the one fell and the other arose at one and the same moment...

3...Babylon thus had almost reached the 1164th year from her foundation, when she was despoiled of her wealth by the Medes and Arbatus, king of the Medes and prefect of Babylon, and deprived of both king and kingdom. The city herself, however, remained safe and sound for some time afterward [until her overthrow by Cyrus]. Likewise, after the same amount of time, that is almost 1164 years after her foundation, Rome too was invaded by the Goths and Alaric, king of the Goths and a count of Rome. The city was despoiled of her wealth but not of her kingdom and remains to the present safe and sound, exercising her rule. Although the hidden decrees of God have preserved the parallelism between the two cities to such an extent that, at Babylon, her prefect Arbatus occupied the city, and, at Rome, her prefect Attalus attempted to exercise power, yet only at Rome, by merit of a Christian emperor, was the impious attempt brought to naught.

And so I have been of the belief that these events deserve special mention so that those who grumble quite senselessly about Christian times may, with the great secret of God's inexplicable judgments partially revealed, know that the one God has directed the course of history, both in the beginning for the Babylonians and in the end for the Romans, and that it is through His forbearance that we live and through our own excess that we live wretchedly.

Mark well that Babylon and Rome had similar origins, similar power, similar size, similar times, similar advantages, and similar evils. Yet the outcome was not similar nor was the failure the same. For Babylon lost her rule but Rome preserves hers; Babylon was bereft by the murder of her king but Rome is safe with her emperor unharmed. And why is this? Because in Babylon the punishment for disgraceful passions was visited upon the king; in Rome the most restrained moderation of the Christian faith was preserved in the person of the king. In Babylon madness permitted the desire for pleasure to be fully satisfied without respect for religion, but in Rome there were Christians to give mercy and Christians to whom they gave mercy and Christians on account of whose memory and in remembrance of whom mercy was given...

## BOOK VII

2. At the beginning of the second book I touched lightly upon the period of the founding of Rome and there I consistently noted many points of similarity between the Assyrian city of Babylon, then first among the nations, and Rome, now holding the same position of primacy. I showed that Babylon was the first, Rome the last empire; that Babylon grew weak little by little, while Rome gradually waxed strong; that Babylon lost her last king at the same time that Rome crowned her first; and that Babylon was attacked and captured by Cyrus and fell dying, just as Rome, rising confidently after the expulsion of the kings, began to enjoy the freedom of ruling herself...

Furthermore, I have said that there intervened between the Babylonian Empire which was in the East and the Roman Empire which arose in the West and was nourished by the legacy of the East, the Macedonian and African Empires. These empires may be regarded as playing the role of a guardian and trustee for brief intervals in the North and in the South. To my knowledge no one had ever doubted that the Babylonian and the Roman empires are rightly called that of the East and that of the West. That the Macedonian Empire was in the North is obvious both from its geographical position and the altars of Alexander the Great which stand to this day near the Riphaean mountains. Carthage, on the other hand, ruled over the whole of Africa and extended the boundaries of her empire not only to Sicily, Sardinia, and other adjacent islands but even to Spain, as is shown by the records of history and by the remains of cities. I have also stated that after each city had stood for the same number of years Babylon was sacked by the Medes and Rome taken by the Goths.

To these arguments, I now add the following proofs to make it clearer that God is the sole ruler of all the ages, kingdoms, and regions. The Carthaginian Empire, from its founding to her overthrow, lasted a little more than seven hundred years; the Macedonian, from Caranus to Perses, a little less than seven hundred. Both, however, came to an end in the number seven, by which all things are decided. Rome herself endured to the coming of the Lord Jesus Christ with her empire unbroken. Nevertheless she too suffered somewhat when she arrived at that same number. For in the seven hundredth year after the founding of the City a fire of unknown origin consumed fourteen districts. According to Livy a worse conflagration never visited Rome. So great were its ravages that some years later Caesar Augustus granted a large sum of money from the public treasury for the reconstruction of the burnt areas. If I were not restrained by a consideration of the present state of affairs, I could also show that Babylon had existed for twice that length of time when, more than fourteen hundred years after her founding, she was finally captured by King Cyrus....

*Chapters 3-31 survey Roman history from the time of Christ and Augustus, the first emperor, to the reign of Jovian.*

## Reign of Valentinian I, a. 364-75

32. In the 1118th year from the founding of the City [of Rome], Valentinian [I], the thirty-eighth emperor, was proclaimed emperor at Nicaea by agreement of the soldiers. He held office for eleven years. Though a Christian, Valentinian, without violating his faith, had performed military duty under the emperor Julian as tribune of the regiment of *scutarii*...

Later he made his brother Valens joint emperor [a. 364-378], and subsequently killed the usurper Procopius and many of the latter's followers...Valens was baptized and converted by the bishop Eudoxius, a supporter of Arian views, and thus he fell into most terrible heresy...

In the third year of the reign of these brothers, Gratian, the son of Valentinian, was made emperor [a. 367-383]. In the same year in the territory of the Atrebates, real wool, mixed with rain, fell from the clouds.

Moreover, Athanaric, king of the Goths, with the greatest cruelty persecuted the Christians living among his own people and raised many of the barbarians to the crown of martyrdom by putting them to death for their faith. There were many who, because they acknowledged Christ, had to flee to the territory of the Romans. They went, not apprehensively as if going to enemies, but with assurance as to brethren.

The Saxons, a people living on the shores of the Ocean in inaccessible marshes and dreaded for their bravery and rapidity of movement, planned a dangerous raid in full force against Roman possessions, but they were crushed by Valentinian in the very territories of the Franks.

Likewise, the Burgundians, a new enemy with a new name, numbering, it is said, more than eighty thousand armed men, settled on the banks of the Rhine. They had been stationed in fortresses in earlier times when the interior of Germany had been subjugated by Drusus and Tiberius, the adopted sons of Caesar. Later they united to form a great people. They took their name from their service, for the stations placed at frequent intervals along the frontier are commonly called *burgi*. That their power is imposing and destructive is attested even today in the Gallic provinces where their residence is now taken for granted. Nevertheless, through the providence of God they have all recently become Christians, embracing the Catholic faith and acknowledging obedience to our clergy, so that they live mild, gentle, and upright lives, regarding the Gauls not as their subjects but in truth as their Christian brethren...

Valentinian was succeeded as emperor of the West by his son Gratian, while Valens, the latter's uncle, ruled in the East. Gratian shared his throne with his brother Valentinian [II].

## Reign of Valens, a. 375-378

33. In the 1128th year from the founding of the City [a. 375], Valens, the thirty-ninth emperor, ruled for four years after the death of Valentinian [I], who alone had been able to make him blush for his impious deeds. Immediately, as if his shameless boldness knew no bounds, he made a law requiring military service of monks. These men were Christians who had given up pursuing secular matters in their various forms and were devoting themselves solely to the work of the Faith. The vast solitudes of Egypt and its stretches of sand, which were unfit for human use because of their aridity, barrenness, and the extreme danger from numerous serpents, were filled and inhabited at that time by great numbers of monks. Tribunes and their soldiers were sent there on a new type of persecution to drag away to other places the saintly and true soldiers of God. Many companies of saints suffered death there. As for the measures taken against the Catholic churches and orthodox believers throughout the various provinces under these and similar orders, let my decision to be silent be sufficient indication of their nature.

*Count Theodosius, father of the future emperor of the same name, crushed the revolt of Firmus in North Africa and, after receiving Christian baptism, was himself executed.*

Meanwhile the emperor Gratian, who was still a youth, saw countless multitudes of enemies invade the Roman domain. Relying on the power of Christ, he met them with far inferior forces and, in a battle at the Gallic town of Argentaria, straightway by a wonderful stroke of good fortune brought to an end a most formidable war. More than thirty thousand of the Alamanni, according to report, were killed there with but slight loss on the Roman side.

In the thirteenth year of the reign of Valens, that is in the short interval of time that followed the wrecking of the churches by Valens and his slaughtering of the saints throughout the East, that root of our miseries simultaneously sprouted a great many shoots. The Huns, a people long shut off by inaccessible mountains, broke out in sudden rage against the Goths and drove them in widespread confusion from their old homes. The Goths fled across the Danube and were received by Valens without a treaty of agreement. They did not even surrender their arms to the Romans, an act that might have made it easier to trust the barbarians. But the general Maximus by his unbearable avarice brought famine and injuries upon the Goths and drove them to arms and rebellion. After defeating an army of Valens, they overran Thrace and swept the whole country with fire, murder, and rapine. When Valens had left Antioch and was going to his doom in that ill-fated war, he was pricked with tardy remorse for his heinous sin and gave orders for the recall of the bishops and other dignitaries.

In the fifteenth year of his reign, Valens fought that lamentable battle in Thrace [at Adrianople, a. 378] against the Goths, who by that time were well prepared in the matter of military training, and who had an abundance of resources...The emperor himself, wounded by an arrow, turned to flight and was with difficulty brought to a cottage on a small farm. While he was hiding there the pursuing enemy came upon him. They set fire to the building, and Valens perished in the flames. In order that the punishment visited on him — this manifestation of divine wrath — might serve all the more as a dreadful example to posterity, he was not even given a common burial.

The wretched and obstinate heathen may find comfort in this one fact alone: these great disasters in Christian times and under Christian rulers (the ruin of the provinces, the destruction of the army, and the burning of the emperor) occurred all at once and bowed down the neck of the state already sore oppressed. This indeed grieves us much and is all the more lamentable for being so unprecedented. But how does it serve to comfort the pagans who can plainly perceive that in this case a persecutor of the churches was also punished? The one God handed on one faith and spread one church over all the world. It is this church that He beholds, that He loves, that He defends; and under whatever name a person conceals himself, he is an alien if he is not associated with this church, and an enemy if he attacks her. Let the heathen take what comfort they may in the suffering of the Jews and the heretics, but only let them confess that there is one God and that He is no respecter of persons as is most conclusively proven by the destruction of Valens. The Goths had petitioned through ambassadors that bishops be sent to them from whom they might learn the rule of the Christian faith. In fatal perverseness the emperor Valens sent teachers of the Arian doctrine, and the Goths continued to believe what they first learned concerning the basic principles of the faith. Therefore, by the just judgment of God Himself, Valens was burned alive by the very men who, through his action, will burn hereafter for their heresy.

## Reign of Gratian, a. 378-83

34. In the 1132nd year from the founding of the City, Gratian the fortieth emperor in succession from Augustus became emperor...Seeing the distressed and almost ruined condition of the state, he exercised the same foresight which led Nerva, in a former time, to choose the Spaniard Trajan, who restored the state. Gratian in his turn chose Theodosius [I, 379-395], likewise a Spaniard, invested him with the purple at Sirmium for the necessary work of reestablishing the government, and made him ruler of the East and of Thrace as well...

Theodosius believed that the state, which had been brought low by the wrath of God, would be restored by His mercy. Putting all his trust in the help of Christ, he attacked without hesitation those mighty Scythian peoples, which had been the dread of all earlier ages and had been avoided even by Alexander the Great, as Pompeius [Trogus] and Cornelius [Tacitus] declare. These peoples were equipped with Roman horses and arms, now that the Roman army had been destroyed, yet he defeated them, that is the Alans, Huns and Goths, in a series of great battles. He entered the city of Constantinople as a victor, and made a treaty with Athanaric, king of the Goths, so that he might not exhaust the small body of Roman troops by continual campaigning. Athanaric, however, died immediately after reaching Constantinople. Upon the death of their king, all the Gothic peoples, on seeing the kindness and bravery of Theodosius, submitted to Roman rule [a. 382]. At the same time the Persians voluntarily sent ambassadors to Theodosius at Constantinople and humbly begged for peace...

In the meantime, by subjugating the barbarian peoples in the East, Theodosius finally freed the Thracian provinces from the enemy. He made his son Arcadius associate emperor. The army in Britain proclaimed Maximus emperor against his will. Maximus was an energetic and able man and one worthy of the throne had he not risen to it by usurpation, contrary to his oath of allegiance. He crossed into Gaul where he treacherously killed the emperor Gratian [25 August 383], who, in his fright at the sudden invasion, was planning to go to Italy. He drove Gratian's brother, the emperor Valentinian, from Italy. The latter took refuge in the East with Theodosius, who received him with a father's affection and soon even restored him to his imperial dignity.

## Reign of Theodosius I, a. 384-395

35. In the 1138th year of the City, after Gratian had been killed by Maximus, Theodosius, the forty-first emperor, became ruler of the Roman world. He remained in office for eleven years. He had already reigned in the East for six years during Gratian's lifetime. The demands of justice and necessity persuaded him to engage in civil war, since, of the two imperial brothers, the blood of the one slain demanded vengeance and the misery of the other in exile pleaded for restoration to his former position. Theodosius therefore put his trust in God and hurled himself against the usurper Maximus with no advantage but that of faith, for he was inferior in every point of military equipment...Thus Theodosius crossed the undefended Alps without being noticed, much less opposed, by anyone, and arrived unexpectedly before Aquileia. His mighty enemy Maximus, a stern ruler who exacted taxes even from the savage Germanic peoples by the mere terror of his name, was surrounded, captured, and put to death without recourse to treachery and without a contest [28 August 388]. Valentinian, after receiving the imperium, attempted to gain control over Italy. On learning of the death of Maximus, Count Andragathius threw himself headlong from his ship into the sea and was drowned. Thus under God's guidance Theodosius gained a bloodless victory.

Observe how, under Christian rulers and in Christian times, civil wars are settled when they cannot be avoided. The victory was won, the city was stormed, the usurper was seized. And this is not half the story. Look elsewhere and see a hostile army vanquished, a count in the service of that usurper — he was more violent than the usurper himself — forced to take his own life, many ambuscades broken up or evaded, countless preparations rendered useless. Yet no one planned stratagems, no one drew up a line of battle, and, lastly, no one, if I may use the expression, even unsheathed his sword. A most formidable war was brought to a victorious conclusion without bloodshed and with the death of but two persons on the occasion of the victory itself. Now, to prevent anyone from regarding this as the result of chance, let me produce testimony to God's power, which orders and judges the universe, so that its revelation may either confound the objectors or force them to believe. I mention, therefore, a circumstance unknown to all and yet known to all. After this war in which Maximus was slain, many wars, both domestic and foreign, have indeed been the lot of Theodosius and his son Honorius up to the present day, as we all recollect, and yet almost all have ended either without bloodshed or, at least, with very little, as a result of a decisive victory due to divine influence.

After the destruction of Maximus and of his son Victor, whom Maximus had left among the Gauls as their emperor, Valentinian the Younger, now restored to his realm, passed over into Gaul. While living there peacefully in a country then tranquil, so the story goes, he was treacherously strangled to death at Vienne by his count Arbogast. Valentinian was hanged by a rope so that it might appear he had taken his own life.

Soon after the death of the Augustus Valentinian [a. 392], Arbogast ventured to set up the usurper Eugenius, choosing him as a figurehead on whom to bestow the imperial title, but intending to manage the government himself. Arbogast was a barbarian who excelled in spirit, counsel, bravery, boldness, and power. He gathered together from all quarters enormous forces as yet unconquered, intending to seize the sovereignty. He drew partly on the Roman garrisons and partly on the barbarian auxiliaries, in the one case by virtue of his power and in the other on account of his kinship. It is not necessary to dilate in words upon events that many have seen with their own eyes and of which they as spectators have a better knowledge. In every respect the career of Arbogast clearly shows that Theodosius was always victorious through the power of God. At the time when he was loyal to Theodosius, Arbogast, in spite of his own slender resources, captured the strongly supported Maximus. But when he clashed with Theodosius, though aided by the united strength of the Gauls and Franks and though also relying upon his devoted worship of idols, he was nevertheless defeated with great ease...

The moment that the forces came within fighting distance [6 September 394], an indescribably great windstorm suddenly began to blow violently into the faces of the enemy. The darts of our men flew through the air and were carried over a great distance, farther than any man could throw, and they fell scarcely anywhere without striking their mark. Furthermore, the force of the unabating gale now dashed the shields of the enemy so heavily against their own faces and breasts as to strike them repeatedly, now pressed their shields so close as to take away their breath, now tore away their shields so violently as to leave them unprotected, now held their shields so steadily against them as to force them backward. Even the weapons that they had hurled with all their might were caught by the wind and driven back to transfix the unfortunate throwers... Eugenius was captured and killed, and Arbogast destroyed himself by his own hand. Thus in this case too, the fires of civil war were quenched by the blood of two men, leaving out of account the ten thousand Goths, who, it is said, were sent ahead by Theodosius and destroyed to a man by Arbogast; for the loss of these was certainly a gain and their defeat a victory. I do not taunt those who disparage us. Let them point out a single war in the history of Rome undertaken from such conscientious and compelling motives, carried out with such divine good fortune, stilled with such merciful kindness, one in which the battle did not entail heavy losses nor the victory a bloody revenge...

## Reigns of Arcadius, a. 395-408, and Honorius, a. 395-423

36. In the 1149th year of the City, Arcadius Augustus, whose son Theodosius [II] now rules the East, and Honorius Augustus, his brother, by whom our state is now completely supported, occupied the forty-second place in the imperial line and began to exercise a joint sovereignty, but in different capitals. Arcadius lived for twelve years after his father's death, and, when he died, left the supreme power to his son Theodosius, who was still very young.

Meanwhile Count Gildo, who was in charge of Africa at the beginning of his brother's reign, revolted as soon as he learned that Theodosius had died. Induced by some sort of envy, according to some, he planned to add Africa to the districts of the Eastern Empire; according to another view, he was influenced by the belief that there would be little hope for the young rulers, since, except for them, hardly any young boy who inherited the throne had ever before reached full manhood. This, indeed, was almost an unparalleled instance in which youths, separated and forsaken, prospered under the guardianship of Christ on account of their own and their father's remarkable faith.

*Suppression of the rebellion in Africa.*

37. Meanwhile the emperor Theodosius the Elder had entrusted the care of his children and the direction of his two courts, respectively, to his two most powerful subjects, Rufinus in the East and Stilicho in the West. What each man did and what he attempted to do, the fates of each made plain. Rufinus, aspiring to the royal dignity for himself, brought in the barbarians; Stilicho, desiring it for his son, gave them support so that the needs of the state in the sudden crisis might veil his wicked aim. I say nothing of King Alaric and his Goths, often defeated, often surrounded, but always allowed to escape. I say nothing of those unhappy doings at Pollentia when the chief command was entrusted to the barbarian and pagan general Saul who wickedly profaned the most solemn days and holy Eastertide and who compelled the enemy, then withdrawing on account of religious scruples, to

fight. The judgment of God soon disclosed not only the power of His favor but also the demands of His vengeance, for although we conquered in fighting we were defeated in conquering. I say nothing of the many internecine conflicts between the barbarians themselves, when two divisions of the Goths, and then the Alans and Huns, destroyed one another in mutual slaughter.

Radagaisus, by far the most savage of all our enemies, past or present, inundated all Italy [a. 405] by a sudden invasion with an army reported to number more than two hundred thousand Goths. Aside from the fact of his own dauntless courage and the support of the vast multitude, he was a pagan and a Scythian, who, according to the custom of the barbarous tribes, had vowed the blood of the entire Roman race as an offering to his gods. Consequently, when he threatened the defenses of Rome, all the pagans in the City flocked together, saying that the enemy was powerful, not merely because of the size of his forces, but especially because of the aid of his gods. They also said that the City was forsaken and would soon perish because it had completely abandoned its gods and its sacred rites. Great complaints were raised everywhere. The restoration and celebration of sacrifices were at once discussed. Blasphemies were rife throughout the City, and the name of Christ was publicly loaded with reproaches as if it were a curse upon the times.

Since in a mixed people the pious deserve grace and the impious punishment, according to God's inscrutable judgment, it was deemed just to allow such enemies to chastise the altogether stubborn and refractory City with a scourge of unusual severity, but not to permit them to destroy everything indiscriminately. At that time there were roaming wildly through the Roman provinces two Gothic peoples, led by two powerful kings. One of these kings was a Christian and more like a Roman, a man, who, through the fear of God, as the event showed, inclined to spare men's lives. The other was a pagan, barbarian, and true Scythian, who in his insatiable cruelty loved not so much the fame or the rewards of butchery as he did slaughter itself. And this man had already reached the heart of Italy and was causing nearby Rome to shake with fright. If, then, he had been the chosen instrument of vengeance — the Romans feared him especially because he courted the favor of the gods with sacrifices — the slaughter would have been more unrestrained without effecting any reform. Thus the last error would have been worse than the first; for had they indeed fallen into the hands of a pagan and an idolater, not only would the remaining pagans have been firmly persuaded to restore idolatry, but the Christians would to their peril have become confused — the latter terrified by the warning, the former encouraged by this precedent. Hence God, the just steward of the human race, willed that the pagan enemy should perish and allowed the Christian enemy to prevail, in order that the pagan and blaspheming Romans might be thrown into confusion by the death of the one and punished by the invasion of the other. In particular, the holy faith and continence of the emperor Honorius, remarkable in a ruler, merited no small measure of divine mercy.

Against Radagaisus, our most savage enemy, God granted that the minds of our other enemies should be disposed to help us with their forces. Uldin and Sarus, leaders of the Huns and of the Goths, came to the aid of the Romans. But God did not allow the workings of His power to appear as the valor of men, particularly when they were our enemies. He smote Radagaisus with supernatural terror, drove him into the mountains of Fiesole, bottled up his two hundred thousand men — this number is the lowest estimate cited — without food or resource on a rough and arid ridge. Weighted down with apprehension, the band that had but lately found Italy too small was crowded upon one small summit, where it hoped to lie concealed. Why delay the tale? No army was arrayed for battle; no fury or fear prolonged the uncertainties of the fight; no killings were done; no blood was shed; nor finally was there that which is usually considered a reason for congratulations, namely, a loss in battle compensated by the fruits of victory. While our men were eating, drinking, and making merry, the enemy, so numerous and so savage, were worn out by hunger, thirst, and exhaustion. All this would matter little if the Romans did not know that the man whom they feared had been captured and subdued and if they did not see that idol worshipper, whose sacrifices they pretended to dread more than his arms, defeated without a battle, sent under the yoke, and exposed to their contempt as a prisoner in chains. So King Radagaisus secretly deserted his men, hoping to escape by himself, but he fell into the hands of our soldiers. He was captured by them, held for a while, and then put to death [23 August 406]. The Gothic captives are said to have been so numerous that droves of them were sold everywhere like the cheapest cattle for a gold coin apiece.

But God did not allow anything to be left of this people; for immediately all those who had been bought died, and what the hard bargainers had shamefully saved in price was mercifully spent on their burial. Thus ungrateful Rome, which now felt the indirect mercy of her God and Judge, not for the pardoning but for the checking of her bold idolatry, was also soon to suffer the wrath of God, although not in full measure on account of the pious remembrance of the saints, both living and dead. If by some chance she should repent in her bewilderment and learn faith through experience, she would be spared for a short space of time from the invasion of Alaric, a hostile but a Christian king.

38. Meanwhile Count Stilicho, who was sprung from the Vandals, that unwarlike, greedy, treacherous, and crafty race, thought it insufficient that he

had imperial power under the nominal emperor, and tried by every possible means to place upon the throne his own son Eucherius. According to common report, the latter had been planning the persecution of the Christians from the time when he was a boy and still a private citizen. Hence, when Alaric and the whole Gothic nation begged humbly and straightforwardly for peace on very favorable terms and also for some place to settle, Stilicho supported them by a secret alliance, but in the name of the state refused them the opportunity of either making war or peace, reserving them to wear down and to intimidate the state. Moreover, other nations irresistible in numbers and might who are now oppressing the provinces of Gaul and Spain (namely, the Alans, Sueves, and Vandals, as well as the Burgundians who were driven on by the same movement) were induced by Stilicho to take arms on their own initiative and were aroused when once their fear of Rome was removed. Stilicho's plan was to batter the Rhine frontier and strike against Gaul. This wretched man hoped that in this dangerous situation he could thereby wrest the imperial dignity from his son-in-law and give it to his son, and that it would be as easy to repress the barbarian nations as it was to arouse them. When the character of these crimes was openly revealed to the emperor Honorius and to the Roman army, the soldiers very properly mutinied and killed Stilicho, who, in order to clothe one boy with the royal purple, had imperiled the blood of the whole human race. Eucherius was also slain, who for the sake of gaining the favor of the pagans had threatened that he would celebrate the beginnings of his reign by the restoration of the temples and by the overthrow of the churches. Several accomplices also were punished for their wicked plots. Thus the churches of Christ and the devout emperor were freed as well as avenged with very little trouble and with the punishment of but a few persons. Therefore, after this great increase of blasphemies without any evidence of repentance, the final, long-impending doom overtook the City.

39. Alaric appeared before trembling Rome, laid siege, spread confusion, and broke into the City [24 August 410]. He first, however, gave orders that all those who had taken refuge in sacred places, especially in the basilicas of the holy Apostles Peter and Paul, should be permitted to remain inviolate and unmolested; he allowed his men to devote themselves to plunder as much as they wished, but he gave orders that they should refrain from bloodshed. A further proof that the storming of the City was due to the wrath of God rather than to the bravery of the enemy is shown by the fact that the blessed Innocent, the bishop of Rome, who at that time was at Ravenna, through the hidden providence of God, even as Lot the Just was withdrawn from the Sodomites, did not witness the destruction of the sinful populace.

While the barbarians were roaming through the City, one of the Goths, a powerful man and a Christian, chanced to find in a church building a virgin advanced in years who had dedicated herself to God. When he respectfully asked her for gold and silver, she declared with the firmness of her faith that she had a large amount in her possession and that she would bring it forth at once. She did so. Observing that the barbarian was astonished at the size, weight, and beauty of the riches displayed, even though he did not know the nature of the vessels, the virgin of Christ then said to him: "These are the sacred plate of the Apostle Peter. Presume, if you dare! You will have to answer for the deed. As for me, since I cannot protect them, I dare not keep them." The barbarian, stirred to religious awe through the fear of God and by the virgin's faith, sent word of the incident to Alaric. He ordered that all the vessels, just as they were, should be brought back immediately to the basilica of the Apostle, and that the virgin also, together with all Christians who might join the procession, should be conducted thither under escort. The building, it is said, was at a considerable distance from the sacred places, with half the city lying between. Consequently the gold and silver vessels were distributed, each to a different person; they were carried high above the head in plain sight, to the wonder of all beholders. The pious procession was guarded by a double line of drawn swords; Romans and barbarians in concert raised a hymn to God in public. In the sacking of the City the trumpet of salvation sounded far and wide and smote the ears of all with its invitation, even those lying in hiding. From every quarter the vessels of Christ mingled with the vessels of Peter, and many pagans even joined the Christians in making profession, though not in true faith. In this way they escaped, but only for a time, that their confusion might afterward be the greater. The more densely the Roman refugees flocked together, the more eagerly their barbarian protectors surrounded them. O sacred and inscrutable discernment of the divine judgment! O holy and saving river, which begins its course at a small house and, as it flows in its blessed channel to the abode of the saints, bears wandering and imperiled souls to the harbor of salvation by its pious power of drawing them to it! ...

The third day after they had entered the City, the barbarians departed of their own accord. They had, it is true, burned a certain number of buildings, but even this fire was not so great as that which had been caused by accident in the seven hundredth year of Rome. Indeed, if I review the conflagration produced during the spectacles of Nero, her own emperor, this later fire, brought on by the anger of the conqueror, will surely bear no comparison with the former, which was kindled by the wantonness of the prince. Nor do I need in a comparison of this sort to mention the Gauls, who, after burning and sacking the City, camped upon her ashes for almost an entire year. Moreover, to remove all doubt that the enemy were permitted to act in this manner in order to chastise the proud, wanton, and blasphemous City, it may be pointed out that her most magnificent sites, which the Goths were unable to set on fire, were destroyed at this time by lightning.

40. It was in the 1164th year of the City that Alaric forced his way into Rome. Although the memory of the event is still fresh, anyone who saw the numbers of the Romans themselves and listened to their talk would think that "nothing had happened," as they themselves admit, unless perhaps he were to notice some charred ruins still remaining. When the City was stormed, Placidia, the daughter of the princely Theodosius and sister of the emperors Arcadius and Honorius, was captured and taken to wife by Alaric's kinsman, as if she had been a hostage given by Rome as a special pledge, according to divine decree; thus, through her alliance with the powerful barbarian king, Placidia did much to benefit the state.

Meanwhile, two years before the taking of Rome, the nations that had been stirred up by Stilicho, as I have said, that is, the Alans, Sueves, Vandals as well as many others with them, overwhelmed the Franks, crossed the Rhine, invaded Gaul, and advanced in their onward rush as far as the Pyrenees. Checked for the time being by this barrier, they poured back over the neighboring provinces. While they were roaming wildly through Gaul, Gratian, a townsman of Britain, was set up in that island as a usurper. He was later slain and in his place Constantine, a man from the lowest ranks of the soldiery, was chosen simply from confidence inspired by his name and without any other qualifications to recommend him [a. 407]. As soon as he had seized the imperial dignity, he crossed over into Gaul where, repeatedly tricked by the deceptive alliances of the barbarians, he did much harm to the state. He sent magistrates into Spain where they were obediently received by the provinces. Thereupon two brothers named Didymus and Verinianus, who were young, noble, and wealthy, undertook not only to seize the power of the usurper, but to protect themselves and their country for the lawful emperor against both the usurper and the barbarians. The order of events made this clear; for every usurper swiftly matures his plans for power before he secretly seizes and publicly establishes it. Success lies in being seen with the diadem and the purple before being found out. These men, on the contrary, spent a long time merely in gathering the slaves from their own estates and in supporting them out of their private incomes. Taking no pains to conceal their purpose, they proceeded to the passes of the Pyrenees without alarming anyone.

To oppose them, Constantine sent into Spain his son Constans, who, shameful to say, had been transformed from a monk into a Caesar. With him Constantine sent certain barbarians, who had at one time been received as allies and drawn into military service, and who were called Honoriaci. They were the cause of the first misfortune that befell Spain. After killing the brothers who were trying to defend the Pyrenean Alps with their private forces, these barbarians received permission to plunder the plains of Pallantia as a reward for their victory. Later, after the removal of the faithful and efficient peasant guard, they were entrusted with the defense of the mountains just mentioned and their passes. These Honoriaci, having had a taste of plunder and being allured by its abundance, planned to secure both freedom from punishment for their crimes and a wider scope for their wickedness. Therefore they betrayed their watch over the Pyrenees, left the passes open, and so loosed upon the provinces of Spain all the nations that were wandering through Gaul and even joined them. There, after engaging for some time in bloody raids and inflicting serious damage upon people and property (for which they themselves are now sorry), and after a division had been made of what had been taken, they have remained in possession of their share to the present day.

41. There would be ample opportunity now for me to speak about these things if it were not that, according to all men, the secret voice of conscience speaks in the soul of each and every man. Spain has been invaded and has suffered slaughter and devastation, but this is nothing new. During the last two years, while the sword of the enemy raged, she endured no harsher treatment from the barbarians than that which she had formerly suffered under the Romans for two hundred years, or than that which she experienced when ravaged for almost twelve years by the Germans in the reign of the emperor Gallienus [a. 254-268]. Nevertheless, if a man knows himself, his acts, and his own thoughts, and fears the judgments of God, would he not admit that all his sufferings are just and even insignificant? Or, if he does not know himself and does not fear God, how can he maintain that his sufferings are not just and insignificant? In the light of these truths, God's mercy brought about the result with the same compassion with which it had formerly made the prediction, for in accordance with His incessant warning in His Gospel, "When they shall persecute you in one city, flee into another," whoever wished to go out and depart, found mercenaries, helpers, and defenders in the barbarians themselves. At that time they were voluntarily offering this help; and though after killing everybody they could have carried off everything, they demanded only a trifling payment as a fee for their services and for the transportation of loads. Many persons indeed did take this course. But those who did not believe the gospel of God, being obstinate, doubly obstinate if they had not even listened to it, did not flee the coming wrath and were justly overtaken and overwhelmed by a sudden attack of God's anger. Nevertheless, soon afterward, the barbarians came to detest their swords, betook themselves to the plow, and are affectionately treating the rest of the Romans as comrades and friends, so that now among them there may be found some

Romans who, living with the barbarians, prefer freedom with poverty to trib-ute-paying with anxiety among their own people.

Yet if the barbarians had been let loose upon the Roman lands simply so that the churches of Christ throughout the East and the West might be filled with crowds of Huns, Sueves, Vandals, and Burgundians, and with believers belonging to various and innumerable races, it would seem that the mercy of God ought to be praised and glorified, in that so many nations would be receiving, even at the cost of our own weakening, a knowledge of the truth which they could never have had but for this opportunity. For how does it harm a Christian who is longing for eternal life to be withdrawn from this world at any time or by any means? On the other hand, what gain is it to a pagan who, though living among Christians, is hardened against faith, if he drag out his days a little longer, since he whose conversion is hopeless is des-tined at last to die?

Because the judgments of God are inscrutable and we can neither know them all nor explain those we know, let me state briefly that the rebuke of our Judge and God, in whatever form it may take, is justly undergone by those who know and likewise by those who know not.

42. In the 1165th year of the City, the emperor Honorius, seeing that nothing could be done against the barbarians when so many usurpers were opposed to him, ordered that the usurpers themselves should first be destroyed. Count Constantius was entrusted with the command of this cam-paign. The state then finally realized what benefit it derived from having a Roman general at last and what ruinous oppression it had been enduring for years from its subjection to barbarian counts. Count Constantius then advanced with his army into Gaul and at the city of Arles besieged, captured, and slew the emperor Constantine [a. 411].

To take up at this point the succession of usurpers as briefly as possible, Constans, the son of Constantine, was killed at Vienne by Gerontius, his count, a worthless rather than an upright man, who replaced Constans by a certain Maximus. Gerontius himself, however, was killed by his own soldiers. Maximus, stripped of the purple and abandoned by the troops of Gaul, which were transferred to Africa and then recalled to Italy, is now a needy exile liv-ing among the barbarians in Spain. Later the tyranny set up by Jovinus, a man of high rank in Gaul, fell as soon as it had been established. His brother Sebastian elected to die as a usurper, for he was slain as he took office. What shall I say of the unlucky Attalus, for whom it was an honor to be slain among the usurpers, and a blessing to die? Alaric, who made, unmade, remade, and again unmade his emperor, doing all this in almost less time than it takes to tell, laughed at the farce and looked on at the comedy of the empire... Attalus, merely a figurehead of sovereignty, was taken by the Goths into Spain; and, having departed thence in a ship for some unknown destination, he was captured on the sea, brought to Count Constantius, and displayed before the emperor Honorius. His hand was cut off, but he was allowed to live.

Meanwhile Heraclian, who had been appointed count of Africa while Attalus was exercising his shadowy rule and who had vigorously defended Africa against the magistrates sent by the latter, obtained the consulship. Puffed up with pride at this honor, he married his daughter to Sabinus, his chamberlain, a man of keen intelligence and skillful enterprise, who might have been called wise if only he had devoted his mental powers to quiet pursuits. Heraclian sided with him when Sabinus was suspected of dangerous designs. After withholding the African grain supply for some time contrary to law, Heraclian set sail in person for Rome, accompanied by a huge fleet, the size of which was unheard of, at least in our times...No sooner had he disembarked with his troops on his way to the capital than he became terrified in an encounter with Count Marinus and took to flight. Seizing a ship, he returned alone to Carthage and was immediately killed by a band of soldiers [a. 413]. His son-in-law Sabinus fled to Constantinople, but was brought back some time afterward and condemned to exile.

This entire series of open usurpers or disobedient generals was, as I have said, overcome by the exceptional piety and good fortune of the emperor Honorius and by the great diligence and quickness of Constantius. Their success was deserved because in those days, by the order of Honorius and the aid of Constantius, peace and unity were restored to the Catholic Church throughout Africa, and the Body of Christ, which we ourselves constitute, was healed by the closing of the [Donatist] schism...

43. In the 1168th year of the City, Count Constantius, who was occupying the city of Arles in Gaul, drove the Goths from Narbonne, and by his vigorous actions forced them into Spain, especially by forbidding and completely cutting off the passage of ships and the importation of foreign merchandise. The Gothic peoples at that time were under the rule of King Athaulf [a. 410-15], who, after the capture of Rome and the death of Alaric, had succeeded him on the throne and had taken to wife, as I said, Placidia, the captive sister of the Emperor. This ruler, an earnest seeker after peace, as was often claimed and finally shown by his death, preferred to fight loyally for the emperor Honorius and to employ the forces of the Goths for the defense of the Roman state. For I have myself, while at the town of Bethlehem in Palestine, heard a certain man of Narbonne, who had served with distinction under Theodosius and who also was a pious, sensible, and serious person, tell the most blessed priest Jerome that he himself had been a very intimate friend of Athaulf at Narbonne, and that he had often heard what the latter, when in

good spirits, health, and temper, was accustomed to answer in reply to questions. It seems that at first he ardently desired to blot out the Roman name and to make all the Roman territory a Gothic empire in fact as well as in name, so that, to use the popular expressions, Gothia should take the place of Romania, and he, Athaulf, should become all that Caesar Augustus once had been. Having discovered from long experience that the Goths, because of their unbridled barbarism, were utterly incapable of obeying laws, and yet believing that the state ought not to be deprived of laws without which a state is not a state, he chose to seek for himself at least the glory of restoring and increasing the renown of the Roman name by the power of the Goths, wishing to be looked upon by posterity as the author of Rome's restoration, since he could not be its transformer. On this account he strove to refrain from war and to promote peace. He was helped especially by his wife, Placidia, who was a woman of the keenest intelligence and of exceptional piety; by her persuasion and advice he was guided in all measures leading to good government. While he was thus eagerly occupied in seeking and offering peace, he was slain at the city of Barcelona in Spain by the treachery, it is said, of his own men.

After him Segeric was proclaimed king by the Goths, and, although he likewise was inclined towards peace by the will of God, he too was nevertheless killed by his own men.

Thereupon Wallia succeeded to the kingdom [a. 415-18], having been chosen by the Goths to break the peace, but appointed by God to establish it. He was especially terrified by God's judgment, because a large band of Goths, provided with arms and ships, had tried to cross into Africa a year before but had been caught in a storm within twelve miles of the Strait of Gades and had perished miserably. He also remembered that disaster suffered under Alaric when the Goths had attempted to cross into Sicily but were shipwrecked and drowned within sight of their comrades. These fears caused him to conclude a very favorable peace with the emperor Honorius giving hostages of the highest rank; he restored Placidia, whom he had treated with decency and respect, to her imperial brother. To ensure the security of Rome he risked his own life by taking over the warfare against the other peoples that had settled in Spain and subduing them for the Romans. However, the other kings, those of the Alans, the Vandals, and the Sueves, had made a bargain with us on the same terms, sending this message to the emperor Honorius: "Be at peace with us all and receive hostages of all; we struggle with one another, we perish to our own loss, but we conquer for you, indeed with permanent gain to your state, if we should both perish." Who would believe these things if they were not proven by the facts? Thus it is that we are informed by frequent and trustworthy messages that warfare among the barbarian nations is now being carried on daily in Spain and that much blood is being shed on both sides; especially is it reported that Wallia, the king of the Goths, is intent upon bringing about peace. In view of these things I am ready to allow Christian times to be blamed as much as you please, if you can only point to any equally fortunate period from the foundation of the world to the present day. My description, I think, has shown no more by words than by my guiding finger, that countless wars have been stifled, many usurpers destroyed, and the most savage peoples checked, confined, incorporated, or annihilated with little bloodshed, no real struggle, and almost without loss. It remains for our detractors to repent of their endeavors, to blush on seeing the truth, and to believe, to fear, to love, and to follow the one true God, who can do all things and all of whose acts (even those that they have thought evil) they have found to be good.

I have set forth with the help of Christ and according to your bidding, most blessed father Augustine, the passions and the punishments of sinful men, the tribulations of the world, and the judgments of God, from the Creation to the present day, a period of five thousand six hundred and eighteen years, as briefly and as simply as I could, but separating Christian times from the former confusion of unbelief because of the more present grace of Christ. Thus I now enjoy the sure reward of my obedience, the only one that I have a right to enjoy; for the quality of my little books, you who asked for this record will be responsible. If you publish them, they must be regarded favorably by you; if you destroy them, they must be regarded unfavorably.

# CHAPTER THREE

# THREE GALLIC COURTIERS AND POETS:
# THOUGHTS ON LIFE, LOVE, AND
# PATRIOTISM

## A. AUSONIUS OF BORDEAUX

*Ausonius was born of modest background in Bordeaux, the capital of Aquitania secunda, ca. 310. He married well, but his wife Sabina, for whom he expressed great affection, died quite young ca. 343 in her twenty-eighth year; he never remarried. After practising some law and teaching in the famous school of his native city, he was called to the imperial court in Trier sometime in the 360s to be the tutor of Gratian, the son of Emperor Valentinian I (a. 364-75). Imperial service led to a series of prestigious positions: quaestor, praetorian prefect of the Gauls, praetorian prefect of Italy and Africa, and consul in 379. His friends and relations also benefited greatly from his political influence, but this was on the wane after his consulship. He weathered the storm of Magnus Maximus's usurpation (a. 383-88) and, retiring to Bordeaux, died sometime after 393. He was a Christian.*

*Ausonius was the author of a wide range of poetry. "Nothing is too mean for his verse; anything that scanned was suitable," is how his most recent editor describes his tastes. Though Ausonius tells us much about the social and intellectual milieu in which he lived, the most intriguing subject of his poetry is often the poet himself.*

Source: *Ausonius*, ed. and trans. Hugh G. Evelyn White, 2 vols. (Cambridge, MA./London, 1919-21). I have revised and modernized the translation, using the edition of R.P.H. Green, *The Works of Ausonius* (Oxford, 1991), and have included a few pieces that White left in the original Latin. In the case of the epigrams, the number references are those of White followed by those of Green in parentheses.

## 10. *A RANKING OF FAMOUS CITIES*, ca. 390

*The Roman Empire was made up of cities, which were the focus of patriotism and the seats of local government. When imperial structures eventually broke down and were replaced, the city remained the foundation of the kingdoms that followed Roman rule in Gaul. In Roman times and later the city was not only the urban area but also the dependent territory and its people.*

*In this famous poem, written near the end of his life, Ausonius sets out to rank renowned cities, whose claim to prominence might depend on their former glories as well as their current importance. There is no mistaking that the poem was written by a Gaul. The attempt at ranking is not very rigorous after the mid point in the list, but the main points in the series in any case are the first and last: Rome and Bordeaux.*

## Rome

First among cities, the home of gods, is golden Rome.

## Constantinople and Carthage

Carthage yields precedence in rank to Constantinople, but will not stand a full step lower; for she scorns to be counted third, yet dares not hope for second place, which both have held. One has the advantage in her ancient wealth, the other in her new-born prosperity: the one has seen her day, the other is now rising and by the loftiness of new achievements eclipses old-time renown, forcing Elissa to give place to Constantine. Carthage reproaches the gods, now full of shame, if this time also she must give place, having scarcely brooked the pre-eminence of Rome.

Let ancient fortune settle your jealousies. Be off now as equals, mindful finally that it was through the power of the gods you both changed your limited influence and your names — when one of you was Byzantine Lygos and the other, Punic Byrsa.

## Antioch and Alexandria

*In Daphne, near Antioch, there was a famous laurel grove containing a temple of Apollo.*

Third would be Antioch, the home of Phoebus's laurel, if Alexander's settlement were willing to be placed fourth: both hold the same rank. Frenzied ambition also drives these two to rival each other in vices: each is disordered with her mob and half-crazed with the riots of her frantic populace. One, fertile and secure, excels because she has the Nile for a bulwark and is located deep in a sheltered site; the other, because she stands confronting the faithless Persians.

The both of you, too, be off now as equals and uphold the Macedonian name. Great Alexander founded one of you; while the other claims Seleucus whose birthmark was an anchor, the branded likeness of which is customarily the sure token of his lineage; for through the whole line of his successors this natal sign has run.

## Trier (Treveris)

*An imperial residence since the time of Constantine.*

Long has Gaul, mighty in arms, yearned to be praised, as does the imperial city of the Treveri, which, though right next to the Rhine, reposes unalarmed as if in the bosom of deep profound peace, because she feeds, because she clothes and arms the forces of the Empire. Her broad walls stretch forward over a spreading hill; the bounteous Moselle glides past, her current peaceful, carrying merchandise brought from afar from all kinds of lands.

## Milan

At Milan also all things are wonderful, with an abundance of wealth, countless stately houses, men naturally eloquent, and customs cheerful; then, there is the beauty of the site, enlarged by a double wall; the Circus, her people's joy; the wedge-shaped mass of the enclosed theater; the temples; the imperial citadels; the wealthy mint; and the quarter renowned under the title of the Herculean Baths. All her colonnades are adorned with marble statuary and her walls are set round her circumference like a rampart. All these structures, rivals, as it were, in the vast masses of their workmanship, are excellent; nor does the close proximity of Rome humble them.

## Capua

*The historical references are to the Second Punic War.*

Nor shall I leave unsung Capua, mighty in the expanse of its fields and fruits, in its luxuries, wealth, and earlier renown, who, despite changes in fortune, relied on her prosperity and knew not how to keep the mean. Now she, once rival, is subject to Rome; now she keeps faith. Once she was faithless, when, undecided whether to flout or court the senate, she dared to hope for magistrates chosen under Campanian auspices, and that, with one consul from among her sons, she might take up the empire of half the world. But she attacked the mistress of the world, the mother of Latium, trusting not in leaders who wore the toga. Sworn to Hannibal's allegiance, she was tricked and, though seeming to be mistress, passed foolishly into slavery to a foe, so that, soon, they were driven to their fall by the failings of them both, and came to ruin, the Carthaginians through luxury, the Campanians through pride. Never does arrogance find a firm-fixed throne! That city, with her power and might of wealth, once a second Rome, her heights adorned with just as lofty peaks, was thrust backwards and scarce can manage to keep eighth place.

## Aquilea

*The Maximus referred to is Magnus Maximus the usurper, who was responsible for Gratian's death (a. 383) and later met his end at the hands of Theodosius at Aquilea in 388. Rutupiae (Richborough) is in Britain.*

This was not your place, but, raised of late by good service, you shall be named ninth among famous cities, Aquilea, colony of Italy, facing toward the mountains of Illyria and most famous for your walls and harbor. But you are even more distinguished because in quite recent days Maximus, the former sutler, posing as a soldier, chose you, after five years had passed, to receive his late expiation. Happy were you, the glad witness of so great a triumph, who punished with Ausonian Mars the Rutupian brigand.

## Arles

Two-fold Arles, open your harbors with a gracious welcome. Arles, the little Gallic Rome, to whom Martian Narbonne, to whom Vienne, rich in Alpine peasants, is neighbour, divided by the flowing water of the headlong Rhône in such a way that you make your central street a bridge of boats. There, enriching other peoples and towns, you take in, but do not hinder, the merchandise of the Roman world enjoyed by Gaul and the broad heartland of Aquitaine.

## Seville (Hispalis)

*At this time Seville may have been the headquarters of the vicarius, the deputy praetorian prefect of the Gauls. The notable omission in this subsidiary Spanish list is Merida (Emerita). The comment on Braga suggests a good deal of ignorance on Ausonius's part. Only Seville is being ranked.*

After these cities, you shall be celebrated, Hispalis, a Spanish name, famous to my ears; a river on the way to the sea flows by you. To you all Spain sends off her magistrates. Not Cordova, not Tarragona with its strong citadel contends with you, nor wealthy Braga, lying proudly in her bay beside the sea.

## Athens

*The references are to the mythological and legendary history of early Athens.*

Now let us also mention Athens, with earth-born ancestors, the stronghold for which Pallas and Consus [Poseidon] once contended, and to where the

44

peace-bearing olive tree first belonged. Hers is the pristine glory of eloquence in the Attic style. From there a Grecian band went abroad and
throughout the peoples of Ionia and the Achaean world poured into a hundred cities.

## Catana and Syracuse

*More legendary and mythological references. The brothers saved their parents from the
fires of Aetna; Arethusa was a nymph pursued by the river God Alpheus.*

Who could be silent about Catana? Or about four-fold Syracuse? — the former renowned for the devotion of the fire-scathed brethren, the latter
embracing the marvelous fount [of Arethusa] and river [Alpheus]: there, flowing beneath the salt waves of the Ionian Sea, they join in fellowship their
sweet waters in the abode which pleases them, exchanging there the kisses of
their waters untainted by the brine.

## Toulouse

*The four cities are suburbs, probably within Toulouse's ample walls.*

Never will I leave unmentioned Toulouse, my nurse, girt round with a vast
circuit of brick walls, by whose side the lovely stream of the Garonne glides
past, home of uncounted people, lying hard by the barriers of the snowy
Pyrenees and the pine-clad Cevennes, between the peoples of Aquitaine and
the land of Iberia. Lately Toulouse has poured forth four cities, but feels none
of the losses of a drained populace, enfolding in her bosom as inhabitants all
whom she has brought forth.

## Narbonne

*Narbonne's subjugation to the Romans went back to 121 B.C.*

You shall not be left out, Martian Narbonne, by whose name *Provincia*
(Provence), once extending over a vast realm, held the right to rule over
numerous inhabitants. Where the Allobroges encroach upon the regions of
the Sequani and the Alpine peaks shut out Italy, where the Iberians are parted
from you by Pyrenean snows, where the Rhône sweeps headlong from its sire
[Lake] Lemannus, and the Cevennes press deep into the countryside of
Aquitaine, right on to those rustic names, the Volcae-Tectosages — all this
was Narbonne. You were the first in Gaul to raise up the fasces of the
Romans under an Italian proconsul.

What shall I tell of your harbors, mountains, and lakes? What of your people with their various forms of dress and speech? Or what of that temple of Parian marble, once yours, so vast in bulk that ancient Tarquin would not have scorned it, nor again Catullus, nor even the last to raise the golden roofs of the Capitol, Caesar himself? You the merchandise of the eastern sea and the Spanish main enriches, as do fleets of the Libyan and Sicilian deeps, and whatever is conveyed by various routes on river and sea: from everywhere in the world comes a laden ship destined for your shores.

## Bordeaux

*Euripus was a famous channel between Boeotia and Euboea; the word came to mean channel or aqueduct. Some commentators regard Ausonius as expressing at the end a loyalty that is divided not dual.*

Long have I censured my unpatriotic silence in not mentioning among the foremost cities you, my country, famed for your wine, rivers, famous men, the virtue and the intelligence of your people, and your senate of nobles, as if I were of a mind that you are a little town and I hesitated to handle praises that were undeserved. I am not ashamed of this, for mine is neither a barbarous land on the Rhine, nor an icy home on frozen Haemus.

Bordeaux is my native land, where skies are temperate and mild and gentle well-watered lands are expansive; where spring is long and winter warm with the new sun, and the rivers are tidal, their flood foaming beneath vine-clad hills, mimicking the sea's ebb and flow.

The square shape of her walls rises so high with lofty towers that the tops pierce the floating clouds. Within the city, you may marvel at diverse streets and the layout of the houses, at how the broad avenues are true to their name (*plateae*), and then at the gates facing each other along intersecting streets; and in the midst of the city, you shall behold in the channel of the spring-fed stream, when father Ocean fills it with his flowing tide, "a whole sea gliding onward with its fleets [Aeneid X 269]."

What shall I recount of that fountain, covered with Parian marble, foaming in the strait of its Euripus? How deep its waters! How swelling the stream! With what force does its headlong course plunge through the twelve openings of its extended brim, never failing to meet the countless needs of the inhabitants? This would you have longed to get your hands on with your forces, King of the Medes, when streams were consumed and rivers failed, and to carry waters of this source through strange cities, you who were accustomed to drink before all others only the water of the Choaspes river.

Hail, fountain with source unknown, holy, refreshing, transparent, unfailing, sparkling, deep, gurgling, clear and shady! Hail, guardian deity of our city, of whom we may drink health-giving draughts, you are Divona in the language of the Celts, a fountain added to the gods! Neither Aponus in taste, nor Nemausus in glassy sheen is more pure, nor with its sea-like surge is Timavus more plentiful.

Let this last task conclude the muster of famous cities. And while illustrious Rome leads the list, so, at the other end let Bordeaux establish her place, there being a twofold precedence. Bordeaux is my home country (*patria*); but Rome surpasses all home countries. I love Bordeaux, Rome I venerate; in the former I am a citizen, in both I am a consul; in Bordeaux was my cradle, in Rome my curule chair.

## II. *BISSULA*

*Bissula was the name of a Suebian captive, freed and raised in Ausonius's household. She may have been captured in 368, when Ausonius and the prince Gratian accompanied Valentinian I on an expedition against the Germans. Ausonius dedicated a collection of little poems about her to his friend Paulinus. Only the introductory material and four relatively short pieces are extant. There is no clear indication of the date of the poems; Bissula seems to have been thoroughly Romanized, however, by the time of their composition.*

*I give the preface to the general reader and two of the poems. Thymele of the preface was a mime mentioned by Martial and Juvenal, an allusion that might suggest that the poems were a little more risqué than the extant pieces suggest. Cratinus, which is an emendation, was an old comic poet famous for his drunkenness. The ellipsis stands in place of a corrupt phrase and likely a lacuna.*

### 2

Reader of this little work of unpolished verse, don't furrow your brows at it. Screw up your face when you ponder weighty poems: I follow Thymele. Bissula is the subject of this verse, and like Cratinus I advise you to have a drink first. I don't write anything for those fasting. If anyone reads me after a few drinks, he will be wise. But he would be wiser still to sleep and think this is a dream sent to him.

### 3

Bissula, born and bred across the chilly Rhine, Bissula, privy to the rising of the Danube, made captive but set free, she is mistress of the pleasures of him whose spoil of war she was. Lacking a mother, in need of a nurse ... and, being immediately freed before experiencing servitude, she felt not the disgrace of her lot and of a lost homeland. Though transformed by Roman blessings, still she remains in appearance German, blue-eyed and fair haired. Speech and looks create quite different impressions of the girl: the latter proclaim her a child of the Rhine, the former a child of Rome.

4

Pleasure, delight, sport, love, and desire! A barbarian, but as a fosterling you surpass Roman girls. Bissula, a crude little name for a delicate lass and a little uncouth to those not used to it, but charming to your master.

## 12. FROM THE *EPIGRAMS*

*Epigrams were short pungent poems on a single theme, incident, or person. Roman epigram had a tendency to run to satirical, comical, and amatory topics. Ausonius's contribution to the genre is heavily influenced by Greek models, but his coarse jokes, combined with romantic and moralizing sentimentalism, and just a touch of cruelty, are Roman enough and a reflection of his own milieu. Such sentiments seem more interesting than those of the mythological and imperial commonplaces I have left out.*

*There is no sure way to date the epigrams. Individual pieces may have been composed at different times; they seem meant to refer to different periods in Ausonius's life. I have added headings.*

### Agathocles's Roots (2 [9])

*Agathocles was ruler of Sicily in the decades around 300 B.C.*

There's a tale about King Agathocles dining off earthen plates and often loading his sideboard with Samian ware; all the while he would be laying out rustic trays with jewelled cups, and so mingling wealth and poverty together.

To one who asked the reason, he responded, "I who am king of Sicily was born a potter's son."

Bear good fortune modestly, if you are someone who from a lowly place rises suddenly to riches.

### The Learned Philomusus (7 [44])

*Philomusus is a stock name.*

Because your library is stuffed with books you bought, do you think you are learned and scholarly Philomusus? By this measure, were you to lay up strings, plectra and lyres, having purchased everything, tomorrow you would be a cithara player.

## The Poet's Friend Galla (34 [14])

I used to say to you, "Galla, we are growing older. Time flies. Make use of your youth. A virtuous lass is an old maid."

You scorned this. Age has crept upon you unperceived and you cannot call back the days that are gone. Now you are sorry and complain that either then you did not have the desire or now you no longer have your former beauty.

Yet give me your embrace and bring together joys forgotten. Give for me to enjoy, even if not what I want, but what I wanted.

## Pergamus, a Runaway Scribe (36 [16])

*The runaway is a slave. The brand would read FUG, for fugitivus.*

As lazy a scribe as you are a sluggish runner, Pergamus, you ran away and were caught on the first lap. For that reason, you have felt letters branded on your face, Pergamus, and what your right hand neglected, your brow endures.

## Myron and Laïs (38 [18])

*The source for this is probably Greek. Laïs was famous as a prostitute and Myron renowned as a sculptor in fifth-century Greece.*

Grey-haired Myron asked to spend the night with Laïs and was refused outright. He sensed the reason and dyed his white head with black soot. Myron, with the same face but not the same hair, requested what he had requested before.

Comparing his features and his hair, and not thinking it him, but noting the resemblance (or perhaps recognizing him and wishing to play a joke), Laïs addressed the artful Myron like this: "Fool, why do you ask what I have refused? I have already rejected your father."

## A Wife's View of The Poet (39 [19])

Whenever my wife would read in my verse the names of those characters from dirty stories, Laïs and Glyceras, she said I was kidding around and pretending to find pleasure there as a joke. Such is her faith in my decency.

## The Poet's Wife (40 [20])

Wife, let us live as we have lived and hold on to the names we first adopted in the marriage bed, and let the time never come that age changes us. But I shall be your young man and you shall be my girl.

Though I should outlive Nestor, and you outstrip in years Deïphobe of Cumae, may we not experience the meaning of ripe old age. It is better to know the rewards of time than to count the years.

## A Rich Phony (45 [26])

A certain fellow proud of his wealth and swollen with arrogance, noble only in words, scorns the famous names of the present age; snatching at ancient genealogies, he announces that Mars, Remus, and the founder Romulus are his own ancestors. He has them woven into his garments of silk. He engraves them on weighty silver plate, and paints them in encaustic on the threshold of his entrance-ways and on the panels of his halls. I do believe he doesn't know who his father was. As for his mother, she was a whore.

## Three's Company (59 [43])

"Three in one bed: two submit to debauchery, and two perpetrate it."

"By my reckoning, there are four."

"You missed the point. Ascribe single offenses to the ones at each end, and count two for the one in the middle, because he does it and submits to it."

## Pythagoras's View of a Late Pedophile (77 [73])

*The poem alludes to the Pythagorean doctrine of the transmigration of souls. Lucilius was a Roman poet who died 102/1 B.C.; the line in which his name appears is uncertain. A hippocamel is an invented creature.*

"Pythagoras, Euphorbus's son, who renews the seeds of nature and assigns souls brought back from death to new bodies, tell me, what will become of Marcus, who has now felt fate's final stroke, if he returns again to live in the world?"

"Who's Marcus?"

"One lately said to prey upon children; he has debauched the entire male sex, a bum-digging laborer in the service of a twisted Venus, a ... pederast, as the poet Lucilius says."

"Not a bull or a mule shall he be, not a hippocamel, or a goat or a ram. No, he shall be a dung beetle."

## Castor and His Wife (78 [74])

*The word* castor *means beaver, an animal thought to have no testicles.*

When Castor wanted to lap up the middle parts of men and was ill-provided with a crowd like this at home, he discovered that for a cocksucker no groin goes to waste: he started to lick the parts of his own wife.

## Crispa (88 [88])

Some people say that you are misshapen, Crispa. That I know not, for, if in my judgment you are beautiful, that is enough. Indeed, since jealousy is joined to love, I also wish that you seem ugly to others, and comely to me.

## The Ideal Mistress (89 [89])

As a mistress, I would have someone who would lightly start quarrels, and she would make no effort to talk like a chaste woman. Pretty, bold, with a ready hand, someone who would take blows and return them, and, if beaten, would take refuge in kisses. For if she does not behave like this, but, chaste and virtuous, acts modestly, she will be — I shudder to say it — a wife.

## A Lawyer with His Own Tastes in the Law (92 [99])

*This poem mentions old Roman statutes of the late Republic and early Empire: the* lex Papia *which encouraged marriage; the* lex Julia *which punished husbands who acquiesced in the adultery of their wives; the* lex Scantinia *against homosexuality, and the* lex Titia *by which provincial magistrates appointed guardians for orphaned minors.*
*The term 'half a man'* (semivir), *appearing here and below (94), is applied by Sidonius Apollinaris to Valentinian III (cf.* **34 a***).*

A lawyer who had an adulterous wife liked the Papian statute, but didn't much care for the Julian.
Why this difference, you ask?
Being half a man himself and fearing the Scantinian statute, he had no fear of the Titian.

## Suspicious Toiletries (93 [100])

*Although the meaning of Clazomenae should be evident, the reason why this Greek town should stand for this particular part of the body is not.*

When you make your groin smooth with a warm depilatory, this is the reason: smooth parts excite shorn whores. But when you soak your anus, plucking out the hairs and rubbing your innermost Clazomenae with pumice, the reason remains hidden: unless it is because pathic submission longs for the vice that looks out in two directions, and you are a woman from the back and a man from the front.

### For Love and Money (94 [101])

*Zoïlus is probably a stock name.*

Half a man as you are, Zoïlus, you have taken a fornicator for a wife. How much trade will be conducted by both of you at home, when the fellow who grinds you pays out to your wife and the adulterer of your wife pays out to you as much as those caught in the act put out to compensate sexual offenses! But lust, which now seems profitable to you, will have its expenses, when age creeps up. Mercenary sluts, whom that procuress, youth, now keeps generous, will begin to sell their services.

## 13. FROM THE *NUPTIAL CENTO*: THE DEFLOWERING OF THE BRIDE

*A Cento was a form of poem composed of fragments, mainly half lines, drawn from other poems, brought together to make a new and harmonious composition; Virgil's* Aeneid *served as the principal source of Ausonius's effort, supplemented by the Georgics and Eclogues. The amusing attraction of the work depends on the ingenuity with which poetic elements can be borrowed from their original context and made to serve a new situation. It was written at the command of Valentinian I, "a learned man, in my opinion," says Ausonius, and one who had himself tried his hand at a similar piece and wanted some competition.*

*Ausonius's Cento is a description of a wedding, beginning with the marriage feast and ending with the couple's entry into the bridal chamber and the deflowering of the bride. Although the Cento originated at court, in its final form it was addressed to Ausonius's friend in Bordeaux, Paulinus, some time later. Gratian's wedding in 374 is a possible occasion for the original composition, though there is no direct allusion to the prince in the poem.*

*Modern opinion of the Cento tends not to be high, not only because of the artificiality of the genre, but also because of the poem's closing section, which is translated here. Hugh Evelyn White, Ausonius's English translator, thought the Cento a "literary outrage," unredeemed by its ingenuity and "disgraced by the crude and brutal coarseness of its closing episode," which he left untranslated. The most recent editor wonders if the violence of the conclusion was a concession to Valentinian's tastes. Ausonius was quite prepared to see its publication.*

*The allegory, which begins as martial, is hardly consistent; the reference to 'ribs' is musical, referring to the curving arms of the lyre supporting crossbar and strings, and there are also nautical and racing allusions. The subject of the last line of the Deflowering is the bride, to judge by its Virgilian source. After the little poetic tag that follows it, Ausonius reverts to prose.*

*The Digression, which is in prose, begins after the bride has requested that the marriage remain unconsummated for the first night only.*

## Digression

So far, to suit chaste ears, I have wrapped the mystery of wedlock in a veil of roundabout and indirect expression. But since the concourse at a wedding loves Fescennine songs, and also that well-known form of merriment furnishes an old-established precedent for freedom of speech, the remaining secrets of bedchamber and couch will also be divulged in a selection from the same author [Virgil], so that I have to blush twice over, since I make Virgil also immodest. Those of you who so choose, set here and now a term to your reading: leave the rest to the curious.

## The Deflowering

After they engaged in the darkness of the lonely night and Venus herself provided the inclination, they try out unusual forms of combat. He lifts himself up aroused, trying many a stratagem in vain, attacking the mouth and face and hotly pressing foot to foot. The deceiver heads for deeper regions; while their feet are intertwined, he snatches from his thigh his rod lying hidden in his robe, reddened with blood-coloured elderberries and vermilion, an awful monster, misshapen, huge, deprived of light, its head bared, and presses in on his trembling foe. In a recess, to which leads a narrow pathway, there is a fiery palpitating fissure; from its darkness it gives forth a pestilential vapour. It is not right for the pure to cross its impious threshold. The pit here is fearful, such is the vapor pouring forth from its black throat and reaching the nostrils with its scent. Here the youth advances along a known road, and, leaning from above and exerting all his strength, impels his knobby spear still unstripped of its bark. It lodges and, driven deep, drinks the virgin's blood. The cavities sound and give forth a groan. Dying, she pulls at the weapon with her hand, but between the bones the point remains lodged deep within the living wound. Three times she rises up, resting on her elbow. Three times she falls back upon the bed. Undaunted he remains. There is no delay or rest. He remains fixed firmly on his course, never letting go, and keeping his eyes uplifted to the stars. Back and forth along the road he goes many times, and, as the womb reverberates, pierces through the ribs and strikes with his ivory plectrum. Now with the course almost complete, as they approach the very end exhausted, rapid panting then convulses their limbs and parched mouths. Streams of sweat flow everywhere. Bloodless she sinks, fluid trickling down from her groin.

> With this off-colour page
> Be satisfied, dear Paul,
> Nothing else do I ask
> But laughter, that's all

But when you have done reading, stand by me to face those who, as Juvenal says, "put on the airs of Curius and live like the Bacchanals," in case, perhaps, they picture my life in the colors of my poem. As Martial said, "Foul is my page, but honorable is my life." And let them remember, learned as they are, that Pliny, a most honorable man, shows prurience in his verse, rigor in his private life; that Sulpicia's little work is wanton, her outlook prim; that Apuleius in life was a philosopher, in his epigrams a lover....*A list of more authors, including Virgil, follows.*

And if the primly-draped propriety of certain folk condemns anything in my playful piece, let them know that it is taken out of Virgil. So anyone who disapproves of this farce of mine should not read it, or once he has read it, let him forget it, or if he has not forgotten it, let him pardon it. For as a matter of fact, it is the story of a wedding, and, like or dislike it, the rites are exactly as I have described.

# B. RUTILIUS CLAUDIUS NAMATIANUS

## 14. FROM *HIS VOYAGE HOME*

*Rutilius was a native of Gaul, very likely Toulouse. He held high positions under Honorius, including those of master of the offices in 412, and urban prefect of Rome in 414. His father before him had held important offices including the urban prefecture.*

*Rutilius's only surviving work is the famous* His Voyage Home, *in which he describes his journey back to Gaul along the Italian coast in the fall of 417. The poem is more than a description of his itinerary but an occasion for discourses on a variety of subjects. It survives as a fragment, breaking off at the beginning of Book II. Rutilius may be the patron of the playwright who wrote* Querolus *(see **30**). Most commentators regard him as a pagan.*

Source: *De Reditu suo sive Iter Gallicum*, ed. Ernst Doblhoffer, 2 vols. (Heidelberg, 1972-77). Translation by A.C. Murray.

### a. In Praise of Rome

*Before Rutilius departs, he praises Rome. The city had been sacked in 410 by the Goths, who had now moved on to Gaul. The term Assyrian applies to the Persians and the Seleucid kings of Syria.*

Listen, fairest queen of your world, Rome, you who have been received among the starry heavens, listen, mother of mortals and mother of gods, in whose temples we are not far from heaven. We sing of you and always shall as long as the fates permit it. No one can be safe who is forgetful of you. Profane forgetfulness shall sooner obliterate memory of the sun than shall the honor with which you are held depart from our heart. Like the sun's rays, you spread your benefits as far as the rising swells of the encircling Ocean. Phoebus, who holds all together, revolves for you; in your domains his horses arise, and in your domains he also puts them away. Libya has not stopped you with its burning sands; the Bear armed with her icy coldness has not driven you back. As far as living nature stretches from pole to pole, there the land makes way for your strength. You have provided disparate peoples with a single homeland (*patria*). Under your dominion, captivity has made those who were unjust better. And by allowing the conquered to share in your own law, you have made a city of what was once the world.

We attest that your descent is to be traced from Venus and Mars — one the mother of the descendants of Aeneas and the other the father of the descendants of Romulus. Forbearance in victory tempers armed might; the character of both divinities are expressed in your conduct. From this comes that noble pleasure you take in struggling and in proffering clemency: it conquers those whom it has feared; and loves those whom it has conquered.

She who discovered the olive [i.e. Minerva] is cherished, and so too are he who found wine [i.e. Bacchus] and the boy who first plowed the earth [i.e. Triptolemus]. Because of the healing art of Paean [i.e. Apollo], altars have been raised to medicine; [Hercules] the descendant of Alceus was made a god as well because of his fame. You also, who have embraced the world with law-giving triumphs, make all things to live by a common compact.

Every corner of the Roman world celebrates you, goddess, and bears your peaceful yoke with necks that are free. All the stars which maintain their perpetual motion never looked upon an empire more fair. Are the military feats of the Assyrians at all comparable? The Medes subdued their own neighbours; the great kings of the Parthians and the tyrants of the Macedonians dictated terms to each other at various times. It is not that you had more bodies and souls at your disposal when you were born, but more purpose and judgment. Through wars waged with just cause and by peace imposed without arrogance, your celebrated glory achieved tremendous power. That you rule is less significant than that you deserve to rule: by what you have done you transcend mighty deeds...

*The poet recounts Rome's recoveries from defeat from the Gallic invasion of 390 B.C. to the Punic wars. The date given below is calculated from one of the traditional dates for the founding of the city of Rome.*

Extend forth the laws that shall prevail throughout the ages of Rome and alone fear not the distaffs of the fates, though you are in your one thousand one hundred and sixty-ninth year [a. 417]. The time that remains is subject to no limits as long as lands endure and the heavens support the stars. What has caused other realms to fall to pieces restores you. The ability to grow strong in misfortune is the prescription for being reborn.

### b. Trouble in Armorica

*As the poet gets his journey underway, he takes leave of a kinsman and fellow Gaul, Palladius. Exuperantius, a native of Poitiers, was praetorian prefect of Gaul in 424; cf. 17, s.a. 425; 18, s.a. 424; and 30.*

On the eve of my departure, I send Palladius back to his studies and the city. The hope and glory of my family, he is an eloquent youth lately sent from the lands of the Gauls to learn the law. He is the dear subject of my concern, a kinsman by blood, whom I love like a son. His father Exuperantius now teaches the inhabitants of the Armorican regions to love the recovery (*postliminium*) of peace; he re-establishes laws, restores freedom, and prevents them from being slaves to their own servants.

### c. Judaism

*The poet sails north along the Italian coast, making stops, and observations, along the way. Just past the island of Elba his company reaches Faleria (Falese) around noon.*

*Antiphates was the king of the Laestrygones who devoured one of Odysseus's men and sank his ships. Pork was something of a Roman staple.*

Neighboring Faleria checks our weary voyage, though Phoebus's course had scarcely reached the midway point. At this time, it so happened that rejoicing country folk soothed their weary spirits with merriment at rural crossroads. In fact it was the day when Osiris, restored at last, rouses joyous seeds to produce anew.

We landed, sought lodging in a villa, and wandered through a wood, pleased with the delightful pools and their enclosed fishpond. The generous waters of the confined flood allow the fish to frisk and play within their preserves.

But we were made to pay dearly for the repose of this lovely way station by a landholder who was a harsher host than Antiphates. For a complaining Jew ran the place — a creature with no liking for human grub. He charged for damaging his bushes and disturbing the seaweed and loudly proclaimed his losses for the water we drank. We tendered him the abuse that is due a disgusting people that shamefully crops the head of the male member. They are the root of stupidity; dear to their hearts are cold sabbaths, but their hearts are yet colder than their religion. Each seventh day is consigned to disgraceful inertia, just as if it were an unmanly replication of their tired god. Not even children, I believe, could put faith in the other absurd merchandise these dealers put on sale. It would have been better if Judea had never been conquered in the wars waged by Pompey [63 B.C.] and in the campaign led by Titus [a. 70]. The infection of a disease once cut out is now spreading too widely and a conquered people bears down on its victors.

### d. Monasticism

As the voyage continues, Capraria now appears. The island is a mess, filled with men who flee from the light. They call themselves 'monks,' a Greek name, because they want to live by themselves, with no one to see them. They are afraid of fortune's gifts, even while they fear the harm she causes. Who would avoid being miserable by choosing to be miserable? What twisted mind came up with such lunacy as to reject good things as long as you are in fear of evil ones? I don't know whether they are trying to punish themselves for their deeds with a prison or whether their melancholy insides are swollen with black bile. In the same way, Homer attributed the cares of Bellerophon to the malady of too much bile; for it is said that the embittered youth took a dislike for the human race after being wounded by dire sorrow.

*The poet returns to the theme once again when he nears the island of Gorgona.*

Gorgona arises surrounded by water in the midst of the sea flanked by Pisa and Corsica. I turn away from the cliffs, monuments of a recent calamity. Here a fellow countryman was lost in a living death. For not long ago one of our youths, rich in ancestry with property and a wife to match, was driven by furies to abandon home and society and entered a shameful retreat, a credulous exile. The unfortunate fellow thought that filth is conducive to heavenly endeavors and inflicted on himself more cruelty than would offended gods. I ask you, is this not a sect more harmful than the poisons of Circe? In her times bodies were transformed, these days it is minds.

### e. Stilicho

*Sight of the Apennines near Pisa prompts a description of Italy's geography, and the role mountains play in her defense.*

    *Exactly what Rutilius meant by the empire's* arcanum *is debatable; I have translated the term as 'sanctuary' without intending this meaning to be taken literally; a common translation is 'secret.' The allegation that Stilicho burned the Sibylline books is made only by Rutilius. Althea destroyed her son by burning the firebrand on which his life depended; and similarly Scylla killed her father Nisus by removing a lock of hair.*

Nature feared there would be jealousy [of Italy]. Just as she shielded vital organs with many other parts and covered valuable members more than once, she regarded it an insufficient protection to set only the Alps in opposition to threats from the north. Even then the Rome that was to be deserved to be surrounded by multiple defenses and to have gods concerned for her.

    The more bitter then is the crime of the cursed Stilicho, because it was he who betrayed the sanctuary (*arcanum*) of the empire. As he endeavoured to survive the destruction of the Romans, cruel frenzy turned the world upside down. And although he feared the means he had previously used to make himself feared, he let loose the javelins of the barbarians for the destruction of Latium. He established an armed enemy in its exposed vitals by a readier scheme than inflicting a defeat. Rome itself was exposed to his hide-clad dependents and was a captive even before she was taken. The traitor struck not only by means of Getic [i.e. Gothic] arms; earlier he burned the decrees of the Sibylline prophecies. We hate Althea for consuming the brand with fire; birds are thought to weep for Nisus's lock of hair. But Stilicho tried to cast down prophetic pledges of eternal rule and distaffs still full. Let the tortures of Nero in hell all come to a halt; let a more melancholy spirit exhaust the flames of Stygian torches. Nero brought down a mortal; Stilicho, an immortal. Nero struck down his own mother, Stilicho overthrew the mother of the world.

# C. PAULINUS OF PELLA

## 15. FROM THE *THANKSGIVING* *(EUCHARISTICUS)*

*From the evidence of his poem, Paulinus was born ca. 376 at Pella in Macedonia, where his father held the important post of vicar. While still a child of three, he was brought home to Bordeaux and there met his grandfather, who was consul for that year (a. 379). His grandfather must therefore have been Ausonius (above, A). Paulinus was count of the private largesse under the usurper Attalus.*

*Paulinus's only surviving work is the* Eucharisticus, or Thanksgiving, *which he wrote in his eighty-third year (ca. 459/60). By this time most of his considerable property had been lost, and his wife and sons had died. The 'thanksgiving' is to Christ and takes the form of a sketch of the poet's life and the true blessings he received from God. Paulinus seems to have had religious inclinations from an early age and considered becoming a monk around 421 when he was forty-five and still had a wife, mother, mother-in-law, and children. His last years were eased by the sale of his remaining property in Marseilles to a Goth.*

*For Paulinus's public career, see* **28**. *The present selection opens when Paulinus was about seventeen, ca. 393.*

Source: two editions of the *Eucharisticus* were used: (1) *Poetae christiani minores*, ll. 154-245, ed. Wilhelm Brandes, Corpus Scriptorum Ecclesiasticorum Latinorum 16 (Vindobonae, 1888), pp. 263-334; (2) Paulin de Pella, *Poème d'action de grâces et prière*, ll. 154-245, ed. and trans. Claude Moussy, Sources Chrétiennes 209 (Paris, 1974). Translation by A.C. Murray.

I wavered among worldly enticements and my parents' wishes that were forever set on my continuing our line. At last, I was roused fairly late for my time of life and erupted with new desires for the youthful pleasures that earlier, as a boy, I thought I could guard against. But in so far as prudent restraint could curb and rein in sexual license and prevent me from including more serious offenses among my faults, as a means of correction, I checked my passions with these guiding principles. I would not go after a woman who would not have me, or if she was under another's authority. Remembering to preserve my cherished propriety, I would guard against giving in to the freeborn, even if they made the offer themselves. I would be satisfied with making use of the servile attractions of the household, preferring to be guilty of a fault rather than a crime and fearing damage to my reputation. I shall also not pass over among my deeds the fact that I knew of one son that was born to me at the time. But I never saw him, since he soon died, nor any bastard of mine after that. At a time when freedom, allied with the sexual inducements of youth, could have ruled me and done me serious injury, even then, you, Christ, took care of me.

Such was the life I led from about the time I was seventeen until I was twenty. Finally my parents' sense of responsibility compelled me, against my will, I confess, to give up the allurements of the soft life and forced me to take a wife. The ancient name of her house was more impressive than its estate, which at the time was burdened with problems because of lack of attention from its aged owner. A young grandchild who had survived her father succeeded to it, and later yielded to my nuptial torches.

Once I had decided to bear the burden laid upon me, in only a few days I was content, aided by the ardor of youth and a zealous spirit, to enjoy the establishment I had acquired. Quickly I forced myself and my people to exchange seductive idleness for unaccustomed activity. Some of them I challenged with the example of my own labor, but others I compelled against their will with the severity of a master. And so, actively pursuing the duties of my new situation, I immediately took action to bring the fallow lands under cultivation and to renew the exhausted vineyards with prompt attention, once I had learned how. And I was first to pay my tax obligations at the appointed time, willingly and of my own accord — something that seems to many a particularly bitter pill to swallow; but thereby I quickly assured myself of leisure to expend later upon private relaxation.

*Paulinus describes the luxury of his household.*

As much as I enjoyed pleasing and welcome amenities, the great devotion I had for my parents was dearer still and outweighed them all. It bound me with a tie of overwhelming love, so that for the greater part of a year we kept them company, an arrangement we all wanted and found rewarding.

Would that this way of life granted to us might have lasted longer by the bountiful gift of Christ and that also the earlier period of peace might have continued. In so many ways my youth could have done with the constant attention of my father's experience, and my education could have been furthered by good models. But the completion of the third decade of life [a. 406] was marked by the unhappy onset of two afflictions. In a public catastrophe mourned by everyone, enemies were poured into the guts of the Roman realm. This coincided with a private misfortune, the death and funeral of my father. For the last days of the end of his life accorded almost exactly with the time when the peace was broken. But for me the destruction caused to my home by the ravages of the enemy, though in itself considerable, was lighter by far than the immeasurable grief caused by the death of my father. He made both homeland and home itself dear to me. For we had such genuine mutual respect for each other that we lived as if there were no age difference between us and our friendship surpassed that of friends of the same age.

# CHAPTER FOUR

## THE ANTIQUE CHRONICLE TRADITION
## IN THE FIFTH AND SIXTH CENTURIES

*There are no extensive narrative histories for the fifth century. Contemporary historians did deal with events under the western emperors during this period, but their works, sometimes of eastern provenance, survive as fragments embedded in later sources (see* **25, 27, 31**). *For complete examples of western historical writing in the fifth century — and for many of that period's events and much of its chronology — we have to look to chronicles.*

*Chronicles became a significant form of historical writing in the western empire in the fourth century under the influence of the work known as Eusebius-Jerome. This was a world chronicle, setting out in tabular form biblical, secular, and ecclesiastical history from Abraham to the present. The original version was written in Greek by the celebrated church historian Eusebius (ca. 260-340), bishop of Caesarea; it survives now only in fragments and in Armenian and Latin translations. In 380, Saint Jerome (ca. 345-420), adapted an edition of Eusebius's work that ended in A.D. 325, translating it into Latin and bringing events down to the year 378. It was Jerome's Latin version that became influential in the west, and his effort to bring the chronicle up to date became a model for western practitioners of chronicle historiography. The main chronicles translated here are all continuations of Jerome and record people and events of recent history.*

*They often do so in a deliberate fashion that belies their appearance as sterile compendia of haphazard data. The chronicle form may not immediately invite reflective reading, but modern scholarship has shown how the genre in its late antique and early medieval form deserves to be treated as the purposeful construct of authors with distinct intentions. For this reason, not to mention the intrinsic interest and sometimes unique value of their contents, I have included large excerpts from the chronicles and attempted completeness over a substantial range of entries.*

*I have also kept some, though not all, chronological trappings of the chronicles. Retention of contemporary dating conventions is often a necessity: not all chronicle entries can be reduced to simple, standard* anno domini *dating. Readers should also be aware of the number of chronological systems available to those recording events; for chronology was, among other things, an aspect of historical self-consciousness and a reflection of the the public face of the Roman state. Finally, some understanding of the variety of systems in use in the fifth and sixth centuries, and their imperfections, may help readers understand the practical problems faced by modern and ancient scholars trying to reconstruct a chronological framework for historical narrative.*

# ·16. PROSPER OF AQUITAINE

*Prosper of Aquitaine (or Prosper Tiro) was a native of Gaul who spent much of his adult life in Rome. He may have held an important position in papal circles, possibly dying in 463. Prosper was deeply involved in the theological disputes of his day in both Gaul and Rome, especially those concerning grace and free will. His chronicle is just one of his works. It was conceived as an abbreviation of the famous chronicle of Jerome, with an original continuation by Prosper himself that began in 378; it was composed in a number of editions between 433 and 455.*

*Prosper's chronicle was influenced by another form of contemporary historical record-keeping, consular annals. Since Republican times, the year in Roman practice had been named after the two consuls who took office on 1 January; by late imperial convention, one consul was named from the West and one from the East. Lists of these consuls circulated, often with occasional and brief annotations that might be used by chroniclers or historians; surviving examples of annals sometimes contain precise dates for important public events. Prosper adopted consular chronology for his chronicle, combining it with a system of his own devising that numbered years from Christ's crucifixion.*

*In the excerpts below, a selection of the years for the earlier portions of Prosper's continuation is given. From the year 409 the chronicle is complete; the years with consuls but no events given in Mommsen's edition have been omitted. No attempt has been made to distinguish various recensions, but in a couple of cases I have given variants. I have combined the dating schemes into one line: the number of the years from Christ's passion, followed by the names (usually two) of the consuls for the year in question. Prosper's dating can readily be incorporated into the later anno domini scheme of dating, which has been placed in the margin.*

Source: *Prosperi Tironis epitoma chronicon*, ed. Th. Mommsen, *Chronica Minora* 1, MGH AA 9 (1892), pp. 385-485. Translation by A.C. Murray.

a. 379  Year 352 [from Christ's passion]. Ausonius and Olybrius [consuls].
...In this period, Priscillian, bishop of Gallaecia, established from the dogma of the Manichees and Gnostics the heresy bearing his name.

a. 381  Year 354. Syagrius and Eucherius.
Martin, bishop of the city of Tours in Gaul, was famous for many examples of miracles...

a. 382  Year 355. Antonius and Syagrius.
Athanaric, king of the Goths, was killed at Constantinople on the fifteenth day after he had been received there...

a. 384  Year 357. Richomer and Clearchus.
Honorius, the son of Theodosius was born.

Siricius presided over the Roman church after Damasus as the thirty-sixth bishop.

In Britain Maximus was made emperor by a mutiny of the soldiers. He soon crossed over to Gaul. Gratian was defeated at Paris through the treachery of the master of the soldiers, Merobaudes, and fleeing was captured and killed at Lyons. Maximus made his son Victor his colleague in power.

Valentinian [II], forty-second emperor, reigned for 8 years with Theodosius.

a. 385    Year 358. Arcadius and Bauto.

...Priscillian, knowing he would be condemned at the Synod of Bordeaux, appealed to the emperor [Maximus]. He was tried at Trier and, along with Euchrotia, wife of Delfidius the teacher of rhetoric, Latronianus, and other partners in his error, was put to death by Euvodius, Maximus's praetorian prefect. At Bordeaux a certain disciple of Priscillian called Urbica was stoned to death on account of her obstinate impiety by an unruly mob.

a. 388    Year 361. Theodosius for the second time and Cynegius.

The usurper Maximus, despoiled of his royal garments, appeared before Valentinian and Theodosius at the third milestone from Aquilea and was condemned to death. His son Victor was killed in Gaul by Count Arbogast in the same year.

a. 389    Year 362. Timasius and Promotus.

Bishops Itacius and Ursacius, on account of the destruction of Priscillian, whose accusers they were, were deprived of the communion of the church.

a. 392    Year 365. Arcadius for the second time and Rufinus.

The extreme severity of Arbogast, master of the soldiers, drove Valentinian into committing suicide at Vienne by hanging himself. On the death of Valentinian, Arbogast, who was burdened with the way the emperor died, as commander of the army, made Eugenius emperor in Gaul.

Theodosius, forty-third emperor, already in power for 14 years, reigned for 3 years with his sons Arcadius and Honorius.

a. 394    Year 367. Arcadius for the third time and Honorius for the second.

John the hermit monk was renowned. He had been granted the gift of prophecy and predicted that Theodosius, who was consulting him on the outcome of the campaign he was mounting against Eugenius, would be victorious.

a. 395   Year 368. Olybrius and Probinus.

Theodosius defeated and killed Eugenius.

Augustine, the disciple of the blessed Ambrose and eminent in eloquence and learning, was made bishop at Hippo in Africa.

At this time, Claudian, the distinguished poet, became well known.

Theodosius died at Milan.

Arcadius, forty-fourth emperor, already in power for 12 years, reigned 13 years with his brother Honorius...

a. 406   Year 379. Arcadius for the sixth time and Probus.

Vandals and Alans crossed the Rhine and entered Gaul on December 31.

a. 407   Year 380. Honorius for the seventh time and Theodosius for the second.

Constantine arose in Britain as a usurper and crossed to Gaul.

a. 408   Year 381. Bassus and Philippus.

Arcadius died in Constantinople.

Honorius, forthy-fifth emperor, reigned for 15 years with Theodosius [II], the son of Honorius's brother.

a. 409   Year 382. Honorius for the eighth time and Theodosius for the third.

The Vandals took Spain.

Attalus was made emperor at Rome. He was soon deprived of power but remained connected with the Goths.

a. 410   Year 383. Senator Varanes.

Rome was captured by the Goths under the command of Alaric, and for this reason there was only a consul for the east, a practice followed the next year as well.

a. 411   Year 384. Augustus Theodosius for the fourth time.

Constantine was defeated and captured by Honorius's generals, Constantius and Ulfila, at the town of Arles. Count Gerontius killed Constantine's son Constans, who had begun his rule in Spain, passing the usurper's role to a certain Maximus.

a. 412   Year 385. Honorius for the ninth time and Theodosius for the fifth.

In Spain Maximus was removed from power and was granted his life because the moderation and insignificance of the man did not merit ill-will toward his affectation of authority.

The Goths entered Gaul under King Athaulf.

At this time, Heros, a holy man and disciple of blessed Martin, was driven out of Arles by its people while he presided over the city as bishop; he was guiltless and not subject to any charge. In his place was ordained Patroclus, friend and acquaintance of Constantius, master of the soldiers, whose favor he procured. This affair was a subject of great disagreements among the bishops of the region.

a. 413  Year 386. Senator Lucius.

His colleague in the consulship was Heraclian, who was responsible for revolution in Africa and deprived of his honor and his life.

The Burgundians acquired part of Gaul near the Rhine.

The brothers Jovinus and Sebastian seized power in Gaul and were killed.

At that time the Briton Pelagius set forth the doctrine bearing his name against the grace of Christ; Caelestius and Julian [of Eclanum] were his assistants. He attracted many people to his erroneous views. He proclaimed that each person is guided to righteousness by his own will and receives as much grace as he deserves, since Adam's sin injured only himself and did not also bind his descendants. For this reason it would be possible for those so wishing to be completely without sin and for all little children to be born as innocent as was the first man before transgression; nor are children to be baptized so they can be divested of sin but so they can be honored with the sacrament of adoption.

a. 414  Year 387. Constantius and Constans.

Attalus on the advice of the Goths and with their help resumed the role of usurper in Gaul.

a. 415  Year 388. Honorius for the tenth time and Theodosius for the sixth.

Attalus was abandoned by the Goths, who removed themselves to Spain, and, deprived of their support, was captured and presented alive to Constantius the patrician.

Athaulf, wounded by one of his own men, died, and Wallia seized his kingdom after destroying those who were thought to want the same thing.

a. 416  Year 389. Theodosius for the seventh time and Palladius.

Seeking peace with Honorius, Wallia restored the daughter of the emperor Theodosius [I], Placidia, whom the Goths had captured and whom Athaulf had married, and Constantius won her hand in marriage.

Zosimus took up the episcopal office of the Roman church. He was the thirty-ninth bishop.

At this time the Pelagians, already condemned by Pope Innocent, were resisted by the diligence of the Africans and especially by the knowledge of Bishop Augustine.

a. 417  Year 390. Honorius for the eleventh time, Constantius for the second.

Honorius entered Rome in a triumph with Attalus walking ahead of his chariot. Honorius ordered him to live in exile on the island of Lipara.

a. 418  Year 391. Honorius for the twelfth time and Theodosius for the eighth.

At this time Constantius, a servant of Christ, and former vicar, living at Rome, most devoutly resisted the Pelagians on behalf of the grace of God. The many things he endured at the hands of their faction placed him among the holy confessors.

A council was held at Carthage and the synodal decrees of the two hundred and fourteen bishops were conveyed to Pope Zosimus. They were approved and the Pelagian heresy was condemned throughout the whole world.

Valentinian, the son of Constantius and Placidia, was born on 2 July.

a. 419  Year 392. Monaxius and Plinta.

At Rome Boniface took up the episcopal office, the fortieth bishop of the Roman church.

Constantius the patrician made peace with Wallia and gave him the province of Aquitania secunda to live in and certain cities of neighboring provinces.

a. 420  Year 393. Theodosius for the ninth time and Constantius for the third.

Constantius was taken as a colleague in power by Honorius.

Jerome the priest died at the age of ninety-one on 30 September.

a. 421  Year 394. Agricola and Eustathius.

Emperor Constantius died.

a. 422  Year 395. Honorius for the thirteenth time and Theodosius for the tenth.

At this time an army was sent to Spain against the Vandals under the command of Castinus. By a senseless and wrongful order, he made Boniface, a man quite famous in the arts of war, averse to participating in his expedition. And Boniface, reckoning that to follow Castinus, whom he had found disagreeable and proud, would be dangerous to himself and degrading, rushed off to Portus and from there to Africa. That was the beginning of many difficulties and subsequent evils for the state. [Cf. **18**, Hydatius, s.a. 422.]

a. 423  Year 396. Marinianus and Asclepiodotus.

Augusta Placidia, driven away by her brother Honorius, went to the east with her children Honoria and Valentinian.

Celestine was set over the Roman church as its forty-first bishop.

Honorius died and John took his imperial authority. It was thought that Castinus, who commanded the army as master of the soldiers, pretended to look the other way.

Theodosius [II] held the Roman empire as forty-sixth emperor.

a. 424  Year 397. Castinus and Victor.

Exuperantius of Poitiers, praetorian prefect for Gaul, was killed in the city of Arles by a mutiny of the soldiers, and this deed was not avenged by John.

Theodosius made his cousin Valentinian [III] Caesar and sent him along with the Augusta, his mother, to take back the western empire. At the time, John's defenses were made weaker because he tried to recapture Africa, over which Boniface was maintaining his hold.

a. 425  Year 398. Theodosus, for the eleventh time, and Caesar Valentinian.

Augusta Placidia and Caesar Valentinian with astonishing good fortune crushed the usurper John and as victors regained royal power. Pardon was given to Aëtius, because the Huns he had brought in on behalf of John were turned back home by his efforts. Castinus, on the other hand, was sent into exile, because it seemed as if John would not have been able to take over the kingdom without his connivance.

*The manuscripts offer two slightly different versions of the next entry:*

*1.* Valentinian was hailed as Augustus by a decree of Theodosius.

*2.* Valentinian was hailed as Augustus by the army.

Arles, noble city of Gaul, was assailed by the Goths with great violence, until, threatened by Aëtius, they withdrew not without losses.

a. 426  Year 399. Theodosius for the twelfth time and Valentinian Augustus for the second.

Patroclus, bishop of Arles, was wounded many times and killed by a tribune, a certain Barnabus. This crime was blamed on the orders of Felix, master of the soldiers, at whose instigation the deacon Titus, a holy man distributing money to the poor at Rome, was also killed.

a. 427  Year 400. Hierius and Ardabur.

Due to the decision of Felix, war was waged against Boniface in the name of the state by the generals Mavortius, Gallio, and Sanoeces. Boniface's power and fame were growing in Africa and he had refused to come to Italy. The generals beseiging Boniface were killed, betrayed by Sanoeces, and soon he who had betrayed them was himself killed. Thereafter access to the sea was gained by peoples who were unacquainted with ships until they were called in by the rival sides to give assistance. The conduct of the war undertaken against Boniface was transferred to Count Sigisvult.

The Vandal people crossed from Spain to Africa.

a. 428 Year 401. Felix and Taurus.

Nestorius, bishop of Constantinople, tried to introduce a new error into the churches. He proclaimed that Christ was born of Mary as a man only, not also as God, and divinity was conferred upon him because of his merit. The diligence of Bishop Cyril of Alexandria in particular and the authority of Pope Caelestinus opposed this impiety.

Part of Gaul near the Rhine seized by the Franks was recovered by the forces of Count Aëtius.

a. 429 Year 402. Florentius and Dionysius.

Felix was promoted to the office of patrician and Aëtius was made master of the soldiers.

Agricola the Pelagian, the son of Bishop Severianus the Pelagian, corrupted the churches of Britain by introducing his own doctrine. On the recommendation of the deacon Palladius, Pope Celestine sent Germanus, bishop of Auxerre, as his representative, and when the heretics had been cast down, he guided the Britons to the Catholic faith.

a. 430 Year 403. Theodosius for the thirteenth time and Valentinian for the third.

Aëtius killed Felix and his wife Padusia and the deacon Grunitus, sensing that they were plotting against him.

Aurelius Augustine, a bishop most outstanding in evey respect, died 28 August. In his very last days he was responding to the books of Julian [of Eclanum] amidst the attacks of besieging Vandals and persevering gloriously in defense of Christian grace.

a. 431 Year 404. Bassus and Antiochus.

A synod of more than two hundred bishops gathered at Ephesus. Nestorius was condemned along with the heresy bearing his name and many Pelagians who supported it because the doctrine was related to their own.

Palladius, having been ordained by Pope Celestine, was the first bishop sent to the Scots believing in Christ.

a. 432 Year 405. Aëtius and Valerius.

Sixtus was set over the Roman church as the thirty-second bishop. The whole city remained peaceful in wonderful harmony.

Boniface received the office of master of the soldiers and came from Africa to Italy by way of Rome. Although he fought a battle with Aëtius, who was opposing him, and defeated him, he died a few days later from illness. Aëtius, who had surrendered power, resided on his country estates and there some of his enemies tried to crush him in a sudden attack. Fleeing to Rome and from there to Dalmatia, he thereafter reached the Huns through Pannonia. He used their friendship and assistance to obtain the peace of the emperors and get his power restored.

a. 433     Year 406. Theodosius for the fourteenth time and Maximus.

All the years calculated up to the fourteenth consulship of Theodosius and that of Maximus:

From the fifteenth year of Tiberius and the passion of the Lord, 406 years.

From the restoration of the temple under Darius, 1054 years.

From the first Olympiad and Isaia the prophet, 1210 years.

From Solomon and the first building of the temple, 1466 years.

From Moses and Cecrops, king of Attica, 1965 years.

From Abraham and the rule of Ninus, 2450 years.

Now from the flood to Abraham there are 942 years, and from Adam to the flood 2242 years. Thus from Adam to the time of the consuls mentioned above, the years amount to 5634.

a. 435     Year 408. Theodosius for the fifteenth time and Valentinian for the fourth.

Peace made with the Vandals by Trigetius at Hippo on 11 February. The Vandals were given a part of Africa to live in.

At the same time Aëtius crushed Gundichar, who was king of the Burgundians and living in Gaul. In response to his entreaty, Aëtius gave him peace, which the king did not enjoy for long. For the Huns destroyed him and his people root and branch.

a. 436     Year 409. Isidorus and Senator.

The Goths confounded the peace agreements and seized many towns in the vicinity of their settlements, attacking the city of Narbonne most of all. When it had suffered for some time from siege and hunger, the city was saved from both dangers by Count Litorius. For he put the enemy to flight and filled the city with grain, having each of his troopers bring along two measures of wheat.

a. 437     Year 410. Aëtius for the second time and Sigisvult.

War was waged against the Goths with the help of the Huns.

In Africa, Gaiseric, king of the Vandals, wanted to use the Arian impiety to undo the Catholic faith within the regions where he resided. He persecuted some of our bishops, of whom the most famous were Posidius, Novatus, and Severianus, to the extent that he deprived them of their right to their churches and even drove them from their cities, for their steadfastness would not yield to the terrors of that most proud king.

The Augustus Valentinian went to the emperor Theodosius at Constantinople and married his daughter.

In the same period, four Spaniards, Arcadius, Paschasius, Probus, and Eutychianus were formerly considered by Gaiseric to be valued and distinguished by virtue of their wisdom and faithful service. To make them even more esteemed, he commanded them to convert to the Arian heresy. But as they most steadfastly rejected this wickedness, the barbarian was roused to a most furious anger. First their property was confiscated, next they were driven into exile, then tortured severely, and, finally, suffering death in various ways, they succumbed wonderfully to a most glorious martydom. A boy called Paulillus, the brother of Eutychianus and Paschasius, was very dear to the king on account of his fine body and refined nature; since he could not be separated by threats from his acknowledgment and love of the Catholic faith, he was beaten for some time with rods and condemned to the meanest servitude. He was not killed, it seems, so that youth should not also take glory in overthrowing the savagery of an impious man.

In the same year barbarian deserters of the federates took to piracy.

a. 438   Year 411. Theodosius for the sixteenth time and Faustus.

In this year too the same pirates plundered many islands, especially Sicily. Measures against the Goths in Gaul went well.

a. 439   Year 412. Theodosius for the seventeenth time and Festus.

Litorius, who led Hun auxiliaries, second in command after Aëtius, rashly joined battle with the Goths, striving to surpass the glory of Aëtius and trusting in the oracles of diviners and the portents of demons. He made us understand the success the band that perished with him might have achieved, had he chosen to follow a course better than his own foolhardiness; for he inflicted such losses on the enemy that, if he had not fallen into captivity by fighting heedlessly, it would have been doubtful to what side victory should properly have been ascribed.

At this time, Julian of Eclanum, a most boastful defender of the Pelagian error was aroused by an immoderate longing for a formerly lost bishopric. By the varied art of deceiving, and exhibiting the pretence of having amended his ways, he endeavored to insinuate himself into the communion of the church. But Pope Sixtus, with the urging of Leo the deacon, opposed these tricks and allowed no approach to lie open to these pestilential efforts, and he caused all Catholics to rejoice in throwing back the deceitful beast, as if the apostolic sword then for the first time beheaded the most proud heresy.

In the same period, Vitericus was considered loyal to our state and renowned for the frequent demonstration of his skill in war.

Peace made with the Goths, for they sought it more humbly than ever before after the lamentable trial of an inconclusive war.

Since Aëtius was concerned with matters that were being settled in Gaul, Gaiseric had nothing to fear from losing his friendship. On 19 October, he took advantage of the peace and seized Carthage. He put its citizens to various kinds of torture and took all of their wealth as his own. Nor did he refrain from despoiling the churches. Emptying them of their sacred vessels, and depriving them of the attention of their priests, he ordered that they no longer be places of divine worship but quarters for his people. He was harsh towards the entire captive population but particularly hostile to the nobility and clergy so that no one could tell whether he was waging war more against man or God. Carthage suffered this captivity in the 585th year after it had become Roman.

a. 440 Year 413. Valentinian Augustus for the fifth time and Anatolius.

When Bishop Sixtus died, the Roman church was without a bishop for more than forty days, awaiting with wondrous peacefulness and forbearance the arrival of Deacon Leo, who was detained in Gaul restoring the friendship between Aëtius and Albinus. It was as if he had been removed quite a distance so that both the merit of him chosen and the judgment of those choosing might be tested. Then Deacon Leo, summoned by a civic legation and delivered to his rejoicing home city, was consecrated the forty-third bishop of the Roman church.

While Gaiseric was inflicting serious damage on Sicily, he received word that Sebastian [the son-in-law of Boniface] was crossing from Spain to Africa and quickly returned to Carthage. Gaiseric thought it would be dangerous to himself and his people if a man skilled in war was bent upon retaking Carthage. But Sebastian, wishing to be regarded as a friend rather than as an enemy, found everything in the mind of the barbarian contrary to what he had supposed. That hope was to him a cause of the greatest calamity and an unhappy death. [Cf. **18**, Hydatius, s.a. 444, 445, 449.]

a. 441 Year 414. Cyrus.

Theodosius opened hostilities with the Vandals by sending the generals Ariobindus, Ansila, and Germanus with a large fleet. They deferred the business with long delays and proved to be more of a burden to Sicily than a help to Africa.

a. 442 Year 415. Dioscorus and Eudoxius.

As the Huns were laying waste to Thrace and Illyricum with savage plundering, the army that was delaying in Sicily returned for the defence of the eastern provinces.

The Augustus Valentinian made peace with Gaiseric and Africa was divided between the two into distinct territories.

Some of Gaiseric's magnates conspired against him because he was proud, even among his own people, due to the successful outcome of events. But when the undertaking was discovered, they were subjected to many tortures and killed by him. Whenever others seemed to venture the same thing, the king's mistrust served to destroy so many that he lost more men by this anxiety of his than if he had been overthrown in war.

a. 443 Year 416. Maximus for the second time and Paterius.

At this time it became clear to the diligent perception of pope Leo that many Manichees were taking refuge in the city. He rooted them out from their hiding places and revealed them to the eyes of the whole church; he caused them to censure and report all the deformities of their doctrine and had great piles of books that had been seized burned. This concern, inspired in the holy man, it seems, by God, was of the greatest benefit not only to the city of Rome but also to the whole world, inasmuch as the confessions of those arrested in Rome might reveal the identity of their teachers, bishops or priests, and the provinces or cities in which they lived. Many bishops in the east imitated the energy of the apostolic governor.

a. 444 Year 417. Theodosius for the eighteenth time and Albinus.

In this year Easter was celebrated on 23 April. This was not an error, for the day of the passion was on 21 April. Out of respect, the anniversary of the City [on 21 April] passed without circuses.

Attila king of the Huns killed Bleda, his brother and co-ruler, and forced his people to submit to him.

a. 448 Year 421. Postumianus and Zeno.

At this time the Eutychian heresy arose. It was created by Eutyches a certain priest who presided over a renowned monastery in Constantinople. He proclaimed that Jesus Christ, our Lord and son of the blessed Virgin Mary, had no maternal substance, but only the nature of God's word was in him in the likeness of a human. On account of this impiety he was condemned by Flavian, bishop of the same city, for he would not be corrected. But relying on royal friendship and the favor of courtiers, he asked to be heard by a universal synod. Theodosius gave his consent and ordered all the bishops to assemble at Ephesus in order to withdraw this condemnation. In this council, Eutyches was absolved and Dioscurus, bishop of Alexandria, claiming primacy for himself, proposed a sentence of condemnation against Flavian, bishop of Constantinople. This was done over the objections of Hilarus, deacon of the church of Rome, who had been sent from the apostolic see along with Julius the bishop to Pozzuoli to represent the holy Pope Leo. For all the bishops who made up the council were compelled to render consent to this heresy by force and fear of counts and soldiers whom the emperor had assigned to Dioscorus, bishop of Alexandria; but the aforesaid deacon, amid serious danger to his life, called out his objection although the fury this caused threatened to destroy him. Leaving all his own people there, he secretly departed so he might lay before the aforesaid pope and other Italian bishops an accusation of how the Catholic faith was violated at the council. The holy Flavian passed on to Christ, ending his life in a most glorious fashion, while in the hands of those who led him into exile.

a. 450    Year 433. Valentinian for the seventh time and Avienus.

When Theodosius had died and the chamberlain Chrysaphius, who had misused the friendship of the emperor, had been killed, Marcian received the kingdom with the agreement of the whole army. He was a most impressive man, indispensible to not only the state but also the church.

By his edicts, which complied with the authority of the apostolic see, the synod of Ephesus was condemned, and it was decided that an episcopal council should be held at Chalcedon, so that forgiveness might heal the reformed and the intransigent might be driven out with their heresy.

a. 451    Year 434. Augustus Marcian and Adelphius.

After killing his brother, Attila was strengthened by the resources of the deceased and forced many thousands of neighboring peoples into a war. This war, he announced as guardian of Roman friendship, he would wage only against the Goths. But when he had crossed the Rhine and many Gallic cities experienced his savage attacks, both our people and the Goths soon agreed to oppose with allied forces the fury of their proud enemies. And Aëtius had such great foresight that, when fighting men were hurriedly collected from everywhere, a not unequal force met the opposing multitude. Although the slaughter of all those who died there was incalculable — for neither side gave way — it appears that the Huns were defeated in this battle because those among them that survived lost their taste for fighting and turned back home.

a. 452    Year 425. Senator Herculanus and Sporacius.

Attila restored the forces he lost in Gaul and tried to enter Italy by way of

Pannonia. Our commander Aëtius made no provision following the exertions of the previous war and failed to make use of the barriers of the Alps by which the enemy could have been checked. He believed his only hope lay in a full retreat from Italy along with the emperor. But since this course seemed disgraceful and fraught with danger, a sense of shame restrained fear and the widespread overthrow of so many of the noble provinces was used to satiate the savagery and greed of the enemy. Of all the plans of the emperor, senate, and people of Rome, none seemed sounder than to send envoys to seek peace from this most fierce of kings. The blessed Pope Leo, supported by the help of God, whom he knew never neglects the labors of the devout, took up this matter along with Avienus, a man of consular rank, and Trygetius, a man with the rank of prefect. Nor was the result other than what faith had taken for granted. For when the entire delegation was honorably received, the king was so delighted with the presence of the chief bishop that he ordered the war to be halted and, having promised peace, retired beyond the Danube.

a. 453    Year 426. Senator Opilio and Vincomalus.

The Synod of Chalcedon ended. Eutyches and Dioscorus were condemned. All who disassociated themselves from them were received into communion. Universally confirmed was the faith that was proclaimed by holy Pope Leo with respect to the incarnation of the Word, according to the evangelic and apostolic doctrine.

Attila died in his own territory. At first great struggles over succession to the kingship broke out among his sons; then a few of the peoples that used to obey the Huns tried to revolt and created conditions and opportunities for wars. In these the fiercest peoples were consumed by attacks upon one another.

Among the Goths residing in Gaul, dissension arose among the sons of King Theodoric, the eldest of which, Thorismund, succeeded his father. When the king tried to act against both the Roman peace and the repose of the Goths, he was killed by his brothers, for he pressed on uncontrollably with harmful measures.

a. 454    Year 427. Aëtius and Studius.

Ominous enmities grew stronger between the Augustus Valentinian and the patrician Aëtius, even after oaths promising mutual loyalty and after an agreement to join their children in marriage. Where the kindness of affection ought to have been strengthened, there the tinder of hatred burst into flame at the instigation, so it was believed, of Heraclius the eunuch. By insincere devotion, he gained such influence over the emperor's thinking that he could easily push him into doing whatever he wished.

*The manuscripts contain two versions of subsequent events:*

*1.* Since Heraclius persuaded the emperor of all manner of wickedness on Aëtius' part, there was thought to be just one course of action available to save the emperor: get his enemy before he got him. As a result Aëtius was cruelly put to the sword within the recesses of the palace at the hands of the emperor and his entourage.

*2.* And so while Aëtius more vehemently sought agreements and more passionately pressed the case of his son, he was cruelly put to the sword within the recesses of the palace at the hands of the emperor and his entourage.

Boethius, the praetorian prefect, was killed at the same time; he was connected to Aëtius by great friendship.

a. 455  Year 428. Valentinian for the eighth time and Anthemius.

The death of Valentinian followed not long after the death of Aëtius. So imprudently was it not avoided that the killer of Aëtius associated with the man's friends and retainers. They found the right time for their crime and, secretly stalking the prince when he left the city and was awaiting a display of arms, stabbed him unexpectedly. Heraclius was killed at the same time, as he was next to the emperor, and no one of that royal host was incited to take revenge for so great a crime.

As this murder was carried out, moreover, Maximus, twice possessor of the consulship and holder of the patrician dignity, took up the imperial power. Although people believed he would be in every way beneficial to the endangered state, it did not take long for him to show by example the kind of mind he had. Not only did he not punish the killers of Valentinian, but he received them as friends; and he forbade the Augusta, Valentinian's wife, to mourn the loss of her husband and within a few days forced her to marry him. But he was not to indulge this lack of restraint for long. After another month he got news of the arrival of Gaiseric from Africa, and many nobles and commoners fled the city. When he gave permission for everyone to leave and wished himself to get away in haste, on the seventy-seventh day after his seizure of power, he was torn to pieces by the royal slaves; thrown in pieces into the Tiber, he was even deprived of burial. After this end to Maximus, a Roman captivity, deserving of many tears, immediately followed, and Gaiseric obtained the city devoid of all protection. Holy Bishop Leo met him outside the gates and his supplication mollified him through the power of God to such an extent that, when everything was given into his hands, he was held back nevertheless from burning, killing, and torture. Then for fourteen days, through an untrammeled and open search, Rome was emptied of all its wealth, and many thousands of captives, all that were satisfactory as to age or occupation, along with the queen and her children, were taken away to Carthage.

In the same year Easter was celebrated on 24 April, according to the stubborn assertion of the bishop of Alexandria, with whom all the easterners think they should agree, even when holy Pope Leo protested that it should rather be observed on 17 April. On that day there was no error in the calculation of the full moon or in the demarcation of the first month. There exist letters of the same pope sent to the most merciful prince Marcian, in which the calculation of the true date is laid out carefully and plainly and in which the Catholic church can be instructed. Though the opinion of easterners was tolerated out of a desire for unity and peace rather than approved, it must by no means go on being imitated, since an opinion that has brought destructive offense should forever lose authority.

## 17. THE *GALLIC CHRONICLE OF* 452

*This chronicle is the work of an anonymous Gaul, writing very close to the year 452. Nothing is known of the author but what can be inferred of his views from the contents of his chronicle. His perspective is sufficently clear to suggest interesting points of contrast with that of his contemporary Prosper. Like Prosper's work, the* Gallic Chronicle of 452 *was a continuation of an epitome of Jerome's translation of Eusebius, and begins where Jerome left off in 378. I give the continuation in its entirety from 379.*

*The chronicler's treatment of years and dates contains a number of errors, traceable in part to the sources he used, which are only reasonably detectable in the earlier portions of the chronicle. Not only did the chronicler work with incorrect regnal year counts for the reigns of Gratian, Theodosius I, and Honorius, but his relative placement of events is not always accurate. Following Mommsen's edition, I have added* anno domini *dates sparingly up to the end of Honorius's reign. After 424 the number of regnal years is correct, and it is possible to equate these with* anno domini *dates, but readers should be aware that doing so does not preclude misdating, intentional or otherwise, by the chronicler. The* Chronicle *is correct in the last few years after 447. Where the* Chronicle *shows 'double dating' — that is the spread of what might be construed as one entry over more than a single year — I have grouped the years together rather than assuming a blank year. Finally, it should be noted that, following Jerome, not only does the chronicler date events by the regnal years of emperors, but he also introduces Olympiads every four years and the years of Abraham every decade; I have omitted the latter two modes of dating.*

*In the translation,* anno domini *dates are placed in the left margin. The year numbers of the emperor's reign are in boldface Arabic numerals set next to the first entry of the year, and the number in brackets at the end of each entry corresponds to the numbering of Mommsen's edition. The headings are those of the chronicle.*

Source: *Chronica Gallica A. CCCCLII*, ed. Th. Mommsen, *Chronica Minora* 1, MGH AA 9 (1892), pp. 646-662; and cf. Steven Muhlberger, *The Fifth-Century Chroniclers: Prosper, Hydatius, and the Gallic Chronicler of 452* (Leeds, 1990), pp. 137-152. Translation by A.C. Murray.

## Gratian reigned for 6 years [a. 379-383]

379  1  Gratian, since he had quite a young brother as a royal colleague, admitted a man of suitable age, Theodosius, into partnership in the kingdom.[2]

Gratian was much inclined to religion and well disposed toward the churches in all matters.[3]

Martin, bishop of Tours, was regarded as outstanding for his apostolic powers.[4]

2  Theodosius restored the exhausted state in the regions of the East.[5]

3  In Britain Maximus was set up as usurper by the soldiers.[6]

4  Maximus vigorously overcame invading Picts and Scots.[7]

5  Ambrosius wrote most splendid books against the faithlessness of the Arians for the Augustus Gratian.[8]

383  6  Maximus crossed the channel and, after a clash with Gratian, killed the emperor as he fled to Lyons.[9]

## Theodosius reigned for 11 years [a.384-395]

1  Maximus, out of fear of the leader of the eastern empire, Theodosius, entered into a treaty with Valentinian [II]. [11]

At Trier, Manichees were detected and destroyed owing to the utmost zeal of Maximus. [12]

2  Justina, the mother of Valentinian, favored the Arians and heaped various types of injustices upon Ambrose and the entire church of Milan. [13]

Relics of the martyrs Gervasius and Protasius first discovered by Ambrose at Milan.[14]

Ambrose's hymns composed; they were sung in a form never before heard in Latin churches. [15]

3  Maximus, saying that an unworthy action had been taken against the position of the church, discovered a way to break the treaty he had made with

Valentinian. Valentinian, fearing the usurper, who was already a threat to his life, fled to Theodosius.[16]

Augustine, while at first teaching rhetoric at Milan, gave up the classroom and converted to the true faith, for previously he was a Manichee. [17]

a. 388   **4**   Theodosius came over to Italy with an army, killed Maximus, and restored Valentinian to his kingdom. [18]

Justina, who had afflicted the churches, was prevented by death from getting back the kingdom with her son.[19]

The devout emperor expunged the monstrous act committed in Thessalonica by an extraordinary example of repentence for the people he massacred.[20]

Heresy of the Apollinarians begun by Apollinaris. [21]

**5**   The Arians, who polluted almost the entire East and West, were, by an edict of the devout emperor, despoiled of their churches, which were assigned to Catholics.[22]

**6**   John, an Egyptian monk, was regarded as famous because he earned the gift of prophecy from the Lord owing to the purity of his life.[23]

**7**   After Damasus, Siricius was the thirty-sixth bishop to take up direction of the Roman church. At Alexandria, on the death of Peter, Timotheus, and after him, Theophilus were made bishops. At Jerusalem, after Cyril, John received the church. At Antioch, on the death of Miletius, Flavianus took his place.[24]

A huge dispute arose among us. The bishops who had been driven out by heretics wanted none but themselves to fill the priestly office now that the heretics had been removed by the emperor.[25]

A terrible portent, resembling in every respect a column, appeared in the sky.[26]

**8-9**   Temples were destroyed in Alexandria, among them the very ancient and famous temple of Serapis, which, like some column, was keeping idolatry from falling.[28]

a. 392  **10**   Valentinian was eliminated at Vienne by Arbogast, his own count. Eugenius took the emperor's place, seizing power as a usurper.[29]

**11**   To revenge Valentinian's death and crush the usurpation of Eugenius, Theodosius crossed over into Italy; the favor of God was revealed when the elements conspired to assist that very endeavor.[30]

395    After Eugenius had been overcome, Theodosius reached the end of his life in the seventeenth year of his reign.[31]

## Arcadius and Honorius reigned for 32 years
### [Arcadius, a. 395-408, Honorius, a. 395-423]

1   Constantinople, in fear of God's anger revealed in fire flashing dreadfully above the clouds, escaped by turning to penance with its whole heart.[33]

395    Stilicho killed Rufinus of the Bosphorus region after overcoming the guard of Huns that supported him, because Rufinus reached the summit of imperial service but could not abide that Stilicho was preferred to him.[34]

2   Claudian the poet was considered worthy of admiration.[35]

397    Gildo stirred Africa into rebellion and withdrew the usual taxes from the Romans.[36]

Prudentius, our [i.e. Christian] lyric poet, a Spaniard by his illustrious birth, developed the strength of his talents.[37]

3   Stilicho, master of the soldiers, killed Gildo in Mauretania and restored Africa to its former status.[38]

Innocent was the thirty-seventh bishop to occupy the throne of the Roman church. [39]

4   Temples of the ancient superstition destroyed over the whole Roman world.[40]

Paulinus of Nola, later a bishop, sold everything as an admirable example, for he was the master of innumerable estates, and unimpeded chose the religious life.[41]

5   John [Chrysostom], bishop of Constantinople, shone in word and deed.[42]

Martin, after living an extraordinary life, put aside his [mortal] body.[43]

6   The insane Pelagius tried to soil the churches with his purulent doctrine.[44]

7   A synod at Alexandria was convened to deal with a dispute arising from the doctrine of Origen. This decision emerged from it: that whoever approved of the works of the above mentioned Origen should be placed outside the church.[45]

8   There was an eclipse of the sun.[46]

Augustine treated a great many matters in countless books.[46]

9  In three books Severus used examples of the saint's holiness to give us a life of Martin.[48]

10-11  A savage storm of barbaric disturbance lay over Italy. For Radagaisus, king of the Goths, crossed the frontier of Italy to plunder.[50]

As a consequence of this, the Arians who had been driven some distance from the Roman world began to take encouragement from the protection of the barbarian peoples to whom they had turned.[51]

a. 405  12  Radagaisus laid many cities waste before he fell: his division of his army into three parts under different leaders opened up to the Romans some means of resisting. Stilicho wheeled around his Hun auxiliaries and annihilated a third part of the enemy force in a notable victory. [52]

a. 408  Arcadius, ruler of the east, died leaving quite a small son, Theodosius, as his successor to the empire.[53]

Caelestine was the thirty-eighth bishop to govern the Roman church.[54]

13  The fury of various peoples began to tear Gaul to pieces. Stilicho set them loose as much as he could, indignant that his son had been denied the kingdom.[55]

14  At Utica the land in the forum of Trajan let out a bellowing noise for seven days.[56]

a. 408  Many advised, among other things, the death of Stilicho in the interests of the state, because he was devising plots against the well-being of the emperor.[57]

Nestorius, bishop of Constantinople [a. 428-431], turned to a heresy that separates God from man in [the person of] Christ.[58]

15  John, count of Africa, was killed by the people.[59]

Proculus, bishop of Marseilles, was considered a man of renown: he agreed to an extensive investigation being conducted into the suspected adultery of bishop Remedius [Remigius].[60]

16  At this time, as the host of enemies grew stronger, the powers of the Romans were weakened to their very foundation.[61]

The British provinces were laid waste by an invasion of Saxons.[62]

The Vandals and Alans ravaged part of Gaul; Constantine the usurper took possession of what was left.[63]

The Sueves took over the greater part of Spain.[64]

410      Finally, the capital of the world, Rome herself, was most foully exposed to sack at the hands of the Goths.[65]

411 **17**  Constantine the usurper was killed.[66]

**18**  Again another looting of Gaul, by the Goths who, under the command of Alaric, had taken Rome and had then crossed the Alps.[67]

**19**  Jovinus seized power as a usurper after Constantine.[68]

    By the diligence of a vigorous man, Dardanus, who was the only one not to submit to the usurper, Athaulf, who was in command of the Goths after Alaric, was turned away from an alliance with Jovinus.[69]

    Sallustius as well as Sebastian [brothers of Jovinus] were killed.[70]

    Valence, the noblest city of Gaul, was stormed by the Goths; Jovinus had gone there in flight.[71]

**20**  Enormous famine in Gaul.[72]

    Aquitaine given over to the Goths.[73]

    Patroclus, bishop of Arles, dared to conduct a disreputable trade in the sale of episcopal offices.[74]

    Heraclian, count of Africa, who rendered vigorous service in the restoration of the Roman world, was killed when he attempted a revolution.[75]

**21-22**  Placidia, the emperor's sister, who was a captive for a long time, and then wife

416  of a king, married Constantius, after the king was killed by deception.[77]

    The Goths were driven back by an attack of Constantius when they moved again after the death of Athaulf.[78]

**23-25**  The heresy of the *praedestinati*, said to have started with Augustine, began to spread in this period.[81]

**26**  There was an eclipse of the sun.[82]

    Sixtus was the thirty-ninth bishop to direct the Roman church [a. 432-440].[83]

**27**  A wonderful portent appeared in the sky.[84]

    Maximus the usurper took control of Spain by force.[85]

**28**  Honoratus, Minervius, Castor, and Jovian, the heads of different monasteries, flourished in Gaul.[86]

29-30  The imperial dignity was conferred on Constantius at the wishes of Hono-
420-21 rius. Constantius exercised it for scarcely eight months and died, leaving an
eight year-old son Valentinian.[88]

    The usurper Maximus was toppled from power and taken to Ravenna
where he was put on display before the emperor during the celebrations of
Honorius's thirtieth anniversary.[89]

31  Placidia was discovered plotting against her brother and exiled to Rome.[90]

a. 423  32  Honorius died at Ravenna.[92]

    John, a former chief of the bureau of notaries, assumed power, though he
had no right to it.[92]

    Honorius left an empire severely weakened by many crises.[93]

## Theodosius [II] reigned for 27 years [a. 424-450]

a. 424  1  Placidia sent a message to Theodosius begging help.[95]

    Sigisvult hastened to Africa against Boniface.[96]

a. 425  2  In Gaul, the [praetorian] prefect Exuperantius was killed by the soldiers.[97]

    Carthage was surrounded with a wall. From the time when the ancient
city had been destroyed, Carthage was not allowed to be fortified by walls by
decree of the Romans in case it sheltered rebellion.[98]

    John was defeated by the army of the east and killed. Ravenna then was
laid waste by looting.[99]

    Aëtius, the son of Count Gaudentius who was killed by the soldiers in
Gaul, entered Italy with Huns in order to support John.[100]

a. 426  3  Valentinian [III] was made emperor at Rome.[101]

a. 427  4  Arles was freed from the Goths by Aëtius.[102]

a. 428  5  At last Placidia was brought to the power she wished for.[103]

a. 429  6  Cassian set forth in books distributed to a great many people the lives of the
fathers, their teachings and rules, which he had learned in Egypt.[104]

a. 430 7-8  Aëtius tried to bring about the destruction of the Juthungi.[106]

    Massacre of almost 20,000 troops fighting in Spain against the Vandals. [Cf.
**16**, Prosper, s.a. 422; **18**, Hydatius, s.a. 422.][107]

The Vandals crossed the strait to Africa and, having torn the province to pieces, inflicted an immense disaster on the Romans.[108]

432   **9**   After his consulate had been proclaimed, Aëtius, turning to better protection, gave way to Boniface, who had come from Africa on the summons of the queen.[109]

There was severe cold that was also ruinous to the health of a great many people.[110]

Boniface was wounded in a battle he won against Aëtius but retired from it to die.[Cf. **16**, Prosper, s.a. 432.][111]

433   **10**   After the battle, Aëtius turned to the Huns, who at the time were led by Rugila, and returned to Roman territory with the help he had asked for.[112]

The Goths were summoned by the Romans to bring help.[113]

Germanus the bishop of Auxerre became renowned for his miraculous powers and the strictness of his life.[114]

434   **11**   Aëtius was received into favor.[115]

Rugila, king of the Huns, with whom peace had been made, died. He was succeeded by Bleda.[116]

435   **12**   Farther Gaul followed Tibatto, the leader of a rebellion, and separated from Roman society. This was only the beginning of almost all the servile order [servitia] of Gaul coming into accord in a Bacaudic revolt (Bacauda).[117]

436   **13**   A memorable war against the Burgundians broke out in which almost the entire people with their king were destroyed by Aëtius.[118]

437   **14**   After Tibatto was captured and the other leaders of the revolt were put in bonds or killed, the commotion of the Bacaudae quietened down.[119]

438   **15**   The Theodosian book bringing together all the laws of legitimate emperors for the first time was issued in this year.[120]

[Polemius] Silvius, who was quite mentally disturbed, composed some writings on religion after he completed his duty serving in the palace.[121]

439   **16**   Leo was the fortieth bishop to take up leadership of the Roman church.[122]

440   **17**   Having pacified disturbances in Gaul, Aëtius returned to Italy. [123]

Abandoned country properties of the city of Valence were given over for division to the Alans who were led by Sambida.[124]

**18-19**
a. 441-42  The British provinces, which up to this time had endured a variety of disasters and misfortunes, were subjected to the authority of the Saxons.[126]

The lands of Farther Gaul were handed over by the patrician Aëtius to the Alans to be divided with the inhabitants. They subdued those who opposed them with arms, drove out the owners, and obtained possession of the land by force.[127]

a. 443  **20**  Sapaudia was given to the remnants of the Burgundians to be divided with the native inhabitants.[128]

a. 444  **21**  Carthage was captured by the Vandals [a. 439] and along with all Africa cast off the might of the Roman Empire with lamentable harm and injury. For thereby it became a possession of the Vandals.[129]

a. 445  **22**  Thrace was shaken by an attack of the Huns.[130]

a. 446  **23**  Bleda, king of the Huns, was struck down through the deceit of his brother Attila, who succeeded him.[131]

a. 447  **24**  New destruction broke out in the East. No less than seventy cities were laid waste by the plundering of the Huns, for no assistence was brought from the West.[132]

a. 448  **25**  Eudoxius, a physician by profession and of perverse, if well-developed, talents, fled to the Huns when implicated in the *Bacauda* that took place at that time.[133]

a. 449  **26**  Eucherius, bishop of Lyons, and Hilary of Arles died, bringing to a close their extraordinary lives.[134]

a. 450  **27**  An abominable heresy was stirred up by a certain abbot [Eutyches]. Theodosius, who provided him with support, died in July, having completed over forty years in power. Marcian succeeded him.[135]

Placidia also died in this year, after a life that was irreproachable following her conversion, and while her son completed his twenty-fifth year in power.[136]

## Valentinian [III, †a. 455] and Marcian

451   1   At this time the pitiable condition of the state was quite evident, for there was no province without a barbarian settler, and the unspeakable heresy of the Arians, which had permeated the barbarian nations, spread over the whole world and laid claim to the name Catholic.[138]

     Attila entered Gaul as if he had the right to ask for a wife that was owed to him. There he inflicted and suffered defeat and then withdrew to his homeland.[139]

450   2   In this year a great many portents appeared.[140]

     As he had suffered an unexpected defeat in Gaul, Attila, enraged, attacked Italy, which the inhabitants, alarmed by fear alone, had stripped of its protection.[141]

# 18. FROM THE *CHRONICLE* OF HYDATIUS

*Most of what we know of Hydatius depends on the testimony of his own chronicle. He was born in Lemica (the area around present-day Ginzo de Limia in north-western Spain) in the province of Gallaecia (Galicia, the modern name, refers to a smaller area than its fifth-century equivalent); Gallaecia was the home country of Theodosius the Great. As a child Hydatius travelled to Palestine, probably in 407, where he saw, among other church luminaries, Saint Jerome. We can infer that he came from a well-to-do, and well-connected, Christian family. He tells us that he became a bishop in 428 but does not explicitly tell us the city, though it was likely Chaves in modern Portugal.*

*His* Chronicle, *which he completed writing around 470, is a continuation of the Eusebius-Jerome world chronicle. It is preserved in later epitomes, and a nearly complete version of it survives in one Carolingian MS. For the period following the close of Orosius's* Histories, *it is the fundamental source for Iberian history and the only major example of Spanish historiography prior to the late sixth century. But these are not the reasons the* Chronicle *is quoted at length here (in fact much of Hydatius's account of strictly local affairs, especially concerning the Sueves, has had to be omitted in this translation). Hydatius was also deeply interested in events elsewhere in the Roman world, especially in Gaul and Italy. In Hydatius's day the Iberian peninsula was still supposed to be part of the Gallic prefecture and the Goths, operating out of southern Gaul at the behest of the imperial government, were beginning their profound impact upon the course of Spanish history.*

*Unfortunately Hydatius's version of events is often complicated by chronological problems, which are especially evident in his valuable account of the period after 455. Events in the* Chronicle *are dated by regnal years of emperors, but these cannot always be readily brought into harmony with calendar years or fitted easily into our conventional* anno domini *dating scheme; for instance, Hydatius assigns three years to the emperor Avitus, whose reign is known to have lasted from July 455 to October 456. Scholars are divided on the extent to which the errors and peculiarities of chronology are due to Hydatius himself or later reworkings of his chronicle.*

*In this translation I follow the regnal year numbers and* anno domini *equivalents proposed in the latest edition of the* Chronicle. *I have omitted other extra-textual chronological markers: four-year Olympiads and the years of Abraham, counted by decades, carried over from Jerome; and Spanish aeras, a local method of dating that counted years from Augustus's conquest of Spain in 38 B.C. (though for an example of this in the text, see s.a. 409). Following the most recent edition, I have noted (in the text s.a. 432, not in the margin) reference to the eighth Jubilee. Jubilees were fifty-year periods, connected with the belief that nine such periods would transpire between the resurrection and the second coming.*

*Anno domini dates are placed in the margin. They are followed by the regnal year used by Hydatius, indicated here by an Arabic numeral in bold face; I give the reign of the emperor to whom these year numbers apply as a subheading. The excerpts begin with the year 409.*

Source: *The Chronicle of Hydatius and the Consularia Constantinopolitana,* ed. and trans. Richard W. Burgess (Oxford, 1993). Translation by A.C. Murray.

## The Reign of Honorius, a. 395-423

a. 409 **15** The Alans, Vandals, and Sueves entered the Spanish provinces in year 447 [according to Spanish chronology]. Some record 28 September, others 12 October, on a Tuesday, in the year when Honorius was consul for the eighth time and Theodosius, the son of Arcadius, consul for the third time.

Alaric, king of the Goths, entered Rome. Although killing took place inside and outside the city, all who sought sanctuary in the holy places were spared.

[Galla] Placidia, the daughter of Theodosius, the sister of the emperor Honorius, was captured in the city.

Alaric died. Athaulf succeeded him to the kingship.

The barbarians who entered the Spanish provinces plundered them in a murderous fashion.

No less virulent was the effect of disease.

a. 410 **16** As the barbarians rampaged out of control through the Spanish provinces and disease caused no less an affliction, the wealth and resources safely stored in the cities were snatched away by the tyrannical tax-collector and used up by the soldiers. Severe hunger spread so that human beings, compelled by hunger, consumed human flesh. Mothers even fed upon the bodies of their own children, whom they had killed and cooked with their own hands. Animals accustomed to the bodies of those killed by the sword, by hunger, or by disease, killed any people who still had some strength left and, feeding on their flesh, everywhere turned savagely to the destruction of the human race. And so with the four misfortunes of sword, hunger, disease, and beasts raging everywhere throughout the world, the predictions foretold by the Lord through his prophets were fulfilled.

411 **17** When the provinces of Spain had been overthrown by the spread of the misfortunes just recorded, the Lord took mercy, and the barbarians were turned toward establishing peace. They partitioned the territories of the provinces among themselves in order to settle down. The Vandals took Gallaecia and the Sueves the portion located on the western edge of the Ocean sea. The Alans obtained the provinces of Lusitania and Carthaginiensis, and the Vandals called Silings, Baetica. In towns and fortresses the Spaniards surviving the misfortunes submitted to the servitude of the barbarians, who were ruling throughout the provinces.

In the Gallic provinces, Constantine was killed by Honorius's general, Constantius, after having usurped authority for three years.

412 **18** In Gaul, the brothers Jovinus and Sebastian, and in Africa, Heraclian, were puffed up with the same mad desire to usurp power...

413 **19** Jovinus and Sebastian were overwhelmed by Honorius's generals and killed at Narbonne.

The Goths entered Narbonne at the time of the vintage...

414 **20** Athaulf married [Galla] Placidia at Narbonne. The prophecy of Daniel was thereby thought to be fulfilled. The prophecy says that the daughter of the king of the south would unite with the king of the north, although he would have no progeny by her...

416 **22** Athaulf, forced by the patrician Constantius to abandon Narbonne, made for the Spanish provinces. He was assassinated in Barcelona by a certain Goth during private discussions. Wallia succeeded him to the kingship. He soon made peace with Constantius, the patrician, and turned against the Alans and Siling Vandals residing in Lusitania and Baetica...

Constantius married [Galla] Placidia.

a. 417 **23** On behalf of Rome, Wallia, king of the Goths, brought about a great slaughter of barbarians in the Spanish provinces...

a. 418 **24** All the Siling Vandals in Baetica were annihilated by King Wallia.

The Alans, who were ruling over Vandals and Sueves, were cut up so badly by the Goths that the few who survived when their king Addax was eliminated forgot about their independence and submitted to the protection of Gunderic, king of the Vandals, who had taken up residence in Gallaecia.

The Goths interrupted the war they were waging on behalf of Constantius when they were recalled to the Gallic provinces to receive homes in Aquitaine from Toulouse to the ocean.

Their king Wallia died, and Theoderic succeeded to the kingdom.

a. 419 **25** ...Valentinian, the son of Constantius and [Galla] Placidia, was born.

The many terrifying signs that occurred in the region of Gaul in the city of Biterrae [Béziers] were described by Paulinus, bishop of the same city, in a letter that was widely circulated...

a. 422 **28** In Baetica, Castinus, master of the soldiers in command of a good-sized force and Gothic auxiliaries, waged war on the Vandals [who had moved from Gallaecia]. When he had reduced them to starvation by seige so that they were prepared to surrender, he precipitously engaged them in open battle and, being betrayed by his auxiliaries, suffered defeat and fled to Tarragona.

a. 424 **30** Honorius died at Ravenna after his thirtieth anniversary celebrations.

After the death of his paternal uncle Honorius, Theodosius [II], the son of Arcadius, ruling for some time previously in the eastern parts since the death of his father, held sole rule of the empire, forty-first emperor of the Romans, when he was twenty-two years old.

John usurped authority [in Rome].

### Reign of Valentinian III, a. 425-55

a. 425 **1** In Constantinople Theodosius made Valentinian, the son of his aunt [Galla] Placidia, Caesar and sent him against John. The generals under Valentinian's command, sent by Theodosius to accompany the Caesar, killed John at Ravenna in the first year of his usurpation of authority; Felix was appointed patrician and master of the soldiers.

Valentinian, who was Caesar, was hailed Augustus at Rome.

The Vandals plundered the Balearic Islands. When they had overthrown Spanish Carthage and Hispalis [Seville] and plundered Spain, they invaded Mauretania...

428   **4**   Gunderic, king of the Vandals, captured Hispalis. Carried away with impiety, he reached his hand into the church of that city and was soon seized by a demon according to the judgment of God and perished. His brother Gaiseric succeeded him to the kingship. According to a story told by some, Gaiseric is supposed to have apostasized and converted from the Catholic faith to the Arian heresy.

429   **5**   Gaiseric, king of the Vandals, abandoned the Spanish provinces in the month of May, crossing along with all the Vandals and their families from the coast of the province of Baetica to Mauretania and Africa...

430   **6**   ...Not far from Arles some bands of Goths were annihilated by Count Aëtius, and Anaolsus their leader was captured.

      Juthungi as well as Nori were vanquished by him in the same way.

      Felix, who was called patrician, was killed at Ravenna in a mutiny of the troops.

431   **7**   Aëtius, general of both services, subdued the Nori, who were in rebellion.

      Again, as soon as the opportunity presented itself, the Sueves broke the peace they had made with the Gallaecians. On account of their plundering, Bishop Hydatius led an embassy to General Aëtius, who was conducting a campaign in Gaul.

432   **8**   Eighth Jubilee after the Lord's ascension.

      When the Franks had been defeated in a war and were received on peaceful terms, Count Censorius was sent as an envoy to the Sueves, and the above-mentioned Hydatius returned with him...

436   **12**   Siege of Narbonne begun by Goths.

      The Burgundians, who had rebelled, were defeated by the Romans under the general Aëtius.

437   **13**   Narbonne freed from the seige.

      Slaughter of twenty thousand Burgundians by Aëtius, general and master of the soldiers...

438   **14**   Slaughter of eight thousand Goths under general Aëtius...

439   **15**   When Gaiseric's trickery had brought about the fall of Carthage on 19 October, he seized all [the diocese of] Africa.

      In a war against the Goths under King Theoderic at Toulouse, the Roman general Litorius took it upon himself to attack with a band of Huns as auxiliaries. These were slaughtered, and he himself was wounded and captured. A few days later he was killed.

Peace was made between the Romans and Goths.

King Gaiseric, carried away by impiety, drove the bishop and clergy of Carthage from the city and, in accordance with the prophecy of Daniel, filled their positions again, handing over the Catholic churches of the saints to the Arians.

Rechila, king of the Sueves, entered Emerita.

a. 441 **17** ...King Rechila took Hispalis and reduced the provinces of Baetica and Carthaginiensis to his authority...

Asturius, a general of both services, was sent to the Spanish provinces and slaughtered the Bacaudae of Tarraconensis in large numbers...

a. 443 **19** Merobaudes, the son-in-law of the master of the soldiers Asturius, was sent as his successor. Merobaudes was of noble birth and his eloquence, and especially his poetry, deserves comparison with that of the ancients. Statues have even been erected in his honor. In the short time he held command, he crushed the arrogance of the Bacaudae of Aracelli. He was soon recalled to Rome by an imperial order at the urging of some jealous people.

a. 444 **20** Sebastian [the son-in-law of Boniface] was detected in his refuge and fled from Constantinople after being warned that measures were being taken against him. When he came to King Theoderic and was treated as a public enemy, he managed to reach Barcelona and enter the city.

a. 445 **21** In the city of Asturica in Gallaecia, certain Manichees who had been in hiding for some years were uncovered due to episcopal reports sent to Antoninus, bishop of Emerita, by Bishops Hydatius and Thoribius, who had previously interrogated them...

Sebastian fled Barcelona and went over to the Vandals.

Reports on Manichees were circulated around the provinces by the bishop presiding in Rome at the time.

a. 446 **22** Vitus was made master of both services and sent to Spain with the support of a not insubstantial force. He harried the people of Carthaginiensis and Baetica, but fled in pitiful terror when the Sueves arrived under their king and when the Goths who had come to help him in his depredations were also beaten in the fighting. The Sueves then brought these provinces to ruin with widespread plundering.

447 **23** Leo, the forty-second bishop, presided over the Roman church; his writings against the Priscillianists were presented to the Spanish bishops by Pervincus, deacon of Bishop Thoribius. Among these works a full discussion of the rites the Catholic faith and blasphemies of heresies was sent to bishop Thoribius. It was approved for deceitful reasons by some Gallaecians...

448 **24** Rechila, king of the Sueves, died a pagan in Emerita in August. Rechiarius, his son and a Catholic, soon succeeded him to the kingship, though not without some secret rivals among his people...

449 **25** ...Rechiarius received the daughter of King Theoderic as his wife, and having begun his reign well, plundered Vasconia in February.

To show his outstanding daring, Basilius gathered together Bacaudae and killed federates in the church of Tyrasso...

449 **26** ...Forced into exile, Sebastian sought refuge under Gaiseric's protection, a ruinous expedient as the outcome showed. A short time after his arrival Gaiseric had him killed.

Letters of Bishop Flavian sent to Bishop Leo along with the writings of Cyril, bishop of Alexandria, to Nestorius of Constantinople on the subject of the Ebionite heretic Eutyches were brought from the Gallic provinces, as was Bishop Leo's reply to Flavian. These along with the reports and writings of other bishops were circulated among the churches.

450 **27** The emperor Theodosius died [28 July] in Constantinople at the age of forty-nine.

After him Marcian was immediately made the forty-second emperor at Constantinople by the soldiers and army, and at the urging also of Theodosius's sister, Queen Pulcheria. Marcian married her and ruled the eastern parts [of the empire].

451 **28** The mother of Emperor Valentinian died at Rome.

In Gallaecia there were constant earthquakes and a number of signs appeared in the sky. On Tuesday 4 April, after sunset, the northern heavens grew red like fire or blood; within the firey redness were brighter streaks resembling glowing red spears. This portent lasted from nightfall until almost the third hour of the night. It was soon explained by a momentous event.

The Huns broke the peace and plundered the Gallic provinces. A great many cities were taken. On the Catalaunian plains, not far from the city of Metz, which they had taken, the Huns were cut down in open battle with the aid of God and defeated by General Aëtius and King Theoderic, who had made a peace treaty with each other. The darkness of night interrupted the fighting. King Theoderic was laid low there and died. Almost 300,000 men are said to have fallen in that battle.

Many signs appeared in the year. On 26 September the moon grew dark in the east. That certain phenomena were seen in the sky over regions of Gaul around the following Easter time is clearly shown by a letter about them by Eufronius, bishop of Autun, addressed to Count Agrippinus. A comet began to appear from 18 June; by the 29th it it could be seen at dawn in the east, and was soon spotted in the west after sundown. By [16 July/1 August], it could be seen only in the west.

On the death of Theoderic, his son Thorismund succeeded to the kingship.

The Huns under their king Attila left Gaul after the battle and made for Italy.

a. 452-3 **29** In the second year of the reign of Emperor Marcian, when the Huns who were plundering Italy had also taken some cities by storm, they were struck through divine providence by heaven-sent disasters, some with hunger and some with a disease. They were also slaughtered by auxiliaries sent by Marcian and commanded by Aëtius and, at the same time, were subdued in their homelands by the heaven-sent disasters as well as by the army of Marcian. And so, subdued, they made peace with the Romans and all returned to their homelands. Their king, Attila, died there soon after his return.

Mansuetus, count of Spain, and Fronto, also a count, were sent as envoys to establish peace with the Sueves and they got the terms with which they had been charged.

Thorismund, king of the Goths, whose intentions were hostile, was assassinated by his brothers Theoderic [II] and Frederic. Theoderic [II] succeeded Thorismund to the kingship.

a. 453-4 **30** In the third year of of the reign of Emperor Marcian, in the month of July, Queen Pulcheria died.

The Bacaudae of Tarraconensis were slaughtered by Frederic, the brother of King Theoderic [II], representing the Roman government.

In Gallaecia there was an earthquake, and a sign appeared on the sun when it rose, as if in contention with it.

Aëtius, general and patrician, summoned alone to the palace on false pretences, was killed by the hand of Emperor Valentinian himself, and a number of distinguished citizens (*honorati*) were murdered along with him by the emperor's swordbearer as they were let in one at a time. When these deeds were done, Valentinian sent envoys to the [barbarian] peoples. Justinianus was the envoy that came to the Sueves.

455  **31**  In the fourth year of the reign of Emperor Marcian, Valentinian, emperor at Rome, was killed on the field in the midst of his army by two barbarian intimates of Aëtius. The emperor was aged thirty six in the thirty-first year of his reign.

After him, [Petronius] Maximus, a former consul, was soon hailed as forty-third Augustus at Rome. Tormented by serious disturbances, which he feared, he married Valentinian's widow when he was made emperor and gave Valentinian's daughter in marriage to his own son from a previous marriage, Palladius, whom he had made Caesar. In seeking imperial power himself he had wickedly contrived the plan for the destruction of those killed by Valentinian and of Valentinian himself. For those reasons, he was killed in that city by an uprising of the people and a mutiny of the troops at the completion of scarcely four months of his reign, and while he was attempting to abandon imperial rule and Rome.

The same year in Gaul, Avitus, a Gallic citizen, was hailed by the army of Gaul and by distinguished citizens (*honorati*) as Augustus, first at Tolouse, then at Arles. He went to Rome and was accepted [as emperor].

Down to Valentinian the line of Theodosius held imperial power.

Marcian in the fourth year of his reign acquired the position of sole ruler, forty third [emperor] of the Romans.

Avitus, who had been both called upon and accepted by the Romans, sent envoys to Marcian to acquire the agreement of the empire.

Before Avitus was made Augustus, Gaiseric entered Rome — at the invitation of Valentinian's widow, according to a lying rumor that was spread about. He plundered the wealth of the Romans and returned to Carthage, taking with him Valentinian's widow, his two daughters, and Gaudentius, the son of Aëtius.

The Sueves plundered the regions of Carthaginiensis that they had restored to the Romans.

### Reign of Avitus, a. 455-456

456  **1**  Marcian and Avitus harmoniously exercised imperial authority.

Count Fronto was sent to the Sueves as an envoy by the Augustus Avitus. Likewise, Theodoric [II], king of the Goths, since he was loyal to the empire, sent envoys to the Sueves so that the latter would preserve the promises of the sworn treaty with respect to him as much as to the empire, since they had joined in one peace treaty. The envoys of both parties were sent back; every oath was violated, and the Sueves fell upon the province of Tarraconensis, which was subject to the Roman empire.

A fair sized force of Heruli landed in seven ships on the shore of Lucus.

When they were attacked by a host that had gathered [to oppose them], the light armed Heruli, numbering almost four-hundred men, got away with only two of their number dead. Returning home, they savagely plundered the coastal regions of Cantabria and Vardullia.

a. 456-7 **2** Envoys of the Goths came to the Sueves again; after their arrival, Rechiarius, king of the Sueves, with a large force of his own men, attacked regions of the province of Tarraconensis. Plundering them, he led off large numbers of captives to Gallaecia.

Soon Theoderic [II], king of the Goths, entered Spain with a huge army in accordance with the desires and instructions of Emperor Avitus. King Rechiarius met him with a host of Sueves at the twelfth milestone from the city of Asturica on the river Urbicus, on 5 October, a Friday. Battle began right away and Rechiarius was defeated. His forces were cut down, a good number were taken prisoner, and a great many fled; the king, wounded and a fugitive, barely escaped to the most distant of his possessions in Gallaecia.

King Theoderic [II] pushed on with his army to Braga, the farthest city of Gallaecia; the sacking of the city — still sad and lamentable, even if no blood was shed — took place on 28 October, a Sunday. A great many Romans were taken captive. The churches of the saints were broken into; altars were lifted up and broken; even virgins of God were taken away, but were not violated. The clergy were stripped right down to their private parts. Everyone was dragged from the refuge of the holy places, both sexes without distinction along with children. The holy places were desecrated by beasts of burden, cattle, and camels. The sack to a certain extent gave new meaning to the scriptual examples of heavenly anger against Jerusalem.

Rechiarius who had fled to the place called Portus Cale was taken prisoner and delivered to King Theoderic [II]. He was put under guard. Other Sueves who had survived the earlier battle surrendered, although a good number were killed nevertheless. Thus the kingdom of the Sueves was destroyed and brought to an end.

In those days King Theoderic [II] heard the news that a great host of Vandals, which had sailed from Carthage with sixty ships to Gaul and Italy, had been slaughtered by Avitus due to a strategem of Count Ricimer.

The tribune Hesychius, dispatched as an envoy to Theoderic [II] with imperial gifts, came to Gallaecia with news of the above slaughter of the Vandal host in Corsica and with the announcement that Avitus had passed from Italy to Arles in Gaul. Easterners whose ships docked at Hispalis reported a bloody victory by the army of Marcian.

Rechiarius was killed in the month of December and King Theoderic [II] passed from Gallaecia to Lusitania...

The Sueves who remained in the most distant region of Gallaecia set up Massilia's son, called Maldras, as king.

Theoderic as he set about plundering Emerita took fright at the portents of the blessed martyr Eulalia.

. 457   **3**  In the third year after he had been made emperor by the Gauls and the Goths, Avitus lost the imperial power, and, deprived of the help promised by the Goths, he also lost his life.

In the eastern parts, Marcian died in the seventh year of his imperial rule [26 January].

In Italy Majorian was hailed as Augustus [1 April], forty-fourth emperor of the Romans, and Leo was hailed Augustus [7 February] in Constantinople.

### Reign of Majorian, a. 457-461

  **1**  Theoderic [II], frightened off by bad news, left Emerita soon after Easter, which was on 31 March [a. 457], to return to Gaul. Part of the host he commanded, which was composed of various nations, he sent to the plains of Gallaecia under his generals. They were versed in deceit and perjury. Under cover of a peace feigned with the usual kind of faithlessness and following the orders they had been given, they marched into Asturica, which Theoderic's looters had already entered under the guise of a Roman commission, and falsely claimed that they had been ordered to undertake a campaign against the Sueves that remained. They found a multitude of different kinds of people there and wasted no time in cutting them down. They broke into the holy churches, seized and destroyed the altars, and carried off every sacred furnishing and service. They found two bishops there and took them away into captivity with their clergy. Weaker persons of both sexes were taken into a miserable captivity. They burned the remaining empty houses of the town and devastated the establishments in the countryside. The city of Palentia suffered a similar destruction as Asturica at the hands of the Goths. One fortress, Coviacum, at the thirtieth milestone from Asturica, was worn down by a long siege of the Goths but, with God's help, resisted the enemy and prevailed. When a large number of their band had been killed, the rest of the enemy returned to Gaul...

. 458   **2**  The Gothic army, dispatched to Spain by King Theoderic [II] under its general Cyril, reached Baetica in the month of July...

Sabinus, bishop of Hispalis, returned to his own church from Gaul after struggling in exile for twenty years.

a. 459  3  Theoderic [II] sent to Baetica a fair sized detachment of his army under his general Suniericus. Cyril was recalled to Gaul. Nonetheless some of the Sueves under Maldras plundered parts of Lusitania, and some under Rechimundus parts of Gallaecia.

The Heruli savagely fell upon some coastal settlements in the territory of Lucus as they were making their way to Baetica...

Envoys dispatched by Nepotianus, master of the soldiers, and by Count Suniericus came to the Gallaecians announcing that Augustus Majorian and King Theoderic [II] had most firmly ratified terms of a peace treaty between themselves, since the Goths had been defeated in a certain battle...

a. 460  4  ...In the month of May, Emperor Majorian entered Spain. As he was proceeding to the province of Carthaginiensis, a number of ships that he was outfitting to take him against the Vandals were snatched away from the coast of Carthaginiensis by Vandals given information by traitors. His plans frustrated, Majorian returned to Italy.

Part of the Gothic army sent to Gallaecia by Counts Suniericus and Nepotianus plundered the Sueves living in Lucus. Betrayed by the informers Dictynius, Spinio, and Ascanius, who spread the poison of their faithlessness to create terror, the army turned back to where it came from. And urged on by the same informers above, Frumarius with a force of Sueves under his command, soon took Bishop Hydatius captive in the church of Aquae Flaviae [Chaves] on 26 July and inflicted massive ruin upon the same district...

The above Hydatius, after completing three months of captivity, by the grace of the compassionate God, returned to Aquae Flaviae in November against the wishes and plans of the above informers...

King Gaiseric through envoys asked peace from Emperor Majorian.

a. 461  5  Ricimer, moved by spite and supported by the advice of jealous men, trapped Majorian and treacherously killed him as the emperor was returning from Gaul to Rome and planning necessary measures for the empire and its prestige.

Severus was hailed Augustus by the senate at Rome [19 November], forty-fifth [emperor] of the Romans, in the fifth year of the imperial rule of Leo.

### Reign of Severus a. 461-465

a. 462  1  ...Gaiseric sent Valentinian's wife back to Constantinople. One of her daughters married Gento, Gaiseric's son, and another married Olybrius, senator of the city of Rome.

The Gaul Agrippinus, a count hostile to his fellow-countryman the distinguished Count Aegidius, handed the city of Narbonne over to Theoderic [II] in order to gain the help of the Goths...

a. 463    **2**    In Armorica, Frederic, the brother of King Theoderic [II], rose up against Aegidius, count [and master] of both services, a man who enjoyed an excellent reputation and who pleased God with his good works. Frederic and his men were defeated and killed. [Cf. **19**, Leo 3; **20**, s.a. 463; and **35**.]...

464-5    **3**    ...In the month of May, envoys of the above-mentioned Aegidius sailed by way of the Ocean to the Vandals and returned to where they came from in September by the same route...

The Vandals were slaughtered in Sicily and driven from the island.

Aegidius died as a result of deception: some say that he was the victim of a trap, some that he was poisoned. With him gone, the Goths soon fell upon the regions he had protected in the name of Rome...

465-6    **4**    ...Envoys of the Sueves announced that Severus had died in the fourth year of his imperial rule [14 November 465]...

Ajax, a Galatian by birth, who had ended up an apostate and a leading Arian, emerged among the Sueves with the help of their king as an enemy of the Catholic faith and the divine trinity. This disease-bearing poison of the enemy of man was conveyed from the Gallic home of the Goths...

Anthemius, brother of Procopius, set out from Constantinople. By God's will, he, along with Marcellinus and other selected counts as well as a numerous army of soldiers, were sent to Italy by the Augustus Leo.

Anthemius was hailed Augustus, forty-sixth emperor of the Romans, at the eighth milestone from Rome, in the ninth year of the emperor Leo, in the month of August [12 April 467].

## The Reign of Anthemius, a. 467-472

466-7    **1**    An expedition to Africa planned against the Vandals was called back because of a change in the weather and poor sailing conditions.

Salla was sent as an envoy by Theoderic [II] to Remismund king of the Sueves. When he returned to Gaul he found Theoderic [II] had been killed by his brother. [Cf. **19**, s.a. 466; **20**, s.a. 467.]

Euric succeeded to the kingship by committing the same crime as his brother. Exalted by the office of king and by his criminal act, he sent envoys to the emperor and to the king of the Sueves. Without delay they were sent back by Remismund, who dispatched his own envoys to the emperor, the Vandals and the Goths...

Envoys on their return from the Goths relate that a number of portents were seen in Gaul...When the Goths had gathered one day for their assembly, the metal blades or edges of the spears they held in their hands for a while no longer preserved the natural appearance of iron but changed colour, some to green, some to red, some to yellow and some to black. In the middle of the city of Toulouse in the same period blood spurted from the ground and flowed throughout the course of a day.

a. 468    **2**    ...Envoys who had been sent to the emperor came back announcing that in their very presence an extremely large army had set out against the Vandals under three generals chosen by Leo; that Marcellinus had likewise been sent by Emperor Anthemius with a large force in alliance with this army; that Ricimer had been made the son-in-law of Emperor Anthemius and appointed patrician; that Asper had been reduced to private life, and his son killed, since they had been prosecuted and exposed for taking the part of the Vandals against the Roman empire...

*Hydatius's chronicle ends in the second year of Anthemius, a. 468, with more accounts of raids, envoys, and portents.*

## 19. THE *GALLIC CHRONICLE* OF *511*

*This chronicle is another continuation of Jerome-Eusebius, preserved in a unique MS in epitome form. The author, who is anonymous, wrote in Gaul in 511 and made use of the* Gallic Chronicle of 452 *and Hydatius. I give only the entries following the death of Avitus. Neither the chronicle's count of regnal years nor its placement of events is always accurate. The year numbers of the emperor's reign are in boldface Arabic numerals. I have placed* anno domini *dates in the left margin. The headings are those of the chronicle.*

Source: *Chronica Gallica DXI*, ed. Th. Mommsen *Chronica Minora* 1, MGH AA 9 (1892), pp. 664-666. Translation by A.C. Murray.

### Leo [a. 457-474] reigned at Constantinople 21 years, Majorian [a. 457-461] at Rome 3 years, 6 months, with Leo.

**3**    Majorian entered Arles.

He wanted to set out for Africa, but his ships were captured in Spain by the Vandals near Spanish Carthage [Cartagena].

461     Having set out for Italy, he was killed at Tortona [Dertona] by the patrician Ricimer.

Severus from Lucania was raised up as emperor [a. 461-465] and consul.

5    Frederic, the brother of King Theuderic, was killed on the Loire fighting with the Franks. [Cf. **18**, s.a. 463; **20**, s.a. 463; and **7.11.**]

a. 466   10   Theuderic, king of the Goths, was killed by his brother Euric at Toulouse.

a. 465          The emperor Severus died, and Anthemius [a. 467-72] was raised up at Rome and reigned for 5 years.

13   Anthemiolus was sent by his father Emperor Anthemius to Arles along with Thorisarius, Everdingus, and Hermianus, count of the stables. Euric crossed the Rhône to meet them, killed the commanders, and laid everything waste.

a. 472   15   Emperor Anthemius was killed by his son-in-law Ricimer and Gundobad, when a civil war was fought in the City.

16   Gauterit, a count of the Goths, occupied Spain in the region around Pamplona, Caesaraugusta [Saragossa] and neigbouring towns.

Heldefred with Vincent, duke of the Spains, besieged Tarragona and took the coastal cities.

But Vincent was dispatched as master of the soldiers by Euric and was killed in Italy by counts Alla and Sindila.

20   Arles was taken by Euric along with Marseilles and other strongpoints.

## Augustus Zeno [a. 474-491] reigned 13 years.

a. 484   7   Euric died at Arles and his son Alaric was installed as king.

11   Theoderic [the Great], driven out by Emperor Zeno, entered Italy, put Unulf to flight, and killed Odoacer.

## Augustus Anastsius [a. 491-518] reigned 19 years.

a. 507   15   Alaric, king of the Goths, was killed by the Franks.

Toulouse was burned by the Franks and Burgundians, and Barcelona was taken by Gundobad, king of the Burgundians. King Gesalicus returned to Spain, his forces having experienced their worst defeat.

19  Of Anastasius; the consuls were Felix [in the West] and Secundinus [in the East]. The indiction was the fourth, the era 5477. [= a. 511]

## 20. THE CHRONICLE OF MARIUS OF AVENCHES

*Marius was bishop of Avenches probably from ca. 574 to 594. Avenches was in the Burgundian kingdom, near Lake Neuchâtel. Marius's chronicle (his only known work) is preserved in a single manuscript of Carolingian date, where it appears as a continuation of Jerome's chronicle, the* Gallic Chronicle of 452 *and the last years of Prosper's chronicle. Among his sources, Marius made use of consular and Gallic annals, including annals resembling those that must have been used by Gregory of Tours. In this translation I have noted parallels and analogues with sources that appear elsewhere in this Reader but not with Italian and eastern annals.*

*Marius dates his events by means of consular years. At the time of writing, the old consular system had finally broken down. The last annual consulship was that of Basilius in 541. The years following were dated from his consulship (the period being called his post-consulship), until the consulship was finally appropriated as part of the imperial title. A peculiarity of Marius's chronology is that an extra post-consulship of Basilius was added at the year 566 combined with a misdating of Justinian's death; thereafter the yearly numbering of the imperial consulship is off by a year.*

*A temporary interruption of the yearly appointment of consuls, with a consequent post-consulship, also occurred in 531.*

*Starting in 523 Marius includes indictions in his dating scheme. At one time the term indiction meant a fiscal cycle of fifteen years beginning with the year 312, but eventually each of the years within the cycle itself came to be called an indiction, numbered from I to XV. The indiction began on 1 September, and so overlapped two consular years, but for purposes of calculation was normally identified with the consular year in which most of its months fell. In the one instance where Marius does not merely include notice of the indiction but precisely dates an event by month and indiction (s.a. 581), the event obviously falls in the previous consular year. There are other examples where the indictions are right, though events are placed under the wrong consular year. Unlike the consular dates, the indictions for the reign of Justin fall in the correct year.*

*I give only those years in which events have been entered, though these are complete, and the year of Justin's imperial consulship, which the manuscript marked with capital letters. The use of dating by consulship allows us readily to give* anno domini *equivalents, which in the translation are placed in the margin. Cross references to* Hydatius *and the* Chronicle of 511 *can be found in documents* **18** *and* **19** *respectively. The abbreviation* Hist. *refers to the* Histories *of Marius's contemporary, Gregory of Tours; see* **46-49**, *where most (but not all) these cross references will be found.*

Source: Two editions were used for this translation. (1) *Chronica a. CCCCLV–DLXXXI*, ed. Th. Mommsen, *Chronica Minora* 2, MGH AA 11 (1894), pp. 225-39. (2) *La Chronique de Marius d'Avenches (455-581)*, ed. and trans. Justin Favrod, 2nd. ed. (Lausanne, 1993); this has a photographic facsimile of the MS. Translation by A.C. Murray.

a. 455   Consuls Valentinian, for the eighth time, and Anthemius.

    *The final year of Prosper's chronicle follows (as above 16).*

    Prosper ends at this point and Bishop Marius begins.

    In the year of the above consul[s], Avitus was raised up as emperor in Gaul, and Theoderic, king of the Goths, entered Arles in peace with his brothers.

a. 456   Consuls John and Varanes.

    In the year of their consulships, Emperor Avitus was toppled by Majorian and Ricimer at Placentia and made bishop for the city.

    In this year the Burgundians took part of Gaul and divided the lands with the Gallic senators.

a. 460   Consuls Magnus and Apollinaris.

    In the year of their consulships, Emperor Majorian went to Spain.

    In this year ships were captured by the Vandals at Elche near Spanish Carthage. [Cf. **18**, s.a. 463; **19**, Leo 3.]

a. 461   Consuls Severinus and Dagauulf [Dagalaiphus].

    In the year of their consulships, the emperor Majorian was toppled from power at Tortona by the patrician Ricimer and killed on the river Scrivia. Severus was raised up as emperor at Ravenna.

a. 463   Consuls Basilius and Vivianus.

    In the year of their consulships, a battle was fought between Aegidius and the Goths between the Loire and the Loiret near Orleans, and there Frederic, king of the Goths, was killed. [Cf. **18**, s.a. 463; **19**, Leo 5; and **35**]

    Consuls Pusaeus and John.

a. 467   In the year of their consulships, Anthemius was raised up as emperor.

    In this year Theoderic, king of the Goths, was killed by his brother Euric at Toulouse. [Cf. **18**, s.a. 466-67; **19**, Leo 10.]

a. 473   Leo, consul for the fifth time.

    In the year of his consulship, Glycerius was raised up at Ravenna as emperor.

a. 474    Leo, junior.

In the year of his consulship, Glycerius was deposed from the imperial office, and Nepos was raised up as emperor.

a. 476    Consuls Basiliscus and Armatus.

When they were consuls, Odoacer was raised up as king.

a. 489    Consuls Probinus and Eusebius.

In the year of their consulships, Theoderic [the Great], king of the [Ostro]goths, entered Italy at Bridge of the Isonzo [Mainizza].

a. 493    [Consuls Eusebius, for the second time, and Faustus Albinus]

In the year of their consulships, King Odoacer was killed by King Theoderic at [the palace of] Lauretum.

a. 500    Consuls Patricius and Hypatius.

In the year of their consulships, a battle was fought at Dijon between the Franks and Burgundians, due to the deceitful machinations of Godigisel against his brother Gundobad. In the battle Godigisel along with his followers fought alongside the Franks against his brother Gundobad. After Gundobad fled, Godigisel obtained his brother's kingdom for a little while, and Gundobad took refuge in Avignon. [Cf. *Hist.* II 32.]

In this year Gundobad regained his strength and surrounded Vienne with an army. He took the city, killed his brother, and condemned to death by many refined tortures a good number of magnates and Burgundians who had been in agreement with Godigisel. Gundobad recovered the kingdom he had lost along with that which his brother had held and ruled successfully down to the day of his death. [Cf. *Hist.* II 33.]

In this year Odoin was killed at Rome.

a. 509    Consul Inportunus.

In the year of his consulship, Mammo, a duke of the [Ostro]goths plundered part of Gaul

a. 515    Consuls Florentius and Anthemius.

In the year of their consulships, the monastery at Agaune was built by Sigismund. [Cf. *Hist.* III 5.]

a. 516    Consul Peter.

In the year of his consulship, King Gundobad died, and his son Sigismund was raised up as king. [*Hist.* III 5.]

a. 522   Consuls Symmachus and Boethius.

In the year of their consulships, Segeric, the son of Sigismund, was unjustly killed by order of his father. [Cf. *Hist.* III 5.]

a. 523   Consul Maximus, Indiction I.

In the year of his consulship, Sigismund, king of the Burgundians, was surrendered by the Burgundians to the Franks, led into Francia dressed as a monk, and there thrown into a well with his wife and children. [Cf. *Hist.* III 6.]

a. 524   Consuls Justin and Opilio, Indiction II.

In the year of their consulships, Godomar, the brother of Sigismund, was appointed king of the Burgundians. [Cf. *Hist.* III 6.]

In this year, he fought against Chlodomer, king of the Franks, at Vézeronce and there Chlodomer was killed. [Cf. *Hist.* III 6.]

In this year, Boethius the patrician was killed in the territory of Milan.

a. 525   Consuls Probus junior and Philoxenus, Indiction III.

In the year of their consulships, Symmachus the patrician was killed at Ravenna.

a. 526   Consul Olybrius, Indiction IV.

In the year of his consulship, Theoderic, king of the [Ostro]goths died in the city of Ravenna, and Athalaric, his grandson, was raised up as king.

a. 532   Second year of the post-consulships of Lampadius and Orestes, Indiction X.

In this year of their consulships, Hypatius the patrician was raised up as emperor in an uprising of the people and was killed at the order of the Augustus Justinian. Pompeius and almost 30,000 people were put to the sword along with Hypatius in the circus.

a. 534   Consuls [Justinianus the Augustus, for the fourth time, and] Paulinus junior, Indiction XII. [*Paulinus was the last western consul.*]

In the year of their consulships, the kings of the Franks, Childebert, Chlothar, and Theudebert, took hold of Burgundy and, when they had put King Godomar to flight, divided his kingdom. [Cf. *Hist.* III 11]

In this year, Africa was restored to the Roman empire after ninety-two years by Belisarius the patrician. Gelimer, king of the Vandals, was delivered a captive to Constantinople and presented with his wife and treasure to the Augustus Justinian by the above mentioned patrician.

a. 535  Consul Belisarius, Indiction XIII.

In the year he was consul and gave consular games, he landed in Sicily and restored it to the Roman empire.

a. 538  Consul John, Indiction I.

In the year he was consul, Milan was stormed by the [Ostro]goths and Burgundians, and there senators and priests along with other people were killed even in the holy places, so that the altars were stained with their blood.

a. 539  Consul Apio, Indiction II.

In the year he was consul, Theudebert, king of the Franks, entered Italy and wasted Liguria and Aemilia. His army caught the sickness of the region and was greatly afflicted.

a. 540  Consul Justin, Indiction III.

In the year he was consul, the Persians ravaged Antioch and laid waste all of Syria.

In this year, Belisarius the patrician took away Witigis as a captive from Ravenna and presented him along with his wife and treasure to the Augustus Justin[ian] at Constantinople.

a. 547  Sixth year of the post-consulship of Basilius, Indiction X.

In this year, Vigilius the Roman pope hastened to Constantinople.

In this year, Baduila [Totila], king of the [Ostro]goths, took Rome and laid it waste. He pulled down the walls and set part of the city on fire.

In this year, General Belisarius restored his forces and brought the city of Rome back under Roman rule.

a. 548  Seventh year of the post-consulship of Basilius, Indiction XI.

In this year, Theudebert, the great king of the Franks, died, and his son Theudebald replaced him in the kingship. [Cf. *Hist.* III 36, 37.]

In this year, Lanthacarius, a duke of the Franks, died, stabbed during the Roman war.

a. 553  Twelfth year of the post-consulship of Basilius, Indiction I.

In this year, Baduila [Totila], king of the [Ostro]goths, was killed by an army of the Roman state under Narses, a eunuch secretary (*chartularius*). Teias received Baduila's kingdom.

a. 554  Thirteenth year of the post-consulship of Basilius, Indiction II.

In this year, Teias, king of the Goths, was killed by the above mentioned Narses.

a. 555   Fourteenth year of the post consulship of Basilius, Indiction III.

In this year, Theudebald, king of the Franks, died, and Chlothar the paternal uncle of his father took control of his kingdom. [Cf. *Hist.* IV 9.]

In this year, Chramn, the son of King Chlothar, was induced by his paternal uncle Childebert to take refuge with him. [Cf. *Hist.* IV 16.]

In this year, the Saxons rebelled, and Chlothar fought against them with a major force: a host of Franks and Saxons fell in the fighting but Chlothar went away the victor. [Cf. *Hist.* IV 10, 14.]

In this period, Buccelin, a duke of the Franks, perished in the Roman war along with all of his army. [Cf. *Hist.* IV 9.]

a. 556   Fifteenth year of the post-consulship of Basilius, Indiction IV.

In this year, the Saxons rebelled again and King Chlothar engaged them in battle where the larger part of the Saxons fell. [*Hist.* IV 10, 14.]

In this year, the Franks devastated all of Thuringia because it had conspired with the Saxons. [*Hist.* IV 10, 14.]

At the same time, Chramn gathered an army and laid waste the territory of his father. [*Hist.* IV 17.]

In this year, Frankish forces devastated the forces of the Roman state, put them to flight...[*lacuna or corrupt text* ]...and took away much wealth.

In this year, when their strength was restored, the forces of the Roman state took possession of the part of Italy that King Theudebert had acquired.

a. 558   Seventeenth year of the post-consulship of Basilius, Indiction VI.

In this year, Childebert, king of the Franks, passed away, and his brother King Chlothar took possession of his kingdom. [Cf. *Hist.* IV 20.]

a. 560   Nineteenth year of the post-consulship of Basilius, Indiction VIII.

In this year the sixteenth moon was darkened in the clear sky amidst the shining stars and could scarcely be seen.

In this year, Chramn, after giving oaths to his father, went to the Bretons and, attempting to seize his father's kingdom, dared to move against him, severely plundering many districts. To stop his son's madness, the father quickly brought up an army and killed the count of the Bretons. He took Chramn alive, burned him along with his wife and children, and put an end to the destruction of the whole region. [Cf. *Hist.* IV 20.]

a. 561   Twentieth year of the post-consulship of Basilius, Indiction IX.

In this year, King Chlothar died and his sons — that is Charibert, Guntram, Chilperic, and Sigibert — divided his kingdom. [Cf. *Hist.* IV 21, 22.]

a. 563 Twenty-second year of the post-consulship of Basilius, Indiction XI.

In this year, the powerful mount of Tauredunum in the territory of Valais collapsed so suddenly that it crushed the fortress which was nearby and the villages along with all their inhabitants. It set in motion the whole lake sixty miles long and twenty miles wide so that the outpouring of water devastated the ancient villages on both banks with their inhabitants and herds and also demolished many holy places with their servants. The force of the water brought down the bridge at Geneva, mills and people, and the flood pouring into the city of Geneva killed a great many people. [Cf. *Hist.* IV 31.]

a. 565 Twenty-fourth year of the post-consulship of Basilius, Indiction XIII.

In this year, the monks of Agaune, roused by the spirit of anger, stormed the church house at night, trying to kill their bishop Agricola and the clergy and citizens who were with him. While the clergy and citizens strove to protect their bishop, they were seriously wounded by those monks.

In this year Magnachar, a duke of the Franks, passed away. [Cf. *Hist.* IV 25; V 17, 20.]

a. 566 Twenty-fifth year of the post-consulship of Basilius, Indiction XIV.

In this year, a sign appeared in the sky for seventy days.

In this year Augustus Justinian died [a. 565], and his nephew Justin took up the imperial office.

In this year, the winter was very severe, so that for five or more months the land could not be seen owing to the great amount of snow. These harsh conditions killed many animals.

In this year, Sindual the Herul usurped power but was killed by Narses.

a. 567 First Year of the consulship of the Augustus Justin II [a. 566], Indiction XV. From the beginning of the world to this consul the years amount to 5,718.

a. 568 Second Year of the consulship of Augustus Justin II, Indiction I.

After Narses, former superintendent [of the sacred bedchamber] and patrician, had laid low so many usurpers — that is Baduila [Totila] and Teias, kings of the Goths; and Buccelin, a duke of the Franks; as well as Sindual the Herul — he was recalled from Italy in this year by the above-mentioned Augustus, having commendably restored Milan and other towns the [Ostro]goths had ruined.

a. 569 Third year of the consulship of Augustus Justin II, Indiction II.

In this year, the king of the Lombards Alboin, with all his forces, left and burned his homeland Pannonia, and, in an expedition that included wives and his entire people, took possession of Italy; there some died by disease, some by hunger, and not a few by the sword. [Cf. *Hist.* IV 41.]

In this year also, they dared to enter the adjoining districts of Gaul, where a large number of them were captured and put up for sale.

a. 570 Fourth year of the consulship of Augustus Justin II, Indiction III.

In this year, a severe illness accompanied by diarrhea and pustules struck Italy and Gaul severely, and cattle in particular perished throughout the above-mentioned regions.

In this year, Celsus the patrician died. [Cf. *Hist.* IV 42.]

a. 571 Fifth year of the consulship of Augustus Justin II, Indiction IV.

In this year, an unspeakable disease of the groin called the pox (*pustula*) ravaged countless people in the above-mentioned districts. [Cf. *Hist.* IV 31.]

a. 572 Sixth year of the consulship of Augustus Justin II, Indiction V.

In this year, Alboin, king of the Lombards was killed at Verona by his own followers — that is Helmichis and others — with the agreement of the king's wife. And the above-mentioned Helmichis, in company with the aforesaid wife, whom he married, surrendered himself at Ravenna to the Roman state along with part of the army and all the treasure brought from Pannonia as well as that accumulated in Italy.

a. 573 Seventh year of the consulship of Augustus Justin II, Indiction VI.

In this year, a duke of the Lombards called Cleph was appointed king of that people, and many magnates and those of moderate rank were killed by him.

In this year, Vaefarius, a duke of the Franks, died, and Theudefred was appointed duke [of the Transjuran region] in his place.

a. 574 Eighth year of the consulship of Augustus Justin II, Indiction VII.

In this year, Cleph, king of the Lombards, was killed by one of his own retainers.

In this year, the Lombards again invaded Valais and took possession of Clusae. They lived in the monastery of the saints of Agaune for many days, and afterward engaged an army of the Franks in battle at Bex, where they were killed almost to a man; a few escaped by flight. Moreover Mauri and other peoples were defeated by the same Franks for venturing to invade their territory of Provence.

a. 576 Tenth year of the consulship of Augustus Justin II, Indiction IX.

In this year, Sigibert, king of the Franks, began hostilities against his brother Chilperic, and when he had already boxed him in and was contemplating killing him, he was killed by Chilperic's men through deception. Sigibert's son Childebert took up the kingship. [Cf. *Hist.* IV 51, s.a. 575.]

a. 577 Eleventh year of the consulship of Augustus Justin II, Indiction X.

In this year died the royal and distinguished youths Chlothar and Chlodomer, the sons of king Guntram. [Cf. *Hist.* IV 25; V 17, s.a. 577.]

a. 578 Twelfth year of the consulship of Augustus Justin II, Indiction XI.

In this year, Merovech, the son of King Chilperic was killed. [Cf. *Hist.* V 18, s.a. 577.]

a. 579 Thirteenth year of the consulship of Augustus Justin II, Indiction XII.

In this year the two brothers Bishops Salonius and Sagittarius were removed from the dignity of the episcopal office for various crimes by a council that gathered at Chalon-sur-Sâone. [Cf. *Hist.* V 27, s.a. 579.]

In this year, the Augustus Justin died and Tiberius succeeded him [8 October 578].

a. 580 First year of the consulship of Augustus Tiberius Constantinus, Indiction XIII.

In this year, in the month of October, the Rhône so overflowed its banks in the territory of Valais that it impeded the gathering of the harvest. And in Italy the rivers so overflowed that the farmers suffered losses. [Cf. *Hist.* V 33, s.a. 580.]

a. 581 Second year of the consulship of Augustus Tiberius Constantinus, Indiction XIV.

In this indiction, in the month of September [= a. 580], Queen Austrechild died; because of her passing, two doctors, Nicolaus and Donatus, were killed. [Cf. *Hist.* V 35, s.a. 580.]

In this year, Mummolus the patrician took refuge in the border country of king Childebert, that is Avignon, taking with him his wife and children, a host of household servants, and much wealth. [Cf. *Hist.* VI 1, s.a. 581.]

# CHAPTER FIVE

# SALVIAN OF MARSEILLES ON GOD'S JUDGMENT

*Salvian was born of a noble family ca. 400 and died ca. 480. His birthplace is generally thought to have been northern Gaul, probably Trier or Cologne. He married (his wife's name was Palladia) and had a daughter, but, after her birth, he and his wife adopted religious lives and separated. Salvian entered the monastery of Lérins ca. 424 and moved to Marseilles in the 430s; by this time he had become a priest. A number of his works survive: a treatise against avarice written under the pseudonym Timothy, a handful of letters, and the work for which he is renowned,* On the Governance of God.

*On the Governance of God, the main argument of which is excerpted here, maintains that God's judgment is immanent. In so doing, it provides a theological explanation for the poor fortunes of the Roman state. Written in the 440s, the work is notable for its references to contemporary and near contemporary conditions and society, both Roman and barbarian, but readers should beware. Salvian does not attempt to describe society, nor strictly speaking does he provide a commentary on it; his subject is morality, his aim is the reform of human behavior, and his method is an indictment of the private and public morals of the Roman elite.*

*To facilitate reading and reference, I have added two levels of subheadings.*

Source: *The Writings of Salvian the Presbyter*, trans. Jeremiah F. O'Sullivan, (New York, 1947), with some minor revisions.

## 21. ON THE GOVERNANCE OF GOD

### BOOK I

#### 1. God's Judgment and God's Governance

Some men say that God is indifferent and, as it were, unconcerned with human acts, inasmuch as He neither protects the good nor curbs the wicked. They say that in this world, therefore, the good are generally unhappy; the evildoers, happy. Because I am addressing Christians, the holy scriptures alone should suffice as a refutation of this charge. But, because many have some pagan disbelief in them, perhaps they can also be enticed by proofs taken from chosen and learned pagans.

*The views of Pythagoras, Plato, and the Stoics are considered.*

Therefore when all men, even those not of our faith, under the compulsion of sheer necessity, have proclaimed that the universe is known and moved and ruled by God, how can He at the present day be thought indifferent and unconcerned?...I am unable to find any who differ in judgment from them beyond the absurdities of the Epicureans and some of the would-be Epicureans...

(2)...They say that God, since He neither protects the good nor punishes the wicked, is disinterested in all things; that in this world therefore, the status of the good is decidedly worse than that of the evil. They say that the good, of a certainty, live in poverty, the wicked in plenty; the good in sickness, the wicked in health; the good in sorrow, the wicked in joy; the good in misery and low estate, the wicked in prosperity and high estate...

No one is unhappy because another thinks he is, but only because he himself thinks himself so...Holy men are humble because such is their wish. They are poor because they delight in the practice of poverty. They are without desire for display before others because they scorn it. They are without honors because they flee from honors. They mourn and exult in mourning. They are weak and rejoice because they are infirm...

Perhaps we are to think that the Fabii, Fabricii and Cincinnati, those past masters of the virtues of olden time bore a heavy burden in being poor, when they did not wish to be rich. All these men devoted their full energies and efforts to the advantage of all, and by their personal poverty enriched the increasing wealth of the state...Poverty was not an object of contempt. Wearing one short and rough garment, men were fetched in those days from the plow to the fasces; perhaps, as they were being garbed in the consular robes, they wiped their dusty sweat with the imperial robes in which they were about to be garbed. Then, magistrates, though poor, had a rich state. Now the power of the rich makes the state poor. I ask: what blindness and insanity make men believe that large private wealth can remain, while the state is impoverished and needy? Such then were the Romans of old, and as they, not knowing God, condemned wealth, so do those who follow the Lord today spurn it...

(4) But you say, perhaps there are other and greater sufferings [than poverty and bodily infirmity], that is the holy suffer many hard and bitter trials in this life: they are captured, tortured and cut to pieces...Perhaps you say this is additional proof for you that God neglects everything in this world and reserves all for judgment in the next, since at all times the good have suffered all the evils while the wicked have done them all. This does not seem to be

the statement of an unbeliever, especially since it acknowledges a future judgment by God.

But we say the human race is to be judged by Christ in such a way that we also now believe that God rules and dispenses all thing in accordance with His reason. As we now affirm belief in God's future judgment, so do we now teach that God is always our judge in this life. While God governs us, He judges us, because his governance is His judgment.

*Proofs of this by reason, example, and authority follow.*

## BOOK IV

### 2. The Infidelity of Christians

Let us put aside the prerogative of the name of Christian, of which I have already spoken [in Bk III]. On the basis of that prerogative we think that, because we are more religious than all other peoples, we must also be stronger. For as I have said, since the faith of the Christian is to believe with faith in Christ and this faithful belief in Christ is to keep His commandments, it follows, without doubt, that neither does he possess faith who lacks faith nor does he who tramples on the mandates of Christ believe in Him. Therefore the whole question turns on this, that he who does not perform the work of a Christian does not appear to be a Christian, because the name without practice and functions is as nothing...

In short, whoever wishes to know more fully that words without substance are as nothing, let him observe the countless peoples who, when their merit ceased, lost even their names. The twelve Hebrew tribes, when they were chosen by God of old, received two holy names, being called the People of God and the People of Israel...They who have long since put aside the worship of God cannot be called the people of God. Neither can that people be said to see God who have denied the Son of God, as it is written: "Israel has not known me, and my People has not understood."... Indeed, I fear that what could be said of them then, the same can be said of us now, because we do not obey the words of the Lord...

*Slaves and Christians*

(2)...Our miseries, infirmities, destruction, captivities and punishment of our wicked servility are proofs that we are bad servants of a good master...

I know very well that it is unpleasant for us when we are struck down. Why are we surprised that God scourges us when we sin, when we ourselves flog our little slaves who transgress? We are unjust judges. We, little men, do not wish to be flayed by God, when we ourselves whip men who are of our own status. I do not wonder that we are unjust in this matter. In us, nature and wickedness are both servile. We wish to sin but not to be punished...

(3) Some among the rich say: "We do not do the same things that slaves do. Slaves are thieves and runaways, slaves are constantly catering to their palates and stomachs." It is true these are the vices of slaves, but the masters, though not all of them, have more and greater vices...

First of all, if slaves are thieves, they are perhaps forced to steal through want. Even though the customary allowances are given, these allowances satisfy custom rather than sufficiency and thus fulfill the law without fulfilling the need. Their indulgence makes their fault less blameworthy, because the guilt of the thief who is unwillingly forced into the theft is excusable. Holy scripture seems to excuse in part the offense of the needy when it says: "the fault is not so great when a man has stolen; for he steals to feed his hungry soul." He steals to fill his hungry soul. For this reason, they who are excused by the Divine Word are not very well to be accused by us.

What has been said of theft by slaves, the same can be said about their running away. This much can be said more correctly about their flight, they are driven to flight, not only by their wretched condition, but by their punishments. They dread their drivers, they dread the confidential domestic servants, they dread their stewards, so that, in the midst of all these overseers, they are almost nobody's slaves, rather than their real master's. They are beaten by all; they are tread upon by all. What more can be said? Many of them take refuge with their masters in fear of their fellow slaves...

They are also said to be liars. Nevertheless, they are compelled to lie by the brutality of impending punishment. Indeed, they lie because they wish to escape torture. Why is it is strange that a slave, in his fear, should prefer to lie rather than to be flogged? They are accused of being greedy of gullet and stomach, but that is nothing new. A man who has often endured hunger has a greater longing for a full stomach. Granted, he may not be hungry for bread, yet he may hunger after tasty morsels, and, therefore, must be pardoned if he seeks all the more avidly what he is constantly without.

But you, the noble and rich, who have an overflow of all good things, who, because of this, should honor God by your holy works because you enjoy His blessings unceasingly, let us see whether your actions are, I do not say holy, but at least harmless. And, as I have said before, who among the rich, with a few exceptions, is not tinged with all manner of crime?...

...If a slave is a runaway, so are you also, O rich and noble, for all who forsake the Law of their Lord are runaways from their Master...

## Crimes of the Rich and Powerful

(4) Why did I go into such minute details about these things and speak, as it were, allegorically, when not only the thefts but the robberies of the rich are acknowledged in the most open of crimes? Where can you find any one living beside a rich man who has not been driven or reduced to poverty? By the encroachments of the powerful the weak lose their belongings or even themselves along with their belongings. Not unrightly does the holy Word apply to both when it says: "the wild ass is the lion's prey in the desert: so also the poor are devoured by the rich." For, not only the poor, but almost the whole human race, is suffering from this tyranny.

As regards people in high places, of what does their dignity consist but in confiscating the property of the cities? As regards some whose names I do not mention, what is a prefecture, but a kind of plunder? There is no greater pillaging of the poor than that done by those in power. For this, office is bought by the few to be paid for by ravaging the many. What can be more disgraceful and wicked than this? The poor pay the purchase price for positions which they themselves do not buy. They are ignorant of the bargain, but know the amount paid. The world is turned upside down that the light of a few may become illustrious. The elevation of one man is the downfall of all the others. The cities of Spain know all about this, for they have nothing left them but their name. The cities of Africa know it — and they no longer exist. The cities of Gaul know it, for they are laid waste, but not by all their officials. They still hold a tenuous existence in a very few corners of the land, because the honesty of a few has temporarily supported those provinces which the ravages of the many have made void.

(5) I have been compelled by sorrow to wander from my subject. Therefore, let me return to my former topic. In what sense are the vices with which the nobles are stained any different from those of slaves, unless, perhaps, it is that those faults, for which they punish slaves, they themselves commit as though they were allowed? A slave is not allowed to have access to those ravages which the above-mentioned nobles perpetrate. It may be that I am exaggerating, because certain slaves, having become noble, committed equal or greater crimes. But it can by no means be imputed to slaves as a body that the servile condition turned out so happily for those few.

Murder is rare among slaves because of their dread and terror of capital punishment, but it is common among the rich because of their hope and trust in impunity. Perhaps we are wrong in putting in the category of sins what the rich men do, because, when they kill their slaves, they think that it is legal and not a crime. Not only this, they abuse the same privilege even when practicing the filth of unchastity. How few among the rich, observing the sacrament of marriage, are not dragged down headlong by the madness of lust? To how few are not home and family regarded as harlots? How few do not pursue their madness toward anybody on whom the heat of their evil desires centers? It was about such men that the Divine Word said: "they are become as stallions rushing madly on the mares."...

(6) Doubtless, many of those who are nobles or who wish to appear as nobles listened with haughtiness and contempt to a consideration of those things of which I have spoken, namely, that some slaves are less dissolute than their masters. When I predicate this not about all of them but only about those it fits, no one should be angry who fails to recognize himself as such, lest by the fact that he is angry he himself appear one of them. Rather, any nobleman who detests these evils should be angry at these men, because they defile the name of nobility by their base crimes. Though such men weigh heavily on all Christians, they especially defile by their baseness those who are said to belong to their class.

Therefore I have said that certain nobles are worse than slaves, and I have spoken objectionably, if I do not prove my statements. From the following crime, a very great one, almost the whole slave class is immune. Which of the slaves has a crowd of concubines? Which of them is defiled by the crime of having many mistresses, and, like dogs or pigs, thinks that he can have as many of them as he can subject to his lust?

The answer seems to be that it is not lawful for slaves to do those things; indeed, they would if they could. I believe this, but, what I do not see being done, I cannot hold as being done. No matter how base his mind, no matter how evil his desires, nobody is punished for a crime of which he is not guilty. Certainly, slaves are bad and worthy of contempt. However, the freeborn and nobles are the more to be reproached if, in their more honored place in society, they are worse than the slaves. Hence it happens that it is necessary to arrive at the conclusion not that slaves are to be absolved from the guilt of their wrong-doing, but that the majority of the rich are more to be condemned than the slaves.

*Unjust Remission of Taxation*

Now who can speak eloquently about the following robbery and crime: because the Roman state, if not already dead or at least drawing its last breath where it still has a semblance of life, is dying, strangled by the chains of taxation as if by the hands of brigands, a great number of rich can be found whose taxes are borne by the poor; that is to say there is found a great number of rich whose taxes kill the poor. I say many can be found. I am afraid I should more truly say all. So few, if there are any at all, are free from this crime that we can find almost all the rich in the category in which I said there were many.

Consider the remedies recently given to some cities. What this accomplished was to make all the rich immune and pile more taxes on the wretched poor. The old taxes were remitted for the benefit of the rich and new taxes imposed on the poor. The cancellation of the least type of taxation enriched the wealthy; the increase of the heaviest has made the poor suffer. The rich have become richer by lessening the obligations which they bore lightly; the poor are dying from the multiplication of the burdens which they were already unable to bear. Thus, the great remedy most unjustly exalted the one and most unjustly killed the other; to one it was a most wicked reward, to the other a most wicked poison. Hence it is I make the observation that there is nothing more vicious than the rich who are destroying the poor by their remedies, and none more unfortunate than the poor whom those things kill which are given as a remedy to all.

*Disparagement of the Clergy*

(7) Indeed, what kind of state of affairs is this, how can it be holy, if a noble begin to be converted to God and immediately loses his rank among the nobility? In what account is the honor of Christ held among a Christian population where religion socially degrades a man?...

...When a man changes his garments, he immediately changes his rank. If he were of high rank, he is become worthy of contempt. If he were most exalted, he is become most base. If he were completely honored, he is become altogether wretched. Yet certain worldly and unbelieving men wonder why they are afflicted by God's anger and wrath, when they persecute Him in the person of all His holy men...

### 3. Romans and Barbarians Compared

(12) [Those who assert nothing is seen by God] say that if God watches over human affairs, if He cares for and loves and rules, why does He permit us to be weaker and more wretched than all other peoples? Why does He allow us to be conquered by the barbarians? Why does He allow us to be subject to the law of the enemy? Very briefly, as I have said before, He allows us to bear these evils because we deserve to suffer them...

Someone says, so be it! Certainly we are sinners and evil. What cannot be denied is that we are better than the barbarians. By this also it is clear that God does not watch over human affairs, because, although we are better, we are subject to those who are worse. We will now see whether we are better than the barbarians. Certainly, there is no doubt that we should be better. For this very reason we are worse, if we who should be better are not better. The more honorable the position, the more criminal the fault. If the person of the sinner is the more honorable, the odium of his sin is also greater...

(13)...Therefore, because some men think it is unbearable that we are judged worse, or not even much better than the barbarians, let us see how, and of which barbarians we are better. For there are two kinds of barbarians in every nation: heretics and pagans. I say we are incomparably better than all these, therefore, insofar as it pertains to divine Law. In what pertains to life and the acts of life, I sorrow and weep that we are worse.... It profits us nothing that the Law is good if our life and way of life are not good. That the Law is good is a gift of Christ, but that our life is bad is the product of our own sin...

(14) Having put aside the prerogative of the Law, which either helps us not at all or condemns us by a just condemnation, let us compare the pursuits, morals, and vices of the barbarians with ours. The barbarians are unjust, and so are we. The barbarians are avaricious, and so are we. The barbarians are unfaithful, and so are we. The barbarians are greedy, and so are we. The barbarians are lewd, and so are we. The barbarians have all manner of wickedness and impurities, and so do we...

But, you say, the barbarians commit the same evils, yet they are not as wretched as we. There is this difference. If the barbarians do the same things as we do, we, however, sin with a greater displeasure to God. For ours and the vices of the barbarians can be equal, but in these same vices our sins must be greater.

### Comparison with Pagans

Since all the barbarians, as I have already said, are either pagans or heretics, I shall discuss the pagans first, for theirs is the prior mistake. The Saxons are savage. The Franks are treacherous. The Gepidae are ruthless. The Huns are lewd. In short, the life of all barbarian nations is corruption itself...

Is it any wonder that the barbarians, who do not know the Law and God think in this way, when well nigh the greater portion of Romans think the same way and know they are sinning? So that I will not speak of any other type of men, let us consider only the crowds of Syrian merchants who have occupied the greater part of nearly all cities. Let us consider whether their life is anything other than plotting artifice and wearing falsehood thin. They think their words are wasted, so to speak, if they are not profitable to those who speak them. So great among them is the honor of God, who prohibits oath-taking, that they think all perjury is a particular gain for them...

And by this we understand, as I have said above, that we who have and spurn the Law of God are much more culpable than those who neither have it nor know it at all. Nobody despises things which are unknown to him... But we are scorners as well as transgressors of the Law and, accordingly, are worse than the pagans, for they do not know the commandments of God and we do. They do not have them, but we do. They do not follow commands which are unknown to them, but we trample underfoot what we know. Therefore, ignorance among them is transgression among us, because it is being guilty of a lesser crime to be ignorant of the commandments of God than to spurn them...

## BOOK V

### Comparison with Heretics

(2) I have already mentioned above that there are two kinds of sects of barbarians: pagans and heretics. Since I think I have said enough about the pagans, let me add, as the exposition demands, something also about the heretics. Someone may say: "Although the divine Law does not demand from pagans that they keep the commandments of which they are so ignorant, certainly the divine Law does demand their observance from heretics, who are not ignorant. It can be said they read the same things we read. They have the same prophets of God, the same apostles, the same Gospels as we. Therefore, the Law is not less neglected by them than by us, or it is even much more so, because, although they read the same scriptures as we, they do worse things than we." Let us look at both sides.

You say they read the same writings which are read by us. How are those writings the same which are badly interpolated and badly translated by authors formerly evil? Therefore they are not the same, because those things cannot be said to be whole which are corrupted in any part. Writings which have lost their fullness are lacking in perfection, and those writings do not preserve their complete value which are deprived of the power of being holy. Only we, therefore, have the sacred scriptures full, uncorrupted, and complete. We either imbibe them at their source or assuredly drink them drawn from the purest source through the medium of correct translation. Only we read them well, and would that we fulfilled them as well as we read them!...

Indeed, barbarians, being strangers to Roman, in fact to human learning, know nothing unless they hear it from their teachers. Thus, they follow what they hear, and they who are ignorant of all literature and knowledge and know the mystery of the divine Law by teaching rather than by reading must necessarily retain the teaching rather than the Law. Thus, to them, the tradition of their teachers and their long-standing doctrines are, so to say, law for them because they know only what they are taught.

Therefore, they are heretics, but not heretics knowingly. Indeed, with us they are heretics, but in their own opinion they are not. So much do they judge themselves Catholics that they defame us with the title of heresy. What they are to us, therefore, we are to them. We are certain that they do injury to the divine begetting because they say the Son is less than the Father. They think we injure the Father because we believe the Father and Son are equal. We possess the truth, but they think they have it. We honor the Godhead, but they think their belief is the honor of His divinity.

They are unobservant of their obligations, but to them this is the highest duty of their religion. They are ungodly, but they think that is true godliness. Therefore, they are in error, but they err with a good heart, not in hatred but in love of God, believing that they honor and love God. Although they possess not the true faith, they think they possess the perfect love of God. In what manner, for this erroneous and false belief, they are to be punished on the day of judgment, nobody can know but the Judge.

I think God bears patiently with them in the meantime because He sees that, although their belief is incorrect, they err through the acceptance of a seemingly correct opinion. He knows that they act in this manner because they are ignorant. However, He knows that our people neglect their own beliefs. Therefore, the barbarians sin through the wickedness of their teachers, but we through our own wickedness. They sin through ignorance; we, through knowledge. They do what they think is right; we, what we know is wrong. Therefore, with just judgment the patience of God sustains them, but reproachfully chastises us, because ignorance can be overlooked for a time, but contempt does not deserve pardon...

(3)...But all those of whom I speak are either Vandals or Goths. I say nothing about the Roman heretics, of whom there is a huge multitude. Nor do I compare the latter either with other Romans or the barbarians, because they are worse than the Romans through their lack of faith and more base than the barbarians in the foulness of their lives. This not only does not help us, but, beyond even that, it grieves us that we are hurt by our own people, because those whom I say are like this are Romans. Hence, we can understand what the whole Roman state deserves when one group of the Romans offend God by their way of living, another by their lack of faith as well as their way of living. Furthermore, even the very heresies of the barbarians at one time stemmed from the perverseness of a Roman teacher; hence, it is even our crime that the barbarian peoples began to be heretics.

(4) Furthermore, insofar as it pertains to the way of life among the Vandals and Goths, in what way are we better than they, or can even be compared

with them? First, let me speak of their love and charity which the Lord teaches is the chief of virtues and which He not only commends throughout sacred scriptures but even in His own words: "by this shall it be known that you are my disciples, that you love one another." Almost all barbarians, at least those who are of one people under one king, love one another; almost all Romans persecute each other...

### Taxation Again, Desertion to Barbarians, and Bacaudae

What kind of situation is this, how cruel, how derivative of this very wickedness, how foreign to barbarians but how familiar to Romans — to ruin one another with exactions? Indeed, not each other, for this would be almost more tolerable if each would endure what he inflicts on others. It is a more serious situation that the many are ruined by the few, to whom public requisitions are their private booty, who make the bills of the fiscal debt into private gain. And not only the highest officials, but often the least officials do this; not only judges, but even the underlings of the judges.

What towns, as well as what municipalities and villages are there in which there are not as many tyrants as towns councillors (curiales). Perhaps they glory in this name of tyrant because it seems to be considered powerful and honored. For, almost all robbers rejoice and boast if they are said to be more fierce than they really are. What place is there, as I have said, where the bowels of widows and orphans are not devoured by the leading men of the cities (principales), and with them those of almost all holy men? For, they consider the latter as widows and orphans because they are either unwilling to protect themselves in their zeal for their profession, or they cannot protect themselves because of their simplicity and humility. Not one of them, therefore, is safe, nor is anyone, except for the very powerful, completely safe from devastating brigandage, unless they are like robbers themselves. To this state of affairs, indeed, to this crime has the world come that, unless one is bad, he cannot be safe.

(5) Since there are so many who despoil the good, perhaps there are some who bring aid in this despoliation, who, as it is written, snatch the needy and poor from the hand of the sinner. "There is none who does good, there is almost not even one." The prophet said "almost not even one" [Ps. 13:3] because, such is the rarity of good men, there seems to be scarcely one of them. Who gives help to the distressed and those that labor, when even the Lord's priests do not resist the violence of wicked men? Either most of them are silent or, even though they speak, they are like those who are silent, and many do this not from lack of resolution, but, as they think, with considered discretion...

All the while, the poor are despoiled, the widows groan, the orphans are tread underfoot, so much so that many of them, and they are not of obscure birth and have received a liberal education, flee to the enemy lest they die from the pain of public persecution. They seek civilized treatment among barbarians because they cannot bear barbarous treatment among Romans. Although the Romans differ in religion and language from the barbarians to whom they flee, and, if I may say so, find the offensive smell of their bodies and of barbarian clothing disagreeable, nevertheless, they prefer to bear among the barbarians habits unlike their own rather than rampant injustice among the Romans. Thus, far and wide, they migrate either to the Goths or to the Bacaudae, or to other barbarians everywhere in power; yet they do not repent having migrated. They prefer to live as free people under an outward form of captivity than as captives under an appearance of liberty.

Therefore, the name of Roman citizens, at one time not only greatly valued but dearly bought, is now repudiated and fled from, and it is almost considered not only base but even deserving of abhorrence. And what can be a greater testimony of Roman wickedness than that many people, upright and noble and to whom the position of being a Roman citizen should be considered as of the highest splendor and dignity, have been driven by the cruelty of Roman wickedness to such a state of mind that they do not wish to be Romans? Hence, even those who do not flee to the barbarians are forced to be barbarians. Such is a great portion of the Spaniards and not the least portion of the Gauls, and, finally, all those throughout the whole Roman world whom Roman wickedness has compelled not to be Romans.

*Bacaudae*

(6) I am now about to speak of the Bacaudae who were despoiled, oppressed and murdered by evil and cruel judges. After they had lost the right of Roman liberty, they also lost the honor of bearing the Roman name. Their misfortune is blamed on themselves. We ascribe to them a name which signifies their downfall. We ascribe to them a name of which we ourselves are the cause. We call them rebels. We call incorrigible those whom we compelled to live as criminals.

For, by what other ways did they become Bacaudae, except by our wickedness, except by the dishonesty of judges, except by confiscation and the pillage of those who have turned tax collection for the state into the acquisition of profits for themselves and have made the tax levies their personal plunder? Like monstrous beasts, they did not rule but devoured their subjects, and feasted not only on the spoils of men, as most robbers are wont to do, but even on their torn flesh and, as I may say, on their blood. Thus it happened that men, strangled and killed by the robberies of judges, began to live as barbarians because they were not permitted to be Romans. They became satisfied to be what they were not, because they were not permitted to be what they were. They were compelled to defend their lives at least, because they saw that they had already completely lost their liberty.

Is the situation any different today than it was then if those who are not yet Bacaudae are now being compelled to be so? Insofar as force and injuries go, they are now being driven to want to become Bacaudae, but are prevented by weakness from doing so. They are like captives forced beneath the yoke of the enemy bearing the penalty out of necessity not choice. In their hearts they desire liberty, but undergo the greatest of slavery.

*Taxation an Unequal Burden*

(7) This is how it is with almost all the lower classes...But what else can these wretched people wish for, they who suffer incessant and even continuous destruction due to the collection of taxes? To them there is always imminent a heavy and relentless proscription. They desert their homes, lest they be racked in their very homes. They seek exile, lest they suffer torture. The enemy is more lenient to them than the tax collectors. This is proved by the very fact that they flee to the enemy in order to avoid the force of the tax levy. This very tax levy, although hard and inhuman, would nevertheless be less heavy and harsh if all would bear it equally and in common.

Taxation is made more shameful and burdensome because the burden of all is not borne by all. The tax of the rich presses upon the poor, and the weaker carry the load for the stronger. There is no other reason they cannot bear it than that the burden imposed on the wretched is greater than their resources. They endure envy and want, misfortunes most diverse and unlike: there is envy when they pay and want in their ability to pay. If you look at what they pay, you will think them abundant in riches, but if you look at what they actually possess, you will find them poverty-stricken. Who can evaluate this degree of iniquity? They make payments as though they were rich and endure the poverty of beggars. Much more serious is the following: the rich themselves occasionally devise supplementary contributions which the poor pay.

But, you say, when the highest assessments belong to the rich and their payments are the heaviest, how does it happen that they themselves wish to increase the amount owed? I do not say that they increase it for themselves. For they increase it because the increase does not affect them. I will tell you how this is done. Commonly, new envoys come, new bearers of letters sent from the top imperial officials, and those men are commended to a few men of illustrious rank for the destruction of many. For them new burdens are decreed, new tax levies are decreed. The powerful decree what the poor are to pay, the favor of the rich decrees what the multitude of the wretched are to lose. They themselves feel nothing of what they decree.

Those who were sent by our superiors cannot, you say, not be honored and generously entertained. Well then, rich men, you who are the first to issue a decree, be the first to give. Be the first in generosity of goods, you who are the first in profusion of words. You who give of mine, give of thine. Most justly, whoever you are, you who alone wish to receive favor, you alone should bear the expense. But to your will, rich men, we the poor accede. What you, the few, order, we all pay. What is more just, more humane? Your decrees burden us with new debts; at least make the debt common to both of us. What is more wicked and more unworthy than that you alone are exempt from the debt, you who make everyone debtors?

Indeed, the most wretched poor thus pay all that I have mentioned, but for what cause or for what reason they pay, they are completely ignorant. For, to whom is it lawful to discuss why they pay; to whom is permitted to find out what is owed? Revelation of this is forthcoming only when the rich get angry with each other, when some of them get indignant because some decrees are issued without their advice and handling.

Then you may hear it said by some of them, "What an unworthy crime! Two or three decree what kills many; what is paid by many wretched men is decreed by a few powerful men." Each rich man maintains his honor by being unwilling that anything is decreed in his absence, yet he does not maintain justice by being unwilling that evil things be done when he is present. Lastly, what these very men consider base in others they themselves later establish, either out of vengeance for past scorn or in proof of their power. Therefore, the most unfortunate poor are, as it were, in the midst of the sea, between conflicting, violent winds. They are swamped by the waves rolling now from one side, now from the other.

(8) But, surely, those who are wicked in one way are found moderate and just in another, and compensate for their baseness in one thing by goodness in another. For, just as they weigh down the poor with the burden of new tax levies, so they sustain them by the assistance of new tax reliefs; just as the lower classes are completely overwhelmed by new taxes, so they are relieved to the full by the remission of taxes. On the contrary, there is equal injustice is in both cases. For, as the poor are the first to be burdened, so they are the last to be relieved.

If when, as has happened lately, the highest powers decide to have regard for the cities in default and to lessen the burdens of taxation somewhat, the rich alone instantly divided among themselves the remedy given to all. Who, then, remembers the poor? Who calls the poor and needy to share in the common benefit? Who permits him who is first in bearing the burden even to stand in the last place for receiving redress? What more is there to say? In no way are the poor regarded as taxpayers, except when the mass of taxes is imposed upon them; they are not reckoned among the number of taxpayers when relief is apportioned.

Do we think we are unworthy of the punishment of divine severity when we thus constantly punish the poor? Do we think, when we are constantly wicked, that God should not exercise His justice against all of us? Where or in whom are evils so great, except among the Romans? Whose injustice so great except our own? The Franks are ignorant of this crime of injustice. The Huns are immune to these crimes. There are no wrongs among the Vandals and none among the Goths. So far are the barbarians from tolerating these injustices among the Goths, that not even the Romans who live among them suffer them.

Therefore, in the districts taken over by the barbarians, there is one desire among all the Romans, that they should never again find it necessary to pass under Roman jurisdiction. In those regions, it is the one and general prayer of the Roman people that they be allowed to carry on the life they lead with the barbarians. And we wonder why the Goths are not conquered by our portion of the population, when the Romans prefer to live among them rather than with us. Our brothers, therefore, are not only altogether unwilling to flee to us from them, but they even cast us aside in order to flee to them.

### Patronage (Patrocinium)

It would be a wonder to me that every last poor and needy taxpayer did not flee but for one reason only. They do not do it because they cannot carry with them their few little possessions, households, and families. For, when many of them would leave behind their little plots of land and cottages in order to avoid the force of tax collection, how could they not wish to take with them, if there were any possibility of doing so, those things which they are compelled to leave behind? Therefore, because they are incapable of doing what they really prefer, they do the one thing of which they are capable. They give themselves to the upper classes in return for care and protection. They surrender themselves as captives to the rich and, as it were, pass over into their jurisdiction and authority.

However, I would not consider this serious or unbecoming, indeed, I would rather thank this public spirit of the powerful to whom the poor entrust themselves, if they did not sell their patronages, if, when they say they are defending the poor, they were contributing to humanity and not to greed. It is harsh and severe that the poor are protected by this arrangement to be despoiled, and that they defend the poor by this arrangement in order to make them more wretched by defending them. For, all those who are defended make over almost all their goods to their defenders before they are defended; thus, in order that the fathers may have defense, their children lose their inheritance. The preservation of the parents is secured by beggaring the offspring.

Look at what the assistance and patronages of the great really are! They give nothing to those whom they have received, but give only to themselves. By this agreement something is given temporarily to the parents that will be completely taken away from the children in the future. And so they sell, indeed some great men sell for the highest price, everything they warrant. Have I said they sell? If only they would sell according to the accustomed and common usage, something, perhaps, might remain to the buyers. This is truly a new kind of buying and selling. The seller gives nothing and gets everything; the buyer gets nothing and loses everything completely. Whereas a feature of almost every transaction is that desire should be on the part of buyer and need on the part of the seller — for the buyer purchases to increase his substance, the seller sells to diminish his — but this is an unheard of kind of trade: wealth increases for the sellers and nothing remains to the buyer except beggary alone.

Now the following is unbearable and monstrous, something human sensibility, I will not say can hardly bear, but can hardly even listen to: most of the poor and wretched, despoiled of their few possessions and evicted from their little plots of land, though they have lost their property, nevertheless bear the taxes on the property they have lost. Though possession has been removed from them, tax liability has not. They lack property rights but are overwhelmed by tax contributions! Who can estimate the extent of this evil! Expropriators occupy their property and the wretches pay the taxes on behalf of the expropriators. After the death of the father, children have no claim by right to the plots of land and are killed off by obligations attached to the fields. In crimes such as these, what is the point at issue but that those stripped naked by private expropriation die from public exaction; plundering carries off their property and the exaction of taxes takes their lives?

And so when they lose their homes and fields to expropriators or abandon them in flight before the tax collectors since they cannot hold them, some of those of whom I speak, who are either more knowledgeable or made so by necessity, seek out the estates of the great and become *coloni* of the rich. Just as they who, when driven by the terror of the enemy, flee to the forts, or they who, when the security of free-born status is lost, flee in desperation to some asylum, in like manner the poor, because they can no longer protect either the dwelling or the honorable status of their birth, give themselves over to the ignoble yoke of the *inquilinus*. They are reduced to these straits: not only driven from their wealth but even from their social status, exiles not only from their property, but even from themselves, losing everything they have with them, they lack property rights and lose the right of liberty.

(9) Indeed, because unhappy necessity thus compels them, their extreme lot would be bearable to a certain extent, if there were not something more extreme. What is more grievous and bitter is that a more cruel evil is added to this evil. They are received as newcomers. They become natives by the legal consequence of their dwelling place and, following the example of that powerful enchantress who was said to change men into beasts, so all these men who are received within the estates of the rich are changed, as it were, by the transformation of Circe's cup. Those whom the rich receive as outsiders and newcomers they begin to consider as their own. Those who were known to be freemen are turned into slaves.

### 4. The Judgment of God by Means of the Barbarians

And we wonder why the barbarians capture us when we make our own brothers captives. There is nothing strange that there are invasions and the destruction of states. We have for a long time been striving toward this by the oppression of the many, so that by capturing others even we ourselves have begun to be captives. For we feel, although much later than we deserve, we feel at length those things which we have done to others, and according to the words of holy scripture we are eating the labor of our own hands, and under a just Judge, God, we are paying back what we owe.

Indeed, we have not been merciful to the exiled, and behold, we ourselves are exiles. We defrauded wanderers; behold, we ourselves are wanderers and are cheated. We circumvented men of freeborn status by taking advantage of the ruinous circumstances of the times; behold, we ourselves have recently begun to live on foreign soil and we already fear the same ruinous circumstances. How great is the faithless blindness of evil-minded men! We are carrying out the condemnation of a God who judges, but we do not acknowledge that we are being judged...

#### Culpability of the Clergy

(10)...Is this true of laymen only, and not of some of the clergy? Is this true of men of the world only, and not of many religious also, or rather those given over to worldly vices under the appearance of religion? These, after shameful deeds and past crimes, have appropriated for themselves the title of holiness but have only professed the name not transformed their lives. They think that the height of divine worship consists in their attire rather than in their deeds, and have cast off their garments, but not their minds...

This is certainly a new kind of conversion. They refrain from lawful acts and commit unlawful ones. They abstain from lawful sexual intercourse, but not from plunder. What are you doing in your foolish delusions? God forbade sin, not marriage. Your deeds do not fit your exertions. You should not be the friends of crime, you who call yourselves strivers after virtues. What you do is absurd. This is not conversion, but aversion....

## Book VI

### 5. More Sins of the Romans

*Public Entertainments and Displays*

(2) I ask: What hope of betterment is there for us, who are induced to evil not by error of belief, but who strive with the zeal of our evil purpose, so that we seem to be always worse? ...

In the first place, there is almost no crime or vice which is not to be found at the games. There it is the height of pleasure to see men die, or, what is worse and more cruel than death, to see them torn to shreds; to see the bellies of wild animals filled with human flesh; to see men eaten for the entertainment of those standing around; to see the pleasure of the onlookers, that is, to be devoured almost no less by the looks of men than by the teeth of beasts. And for this to be done, there is a world of expense. With great care and pains are the preparations made. Hidden places are approached, impassable ravines are searched, impenetrable forests are wandered through, the cloudy Alps are climbed, the deep valleys are probed. In order that the bowels of men may be devoured by wild animals, nature is not allowed to hold anything in secret.

But, you say, these things are not done all the time. This is correct. That they are not always done is an excellent excuse for wrongdoing! As if, indeed, we should let acts which injure God be done constantly, or let acts which are bad be done well because they are not done all the time. Murderers do not always kill. Yet they are murderers even when they are not killing, because all the while they are stained with murder. Robbers do not always rob. Yet they do not cease to be robbers, because even when they are not actually committing robbery they do not put the thoughts of robbery from their minds. In like manner, all those who delight in games of this sort are not mentally blameless of the guilt involved in looking at the games even when they are not looking, because they would always look if they could.

Nor is this the only sin. There are others greater. What are they? Are not hens fed by the consuls according to the custom of the old pagan profanations? Are not the auguries of the flying bird sought? Almost all those sacrifices are performed which the pagans of old thought foolish and laughable. When the very consuls do all those things, those men who give their names to the years and from whom the years themselves take their beginning, are we to believe that those years can proceed well for us which are begun with such ceremonies? Would that just as these things are done only for the consuls, so they would infect those only on whose account they are done.

It is most deadly and serious that, while these ceremonies are done with public consent, the honor of a very few becomes the crime of all, and thus, since two are placed in office each year, scarcely anyone anywhere escapes contamination.

(3) Let us presume that enough has been said about the games which, as you make excuse, are not performed all the time. However, let us speak about the daily obscenities. These the legions of devils have devised, of such a nature and so innumerable that even honest and upright minds can hardly overcome them all completely, although they can scorn and tread underfoot some of them. Armies about to fight are said either to cut up with pitfalls, or fix with pilings, or sow with cavalry obstacles those places through which they know the enemy troops will come, so that, although some do not fall into all these traps, none fully escapes. In the same way, the demons have prepared so many alluring ambushes for the human race in this life that, even though one avoids most of them, he is, however, caught by one or another.

Indeed, because it would take long to speak about all these snares now, namely the amphitheaters, music halls, public processions, jesters, athletes, tumblers, pantomimes, and other monstrosities, which disgust me to talk about, and because it is disgusting to have knowledge of such evil, I will speak only about the impurities of the circuses and theaters. Such things are done there that nobody can speak about them, let alone think of them, without being tainted.

For the most part, other vices claim for themselves particular portions of us: filthy thoughts affect our minds; immodest glances, our eyes; evil language, our ears. When one of these functions has gone astray, the rest can be without sin. But in the theaters none of our senses is free from guilt, because our minds are stained by evil desires, our ears by hearing, our eyes by seeing. Indeed, all these scenes are so disgraceful that a person cannot even describe them and talk about them without shame...

Thus, there comes something new for the prosecutor when he discusses the baseness of these crimes, so that, although without doubt he who wishes to bring the charge is upright, he cannot speak and denounce these obscenities and his character remain whole. All other evils taint those who perform them, not those who see or hear them. Though you hear someone blaspheme, you are not tainted by the sacrilege because you mentally disagree. And if you come upon a robbery, you are not made evil by the act, because you abhor it in your mind.

The impurities of the games are unique, because, in a way, they make the crime one, both for those who perform them and those who watch them, For, while the spectators approve and gladly watch them, all perform them through sight and consent... Therefore, in these representations of fornication the whole audience mentally commits fornication, and those who, perhaps, came in purity to the games, return from the theaters in adultery...

We love things and worship things. God alone, in comparison with all other things, is vile to us. Besides other instances which prove it, one particular illustration establishes the point I am making. If, when it should happen — because it often does happen that on the same day on which an ecclesiastical feast occurs the public games are performed — I ask of everybody's conscience what place has greater crowds of Christian men: the spectators' benches at the public games or the entrance to the house of God? Do the crowds prefer the temple or the theater? Do they love more the teachings of the Gospel or the theatrical musicians; the words of life or the words of death; the words of Christ or the words of the mime?

There is no doubt that we love more that which we prefer. For, on every day of these fatal games, whatever feast of the Church it may be, not only do those who say they are Christians not come to the church, but, if any come perhaps unwittingly, if they hear the games being performed, while they are already in the church, they leave the church. They spurn the temple of God in order that they may run to the theater...

(8) But it can be answered that these performances are not enacted in all Roman cities. That is true. I also add that they are not now done in those places where they were done formerly. They are not now done in the city of Mainz, but that is because it is ruined and destroyed. They are not performed at Cologne, but that is because it is filled with the enemy. They are not done in the most excellent city of Trier, but that is because it is laid low by invasion, four times repeated. They are not done in most of the cities of Gaul and Spain.

Therefore, woe to us and our iniquities; woe to us and our impurities! What hope is there for the commonalty of Christians in the sight of God, when these evils cease to exist in Roman cities only from that time when they began to be under the law of the barbarians? Vice and impurity are, as it were, native characteristics of the Romans, and are, as it were, their mind and nature. Wherever there are Romans, there is much vice...

We must consider why these towns are still the sites and lodging places of the games, though the games have ceased to exist. They are still the sites and homes of vices because all manner of impure actions were done in them formerly. The games themselves are not now performed, since they cannot be performed because of the misery and poverty of our time. That they were formerly enacted was due to depravity. That they are not enacted now is due to necessity...

...Finally, when the residents of any town come to Ravenna or Rome, a part joins the Roman people in the circus and a part joins the people of Ravenna in the theater. Therefore, let nobody think himself excused because of place or absence. All who are joined to each other in their will to do base actions are one in the baseness of their actions. We flatter ourselves especially on the probity of our way of life. We flatter ourselves on the rarity of our vices!...

(12) But, of course, we who are corrupted by prosperity are corrected by adversity and we, whom a long peace has made profligate, strife makes us temperate. Have the peoples of the cities who were lewd in prosperity begun to be chaste in adversity? Has drunkenness, which increased with peaceful and abundant years, ceased immediately with the plundering done by the enemy?

Italy has already been laid waste by many calamities. Have the vices of the Italians ceased on that account? The city of Rome has been besieged and taken by storm. Have the Romans ceased to be frenzied and blasphemous? Barbarian nations have overrun Gaul. Insofar as it pertains to evil living, are the crimes of the Gauls not the same as they were? The Vandals have crossed into Spanish territory. The lot of the Spaniards is indeed changed, but their wickedness is not changed.

Lastly, lest any part of the world be immune from fatal evils, wars have begun to cross over the seas. They have laid waste and overthrown cities which were cut off by the sea in Sardinia and Sicily, the imperial storehouses. The vital blood vessels, as it were, being cut, they have captured Africa itself, which is, so to say, the heart of the Empire. And then what? When the barbarians entered these lands, did the inhabitants cease in their vices, perhaps in fear? Or, as even the worst of slaves are wont to be corrected for the moment, did terror immediately wrest modesty and restraint from them?

Who can judge the enormity of this evil? The barbarian peoples were sounding their arms around the walls of Cirta and Carthage, and the Christian population of Carthage still went mad in the circuses and reveled in the theaters. Some were strangled outside the walls; others were committing fornication within. A portion of the people was captive of the enemy without the walls and a portion was captive of vice within the walls...

*Cities of Gaul*

(13) Why do I speak about things that are far away and are, so to say, removed into another world, when I know that in my own native country and in the cities of Gaul almost all the more excellent men have been made worse by their misfortunes. Indeed, I myself have seen at Trier men, noble in birth and elevated in dignity, who, though already despoiled and plundered, were actually less ruined in property than in morality. Though they were despoiled and stripped, something of their property still remained to them, but nothing whatsoever of self-restraint. They were more dangerous enemies in themselves than the enemy outside, so that, though they were overthrown by the barbarians from without, they were still overthrown more by themselves. It is sad to refer to what I saw there. Honored old men, tottering Christians, the ruin of their city already imminent, tended slavishly to their palates and lusts...

The leading men in the city lay down at banquets; they forgot honor; they forgot age; they forgot religion; they forgot the dignity of their name. They were stuffed with food, lax from wine-bibbing, frantic from shouting, frenzied with revelry. They were bereft of no less than their senses. Indeed, because they were almost constantly like this, they no longer had senses. Though these were the actual circumstances, what I am about to say is much worse. Not even the ruin of their cities put an end to this waywardness.

The wealthiest city of Gaul was taken by storm four times. It is easy to know of which one I speak. The first captivity should have sufficed for amendment, so that the repetition of their sins would not renew destruction. What followed? What I say is incredible. The continuance of calamities in that city caused an increase of crimes there. Like the serpentine monster which multiplied when killed, as the fables have it, so even in the most excellent city of Gaul crimes increased by the very blows with which crimes were checked so that you would think that the punishment of crime was, as it were, the mother of vice...

What about another city, not far distant, but almost of the same magnificence? Is there not the same destruction of both property and morals? Beyond the fact that the two common evils, avarice and drunkenness, had there destroyed all, it came to this at least that the leaders of that very city, in their avid greed for wine, did not arise from their feasting when the enemy was entering the city. I believe God clearly wished to show them why they were perishing, since at the actual moment of perishing they were doing that very thing through which they had come to final perdition. I saw there tear-inspiring sights. It did not matter whether they were boys or old men. There was one buffoonery, one levity. All kinds of evil went on at the same time: luxury, drinking to excess, immorality. All were doing everything alike: they played, drank, and committed adultery...

(14) I have spoken about the most famous cities. What about other cities in other parts of Gaul? Have they not fallen because of similar vices of their inhabitants? Their crimes possessed them in such a way that they did not fear danger. Their captivity was foretold them and they were not afraid. Indeed, fear was taken away from the sinners to obviate the possibility of caution. Thus, when the barbarians were located almost in plain sight of all, there was neither fear of men nor protection of cities. So great was the blindness of soul, or rather so great was the blindness of sins, that, without doubt, nobody wished to perish, yet nobody did anything to prevent his perishing...

(15) Perhaps you are saying that these things happened in the past, or no longer exist, or will forever cease. If today any city or province is struck down by heavenly blows, or is overrun, humbled, converted, and corrected by a hostile population, if practically all peoples who bear the Roman name prefer to perish rather than be corrected, it is easy to see they prefer to die rather than live without their vices. This can be proved in a few words by the fact that the greatest city of Gaul was destroyed three times by successive captures, and, when the whole city had been burned, evil increased after its destruction.

Those whom the enemy did not kill in the city's ruin, disaster overwhelmed after its ruin. They who escaped death in the city's destruction did not survive disaster after its fall, for wounds, struck deeply, killed some with lingering deaths. Others were burned by the flames of the enemy or even suffered the pain of torture after the flames were extinguished. Some died of hunger, some of nakedness, and some wasted away. Others were numbed with cold. Thus, they hastened through different ways of dying into a single door of death.

What followed? Other cities were also afflicted by the destruction of one town. Here and there — something that I myself have seen and experienced — lay the naked and torn bodies of both sexes, infecting the eyes of the city as they were torn to pieces by birds and dogs. The deadly stench of the dead brought death to the living. Death was breathed from death. And thus even those who escaped the destruction of the aforementioned city suffered the evils of another destruction.

What happened after this, I ask? Who can judge this kind of madness? A few nobles who survived destruction demanded circuses from the emperors as the greatest relief for the destroyed city...O people of Trier, do you therefore long for circuses, and this when you are devastated and knocked out, after you have suffered disaster and bloodshed, punishment and captivity, after so many destructions have overrun your city? What is more tearful than this foolishness, what is more mournful than this madness? I confess, I believed you were most wretched when you were suffering destruction, but I see you are more wretched still when you asked for public spectacles. I thought that in destruction you had lost only your property and goods; I did not know you had also lost your senses and intelligence...I do not wonder at all, I do not wonder that the evils which took place have happened to you, for, since three destructions did not correct you, you deserve to perish by a fourth...

Nothing is left of our peace and former prosperity except our crimes alone and in full. Our crimes which have ended our prosperity are left. Where are the old resources and dignities of the Romans? Formerly, the Romans were most strong; now they are without strength. The old Romans were feared; we are afraid. The barbarian people paid them tribute; we are tributary to the barbarians. The enemy sells us the enjoyment of daylight. In a way, our entire welfare is at a price...

## Book VII

### 6. Sexual Morality of Romans and Barbarians

(2) Perhaps you are thinking that, since I have spoken at length about public games and public immorality, in this respect only are we worse than the barbarians, as they do not commit these offenses but we do; yet we are not so stained with the sin of carnal lust and the filth of deadly fornication. If you will, let me also compare the Romans with other nations in respect to this point. Indeed, I do not know a better comparison than with those barbarians whom, placed as possessors in the very bosom of the state, God has made the masters of the Roman soil...

*Aquitaine*

Nobody doubts that the Aquitanians and the Nine Peoples possessed the most delicious bit of almost all Gaul, and a fruitful udder of plenty, and not only plenty, but pleasantness, beauty, and luxury, which are sometimes preferred to plenty...What came of all these gifts?... In all Gaul, just as men were first in riches, so they were first in vice

(3)...However, exception must be made for a very few holy and distinguished men who, as one of their number has said, "have redeemed their crimes by scattering their wealth."...

But among the Aquitanians, what city, in its richest and most noble section, was not like a brothel? Who among the noble and rich did not live in the mire of lust? Who among them did not immerse himself in the abyss of the most sordid whirlpool of vices? Who among them gave to his wife the faith of a husband? And as concerns promiscuous lust, who did not reduce his wife to one of his maidservants and so degrade the vows of marriage that no woman seemed more lowly in his household because of the disparagement of marriage than she who was first in rank by the dignity of marriage.

(4) Perhaps someone is thinking that my accusations are not altogether correct, because it is true that the mothers of households in Aquitaine had their rights and held the honor and power of being mistresses over the home. Indeed, many held the right of ruling the house unimpaired, but almost none possessed her matrimonial rights unsullied. Just now I am not inquiring into the power exercised by the wives, but how corrupt was the way of life of their husbands. I should say that mothers did not even possess their power unimpaired in that sphere, because any woman who has not her rights of marriage inviolate and safe does not possess intact the right of government over the household. The mother of the house is not far removed from the lowliness of female slaves when the father of the house is the husband of maids...

(5) You may be saying that it is difficult to prove these charges and that there are no traces extant of past turpitudes and vices. Look! Even now, many of these men, although they are without a homeland and live as paupers in comparison with their past opulence, are for the most part worse than they were. They are not worse for the simple reason that their actions are the same as before, but are worse because they do not cease from crime. Indeed, their evil deeds, although they are not greater in kind, are yet more numerous. In this way, although they do not increase the novelty of their crimes, their crimes are piled up in plurality...

(6)...Among chaste barbarians, we are unchaste. I say further: the very barbarians are offended by our impurities. It is not lawful to be a whoremonger among the Goths. Only the Romans living among them are allowed to be impure by right of nationality and name. I ask: What hope is there for us before God? We love impurity; the Goths abominate it. We flee from purity; they seek it. Fornication among them is a crime; with us a distinction and an ornament...

*Spain*

(7) Perhaps, this was the case in Aquitaine only. Let me cross over to other parts of the world, lest I seem to give all my attention to Gaul. Have not the same or perhaps greater vices destroyed Spain? Indeed, even if the heavenly anger had handed Spain over to other barbarians, the enemies of purity there would have suffered tortures worthy of their crimes, but just for good measure, to make the condemnation of impurity manifest, that country was delivered to the Vandals, that is, to chaste barbarians. By the captivity of the Spaniards, God wished to show in two ways how much He hated carnal

lewdness and loved chastity, when He put the Vandals in command solely on account of their great chastity and subjugated the Spaniards solely on account of their great impurity.

Why did God act thus? Were there not in the whole world stronger bar-barians to whom the Spaniards might be delivered? Doubtless, there were many stronger. Indeed, if I am not mistaken, all were stronger. God gave all to the weakest enemies to show that it was not resources but the cause that con-quers...

### Recent War with the Visigoths, a. 436-39

(9)...God says that all who presume they can be liberated by their own resources speak against Him. Who is there among the Romans who does not talk like this? Who is there among them who does not feel this way? Who is there among us who does not almost constantly blaspheme in this respect? It is common knowledge that the state has no resources, and, indeed, we do not acknowledge to whose favor we are indebted for being still alive.

When God gives us some measure of prosperity beyond our hope and merit, one man ascribes it to fate, another to chance, another to the plans of the leaders, another to foresight, another to the magistrates, another to his patron. Not one ascribes it to God. And we are amazed if His heavenly hand does not give us something, while we disparage it for what it has given us. For is that not what we are doing when we attribute the good it gives us to the chance of events, to the qualities of generals, or to other frivolous causes?...

Not thus do the Goths behave, not thus do the Vandals act, though trained by evil teachers. They are better than we in this respect. I suspect some are offended by what I say, but, because truth must be considered more than offense, I will say it and say it often. Not thus do the Goths behave, not thus do the Vandals act, who at moments of crisis demand help from God and call their prosperity the gift of God.

In fact our misfortune in the last war [a. 436-39] proved this. When the Goths were apprehensive, we dared to put our hope in the Huns; they in God. When they sought peace, we refused them peace. They sent bishops as intermediaries and we turned them away. They honored God even in foreign priests; we have contempt for Him even in our own. Accordingly, the end of the affair corresponded to the actions of both parties. In extreme fear, they were given the palm of victory. We, in extreme exaltation, were given confu-sion. Truly in us and in them was clearly proved that saying of our Lord, "For whoever exalts himself shall be humbled, and he who humbles himself shall be exalted."...

(10) This the general of our forces [Litorius] learned. He entered that same enemy town as a captive on the day he had presumed he would enter it as a victor. He proved what the prophet said: "for a man's way is not his own, nor is it in the power of man that he walk and direct his steps." ...Apart from the unfortunate turn of events, in this very man was disclosed the immediate judgment of God, for he himself has suffered all that he presumed he would do to others. Because he believed that he would capture the enemy without the help of the Divinity and the consent of God, he himself was captured. He presumed he had superb judgment and wisdom, and incurred disgrace for his rashness. The bonds he had prepared for others he himself had to bear. What, I ask, could be more obviously the judgment of God than that he who had the assurance of a plunderer should become plunder? He who anticipated a triumph was a triumph. He was surrounded, seized, and fettered. His arms were tied behind his back. The hands which he thought valorous he saw bound. He became a public spectacle for boys and women. He saw barbarians making sport of him. He bore the ridicule of both sexes. He who had the great pride of a strong man endured the death of a craven. Would that this amounted to a speedy cure for his wrongs and not a long drawn out burden. But, as far as the extent of the penalties he suffered is concerned, he was wasted by a long captivity and by long drawn out sickness in a barbarian prison and was reduced to such a wretched state that he became an object of pity to the enemy. Most men think this is more difficult and bitter even than the punishment itself.

Why did all this happen? Why, doubtless, unless as I said, the enemy were humble before God and we were rebellious. They believed that victory was in the hand of God. We believed that it was in our own hand... Finally, as the affair showed and demonstrated, the enemy's king, stretched on a goat-hair cloth, poured out prayers up to the day of the battle. Before the battle he threw himself on the ground in prayer and arose from prayer to the battle. Before he took command in the battle he fought by prayer, and proceeded confidently to the fight because he had already merited victory by his prayers.

### Africa and the Vandals

(11) The situation is not unlike this even among the Vandals. When our armies marched against them in Spain, our forces had as much presumptive faith to crush them as even recently against the Goths. Our soldiers were brought low by a similar disdaining pride and by a like outcome...

(13) The Vandals could have remained in Gaul and they were not afraid. Indeed, that heavenly hand which drew them to Spain to punish the sins of

her inhabitants compelled them to pass on to Africa to devastate that country. They themselves confessed that they were not doing their own will, for they say they were activated and driven by a divine command...

As all dirt flows into the bilge in the hold of a ship, so vices flowed into the African way of life, as if from the whole world. I know of no baseness which did not abound there, whereas pagan and wild peoples at least have their own peculiar vices, even if all of these do not merit reproach.

The Gothic nation is treacherous, but chaste. The Alani are unchaste, but less treacherous. The Franks are liars, but hospitable. The Saxons are savage in their cruelty, but admirable in their chastity. In short, all peoples have their own particular bad habits, just as they have certain good habits. Among almost all Africans, I know not what is not evil. If the charge is inhumanity, they are inhuman; if drunkenness, they are drunkards; if forgery, they are the greatest of forgerers; if deceit, they are the most deceitful; if greed, they are the most greedy; if treachery, they are the most treacherous. Their impurities and blasphemies must not be mentioned here, because in the evils about which I have just spoken they have surpassed the evils of other peoples, but in impurity and blasphemy they have even surpassed themselves...

(17)...I will say much more. Would...that the impure had been content to be defiled solely by the fornication of fallen women! More grave and criminal was the fact that those vices, about which the blessed apostle Paul complained with the greatest lament of his soul, were almost all practiced in Africa: men, having put aside the natural use of woman, burned in their desires for one another; men doing base things with men, and receiving to themselves the due reward of their error. Just as they do not approve having knowledge of God, God handed them over to a distorted mentality to do what was inappropriate [Rom. 1: 27-28].

(18) ...Then, as if their fault was not bad enough if only the authors of the evils were sullied by the evil, it became the sin of the whole city, because of public acknowledgment of the vice. The entire city saw and allowed it to continue. The judges saw and were quiet. The people saw and applauded. Thus the fellowship of vice and crime was diffused throughout the entire city. Consent made it common to all, though its performance was not common to all...

(22) ...I have stated that the cities of Africa were filled with monstrous impurities, especially with the queen and mistress as it were of other vices, but the Vandals were not stained by all this. The barbarians were unlike the Romans about whom I have spoken; the barbarians set themselves to correct the stain of our baseness. They removed from every place in Africa that lowly vice of effeminate men. They even abstained from contacts with prostitutes and, not only have they abstained from or removed prostitution for the time

being, but they have made it completely cease to exist...

They ordered and compelled all prostitutes to enter the married state. They turned harlots into wives, fulfilling that saying and command of the apostle, that every woman should have her own husband and every man his own wife [I Cor. 7.2]; that since incontinence cannot be restrained without this yielding to carnal usage, in this way natural desire should receive a legitimate outlet, so that there would not be sin by incontinence...

For the suppression of lust the Vandals also added severe ordinances for chastity. They repressed impurity with the sword of legal decrees, so that marital affection at home and the fear of the law in public preserved the purity of both sexes. Thus, morality rested upon a double defense, since it had love indoors and fear outdoors...They directed their laws according to the rule of divine Law, so that they believe nothing is lawful in this matter which God does not wish to be lawful. They thought that no man should permit himself anything unless it is permitted to all by God.

(23) I know what I say seems intolerable to some, but I must act according to the reason of things, not to the whims of desire...I ask: What hope can there be for the Roman state when the barbarians are more chaste and more pure than the Romans?...I say: Let us be ashamed and confused. Among the Goths, no one is unchaste but the Romans, and among the Vandals not even the Romans. Among them, so much has the eagerness for chastity and the severity of discipline profited them that not only are they themselves chaste, but let me say something novel and unbelievable, something almost even unheard of, they have even made the Romans chaste...

# CHAPTER SIX

# PRISCUS OF PANIUM ON ATTILA THE HUN

*Groups of Huns alternated as enemies and allies of Rome from the late fourth century onward. During Aëtius's ascendancy, they had a not insignificant role to play in the history of Gaul, serving the imperial authorities. The rising power of Attila in the 440s gradually changed the nature of the relationship. Under his leadership the Huns attacked the eastern empire, draining its resources and subjecting it to tribute, and, in 451, Attila turned on the West. Although Attila's direct impact on western affairs was short lived, his reputation and his invasion of Gaul in 451, and of Italy in the following year, left a remarkable imprint on imaginative literature, from popular tales to saints' lives.*

*The major historical source for Attila's career is the work of the rhetor and sophist Priscus of Panium, who was born in Thrace, perhaps between 410 and 420. Priscus was the author of a Greek history of his times in eight books in which Attila and the Huns had a prominent role; if, as seems likely, it covered the reigns of Theodosius II, Marcian, and Leo, it ended about 474. It survives only in the works of later authors; most of these fragments cover the years 447-450 and deal with the Huns.*

*The fragments below are derived from the following sources: (1) the* Excerpta de Legationibus, *a tenth-century collection of extracts on diplomatic subjects; (2) Jordanes,* Getica, *a Latin history of the Goths written in Constantinople ca. 550; and (3) John of Antioch, a seventh-century compiler of a universal chronicle. In citing sources I have given the fragment number as found in R. C. Blockley,* The Fragmentary Classicising Historians of the Later Roman Empire: Eunapius, Olympiodorus, Priscus and Malchus, *2 vols. (Liverpool, 1983).*

## 22. AN EMBASSY TO THE COURT OF ATTILA, a. 449

*In 449 Priscus was asked by his friend Maximin to accompany him on an embassy he was leading to the court of Attila. The interpreter on the embassy was Bigilas, who had previous experience in diplomatic contacts between the Constantinopolitan and Hunnic courts. The embassy was to travel with two Hun ambassadors, Edeco, one of Attila's chief followers, and Orestes, Attila's secretary and a Roman in origin; they had met earlier with the emperor, Theodosius II. Prior to departure, Chrysaphius, the imperial chamberlain, in a secret meeting enlisted Edeco, one of the Hun ambassadors, to arrange for the assassination of Attila. Though Bigilas the interpreter was privy to this plot, the other members of the embassy, including its leader Maximin, were not. In the selection below, the cool reception the east Roman embassy receives from Attila can be accounted for by Edeco's informing Attila of the plot as soon as he had reached his master's court.*

*Priscus's account is justly famous for its detailed description of Attila and the Hun court. The celebrated exchange between Priscus and a Greek-born soldier serving the Huns on the relative merits of the Roman and barbarian way of life should not be read, however, as straight reportage; readers should also be warned against readily accepting the debate as an uncomplicated expression of contradictory viewpoints. Priscus's account is also suggestive of the relations between western Roman leadership and the Huns in the period prior to the embassy.*

*Attila's secretary Orestes later became patrician and master of the soldiers in the West. He made his son Romulus Augustulus emperor in 475 and was himself killed in August 476 by Odoacer, who soon afterwards deposed his son. Some scholars identify the Edeco of Priscus with the father of Odoacer.*

Translation: J.B. Bury, *History of the Later Roman Empire* (London, 1889; Dover PB edition, New York, 1958) 1: 279–88; I have made minor revisions and additions, and supplied sub-headings. The fragment is from the *Excerpta de Legationibus* = Blockley, Priscus Frag. 11.

## The Journey Begins

We set out with the barbarians and arrived at Sardica, which is thirteen days for a fast traveler from Constantinople. Halting there we considered it advisable to invite Edeco and the barbarians with him to dinner. The inhabitants of the place sold us sheep and cattle, which we slaughtered, and we prepared a meal. In the course of the feast, as the barbarians lauded Attila and we lauded the emperor, Bigilas remarked it was not fair to compare a man and a god, meaning by the man Attila and by the god Theodosius. The Huns grew excited and hot at this remark. But we turned the conversation in another direction, and soothed their wounded feelings; and after dinner, when we separated, Maximin presented Edeco and Orestes with silk garments and Indian gems...

When we arrived at Naissus we found the city deserted, as though it had been sacked; only a few sick people lay in the churches. We halted a short distance from the river, in an open space, for all the ground adjacent to the bank was full of the bones of men killed in the fighting. On the morrow we came to the station of Agintheus, the commander-in-chief of the Illyrian armies [*magister militum per Illyricum*], who was posted not far from Naissus, to announce to him the imperial commands and to receive five of those seventeen deserters [being returned to Attila by the emperor]. We had an interview with him, and having treated the deserters with kindness, he committed them to us.

The next day we proceeded from the district of Naissus towards the Danube; we entered a covered valley with many bends and windings and circuitous paths. We thought we were traveling due west, but when the day dawned the sun rose in front; and some of us unacquainted with the topography cried out that the sun was going the wrong way, and portending unusual events. The fact was that that part of the road faced the east, owing to the irregularity of the ground. Having passed these rough places we arrived at a plain which was also well wooded. At the river we were received by barbarian ferrymen, who rowed us across the river in boats made by themselves out of single trees hewn and hollowed. These preparations had not been made for our sake, but to convey across a company of Huns which had just met us on the road; for the royal Scythian [Attila] pretended that he wished to hunt in Roman territory, but his intent was really hostile, because all the deserters had not been given up to him.

Having crossed the Danube and proceeded with the barbarians about seventy stadia, we were compelled to wait in a certain plain while Edeco's party went ahead to inform Attila of our arrival. As we were dining in the evening, we heard the clatter of horses approaching, and two Scythians arrived with instructions that we were to set out to Attila. We asked them first to partake of our meal, and they dismounted and made good cheer.

## Attila's Camp

On the next day, under their guidance, we arrived about three o'clock at the tents of Attila, which were numerous, and when we wished to pitch our tent on a hill the barbarians who met us prevented us, because the tent of Attila was on low ground, so we halted where the Scythians desired...

*Attila, now aware of the plot against his life, refused to meet personally with the embassy and ordered it to leave. Edeco had informed Attila, Priscus surmises, either because he was from the beginning insincere in his dealings with Chrysaphius, or else he now feared that Orestes, who was excluded from the private meeting with the chamberlain, would report it to Attila.*

When I saw that Maximin was very dejected, I went to Scottas [brother of Attila's confidant, Onegesius, who was absent on an expedition with Attila's son], taking with me Rusticius, who understood the Hun language. He had come with us to Scythia, not as a member of the embassy, but on business with Constantius, an Italian whom Aëtius had sent to Attila to be that monarch's private secretary. I informed Scottas, Rusticius acting as interpreter, that Maximin would give him many presents if he would procure him an interview with Attila; and, moreover, that the embassy would not only conduce to the public interests of the two powers, but to the private interest of Onegesius, for the emperor desired that he should be sent as an ambassador to Byzantium to arrange the disputes of the Huns and Romans, and that there he would receive splendid gifts. As Onegesius was not present it was for Scottas, I said, to help us, or rather help his brother, and at the same time prove that the report was true which ascribed to him an influence with Attila equal to that possessed by his brother. Scottas mounted his horse and rode to Attila's tent, while I returned to Maximin and found him in a state of perplexity and anxiety, lying on the grass with Bigilas. I described my interview with Scottas and bade Maximin make preparations for an audience with Attila...

## First Meeting With Attila

As we were considering what to say to Attila, and how to present the emperor's gifts, Scottas came to fetch us, and we entered Attila's tent, which was guarded by a ring of barbarians. We found Attila sitting on a wooden chair. We stood at a little distance and Maximin advanced and saluted the barbarian, to whom he gave the emperor's letter, saying that the emperor prayed for the safety of him and his followers. The king replied may the Romans have what they wished for him and immediately addressed Bigilas, calling him a shameless beast, and asking him why he ventured to come when all the deserters had not been given up.

*Attila berated Bigilas furiously for the failure of the Romans to turn over deserters, whose names he had read out, claiming that only Bigilas' status as an ambassador was saving him from being impaled. Neither Priscus nor Maximin could figure out why Attila was so angry and even Bigilas, who alone among the Romans was privy to the arrangement with Edeco, still believed that Attila was unaware of the plot. Attila sent Bigilas back to the empire to get deserters and kept the rest of the Roman embassy with him. Edeco pretended to Bigilas that the plot was still secret.*

## A Journey North To Attila's Residence

After the departure of Bigilas, who returned to the empire, we remained one day in that place, and then set out with Attila for the northern parts of the country. We accompanied the barbarian for a time, but when we reached a certain point took another route by the command of the Scythians who conducted us, as Attila was proceeding to a village where he intended to marry the daughter of Eskam, though he had many other wives, for the Scythians practise polygamy.

*The Romans camped by a lake near a village but in the night were scattered by a terrible thunderstorm that overthrew their camp and dispersed their belongings. They made for the village in the dark.*

But we all reached the village by different ways and raised an alarm to obtain what we lacked. The Scythians of the village sprang out of their huts at the noise, and, lighting the reeds which they use for kindling fires, asked what we wanted. The barbarians with us replied that the storm had alarmed us; so they invited us to their huts and provided warmth for us by lighting large fires of reeds.

The lady who governed the village — she had been one of the wives of Bleda [Attila's brother] — sent us provisions and good-looking girls to console us (this is a Scythian compliment). We treated the young women to a share in the eatables, but declined intercourse with them. We remained in the huts till day dawned and then went to look for our lost utensils, which we found partly in the place where we had pitched the tent, partly on the bank of the lake, and partly in the water. We spent that day in the village drying our things; for the storm had ceased and the sun was bright. Having looked after our horses and baggage animals, we directed our steps to the princess, to whom we paid our respects and presented gifts in return for her courtesy. The gifts consisted of things which are esteemed by the barbarians because not produced in the country — three silver bowls, red skins, Indian pepper, palm fruit, and other delicacies.

### A West-Roman Embassy

Having advanced a distance of seven days farther, we halted at a village; for as the rest of the route was the same for us and Attila, we had to wait, so that he might go in front. Here we met with some of the western Romans, who had also come on an embassy to Attila — the count Romulus, Promotus governor of Noricum, and Romanus a military officer. With them was Constantius, whom Aëtius had sent to Attila to be his secretary, and Tatulus, the father of Orestes who was with Edeco; they were not connected with the embassy, but were friends of the ambassadors. Constantius had known them of old in Italy, and Orestes had married the daughter of Romulus.

The object of the embassy was to soften the soul of Attila, who demanded the surrender of one Silvanus, a dealer in silver plate in Rome, who had received golden vessels from a certain Constantius. This Constantius, a native of Gaul, had preceded his namesake in the office of secretary to Attila. When Sirmium in Pannonia was besieged by the Scythians [ca. 441-42], the bishop of the place consigned the vessels to Constantius's care, so that, if the city were taken and he survived, they might be used to ransom him; and in case he were slain, to ransom the citizens who were led into captivity. But when the city was enslaved, Constantius ignored the rights of the Scythians, and, as he happened to be at Rome on business, pawned the vessels to Silvanus for a sum of money, on condition that, if he gave back the money within a prescribed period, the dishes should be returned but otherwise should become the property of Silvanus. But then Constantius, suspected of treachery, was crucified by Attila and Bleda; and afterwards, when the affair of the vessels became known to Attila, he demanded the surrender of Silvanus on the ground that he had stolen his property. Accordingly Aëtius and the emperor of the western Romans sent envoys to explain that Silvanus was the creditor of Constantius, the vessels having been pawned and not stolen, and that he had sold them to priests and others for sacred purposes; for it was not right for people to use as their own vessels dedicated to god. If, however, despite this just reason and respect for divinity, Attila refused to desist from his demand, he, the emperor, would send him the value of the vessels, but would not surrender the innocent Silvanus.

## At Attila's Residence

Having waited for some time until Attila advanced in front of us, we proceeded, and having crossed some rivers we arrived at a large village, where Attila's house was said to be more splendid than his residences in other places. It was made of polished boards and surrounded with a den enclosure, designed, not for protection, but for appearance. The house of Onegesius was second to the king's in splendor, and was also encircled with a wooden enclosure, but it was not adorned with towers like that of the king. Not far from the enclosure was a large bath which Onegesius —who was the second in power among the Scythians — built, having transported the stones from Pannonia; for the barbarians in this district had no stones or trees, but used imported material. The builder of the bath was a captive from Sirmium, who expected to win his freedom as payment for making the bath. But he was disappointed, and greater trouble befell him than mere captivity among the Scythians, for Onegesius appointed him bathman, and he used to minister to him and his family when they bathed.

## Attila's Welcome

When Attila entered the village he was met by girls advancing in rows, under thin white canopies of linen, which were held up by the outside women who stood under them, and were so large that seven or more girls walked beneath each. There were many lines of damsels thus canopied, and they sang Scythian songs.

When Attila came near the house of Onegesius, which lay on his way, the wife of Onegesius issued from the door, with a number of servants bearing meat and wine, and saluted him and begged him to partake of her hospitality. This is the highest honor that can be shown among the Scythians. To gratify the wife of his friend, he ate, just as he sat on his horse, his attendants raising the tray to his saddlebow; and having tasted the wine, he went on to the palace, which was higher than the other houses and built on an elevated site.

## At the House of Onegesius

But we remained in the house of Onegesius, at his invitation, for he had returned from his expedition with Attila's son. His wife and kinfolk entertained us with dinner, for he had no leisure himself, as he had to relate to Attila the result of his expedition and explain the accident which had happened to the young prince, who had slipped and broken his right arm.

After dinner, we left the house of Onegesius and took up our quarters nearer the palace, so that Maximin might be at a convenient distance for visiting Attila or holding intercourse with his court.

The next morning, at dawn, Maximin sent me to Onegesius, with presents offered by himself as well as those which the emperor had sent, and I was to find out whether he would have an interview with Maximin and at what time.

## Debate with a Defector

When I arrived at the house, along with the attendants who carried the gifts, I found the doors closed, and had to wait until some one should come out and announce our arrival. As I waited and walked up and down in front of the enclosure which surrounded the house, a man, whom from his Scythian dress I took for a barbarian, came up and addressed me in Greek, with the greeting "Hail!" I was surprised at a Scythian speaking Greek. For the subjects of the Huns, swept together from various lands, speak, besides their own barbarous tongues, either Hunnic or Gothic, or — as many as have commercial dealings with the western Romans — Latin; but none of them easily speak Greek, except captives from the Thracian or Illyrian sea-coast; and these last are easily known to any stranger by their torn garments and the squalor of their heads, as men who have met with a reverse. This man, on the contrary, resembled a well-to-do Scythian, being well dressed and having his hair cut in a circle in Scythian fashion.

Having returned his salutation, I asked him who he was and where he had come from to take up Scythian life in a foreign land. When he asked me why I wanted to know, I told him that his Hellenic speech had prompted my curiosity. Then he smiled and said that he was born a Greek and had gone as a merchant to Viminacium, on the Danube, where he had stayed a long time and married a very rich wife. But the city fell prey to the barbarians, and he was stript of his prosperity and, on account of his riches, was allotted to Onegesius in the division of the spoil, as it was the custom among the Scythians for the chiefs to reserve for themselves the rich prisoners. Having fought bravely against the Romans and the Acatiri, he had paid the spoils he won to his master and so obtained freedom. He then married a barbarian wife and had children, and had the privilege of eating at the table of Onegesius.

He considered his new life among the Scythians better than his old life among the Romans, and the reasons he gave were as follows: "After war the Scythians live in inactivity, enjoying what they have got and not at all, or very little, harassed. The Romans, on the other hand, are in the first place very liable to perish in war, as they have to rest their hopes of safety on others, and are not allowed, on account of their tyrants, to use arms. And those who use them are injured by the cowardice of their generals, who cannot support the conduct of war. But the condition of the subjects in time of peace is far more grievous than the evils of war, for the exaction of taxes is very severe, and unprincipled men inflict injuries on others, because the laws are not applied to all. A wrongdoer who belongs to the wealthy classes is not punished for his injustice, while a poor man, who does not understand the matter, undergoes the legal penalty, that is if he does not depart this life before the trial, since the course of lawsuits is so protracted and so much money is expended on them. The climax of the misery is to have to pay to get justice. For no one will grant a hearing to the injured man unless he pay a sum of money to the judge and his officials."

In reply to these and other complaints, I asked him to be good enough to listen with patience to the other side of the question: "The creators of the Roman system," I said, "who were wise and good men, in order to prevent things from being done haphazardly, made one class of men guardians of the laws and appointed another class to the profession of arms, who were to have no other object than to be always ready for battle and to go forth to war without dread, as though to a familiar exercise, having by practice exhausted all their fear beforehand. Others again were assigned to attend to the cultivation of the ground, to support both themselves and those who fought in their defense, by contributing the military grain tax... To those who protect the interests of the litigants a sum of money is paid by the latter, just as a payment is made by the farmers to the soldiers. Is it not fair to support him who assists and requite him for his kindness?... And as to the long time spent on lawsuits, if such is the case, that is due to concern for justice, so that judges may not fail in passing correct judgments by having to give sentence in an offhand fashion; it is better that they should reflect and conclude the case more tardily than that, by judging in a hurry, they should both injure man and offend the Deity, the founder of justice. The laws apply to all, and even the emperor obeys them. And it is not a fact, as was part of his charge, that the rich get away with violence against the poor, unless one of them avoids justice by escaping detection...As for your freedom, you should give thanks to fortune rather than your master...The Romans treat their servants better. They deal with them as fathers or teachers, admonishing them to abstain from evil and to follow the lines of conduct which they have esteemed honorable; they reprove them for their errors like their own children. They are not allowed, like the Scythians, to inflict death on them. They have numerous ways of conferring freedom; they can manumit not only during life, but also by their wills, and the testamentary wishes of a Roman in regard to his property are law."

My interlocutor shed tears, and confessed that the laws and constitution of the Romans were fair, but deplored that the authorities, not possessing the spirit of former generations, were ruining the state.

## A Meeting with Onegesius

As we were engaged in this discussion a servant came out and opened the door of the enclosure. I hurried up, and inquired how Onegesius was engaged, for I desired to give him a message from the Roman ambassador. He replied that I should meet him if I waited a little, as he was about to go forth.

And after a short time I saw him coming out, and addressed him, saying, "The Roman ambassador salutes you, and I have come with gifts from him and with the gold which the emperor sent you. The ambassador is anxious to meet you and begs you to appoint a time and place." Onegesius bade his servants receive the gold and the gifts and told me to announce to Maximin that he would go to him immediately. I delivered the message, and Onegesius appeared in the tent without delay.

He expressed his thanks to Maximin and the emperor for the presents and asked why he sent for him. Maximin said that the time had come for Onegesius to have greater renown among men by going to the emperor to settle, by his wisdom, the disputes between the Romans and Huns and to establish concord between them; and thereby he would procure many advantages for his own family, as he and his children would always be friends of the emperor and the imperial family.

Onegesius inquired what measures would gratify the emperor, and how he could arrange the disputes.

Maximin replied, "If you cross into the lands of the Roman empire you will lay the emperor under an obligation, and you will arrange the matters at issue by investigating their causes and deciding them on the basis of the peace."

Onegesius said he would inform the emperor and his ministers of Attila's wishes, but the Romans need not think they could ever prevail on him to betray his master or neglect his Scythian training and his wives and children, or to prefer wealth among the Romans to bondage with Attila. He added that he would be of more service to the Romans by remaining in his own land and softening the anger of his master, if he were indignant about anything with the Romans, than by visiting them and subjecting himself to blame if he made arrangements that Attila did not approve of. He then retired, having consented that I should act as an intermediary in conveying messages from Maximin to himself, for it would not have been consistent with Maximin's dignity as ambassador to visit him constantly.

## A Visit to Attila's Compound

The next day I entered the enclosure of Attila's palace, bearing gifts to his wife, whose name was Hereka. She had three sons, of whom the eldest ruled the Akatiri and the other nations who dwell in Scythia by the Black Sea. Within the enclosure were numerous buildings, some of carved boards beautifully fitted together, others of boards planed straight and fastened on round wooden blocks which rose to a moderate height from the ground.

Attila's wife lived here, and, having been admitted by the barbarians at the door, I found her reclining on a soft couch. The floor of the room was covered with woollen mats for walking on. A number of servants stood round her, and maids sitting on the floor in front of her embroidered with colours linen cloths intended to be placed over the Scythian dress for ornament.

Having approached, saluted, and presented the gifts, I went out and walked to another house, where Attila was, and waited for Onegesius, who, as I knew, was with Attila. I stood in the middle of a great crowd — the guards of Attila and his attendants knew me, and so no one hindered me. I saw a number of people advancing, and a great commotion and noise, Attila's egress being expected. And he came forth from the house with a dignified gait, looking round on this side and that. He was accompanied by Onegesius and stood in front of the house; and many persons who had lawsuits with one another came up and received his judgment. Then he returned into the house and received ambassadors of barbarous peoples.

As I was waiting for Onegesius, I was accosted by Romulus and Promotus and Romanus, the ambassadors who had come from Italy about the golden vessels; they were accompanied by Rusticius and by Constantiolus, a man from the Pannonian territory, which was subject to Attila. They asked me whether we had been dismissed or had to remain, and I replied that it was just to learn this from Onegesius that I was waiting outside the palace. When I inquired in my turn whether Attila had granted them a kind reply, they told me that his decision could not be moved, and that he threatened war unless either Silvanus or the drinking-vessels were given up...

As we were talking...Onegesius came out; we went up to him and asked him about our concerns. Having first spoken with some barbarians, he bade me inquire of Maximin what consular the Romans were sending as an ambassador to Attila.

When I came to our tent I delivered the message to Maximin, and deliberated with him what answer we should make to the question of the barbarian. Returning to Onegesius, I said that the Romans desired him to come to them and adjust the matters of dispute, otherwise the emperor will send whatever ambassador he chooses. He then bade me fetch Maximin, whom he conducted to the presence of Attila. Soon after Maximin came out, and told me that the barbarian wished Nomus or Anatolius or Senator to be the ambassador, and that he would not receive any other than one of these three; when Maximin replied that it was not meet to mention men by name and so render them suspected in the eyes of the emperor, Attila said that if they did not choose to comply with his wishes the differences would be adjusted by arms.

## A Banquet with Attila

When we returned to our tent the father of Orestes came with an invitation from Attila for both of us to a banquet at three o'clock. When the hour arrived we went to the palace, along with the embassy from the western Romans and stood on the threshold of the hall in the presence of Attila.

The cup-bearers gave us a cup, according to the national custom, that we might pray before we sat down. Having tasted the cup, we proceeded to take our seats; all the chairs were ranged along the walls of the room on either side. Attila sat in the middle on a couch; a second couch was set behind him, and from it steps led up to his bed, which was covered with linen sheets and wrought coverlets for ornament, such as Greeks and Romans use to deck bridal beds. The places on the right of Attila were held chief in honour, those on the left, where we sat, were only second. Berichus, a noble among the Scythians, sat on our side, but had the precedence of us. Onegesius sat on a chair on the right of Attila's couch, and over against Onegesius on a chair sat two of Attila's sons; his eldest son sat on his couch, not near him, but at the extreme end, with his eyes fixed on the ground, in shy respect for his father.

When all were arranged, a cup-bearer came and handed Attila a wooden cup of wine. He took it and saluted the first in precedence, who, honored by the salutation, stood up and might not sit down until the king, having tasted or drained the wine, returned the cup to the attendant. All the guests then honored Attila in the same way, saluting him, and then tasting the cups; but he did not stand up. Each of us had a special cupbearer, who would come forward in order to present the wine, when the cup-bearer of Attila retired. When the second in precedence and those next to him had been honored in like manner, Attila toasted us in the same way according to the order of the seats. When this ceremony was over the cup-bearers retired, and tables, large enough for three or four or even more to sit at, were placed next to the table of Attila, so that each could take of the food on the dishes without leaving his seat. The attendant of Attila first entered with a dish full of meat, and behind him came the other attendants with bread and cooked foods, which they laid on the tables. A luxurious meal, served on silver plate, had been made ready for us and the barbarian guests, but Attila ate nothing but meat on a wooden trencher. In everything else, too, he showed himself temperate; his cup was of wood, while to the guests were given goblets of gold and silver. His dress, too, was quite simple, affecting only to be clean. The sword he carried at his side, the latchets of his Scythian shoes, the bridle of his horse were not adorned, like those of the other Scythians, with gold or gems or anything costly. When the viands of the first course had been consumed, we all stood up and did not resume our seats until each one, in the order before observed, drank to the health of Attila in the goblet of wine presented to him. We then sat down, and a second dish was placed on each table with eatables of another kind. After this course the same ceremony was observed as after the first.

When evening fell torches were lit, and two barbarians coming forward in front of Attila sang songs they had composed, celebrating his victories and deeds of valour in war. And of the guests, as they looked at the singers, some were pleased with the verses, others reminded of wars were excited in their souls, while yet others, whose bodies were feeble with age and their spirits compelled to rest, shed tears.

After the songs, a Scythian, whose mind was deranged, appeared and by uttering outlandish and senseless words forced the company to laugh. After him Zerkon, the Moorish dwarf, entered. He had been sent by Attila as a gift to Aëtius, and Edeco had persuaded him to come to Attila in order to recover his wife, whom he had left behind him in Scythia; the lady was a Scythian whom he had obtained in marriage through the influence of his patron

Bleda. He did not succeed in recovering her, for Attila was angry with him for returning. On the occasion of the banquet he made his appearance, and threw all except Attila into fits of unquenchable laughter by his appearance, his dress, his voice, and his words, which were a confused jumble of Latin, Hunnic, and Gothic. Attila, however, remained immovable and of unchanging countenance, nor by word or act did he betray anything approaching a smile of merriment except at the entry of Ernach, his youngest son, whom he pulled by the cheek, and gazed on with a calm look of satisfaction.

I was surprised that he made so much of this son and neglected his other children; but a barbarian who sat beside me and knew Latin, bidding me not reveal what he told, gave me to understand that prophets had forewarned Attila that his people would fall but would be restored by this boy.

When the night had advanced we retired from the banquet, not wishing to assist further at the potations.

*More feasting and diplomatic exchanges took place before the Roman embassy was dismissed. The embassy successfully pleaded for, and paid for, the release of a certain woman and her children captured by the Huns. There was a banquet with Attila's wife and again with Attila. He told the embassy that the Romans must settle a complaint his secretary Constantius had with the emperor over the emperor's failure to provide Constantius with a suitably rich bride.*

*Epilogue. On Bigilas' return to Scythia, Attila extracted a huge sum of gold from him for his involvement in the plot against his life and demanded the surrender of the chamberlain Chrysaphius.*

## 23. ATTILA AND THE WEST, a. 450-52

*The following account should be compared with western sources **16-18**.*

### a. Attila and Honoria

*The news described below reached Constantinople in June 450. Attila's claim on Honoria is alluded to in **17**, s.a. 451.*

Source: C.D. Gordon, *The Age of Attila* (Anne Arbor, 1960), pp. 104-05. This fragment of Priscus is from John of Antioch = Blockley, Priscus 17.

[A messenger arrived at Constantinople from the west] announcing that Attila was involved with the royal family at Rome, since Honoria, the sister of Valentinian [III], had summoned him to her help. Honoria, though of the royal line and herself possessing the symbols of authority, was caught going secretly to bed with a certain Eugenius, who had the management of her affairs. He was put to death for his crime, and she was deprived of her royal position and betrothed to Herculanus, a man of consular rank and of such good character that it was not expected that he would aspire to royalty or revolution. She brought her affairs to disastrous and terrible trouble by sending Hyacinthus, a eunuch, to Attila so that for money he might avenge her marriage. In addition to this she also sent a ring pledging herself to the barbarian, who made ready to go against the western empire. He wanted to capture Aëtius first, for he thought he would not otherwise attain his ends unless he put him out of the way.

When Theodosius [II] learned of these things, he sent word to Valentinian to surrender Honoria to Attila. Valentinian arrested Hyacinth and examined the whole matter thoroughly; after inflicting many bodily tortures on him, he ordered that he be beheaded. Valentinian granted his sister Honoria to his mother [Galla Placidia] as a boon, since she persistently asked for her. And so Honoria was freed from danger at this time.

*Theodosius, after falling off his horse, died in late July 450 and was succeeded by Marcian in August of the same year.*

Translation: C.D. Gordon, *The Age of Attila* (Anne Arbor, 1960), pp. 105–06. The fragment is from *Excerpta de Legationibus* = Blockley, Priscus 20.1.

When it was announced to Attila that Marcian had come to the Roman throne in the east after the death of Theodosius, the Hun told him what had happened in the matter of Honoria. And he sent men to the ruler of the western Romans to argue that Honoria, whom he had pledged to himself in marriage, should in no way be ill-treated, for he would avenge her if she did not receive the scepter of sovereignty. He sent word also to the eastern Romans concerning the appointed tribute, but his ambassadors returned from both missions with nothing accomplished.

The Romans of the west answered that Honoria could not come to him in marriage, having been given to another man, and that the royal power did not belong to her, since the control of the Roman empire belonged to males not to females.

And the Romans of the east said that they would not submit to paying the tribute which Theodosius had arranged: to one who was peaceful they would give gifts, but against one threatening war they would let loose arms and men inferior in no way to his power.

Attila was of two minds and at a loss which [part of the empire] he should attack first, but finally it seemed better to him to enter on the greater war and to march against the West, since his fight there would be not only against the Italians but also against the Goths and Franks — against the Italians so as to seize Honoria along with her money, and against the Goths in order to earn the gratitude of Gaiseric, the Vandal king.

## b. Vandals and Huns

*This explanation in Jordanes for Vandal support of Attila may come from Priscus. After repudiating Theoderic's daughter, Huneric betrothed Eudocia, daughter of Valentinian III, and married her soon after 455.*

Source: Jordanes, *Getica*, ed. Th. Mommsen, MGH AA 5.1 (1882), c. 184 = Blockley, Priscus, 20.2. Translation by A.C. Murray.

When Gaiseric, king of the Vandals, learned that Attila had made up his mind to lay waste the whole world, he hastened on the war against the Visigoths by sending many gifts. For he feared that Theoderic, king of the Visigoths, would try to take revenge for the harm done his daughter. She had been married to Huneric, Gaiseric's son, and was at first happy in such a marriage. But afterwards, as he was a brute even to his own family, on the merest suspicion of her preparing poison, he had her nose slit and ears cut off, ruining her natural beauty, and sent her back to her father in Gaul. As a result the miserable woman constantly presented an awful spectacle and the cruel deed, which moved even strangers, was a most powerful inducement to her father taking revenge.

## c. Attila and the Franks

*The identity of the Frankish king in this passage has long excited speculation. Gibbon thought the king was Chlodio; many have thought that the king is Merovech and that the son who visited Rome is Childeric. Cf. **34b** and **78**; and for the existence of late stories about Childeric and the Huns, see **87**.*

Source: C.D. Gordon, *The Age of Attila* (Anne Arbor, 1960) p. 106. The fragment is from the *Excerpta de legationibus* = Blockley, Priscus 20.3.

Attila's excuse for his war against the Franks was the death of their king and the disagreement of his children over the rule, the elder, who decided to bring Attila in as his ally, and the younger, Aëtius. I saw this boy when he was at Rome on an embassy, a lad without down on his cheeks as yet and with fair hair so long that it poured down around his shoulders. Aëtius had made him his adopted son, along with the emperor given him very many gifts, and sent him away in friendship and alliance.

## d. Attila's Terms

Source: continuation of above.

For these reasons Attila was making his expedition, and again he sent certain men of his court to Italy that the Romans might surrender Honoria. He said she had been joined to him in marriage, and as proof he dispatched the ring sent by her in order that it might be shown. He also said that Valentinian should withdraw from half of the empire in his favor, since Honoria had received its control from her father and had been deprived of it by the greed of her brother. When the western Romans held their former opinion and paid no attention to his proposal, he devoted himself eagerly to preparation for war and collected the whole force of his fighting men.

## e. Attila Meets the Pope

*After his unsuccessful invasion of Gaul in 451, Attila invaded Italy in 452, where he was met by an embassy sent from Rome. The pope's participation in the embassy was soon the subject of legendary embellishment. Modern historians have often seen it as a sign of rising temporal powers on the part of the papacy, though in similar situations bishops had long undertaken embassies on behalf of their cities.*

Source: Jordanes, *Getica*, ed. Th. Mommsen, MGH AA 5.1 (1882), c. 223 = Blockley, Priscus 22.1. Translation by A.C. Murray.

Though Attila had his heart set on going to Rome, his men, as the historian Priscus relates, kept him away, not out of consideration for the city — to which they were hostile — but by holding up the example of Alaric, one time king of the Visigoths. They were afraid for the good fortune of their own king, for Alaric had not long survived the capture of Rome, but had at once died. While Attila's intentions wavered back and forth between going or not and he was delaying while he considered the matter, a peace mission reached him from Rome. For Pope Leo himself came to him in the district of Ambuleium in Venetia where the Mincius River is commonly crossed by travelers. Attila soon laid aside his usual fury and, returning from where he had come from, departed beyond the Danube with the promise of peace. Issuing threats, he declared above all that he would inflict heavier penalties on Italy if Honoria, the sister of the emperor Valentinian and daughter of Galla Placidia Augusta, were not sent to him along with the share of the royal wealth due her.

## 24. ATTILA'S DEATH, a. 453

Source: Jordanes, *Getica*, ed. Th. Mommsen, MGH AA 5.1 (1882), c. 223 = Blockley, Priscus 24.1. Translation by A.C. Murray.

Priscus the historian relates that Attila at the time of his death took to wife a beautiful girl by the name of Ildico, having countless other wives, as was the custom of that people. Rather overdoing the celebrations at the wedding, he lay down on his back, overcome by wine and sleep. An excess of blood that would normally have spilled out through his nose drained back in a deadly stream into his throat, as it could not flow out by the usual passages, and killed him. And so drunkenness brought about a shameful end to a king renowned in war.

The dawn came, and after a good part of the day had passed, the servants of the king, fearing something was wrong, after loudly shouting outside the room, broke in. They found Attila already dead from the hemorrhage and without a wound, and the girl, her head downcast, weeping beneath her veil. Then, as is the custom of that people, they cut off part of their hair and disfigured their hideous faces with deep wounds to mourn the famous warrior, not with womanly wailing and tears but with manly blood.

With respect to this event, the following marvel took place: Marcian, emperor of the east, who was anxious about so fierce an enemy, dreamt that the divinity stood beside him on that very night and showed him the bow of Attila, broken — for the Huns owe much to that weapon. The historian Priscus says he verified this story with truthful testimony. For Attila was viewed by the great empires as so terrifying that the powers above granted rulers signs of his death.

We shall not pass over telling a few of the many ways his body was honored by his peoples. The corpse was placed in a silken tent in the middle of a plain and a marvelous spectacle solemnly enacted. For in the place he had been laid the most select horsemen of the entire nation of the Huns rode around in circles in the fashion of the circus games, reciting his deeds in a funeral chant in the following way:

"Attila, chief king of the Huns, the son of Mundzuc, lord of the bravest peoples, who alone possessed Scythian and Germanic realms with powers unheard of before his time, who also terrified both empires of Rome by capturing its cities and, placated by entreaties, received an annual tribute to prevent his plundering the rest. When he had done all these deeds as a result of good fortune, he died, not by the wounds of foes, not by the treachery of his own followers, but painlessly and happy amidst rejoicing, his nation safe. Who can believe he has passed away for whom no one thinks to take vengeance?"

After he was mourned with such dirges, they celebrated over his tomb what they call a *strava* with great revelry, and, giving way to contrary emotions in turn, they displayed a mixture of funeral grief and joy. The corpse was buried in the earth in the secrecy of night. They bound the coffins, the first with gold, the second with silver, and the third with the strength of iron, symbolizing by this means all that befitted a most powerful king: iron, because he subdued peoples; gold and silver because he received the trappings of both empires. They added equipment taken from slain enemies, costly fittings gleaming with a variety of gems, and badges of various kinds by which princely state is maintained. And to preserve such wealth from human curiosity, they paid a hateful reward to those assigned the task by cutting them down, and sudden death engulfed the buriers and the buried alike.

# CHAPTER SEVEN

# FRAGMENTS AND SCRAPS OF FIFTH-CENTURY HISTORY

## 25. THE FRANKS AND IMPERIAL POLITICS, a. 388-420

*The role of the Franks in the events of the late fourth and early fifth centuries is illuminated in excerpts from two contemporary histories and a passage from the poetry of Claudian. The historical excerpts were culled from the works of Sulpicius Alexander and Renatus Profuturus Frigeridus by the sixth-century bishop and historian, Gregory of Tours, who was looking for early references to Frankish kings. All that survives of Sulpicius's and Renatus's histories are the excerpts in Gregory's work.*

Sources: (1) Gregory of Tours, *Historiarum libri X*, ed. Bruno Krusch and Wilhelm Levison, MGH SRM I/1, 2nd. ed.; and *Zehn Bücher Geschichten*, ed. R. Buchner (Berlin, 1955) vol. 1: Bk. II 9. Translation by A.C. Murray. (2) *Claudian*, trans. Maurice Platnauer (Cambridge MA./London, 1923) 1: 379-383.

### A. SULPICIUS ALEXANDER

*Sulpicius's history likely ended in the very last years of the fourth century. The following excerpt refers to Frankish raids of 388. Maximus is Magnus Maximus, the usurper (a. 383-88), then at Aquilea. Nanninus also appears in Ammianus's history (31.10, 38.5)*

At that time under the dukes Genobaud, Marcomer, and Sunno, the Franks broke into the province of Germania. After forcing the frontier, they killed large numbers of people, ravaging the fertile districts in particular, and struck terror even into Cologne. When news of this reached Trier, Nanninus and Quintinus, masters of the soldiers, to whom Maximus had entrusted his young son and the defense of Gaul, gathered their forces and assembled at Cologne. But the enemy, having pillaged the richest parts of the provinces, crossed the Rhine, laden with plunder. They left a good number of their men behind on Roman soil, ready to lay waste again. Fighting them suited the Romans, and many Franks were put to the sword in the Carbonarian forest.

There was debate whether this favorable outcome justified the Romans crossing over into Francia. Nanninus refused, knowing that the enemy were not unprepared and would doubtless be even tougher on home ground. This viewpoint displeased Quintinus and the other officers, and so Nanninus withdrew to Mainz. Quintinus led the army across the Rhine near the fortress of Neuss and, after two days' march, came across empty houses and large townships which had been deserted. For the Franks, pretending to be afraid, had retired into the more remote reaches of the countryside, and prepared abattis at the edges of the woods. The Roman troops burned all the houses, thinking in their cowardly stupidity that venting their rage on these would bring victory; they passed an anxious night under arms.

At dawn, Quintinus led them into the bush, and they ranged all over until almost midday, taking the wrong paths. At length, finding everything completely blocked off by great fences, they tried to make their way out into the marshy flats adjoining the woods. The enemy, making use of the tree trunks and standing on the abattis, showed themselves here and there, and, as from the heights of a tower, discharged arrows like ballistae, smeared with poison, so that mere flesh wounds or those not normally lethal proved fatal. Then the army, surrounded by even greater numbers of the enemy, eagerly streamed into the open ground left unoccupied by the Franks. The horsemen were the first swallowed up in the morass, men and horses in confusion bearing each other down in one common disaster. The foot-soldiers, though not trampled under the weight of the horses, were also stuck in the mud and had trouble extricating their feet. Though they had only come out in the open a short while before, in panic, they retreated to hide in the woods. With their ranks thrown into disorder, the legions were cut to pieces. Heraclius, tribune of the Jovian legion, and almost all the officers were killed; only the darkness of night and the recesses of the forest offered a few complete safety.

*Sulpicius also deals with events following the suppression of Maximus by Theodosius. Arbogast, a Frank by birth, was one of Theodosius' generals.*

At this time Carietto and Syrus replaced Nanninus and were stationed in the province of Germania with an army to oppose the Franks...

[*Following plundering by the Franks.*] Arbogast was unwilling to countenance any delay and urged the emperor to exact just retribution from the Franks, unless they immediately restored all they had taken the previous year when the legions were cut up, and unless they surrendered those responsible for the war who were to blame for treacherously violating the peace...

A few days afterwards, a hurried conference was held with Marcomer and Sunno, petty kings (*regales*) of the Franks; hostages were demanded as usual and Arbogast retired to winter quarters at Trier.

*Arbogast served as master of the soldiers in Gaul under Valentinian II from 388 to 392. Subsequently he promoted the usurper Eugenius, committing suicide soon after the latter's execution in 394.*

While in the east various events occurred in Thrace, in Gaul the state was thrown into confusion. Emperor Valentinian was shut up in the palace at Vienne and reduced almost to the level of a private citizen; the management of military affairs was given over to Frankish followers; even civil administration passed into the control of Arbogast's faction. Among all those bound by the military oath, no one could be found who dared obey the personal orders or commands of the emperor...

In the same year Arbogast, pursuing the Frankish petty kings Sunno and Marcomer with a kind of family (*gentilis*) hatred, came to Cologne in the depths of winter, knowing that all the retreats of Francia could be penetrated and burned now that the leaves had fallen and the bare woods could no longer conceal ambushes. He gathered his forces and crossed the Rhine, plundering the country of the Bructeri, which was next to the river, and the region inhabited by the Chamavi. He encountered no opposition. Only a few Ampsivarii and Chatti, under the command of Marcomer, appeared on the farthest ridges of the hills...

Then the usurper Eugenius undertook an expedition to the borders of the Rhine to renew in the usual way the old treaties with the kings of the Alamanni and the Franks and to show to the wild peoples an army of immense size for that time.

## B. CLAUDIAN ON THE CONSULSHIP OF STILICHO, a. 400

*Claudian, a Greek-speaking Egyptian by birth, turned his hand to Latin on his arrival at the court of Milan around 395. He became the mouthpiece of his patron, Stilicho, general of the western armies and guardian of the emperor Honorius. The following excerpt from a poem celebrating Stilicho's first consulship in the year 400, deals in a tendentious fashion with the general's tour of the Rhine frontier in 396.*

Do we wonder that the foe so swiftly yields in battle when they fall before the sole terror of his name? We did not declare war on the Franks; yet they were overthrown. We did not crush in battle the Suebi on whom we now impose our laws. Who could believe it? fierce Germany was our slave before ever the trumpets rang out. Where are now thy wars, Drusus, or thine, Trajan? All that your hands wrought after doubtful conflict that Stilicho did as he passed along, and o'ercame the Rhine in as many days as you could do in years; you conquered with the sword, he with a word; you with an army, he single handed. Descending from the river's source to where it splits in twain and to the marshes that connect its mouths, he flashed his lightening way...The speed of the general outstripped the river's swift course, and Peace, starting with him from Rhine's source, grew as grew Rhine's waters. Their names once remarkable, kings with flaxen hair, whom neither gifts nor prayers could win over to obedience to Rome's emperors, hasten at his command and fear to offend by dull delay. Crossing the river in boats they meet him wheresoever he will. The fame of his justice did not play him false: they found him merciful, they found him trustworthy. Him whom at his coming the German feared, at his departure he loved. Those dread people, whose wont it was ever to set a price on peace or let us purchase repose by shameful tribute, offered their children as hostages and begged for peace with such suppliant looks that one would have thought them captives, their hands bound behind their backs, and they mounting the Tarpeian rock with the chains of slavery upon their necks. All those lands that lie between Ocean and the Danube trembled at the approach of one man. Boreas was brought into servitude without a blow; the Great Bear was disarmed.

In so short a time didst thou win so many battles without loss of blood, and, setting out with the moon yet new, thou didst return before it was full; so didst thou compel the threatening Rhine to learn gentleness with shattered horns, that the Salian now tills his fields, the Sygambrian beats his straight sword into a curved sickle, and the traveler, as he looks at the two banks, asks over which Rome rules. The Belgian, too, pastures his flock across the river and the Chauci heed it not; Gallic herds cross the middle Elbe and wander over the hills of the Franks. Safe it is to hunt amid the vast silence of the distant Hercynian forest, and in the woods that old-established superstition had rendered awful our axes fell the trees the barbarian once worshipped and nought is said.

Nay more, devoted to their conqueror they offer arms in his defense. How often has Alamannia begged to add her troops to thine and to join her forces with those of Rome! Nor yet was she angered when her offer was rejected, for though her aid was refused her loyalty came off with praise. Provence will sooner drive out the governor thou sendest than Francia will expel the kings thou has given it. Not to rout rebels in the field but to punish them with chains is now the law; under our judge a Roman prison holds inquest on the crimes of kings. Marcomer and Sunno give proof: the one underwent exile in Etruria, the other, proclaiming himself the exile's avenger, fell beneath the swords of his own soldiers. Both were eager to arouse rebellion, both hated peace — true brothers in character and in a common love of crime.

## C. RENATUS PROFUTURUS FRIGERIDUS

*Renatus probably wrote in the middle part of the fifth century: he seems to have covered events from around the first years of the fifth century to at least some time after the early career of Aëtius (cf. below, 31).*

*Gregory seems to place the following events around 410, but they are better regarded as part of the preliminaries to the invasion of 406. Goar, a king of the Alans, later supported the usurper Jovinus and appears in Roman service in Constantius's Life of St. Germanus (below, 33 and cf. 28). The Vandal king Godigisel was the father of Geiseric.*

Meanwhile, Goar went over to the Romans, and Respendial, king of the Alans, wheeled the line of march of his forces away from the Rhine. The Vandals were getting the worst of it in fighting against the Franks, their king Godigisel having been killed and an army of about twenty thousand men destroyed. The Vandals were on the point of total extermination when the forces of the Alans came to their aid in the nick of time.

*The Constantine in the following passage is the famous usurper and ruler of Gaul and Spain, proclaimed emperor in Britain in 407 and temporarily recognized by Honorius. He was beheaded in 411.*

The usurper Constantine summoned his son Constans, also a usurper, from Spain to consult with him on affairs of state. And so Constans left the paraphernalia of his court and his wife at Saragossa and, entrusting all his interests in Spain to Gerontius, traveled without a pause to meet his father. When they met and a good number of days passed without any bad news from Italy, Constantine gave himself over to gluttony and drunkenness and told his son to return to Spain. Constans had sent his forces on ahead and was staying behind with his father when news came from Spain that one of his dependents, Maximus, had been made emperor by Gerontius and was arming himself with a following of barbarian peoples. Taking fright at this news, Constans and Decimius Rusticus, now prefect but formerly master of the offices, sent Edobech on ahead to the peoples of Germania, and they themselves set out for the Gallic provinces, intending to return right away to Constantine with Franks, Alamanni, and all available soldiers...

*The siege here is that of Arles in 411. Honorius's forces were commanded by Constantius. Jovinus was proclaimed emperor in 411 and beheaded in 412.*

The siege of Constantine was just entering its fourth month when news suddenly arrived from Farther Gaul that Jovinus had assumed the imperial insignia and was threatening the besiegers with Burgundians, Alamanni, Franks, Alans, and all his forces. Siege operations were expedited, the gates were opened, and Constantine was given up. He was immediately sent to Italy, but he was met by executioners sent by the emperor and beheaded on the river Mincio...

In those same days Decimius Rusticus, prefect of the usurpers, Agroetius, formerly chief of the secretaries of Jovinus, and many nobles were captured in the Auvergne by the generals of Honorius and cruelly put to death. The city of Trier was plundered and burned by the Franks; this was their second attack.

*The following event took place between 420 and 422. For Castinus see 16 and 18, s.a. 422.*

At the same time Castinus, count of the domestics, was sent to Gaul, where an expedition against the Franks had been undertaken.

## 26. AN ANONYMOUS SKETCH OF THE REIGN OF HONORIUS

*An unflattering view of Honorius and Galla Placidia from one of a series of slight imperial biographies written by an unknown westerner in the second quarter of the fifth century.*

Source: *Narratio de imperatoribus domus Valentinianae et Theodosianae*, ed. Th. Mommsen, *Chronica Minora* 1 MGH AA 9 (1892), pp. 629-30. Translation by A.C. Murray.

Honorius ruled 32 years...The state suffered many severe wounds during his reign. The most biting was the capture and ruin of the city of Rome by Alaric, king of the Goths. The sister of the emperor, the Augusta Placidia, at first a captive and then, it is true, the wife of a king, but a barbarian one, is a blot on the public life of the times. Gaul and Spain were ravaged by barbarian peoples, the Vandals, Sueves, and Alans, and thoroughly destroyed. The British provinces were forever removed from the Roman name. Yet, while this same emperor accomplished nothing worthwhile against external enemies, he enjoyed the utmost fortune in the destruction of usurpers. Most of them — Constantine and his sons; Jovinus and his brother Sebastian; Attalus, propped up by Gothic power; Maximus, purple-clad in Spain; and several others — he defeated, seized, and destroyed.

# 27. OLYMPIODORUS ON GALLA PLACIDIA AND THE GOTHS

*Olympiodorus, a pagan from Thebes in Egypt, was author of a history in twenty-two books covering the reigns of Honorius and Theodosius II down to the proclamation of Valentinian III as emperor in 425. It was written in Greek at Constantinople, probably soon after 440, and dedicated to the emperor Theodosius II. Though the history is no longer extant, excerpts survive in other works. All of the following excerpts are from the* Bibliotheca *of Photius, the celebrated ninth-century Byzantine scholar and patriarch.*

Source: R.C. Blockley, *The Fragmentary Classicising Historians of the Later Roman Empire: Eunapius, Olympiodorus, Priscus and Malchus*, vol. 2 (Liverpool, 1983).

### Fragment no. 22.1

When Athaulf was asked to return Placidia, he demanded the grain which had been promised. Although they could not fulfill their promises, they nevertheless swore to deliver it, if they received Placidia. The barbarian pretended to agree and advanced to the city named Marseilles, which he hoped to capture by treachery. There he was wounded by a blow from the most noble Boniface and, barely escaping death, he retired to his own tent, leaving the city rejoicing and full of praise and acclaim for Boniface.

### Fragment no. 24

With the advice and encouragement of Candidianus, Athaulf married Placidia at the beginning of the month of January in the city of Narbo[nne] at the house of Ingenuus, one of the leading citizens of the place. There Placidia, dressed in royal raiment, sat in a hall decorated in the Roman manner, and by her side sat Athaulf, wearing a Roman general's cloak and other Roman clothing. Amidst the celebrations, along with other wedding gifts Athaulf gave Placidia fifty handsome young men dressed in silk clothes, each bearing aloft two very large dishes, one full of gold, the other full of precious — or rather, priceless — stones, which had been carried off by the Goths at the sack of Rome. Then nuptial hymns were sung, first by Attalus, then by Rusticius and Phoebadius. Then the ceremonies were completed amidst rejoicings and celebrations by both the barbarians and the Romans amongst them.

### Fragment no. 26

When Placidia had borne him a son, whom he named Theodosius, Athaulf became even more friendly towards the Romans. But his and Placidia's desires remained unfulfilled in the face of the opposition by Constantius and his supporters. When the child died, his parents grieved for him greatly and buried him in a silver coffin in a chapel outside Barcelona. Then Athaulf himself was killed while, as was his custom, he was spending some time in the stable inspecting his horses. His slayer was one of his own dependents, Dubius by name, who had been waiting the chance to avenge an old grudge. For long ago his master, a king of part of the Goths, had been slain by Athaulf, who afterwards took Dubius into his own service. So in killing his second master Dubius avenged the first.

On his deathbed Athaulf told his brother to hand back Placidia and, if they could, ensure Roman friendship toward themselves. But Singeric, the brother of Sarus, by conspiracy and coup rather than by the Gothic law of succession, became his successor and he killed Athaulf's children by his first wife, tearing them by force from the arms of the bishop Sigesarus. To spite Athaulf he ordered his queen, Placidia, to walk before his horse with the rest of the prisoners for a distance of twelve miles from the city. After a reign of seven days Singeric was killed and Wallia was declared leader of the Goths.

### Fragment nos. 29.1, 2

The Vandals call the Goths *Truli* because when they were oppressed by hunger they bought grain from the Vandals at one solidus per *trula* [scoop].

When the Vandals overran Spain and the Romans fled to their walled cities, such famine afflicted them that they were reduced to cannibalism. A woman who had four children ate them all, in each case giving as her excuse the nourishment and survival of those remaining. Finally, when she had eaten them all, the people stoned her to death.

### Fragment no. 30

Euplutius the *agens in rebus* was sent to Wallia, who had been proclaimed tribal leader of the Goths, to negotiate a peace treaty and the return of Placidia. He was readily received, and when 600,000 measures of grain had been sent, Placidia was freed and handed over to Euplutius for Honorius, her brother.

### Fragment no. 33

When Honorius was celebrating his eleventh consulship and Constantius his second, they solemnised Placidia's marriage. Her frequent rejections of Constantius had made him angry at her attendants. Finally, the emperor Honorius, her brother, on the day on which he entered his consulship, took her by the hand, and despite her protests, gave her over to Constantius, and the marriage was solemnised in the most dazzling fashion. Later a child was born to them, whom they named Honoria, and a boy, whom they named Valentinian. While Honorius was still alive he became *nobilissimus* at Placidia's insistence, and after his death and the overthrow of the usurper John he was proclaimed emperor of Rome.

Constantius became co-emperor with Honorius, who appointed him, but rather unwillingly. Placidia was proclaimed Augusta jointly by her brother and husband. The proclamation announcing the elevation of Constantius was then sent to Theodosius [II], Honorius' nephew and the ruler of the eastern empire, but it was not accepted. Constantius fell ill and regretted his elevation, that he no longer had the freedom to leave and go off wherever and in whatever manner he wished and could not, because he was emperor, enjoy the pastimes which he had been accustomed to enjoy. Finally having reigned for seven months, as the dream foretold to him — "six have already been completed, and the seventh begins" — he died of pleurisy. With him died the hostility towards the east and the expedition which he had been preparing because they did not approve his proclamation as emperor.

### Fragment no. 36

He [Olympiodorus] tells a marvelous story about a certain Libanius, an Asian by race, who came to Ravenna during the reign of Honorius and Constantius. According to the historian, he was a consummate magician, able to achieve results even against barbarians without resort to weapons, and this he promised to do. He was given permission to make the attempt, but when his promise and his high repute came to the ears of the empress Placidia, the magician was put to death. For Placidia threatened Constantius that she would break up their marriage if Libanius, a wizard and an unbeliever, remained amongst the living.

### Fragment no. 37

Constantius was an Illyrian by birth, from Naissus, a city of Dacia. From the time of Theodosius the Great he had taken part in many campaigns and, as has been told, was later elevated to the rank of emperor. In addition to his other virtues he was free from greed until he married Placidia. But when he was joined to her, he fell into lust for money. After his death Ravenna was inundated from all sides with suits over his misappropriation of possessions. But Honorius's unresponsiveness and the close relationship of Placidia to him rendered both the complaints and the power of justice ineffectual.

## Fragment no. 38

The affection of Honorius toward his sister grew so great after the death of her husband Constantius that their immoderate pleasure in each other and their constant kissing on the mouth caused many people to entertain shameful suspicions about them. But as a result of the efforts of Spadusa and of Placidia's nurse, Elpidia (to both of whom she paid great attention) and through the co-operation of Leontius, her steward, this affection was replaced with such a degree of hatred that fighting often broke out in Ravenna and blows were delivered on both sides. For Placidia was surrounded by a host of barbarians because of her marriages to Athaulf and Constantius. Finally, as a result of this flare-up of enmity and the hatred as strong as their previous love, when Honorius proved the stronger, Placidia was exiled to Byzantium with her children. Only [the general] Boniface continued loyal to her and from Africa, which he governed, sent whatever money he could and promised other kinds of assistance. Later, he contributed all his resources towards her restoration as empress.

## 28. FROM THE *THANKSGIVING* OF PAULINUS OF PELLA: THE SACK OF BORDEAUX AND THE SIEGE OF BAZAS, a. 414/415

*For Paulinus's life and his* Thanksgiving, *see* **15**. *The following account was written about forty-five years after the events it describes; the sack of Bordeaux took place in 414. Some would identify Paulinus's friend, the Alan king with whom he negotiated outside Bazas in 414/15, as Goar (cf. above,* **25 C**, *and below,* **33**). *The following selection opens with Paulinus's absence from Bordeaux shortly before the events of 414.*

Source: two editions of the *Eucharisticus* were used: (1) *Poetae christiani minores*, ll. 270-402, ed. Wilhelm Brandes, Corpus Scriptorum Ecclesiasticorum Latinorum 16 (Vindobonae, 1888), pp. 263-334; (2) Paulin de Pella, *Poème d'action de grâces et prière*, ll. 270-402, ed. and trans. Claude Moussy, Sources Chrétiennes 209 (Paris, 1974). Translation by A.C. Murray.

And, above all, misfortunes long my due laid a special hold of me. For my second homeland was in the East, where I was born and was a not inconsiderable land holder, and I was delayed against my will on a prolonged journey. The reluctant efforts of my own people were responsible for this in the first instance. But the sometimes conflicting wishes of those dear to me and a mind often struggling to deal with its own desires delayed me, just as much as the recurrent fear of a doubtful outcome happened to keep postponing the making of preparations. On the other hand, I found attractive the habits of ease and the leisure I had known and the many exceptional conveniences of an estate, alas, filled to excess in hard times with very pleasing delights of all kinds and every blessing. At the time it alone even lacked a Gothic guest. Soon afterwards it suffered disastrously as a result. There was no one with a special interest in protecting the place and it was allowed to be given over to pillaging by the forces as they departed. For I know that some Goths with the utmost decency attempted to assist their hosts by giving them protection.

But a new cause of greater trouble was added to the circumstances of my lot as I just described it. In looking for empty support, the usurper Attalus burdened me during my absence with a hollow title of distinction, making me count of the private largesse, a post which he knew had no revenue to support it. By now even he himself had ceased to put much faith in his own rule. Dependent on the Goths alone, he now knew them only too well. He could rely on them at the moment for his life but not also for his imperial authority, and on his own he had no resources that were his nor any military support.

For this reason, I admit that I, and by no means the representatives of a shaky usurper, pursued peace with the Goths. At the time, it was a choice the Goths themselves agreed upon and a little later, though purchased at a price, was ceded to others. And it remains nothing to be ashamed of, since I see that at the present time in our state a good many flourish through the good will of the Goths. However, at an earlier time, many suffered severely and I was a big part of that, being deprived of all my own property and outliving my own homeland.

For you see, when, by a decree of king Athaulf, they were about to head out of the town, the Goths, who had been received on terms of peace, subjected us no less to the bitter usage of war and burnt the whole place. They found me there, then a count of that emperor whose officials they did not acknowledge as their own. They stripped me and my mother both of all our goods, subjecting us to a common fate, but thought to spare us, their prisoners, in one respect — we were free to leave without being hurt. The honor of all the women in our company as well as of the female servants, anyone who had been in the train of our fortunes, was wholly preserved and no one assaulted them. I was spared an even greater concern by the dispensation of God, to whom I owe perpetual gratitude: my daughter, whom I previously married to a husband, missed the disaster visited on us all because she had left her homeland.

But this was not an end to the troubles which I said we had to endure. Driven from ancestral homes consumed by fire, we were immediately caught up in an enemy siege while staying in the neighboring town of Bazas, which was also the homeland of my ancestors. Much more serious than encirclement by the enemy was a party of slaves who had taken up arms for the particular slaughter of the well-born and who were joined by the insane fury of a few good-for-nothing, if freeborn, youths. You, just God, diverted this bloodshed away from the innocent and immediately checked the slaughter with the death of a few of the guilty. Without my knowing it, you had the killer threatening my own life perish at the hands of another avenger. Indeed, you repeatedly made me obliged to you with fresh gifts, so I would know I owed you eternal thanks for them.

I was alarmed by the sudden onset of such danger, which I saw could strike me down within the city, and I, too terrified I admit, made a new mistake. I hoped that with the help of a king [of the Alans] who a short time ago was my friend, and whose forces were inflicting a long siege on us, I could get away from the beleaguered city along with a large group of those dear to me. The hope urging on these preparations of ours was my knowledge that the king was pressing upon our people against his will, compelled by the authority of the Gothic people. I set out from the city intending to investigate and fearlessly made for the king without anyone getting in my way. I was happier, however, before I addressed my friend, whom I thought would be more favorable to my request. When I had scrutinized his intentions as deeply as I could, he said he could not help me if I stayed outside the city; and he disclosed that it would now be unsafe for him to allow me, now that I had been seen, to return to the city, unless he himself were admitted to it right away along with me. In fact, he knew that the Goths were again making ominous threats against me, and he himself wished to free himself of their control.

I was astonished and, I confess, shaken by the proposition he put forward and by extreme fear of the danger this involved. But by the mercy of God, who always and everywhere attends upon the prayers of those who are discouraged, I soon recovered my composure. Though fearful, I myself boldly endeavored in my own interests to further the plan of my still hesitating friend, advising against insurmountable goals that I knew must by all means be rejected, but encouraging action on measures that had to be taken as soon as possible.

These the clever man himself approved and acted on just in time. He personally conferred with the leaders of the town and immediately carried out the scheme in a hurry in the course of one night with the help of God, whose favor he now possessed; for that reason the king was able to help us and his own people. The whole crowd of Alan women, accompanied by their husbands bearing arms, left their positions and assembled together. The king's wife was the first to be handed over to the Romans as a hostage, and with her also the king's dear son, and I myself was restored to my people as part of the terms of the peace that was agreed upon, just as if I had been delivered from our common enemy the Goths. The outskirts of the town were surrounded by a rampart of Alan soldiers. With promises given and received, they were ready to fight for us, whom recently they themselves as enemies had besieged. Marvelous was the appearance of the city: a large unarmed crowd of both sexes encircled its walls on all sides. A barbaric host lay outside, clinging to our walls and surrounded by a rampart of wagons and armed men.

This was part of a not inconsiderable force, and when the crowd of Goths pillaging round about saw that they were separated from it, they immediately felt they could no longer remain there in safety. Now that the guest in their midst had unexpectedly turned on them, the Goths dared try nothing further, and chose to hurry off of their own accord. Our auxiliaries, as we called them, followed their example in good time and departed, prepared to preserve their promise of peace with the Romans wherever their lot was to carry them.

And so a great matter that I undertook rashly turned out well in the end with the favorable help of God, and God turned my mistake into new joys for many as well as myself by lifting the siege.

## 29. THE ESTABLISHMENT OF THE GALLIC COUNCIL OF THE SEVEN PROVINCES, a. 418

*At some point in the first years of the fifth century, the site of the Gallic prefecture was moved from Trier in the north to Arles in the south. In 418, roughly at the time the Visigoths were being located in Aquitaine, a diocesan council was established for the Seven Provinces, which consisted of the southern diocese of Viennensis; the provinces were Novempopuli, Aquitanica I and II, Narbonnensis I and II, Viennensis, and Alpes Maritimae. Provincial councils were a regular feature of late imperial government, but larger diocesan councils seem only to have met occasionally. In the case of the Seven Provinces, the intention was that the council be a permanent institution, for it was to be held every year at Arles under the presidency of the praetorian prefect.*

*The letter below is the official announcement from the emperor Honorius setting up the council as a permanent institution. The reason for establishing the council at this time and its relation to the functioning of the prefecture as a whole are problems about which the letter unfortunately provides no ready answers. The emphasis placed on the commercial benefits accruing to the holding of the council is noteworthy.*

*The 'judges' in the letter are provincial governors. The earlier prefect Petronius held his office between 402 and 408. Praetorian prefects were addressed as 'your magnificence.' The addressee Agricola may have been the father of the later emperor Avitus. The ellipsis stands for the adjective 'notiores,' which is problematic, and has been emended in various ways; I place one such conjecture in brackets.*

Source: W. Grundlach, *Epistolae Arelatenses genuiniae*, in MGH Epistolae 3: Epistolae Merowingici et Karolini Aevi (1892), pp. 13-17. Translation by A.C. Murray.

### [Letter] sent to the illustrious Agricola, prefect of the Gauls

Among matters of state that still required attention, we have found the most sound request of your magnificence clearly instructive. Accordingly we decree a measure for our provincials — that is in the Seven Provinces — that will remain forever in force, as must plainly have been the hope of the provincials themselves.

On account of private and public needs, the well-being of landlords (*possessores*) and the accounting of public burdens demands that dignitaries (*honorati*) assemble and delegates (*legati*) be sent, not just from the provinces but from the various cities, so your magnificence may examine them. For these reasons we judge it especially suitable and expedient that the Seven Provinces commence holding a council; this custom shall be retained each year hereafter, a time having been set in the metropolitan town, that is Arles. In this council, we plainly have regard for the particular and for all in common: in the first instance, so that, by the assembly of the best people (*optimi*) in the illustrious presence of the prefect, discussions of individual matters can be most beneficial, provided this conforms to the orderly management of public business; then, in that whatever was discussed and established, once the accounting has been reviewed, cannot be concealed from the... [more remote?] provinces, and the same kind of fairness and justice must be applied to those not present.

Apart from the requirements of public business, we believe that, by giving orders for there to be a council every year in the city of Constantina [Arles], plainly not a little human benefit will also accompany frequent attendance at it. So suitable is the place, so great the amount of trade, so busy the traffic coming and going there, that goods produced anywhere may be sold there quite easily; for no province so rejoices in the extraordinary bounty of its own products as not to believe that this abundance belongs especially to Arles alone. Whatever the rich East, perfumed Arab or spoiled Assyrian, or what fertile Africa, beautiful Spain or brave Gaul may consider admirable abounds there in such quantity as to make one believe that everything the world agrees is splendid is produced there. Now is the time for the waters of the Rhône and the Tyrrhenian sea to link the lands through which the former flows and around which the latter laps, to make them, so to speak, neighbors.

Since, therefore, whatever excellence the land has serves this city, and whatever is produced in various places is brought to it by sail, oar, and cart, by land, sea, and stream, how then may our Gallic provinces believe that not much has been granted them when we provide for an assembly in that city in which, by a certain divine gift, such favorable conditions for trade and commerce are furnished? If, indeed, the illustrious prefect Petronius by plainly reasonable and proven advice already anticipated instituting this measure, our wisdom, Agricola, dearest and most loving kinsman, causes us to exercise our customary authority to decree that what has been corrupted by the negligence of the times or the slothfulness of usurpers is to be restored.

For which reason, let your illustrious magnificence follow this command of ours and a previous instruction of your office and see to it permanently that dignitaries (*honorati*) or landlords (*possessores*) and judges of each of the provinces know that during the period from the Ides of August to the Ides of September in the city of Arles a council is to be held each year. Provision must be made with regard to Novempopulana and Aquitanica secunda, which provinces are situated some distance away, that if certain business holds back their judges, they must know that legates are to be sent according to custom. By such foresight, we understand that we grant a significant favor and benefit both to our provincials and to the city of Arles, and, we should certainly add, to the city's embellishment — for we are much indebted to the loyalty of the city, according to the attestation and opinion of our relation and patrician.

Let your magnificence know that a judge is to be fined 5 pounds of gold, and a dignitary (*honoratus*) or city councillor (*curialis*) 3 pounds, if he delays coming to the appointed place within the prescribed period.

Given on the 15th day before the Kalends of May [17 April]. Received at Arles 10 days before the Kalends of June [23 May], our lord Honorius being consul for the twelfth time, and Theodosius consul for the eighth.

## 30. FROM THE COMEDY *QUEROLUS*: LAWS OF THE FOREST ALONG THE LOIRE

*Querolus is a fifth-century comedy, the only extant play of the late empire in a genre whose heyday lay six centuries in the past. It enjoyed some popularity in the Middle Ages and in modern times has been mistaken for a reworked play of Plautus.*

*The author is unknown and the play seems to have been designed for private performance in the home of the dramatist's patron Rutilius. If this is the famous poet and urban prefect (a. 414) Rutilius Claudius Namatianus (see 14), as is often supposed, the play would date from early in the century, though its fifth-century date is assured in any case. Rutilius was a pagan. Among other themes, the play deals often in an amusing fashion with a question common to religious and philosophical thinking of the day: why do the wicked seem to flourish and the righteous suffer?*

*The main character is Querolus, which means the complainer or whiner, a rude, weak, bad-tempered fellow, dissatisfied with his life. The following extract is a conversation between Querolus (abbreviated Q in the excerpt) and his* lar familiaris *(abbreviated LF), the god of his household, who has the power to affect, if not completely determine, Querolus's fate. The lar familiaris has been persuading Querolus that he is not so badly off after all. The discussion touches in a satirical vein upon the current situation on the Loire. This reference is commonly thought to pertain to conditions resulting from the Bacaudae rebellion.*

*The word 'oak' in the translation probably refers to a tree, and not an object made from the wood of that tree, but the translation is still problematical. The derivation and meaning of the word* patus *are uncertain, Greek and Celtic origins having been suggested.*

Source: *Querolus (Aulularia),* ed. and trans. Catherine Jacquesmarde-Le Saos (Paris, 1994) pp. 18-20. Translation by A.C. Murray.

LF: Certainly all goes well for you.

Q: I admit that.

LF: What more do you want?

Q: Why does it go better for others?

LF: That is envy speaking.

Q: You bet I'm envious; I am worse off than my inferiors.

LF: What if I show you that you are more fortunate than those you are talking about?

Q: Do that and then Querolus will not allow anyone to complain.

LF: To expedite and clarify matters, I won't bother with arguments. You tell me the lot in life that would please you, and the destiny you wish I shall now deliver. Just remember this: don't suppose that you can complain about anything or exclude something from your choice.

Q: I like the idea of my doing the choosing. Give me wealth and military honors, even of the modest kind.

LF: I can give you that. But consider if you can carry out what you ask.

Q: What?

LF: Can you wage a campaign, parry a sword stroke, break through a battle line?

Q: I have never been able to do that.

LF: Yield the booty and the honors to those who can.

Q: At least give me some post of a municipal nature and quite humble.

LF: So you would want both to exact and pay out all manner of goods?

Q: Good grief, that's out of the question. I now wish to do neither. If you can, household god, make me a private person and a powerful person (*potens*) both.

LF: What kind of power do you want?

Q: I want to be allowed to despoil those who owe me nothing; to strike those that are unnconnected to me; and, as far as neighbors are concerned, to be able both to despoil and to strike them.

LF: (laughing) You don't want power (potentia), you want to commit brigandage (latrocinium). Good god, I don't know how this can be given to you. Unless (pausing), I've got it! Go and live on the banks of the Loire.

Q: What then?

LF: In that place people live by the law of nations. There it's no trick. There capital sentences are issued from an oak[tree] and written on bones. There peasants conduct the pleadings and private persons act as judges. There all is permitted. If you are rich, you shall be called patus — this is what they say in our Greece. O woodlands, O wilderness, who has said that you are free? There are many more important matters about which I shall be silent, but this will do for now.

Q: I am neither rich nor do I wish to make use of an oak[tree]. I don't like these laws of the forest.

LF: Look for some position gentler and nobler if you cannot engage in disputes.

Q: Give to me the kind of position that a lawyer gets, and a shyster at that.

LF: You mean you number lawyers among the fortunate?...

*The* lar familiaris *continues to show Querolus that each lot in life is fraught with unpleasant consequences.*

## 31. RENATUS PROFUTURUS FRIGERIDUS ON AËTIUS

*Renatus has been excerpted from Gregory of Tours's* Histories *(cf.* **25 C**, *above). Gregory's own portrait of Aëtius is hardly as flattering (cf.* Hist. II 8). On the death of Gaudentius, see **17**, s.a. 425.

Source and translation as above **25**.

I think it wrong to be silent about what the history of Renatus Frigeridus recounts about Aëtius. He relates in the twelfth book of his histories how, after the death of Honorius, the young Valentinian [III] was made emperor when only five years old by his cousin Theodosius, and how in Rome the tyrant John had assumed the imperial title and his emissaries were treated with contempt by the emperor. He then adds the following:

While these events were taking place, envoys were sent back to the usurper carrying frightful terms. John was persuaded by these to send Aëtius, at the time holding the post of curator of the palace (cura palatii), with a huge amount of gold to the Huns. They were known to Aëtius from the time he was their hostage and were bound to him by intimate ties of friendship. John's instructions were that as soon as the enemy had entered Italy, Aëtius was to fall on their rear while he himself attacked from the front. And since in what follows much will be recounted about this man Aëtius, it is fitting to outline his origins and character.

His father Gaudentius was someone of the first rank in the province of Scythia who began his military career in the palace and rose to the high position of master of the cavalry [*magister equitum per Gallias*]. His mother was Italian, a wealthy woman of noble birth. The son Aëtius was in boyhood a guardsman and a hostage for three years of Alaric, then of the Huns. Later he became the son-in-law of Carpilio, former count of the household troops, and under John he was a curator of the palace.

He was average in size, manly in appearance with a well-made body that was neither too weak nor heavy. He was quick-witted and agile, a most accomplished horseman, skilled in the use of the bow and no slouch with the lance. Exceedingly proficient in the arts or war, he was renowned for the arts of peace and, possessed of a good heart, was not avaricious and barely affected by immoderate desires. Those who urged perverse actions did not deflect him from his purpose, and he was forbearing of wrongs and eager to take on tasks. Fearless in the face of danger, he could bear hunger, thirst and lack of sleep very well. From an early age he seems to have been given a premonition of the great power to which he was destined by the fates. He shall be praised later in the right time and place.

This is what the above-mentioned historian has to say about Aëtius.

## 32. FROM THE IMPERIAL DECREES OF THE THEODOSIAN CODE AND ITS *INTERPRETATIO*

*The Theodosian Code was drawn up under the eastern emperor Theodosius II in 438 and accepted in the West under Valentinian III in 439. It is not a code in quite the sense moderns would understand the term, that is, a comprehensive survey and classification of an area of law, but is rather a collection of imperial constitutions, or edicts, since the time of Constantine. It was the beginning of state-directed codification in the late empire, though it had precursors in private statute-collections of the second and third centuries. In 506, a version of the Theodosian Code, much abridged but with additions from other sources of Roman law, was issued by Alaric II, the Gothic king of Toulouse. This compilation, known as the Breviary of Alaric, remained an influential repository of Roman law in Gaul throughout the early Middle Ages.*

*Imperial constitutions dealt with any matter of concern to the emperor, and so the Code contains edicts of both narrow and broad application tied, at least originally, to very specific political and social contexts; many circumstantial details were often eliminated in the excerpting process of codification. The Code arranged the constitutions* *chronologically under various titles; it was composed of sixteen books. For an example of a constitution that has come down to us outside the Code, see **29**, above.*

Source: *Theodosiani libri XVI*, ed. Th. Mommsen and Paulus M. Meyer, 3rd ed. (Berlin, 1962). Translation by A.C. Murray.

## a. Ranking Roman Society

*The following constitution, which appears in the title 'Heresy' (XVI 5 54), was issued by Honorius in 414 and concerns the Donatists in north Africa, the losing side in a schism in the African church going back to the persecutions of Diocletian; the measures of Honorius had their effect though the movement was not entirely suppressed. The emperor's edict is excerpted here not for its role in the Donatist controversy, but because its series of fines presupposes a schematic representation of Roman society that is instructive about the terminology used in many late Roman sources. Its terminology should be compared with, among other sources, **29** above, another constitution issued by Honorius.*

*Note that the* Code *retains the address, date, and provenance of the edict, bureaucratic trappings that are invaluable for modern scholars attempting to reconstruct the exact context of the edict or incidental elements of its contents. For example, the addressee, Julianus, was Q. Sentius Fabricius Julianus, memorialized in other constitutions in the* Code *and in two local inscriptions, from which we get his full name.*

*The emperor refers to himself as Our Clemency. Civil priests were no longer priests in a religious sense but were responsible for providing games.* Emphyteusis *was essentially a form of long-term or perpetual leasehold, common on imperial estates. The imperial largesse was a fund within the treasury.* Peculium, *as applied to* coloni, *means their personal property.*

Emperors Arcadius and Honorius to Julian, proconsul of Africa.
We decree that the Donatists and heretics, whom the forbearance of Our Clemency has protected to this point, are to feel the force of the appropriate authority. Let them recognize by a clear order that they are deprived of the right to bear witness and to make a will and of entering into contracts with someone, and must forever be branded by infamy and be separated from the gatherings of decent people and participation in civil life.

*Ecclesiastical property of the Donatists is to be transferred to Catholics; Donatist clergy are to be exiled. Those who harbor fugitives fleeing this penalty will have their property confiscated and suffer the same punishment as the fugitive.*

Moreover We inflict loss of patrimony and fines in a clear fashion, establishing the penalties appropriate to men and women, to individual persons and to high offices (*dignitates*), in accordance with their status.

Therefore anyone who is invested with the rank of proconsul, vicar, or count of the first rank shall be compelled to pay 200 pounds of silver to be added to the resources of our fisc, unless he changes his mind and accepts Catholic practice. No one should suppose this will be enough to check their determination. Let the fine be imposed as often as such a person is convicted of attending a prohibited gathering, and if, after five times he cannot be brought back from his error by fines, let him at that point be referred to Our Clemency for us to pass severer judgment regarding his entire property and his status.

We apply the same kind of penalties to other dignitaries (*honorati*): thus a senator lacking the privilege of holding high office (*dignitas*) and found to be a member of the Donatists shall pay 100 pounds of silver; those with the rank of civil priests (*sacerdotales*) shall pay the same amount; the ten chief town councillors (*curiales*) are to be sentenced to a fine of 50 pounds of silver; and the rest of the decurions of a town shall pay 10 pounds of silver for preferring to remain heretics.

If chief tenants (*conductores*) of the imperial house allow heretical practices on properties belonging to the emperor's estates, they shall be compelled to render as a fine as much as they are accustomed to furnish as rent. Moreover, the same terms of the sacred decree apply to tenants holding by *emphyteusis*.

As for chief tenants (*conductores*) of private persons, if they allow congregations to meet on their properties, or if, through their forbearance, the sacred mystery is defiled, let the judges bring this to the attention of the owners (*domini*), whose concern it is, if they want to avoid the penalty of this sacred order, either to reform those in error or change those who persist in their error and provide those properties with the kind of directors [that is chief tenants] who abide by divine commands of the emperor. Should they fail to carry out their charge, let them furthermore, by authority of the directive that has been issued, be fined the amount of the payments they are accustomed to receive, so that profits that could have been theirs, shall accrue to the sacred treasury.

If members of the office staff of the various judges are caught in this heresy, let them be subject to a payment of 30 pounds of silver as a penalty; if they still will not stay away from error after being condemned five times, let them be beaten and placed in exile.

As for slaves and *coloni*, the severest punishment shall serve to deliver them from such hazardous behaviour. And if a *colonus*, after being beaten, still persists in his resolve, at that point let him be fined one third of his *peculium*.

And everything that can be collected from people and places of this sort shall be sent to the sacred imperial largesse.

Given on the fifteenth day before the Kalends of July, at Ravenna. In the year of the consulships of Constantius and Constans. [17 June 414.]

## b. *Praescriptio Fori*

*A summary, or paraphrase, accompanied the abbreviated text of the Theodosian Code that Alaric II issued in the Gothic kingdom of southern Gaul in 506. This summary, or* Interpretatio, *is thought to be an independent work taken over by Alaric's compilers. The paraphrase of the* Interpretatio *is roughly true to the original but sometimes changes the contents of its model slightly, generalizing the contents or adapting them to current provincial conditions and sub-Roman government.*

*The following brief examples from both the* Code *and the* Interpretatio *concern the legal problem of* praescriptio fori, *the right of individuals, depending on rank, privilege, and circumstance, to have their cases heard before particular courts. In provincial administration, the usual court dealing with important cases was that of the governor, called the judge ordinary. The title judge was also an attribute of other great imperial officials, as it was of the royal officials that replaced imperial administrators in the successor kingdoms. The clerical examples of judicial privilege may be compared with Frankish ecclesiastical and secular legislation (73, 74).*

*[1] From the title 'Accusations and Laying Criminal Charges' (IX 1 1 = Breviary IX 1 1). Senators had the right to be tried before the prefect of the city of Rome.*

Emperor Constantine to Octavian, count of the Spanish provinces.
Anyone of senatorial rank (*clarissima dignitas*) who abducts a virgin, or seizes another person's property, or is apprehended in any offense or crime, shall immediately have the public laws applied to him within the province in which he committed the transgression; his name shall not be brought to our attention, nor shall he be allowed to take advantage of the right to have a trial in the court appropriate to his judicial status (*praescriptio fori*). For a charge rules out all considerations of rank if it is a question of a criminal suit as opposed to a civil or pecuniary matter.

Given on the day before the Nones of December, at Serdica. Received on the fifth day before the Nones of March at Cordova. In the year of the consulships of Gallicanus and Bassus. [4 December 316.]

INTERPRETATIO. Whoever commits a crime worthy of condemnation and punishment cannot say that he must be prosecuted in his own court, that is in the region where he resides, but let vengeance be taken on him by the judges of the region in which the crime was committed, and let his person not be referred to the prince.

*[2] From the title 'Jurisdiction' (II 1 4 = Breviary II 1 4).*

Emperors Valentinian and Valens, Augustuses, to Terentius, governor of Tuscany.

The plaintiff shall follow the forum of the defendant, so that if a senator sues a provincial, the case shall be held before the judge who governs the province. But should a provincial not defend an action, but bring one, the case shall be tried in the court of the urban prefect.

Given on the Kalends of December, at Milan. In the year of the consulship of the divine Jovian and Varronianus. [1 December 364.]

*'Divine' (divus) was the epithet of deceased emperors.*

INTERPRETATIO. If someone decides to sue another person, he should know that the matter must be brought before the judge of the province in which the defendant resides.

*[3] From the title 'Bishops, Churches, and Clerics' (XVI 2 12 = Breviary XVI 1 2).*

The emperors Constantius and Constans [?] to their friend Severus, greetings.

By a law of Our Clemency, we prohibit bishops from being accused in the courts, otherwise the floodgates will be opened to frenzied accusers who count on finding impunity for their charges in episcopal kindness. Therefore if anyone lays a complaint, it is most appropriate that it be investigated before other bishops, so that a timely and suitable hearing may accommodate the concerns of all parties.

Letter, given nine days before the Kalends of October. Received on the Nones of October. In the year of the consulships of Arbitio and Lollianus. [23 September 355.]

*The consul of this year is the same Arbitio, general and master of the soldiers, whom Ammianus implicated in the plot against Silvanus (cf. 3).*

INTERPRETATIO. For anyone to dare to accuse a bishop before public judges is especially prohibited. Instead, let the complainant not delay to bring whatever he thinks is his due, according to the nature of the matter, before a hearing composed of bishops, so that his claim against the bishop can be determined in a court of other bishops.

*[4] From the title 'Bishops, Churches, and Clerics' (XVI 2 23 = Breviary XVI 1 3).*

The emperors Valens, Gratian, and Valentinian, Augustuses, to Artemius, Euridicus, Appius, Gerasimus, and other bishops.

Just as the custom is with temporal [*civilis*] suits, so should it prevail in ecclesiastical affairs: in the case of disputes and minor offenses pertaining to religious practice, they should be judged by local hearings in diocesan synods. Criminal matters are an exception. Criminal procedure requires that they be held before the judge ordinary or before extraordinary judges and authorities of illustrious rank.

Given sixteen days before the Kalends of June, at Trier. In the year of the fifth consulships of the Augustus Valens and the first consulship of the Augustus Valentinian. [17 May 376.]

INTERPRETATIO. Whenever a dispute arises among clerics for any reason pertaining to religion, care must be taken to abide by the following practice. Let the bishop assemble the diocesan priests and settle the matters in dispute by their judgment. Certainly, if a criminal charge is made, let it be brought to the attention of the judge in the city where the action is brought so that what is proved to have been a criminal act may be avenged by his sentence.

## 33. FROM THE *LIFE OF ST. GERMANUS* BY CONSTANTIUS OF LYONS: TAXES, ALANS, AND BACAUDAE IN FARTHER GAUL

*Constantius of Lyons, who was born around 415, wrote his* Life *of St. Germanus around 480, some thirty years after the death of its subject. Germanus was bishop of Auxerre (a. 418-448) and a native of the town. He was educated in the law, a vocation that prepared him for an unknown, but important, civilian (not, as is sometimes believed, military) office, which he held before becoming bishop. The* Life *is most famous for its account of Germanus's visits to Britain to combat Pelagianism, but it also takes incidental notice of people and events in Gaul and Italy in the 430s and 440s.*

Sources: *Vita Germani episcopi Autissiodorensis auctore Constantino*, ed. W. Levison, MGH SRM 7 (1919-20), pp. 247-283. Translation by A.C. Murray.

*Germanus's first expedition to Britain took place in 429 (see* **16**, *s.a. 429).*
(19) On the return of the venerable priests [from Britain], the Gallic provinces rejoiced, the churches celebrated, and the demons trembled. In fact, the blessed Germanus's own city relied on him to represent it, as he had been accustomed to do, in two circumstances — before the divine majesty and when worldly crises struck. Now a tax burden beyond the ordinary and countless other burdens had weighed down upon his citizens, as if they were parentless orphans. Those who had been abandoned received help; he

acknowledged their complaints and felt sympathy for their pain and, for the sake of peace and order, undertook, after the dangers of his sea voyage, the difficulties of a land journey, in order to gain relief for his city.

*Germanus traveled to Arles, effecting various miracles on the way. The praetorian prefect for the Gallic Provinces at the time was Auxiliaris (a. 435/438). Germanus healed the prefect's wife of a quartan fever and gained relief for his city.*

*Germanus then went to Britain a second time to quell a resurgence of Pelagianism. Successful once again, he returned to his diocese.*

*The following events should be compared with* **17**, *cc. 127-133. The likely date of Germanus's death was 448.*

(28) He had scarcely returned from his trip abroad [to Britain] when a delegation from the region of Armorica (*tractus Armoricanus*) solicited help from the weary bishop. The great Aëtius, who directed affairs of state at the time, had been antagonized by the excesses of the proud district. Because its communities had dared to rebel, he had given permission for them to be subdued by Goar, the fierce king of the Alans, who gaped at the prospect with the longing of a greedy barbarian.

And so one old man was matched against a most warlike people and against a king, a servant of idols, but an old man greater and stronger than them all because of the help of Christ. Without delay he went forth immediately, for the forces of war were threatening. By now the Alans had advanced and ironclad cavalry entirely filled the road, but our bishop traveled to meet them, until he neared the king himself, who soon appeared. The march was well advanced when the meeting took place; his opponent was an armed general among his troops. The bishop first begged as a suppliant through an interpreter, then rebuked the king's delay, and finally, reaching out with his hand, grabbed the reins of his horse and, in halting the king, brought the whole army to a standstill. At this the fierce king's anger was, at God's command, exchanged for admiration; the king marvelled at the bishop's resolve, respected his dignity, and was shaken by his insistent authority. Pride was put aside and the accoutrements of war and the turmoil of conflict gave way to the peaceful forum of negotiation. And there was a discussion, not about what the king wanted, but how the bishop's request might be fulfilled. The king and his army set up camp. He solemnly gave an assurance of peace, provided the reprieve that he had granted was confirmed by the emperor or Aëtius. Meanwhile, through the intervention of the bishop and his holy merit, a king was restrained, an army called back, and a province delivered from devastation.

*Germanus then set out for Ravenna to obtain the imperial pardon. Miracles accompanied his journey and his fame preceded him.*

*Peter was bishop of Ravenna a. 433-450. Valentinian was born in 419.*

(35)...Peter [Chrysologos] was at the time presiding as bishop over the church of Christ [in Ravenna] in accordance with apostolic provision. Queen Placidia was also ruling over the Roman empire along with her son Valentinian, who was now a youth. They so loved the Catholic faith that, although they had authority over everyone, they accommodated the servants of God with the deepest humility. They all vied with each other out of divine love in welcoming the venerable Germanus. The chief officials courted him, the great nobles came to meet him, the church embraced him rejoicing. The venerable queen sent to the lodging of the bishop a generous silver platter filled with delicacies, none of them prepared with meat. He accepted the gift and shared it out so that his servants got the food and he took the silver himself, sending back in its place a small wooden dish containing barley bread. The queen clasped both with immense joy, because her silver had passed into the hands of the poor, and she had received the food of the holy man in its humble serving dish. And so she covered the wood with gold and kept the bread for effecting many a cure and healing.

*At Ravenna Germanus healed the sick and freed prisoners.*

(40) With respect to the plight of the district of Armorica, which had made the journey necessary, surely, after gaining a reprieve and continuing assurance, the bishop would have proved the case to his liking, if the faithlessness of Tibatto had not summoned that unstable and disorderly people to a new rebellion. When this happened, even the intervention of the bishop had no effect, and the imperial trust was destroyed by deception. Tibatto, however, soon paid for his many tricks, suffering the penalties of reckless betrayal.

*After a dream in which God announced the bishop's imminent death, Germanus grew sick and died at Ravenna. The empress Placidia visited his death bed and granted his last request to be buried in Auxerre.*

## 34. FROM SIDONIUS APOLLINARIS'S PANEGYRICS ON AVITUS AND MAJORIAN

*Sidonius Apollinaris, who was born ca. 430, is renowned for his letters (see **37**) and his poetry. Among his poems are three imperial panegyrics (for panegyric as a genre, see **2** and cf. **25 B** and **50**). The first was delivered in Rome, 1 January 456, on the occasion of the new emperor Avitus assuming the consulship; Avitus was Sidonius's father-in-law. The second was delivered not long after that, in 458 in Lyons, in honour of the new emperor Majorian, who had helped bring about the fall of Avitus. The third panegyric was delivered 1 January 468 in honor of Anthemius; the circumstances behind this occasion are described in Sidonius's letter to his friend Herenius (**37.9**). Panegyric gave the poet a chance to cast the most favorable light upon the career of the honoree and his* *role in recent events. The following two excerpts are taken from the panegyrics to Avitus and Majorian.*

Translation: Sidonius, *Poems and Letters*, ed. and trans. W.B. Anderson, vol. 1 (Cambridge MA./London, 1936), V, VII.

## a. The Election of Avitus as Emperor

*A revealing account of Avitus's election as emperor in 455, as the somewhat youthful spin-doctor Sidonius would have his audience believe it occurred.*

*The Visigothic king Theoderic II, who figures prominently in Avitus's seizure of power, was also the subject of a famous letter of Sidonius addressed to Agricola, Avitus' son (37.1). The claim of the Arvernians to be of Trojan descent is mentioned by Lucan (I 427 f.), as Sidonius was well aware; Avitus was an Arvernian. The reference to Gergovia recalls events from Julius Caesar's campaign against Vercingetorix.*

*The speaker throughout the excerpt is Jupiter, who at a convention of the gods answers the pleas of Roma for an emperor to surpass Trajan.*

"I have a land which carries its head high as sprung from Latin [=Trojan] blood, a land famed for its men, a land to which Nature, the blessed creator of all things, vouchsafed no peer in days gone by. From the city extend rich and fruitful fields ... O Arvernian, who dwellest therein, sole hope of the world, thou yieldest to none when thou fightest on foot, and on thy steed, thou art a match for any man! Let Fortune, Caesar's attendant goddess, be my witness, who was sore dismayed in this land when his warriors were forced back from Gergovia's hill and scarce halted their flight at their very camp. I ordained that these men should be thus gallant, but all the time I was making ready, O Rome, to present to thee Avitus, whose natal tree, rich in noble branches, hath long shone illustrious..."

*A sketch of Avitus's career follows, beginning with his early exploits in hunting and hawking, and proceeding through his maturer years. His good relations with the Goths and his role in opposing Attila's invasion are stressed. The following selection begins with the death of Aëtius; at this time Avitus, now a former praetorian prefect of the Gallic provinces, was retired.*

"Placidus [Valentinian III], the mad eunuch [*semivir*], slaughtered Aëtius.

"Scarce was the diadem set on the head of Petronius [Maximus], when all at once came a barbarian flood, and the Goths had visions of Rome captured by them and of the whole earth ready to surrender to their frenzy... The Aremorican region too expected the Saxon pirate, who deems it but sport to furrow the British waters with hides, cleaving the blue sea in a stitched boat. The Frank began to lay low the First German [*Germania prima*] and the

Second Belgian [*Belgica secunda*]; the bold Alaman was drinking the Rhine from the Roman bank and proudly lording it on both sides, a citizen or conqueror.

"But Maximus, now emperor, seeing such loss of widespread lands, took the sole availing course in such distress and chose for himself Avitus as Master of Horse and Foot. The tidings of the rank bestowed found him farming, plying the bent mattock's tooth or stooping over the curved plow as he turned up the unsunned clods in his fertile acres. Thus aforetime Cincinnatus came, a poor ploughman, to heal his country's broken fortunes, when his wife put the old robe upon him, standing before the oxen, and his doors of willow-wood now opened for a dictator, who bore back to his dwelling what he had not sowed, and thus the triumphal purple, weighted with a mean load, carried common seed.

"No sooner had he taken up the burden of the office thrust upon him than the Alaman sent envoys to crave pardon for their frenzy, the Saxon's raiding abated and the marshy water of Albis [Elbe] confined the Chattian; and scarce had the moon viewed all this throughout three monthly courses, when he set himself on the march to the peoples and lands possessed by the bold Goth ...

"Here the chiefs of the Visigoths [*Vesi*] were letting loose the war they had planned, when suddenly their fury was checked by tidings that Avitus, armed with an imperial writ, was already entering the home of the Goths and, having laid aside for a little the pomp of the Master's office, had taken upon himself the authority of an ambassador.

"The Scythian [i.e. Gothic] leaders and senate alike were thunderstruck...

"Hereupon, as it chanced, one of the Goths, who had reforged his pruning-hook and was shaping a sword with blows on the anvil and sharpening it with a stone, a man already prepared to rouse himself to fury at the sound of the trumpet and looking at any moment with manifold slaughter to bury the ground under unburied foes, cried out, as soon as the name of the approaching Avitus was clearly proclaimed: 'War is no more! Give me the plow again! If I recall the familiar old days of idle peace, he hath time and again taken the sword from me. O shame! O ye gods above! To think that faithful friendship should have such power! Why dost thou threaten me with tedious treaties, dealing loyally with me to my loss? Thou dost bid us both give to thee and owe to thee the advantages of peace. Who could have believed it? Lo! the Gothic kings are fain to yield obedience, and deem their royal power of less account than that. Nor can I even say that thou dost shun battle to screen a craven spirit; brave art thou, albeit thou lovest peace. Avitus is already ending the strife of parties, and Messianus [Avitus' subordinate] too, sent on before, is curbing the Gothic wrath. Thou hast as yet but sent thine orders, Avitus, and we are laying down our arms. What further power canst thou desire? I count it a small thing that we are not thine enemies; nay, if I have gained a right knowledge of thee in action aforetime, thine auxiliary will I be; thus at least I shall have leave to fight.'

"While the Visigoth revolved these thoughts in his stern heart, they had come into view. The king [Theoderic II] and the Master took their stand together, the Master with confident look, while the other blushed with joy and by his blush sued for clemency. Then Avitus kept on one side of him the king, on the other side the king's brother [Frederic], and with joined hands they entered Tolosa [Toulouse], city of Pallas. Even thus with hand clasped in hand beside the couches of the gods did Romulus and Tatius establish their treaty, when Hersilia on the hill of Pallas thrust the Sabine women between their father's weapons and the husbands who were furiously battling against their kindred.

"Meanwhile, when thou [Roma] wert off thy guard, the Vandal with stealthy arms captured thee, and the Burgundian with his traitorous leadership extorted from thee the panic-fury that led to an emperor's slaughter... Rumor brought to Gothic ears the exile of the senate, the ills of the common folk, the emperor's murder and the captivity of the Empire. At dawn of day a meeting of Gothic elders was assembled in the wonted fashion; there stand they, old in years but hale in counsel; their dress is unkempt, tarnished and greasy are the linen garments on their lean backs; their coats of skin are drawn up high and cannot reach the calf; their knees are bare and their boots of horse-hide are held up by a common knot.

"When this company of elders, venerable for all their poverty, entered the council, and the king called for the proposals of peace, the general said: 'I confess that I would fain have cherished evermore in tranquility among my paternal acres the rest that my toil has earned, now that after holding three commands I have reached a fourth glory and held the supreme honor of the Prefecture. But as Maximus, late sovereign of our western world, after a thousand refusals from our chief men, summoned me, all unsuspecting and far away, to serve amid the clarions of war after controlling the laws, and ordained that I should now hear the blaring trumpets instead of the court-usher's voice, then did I right readily embrace the duty, that I might go as ambassador to you. I crave of you the old treaty, which even now that aged man, my one-time friend [Theoderic I], for whom to follow Avitus was always to grow greater, would be maintaining if only I had bidden him. In former days I was wont to guide the doings of the Goths; thou knowest that my counsel was often acted on before thou wert aware of it. But fate hath taken away from me my guardian-spirit of former days, and all my services have faded from sight along with thy father. He had surrounded Narbo

[Narbonne, a. 437], and it was enfeebled with wasting famine (thou were then a child): hemming in those panic-stricken thousands he had all but driven them to eat of loathsome things, and already he had begun gloomily to think that some of his due spoil would be lost if haply the besieged perished within, when he gave ear to my advice, and withdrawing his arms relieved the walls from war. And thee thyself (See! there are old men to witness it), these hands of mine have held weeping close to this breast, when perchance thy nurse was taking thee away from me to give thee suck and thou wert loth to go. Behold! I come and seek now a fresh pledge of our old love. If thou hast no loyalty, no reverence for thy father, then go thy harsh way and refuse peace.'

"From all the council arose murmurs and shouting; the insurgent crowd, condemning war, raised a friendly uproar.

"Then out spake the king: 'O leader renowned, I have long been blaming thee for begging peace from us when thou hast power to enforce bondage and draw willing peoples to war in thy train. I beseech thee, brand me not with obloquy by bringing up my father's name. What blame can be mine if thou give me no orders? What thou mightest have advised in his day thou needst now but desire; the only hindrance is that the Goths have not learnt what thou wouldst have. Thanks to thee the laws of Rome have long been pleasing to me; when I was a child my father bade me learn lines by heart at thine instruction, that those strains of Virgil's ancient page, taught to thy willing pupil, might soften my Scythian ways; even then thou didst teach me to desire peace. But hear now the terms of my obedience, and perhaps thou wilt be pleased to sanction a compact. I swear, O Rome, by thy name, revered by me, and by our common descent from Mars (for among all things that have been since the beginning of time the world hath naught greater than thee and thou hast naught greater than the senate): I desire to keep the peace with thee and to wipe out the transgressions of my grandsire [Alaric], whose one blot is that he captured thee; but if the gods bless my prayer, the guilt of that ancient destruction can be atoned for by avenging that of to-day — if only thou, renowned leader, shouldst take upon thee the name of Augustus. Why dost thou avert thine eyes? Thine unwillingness becomes thee all the more. We do not force this on thee, but we adjure thee: with thee as leader I am a friend of Rome, with thee as emperor I am her soldier. Thou art not stealing the sovereignty from any man; no Augustus holds the Latian hills, a palace without a master is thine. I protest, it is not enough that I do thee no harm; I would that thine imperial diadem might bring me the means to do thee service. My part is but to urge thee; but if Gaul should compel thee, as she has the right to do, the world would cherish thy sway, lest it perish.'

"He spake, and straightway with his brother gave his solemn pledge in the form of words desired. But thou, Avitus, didst depart in sadness, knowing it could not be hidden from the Gauls that the Goths could be at their service if thou wert emperor. Yea, when it was revealed to the anxious citizens that thou wert carrying back with thee a treaty, they eagerly rushed to meet thee, and without thy knowing it they spread a tribunal for thee beforehand, and when the crowds of nobles deemed they were assembled in sufficient multitude — those on whom the snowy rocks of the Cottian Alps look down, those around whom in their sundry regions wind the waters of the Tuscan sea or the Rhine, and those whom the long ridges of the Pyrenees shut off from Spanish rule — then did that throng approach with joy that man oppressed by a crushing load of care.

"Thereupon the oldest of all those lords, one right worthy to be his country's spokesman, thus began: 'Of the cruel fortune that hath long harassed us with divers hardships under a boy-emperor [Valentinian III], tearing our prosperity to shreds, it would belike be tedious to make plaint, O mighty leader, since verily thou wert the chiefest figure among the mourners, lamenting ever thy country's wounds and tortured by uncontrollable anxieties. Amid these calamities, that universal destruction, to live was death. But as we, taught by our fathers' words, paid homage to idle laws and deemed it a hallowed duty to cling to the old order even through disasters, we endured that shadow of Empire, content to bear even the vices of an ancient stock and to tolerate, more from custom than by reason of just claim, a house that had been wont to be invested with the purple. Of late a golden opportunity shone forth, whereby Gaul might make her own strength felt, while Maximus was possessing himself of the panic-stricken capital; and she might well have possessed herself of the world if with thee as Master she had restored to herself all her rightful lands. 'Tis no secret who of us it was that stirred up the Belgian land, the Aremorican shore and the Gothic fury [against Attila]. In this dread warfare we yielded pride of place to thee, renowned one. Now the supreme office calls for thee; in time of peril a realm cannot be ruled by a poltroon. All ambitious rivalry gives place when extremity calls for men of renown. After the losses of Ticinum and Trebia the trembling republic came in haste to Fabius. By the election of Livius the disaster of Cannae, famous for Varro's rout, was undone; undone too was the Carthaginian, still exulting over the deaths of the Scipios. The world, they say, lies captive in the captive city; the emperor has perished, and now the Empire has its head here. Ascend the tribunal, we beseech thee, and raise up the fainting; this time of peril asks not that some other should love Rome more. Nor do thou by any chance deem thyself unequal to sovereignty. When Brennus's host beset the Tarpeian rock, then, thou knowest, Camillus was himself the whole of our state, and he, the destined avenger of his country, covered the smoking embers of the city with the slaughtered enemy. No gold scattered among the people hath secured for thee the verdict of the centuries; this time no venal tribes bought with plenteous coin rush to give their votes; the suffrages of the world no one can buy. Though a poor man, thou art being chosen; rich art thou in thy deserts, and that suffices in itself. Why dost thou hinder the desires of thy country, when she orders thee to give orders to her? This is the judgment of all: "if thou becomest the master I shall be free.'"

"Then a great clamor filled the hall of Viernum [Beaucaire, near Arles] (for it was in this place, as it chanced, that the senate's devoted throng had brought before him the force of its authority, its desires, and its prayers). Place, hour, and day are declared auspicious for the assumption of empire, and straightway those resourceful nobles joyously order a guard to be set there.

"The third day had spread the sun's light over the retreating stars: the lords of the land assemble in haste and with soldiers all around set him on a mound-platform; there they crown their sorrowing chief with a military collar and present him with the outward emblems of sovereignty (hitherto the only attribute of an emperor he had assumed was his cares)...

"This man I have given thee, Rome, while Gaul throughout her wide plains thunders with plaudits for Augustus, and the north, now stronger, carries the auspicious clamor to the pale-cheeked south [i.e. the Vandals]... But now be of good cheer with such a man for emperor, O Rome, ancient mother of gods; lift up thine eyes and cast off thine unseemly gloom. Lo! a prince of riper years shall bring back youth to thee, whom child-princes have made old."

The great Father had scarce ended his utterance when the gods clapped their hands and a shout of applause rang through the council. The fateful Sisters spun out a happy time for thy rule, Augustus, and for thy consular year they drew out with their whirling spindles a golden age.

### b. Majorian and the Fight at Vicus Helena

*This excerpt concerns incidents in the career of Majorian while he was serving under Aëtius's command, around 447/8, if the attack on Tours was connected with the uprising in Armorica referred to in the* Gall. Chron. 452, s.a. 448 *(17, and cf. 33, above). Vicus Helena, the site of an encounter with the Franks, is usually identified with Hélesmes, Dép. Nord. The Frankish king Cloio is the same as Chlodio of Gregory of Tours's* Histories *(78). Prior to Gregory's writing, the king is mentioned only here. (But cf. 23 c.)*

*The principal speaker in the first part of the panegyric is the goddess Africa, who begs Roma to send Majorian against the Vandals. Africa recounts Majorian's background and exploits and tells how Majorian fell afoul of Aëtius's wife, who divined that Majorian was destined to be emperor. Africa recounts the following speech of Aëtius's wife, who attempts to persuade her husband to kill Majorian. The wife in question would have been Pelagia, Aëtius's second wife and the widow of Boniface; she claimed descent from Gothic kings.*

"'Compared with him [Majorian], Alexander the Great…is an arrant sluggard. What shall I do? What realm shall I win for my son, debarred as I am from a Gothic sceptre, if Rome ignores me and, to crown all, our little [son] Gaudentius is trodden underfoot by this youth's [i.e. Majorian's] destiny? Already Gaul and all Europe sound his praises. He bathes in the icy waters of Rhine, Arar [Saône], Rhône, Mosa [Meuse], Matrona [Marne], Sequana [Seine], Ledus [Laz], Clitis [unknown], Elaris [Allier], Atax [Aude], Vacalis [Waal]; the Liger [Loire] he cleaves with an axe and drinks piece by piece.

"'When he defended the Turoni [the people of Tours], who feared the conflict, thou wast not there; but a little later ye fought together where Cloio the Frank had overrun the helpless lands of the Atrebates [Artois]. There was a narrow passage at the junction of two ways, and a road crossed both the village of Helena, which was within bowshot, and the river, where that long but narrow path was supported by girders. Thou wert posted at the crossroads, while Majorian warred as a mounted man close to the bridge itself. As chance would have it, the echoing sound of a barbarian marriage-song rang forth from a hill near the riverbank, for amid Scythian dance and chorus a yellow-haired bridegroom was wedding a bride of like colour. Well, these revellers, they say, he laid low. Time after time his helmet rang with blows, and his hauberk with its protecting scales kept off the thrust of spears, until the enemy was forced to turn and flee.

"'Then might be seen the jumbled adornments of the barbarian nuptials gleaming red in the waggons, and captured salvers and viands flung together pell-mell, and servants crowned with perfumed garlands carrying wine-bowls on their oily top-knots. Straightway the spirit of Mars waxes fiercer and the nuptial torches are snapped asunder by the more fiery goddess of war; the victor snatches their chariots and carries off the bride in the hour of her bridal.

"'Not so fiercely did Bacchus, Semele's son, embroil Pholoe's monsters and the Thracian Lapithae, when his revels inflamed the Thracian women, stirring up both love and war, and they used for the struggle first of all the bloody meats of the feast, and whirling the wine about deemed their cups weapons; while as the affray grew fiercer, the blood of Centaurs defiled Emathian Othrys.

"'And truly the quarrel of the cloud-born brothers [Centaurs] deserves no more renown; for this youth likewise subdues monsters, on the crown of whose red pate lies the hair that has been drawn towards the front, while the neck, exposed by the loss of its covering, shows bright. Their eyes are faint and pale, with a glimmer of greyish blue. Their faces are shaven all round, and instead of beards they have thin mustaches which they run through with a comb. Close-fitting garments confine the tall limbs of the men; they are drawn up high so as to expose the knees, and a broad belt supports their narrow middle.

"'It is their sport to send axes hurling through the vast void and know beforehand where the blow will fall, to whirl their shields, to outstrip with leaps and bounds the spears they have hurled and reach the enemy first. Even in boyhood's years the love of fighting is full grown. Should they chance to be sore pressed by numbers or by the luck of the ground, death may overwhelm them, but not fear; unconquerable they stand their ground, and their courage well-nigh outlives their lives.

"'Such men he put to flight with thee [Aëtius] to witness and to praise. Who could endure it? All thine exploits he shares, many more he performs without thee. All men fight for their emperor; I fear, alas! he now fights for himself. If he should win the sovereignty, then all the conquests thou makest are victories for him. Here the fates leave no middle course; if thou refuse to be his assassin, thou wilt be his slave...'"

*Aëtius refuses his wife's entreaties to kill Majorian, but agrees to discharge him.*

## 35. FROM LOST ANNALS OF ANGERS: AEGIDIUS, CHILDERIC, AND ODOACER

*Because of its paratactic style, the following excerpt from Gregory of Tours's* Histories *(II 18, 19), completed in 594, has long been accepted as coming from a now lost set of annals from Angers. Gregory's excerpt covers the period from 463 to around 470; he seems to have expunged a yearly dating scheme that clearly accompanied the original annals. It is difficult to say how long after the events the annals of Angers were compiled, but they were certainly not contemporary. Gregory's interest in this particular set of annals probably derives from their mention of Childeric, Clovis's father.*

*The succinctness of the annals makes them difficult to interpret and the basic questions of who is doing what to whom and on whose behalf cannot be answered with absolute confidence. With the exception of the Goths, all the participants may have been ostensibly in Roman service; and so the annals may be recording a falling out among allies, occasioned in part by the succession of the emperor Severus (a. 461-465), and then the death of Aegidius.*

*The battle of Orleans, fought in 463, was a victory over the Goths won by Aegidius. He was master of the soldiers for Gaul 456/7-465, appointed by either Avitus or*

*Majorian; but he was not accepted by the emperor Severus. Childeric was a Frankish king, son of Merovech, and father of Clovis. He is in Roman service in the excerpt. See further,* **18**, *s.a. 462-465;* **19**, *s.a. 5 Leo;* **20**, *s.a. 463; and* **78**. *Not all Franks were subject to Childeric.*

*Odoacer is generally believed to be the commander who deposed Romulus Augustulus in 476 and who ruled Italy from 476-493 as patrician and king, until his death at the hands of Theoderic the Great. Some think he was the son of Edeco (see* **22**) *and came to Gaul after the breakup of Attila's empire. The Saxons whom he commanded in this instance had occupied islands on the Loire as pirates; cf. Sidonius's letter to Namatius,* **37.17**. *It is generally thought that in the excerpt Odoacer and the Saxons begin as Roman enemies and are brought into an alliance by the Franks only at the end; but it is more likely that they had agreements with Roman authorities prior to Aegidius's death.*

*The Britons were in Roman service under a certain Riothamus; see Sidonius,* **37.19**.

*Count Paul is clearly a Roman commander, but his death is problematical. Was he killed by the Saxons? Probably, but the Latin can be construed to mean that Childeric's forces killed him.*

*The reference to the Alamanni has been considered a mistake for the Alani, or misdated. If there is an error here, it is not likely Gregory's.*

*On Aegidius's son Syagrius and Childeric's son Clovis, see* **46**.

Source: Gregory of Tours, *Historiarum libri X*, ed. Bruno Krusch and Wilhelm Levison, MGH SRM I/1, 2nd. ed., Bk. II 18-19. Translation by A.C. Murray.

Then Childeric fought at Orleans [a. 463].

Odoacer came with Saxons to Angers. This was a time when a great epidemic ravaged the population.

Aegidius died [a. 465], leaving a son called Syagrius. After his death Odoacer took hostages from Angers and other places.

The Britons were driven out of Bourges by the Goths, and many of them were killed at Bourg-de-Déols [ca. 468].

Count Paul led Romans and Franks in a campaign against the Goths and carried off plunder.

Odoacer came to Angers. The next day King Childeric arrived and took the city after Count Paul had been killed. On that day the cathedral manse was burned in a violent fire [a. 469?].

After these events there was war between the Saxons and Romans. But the Saxons retreated leaving many of their men to the swords of the pursuing Romans. The Franks captured and ruined their islands, killing a large number of people. In the ninth month of this year, there was an earthquake.

Odoacer entered into a treaty with Childeric and they subdued the Alamanni who had invaded part of Italy.

*The next event Gregory mentions is Euric's establishment of Duke Victorius over the "seven cities," meaning Aquitania prima, in the fourteenth year of the king's reign, that is, a. 479.*

## 36. SALES IN THE CODE OF EURIC, ca. 475

*The Code of Euric is the modern name for a law coded issued by the Visigothic king Euric about the year 475. It survives only in a fragmentary condition on a palimpsest, which is a MS whose original text has been wiped off and replaced with new text. Much of the code has been obliterated, but enough of it survives to show that it was no mean legislative achievement. The code was the basis for the development of Visigothic law, and was influential in later Burgundian and Bavarian codifications, among others. The Code of Euric does not deal in Germanic customary law but in vulgar law and contemporary Roman practices, which it handles quite freely. (The modern term 'vulgar law' is sometimes used to refer to Roman law that no longer corresponded to the forms of classical jurisprudence.)*

*Some of the character of the code is revealed in the following laws about sales. In conformity with contemporary thinking, and late Roman legislation, they treat payment of the purchase price as the principal element in the transaction. The complications of slavery are prominent as in earlier ages. The* scriptura *(translated below as 'bill of sale') recorded not only the agreement but the receipt of the price by the vendor.* Peculium *was property at the disposal of a slave and administered by him; its ownership belonged to the master.*

Source: *El Còdigo de Eurico*, ed. Alvaro D'Ors, Estudios Visigoticos II (Rome and Madrid, 1960) 26-31. Translation by A.C. Murray.

### On Sales

286 A sale that is conducted by means of a bill of sale (*scriptura*) is fully valid. If a bill of sale is not drawn up, the purchase is still valid if witnesses attest to the purchase price being paid. A sale that is extracted by force, that is by threats of death or by confinement, is invalid.

287 If something is procured from a slave without his master's knowledge, if the master refuses to recognize the validity of the sale, let the master return the price to the buyer and let the sale be invalid.

288 If someone sells his slave, and the slave accuses his former master of some offense, let the seller receive back the slave he sold and return the price to

the buyer, so that he may inquire of his slave about the charge that the slave has leveled at him. We order this procedure also to be followed with regard to female slaves.

289 Whenever a dispute arises about property that has been sold and it is established that it belonged to another, let the owner suffer no disadvantage. And let whoever dared sell another's property be compelled to pay the owner double as well as return the price he received to the buyer; and let local judges assess the value of the improvement the buyer may have contributed by his own efforts to the property he acquired, and let fair compensation be rendered to him for his efforts by him who sold property that was not his own.

290 If anyone sells a freeman and the latter proves his freedom, let the party whose person was sold receive a slave or the price of a slave from the seller. The seller is also to be compelled to pay the buyer a double price for what the buyer received. This rule is also to be followed for female slaves.

292 If a slave is purchased by means of his own *peculium*, and it happens that his master is unaware of this, let the slave not leave the power of his master. For the master unknowingly receives not a price but the property of his own slave.

293 Exchange has the same validity as sale.

294 This rule is to be followed with respect to sales: if property, or slaves, or any kind of animal are sold, no one can invalidate the sale by saying the property was sold at a low price.

295 If a seller is not reliable (*idoneus*), he shall furnish the buyer with a surety.

296 If part of the purchase-price is given and part is promised, the sale is not thereby invalidated. But if the buyer does not pay the remaining part of the price on the agreed upon date, let him pay interest on the part he owes, unless an agreement is made for the property that has been sold to be restored.

299 Parents are not permitted to sell, donate, or pledge their children. Whoever receives them will not gain title over anything. Rather, let whoever buys a child from his parents lose the price he paid.

# CHAPTER EIGHT

# THE WORLD OF SIDONIUS APOLLINARIS: FROM ROMAN TO VISIGOTHIC GAUL

*Sidonius Apollinaris was born under the empire around 430, probably at Lyons, and died a subject of the Visigothic king, Euric (a. 466-93), some time between 480 and 490. As a young man, he married Papianilla, the daughter of the future emperor Avitus (a. 455-56) and had a distinguished, if at times rocky, public career. From his marriage he acquired the estate of Avitacum, near Clermont in the Auvergne, which became his "second homeland." He became bishop of Clermont around 470. Greatly admired for his literary talents, he published poetry (cf. 34) and letters. A collection of his letters in nine books survives: Books 1-7 appeared in 477 and two other books were brought out in subsequent years. The following selection of fifty letters comprises about one third of the total.*

*Sidonius's letters are one of the most important sources we have for fifth-century history and culture. Although the letters clearly reflect the great events of the day as well as everyday life, one should keep in mind when reading them that Sidonius undoubtedly reworked them for publication; the publication of letter-collections was a well-developed literary genre of the period and one should not expect ancient writers and readers of these collections to have the same interests as their modern counterparts.*

*Sidonius's letters were not placed in chronological order and often have only the most incidental indications of date. In the following selections, I have tried to group the letters according to a rough chronological sequence. Precise dates are rarely possible, and often contentious; still the main phases of Sidonius's adult life are known and most of the letters can be placed at appropriate stages within very rough limits of accuracy.*

Source: The translation is based on that of O.M. Dalton, *The Letters of Sidonius*, 2 vols. (Oxford, 1915), but with extensive revisions. The Loeb edition of W.B. Anderson (Cambridge MA./London, 1936-65) and the Budé edition of André Loyen (Paris, 1960-70) have been consulted. Book and letter number have been placed after the the name of the addressee; numbers of the present translation are in square brackets before the address.

# 37. FROM THE LETTERS OF SIDONIUS APOLLINARIS

## A. EARLY YEARS, BEFORE 467

### Description of Theoderic II, King of the Visigoths (a. 453-466)

*Agricola, the addressee of this letter, was the son of the emperor Avitus and Sidonius's brother-in-law. The letter seems to be the earliest in the collection and must date between 453 and 466. The Gothic settlement had been in existence for over a generation by the time this letter was written.*

[1] To his friend Agricola (1.2)
Since the reputation of Theoderic as a cultured man commends the Gothic king to everyone, you have often begged for a report of his physical appearance and the character of his life. I gladly accede, as far as the limits of a letter allow, and highly approve so fine and noble a concern.

Well, he is a man worth knowing, even by those who cannot enjoy his acquaintance. For God's judgment and nature's handiwork have endowed him with a perfect combination of qualities and his character is such that not even jealousy of royal power can diminish praise for it.

And first as to his appearance. His body is well-proportioned, and he is shorter than the very tall but taller and more imposing than those of medium height. His head is round, and his hair is gradually curled as it sweeps back from brow to crown. His neck is sinewy. The eyebrows form bushy arches over each of his eyes, and, when he closes his eyelids, the lashes extend some distance onto his cheeks. Strands of hair come down over his ears, as is the fashion of his people. His nose is finely aquiline; his lips, delicate and not distended by a wide mouth. Every day the hair on his upper lip is cut off; facial hair is thick in the hollows of the temples, but his barber always removes the rich growth on the lower part of the face, as if his cheeks were still those of a youth. The flesh of the chin, throat, and neck, which is not fat but full, is milk-white, but, if you look more closely, is imbued with a youthful ruddiness, because he often flushes, not from anger, but from modesty. His shoulders are smooth, upper-arms strong, fore-arms hard, hands broad. His chest is prominent but his waist narrow. His back is divided by the spine lying recessed between the elevated surfaces of the ribs. His sides swell with bulging muscle and vigor reigns in the well-girt flanks. His thighs are hard, like horn; his hams, manly, and knees, graceful and quite without wrinkles. His lower legs are strengthened by sturdy calves, and the feet that bear such mighty limbs are small.

Now you will want to know about the routine of his public life. Before day-break, he goes with a very small suite to attend the service of the priests of his faith. He prays with considerable regularity, but, if I may speak in confidence, one may suspect more habit than conviction in the piety. Administrative duties of kingship take up the rest of the morning. An armed retinue is stationed about the royal seat; a crowd of fur-clad attendants is admitted so that they can be within call, but kept at the threshold for quiet's sake; and so there is the sound of hushed conversation on the other side of the curtains by the doors within the chamber. Meanwhile foreign envoys are introduced. The king hears them out, and says little; if a thing needs more discussion, he puts it off, but accelerates matters ripe for dispatch.

The second hour arrives; he rises from the throne to inspect his treasury or stables. If the chase is the order of the day, he joins it, but never carries his bow at his side, considering this beneath the royal dignity. If chance presents to hand a bird or animal during the hunt or on the road, he puts his hand behind his back and takes from a servant a bow with the string hanging loose; for just as he considers bearing the bow in a quiver childish, so he regards receiving the weapon ready strung to be womanish. When he receives it, he sometimes strings it by bending it from opposite ends, and sometimes sets the knotted end down onto his dangling heel, pushing the drooping loop-end of the string up the bow with his finger. After that, he takes his arrows, strings them, and lets fly. He will ask you beforehand what you would like him to strike; you choose, and he hits. If there is a miss through an error on the part of either of you, the fault will be less likely that of the archer than the perception of the spotter.

On ordinary days, his table resembles that of a private person. If you join him for a meal, the board does not groan beneath a mass of dull and unpolished silver set out by panting servants; the weight lies rather in the conversation than in the plate; there is either sensible talk or none. The hangings and draperies used on these occasions are sometimes of purple silk, sometimes only of linen; art, not costliness, commends the fare, as spotlessness rather than bulk the silver. The servings of cups and bowls of wine are spaced out, so that a thirsty guest has more reason to complain than a drunk one has to refuse another serving. In short, you will find Greek elegance, Gallic abundance, Italian swiftness, public splendor, private attention, and royal order. As to the magnificence of festive days, my report must omit them, for no man is so unknown as not to know of them. But to return to my theme again.

His midday nap after dinner is always brief or passed over completely. When inclined for the board-game, he is quick to gather up the dice, examines them with care, shakes the box with expert hand, throws rapidly, calls upon them jokingly, and calmly waits the issue. Silent at a good throw, he laughs over a bad one, annoyed by neither outcome and always the philosopher. As to second throws, he disdains to fear them or to have recourse to them; he refuses to avail himself of one if offered and ignores those waged against him. If his opponent's piece gets away, he does not stir himself, and, if his piece gets away, there is no collusion [on the part of his opponent]. You might think that he was handling weapons even when he touches gaming-pieces; his one thought is victory. When games are played, he puts off a little of the sternness of kingship, urging freedom and fellowship in playing. I think he is afraid of being feared. He is delighted when his defeated opponent is upset, and he will never believe that his opponents have not let him win unless their annoyance guarantees that he really is the victor. You would be surprised how often the pleasure born of these little happenings may favor the march of great affairs. It is then that petitions long wrecked by inadequate patronage are brought to port with a swift decision. It is then that I myself, when I have a favor to ask, am gladly beaten by him, since my loss at the gaming-board may mean the winning of my cause.

About the ninth hour, the burden of government begins again. Back come the claimants, back come the ushers to remove them; on all sides the round of litigants makes an uproar, which lasts till evening and only grows still when the king takes his supper; even then they only disperse to attend their various patrons among the courtiers and are on alert until the night watches are posted. Sometimes, though this is rare, supper is enlivened by the witticisms of low comics, provided no guest is ever subjected to biting criticism. There is no noise of hydraulic organ, however, or choir with its conductor intoning a set piece; no lyre players or flautists, no master of the music, no girls with cithara or tabor sound forth; for the king cares for no instruments but those which no less charm the mind with virtue than the ear with melody.

When he rises to withdraw, the treasury watch begins its nighttime vigil; armed sentries stand on guard at the entrances to the palace during the first hours of sleep. But I am wandering from my subject. I never promised a whole chapter on his reign, but a few words about the king. I must stay my pen; you asked for nothing more than one or two facts about the person and the tastes of Theodoric; and my own aim was to write a letter, not a history.

Farewell.

### Pleasing Queen Ragnahild

*Recent opinion favors the view that Ragnahild was the wife of Euric (a. 466-93), not Theoderic II (a. 453-66).*

[2] To his friend Evodius (4.8)
I was just setting out for a remote country district when your messenger handed me your letter telling some of your acquaintances in confidence that

you were on the point of visiting Toulouse in obedience to a summons from the king. This gave me an excuse to shake off the embarrassing crowd which delayed my early start and allowed me to give you such reply as a traveler, even one on horseback, could attempt. My servants had gone ahead at dawn to pitch my tent eighteen miles away at a spot with many conveniences for camping, a cold spring issuing from a wooded hill with a meadow of rich grass at the foot; a river in the foreground stocked with waterfowl and fish; and in addition to these advantages, almost on the bank, the new home of an old friend whose unstinting hospitality knows no bounds, whether you refuse it or not. After stopping behind to do what you required, so that the messenger could at least be sent back at once from the outskirts of the town, I found it was already more than four hours after dawn; the sun was well up, and its gathering heat had absorbed the heavy dews of night. The torrid air and our parched throats got worse and worse, and so clear was the sky that the only cloud to give protection from the blazing heat was one of dust. The long road made us groan, stretching in full view for miles in front of us across the grassy plain; before it had time to tire us, it already terrified by its prospect; it meant that our lunch would be late.

All this introduction is to convince you, honored lord and brother, that when I complied with your request, I had small time to spare and little leisure of mind or body. I return now to the substance of your letter. After the usual salutations, you ask me to send an epigram limited to twelve verses and suitable for engraving on a large shell-shaped cup, fluted from foot to rim with six channels by the sides of the handles on both sides. You intend the verses, I suppose, for the hollows of the flutings, or better still, if that seems more suitable, for the ridges between, and, as I gather, you propose to assure yourself an invincible protection for all your plans, actual or prospective, by offering the cup, enriched with this embellishment, to Ragnahild, the queen. I do your bidding, then, not as I could have wished, but as circumstances allowed. Be the first to forgive your own fault in this, for you gave the silversmith time but the poet none, even though you know perfectly well that in the literary smithy the verses forged upon the metric anvil want polishing no less severely than any metal. But all this is by the way. Here, try out the poem!

The shell which bears Cythera behind the fish-tailed Triton, compared with this, must yield its pride of place. Bend your queenly head to our prayer, exalted patroness; accept this humble gift; graciously look down upon Evodius who seeks your favour; make him great, and your own glory shall grow greater. Your sire and your lord's sire were kings; royal too is your lord; may your son also reign as king, both by his father's side and after him. Happy is the water enclosed in this gleaming metal, reflecting a royal face yet brighter! For when the queen shall deign to touch it with her lips, the silver shall draw new splendor from her countenance.

If you love me well enough to make use of such idle stuff, conceal my authorship and properly rely for success on your own part of the offering. For in such a market and venue [as the Visigothic court] my writing will get less praise than the surface you have inscribed it on.

Farewell.

## A Case of Abduction

*There is no indication of date, but the letter seems to come from a time before Sidonius became bishop.*

[3] To his friend Pudens (5.19)
The son of your nurse has abducted the daughter of mine. This is a shameful action, and one which would have made us enemies, had I not known at once that you knew nothing of the man's intention. But though you have cleared yourself of complicity, still you do not scruple to ask that this crying offense should be allowed to go unpunished. I can only agree on one condition: that you promote the ravisher from his hereditary position of *inquilinus* (*originalis inquilinatus*) by changing your relation to him from that of master to that of patron. The woman is already free; but in the end she will only appear to have been properly taken up as a wife, and not to have been turned over to be a subject of sport, when our criminal, whose cause you espouse, ceases to be your tributary (*tributarius*) and becomes your client, assuming the status of a plebeian in place of that of a *colonus*. Nothing short of this kind of compensation and amends will in the least condone the affront to me. I yield to your requests and friendship to this extent — provided a grant of freedom releases the husband, then a penalty of law will not bind the abductor.

Farewell.

## The Value of Office I

*The municipal council in question is probably that of Lyons. The trip to Arles would be to attend the Council of the Seven Provinces (cf. **29**). The date is uncertain.*

[4] To his friend Pastor (5.20)
Your absence from yesterday's business of the municipal council was thought by its important members to have been intentional; they suspect that you wished to avoid the burden of an embassy which might be laid upon your shoulders. I congratulate you on being so eligible a person as to live in con-

stant fear of being elected. Your efficiency commands my applause, your prudence my admiration, your happy fortune my congratulations; in fact, I wish the same lot for all friends for whom I have such fondness.

Many men who are driven by a detestable thirst for popularity take the chief citizens by the hand, lead them away from a meeting, and force kisses on them off to the side, promising services for which no one asked them. To create the impression that giving them a commission will protect public interest, they are prepared to return the postal-warrant entitling them to use public transport and, of their own accord, to refuse expenses. They also secretly canvass every member in turn so that they may be publicly invited by all when the council meets. The consequence is that, though people may decide to accept such free service, more often their inclination favors the choice of a more modest representative, even with the expenses — the shamelessness of the volunteer is that irksome, even though choosing him throws no tax burden on the town.

Since, then, the intentions of our best citizens cannot have eluded you, acquiesce, and meet their wishes. You have given proof enough of modesty; put the warm feelings of those who invite you to the test. Your first failure to appear was put down to discretion; repetition of such conduct would expose you to the charge of indifference.

Remember, too, that if you do go to Arles, you will be able to greet your venerable mother and your affectionate brothers on the way; you will greet your native soil that returns the love you bear it, and is doubly delightful when unexpectedly revisited. Then there is your home; think how convenient it will be to inspect, even in passing, its steward, vines, grainfields, olives, and the house itself. Though our envoy, you will travel for your own benefit; your traveling on city business should, if I am not mistaken, prove such an advantage to you that you will eventually feel as though the city has done you a favor by letting you visit your own people.

Farewell.


## B. SIDONIUS GOES TO ROME, a. 467-68

*On the accession of Anthemius, it was Sidonius who was chosen by his fellow Arvernians to present a petition to the new emperor on an unknown matter. Sidonius's visit to Rome on this occasion coincided with the marriage of the patrician Ricimer to Alypia, the daughter of Anthemius. On 1 January 468 Sidonius delivered a panegyric to celebrate Anthemius's entry into the consulship of that year. He was rewarded with the post of prefect of the city of Rome.*

## The Value of Office II

*These three letters were written after Sidonius had agreed to undertake the trip to
Rome. Gaudentius, the addressee of the first, had been appointed vicar of the Seven
Provinces, probably in 467; the letter survives as a fragment.*

[5] To his friend Gaudentius (1.4)
Congratulations, most honored friend; the rods of office are yours by merit.
To win your dignities you did not parade your mother's income, your ancestral inheritance, your wife's jewels, or your father's fortune. In place of all this,
it was your proven integrity, your respected zeal, and your readily-accepted
companionship that won you favor in the imperial household. Three and four
times happy man! Your promotion means joy to supporters, pain to detractors, and glory to your posterity, to say nothing of the example it provides to
the active and the eager and the spur it applies to the idle and the lazy. Those
who try to compete with you, in whatever spirit, may owe their success to
their own exertions if they overtake you, but will no doubt owe it to your
example that they took up the chase in the first place.

With all due respect to men of character, I can imagine to myself that
cowardess in which detractors take so much pride and that habitual aversion
to public service which you find among the lazy. With no hope of rising
themselves, they crown their cups with sophistries about the charm of a free
life out of office, their motive a base indolence, and not the love of the ideal
which they pretend...

[6] To his friend Philomathius (1.3)
Indict me now by the laws against undue-influence, degrade me from the
senate for my constant concern with attaining a rank that runs in my family;
for my own father and my wife's, my grandfather and great-grandfather held
urban and praetorian prefectships and masterships at court and in the army.

Look at my friend Gaudentius. Up to now only of tribune's rank, he rises
above the slack-jawed idleness of our countrymen by acquiring the vicariate.
Of course our youth grumble at his treading under foot their good birth; but
when a man outstrips his critics, he only feels joy. And they now respect a
man, until yesterday, scorned; they used to look down upon him when he
was a fellow member of the assembly, but now, stunned by the sudden gifts of
fortune, they look up at him as he presides over them. For his part, he uses
his bellowing crier to stun the ears of his snoring detractors, who, though
roused by feelings of animosity towards him, will then be given seats on the
bench reserved for his friends.

You too had best briskly repair the loss of your old post [assessor of the
vicar?] by accepting the position of counselor to the [praetorian] prefect now

offered to you; if you fail to do so, if you come to the council [of the Seven Provinces] without the standing of a counselor, you will be set down as someone who has only carried out the responsibilities of the vicariate.

Farewell.

*The following letter has been dated to Sidonius's trip to Rome in the train of Avitus in 455, to a trip in 460, and more usually to the trip of 467. The Eutropius in question became praetorian prefect of Gaul, probably ca. 470.*

[7] To his friend Eutropius (1.6)

I have long wished to write, but feel the impulse more than ever now, when by Christ's atoning grace, I am actually on the way to Rome. My sole motive, or at least my chief one, is to drag you from the slough of your domestic ease by appealing to you to undertake imperial service...

Moreover, by the goodness of God, your age, your health of body and mind concur to fit you for the task; you have horses, arms, wardrobe, money, and servants; the one thing lacking, unless I am mistaken, is the courage to begin. Although you are energetic enough at home, at the idea of foreign travel a paralyzing melancholy confounds you. But how can it fairly be described as foreign travel for a man of senatorial descent, who must daily encounter the effigies of his ancestors adorned in their consular robes, to visit once, and in the prime of his life, the home of laws, the training-school of letters, the court of honours, the pinnacle of the world, the homeland of freedom, the city unique upon earth, where only barbarians and slaves are foreigners?

Shame on you now if you let yourself be left among cow-keeping rustics or grunting swineherds, as if it were the height of your desires to feel the plow-handle tremble above the cleft furrow, or to despoil the meadow of its flowery wealth, bowed over your scythe, or to hoe the lush vines with your gaze fixed upon the earth. Wake up! Let your mind, wasted and enervated by luxuriant ease, rise to higher things. Is it less a duty in a man of your descent to cultivate himself than his estate? In the end, what you call a young man's exercise is really the repose of veterans whose exhausted hands late in life exchange rusty swords for the mattock.

Suppose you achieve your end: vineyard upon vineyard foams with new wine; granaries burst storing endless piles of grain; your well-fed herdsman drives a crowd of his charges with swollen udders through the stench of the enclosure's gates for milking? What is the use of having enlarged your patrimony by such a sordid accumulation and of having not only lived as a recluse among such employments, but, what is worse, for the sake of them? Will it not be a shame if one day, when the council meets, you are there, an inglorious old farmer, required to stand in obscurity behind your juniors, who have

seats and express their opinion, and forced to bear the burden of some pro-
nouncement of a poor man who has attained high office; and all the while,
with anguish you see yourself surpassed by men who once would have been
considerd unworthy of following in our footsteps?

But why say more? If you take my advice you shall find me your ally,
assistant, guide, and partner in all your efforts. But if you let yourself be
caught in the alluring nets of pleasure and prefer to be coupled, as the saying
goes, to the tenets of Epicurus, who sacrifices virtue and defines the chief
good as physical gratification, then, with our ancesters and posterity as witnesses, I will have nothing to do with the offense.

Farewell.

## The Journey to Rome

[8] To his friend Herenius (1.5)
Your letter finds me at Rome. You are anxious to know whether the affairs
which have brought me so far go forward as we hoped; what route I took,
and how I fared on it; what rivers celebrated in song I saw, what towns famed
for the placement of their fortificiation, what mountains reputed as the haunt
of gods; and what battlefields were worth seeing (for you find great satisfaction in checking your reading against the more accurate relation of those
who have seen the site). I rejoice that you inquire about my doings, because I
know that your interest springs from the heart. Well then, though little acci-
dents there were, I will begin, under kind providence, with things of good
event; it was the practice of our ancestors, as you know, to develop even a tale
of mishap from fortunate beginnings.

As someone summoned by imperial letter, I was able to avail myself of the
public post once I had left behind the walls of our beloved Lyons. My route
lay alongside the homes of acquaintances and relations, and I lost less time
from scarcity of horses than from multiplicity of friends, who warmly
embraced me, and whose prayers vied with one another in wishing me a
happy journey and safe return.

In this way I drew near the Alps, which I ascended easily and without
delay; formidable precipices rose on either side, but the snow was hollowed
into a track, easing the progress of our journey. Such rivers, too, as could not
be crossed in boats, had convenient fords or traversable bridges, built in
antiquity from their foundations to the cobbled road resting on vaulted
arches. At Ticinum [Pavia] I boarded the packet known as the *cursoria*, which
soon bore me to the Po, where I laughed over those convivial songs of
ours about Phaethon's sisters and their unnatural tears of amber gum.
I explored a little the mouths of those tributaries descending from Ligurian
or Euganean heights, the sedgy Lambro, the blue Adda, the swift Adige, the

slow Mincio; their shorelines and high banks were clothed with groves of oak and maple. Everywhere resounded sweetly the harmony of birds, whose loose-piled nests swayed sometimes on hollow reeds, or sometimes on rushes and smooth reed-grass luxuriantly flourishing in the moisture of the wet riverain soil.

The way led past Cremona, whose nearness once caused the Mantuan Tityrus to sigh so deeply. We just touched at Brescello to take on Aemilian boatmen in place of our Venetian rowers, and, bearing to the right, soon reached Ravenna, where one would find it hard to say whether Caesar's road, passing between the old town and the new port, separates or unites the two. Moreover, a branch of the Po flows through this double city, and a branch flows around it, diverted from its main bed by the state dykes, and drained off by them through channels. The division of the river means that some water flows round the walls, giving them protection, and some penetrates the city, bringing it trade — an admirable arrangement for commerce in general, and especially for bringing in foodstuffs. But the drawback is that, with water all about us, we could not quench our thirst; there was no pure-flowing aqueduct or purified cistern, or bubbling spring, or unclouded well. For on the one side, the salt tides press upon the gates; on the other, the movement of vessels stirs the sediment of sewage in the canals and the slug-gish flow is fouled by the bargemen's poles, piercing the sticky sludge on the bottom.

From Ravenna we came to the Rubicon, which borrows its name from the red color of its gravels and formed the frontier between the old Italians and the Cisalpine Gauls, when the two peoples divided the Adriatic towns. From there I journeyed to Rimini [Arminum] and Fano, the first famed for its association with Caesar's rebellion, the second tainted by the death of Has-drubal; for here flows the Metaurus, renowned through the ages for the out-come of a single day, as if it had never ceased to run red to this hour, bring-ing down the dead on blood-stained waters to the Dalmatian Sea.

After this I lost no time traversing the other towns of the Flaminian Way — in at one gate, out at the other — leaving the Picenians on the left and the Umbrians on the right; and there either Calabrian Atabulus or the dis-ease-ridden Tuscan region infected my body, exhausted by breathing air that was filled with poisionous exhalations and alternating between hot and cold. Fever and thirst ravaged the very marrow of my being; I kept promising to quench their desires with drinks from pleasant fountains or hidden wells, yes, and from every waterway, whether at hand or still to come, water of lake Veli-nus clear as glass, of the Clitumnus ice-cold, of the Anio blue, of the Nar sul-furous, of the Farfa transparent, of the Tiber muddy; I longed to drink, but prudence stayed the craving.

Meanwhile, Rome herself spread wide before my view, and I felt like draining down her aqueducts or even the water of her naval spectacles. Before I reached the city limits, I fell prostrate at the triumphal threshold of the Apostles, and immediately I felt the weariness vanish from my enfeebled limbs. After this proof of celestial protection, I rented lodgings at an inn, and even now I am there trying to get a little rest and lying down as I write.

As yet I have not presented myself at the bustling gates of emperor or court official. For my arrival coincided with the wedding of the patrician Ricimer, who was being married to the emperor's daughter in the hope of securer times for the state. Not individuals alone, but whole classes and parties are given up to rejoicing. It seemed a good idea to your transalpine friend to lie low. While I was writing these very lines, scarce a theater, provision-market, praetorium, forum, temple, or gymnasium but echoed to the Fescennine cry of Thalassio! Even at this hour the schools are closed, no business is doing, the courts are voiceless, missions are postponed; there is a truce to intrigue, and, faced with the buffooneries of the stage, all the serious business of life seems to have taken a leave of absence. Though the bride has been given away, though the bridegroom has put off his garland, the consular his embroidered robe, the brideswoman her robes, the distinguished senator his toga, and the plain man his cloak, yet the noise of the great gathering has not died away in the palace chambers, because the bride still has to move to her husband's house. When this merrymaking has run out its course, you shall hear what remains to tell of my struggles and exertions, if indeed the hectic respite gripping the whole city is ever to end, even when the festivities are over.

Farewell.

## Patronage

*The potential patrons, Avienus and Basilius, were ex-consuls; the former was a member of the Corvini family and the latter of the Decii. Pyrgopolinices and Thraso were boastful soldiers in the comedies of Plautus and Terence respectively.*

[9] To his friend Herenius (1.9)
With the patrician Ricimer being well married, and the wealth of both empires blown to the winds in the process, the community has at last resumed its sober senses and opened door and field again to business. Even before this happened, I had already been made welcome to the home of the former prefect Paul, and enjoyed the friendliest and most hospitable treatment in a house no less respectable for piety than learning. I do not know a man more eminent in every kind of accomplishment than my host. Good heavens, the subtleties he can propound, the rhetorical figures he uses to express his ideas, the balanced phrasing of his verses, the ingenious devices made by his

artful hands — all these are amazing! And over and above all his learning, he has a still better possession, a conscience superior even to this expertise.

Naturally, my first inquiries as to possible avenues to court-favor were addressed to him; with him I discussed the likeliest patrons for the advancement of our hopes. There was, however, little need to hesitate; the number of those whose patronage merited our consideration is so small. There are, indeed, many senators of wealth and birth, ripe in experience, capable of giving good advice, high ranking, and equally worthy of respect. But without disparagement to others, we found two consulars, Gennadius Avienus and Caecina Basilius, in enjoyment of a peculiar eminence and conspicuous above the rest; if you leave out of account the great military officers, these two members of the exalted order easily come next to the emperor himself. Though both of them are to be admired, their characters are different and the resemblance between them hangs more on style than substance.

Let me give you a short description of the pair. Avienus reached the consulate by luck, Basilius by merit. It was observed that the former attained his dignities with enviable rapidity, but that although the latter was slower, he won the greater number of distinctions in the end. If either chanced to leave his house, they were engulfed on all sides by a host of clients forming an escort. So far they were alike, but the spirits and expectations of their friends were quite different. Avienus would do all that he could for the advancement of his sons, or sons-in-law, or brothers, but was so absorbed in family candidates that his energy in the interest of outside aspirants was proportionately impaired. There was a further reason for preferring the Decian to the Corvinian family. What Avienus could only obtain for his own connections while in office, Basilius obtained for strangers while he was in a private station. Avienus revealed his purpose freely, and at once, but little came of it; Basilius rarely and not for some time, but to the petitioner's advantage. Neither of the two was inaccessible or costly of approach; but in the one case cultivation reaped mere affability, in the other, solid gain. After balancing alternatives for some time, we finally compromised in this sense; we would preserve all due respect for the older consular, whose house we were duly frequenting, but devote our energies to being in the circle attending upon Basilius.

Now while, with the assistance of this right honorable friend, I was considering how best to advance the petitions of the Arvernian delegation, the Kalends of January came round, on which day the emperor's name was to be enrolled in the Fasti as consul for a second year [a. 468].

"The very thing," cried my patron. "My dear Sollius, I well know that you are engaged in an exacting duty, but I do wish you would bring out your Muse again in honor of the new consul; let her sing something appropriate to the occasion, even if hastily composed. I will get you in, and be your support as you prepare and as you go along. Take the word of someone with experience in these matters: serious advantages may accrue to you from this little scheme."

I attended to his instructions and he did not fail to follow through on his propositions. He was an invincible ally in the devout performance laid upon me and persuaded my consul to make me the president of his senate [that is, prefect of the city of Rome].

But I expect you are tired to death of this prolix letter and would much rather peruse my little work itself at your leisure. Indeed, I am sure you would, so I have appended the poem itself to my wordy letter. In the meantime, it can converse with you in my place for a few days until I arrive. If you judge my verses worthy of applause, I shall be just as delighted as if a speech of mine in the assembly or from the rostra called forth 'bravos,' not of senators alone but of all the citizens. I warn you and give you notice not to set this slight piece of mine on the same plane as the hexameters of your own Muse, for by the side of yours my lines will suggest the triviality of epitaph-mongers rather than the grandeur of heroic verse.

Rejoice, all the same, with the panegyrist; he cannot claim the credit of a fine performance, but at least he has the reward of one. And so, as long as grave matters are to be enlivened by jokesters, I will imitate the Pyrgopolinices of Plautus and conclude in a pretentious and Thrasonical vein. And since, by Christ's aid, I have got the prefecture by a lucky pen, I bid you treat me as my new state demands; pile up all conceivable felicitations and exalt to the stars my eloquence or my luck, according as I please, or fail to please, your judgment. I can see you laughing when you note my vaingloriousness alongside the wild soldiers of comedy.

Farewell.

## Urban Prefect

*This is the only letter in which Sidonius reveals anything about his duties as prefect of Rome.*

[10] To his friend Campanianus (1.10)
The prefect of the food supply has personally presented the letter in which you commend him, as your old friend, to me, a new judge. I am greatly indebted to him, but most of all to yourself for this evidence of your resolve to assume that my friendship is certain and undiminished. I welcome, I eagerly embrace, this opportunity of acquaintance and of intimacy, since my desire to oblige you cannot but draw closer the bonds which already unite us.

But please also recommend me, by which I mean the defence and preservation of my reputation, to his attention. For I rather fear that there may be an uproar in the theatres over the shortage of food among the Roman people, and that the general hunger will be laid at my door. I am on the point of dispatching him immediately to the harbour in person, because I have news that five ships from Brindisi have put in at Ostia, laden with wheat and honey. If he acts energetically and can get these cargoes ready for distribution in time for the expectant crowds, he would win my favour, I would win the people's, and he and I together would win yours.

Farewell.

## C. FROM PREFECT AND PATRICIAN TO BISHOP

### The Perils of Office I: Arvandus

*Arvandus, praetorian prefect of Gaul from 464-468, was condemned by the Senate in 469 after being removed from office. He was a friend of Sidonius. Arvandus's accusers, Tonantius Ferreolus, Thaumastus, and Petronius, represented the Council of the Seven Provinces and were kinsmen and friends of Sidonius.*

*Trials before the Senate were presided over by the urban prefect. Sidonius, who had left Rome by the time of Arvandus's condemnation, had also presumably left office prior to his departure from the city.*

[11] To his friend Vincentius (1.7)

The case of Arvandus distresses me, and I do not pretend to conceal my distress, for it is our emperor's crowning glory that a condemned prisoner may have friends who need not hide their friendship. I was this man's friend more than was warranted by his light and unstable character, witness the ill-will lately kindled against me on his account, the flame of which has scorched me for a certain lack of foresight. But I owed it to myself to remain his friend, though he on his side is not at all steadfast; I make this complaint to be candid, not to disparage him. For he despised the advice of those loyal to him and made himself a plaything of fortune throughout the affair; the marvel to me is not that he fell at last, but that he ever stood so long. How often he would boast of weathering adversity, when we, with a less superficial sense of things, deplored the sure disaster of his rashness, unable to call any man happy who only sometimes and not always could be said to enjoy that state.

You ask how his condemnation came about. I will tell you in few words but with the loyalty due to a friend, even one brought to ruin.

During his first term as prefect his administration was very popular; the second term was an absolute disaster. Crushed by debt and living in dread of creditors, he was jealous of the magnates who were likely to be his successors. He would mock everyone who conversed with him, profess astonishment at their advice, and spurn their help; if people called on him too rarely, he showed suspicion; if too regularly, contempt. At last the general hate encompassed him like a rampart; before he was well divested of his authority, he was invested with guards, and a prisoner bound for Rome. Hardly had he set foot in the city than he was all exultation over his fair passage along the stormy Tuscan coast, as if convinced that the very elements were somehow at his bidding. At the Capitol, the count of the imperial largesse, Flavius Asellus, acted as his host and jailer, showing him deference for his prefectship, which seemed, as it were, yet warm, so newly had it been stripped from him.

Meanwhile, three envoys from Gaul arrived upon his heels bearing official resolutions and prepared to bring charges in the name of the provinces. They were Tonantius Ferreolus, ex-prefect and grandson on his mother's side of the consul Afranius Syagrius, Thaumastus, and Petronius, men extraordinarily eloquent and experienced and conspicuous ornaments of our country. Among other matters that the provincials had authorized them to pursue, they brought forward an intercepted letter, which Arvandus's secretary, now also under arrest, declared to have been dictated by his master. It was evidently addressed to the king of the Goths [Euric], and was dissuading him from concluding peace with the Greek emperor [Anthemius], urging instead that the king attack the Britons north of the Loire, and asserting that the Gallic provinces ought to be divided between the Visigoths and the Burgundians by the law of nations. There was more in the same mad vein, calculated to inflame a warlike king or shame a peaceful one into action. The lawyers found here a flagrant case of treason.

This interpretation did not escape the excellent Auxanius and myself; whatever the circumstances of our contracting Arvandus's friendship, we both felt that to evade the consequences now in his hour of need would be faithless, barbarous, and cowardly. He suspected nothing of what was going on, and so we informed him of all the manoeuvering taking place round about him that his passionate and ardent opponents were, with consumate skill, planning to keep secret until the time of his trial; since their reckless adversary had rejected the advice of his friends and was rashly trusting to his own devices, they intended to ensnare him when he made some unconsidered reply. We told him what to us and to more secret friends seemed the safe course. We advised him not to make the slightest admission to his opponents, even if it seemed inconsequential and they presented it as a completely trifling matter; the more their pretense created in him a false sense of security, the more dangerous were their intentions.

When he grasped our point, he started forward, suddenly breaking out into abuse.

"Be off, you false and unworthy sons of prefectorian fathers," he cried, "and take your pointless fear with you. Leave this part of the affair to me, since you know nothing about it. For Arvandus it is sufficient that his conscience is clear; it is bad enough that I have to employ lawyers to defend me on charges of extortion."

We came away in low spirits, disturbed less by the insult to ourselves than by a real concern. What right has the doctor to take offense when a man past cure gives way to anger?

Meanwhile, our defendant went off to parade about the capitol square, and in white raiment too; he basked in the sly greetings which he received; he listened with a gratified air to the bubbles of flattery bursting about him. He rummaged through the gems and silks and each of the valuable cases of the dealers, and, as if he were a likely purchaser, examined the merchandize, picking it up, rejecting it, and tossing it back. In the midst of this, he moaned and groaned over the laws, the age, the senate, the emperor, all because they would not vindicate him without a trial.

A few days passed, and, as I learned afterwards (I had left Rome in the interim), there was a full house in the Senate. Arvandus proceeded there freshly primped and groomed. The plaintiffs, drably dressed and unkempt, waited the summons of the ten judges and so, by their intentionally disordered appearance, gained the sympathy given those in mourning clothes and snatched from the defendant the pity that was his due.

The parties were summoned and admitted. As is usual, they took up positions opposite each other. Before the trial began, all those of prefectorian rank were allowed to sit. Even at that point, Arvandus displayed his ill-starred pushiness, stepping forward and forcing himself almost into the very laps of the judges. Ferreolus, with his colleagues at his side, seated himself quietly and modestly at the lowest end of the benches, being mindful of his role as an envoy no less than his rank as senator; he subsequently gained more credit and respect by doing this. While this was going on, the rest of the members of the house came in.

Both parties rose and the envoys set forth their charges. They first produced their mandate from the provinces and then the already-mentioned letter. This was being read out slowly when Arvandus admitted the authorship without even waiting to be asked. The envoys rejoined, rather wickedly, that the fact of his dictation was obvious. And when the madman, blind to the depth of his fall, dealt himself a deadly blow by repeating the avowal two or three times, the accusers raised a shout, and the judges joined in, that he stood convicted of treason out of his own mouth. Besides, he was done in by legal precedents beyond number warranting this verdict.

Then and only then was the afflicted man said to have turned white, belatedly repenting his talkativeness. All too late he realized that it is possible for someone to be convicted of high treason for offenses other than aspiring to the purple.

He was stripped on the spot of all privileges pertaining to his two terms in the prefecture, an office which he administered for five years and whose fasces were renewed once. He was consigned to the public prison as one of plebeian birth — not because he was degraded to that rank but because he was restored to it. According to eye-witnesses, the most wretched feature of the process was that, as a result of his intrusion upon his judges all decked out and spruced up while his accusers were dressed in black, his pitiable plight won him no pity when he was led off to prison a little later. How, indeed, could anyone be much moved at his fate, seeing him carried off to the quarries or hard labour carefully groomed and perfumed?

Judgment was deferred a bare fortnight. He was then condemned to death, and hauled off to the island of the Serpent of Epidaurus, where, deprived of all grace, he is an object of compassion even to his enemies. And there, as if vomited by a sickened Fortune from the land of the living, he now drags out by benefit of Tiberius's law his respite of thirty days after sentence, shuddering through the long hours at the thought of the hook and Gemonian stairs, and the noose of the brutal executioner.

We, of course, whether in Rome or out of it, are doing all we can; we make vows and pile up prayers and supplications that the imperial clemency may suspend the stroke of the sword which is now drawn, and instead bestow upon a man already half dead a penalty of exile with confiscation of property. But whether Arvandus is awaiting the worst or is experiencing it, he is surely the most miserable soul alive if, branded with such marks of shame, he fears anything more than life itself.

Farewell.

## The Perils of Office II: Seronatus

*Two letters on Seronatus, who seems to have been vicar of the Seven Provinces in 469. Although the letters offer only a catalogue of his abuses, he was eventually accused by the Arvernians of being in league with Euric and condemned to death; his fate is mentioned in passing in a later letter to Bishop Graecus (no. 44, below).*

[12] To his friend Pannychius (5.13)

Do you know that Seronatus is coming back from Toulouse? If not (and I suspect you do not), learn it from the following.

Evanthius is hurrying to Clausetia, making the assembled laborers clear the road wherever it is choked with fallen branches. In fact, when he finds potholes, he himself in a panic brings up dirt, fills them in, and levels them off.

Like pilot-fish that lead the lumbering whale among the rocks and shoals, his business is to precede his own monster, guiding him from the valley of the Tarn.

But Seronatus, whose temper is as quick as his ponderous bulk is slow, no sooner appears like a dragon uncoiling from his cave, than he makes immediate descent upon the pallid folk of Javols, whose cheeks are pale with fear. Scattered individually about the countryside, they are sometimes exhausted by his unheard-of impositions; sometimes he snares them in the mesh of false accusations, not even allowing the wretches to return home when they have paid their annual tribute.

Wherever he goes, the sure sign of his impending arrival is the appearance of chain gangs, dragging their shackles. He takes delight in their anguish, he feeds on their hunger, and he finds a special beauty in disfiguring the condemned before punishing them, compelling the men to grow their hair long and cutting off the hair of the women. If now and then a prisoner receives a pardon, it is through his vanity or his corruption, never through his mercy. Neither the prince of orators, Marcus [Cicero] of Arpinum, nor the prince of poets, Publius [Virgil] of Mantua, could adequately describe so dire a creature.

This plague — may God confound his betrayals — is said to be now on his way; anticipate the disease by salutary precautions. Protect yourself against lawsuits, if such are contemplated, by making agreements with those who are litigious; against tax claims, have your receipts handy; do not let this evil man find a way of injuring or benefiting the affairs of good people. Do you want me to sum up my feelings about Seronatus? Others fear suffering injury at his hands; to me even the benefits conferred by a brigand are suspicious.

Farewell.

*Ecdicius was a son of the late emperor Avitus.*

[13] To his [brother-in-law] Ecdicius (2.1)
Your countrymen of Auvergne suffer two evils at once. "What are those?" you ask. Seronatus's presence and your absence.

Seronatus — his very name first calls for notice; I think that when he was so named, a prescient fortune must have played with contradictions, as our predecessors did, who by antiphrasis called wars, which are the foulest of activities, *bella* and, with no less perversity, called the Fates *Parcae*, because they never spare (*parcere*) anyone.

Seronatus, the Catiline of our day, has just returned from the region of Aire where the draught he took of the blood and fortunes of its wretched people was small compared to the concoction he is preparing here. You must know that his long-concealed savagery comes daily further into the light.

His spite is open, his deceit base, and his arrogance servile. He gives orders like a lord, makes exactions like a tyrant, sentences like a judge, and lies like a barbarian. He goes armed the whole day because he is a coward and fasts because he is a glutton. Greed makes him terrifying and vanity cruel. He never ceases to punish theft and, at the same time, to commit it. He openly belches forth nonsense about war to provincials and literature to barbarians, to the laughter of the assembled company. Though he barely knows the alphabet, he has the conceit to dictate letters in public and the audacity to revise them under the same conditions. Everything he covets he makes a show of buying, but he has no intention of paying for it nor any hope of getting proper documents. He lords it over the council [of the Seven Provinces], but when good counsel is required, he is silent. He make jokes in church and preaches at table; passes sentences when he goes to bed but is asleep during judicial examinations. He daily fills the woods with fugitives, the villas with guests (*hospites*), the churches with criminals, and the prisons with clerics. He revels among the Goths and behaves insolently among the Romans. He makes fools of the prefects and makes a killing with the state accountants. He tramples under foot the laws of Theodosius and offers in their place the laws of Theoderic. He goes looking for old charges and new tributes.

Be quick, then, to unravel the tangle of affairs that makes you linger; cut short whatever causes your delay. Our people are at their last gasp and await your coming; freedom is almost dead. Whether a situation is hopeful or hopeless, they want you in their midst to lead them. If the state is unable to provide troops, if, as is the rumor, the emperor Anthemius has no resources, the nobility is determined under your leadership to give up their country or the hair of their heads.

Farewell.

## A New Solon Among the Burgundians

*There is no clear indication of the date of this letter; it could be quite late if written during Sidonius's episcopate. Sidonius had earlier written to the addressee Syagrius, perhaps around 467, chastising him for spending too much time on his farm. Syagrius was now serving the Burgundian regime.*

[14] To his friend Syagrius (5.5)
You are the great grandson of a consul (and in the male line, though that has little bearing on the matter before us). As such, you are the descendant of a poet, whose literary achievement would certainly have honored him with statues had they not been secured for him already by his official honors — the fine verse that he has left us testifies to that. As far as letters are

concerned, the endeavors of his successors have readily matched his standards. But here is a feat that fills me with indescribable amazement — you are picking up a knowledge of the Germanic tongue with the greatest of ease.

I can recall the thoroughness of your education in liberal studies; I know with what fervid eloquence you used to declaim before the rhetor. Such being your training, tell us how you have so quickly absorbed the sounds of a foreign speech, so that, after having your Virgil caned into you and sweating over the opulent and flowing style of the varicose orator of Arpinum [Cicero], you soar out like a young falcon from the ancient eyrie?

You can hardly conceive how amused we all are to hear that the barbarian fears to perpetrate a barbarism in his own language when you are near. Old Germans bowed with age are astounded to see you translating letters; they actually choose you for arbiter and mediator in their disputes. You are the new Solon of the Burgundians in discussing the laws; the new Amphion in tuning the cithara, though it is only three-stringed. You are popular, you attract friends, you are sought out and give delight. You are chosen, you are invited, you decide issues, and are listened to. In body and mind alike these people are stiff and very hard to form. In you they embrace the Roman spirit even as they learn their native tongue.

Let me end with a single caution. Clever as you are, devote whatever time you can spare to reading, and, as you are a cultivated man, preserve a balance between the two languages; keep your own, so you will not be laughed at, and practice the other, so you may do the laughing.

Farewell.

## A Disturbed Burial

*Sidonius's grandfather, Apollinaris, was praetorian prefect of Gaul in 408/409. The mention of tyrants in the poem refers to Constantine and Jovinus. There is no real indication of the letter's date.*

[15] To his nephew Secundus (3.12)
I have dreadful news. Yesterday profane hands all but desecrated the grave where my grandfather and your great-grandfather lies, but God prevented the accomplishment of the impious act. The cemetery had for years been over-crowded with burned and unburned burials, and interment there had long ceased. But snows and constant rains had caused the mounds to settle; the raised earth had been dispersed, and the ground had resumed its former even surface. This explained how it was that some coffin-bearers presumed to profane the spot with their grave-digging tools just as if it were unoccupied by human bodies.

What else is there to say? They had already unturfed the ground, so that the soil showed black, and were piling the fresh sods upon the old grave. By a mere chance I happened to be passing on my way to Clermont and saw this public crime from the top of a neighboring hill. I gave my horse his head and dashed at full speed over the intervening ground, flat or steep was all the same to me; I grudged even those brief moments and, sending a shout before me, stopped the infamy even before I myself reached the scene. Those caught in the crime were still hesitating whether to make off or hold their ground, when I was upon them. I confess my mistake, but I could not stop myself from inflicting punishment on the captives; the brigands were were put to the torture on the very grave of our beloved ancestor, enough to assuage the feelings of the living and to protect the dead.

In reserving nothing in this matter for the judgment of our bishop, I had in mind the strength of my own case and his person, and I took both into consideration: my fear was that the former might be settled with more leniency than was right, or that the latter might inflict a harsher penalty than he should. As one willing to make amends, I did send him an account of the whole affair after I had resumed my journey, and this upright and holy man heaped praise on my indignation, although I was only asking for pardon; he declared that in his opinion it was right that men guilty of such carelessness should have been beaten according to the custom of our ancesters.

The incident should help to prevent any similar mischance in future, and I beg you in my absence to see to it that the disturbed earth is at once raised to a mound again and covered with a smooth flat slab at my expense. I have deposited a sum of money with the venerable Gaudentius to cover the cost of the stone and of the labor. The poem which I enclose was composed last night; it is not polished, I suppose, because I was too busy with preparations for the road. Such as it is, please have it carved on the tomb with the smallest possible delay and be specially careful that the stone-mason makes no errors either by negligence or by intention; for whatever the cause, the captious reader will put it all down to me. If you carry out this pious obligation I shall thank you no less heartily than if you were not certain to receive part of the praise and credit. For were I, your uncle, no longer with you, the whole responsibility of this duty would have devolved on you as the next descendant after myself.

A grandson not all unworthy of such a grandfather, I dedicate to him, though all too late, this epitaph, my father and my paternal uncles being dead, that you, O passer by, may never tread on unmounded earth, unwitting of the reverence due to him who is buried in this grave. Here lies the prefect Apollinaris, who, having ruled Gaul well, was gathered to the bosom of a mourning country. He was a highly skillful and capable toiler in agriculture, in government, and in the forum. A perilous example to others, he dared be a free man under the rule of tyrants. But this stands as his chief title to fame, that of all his line he was the first to purify his brow with the sign of the cross and his limbs with baptismal water and was the first to reject sacrilegious rites. This is the highest glory, this the transcendent virtue, if a man outstrip in hope those whom he equals in honors and is placed by his merits above his fathers, though on earth his titles were the same as theirs.

I know well that this epitaph is unworthy of our accomplished ancestor; yet I think the souls of the lettered do not refuse a poetic tribute. And you should not regard as belated a tribute expended by heirs of the third and fourth degree. How many revolving years rolled by before Alexander celebrated funeral rites for Achilles' shade or Julius Caesar for the shade of that Hector whom he treated as an ancestor of his own?

Farewell.

## A Barbarian Prince

*The Sigismer in this letter is otherwise unkown. He seems to have been a Frankish, or possibly Burgundian, prince.*

[16] To his friend Domnicius (4.20)

You take such pleasure in the sight of arms and those who wear them that I can imagine your delight if you could have seen the young prince Sigismer on his way to the palace of his father-in-law in the guise of a bridegroom or suitor in all the pomp and style of his people. A horse covered in trappings went before, actually I should say horses laden with flashing gems preceded him and even followed after; but a still more handsome sight to be seen was the prince himself, as he marched on foot amid his runners and attendants, dressed in fiery scarlet, ruddy gold, and milk-white silk, while his hair, the blush of his cheeks, and his skin accorded with the three hues of his outfit.

But the princes and allies accompanying him had a frightening appearance, even in peace. Their feet were laced in boots of bristly hide reaching from the toe to the heel; knees, shins and calves were exposed. In addition, they wore high tight tunics of varied color hardly descending to their bare knees, the sleeves covering only the upper arm. They had green mantles with crimson borders; swords, which hung in baldrics that crossed their shoulders, pressed on sides encased in bossed deer-hide.

The very equipment that adorned them defended them; in their right hands they grasped barbed spears and throwing axes; their left sides were guarded by shields, which flashed with tawny golden bosses and snowy silver borders, betraying at once the wearers' wealth and occupation. Though the business in hand was wedlock, Mars was no less prominent than Venus in all this pomp.

Why need I say more? Such a fine show lacked only your presence. For when I realized that you would not be seeing things you love to see, I missed the uncontrolled pleasure you would have taken in the spectacle.

Farewell.

## Chasing Saxons

*The omitted portions of this letter show that it was written after the publication of some of Sidonius's letters; the contents there, however, make it difficult to accept that it was composed by Sidonius the bishop after 477, when the books of letters as we now have them began to be published. As Sidonius seems to have published letters at earlier stages in his career, I have placed this letter before his episcopate.*

*The addressee Namatius, a resident of Novempopulana, was stationed on the Atlantic coast to guard against pirates. The present selection begins after Sidonius has been teasing Namatius about the quality of his hunting dogs.*

[17] To his friend Namatius (8.6)

...Joking apart, do let me know how things go with you and your household. Just as I was on the point of ending this letter, which had rambled on long enough, suddenly a messenger from Saintonges arrived. I spent some time talking with him about you, and he was positive that you had sounded the battle signal to the fleet, and, discharging the duty of sailor and soldier, you were coasting the winding western shores on the look-out for the curved skiffs of the Saxons. In every one of their oarsmen you would think you were looking at an arch-pirate: all of them together issue orders and obey them, giving and taking guidance in the art of robbery. These circumstances provide the best reason for warning you even now to be especially on your guard.

The Saxon is the most ferocious of all foes. He comes on you suddenly; and when you are waiting for him, he slips away. He is contemptuous of those who stand in his way and overthrows the unwary. If he pursues, he overtakes; if he himself takes to flight, he gets away. Shipwrecks to him are no terror, but only so much training. His is no mere acquaintanceship with the perils of the sea; he knows them intimately. A storm serves to put his victims off guard and to prevent his own imminent attack from being seen; the chance of bringing off a surprise attack makes him gladly hazard rough seas and jagged rocks.

Moreover, when the Saxons are ready to unfurl their sails for the voyage home from the mainland and to lift their anchors from the shallows of enemy waters, it is the custom of those going home to put every tenth captive to a torturous death by drowning, in a ritual all the sadder for being due to religion, and to pass this wicked death sentence upon the doomed crowd by means of the perfect equity of casting lots. Those returning are bound by vows which have to be paid in victims. Polluted by sacrilege rather than purified by sacrifices of this kind, these perpetrators of an unpropitious slaughter regard it a religious act to extract agony from a prisoner rather than ransom.

I am full of anxiety and apprehension about these dangers, though, on the other hand, there are good reasons for me to feel encouraged. First, you follow the standards of a victorious people. Second, I dare say that men of prudence, among whose number you may fairly be counted, are not in the habit of leaving anything to chance. Third, good friends who live far from each other are apt to feel alarm even when there is no danger, because it is natural to be apprehensive about distant and unresolved events. You may say perhaps that my fears should not be such a concern. That surely is true, but it is also true that we fear most for those whom we love most. So, as soon as you can, please relieve the fears which your situation has aroused by giving me a favorable account of your fortunes. Until I get good news, I will never wholly be dissuaded from fearing the worst regarding friends who are away from home, especially those whose business is the trumpet and the command of troops.

In accordance with your request, I send you the *Logistoricus* of Varro and the *Chronographia* of Eusebius. If these works reach you safely, and you find a little leisure from the your duties overseeing patrols when you are in camp — the luck of the draw should supply some respite — you will be able, once your arms are furbished, to apply another kind of polish to an eloquence which must be getting rusty.

Farewell.

## Episcopal Appointment at Chalon

*This letter seems to belong to a time before Sidonius became bishop, but when he was connected with the circle of Bishop Patiens of Lyons. Euphronius was bishop of Autun.*

[18] To his friend Domnulus (4.25)
I cannot delay an hour in letting you know of an event which must cause you the greatest pleasure, anxious as you were to learn what success attended the piety and firmness of our metropolitan and father in Christ, Patiens, upon the occasion of his visit to Chalon. He went to ordain a bishop for that town, where discipline had been imperiled after the retirement and subsequent death of the young bishop Paulus. Some of the provincial bishops formed his escort; others had preceded him. When the episcopal council met, it found that the opinion of the citizens was not unanimous, and that there

existed private factions of the kind so ruinous to the public welfare.

The existence of three candidates aggravated these evils. The first had no moral qualification whatever, but only the privilege of ancient lineage, of which he made the most. The second was brought in on the applause of parasites, bribed to support him by the free run of a gourmand's table. The third had a tacit understanding with his supporters that, if he attained the object of his ambition, the plundering of church estates should be theirs.

Seeing this, the holy Patiens and the holy Euphronius were determined that no thought of dislike or popularity should move them from the firmness and severity of the saner judgement. They communicated their intention to their fellow bishops in secret before they made it public. Then, with a complete disregard of the unruly crowd, they seized the holy John, suddenly joining their hands to his. John was a man conspicuous for an honorable, humane, and gentle life, who was without the faintest suspicion of what they proposed or the slightest desire for preferment. He had first been a reader and so had been a server at the altar from his tender years. In the course of time and strenuous duty he became archdeacon, in which office or rank his efficiency kept him back; they would not give him promotion because they did not wish to relieve him of functions he performed so well. This was the man, a priest only of the second order, whom the two bishops consecrated as their colleague, among the competing voices of the factions, who were slow to praise one never even put forward for the office, but who dared not at the same time say anything against a man altogether praiseworthy. And the consecration took place to the stupefaction of intriguers, the shame of the wicked, and the delight of the good, without one dissenting voice.

And now when the monasteries of the Jura, where you love to climb as if in foretaste of a celestial habitation, allow you to return to us, you will be able to rejoice over how these our fathers and protectors agreed in their judgments or, as it were, had judgments that were in agreement. Celebrate too the man whom Euphronius and Patiens consecrated, one by his testimony and the other by laying on of hands, both together by their good judgment. Euphronius acted as befitted his age and also his long tenure of office, and Patiens, for whom no praise could be too high, as suited one who by his ecclesiastical dignity is the chief of our city and, by the priority of the city, of the province.

Farewell.

## D. SIDONIUS THE BISHOP

### Riothamus

*This letter was written at some time after Sidonius became bishop of Clermont around 470. The addressee, Riothamus, was a Breton commander, called "king of the Britons" by Jordanes* (Getica, 237-38). *An ally of Anthemius in the years 467-472, he was defeated by Euric and took refuge with the Burgundians.*

[19] To his friend Riothamus (3.9)

I will write once more in my usual fashion, mixing greetings with complaint. Not that I wish at all to follow up the first words of greeting with disagreeable subjects, but things seem to be always happening which a man of my order and in my position can neither mention without unpleasantness, nor pass over without neglect of duty. Yet I do my best to remember the burdensome and delicate sense of honor that makes you so ready to blush for the faults of others.

The bearer of this is an obscure and humble person, so insignificant and helpless that he brings harm to his own cause; his complaint is that Britons are secretly enticing away his slaves. Whether his charges are justified, I cannot say; but if you can only bring the parties together and fairly air the grievances, I think the unfortunate man may be able to make good his claim. All this is contingent on a poor stranger from the country, alone, insignificant and unarmed, having chance of a fair and decent hearing amidst canny adversaries who are armed, unruly, and insolent by virtue of their courage, their numbers and their fellowship.

Farewell.

### A Count for Autun

*This letter was hardly written to a sixteen-year-old, which would have to be the case if the Attalus in question is the same as Gregory bishop of Langres and the usual dates for his life are accepted: birth, ca. 450; countship of Autun, ca. 466-506; episcopacy, ca. 506-539. The bishop lived until he was ninety, according to Gregory of Tours. There is no clear-cut indication of the letter's date but Sidonius's episcopacy seems most likely.*

[20] To his friend Attalus (5.18)

I was delighted to hear that you have just taken charge of the city of the Aedui [i.e. Autun]. My gladness is fourfold: first, you are a friend; second, you are just; third, you are strict; and fourth, you will be quite near us.

You will now have not only the inclination to render considerable assistance to our people and our affairs, but the duty and the power of doing so.

In my satisfaction at seeing new authority vested in an old acquaintance, I am already looking round for objects on which you may exercise your good offices. For understand, I feel so sure of those, that if I fail to find anything to ask for, I would expect you yourself to find something to grant me.

Farewell.

## Buying Books at Rheims

*The addressee is the Remigius who, according to Gregory of Tours, baptised Clovis and 3000 of his followers and whose own letters are translated at 38, 40, and 44. The date of this letter is uncertain.*

[21] To Lord Bishop Remigius (9.7)

One of our citizens of Clermont went recently on a journey to Belgic Gaul (I know the man but not the business he was on, which is all quite immaterial). When he reached Rheims, he won over your copyist or your bookseller probably by giving him cash or doing him a favor; in any case, he had him part with a complete set of your *Declamations* without your knowledge. After his triumphant return to us and the town with such a rich haul of books, as a citizen he presented them all to us as a gift — a not unworthy act — though we were quite ready to purchase them. I and all those devoted to literature were properly desirous of reading the books, and we at once began to transcribe the whole, committing to memory as much as we were able.

It was the universal opinion that there are few people living now who can write as you do. There are few writers, or none, who can match your abilities to arrange subjects, position letters, or combine syllables; or who can employ illustrations as apposite, statements as trustworthy, epithets as appropriate, allusions as charming, arguments as sound, sentiments as weighty, diction as flowing, and conclusions as resounding as yours. The framework is always stout and firm, its parts tied together securely by delightful transitions, although it is no less easy, smooth and rounded to perfection as a result. It allows reading to proceed gracefully without encountering the obstacle of rough word-connections that cause the tongue to roll around the palate stammering. All is fluent and smooth — as when the finger glides lightly over a surface of polished crystal or onyx without catching its nail, as there is not the slightest crack or fissure to stay its passage.

I have said enough. No work of a present-day orator exists which your masterful skill could not easily surpass and outdo. I almost dare to suspect, lord bishop, that a flow of eloquence so copious and so far beyond my powers of description must sometimes (forgive my audacity) make you vain. Just because you are illustrious for the goodness of your way of life as well as of your literary skills, you must not flee from us. I praise what is well written, even if I do so in a style that itself is not worthy of praise. In future, then, stop evading my judgments, which threaten neither biting criticism nor rebuke. For I must warn you that if you fail to enrich my barren soil with your fluent eloquence, I shall wait for a thieves' hiring fair, and the clever hands of burglars will soon despoil your book-boxes with our connivance and support. If duty does not compel you now to take action to fulfill our request, then you will find that you take action in vain when the thieves have stripped you bare.

Please keep me in your thoughts, my lord bishop.

## Three letters on Episcopal Election in Bourges

*Bourges was the metropolitan city of Aquitanica prima, which included Clermont. The election in Bourges took place in 470/1.*

*The addressee of the first letter, Agroecius, was Bishop of Sens, the metropolitan city of Lugdunensis Senonia.*

[22] To Lord Bishop Agroecius (7.5)

A decree of the citizens has called me to Bourges. The reason for the summons is the tottering condition of the church, which has just been deprived of its bishop; members of both orders have been intriguing for the vacant see, just as if some bugle had sounded for the fray. The people are excited and divided into factions; while only a few are ready to propose others, there are many who do not so much propose as impose themselves. If you make a suggestion as far as is humanly possible in accordance with God and the truth, you run into nothing but frivolity, inconsistency, and falseness, and — how shall I put it? — only presumption itself is straightforward. You may think these complaints exaggerated; but I dare say that there are many here who are of such a rash and perilous frame of mind that they are ready to offer ready money for this holy see and the position that goes with it; the goods might before now have been put up for sale in open market if a vendor could have been found as desperate for the transaction as the purchaser was eager.

Your arrival is anxiously awaited. I beg you to join me and by your help offset my inexperience and reticence in fulfilling the requirements of my office. Though you are in charge of Sens, do not, in such critical times, refuse your help in healing the dissensions of the people of Aquitaine. It is of small consequence that we live in different provinces, when, in the matter of religion, we are joined in the same cause. Moreover, the capital of the Arverni [i.e. Clermont] is the last of all the cities in Aquitanica prima which the fortunes of war have left on the side of the Romans; for this reason, the body of provincial bishops is inadequate to establish a new prelate at Bourges unless restored to health by the support of metropolitans. Rest assured that I have in no way encroached on your prerogative: as yet I have neither nominated, summoned, nor chosen a candidate. I have left the matter absolutely intact for your decision. My only role is to invite you here, to await your decisions, to applaud your judgments, and, when someone has been chosen for the position, to ensure that you issue the command and I proffer obedience.

I do not for a moment suspect that any bad adviser will dissuade you from acceding to this request; but should that prove to be the case, you will find excuses for not coming easier to discover than reasons to avoid blame. On the other hand, your coming will prove that though there may be limits to your diocese, your brotherly love is without bounds.

Please keep me in your thoughts, my lord bishop.

*Euphronius was bishop of Autun. Cf. letter 18.*

[23] To Lord Bishop Euphronius (7.8)
I am now held in the bonds of my clerical duty, but I should regard my undistinguished position as a veritable blessing if only the walls of our cities were as near as the borders of their territories. I would then consult your holiness on all things small and great; my activities would flow like a peaceful and untroubled stream, could they but rise from your advice as from a health-giving spring. They should never know the froth of vain conceit, or the turbid course of pride, or the muddiness of a bad conscience, or the falls of headstrong youth; if defilement and corruption were found in them, they should be washed clean if channeled through your counsel.

But as the distance that divides us prevents the fulfilment of these desires, I earnestly beg you to free me from the perplexing dilemma that confronts me. The inhabitants of Bourges demand the consecration of Simplicius, a man of *spectabilis* rank, as their bishop; I want your decision as to what I should do in such an important matter. I have such high regard for you and you have such authority over others that you will get your way (and you always want what is fair) not by prevailing upon us so much as by commanding us.

As to Simplicius, I must tell you that a great many good things are said about him and by the best people. At the outset of discussions I was inclined to view this testimony with little favor as it seemed to me to suggest favoritism. But when I observed that his rivals could find nothing better to do than to hold their tongues, especially those of the Arian persuasion, when I saw that no irregularity could be alleged to discredit the nominee, though he is not yet in orders, I came to the conclusion that a man against whom the bad citizen could say nothing and on whose behalf the good could never say enough must be regarded as almost a perfect character.

But how foolish I am to make these comments, as if I were giving advice in place of asking it. Rather all matters will be arranged among the clergy as you wish and in accordance with your letter and communicated to the people. We are not so completely devoid of sense as to decide first to invite you to come, if that were possible, and then, failing that, at any rate to solicit your advice, without intending to follow you in all matters.

Please keep me in your thoughts, my lord bishop.

*Perpetuus was bishop of Tours and had asked Sidonius for a copy of his address to the people of Bourges on the occasion of the election of its new bishop. Only excerpts from Sidonius's response are given below.*

[24] To Lord Bishop Perpetuus (7.9)
*The opening of the letter praises Perpetuus's Catholic learning and apologizes for the shortcomings of Sidonius's address.*

So great was the company of the competitors, that two benches would not have held the candidates for the single vacant throne. And every one of these was as pleased with himself as he was critical of his rivals. If the people had not calmed down and thrown over its own right of judgment, subordinating it to that of the bishops, there would have been little chance of coming to a common resolution. As it was, one saw small groups of priests whispering together in corners, though not a word was uttered openly, most of them being just as afraid of their own order as of every other. Since everyone in public was suspicious of everyone else, the result was that they all gave a hearing to a proposal which they did not reject and to which they could then lend their support.

Here, then, is the address, with accompanying rolls. It was written in two vigils of a single summer night, Christ as my witness. I greatly fear that reading it will more readily attest to the haste of its composition than anything I could say.

*The address begins with a self-deprecating introduction.*

The duty [of being an instructor] is in itself impossible enough, but it is made heavier by the reticence which I feel because you have specially authorized me by the mandate of your decretal letter to choose a bishop for you, in the presence of a saintly prelate worthy of the highest pontificate; not only is he the head of a province, but he is my superior in experience, in training, in eloquence, in prestige, in seniority, and in years. Speaking thus about the election of one metropolitan in the presence of another, I, as a junior and provincial bishop, am doubly stigmatized by my inexperience and presumption. But it was your misguided wish that I, a person lacking wisdom, should search on your behalf, with Christ's help, for a wise bishop...

*Sidonius then lists at great length the carping criticism that the choice of various kinds of candidates would likely elicit.*

I shall therefore fulfill a promise which I need to make not so much to people of goodwill as to slanderous folk full of suspicion... In choosing the right man for you, I have been swayed by neither money nor influence. I have weighed with due, in fact with excessive, consideration, the standing of the person and the condition of the times, the city, and the province, and I have come to the belief that the best man is he whose life I shall rather hastily review.

He is the blessed Simplicius, up to now considered a member of your order, but hereafter a member of ours, provided God, through you, approves him. He fits both spheres by his conduct and public life, so that the state finds in him someone to be admired and the church someone to be cherished.

If birth is still to command respect — and the Evangelist shows that it should not be passed over, for Luke, beginning his eulogy of John, accounts it significant that John came from priestly stock and exalts the importance of his family before celebrating the nobility of his life — I will recall the fact that his relatives have presided alike over ecclesiastical see and secular tribunal. His family, distinguished in both walks of life, has been renowned for its bishops and prefects; his ancestors have always been accustomed to administer divine and human laws.

If we exercise a little more circumspection and consider his person, we find him conspicuous among those of *spectabilis* rank. You may say that Eucherius and Pannychius are his betters because they have the rank of *illustris*. They may have been so regarded to this point, but in the matter presently before us they are excluded by the canons, because each of them has married again. If we consider his age, we find that he has the vigor of youth and the wisdom of age. If we compare his learning and his talents, we see nature rivaling knowledge. If simple human kindness is at issue, he gives more than enough to citizen, cleric, and stranger, from the lowest to the highest, and repeatedly it is the person in no position to repay him who receives his bread. When embassies have had to be undertaken, more than once he has represented his city before fur-clad kings and purple-clad emperors. If you ask from what master he learned the rudiments of the faith, I will make the proverbial response, 'his home provided his teacher.'

Finally, dear friends, this is the man who was confined in the darkness of a prison cell and on whose behalf God flung wide the heavily bolted gates of a barbaric prison. This is the man whom, if report be true, you yourselves once shouted out must be called to the priestly office in preference to his father-in-law and father; but at the time he returned home covered with glory, preferring to find honor in the post of his kinsmen rather than in his own.

I had almost overlooked a point which should under no circumstances have been passed over. Under Moses — in days of old, as the Psalmist says — all Israel freely heaped their share of offerings at the feet of Bezaliel in the desert in order to erect the tabernacle of the covenant. Afterwards Solomon, to build his temple in Jerusalem, exhausted the whole strength of his people, though he could combine the captured riches of the Palestinians and the tribute of surrounding kings with the treasures of the Queen of Sheba from the south. On your behalf, Simplicius, by himself and out of his own slender resources, built a church, while he was still a young official under paternal authority, and already himself a father. Neither consideration of his young children nor the steady opposition of his elders could divert him from the fulfilment of his vow. Yet it was his way not to talk about this. For, unless I am mistaken, he is someone who is completely averse to courting popularity; he does not seek the good opinion of everyone, just of the worthiest; he does not degrade himself by undiscriminating familiarity, but makes his friendship even more valuable by according it only after the most careful thought. His manly nature makes him want to help rather than please his rivals, like the stern father who thinks more of his children's best interests than of their desires. He is a man constant in adversity, loyal in danger, and unassuming in prosperity; his clothing is simple, his speech unaffected; in a group, he is not forward, but, when a decision is needed, he stands out from the rest. A friendship of which he knows the worth he will pursue with ardor, hold with constancy, and never abandon; he conducts an open quarrel in an upright fashion, is slow to accede to it, and quick to put it aside. His favor is greatly to be desired because he himself is not one to curry favor. His aim is not to assume the priestly office but to be deserving of it.

But someone will say: "How did you learn so much about him in so short a time?" My answer is that I made acquaintance with men of Bourges long before I knew their city. I have met them on the road and in the civil service; many I have met while conducting business or negotiations; many when they or I have been abroad. Moreover, one can learn a lot of useful information about a person from his reputation, since common report naturally does not limit itself to a man's homeland. So if a city is to be judged less by the circumference of its walls than by the fame of its citizens, I learned first not just who you were but where you stood in the world.

The wife of Simplicius comes from the stock of the Palladii who in both the schools and in the church have occupied the highest positions with the approval of the order in question. To speak of a matron's character demands both brevity and respect; I will only say here that this woman does justice to the priestly office enjoyed by her two families, the one in which she was reared and grew up, and the one she joined on marriage. She and her husband both educate their children on sound and careful principles, so that the father, comparing them with himself, is all the happier for the discovery that he is already being surpassed.

You have sworn to abide by my humble decision in this election — for an oral oath is no less binding than a written one. I pronounce then in the name of the Father, the Son, and the Holy Spirit that Simplicius is the man whom you are to make metropolitan of our province [Aquitanica prima] and chief priest of your city. If you accept the new verdict I give concerning the man of whom I speak, applaud with the harmony your old verdict demands.

### A Tale as Good as an Attic Comedy

*The subject of the following two letters is Amantius, who became a courier between Graecus, the addressee of the letters, and Sidonius. Graecus was bishop of Marseilles and later played a role in negotiations with Euric over the cession of the Auvergne (cf. letters 43 and 44, below).*

*The first letter is Sidonius's original recommendation of Amantius to Graecus. The second letter attempts to clear up some misconceptions resulting from the first.*

[25] To Lord Bishop Graecus (6.8)
The bearer of this letter earns a poor living solely as a trader; he gets no earnings from a craft, no salary from the public service, and no profit from agriculture. Because he is known to hire himself out as a purchasing agent, his reputation has grown, but so too has the wealth of others. People put a lot of faith in him even though his means are small; when a ship's cargo is landed and goes on the market, he attends the sale with other people's money, but he deposits with his creditors, who do well to credit him, no collateral but his own reputation for honesty. These circumstances were brought to my attention as I wrote, but I have no hesitation affirming the truth of what I have heard, because he is on good terms with people who are on quite good terms with me.

Therefore I recommend to you a man who looks delicate but who has had a rough start in life. And since his name has recently been entered into the register of readers, you will see why I owed him not just a letter fit for a citizen about to make a journey, but a canonical letter appropriate to a cleric.

With good reason I think he will soon prove to be a distinguished merchant, if he seeks to serve you and gives up the cold water of a hometown fountain for a source of more discerning taste.

Please keep me in your thoughts, my lord bishop.

*In the following letter, Hippolytus is a fictional character from Greek mythology and tragedy; the term Milesian refers to the racy stories of Aristides of Miletus (ca. 100 B.C.) and tales of a similar character. This letter also attests to the presence of a count of the city in Marseilles.*

[26] To the Lord Bishop Graecus (7.2)
You overwhelm my modesty, most accomplished of bishops, by heaping all kinds of praises on the rustic lines I churn out. I wish I were not guilty of having told you in my first letter a patchwork of lies and half truths, though I myself was deceived; in fact, a crafty traveler imposed upon my innocence.

He asserted that he was only a merchant, and, as a reader, he managed to get out of me a canonical letter, which fittingly should have contained an expression of gratitude. For, as I afterwards learned, he was advanced by the generosity of the people of Marseilles more than one so moderately favored in birth and fortune had reason to expect. How these deeds unfolded would make a fine story, if only there were a narrator good enough to recount it. But as you have asked me for a long and diverting letter, permit me to sketch out the hospitality accorded this messenger of ours, comparable in its way to a scene from comedy; I shall be careful to say nothing to offend someone in your position. And pardon me if I seem to know for the first time a man whom I am now introducing to you for the second time. Usage permits a writer to find his subject-matter wherever he can; why, then, should I go farther afield looking and searching for something to talk about, when the man who is to bear my letter can himself provide the theme of it?

The bearer, then, is a native of Clermont. His ancestors' origins were not lofty but were beyond reproach, and if they had nothing illustrious to boast about, they had no servile background to fear either. They were satisfied with moderate wealth, though it was adequate and unencumbered. Their public career had been pursued in ecclesiastical rather than imperial service. The father was very frugal and not generous enough toward his children; he preferred to benefit his son through excessive miserliness rather than to gratify the desires of youth. In this situation, the boy came to you a little too lightly equipped; and this was no small obstacle to his first undertakings, for a light purse is the heaviest encumbrance on a journey.

Nevertheless his first entry into your city was quite favorable. Your predecessor holy Eustachius immediately conferred on him a two-fold blessing in word and deed. He wanted lodgings right away; they were readily found with the prelate's assistance. He quickly made an appearance and a rental agreement was duly drawn up. At once he set about making the acquaintance of his neighbors, frequently presenting himself and being civilly greeted in return. He treated everyone as befitted their age; he won over the old by being respectful and those of his own age by helping them out. Above all he lived chastely and temperately, showing qualities as admirable as they are rare at his time of life. Ever prowling about at the right time, he gained the recognition, then the acknowledgment, and finally the company of the top people, even the count of the city at the time. And so by applying himself day in day out he advanced to higher circles of associates; the best people competed to support him. Everyone wished him well; there were plenty to offer him good advice. Private individuals made him presents, officials helped him by grants. In short, his prospects and his resources rose by leaps and bounds.

It so happened that near the residence where he had taken up lodgings there resided a lady as well provided with income as with good character; she had a daughter, not quite marriageable, but no longer a child. He charmed the girl with his attentions (given her young age this was still appropriate), presenting her with various trifles and trinkets which delight a young girl's fancy; on such trivial grounds, the heart of the maid became linked strongly to his own.

Time passed and she reached the age of marriage. I will get to the point. This young man, alone, with slender means, a foreigner, a youth still in his father's power, who had left his homeland without his father's leave or knowledge, seeks the hand of a girl equal to himself in birth but superior in fortune. He seeks her hand, and, what is more, he is successful, and he marries her. For the bishop intervened on behalf of his reader, and the count supported his client; the future mother-in-law did not trouble to investigate his means; and the bride approved his person. The marriage contract was written up, and some suburban estate of our little town was entered into the matrimonial settlement and read out with theatrical display. With this legal swindle and fraudulent proceedings completed, the beloved pauper carried off the wealthy bride. He carefully went through and packed up the belongings of his wife's father's and took advantage of the generous easy-going naïvité of his mother-in-law to extract from her a sizable gift; then the imposter sounded the retreat and withdrew undefeated to his homeland [the Auvergne].

After he had gone, the mother of the girl thought of bringing an action against him for restitution on grounds of the exaggerations in the contract. But it was rather late for her to start lamenting the slim contribution of the bridegroom to the marriage, when she was already rejoicing at the bounty of grandchildren. It was with the object of appeasing her that our Hippolytus went to Marseilles when he brought you my first letter of introduction.

That is the story of this extraordinary young man, as good in its way as any out of Attic comedy or Milesian fable. At the same time, excuse me if I have exceeded the acceptable bounds of a letter; I have gone into details so you might have some idea of the man you receive and to whom you have granted the privileges of citizenship; and besides, one naturally has a kindly feeling for those in whom one has taken active interest. You will prove yourself in everything the worthy successor of Eustachius if you pay his clients the legacies of patronage, just as you pay relatives the legacies left to them in a will.

See now, I have obeyed and discharged my duty with my chatter; remember that one who imposes on a man of small descriptive powers a subject calling for great detail, must not complain if the response he gets looks more like chitchat than eloquence.

Please keep me in your thoughts, my lord bishop.

## Renewing an Old Friendship

*Polemius was the last praetorian prefect of Gaul, probably in the years 471-72. The Tacitus mentioned here is the great historian of that name; the German commander is the Batavian Claudius Civilis.*

[27] To his friend Polemius (4.14)
Your ancestor Gaius [Cornelius] Tacitus, a man of consular rank in the times of Trajan, in his history mentions a German general as saying, "My friendship with Vespasian goes back a long time, and, when he was a private person, we were called friends."

You ask the object of this preface: to remind you that your position as a public man ought not to involve neglect of private friendships. For almost two years, my old regard for you, rather than my satisfaction at your new dignity, has led me to rejoice over your elevation to the post of praetorian prefect in Gaul. If the misfortunes of the Roman state allowed it, I would have been displeased that you did not enrich every person, I shall not say province, with various favours. And now that shame prevents me from asking what it is beyond your power to grant, I want you to tell me how your generosity would have been revealed in deeds, when you have proved so stingy with words. For if one compares your skill with that of your ancestors, you can surpass the orators of the Cornelii and the poets of the Ausonii.

Up to now you have been a philosopher; but if suddenly you are seized by a new sense of importance because you exercise power, remember, 'We too have had a taste of fame and glory' [Aeneid II 89]. You may think that the lowliness of our profession deserves scorn because we priests take it upon ourselves to lay bare before Christ, that healer of human lives and fortunes, the ugly sores of the sick spirit — in men of my order these are at least not swollen by pride, even if they still reek to some extent from lack of attention. If this is your view, I would have you know this, that it is one thing to stand before the magistrate in court, and another to stand before the judge of all the world. The offender is condemned who in your presence cannot keep quiet about his deeds; with us the same confession made to God brings the offender absolution. It is evidently unsuitable therefore for those in your position to proclaim the guilt of someone whose case belongs to the tribunal of another.

For this reason you can no longer dismiss my complaining about the pain I feel; whether the success you have come to enjoy makes you forget old friendship, or only neglect it, the result in either case is almost equally bitter to me. If, then, you have concerns about the future, write to me as to a priest; if about the present, write as to a colleague. There is a virtue which never disdains an old friend for a new one; if it was born in you, develop it; if not, at once implant it in your heart. Otherwise you will appear to treat your friends as one does flowers, which are only cherished as long as they are fresh.

Farewell.

### Reconciling a Father with his Son

*Sidonius was a bishop when he wrote this, but otherwise there is no indication of date.*

[28] To his friend Proculus (4.23)
Your son — indeed I should say our son — has taken refuge with me, full of sorrow for having wrongly abandoned you, overwhelmed with shame and repentance for his desertion.

When I heard how he had misbehaved, I rebuked the skulker with sharp words and threatening looks. The voice was mine, but I spoke in your place, as I denounced him as one deserving disinheritance, the cross, the sack, and the other penalties of parricides. He flushed red in his confusion, but made no brazen excuses for his fault; and when I convicted him on every point, such overwhelming floods of tears accompanied his contrition that it was impossible to doubt that he would ever do this again.

I entreat you, therefore, to show mercy on one who is so hard on himself; imitate Christ and do not judge someone guilty who confesses himself worthy of condemnation. Even if you are merciless and subject him to unheard-of punishments, no torture you can apply will inflict more pain than his own shame. Save him from his despairing fears; preserve the confidence I have in you; and — if I am any judge of the nature of a father's love — free yourself from the anguish you must feel in secret at the spectacle of a son crushed by affliction. I shall only have done him great harm if you do him even a little, which I trust you will not do unless you mean to remain as hard as a rock and as impenetrable as a diamond.

If I am right in expecting something better from your character and friendship, forgive him and be generous. In reconciling you, I promise that he will henceforward always be a loyal son. To absolve him promptly of his fault is to bind me by your kindness, for I earnestly beg you not just to pardon him but to do so instantly. I want you, when he returns, not to open to him your door alone, but your heart as well. Great God! what a bright day will dawn for you, what joyous news it will be to me, what gladness will fill his soul, when he casts himself at his father's feet and receives from the lips of the father he injured, those lips which he dreads, not reproaches but a kiss!

Farewell.

## Abduction by *Vargi*

*This letter is important for understanding the role of the bishop's court in settling potential criminal suits; plaintiffs were entitled to bring such matters before secular or ecclesiastical tribunals, each of which provided different remedies. The term* vargus *is most likely Germanic and in later sources means outlaw. Lupus was bishop of Troyes from around 426; he died in 479. The letter may date to an early period in the troubles with the Visigoths referred to in the next section.*

[28] To Lord Bishop Lupus (6.4)

I pay my respects to the incomparable eminence of your apostolic life, a debt that will never be discharged though ceaselessly rendered. But I have a further object, to enlist your old friendship on behalf of the recent distress of the suppliant bearers of this letter. They have journeyed into Auvergne, a great distance especially in these times, and the journey has been undertaken in vain.

A female relative of theirs who had unfortunately been carried off during a raid by *vargi*, as the local brigands are styled, had been brought here a few years ago and sold. When they received trustworthy information about this, they followed her trail, which was clearly marked but cold. As it happened, before their arrival, the unfortunate woman, who had certainly been sold in open market, died in the establishment of my agent and under his control. A certain Prudens (for such is his name), rumored to be now resident in Troyes, had attested the contract for the vendors, who are unknown to me; his signature is to be seen on the agreement of sale as that of a suitable warrantor of the transaction.

The authority of your person and the advantage of your presence, when the parties have been brought face to face, will readily enable you, should you think fit, to investigate the whole course of the outrage. I gather from what the bearers say, that the offense was made even more serious by one of the travelers being killed in the course of the abduction.

Though contemplating a criminal charge, they come seeking the healing prescription and civil remedies of your court. And so your position as well as your character, unless I am mistaken, will cause you to relieve the affliction of one side and save the other from danger, by means of a settlement without condemnation. The moderation of such a salutary decision would diminish the misery of one party and the guilt of the other, and would give both of them a greater feeling of security. Otherwise, given the conditions of the times and the place, the state of the dispute in the end may reach the level it first had at the beginning.

Please keep me in your thoughts, my lord bishop.

## Recommendation for a Jew

*This letter too likely concerns the judicial activities of bishops. Nothing is known about its recipient.*

[30] To Lord Bishop Eleutherius (6.11)
This letter is to recommend to you a Jew, not because I have any liking for a false belief that brings destruction on those it envelops, but because it is not right to pronounce one of them wholly worthy of damnation as long as he still lives. For someone who can be converted still has the prospect of absolution.

It is better for him to go over the details of his troubles personally in your presence; for it is a good idea not to spoil the polished arrangement of proper epistulary style with too many subjects. In any case, since people of this kind often have a just cause as far as earthly affairs and law are concerned, you too can defend the rights of this unfortunate man, even if you oppose the falseness of his faith.

Please keep me in your thoughts, my lord bishop.

## Youthful Weakness and Concubinage

*There is no indication of date in this letter nor do we know the addressee's see. The letter may date from much later in Sidonius's episcopacy.*

[31] To Lord Bishop Ambrosius (9.6)
Your holiness's intercession with Christ on behalf of our beloved friend has had its effect. (Why bother with his name when you will recognize all the particulars?) You used to complain about his youthful weakness, sometimes

openly when you met with those who saw it, sometimes groaning silently to yourself. He has just broken off his association with that shameless slave-girl to whom he had completely subjected himself, a prisoner of filthy intercourse; he has suddenly straightened up and taken thought for his patrimony, his descendants, and his reputation.

When his circumstances were reduced by losses sustained by his family property, he began to understand and reconsider how much of the modest fortune that he had received from his father and grandfather was being wasted by the extravagance of this domestic Charybdis. As soon as he realized this — and it was a late repentance — he finally took the bit in his teeth, threw off the yoke, and, as they say of Ulysses, plugging his ears with wax, fled the allurements of ruinous whoring, deaf to temptation. Now a respectable husband, he has taken in marriage, as is proper, an unsullied girl, distinguished by her character and birth as well as her princely fortune.

It would really have been glorious if he had abandoned sensual pleasure and not taken a wife. But though it may happen that people abandon wicked habits for virtuous ones, few can begin with the most important virtues, and those who have long given in to their passions cannot immediately give up everything all at once.

For this reason it is up to you to busy yourself with prayers to obtain the prospect of children for the couple as soon as possible. When one or two sons are born (and even that is too many), it will be reasonable if this husband, who before marriage thought he could take illicit pleasures, refrains in the future from the pleasures permitted to him. For, though lately married, even the couple themselves behave themselves in such a fashion and with such modesty that, once you see them, you will truly understand the immense difference between the decent love of a wife and the illusory charms of concubinage.

Please keep me in your thoughts, my lord bishop.


## E. BLOCKADE OF CLERMONT, a. 471-74

*Euric's aggressive policy towards Roman power (and that of other players in the new polity of the Gallic provinces) led him in the years 471-474 to mount campaigns against Clermont, which stood in the way of Visigothic expansion. These eleven letters refer in various ways to Clermont's resistance during these years and to those who participated in it.*

*Magnus Felix was a fellow student of the young Sidonius and encouraged him to publish his poems. He held the dignities of praetorian prefect (probably of Gaul, in 469) and patrician.*

[32] To his friend Magnus Felix (3.4)

Gozolas, a Jew by nationality and a client of your excellency — and a person I too should like if I did not despise his religion — brings you my letter, which I wrote with a good deal of anxiety.

Our town is terrified by the peoples that crowd around it under arms as if it were an obstacle to their expansion. We are located between rival forces, a pitiful prey to them, held in suspicion by the Burgundians and near neighbors of the Goths; we are spared neither the fury of our attackers nor the envy of our defenders.

But more about this some other time. Meanwhile, if all is right with you at least, that is good. For at heart I am not the type of person who would not wish things to go well everywhere else, even if we are being openly punished on account of crimes committed in secret. Certainly someone who cannot express well-wishes when times are bad is as much a prisoner of his own vile nature as of his enemies.

Farewell.

*This letter was written when the addressee Ecdicius, son of the late emperor Avitus, was at the Burgundian court, perhaps in 473/74. The events it describes belong to 471. Ecdicius was rewarded eventually with the patriciate in 474 (see letter 42, below).*

[33] To his friend [and brother-in-law] Ecdicius (3.3)

Never have my people of Clermont missed you so much as at present; their affection for you is a ruling passion, and for many reasons: first, because the land of a man's birth rightly claims the chief place in his affection; secondly, because almost alone among mortals of your generation you were a cause of longing in your homeland prior to your birth no less than a cause of joy after you were born. The proof of this claim occurred during your mother's confinement: the citizens kept track of the time as your birth approached, united in their prayers.

I pass over that commonplace, no slight inducement to affection for being so, that here is the sod on which you crawled as an infant; I refrain from saying that here are the first fields you trod, the first rivers you swam, the first woods in which you hunted. I pass over that here you first had sport with ball and dice, hawk and hound, horse and bow. I will ignore how learning from all over the world was assembled to benefit your boyhood years, and that at one time we owed it to you that the nobility were instructed in eloquence and sometimes even in the measures of the muses and were prepared to lay aside rough Celtic speech.

Nothing so kindled everyone's regard for you as this, that after demanding they become Latins, you then prevented them from becoming barbarians. For how can the citizens ever forget how great a man you are when members of both sexes and of every age and rank lately caught sight of you from the half ruined ramparts riding across the gap between the enemy and the walls. Attended by a company of scarcely eighteen troopers, you passed through several thousand Goths not just in broad daylight but out in the open — a feat which posterity will have trouble believing. At the mention of your name and the sight of your person, a seasoned force was overcome by astonishment, and the enemy commanders, taken by surprise, failed to appreciate how many men they had and how few were accompanying you. Immediately all the enemy lines were withdrawn to the brow of a steep hill, and although they had previously been employed in an assault on the town, they were not deployed for combat when they saw you. Meanwhile, you cut down their rearguard, composed of men who were there, not because they were cowardly, but because they were brave and were their best troops. You lost none of your own men in the engagement and were left the sole master of a completely open plain, though you had no more comrades in the fight than you usually have guests at the table.

Imagination may better conceive than words describe the applause and tears of joy that greeted your leisurely return to the city. The courts of your spacious house crammed with people were the auspicious setting for the crowd giving you an ovation on your return. Some kissed away the dust that covered you; some took from the horses the bridles slimed with foam and blood; some removed the sweat-drenched saddles; some undid the flexible cheek-pieces of the helmet you were about to remove; some set about unlacing your greaves; some counted the notches in swords blunted by blows; and others measured with envious fingers the cuts and punctures made in the mesh of the mail shirts. Though many, dancing for joy, embraced your comrades, the full brunt of popular joy was heaped on your shoulders. You were among an unarmed host at last, but weapons would not have availed to extricate you from it. You bore with good grace the boorishness of your well-wishers, and, though you were torn to bits by people madly rushing to embrace you, as a conscientious reader of the state of public enthusiasm you had recognized the necessity of conveying the warmest acknowlegments upon whoever inflicted the worst outrage upon you.

And next I shall say nothing of how you raised what was practically a public force from your private resources, and with little outside help from important people; and of how you curbed the unchecked raids of the enemy, restraining their plundering.

I shall say nothing of the surprise attacks by which you sometimes annihilated whole squadrons of cavalry with the loss of only two or three men on your side. You inflicted such losses on the enemy by these unexpected engagements that they devised a disgraceful plan to conceal the number of their dead. They decapitated all whom they could not bury in the short night-hours, as if it were less revealing to leave a corpse without its head than to let one with long hair be recognized by its locks. When, in the morning light, they saw their efforts to remove the extent of their defeat revealed in all its contemptible savagery, they then turned at last to open obsequies; but they were no more successful in covering their ruse by haste than they were in covering their losses by their ruse. They did not even hurriedly raise a mound of earth over the remains; nor did they consign the bodies to their graves washed and clothed, performing the proper rites due the dead. Bodies were brought in from everywhere, piled on dripping wagons; and since you never paused a moment in pressing home your victory, they were hurriedly placed in buildings that were then set on fire, and the blazing fragments of collapsing roofs became their funeral pyres.

But I chatter on too much; my aim was not to reconstruct the whole story of your achievements, but to recall a few of them, in order to convince you that your absence makes your friends heartsick and that only your return will provide a quick and efficacious remedy. If, then, the entreaties of our people can persuade you, sound the retreat and start homeward at once. Deliver yourself without delay from constant exposure to the dangerous intimacy of kings. The nature of their friendship is rightly compared by those with experience to a flame, which illuminates things at a short distance but consumes them if they come too close.

Farewell.

*The date of this letter is uncertain but its contents may refer to the Visigothic attacks between 471 and 474. Eucherius, the addressee, had been regarded as ineligible for the bishopric of Bourges in 470 because he had been twice married (cf. above, letter 24). According to Gregory of Tours, he was put to death by Duke Victorius (also a correspondent of Sidonius) after the victory of Euric.*

*The Brutus mentioned here is not the assassin of Caesar but a much earlier figure supposedly involved in the expulsion of the Tarquins.*

[34] To his friend Eucherius (3.8)
I respect the ancients, but not so I can denigrate the abilities and achievements of my contemporaries. It may be true that the Roman state has sunk to such extreme misery that it has ceased to reward its loyal servants, but not for that reason does our age not produce a Brutus or Torquatus.

"What are you getting at?" you ask. I am speaking to you and about you, most accomplished sir. The state owes you the rewards which history applauds when paid to the above-mentioned men. For this reason, people with no knowledge of affairs had best suspend hasty judgments and abandon the habit of looking up to the men of the past and down on those of our own day. It is abundantly clear that the state defers its rewards, and that you deserve them.

Yet there is no great wonder in this. A nation of federates not only rudely manages Roman resources but is even destroying them at their very foundations. We have nobles and soldiers, warlike beyond even our hopes and the expectations of the enemy: but what is lacking is not their deeds as much as it is their rewards.

Farewell.

*Mamertus was bishop of Vienne. This letter, which looks back on the events of the blockade, is usually thought to date from about the time of the capture of Arles and Marseilles by the Visigoths in 473.*

[35] To the Lord Bishop Mamertus (7.1)

Rumor has it that the Goths have invaded Roman territory; our unhappy Auvergne is always their gateway on such incursions. We furnish fuel for the fire of our enemy's hatred for a special reason: by Christ's aid, we are the sole obstacle preventing them from establishing their frontier along the course of the Loire from the Ocean to the Rhône. The aggressive pressure of this threatening power has long swallowed up districts surrounding us and whole stretches of territory.

We are not sure that the scorched face of our walls, or the decaying palisade of stakes, or the ramparts worn by the breasts of guards on constant watch, will support our courage, so reckless and so dangerous. We only find comfort in the Rogations which were introduced under your auspices. The Arvernian people have begun to undertake the commencement and organization of these observances and, if not with the same effect [as in Vienne], at least with no less enthusiasm; this is the reason that the Arverni have not yet retreated from the terrors encircling them.

My enquiries did not fail to discover that the city entrusted to you by heaven was, at the time when these prayers were first established, being emptied of its population, who were being terrified by all kinds of signs. Earthquakes shattered the facades of public buildings with frequent shocks. Fires repeatedly broke out, burying fallen rooftops under mounds of ash. Then, deer, bold but inspiring fear by their tameness, provoked astonishment by making their lairs in the forum. In the midst of these signs, as the city became empty with the departure of its leaders and ordinary citizens, your prompt response was to revive the example of ancient Nineveh [cf. Jonah 3:5], so that your despair might not be a reproach to the divine warning. And in fact, you least of all could mistrust God without being sinful, after your own experience of his powers. One time, when a fire had broken out in the city, your faith burned hotter than the flames. In full sight of the terrified crowd, you alone stood forth to stay the fire, which recoiled, its flames curling backwards in retreat. Here was a wonder, terrifying, novel, and strange — a blaze, to which nature imparts no understanding, showed its regard for you by giving way.

First of all, for members of our order, and these few in number, you prescribed fasts, prohibited disgraceful behavior, announced penalties, and promised remedies. You explained to all that punishment was imminent, but so too was pardon. You taught that the threat of destruction which had been revealed was to be averted by frequent prayer. You warned that the constantly raging fires could be extinguished better by the water of tears than of rivers, and that the menacing shock of earthquake could be stilled by the firmness of faith. The lower class immediately followed your advice, and this influenced those of higher rank, who had shown no compunction about running away and were now not ashamed to return. God, who sees into all hearts, was appeased by this piety, and saw to it that your observances would be a salvation for you, an example to be imitated by others, and a defense for both. Thereafter in your city there were no catastrophes to bring disaster nor portents to cause fear.

The people of Clermont, knowing that all these ills that befell your people of Vienne before the Rogations have not befallen them since, are anxious to follow the lead of so holy a plan. And so they solicitously beg you yourself, blessed bishop, to use the advocacy of your prayers in support of those to whom you have already sent copies of the Rogations. In the history of our ancestors, not since the confessor Ambrose found the remains of two martyrs has anyone in the West, except for you, been granted a similar privilege; for you have translated in its entirety the body of Ferreolus along with the head of our martyr Julian, which once upon a time the executioner's bloody hand brought before the raging persecutor. What we ask as compensation is only fair — that a portion of patronage should come to us from Vienne, since a portion of our patron saint came to you from here.

Please keep me in your thoughts, my lord bishop.

*The reference to a treaty in this letter is sometimes thought to refer to the final negotiations with Euric, but without sufficient reason.*

[36] To his friend Calminius (5.12)
It is not pride on my part, but the unruliness of another, that makes my letters so few and far between. Don't expect me to be more explicit about this matter; your own fears, similar to mine, explain the need for silence.

One thing, however, I may openly lament. Sundered as we are by this whirlwind of warring forces, we have practically no chance of meeting one another. You never appear before the anxious gaze of your countrymen, except, as it happens, when at the whim of strangers we are forced to protect ourselves, you in your mail shirt, we behind our ramparts. At such time you are led against this land as a captive, obliged to empty your quiver of arrows and to fill your eyes with tears. We bear you no ill will; we know that your prayers are otherwise directed than your missiles.

Since in the meantime, even though we lack the security of a treaty, truces at least bring a glimmer of hope to brighten our prospects of liberty, I entreat you to write us as often as you can; you may be sure that our besieged citizens preserve in their hearts good feelings towards you and disregard the hateful part you play as their besieger.

Farewell.

*Constantius, the addressee of the next letter, was responsible for encouraging Sidonius to publish his letters. Some would identify him with the author of the* Life of St. Germanus *(see 33).*

[37] To his friend Constantius (3.2)

The people of Clermont salute you, a mighty guest visiting their humble cottages. You do not try to impress us with your retinue but you are pressed round with our affection.

Good God, what joy those afflicted people felt when you set your sacred foot within their half-ruined walls. What mobs crowded round you, males and females of every age and rank! How well did your stimulating speech speak to each and every one of them! How charming the small boys found you, how affable the young men, how serious the old! What tears you shed for buildings, brought down by the flames, and homes half-burned to the ground, as if you had been the father of us all! What grief you showed at the sight of fields buried under the bones of the unburied dead! And afterwards how encouraging you were, and with what spirit you urged us to rebuild!

Over and above all this, you found the city emptied no less by civil strife than by barbarian attack. You urged all to accept peace, and those to whom you brought back love you gave back to their homeland. At your admonition they rejoined a united cause no less than a united city. The restoration of people on the walls is your doing, as is the unanimity among a restored people.

For this reason, one and all well believe that you belong to them and that they belong to you; and they make no mistake as to what is your crowning glory. For day by day they all bear in mind how a person, advanced in years, frail in health, of the highest nobility, and respected for his piety, broke through obstacle after obstacle, simply out of love; one adversity after another stood in the way of your coming: long days treks and days of short duration, heavy snow and light fare, lonely expanses and cramped lodgings, and ruts in the roads, sodden with rain or rigid with frost; add to this, the public highways with their rough stones, rivers slippery with ice, hills with rugged approaches, valleys scoured by continual landslides. Because of all these discomforts, and since you sought no personal advantage, you took away with you the love of a whole city.

In conclusion, we pray to God that you live as long as you wish, tirelessly seeking, winning, and enjoying the friendship of good people; that the affection which you leave behind accompany you wherever you go; and that you long receive recompense for your labor on behalf of peace, whether you lay its foundations or erect the whole edifice.

Farewell.

*Another thank-you letter, possibly to be dated to the period following Sidonius's visit to Lyons in 474 (below, letter 42), but the events it describes could have occurred at an earlier stage in the blockade. Patiens was bishop of Lyons.*

[38] To Lord Bishop Patiens (6.12)
Opinions differ on this subject, but my own belief is that he lives most to his own advantage who lives for others and does heaven's work on earth by pitying the poverty and misfortune of the faithful.

"What are you getting at?" you ask. Most blessed father, my sentiments refer especially to you. Not content just to relieve the distress which you know at first hand, you push your inquiries to the very limits of Gaul and consider each case of want upon its merits without respect of persons. Povery or infirmity preventing someone from making his way to you in person are no hindrance. Your generous hand anticipates the needs of those whose feet are unable to bring them to you. You keep an eye out for provinces other than your own and the breadth of your concern includes relieving the distress of people living far away. And so it happens that, since the reserve of the absent may touch you no less than the pleas of those near at hand, you have often wiped away tears from the eyes of those you have never seen.

I say nothing of the daily labor you undertake to relieve the needs of your impoverished citizens by means of unceasing vigils, prayers, and charity.

I pass over your moderation, which always enables you to be considered as courteous as you are ascetic, so that the king in your parts [that is, Chilperic] is never known to tire of praising your meals and the queen your fasts.

I pass over your adorning of the church entrusted to your care with such good taste that the viewer is left uncertain whether the additions are better than the old fabric which has been repaired.

I pass over how, under your auspices, basilicas rise up from the ground in so many districts, and how their adornments are increased; how the condition of the faith is improved under your administration in so many ways that only the number of heretics is diminished; how, in a kind of apostolic hunt, you catch the wild minds of the Photinians in the spiritual net of preaching; and how barbarians are already your followers and, whenever they are overcome by your eloquence, stick to the trail you have set until you, a fortunate fisher of souls, draw them from the depths of error.

It may be true that some of these good deeds must be shared with colleagues; but there is one which is yours by, as lawyers say, special title, and which your modesty cannot deny. After devastion by the Goths, when the crops were all destroyed by fire, you sent at your own expense free supplies of grain for the general relief of the destitute throughout the ravaged provinces of Gaul, though it would have been relief enough to starving peoples if the product had come to them, not as a gift, but by the usual paths of commerce. We saw the roads crammed with your grain. Along the Saône and Rhône we saw more than one storehouse which you alone had filled.

*Sidonius, recalling tales of Triptolemus and Ceres, suggests that the legends of the pagans have been eclipsed by the deed of Patiens.*

If as an esteemed man of religion you find a comparison drawn from the Achaean superstition of Eleusis inappropriate, let me draw upon the industry of the venerable patriarch Joseph as an historical example (I leave aside the regard due his mystical significance). Because he had foreknowledge, he readily provided a remedy for the famine that was to follow the seven years of plenty. But from a moral pespective, in my opinion, that person is in no way inferior who provides aid in a similar emergency without knowledge of the future.

I cannot exactly tell how much gratitude the people of Arles and Riez, how much the residents of Avignon, Orange, and Viviers, how much the landholders of Valence and Trois Chateaux render to you; it is hard to count up the thanks of people who received provisions of food and had no need to count out a penny. But in the name of the city of the Arverni, I give you all the thanks I can. For you decided to help us despite the fact that we were not part of your province, our cities were not close, no convenient waterway connected us, and no payment had been offered. Through me the Arverni express their boundless thanks to you; with the addition of your supply of bread, they have been able to find enough to feed themselves.

Now that I have properly fulfilled the duty entrusted to me, I will go from being an envoy to a messenger. I would have you know immediately that your fame spreads through all Aquitaine; in the wishes and prayers of all, you are loved and praised, longed for and honored. In these bad times, you are a good priest, a good father, and a good year (as it were) to people to whom the risk of starvation would have seemed a reward had they no other way of experiencing your generosity.

Please keep me in your thoughts, my lord bishop.

*Magnus Felix is the same addressee as in letter 32, above. Licinianus was quaestor sacri palatii under Julius Nepos in 474. Licinianus was sent by the emperor to negotiate with Euric regarding the position of the Arvernians in late 474. He brought with him the letter conferring the patriciate on Ecdicius, referred to in letter 42, below.*

[39] To his friend [Magnus] Felix (3.7)

You have not written for a long time. Each of us is true to his habits: I chatter on, you hold your peace. And since in other obligations of friendship you are beyond reproach, I think your ability not to grow weary of such idleness is itself a kind of virtue. Will no thought of old acquaintance ever lift you from the rut of this interminable silence? Or are you really unaware that it is nothing short of insult to refuse a talkative man an answer? Immersed in your library or business, you give no sign of life, yet all the while expect the attention of a poor line from me, though you know quite well that mine is a ready rather than a gifted pen.

My anxieties at least ought to furnish subject enough for your pen. Mind that you load the hands of travelers with letters to relieve your friends' concerns and waste no time letting them know whether the *quaestor* Licinianus is likely, with God's direction, to open a safe passage out of our mutual state of consternation. He is described as one who has more than fulfilled the expectations formed of him, proving greater on acquaintance than his great repute, a man conspicuously endowed with every gift of nature and good fortune. A model of judgment, adorned with equal discretion and personal charm, this trusty envoy is worthy of the power which he represents. He is quite free from affectation or pretense; there is nothing feigned in the gravity which lends weight to his words. He does not follow the example of most envoys, who deliver their message without assurance and wish to be perceived as circumspect; but it is said that he is not to be numbered among those envoys who sell the secrets of the princes who send them and solicit from barbarians advantage for themselves rather than for their mission. Such is the character of the man as conveyed to us by favorable report.

Let us know at once if the description squares with the truth, so that in the meantime my people may catch their breath from their unceasing vigil. At present neither snowy day nor moonless or stormy night is enough to draw them from their watch upon the walls. Even were the barbarian to withdraw to winter quarters, their fears are too deep to be eradicated and at best can only be suspended. Soothe us with good news, for only our homeland is far away from you, not our cause.

Farewell.

*Julius Nepos overthrew the emperor Glycerius with eastern help and was proclaimed emperor in June 474. These two letters suggest some of the political consequences that attended news of his succession in Gaul. The addressee Apollinaris was Sidonius's uncle, living at the time at Vaison. Sidonius's personal intervention was made possible by the seasonal suspension of hostilities with the Goths. Thaumastus, brother of Apollinaris, had earlier been involved in the impeachment of Arvandus.*

*Chilperic was both master of the soldiers (probably appointed by Glycerius) and, at least by the second letter, king of the Burgundians. The term tetrarch, found in the second letter, seems to be an allusion to Chilperic's three brothers. One of them, Gundobad, was patrician under Olybrius and responsible for the appointment of Glycerius. He ruled as a king of the Burgundians to 516.*

[40] To his friend Apollinaris (5.6)

As soon as summer gave way to autumn and the fears of the Arvernians were brought under control for a time by the season, I journeyed to Vienne and visited your brother Thaumastus, whom I respect as a friend by virtue of our kinship and ages. He was in a very gloomy state of mind. Afflicted already by the recent loss of his wife, he was no less troubled on your account, being fearful and apprehensive that turbulent barbarians or corrupt soldiery might trump up some charge against you.

He is certain that the venomous tongues of certain villains have been secretly at work, whispering in the ear of the master of the soldiers, the ever-victorious Chilperic, that it was chiefly your doing that the town of Vaison was won over to the side of the new emperor. If you or yours are exposed to any suspicion on this score, inform me at once by sending back a personal note, so that you do not lose the benefit of my attention or representation. If you think there is really something to worry about, I shall make it my business either to gain for you good favor that will provide security or to learn the grounds of the anger so you can be more careful.

Farewell.

*The same context as the above letter. It is one of Sidonius's windier pieces, much abbreviated here. Lucumo/Tanaquil, Germanicus/Agrippina are allusions to Chilperic and his wife. The former pair were a legendary king and queen of Rome. Chilperic's queen's name was probably Caretena; Chilperic was the father of Chlothild, who mar-*

*ried Clovis (see 46, and cf. 89, 96). Cibyrates is an allusion to two brothers who helped the governor Verres plunder his province of Sicily in 73-70 B.C.*

[41] To his friend Thaumastus (5.7)

At last I have discovered the identity of those who have accused your brother before our tetrarch of siding with the partisans of the new emperor — unless, indeed, the concealed tracks of informers have escaped the keen senses of my trusty friends. The accusers are people, as you yourself have heard me say, whom Gaul endures with groans these many years, and who make the barbarians themselves seem merciful by comparison.

These are people whom even those who are feared fear. These are people whose peculiar occupation is to make false charges, to denounce, to threaten, and to snatch property. These are people whose efforts you hear praised when it is a time of rest; their spoils you hear about when there is peace, their evasions when there is war, and their victories when they are in their cups. These are people who delay cases when called [to preside over them] and block them when they are passed over; who become haughty if reminded [of their duty] and forgetful if they are enriched. These are people who pay for lawsuits and sell their mediations; who assign arbitrators, dictate their judgments, and tear up their decisions; who drag in litigants and drag out hearings; who drag off the convicted and drag back those whose business is being concluded...

Such are the characteristics of those who are overwhelming a man of outstanding goodness and power. And what can one man do, encompassed on every side by slanderers. What may he do whose nature suits the company of good men but whose life is lived among the wicked whose evil advice would make Phalaris more blood-thirsty, Midas more greedy, Ancus more vain, Tarquin more proud, Tiberius more crafty, Gaius more dangerous, Claudius more dull-witted, Nero more corrupt, Galba more covetous, Otho more reckless, Vitellius more prodigal, Domitian more ferocious?

But the chief consolation in our troubles is this: our Lucumo is restrained by his Tanaquil. With a timely and witty word, she rids her husband's ears of the poisonous tales instilled there by whisperers. You should know that up till now it has been her doing that the mind of our common patron has not been poisoned against the well-being of our brothers by these younger Cibyrates; God willing, that will never happen while the present power rules a Lyonese Germania, and our present Agrippina exerts her moderating influence on her and our Germanicus.

Farewell.

*While at Lyons in the autumn of 474, Sidonius heard news of the arrival of the impe-*
*rial representative, Licinianus. Sidonius's wife would have been still in Clermont. Ros-*
*cia, their daughter, was staying safely with her grandmother and aunts at Lyons. The*
*patriciate, which was now to be awarded to Ecdicius, had already been conferred on*
*Sidonius at some point in his career, probably just about five years before the present*
*letter.*

[42] To his wife Papianilla (5.16)
The moment the *quaestor* Licinianus, on his way from Ravenna, had crossed
the Alps and set foot on Gaulish soil, he sent a message in advance announcing his arrival. In it he declares that he is bearing a commission, which, when
he comes, will confer the title of patrician also on your brother Ecdicius,
whose honors delight you no less than my own. He has attained this distinction very soon, if you consider his age, but rather late if you consider his
achievements. For he paid for this promotion some time ago, not by weighing out payments in gold, but by serving in the field; and as a private citizen
he poured into the public coffers no mere contributions but the spoils of
war.

Julius Nepos, an emperor supreme in character no less than arms, has con-
scientiously discharged the commitment made by the previous emperor
Anthemius to reward your brother's labors. This is an action all the more
commendable for the speed with which the present emperor has made good
on a promise repeatedly given by his predecessor. The result is that hereafter
the best people will be able, and should feel obliged, to devote on behalf of
the state whatever resources they have, for even if an emperor should die, the
empire will always fulfill whatever that prince had promised to those working
in his service.

If I am right about your feelings, I am sure that even in the depths of
adversity you will derive great consolation from this news, and that not even
the dread of an impending siege will divert your thoughts from the joy we
both share. I well know that not even the distinction which was awarded to
me, and in which by law you had a share, pleased you as much as this one; for
though you are a good wife, you are the best of sisters. That is why I have lost
no time in writing a letter of congratulations for the distinction added, with
Christ's blessing, to your family's honors. In doing so, I both relieve your anxiety and make up for your brother's modesty; he would be sure to say nothing of his own promotion, and, even if somehow you were unaware of his
reserve, you would not blame him for his silence.

As for me, I derive great satisfaction from your family's distinctions, which
you have been awaiting with unconcealed impatience; but as great as they are
I take greater pleasure in the friendship which I hope will be maintained in
the future between our children and his. And I pray on behalf of our families

that just as we both, with divine favor, took families of praetorian rank and made them patrician, our children in turn may take patrician rank and make it consular.

Roscia, our joint care, sends you greetings. It may not be a common way to raise grandchildren, but she is being brought up by her grandmother and her aunts who temper their indulgence of her with a discipline that molds her character but is apppropriate to her tender years.

Farewell.

## F. CESSION OF CLERMONT AND THE AUVERGNE

*In 475 Epiphanius, bishop of Pavia (he is not mentioned by Sidonius) concluded an agreement with Euric. In the same year, a committee composed of four Gallic bishops, Basilius of Aix, Graecus of Marseilles, Faustus of Riez, and Leontius of Arles, arranged for the surrender of the Auvergne to Euric. The following two letters were written to members of this committee. Graecus was a frequent correspondent of Sidonius.*

[43] To Lord Bishop Basilius (7.6)

By God's gift our old ties of friendship are an example new to these times. It is true that for some time we have loved one another on equal terms. But as far as our shared spiritual life is concerned, you are the patron and I the client. I presume too much in saying even this. For so great is my unworthiness that even the proven efficacy of your intercession can hardly make headway against my constant backsliding.

Because you are my master twice over, both as patron and as friend, and because I well remember the fiery power of your thoughts and the flood of your words when I saw you pierce with the sword of spiritual testimony Modaharius, that Gothic citizen, who was brandishing the javelins of Arian heresy — for these reasons, and with all due respect and consideration to other bishops, I do no harm in reporting to you tearfully how in this age the wolf that feeds on the sins of lost souls stealthily preys upon the sheep-folds of the church, though the grip of his fangs still goes undetected. For the old enemy finds it easier to leap upon the bleating and abandoned sheep by first threatening the throats of the sleeping shepherds. I am not so oblivious of myself as ever to forget that I am somone whose conscience has yet to be washed clean by many tears; though, by God's grace, its excrement shall at some point be cleared away with the mystic rake of your prayers. But since the public welfare must take precedence over one man's guilty shame, I shall not hesitate to proclaim the cause of truth, even if someone charges me with vanity and criticizes the ardor of my faith.

Euric, king of the Goths, having broken and abrogated the old treaty, either defends or extends by right of arms the boundary of his kingdom. In this world a sinner like me is not allowed to lay a complaint nor a saint like you to carry out an investigation. Rather, if you ask me, it is the rule in this world for the rich to be clothed in purple and fine linen and for Lazarus to be stricken with sores and poverty. It is the rule that, as long as we dwell in this allegorical Egypt, Pharaoh will go with a diadem on his head, and the Israelite with the carrier's basket. It is the rule that, as long as we are burned in the furnace of this symbolic Babylon, we must sigh and groan for the spiritual Jerusalem like Jeremiah, while the Assyrian thunders in his royal pomp and treads the Holy of Holies beneath his feet. Yet when I consider the change from the blessings of this life to those of the life to come, I endure the calamities we all suffer with patience. For, in the first place, when I examine myself, any affliction that might occur seems lighter than what I deserve; then, I know well that the best cure for the inward man is for the outward man to undergo the flails of various sufferings in the threshing floor of this world.

I must confess that as formidable as the Gothic king may be on account of the victories of his forces, I dread Euric less as the assailant of our walls than as the subverter of Christian laws. They say that the mere mention of the name of Catholic so embitters his countenance and heart that one might better take him for chief of his Arian sect than monarch of his nation. Moreover, though he is mighty in war, quick witted, and in the prime of life, he still makes one big mistake — he attributes the success of his undertakings and his plans to the orthodoxy of his belief, whereas it is actually attained by earthly fortune.

For these reasons you should know right away the hidden malady of the Catholic church so that you may take steps to apply an open remedy. Euric has created a spiritual wasteland of considerable extent. Bordeaux, Périgueux, Rodez, Limoges, Javols, Eauze, Bazas, Saint-Bertrand-de-Comminges, Auch, and a much greater number of cities have been deprived of their bishops by death. They have not been replaced, and through them, of course, the ministry of the minor orders receives its appointments. This wasteland spreads day by day as the ranks of priests are diminished by death; congregations are so afflicted with despair at the loss of their bishops and the ruin of their faith that even the heresiarchs of the past (not to mention the heretics of the present) would be moved to pity. There is no administration in dioceses and parishes. You may see the debris of fallen roofs in the churches or doors off their hinges and the entranceways to basilcas blocked by thickets of thorn bushes. Worse still, you may see cattle, not only lying in half-open porticoes, but even eating grass from the sides of overgrown altars. And desolation is not found in country parishes alone; even the congregations of urban churches are thinning out.

What comfort remains to the faithful, when not only the teaching of the clergy perishes but even the memory of it? Of course when one of the clergy dies and a church acknowledges an heir to his office without the accompanying [episcopal] benediction, then the episcopal office has died in that church not just the bishop. And what hope would you say remains when the end of a man's life means the end of religion? Examine more closely the wounds of the spiritual body and you will readily understand that for every bishop snatched away the faith of a congregation is imperiled. I need not mention your colleagues Crocus and Simplicius, removed from the thrones to which they had been appointed and suffering the same exile, if different punishments. For one of them suffers in not being able to see his homeland, and the other suffers in being able to see the home to which he cannot return.

You for your part find yourself associated with the most holy bishops Faustus, Leontius, and Graecus by virtue of your city, your order, and your brotherly affection; through the agency of you bishops, the wretched terms of treaties are passed along; by your hands are conveyed the covenants and agreements of two kingdoms. Try to obtain as a chief article of the peace agreement permission to carry out episcopal ordinations so that we can hold those peoples of Gaul now included within Gothic territory for the faith, even if we do not hold them by the treaty.

Please keep me in your thoughts, my lord bishop.

*The ellipsis in the second sentence marks a lacuna in the text. On Amantius, see letters 25, 26.*

[44] To the Lord Bishop Graecus (7.7)
Here again is Amantius, the bearer of my trifles. He is returning to his beloved Marseilles to bring home, as is his habit, a little plunder from the city, provided... he is favored by an incoming cargo. I could use the opportunity of his journey to chatter on, if one and the same mind could handle joys and endure sadness at the same time. For the state of our unhappy corner of the world is now such that, according to report, conditions were less wretched during the war than they are with peace.

Our enslavement was made the price of another's security. A most grievous enslavement it is, for, if ancient times are recalled, the Arvernians dared to claim that they were brothers to Latium and regarded themselves as people of Trojan descent. If recent events are considered, these are the people who with their own resources halted the advance of enemies of the state. These are the people who, though repeatedly shut up within their walls, showed no fear of the Goths and, in turn, struck fear into the hearts of their attackers as they were stationed within their camp. Yet, they never reaped the benefit of their successes in the field; those served to bring you relief. And when there were reverses, they were the ones crushed by the misfortune. These are the people who, out of devotion to the state, were not afraid to bring to justice Seronatus, who was serving up the provinces to the barbarians; and after his conviction, the state could barely find the courage to execute him.

Is this is to be their reward for enduring scarcity, fire, sword, and disease, for glutting their swords in enemy gore and for fighting on though wasted by hunger? Is this, then, the famous peace we dreamed of, when we tore the grass from crannies in the walls for food; in our ignorance we were often poisoned by deadly grasses, which, being green, we gathered with hands made the same color by starvation and without being able to judge the properties of the leaves or pulp. Is it in return for so many remarkable proofs of our fidelity that we, according to my infornation, have been cast aside?

I hope you are ashamed of this treaty which brings neither honor nor advantage. The legations are channeled through you. Not only are the terms that have been negotiated revealed to you first of all, even though the emperor is not present, but the terms to be discussed are entrusted to you. I ask your pardon for telling you hard truths; distress removes any suspicion of abuse in my remarks. You have too little regard for the common good; when you meet in council, you are less concerned to relieve public dangers than to favor private interests. By the long repetition of such acts you begin to resemble the last instead of the first among your fellow provincials.

How long can sleights of hand like this go on? Our very ancestors will glory in that name not much longer if they begin to have no descendants. Use your advisory powers to try to break the disgraceful conditions of this agreement. If necessary, it will be a joy to endure siege again, to fight again, to starve again. But if we are handed over, we whom force failed to conquer, this is proof that you are the cowardly contrivers of any barbarous condition that you recommend.

But why do I give free rein to so much sorrow? You must make allowance for the afflicted and not blame those who are in mourning. Other regions that are surrendered have to expect servitude; the Auvergne awaits punishment. If you can hold out no help in our extremity, at least bring it about by your unceasing prayer that our blood lives on though our liberty is extinguished. Provide land for the exile, ransom for the captive, expenses for the refugee. If our city gates are to be opened to the enemy, let yours never be closed to your friends.

Please keep me in your thoughts, my lord bishop.

## G. SIDONIUS, A SUBJECT OF EURIC

### Exile and Confinement

*After the cession of Auvergne, Sidonius suffered a brief exile (among other penalties) and was lodged in the fortress of Livia, between Carcassone and Narbonne. The following two letters refer to this period of confinement.*

*The first letter is usually thought to have been written from Bordeaux, where Sidonius stayed for a time following his release from Livia in 476, but it could equally have originated from Livia itself. The letter has also been used to argue for an otherwise unattested exile prior to Sidonius's assumption of episcopal office.*

*The letter's recipient, Faustus, bishop of Riez and former abbot of the monastery of Lérins, may have been of British origin. He was one of the negotiators with Euric in 475 and was himself exiled around 476-484 for opposing Arianism.*

[45] To Lord Bishop Faustus (9.3)

Your old loyalty to a friend and your old mastery of diction are the same as ever, and so I admire your letters for their eloquent skill and for their expression of sincere affection.

But at the present juncture, if you do not mind me saying so, when the roads are no longer secure owing to the movements of peoples, I think the only prudent and safe course is to give up regular correspondence especially between these two cities which are so far apart. We must be less assiduous letter writers for a time and learn the practice of keeping quiet. This is a harsh and bitter deprivation when a friendship is as close as ours, but it is brought about not by casual circumstance, but by many causes at once definite, inevitable, and diverse in their origin.

First among them I must set the examination of letter-carriers by those guarding the highways. There may be no danger since letter-carriers have committed no crime, but they have to put up with endless annoyance, while some vigilant investigator pries into every aspect of their business. At the first sign of a faltering reply to the questions, they are suspected of carrying verbal instructions that have not been committed to writing. For this reason messengers are often made to suffer ill-treatment and the sender suspicion, especially at a time like this, when established treaties of kingdoms long each others rival have been destabilized once more by divisive terms.

Quite apart from this consideration, my mind is depressed by personal losses on every side. I was taken from my homeland under the pretext of performing a service, but actually under compulsion. Banished to this place I am broken by all sorts of of anxieties, since here I endure the hardships of an alien and there [at home] I suffer confiscation of my property. It is therefore by no means the right moment to ask me for letters with some polish, and were I to attempt them, it would be impertinence, for the exchange of a lively or elaborate correspondence is for the fortunate. To me it is a kind immoral barbarism to write jovially with a vexed spirit.

How much better it would be for you to confer the powerful benefits of your unremitting prayers upon a soul conscious of its guilt and trembling hour after hour as it recalls the debts of a sinful career. You are versed in the prayers of the island brotherhood, and you transferred them from the training ground of the hermit congregation and from the assembly of the monks of Lérins to the city where you preside over the sacred rites of the church. For all your episcopal rank, you are an abbot still in spirit and refuse to make your new dignity a pretext for relaxing the rigor of the ancient discipline. As I said, ensure for me by your most potent intercession that my portion is the Lord; that enrolled among the companies of my fellow tribesmen the Levites, I cease to be of the earth, I to whom no earth now belongs; and that I begin to live as much a stranger to the sins of the world as I am to its riches.

The third reason that I began to stop writing you is perhaps the most important. I have a boundless admiration for your tropical figurative style, and for that consummately varied and perfected diction of which your last letter affords such ample evidence...

There you have the causes of my present and future silence; I could not refuse a few words without disobedience, but henceforward I shall hold my peace and learn in silence...

Please keep us in your thoughts, my lord bishop.

*The following letter, recalling his confinement, was written after Sidonius's release from Livia, and after his return to Clermont. Leo was an advisor to Euric, and later Alaric II.*

[46] To his friend Leo (8.3)

I send you, as you ordered, the *Life of Apollonius the Pythagorean*, not as Nichomachus the Elder copied it from a manuscript of Philostratus, but as Tascius Victorianus copied it from a manuscript of Nichomachus. I was so eager to fulfill your wish that the result is a makeshift copy, with a wild, hurried, and rough transcription.

Yet the work took longer than expected, and for this you must not blame me. For as long as I was forced to stay within the walls of Livia — and the end of that inconvenience I owe, next to Christ, to you — my mind was sick with care, and I was really unable to get through your commission even in a desultory manner, being miserable at night and distracted by duties during the day. To make matters worse, when the evening hour recalled me at last from my post to my quarters quite exhausted, I could scarcely get a wink of sleep; a commotion would start near the skylight of my chamber caused by two old Gothic women — and two more drunken, vomiting, and quarrelsome creatures will never be found again.

As soon as my return home gave me a little leisure, I sent the book off, without polish and half-raw, an immature wine, as they say, but in doing so, I thought more of your anxiety to have it than of my own responsibilities.

Now that your wish is gratified, forsake for a while the laurel trees of Apollo, the font of Hippocrene, and those measures of which you alone are absolute master (though these, as is the way of trained poets like yourself, trace their source, not to Delphi, but to dedicated practice in the poetic art). Halt the renowned stream of an eloquence characteristic of you and your family, pouring from your ancestor Fronto through successive generations into your breast.

Lay aside for a moment the acclaimed speeches you compose as spokesman of the king. With these the glorious monarch strikes fear into the hearts of the peoples across the sea, or as victor imposes a treaty upon the barbarians trembling by the Waal, or throughout his expanded realm curbs force by laws as once he curbed peoples by force.

Shake off your endless cares and steal the leisure that belongs to you from the troubles and turmoil of the court. The story you demanded will not be read properly and to advantage unless you surrender yourself wholly to the book and voyage along with our Apollonius to the Caucasus and the Indus, and travel with him among the Gymnosophists of Ethiopia and the Brahmins of India...

*Sidonius concludes with a flattering, and very rough, comparison between Apollonius and Leo.*

Farewell.

## Euric's Court at Bordeaux

*After his release in 476 Sidonius, doubtless still subject to penalties, traveled to Bordeaux to wait, perhaps, on the pleasure of the king and to petition for property belonging to his mother-in-law. Lampridius, the letter's addressee, an old friend, was an orator and teacher at Bordeaux who enjoyed Euric's favor; in another letter Sidonius tells us that Lampridius died at the hands of his own slaves.*

*Sidonius had been cooling his heels for two months at the time this letter was written. Tityrus and Meliboeus are characters from Virgil's first ecologue.*

[47] To his friend Lampridius (8.9)
On my arrival at Bordeaux, your messenger delivered your letter, full of nectar, rich with blooms and pearls. You blame me for my silence and ask for

some of my verses, doing so with your own verses which sing in the mouth with the modulation of a many-holed flute. But you do this while benefiting from the the king's generosity and feel secure after enjoying his favors. Perhaps you have forgotten one satirist's remark about another: "Horace shouts for joy only when he has had enough to eat."

Why say any more? Since you are in a position of ease, you think you can tell me to sing because you are in a mood for dancing. However that may be, I obey, and I do so not only without compulsion but readily; only somehow you must control the stern look of a Cato-like judgment. You know well enough the joy of poets. Their spirits get entangled in grief as fish do in nets; when there is bitterness or sadness, the tender nature of the poet does not readily work itself free from the bonds of anguish. I still have not acquired any part of my mother-in-law's inheritance, even the usufruct of a third at the price of a half.

Meanwhile you can see whether the theme of the poem you demand is such as to please you; but distress will not let me live my life in one mood and write in another. It would not be fair for you to judge the poems we are now exchanging one against the other, as it were. I am troubled; you are happy. I am still an exile; you are now a citizen. This is the reason my verse is not on a level with yours: I ask for the same privileges as you, but do not get equivalent treatment.

If, however, you happen to be kind enough as to accept these trifles which I have composed in the midst of much mental tribulation, you will convince me that they are like the songs of the swan, whose cry is more melodious when it suffers pain; or that they are like the lyre's tightly strung strings, the music of which is sweeter the tighter they are wound. But if verses lacking relief and joy are unable to gain your approval, you will find nothing to please you in the sheet I have attached below. There is another consideration. A piece which you only read and cannot hear is robbed of the help which delivery by the author can give it. Once the work is sent off, there is nothing for even the most musical of poets to do; distance does not allow him to do what pantomime choruses commonly do — make bad verse acceptable by virtue of fine delivery.

> Lampridius, glory of our Thalia, why now do you try to elicit songs
> from Cirrha, or the Boeotian Muses, or Helicon's poetic stream dug by
> neighing Pegasus with a stroke of his hoof? Why do you repeatedly try
> to make me write, as if I had borne the Delphic implements for your
> Delian god, and, myself a new Apollo, controlled the cauldron and
> tripods, the lyre, the quivers, the bows, and gryphons, shaking here the
> berries and there the clusters of a two-fold foliage?
> You, Tityrus, have already regained your lands. You, a musician with

marvelous facility in string, voice, and verse, wander through the groves of plane and myrtle and strike the lyre; your words and music resound together in harmonious measures.

As for me, I am stuck here and have had but one audience, though two new moons have cast their gaze upon me. For even the king himself has little time since a subjugated world awaits his replies. Here we see the blue-eyed Saxon, previously accustomed to the sea, but now afraid of the land. The razor, not content to restrain its bite along the farthest border of his head, pushes back the hair-line; and so, with his hair clipped close to the skin, his head becomes smaller and his face longer. Here we see you, aged Sygambrian, whose head was shaved at the back after your defeat, now grow hair anew on an old neck. Here strolls the grey-eyed Herulian, inhabitant of Ocean's furthest shore, and almost of one complexion with its weedy deeps. Here the seven-foot Burgundian often bends his knee, begging for peace. Under the patronage of these [Visigoths], the Ostrogoth flourishes and repeatedly presses on the neigbouring Huns; submission to his patrons allows him to triumph over the Huns. Here, Roman, you seek protection; if the Great Bear starts a commotion among the hosts of the Scythian regions, your forces, Euric, are requested to oppose them, so that the Garonne, mighty thanks to Mars sojourning on its banks, may protect the meager stream of the Tiber. Here even Arsaces the Parthian asks to hold the lofty palace of Susa under a treaty promising subsidies. For he perceives that the full panoply of war is arising here in support of the Bosphoran regions [i.e. Constantinople] and believes that Persia, already dismayed at the mere sound of conflict, can scarcely rely on Euphrates' bank for protection. Although he fancies himself related to the stars and vaunts his kinship with Phoebus, here he makes supplication as a mere mortal.

Amidst all this, my days go by in fruitless waiting. As for you, Tityrus, stop calling upon me to sing. I feel wonder, not envy. And as I effect nothing and utter fruitless prayers, I have become like Meliboeus.

There is the poem. Read it at your leisure, and like a charioteer already crowned, look down from the podium to the arena where I still struggle in the sweat and dust. Whatever pleasure you derive from this present effort, do not expect me to do the like again, as long as I lament my losses rather than sing my songs.

## H. LAST THOUGHTS ON LATIN CULTURE, HISTORY, AND NOBILITY

### Roman Eloquence on the Moselle

*The addressee Arbogast was a descendent of the famous Arbogast, a Frankish officer who served as master of the soldiers under Valentinian II and Eugenius the usurper in the late fourth century. The Arbogast of the letter was count of Trier. I am inclined to agree with the placement of this letter soon after Sidonius's exile, but it might date much earlier in his episcopal career.*

[48] To his friend Arbogast (4.17)

Your friend Eminentius, great lord, has delivered a letter which you yourself composed, admirable in style, and replete with three shining qualities. The first of its merits is friendliness, which leads you to esteem my lowly talents even though I am a stranger and anxious now to avoid publicity. The second is modesty, which makes you apprehensive for no good reason but wins you the praise you deserve. The third is humor, which makes you wittily accuse yourself of writing trifles, whereas you have drunk at the well-spring of Roman eloquence and, though you drink from the Moselle, the taste of the Tiber is in your mouth; and so you are an intimate of barbarians, yet your speech commits no barbarisms. In eloquence and valor you equal the ancient generals whose right hands could wield the stylus no less skilfully than the sword.

The Roman tongue has long been effaced from Belgic and Rhenish lands; but if its splendor has anywhere survived, it is surely with you; though the authority (*iura*) of Rome has collapsed on the frontier, as long as you live and preserve your eloquence, the language does not falter. For this reason, as I return your greeting, I rejoice that traces of our vanishing literary culture remain in your illustrious breast; continue your assiduous studies and you will find that people with learning are as much above simple folk as humans are above beasts.

As for your desire that an inept exegete like myself should ramble on about the holy scriptures, you would do far better to direct your request to the clergy who live close to you and who are venerable in years, renowned for their faith, known by their works, ready in speech, and endowed with good memories — in sum, in all the sublimer gifts, my superiors. Even if we leave out of account the bishop of your city, a character of supreme perfection, blessed in the possession of every virtue and with a reputation to match, it is far better for you to consult on any problem whatsoever the celebrated fathers and chief priests of Gaul. Lupus [bishop of Troyes] is not too far away and Auspicius [bishop of Toul] is within your reach, and however inquisitive you may be, you will not exhaust a learning such as theirs. In any case, pardon me for disobeying this part of your request, and not just because you are kindly but for good reasons; for it is right that you should escape from incompetence, and it is equally right that I should avoid pretentiousness.

Farewell.

## A Request to Write History

*The addressee is the same Leo who served Euric and helped obtain Sidonius's release.*

[49] To his friend Leo (4.22)

The magnificent Hesperius, a gem in the crowns of friendship and letters, said on his return from Toulouse not long ago that you were advising me to turn my hand to writing history now that my books of letters were completed. I am deeply touched and receive a weighty opinion such as this with the utmost respect; for you proclaim me fit for greater tasks when you think I should abandon lesser ones. But, sorry to say, I find it easier to respect your judgment than to follow your advice.

The task you recommend is worthwhile, but no less so if you do it yourself. Even in ancient times Tacitus made the same suggestion to Pliny and then took his own advice. The precedent shows that such an undertaking has more relevance to you than me; for I yield to Pliny as his pupil, whereas in the old historical style you rightly surpass Tacitus. Were he to come to life in our day and could witness your literary eminence and reputation, he would now truly be the 'silent one' (*tacitus*).

You, therefore, are the man to shoulder the burden of your own proposal; for you have the considerable advantage of immense amounts of information, in addition to remarkable eloquence. Daily, in the council of a powerful king, you become thoroughly acquainted with the whole world's business and laws, its wars and treaties, its regions and distances, and its faults. Who better then could prepare himself for this task than he who has obviously come to know the movements of peoples, various forms of embassies, the deeds of generals, the agreements of rulers, in short the privy affairs of states, and who from his preeminent position has no need to suppress the truth or to manufacture a lie?

How different is my own condition. My recent sojourn in foreign parts was an affliction, and my old reading is of no benefit; moreover religion is my profession, humility my desire, and insignificance keeps me out of sight. My trust is no longer in the matter of the present world, but in the hope of a world to come. Finally, failing strength hampers me and now (or perhaps too late) makes idleness pleasing to me. I am no longer concerned that my literary efforts receive the praise of my own generation or even of the generation to come.

I am determined to seek little glory from history especially because we churchmen are rash if we publish our own affairs and vainglorious if we deal with the affairs of others; we record the past without advantage and the present from imperfect knowledge; we write what is untrue to our disgrace, and what is true at our peril. History is the kind of subject in which you win scant credit for mentioning good men and incur serious disfavor for referring to infamous ones. Thus from the outset the quality and spirit of satire blends with the historian's style. Historical writing, then, is quite incompatible with our religious profession; it begins with ill-will, is carried on through toil, and ends in hatred. But all this is the outcome only when the writers are clerics — the viper's teeth of complainers grips us, and we are called mad if our work is plain, and presumptuous if it is done with precision.

But your fame grants you the power to trample the necks of detractors or the celebrity to transcend their complaints, and so if you readily take upon yourself this subject matter, no one will have written in a more exalted fashion than you, and no one so near the antique manner, even though your theme be the story of our own times. For as you were previously imbued with eloquence and are now well versed in the affairs of the world, you have provided the poisoned fang with no opportunity to lacerate you. And so in years to come your works will be consulted with advantage, heard with delight, and read with the assurance of authority.

Farewell.

## Culture and Nobility

*The addressee of this letter is not otherwise identifiable.*

[50] To his friend Johannes (8.2)
I should hold myself guilty of a crime against learning, most accomplished friend, were I to defer congratulations on your own success in deferring the decease of literature. When she was, as it were, dead and buried, it is your glory to have revived, supported and championed her, and, in the storm of wars, you are the sole teacher in Gaul who has brought the Latin tongue safely into port, though her military forces have suffered disaster.

Our contemporaries and our successors should all with one accord and with fervent gratitude dedicate to you in various locations statues (if permitted) and portraits, as to a second Demosthenes or Cicero. By your teaching these generations have been moulded and educated, and, now in the power of an unconquered but foreign people, they shall preserve this evidence of their ancient birthright. Since the grades of rank are now abolished which once distinguished the high from the low, hereafter the mark of nobility will be the knowledge of letters.

I, above all others, am deeply indebted to the benefits your teaching confers. As it is my habit to write, laboring on something for posterity to read, I am assured at least of your school and its instruction turning out a crowd of qualified readers.

Farewell.

# CHAPTER NINE

# CLOVIS, KING OF THE FRANKS, A. 481/2–511

*Chlodovechus* — *Clovis, according to modern French and English usage, or Louis, in a later medieval form of the name* — *was the founder of a Frankish state that came to include most of the Roman provinces of Gaul, as well as territories across the Rhine. The permanent acquisition by the Franks of territories in southern Gaul dates from Clovis's defeat of Alaric II, king of the Visigoths, at the battle of Vouillé in 507. Clovis's descendants, called the 'Merovingians'* — *a family name derived from the king's grandfather Merovech (see **78–80**)* — *ruled until 751, when they were pushed aside by a new dynasty, the Carolingians. Clovis's father, Childeric, was a king of the Salian Franks in northern Gaul and, ostensibly at least, in Roman service (for the historical sources of his activities, see **35** and cf. **23c**; for the legendary ones, **78–80, 87–8**). The Frankish kingdom that Clovis created is viewed by moderns as laying the foundation of France and Germany.*

*Accounts of Clovis's career have traditionally been based on the famous description of the king's reign in the* Histories *of Gregory, bishop of Tours (**46**, below). But Gregory's history, which is the only source to give us a narrative, was composed some time after the king's lifetime: Clovis died in 511 and Gregory, who was born a generation later, completed writing his history in 594, the year of his own death. Modern scholars have become increasingly skeptical about the biases of Gregory's approach to his subject and, as consequence, have tried to gauge the credibility of the bishop's account against earlier, especially contemporary, sources. For example, a problem recurrent in the modern literature on Clovis is the date of the king's baptism in the Catholic faith, an event often seen as a watershed in European history. Gregory connects Clovis's conversion, and subsequent baptism, to the persuasive efforts of his wife Chlothild, and then to the king's battlefield victory against the Alamanni in 496. The dates for his baptism suggested by modern scholars on the basis of earlier sources range from 496, Gregory's date, to 508, the year after the famous battle of Vouillé, in which Clovis, whom Gregory portrayed as a champion of Catholicism, defeated the Arian king of the Visigoths, Alaric.*

*The following selections are the chief sources for the king's reign, arranged in chronological order. They are, with the exception of Gregory's narrative, all letters of one kind or another. Readers should be aware that the rhetorical and epistolographic conventions of the age, combined with the occasional faulty transmission of the text, make some turns of phrase obscure or ambiguous and that more than one translation can sometimes be supported. Editors have on occasion resorted to emendations (sometimes mistaken for variants by scholars), which in my translation I have tried to keep to a minimum. In a couple of instances where I have found the text unrecoverable in the Epistolae Austrasicae, I have placed ellipses.*

## 38. LETTER OF BISHOP REMIGIUS OF RHEIMS TO CLOVIS, a. 481/2

*In 481 or 482, at the time of his succession to the kingship of his father, Clovis was still a boy, probably of fifteen. There were other kings of the Franks at the time. The following letter is best dated to Clovis's succession, but some would date it following his defeat of Syagrius in 486 (below, **46**, c. 27).*

*The author of the letter, Bishop Remigius, was metropolitan of Belgica secunda. Bishop of Rheims for over seventy years (ca. 458-ca. 532), Remigius outlived Clovis by two decades; he is also the author of a letter on the occasion of the death of the king's sister (**40**, below) and another letter that dates just after the king's death (**44**, below). A letter that Remigius received from Sidonius Apollinaris is also extant (**37.21**).*

Source: *Epistolae Austrasicae,* no. 2, ed. W. Grundlach, MGH Epistolae 3: Epistolae Merowingici et Karolini Aevi 1, with Emendata by Bruno Krusch, pp. 719-20; reprinted (and re-edited in conformity with Krusch's emendations) in CCSL 117, ed. Henri Rochais. Translation by A.C. Murray.

Bishop Remigius to the noted lord, greatly esteemed for his merits, King Clovis.

Great news has reached us that you have taken up the administration of Belgica secunda. It is no surprise that you have begun to be as your parents ever were. You, who have already reached the very top by the practise of humility, must see to it through your merit that God's favorable judgment does not turn from you, for, as the saying goes, the deeds of a man are tested.

You must summon to your side counselors who can enhance your reputation. Your bounty should be pure and decent and you should pay respect to your bishops and always have recourse to their advice; and if there is good agreement between you and them, your province will better endure. Encourage your citizens, give relief to the unfortunate, support widows, and nourish orphans... Let justice issue from your mouth. Expect nothing at all from the poor and strangers in case your desire to receive their gifts or anything else increases. Let your court be open to all, so that no one shall depart from there downhearted. Whatever paternal property you possess, free captives with it and release them from the yoke of servitude. Should anyone come into your presence, let him not feel like a stranger. Joke with the young, hold discussions with elders — if you would reign, render judgments nobly.

## 39. LETTER OF BISHOP AVITUS OF VIENNE TO CLOVIS REGARDING THE KING'S BAPTISM, ca. 496-99(?)

*Avitus, Catholic bishop of Vienne (ca. 494-ca. 518) was the leading religious figure in the Burgundian kingdom. The king for most of his episcopacy was Gundobad († 516), who was an Arian Christian. Avitus was the author of homilies and poems, and a number of his letters are extant; he corresponded with, among others, the son of Sidonius Apollinaris (cf. **46**, c. 37, below), to whom he was related.*

*The most famous, and controversial, of Avitus's letters is the one below to Clovis on the occasion of the king's baptism. Avitus tells us the day of the event, Christmas, but not the year. The circumstance leading to the baptism should be compared with the account of Gregory of Tours (**46**, c. 31, below). Some scholars claim to find in the letter evidence of a pagan, Frankish belief in the divine descent of Clovis's ancestors. The 'prince' at the beginning of paragraph three is best understood as the emperor Anastasius (a. 491-518), whose rule at first promised a return to orthodoxy in the East. I regard the famous Sirmondian version of this passage as a gloss.*

Source: Epist. ad diversos 46, in *Alcimi Ecdicii Aviti Viennensis episcopi opera quae supersunt*, ed. Rudolf Peiper, MGH AA 6.2 (1883), pp. 75-76. Translation by A.C. Murray.

Bishop Avitus to King Clovis.

The followers of all kinds of sects have cast the shadow of the name Christian over your keen intelligence with their views, diverse in their conjecture, various in their great number, and empty as far as truth is concerned. While we consign those views to Eternity and, while we reserve to a future investigation anything each person thinks is right, still, the radiant ray of truth shines forth at the present time. Indeed, divine providence finds in our day a certain arbiter. Though you choose on your own behalf, you make a judgment for us all: your faith is our victory.

In this same issue [of conversion], a great many people — if by the exhortation of priests or at the prompting of associates they are moved to seek out the sanity of believing — are accustomed to adduce as an impediment the customs they inherit with birth and ancestral practices; thus harmfully preferring reverence to salvation, they reveal that they do not know how to choose anything, while preserving, as prisoners of unbelief, useless veneration for their parents. Let harmful shame give up this pretext after the miracle of such a deed. From the entire garland of ancient descent, you are content simply with nobility and have tried to draw from yourself whatever can adorn in its entirety the summit of nobility of your own descendants. You have authors of good deeds [in your lineage]; you have wished to be the author of better ones. You answer to your ancestors by reigning in the world; for the sake of posterity, you make provision to reign in heaven.

By all means let Greece rejoice in having chosen a prince who is one of us [that is, who is Catholic]: but Greece is not alone in deserving the gift of so great a favor. Your world too is illuminated by its own renown, and, in the western regions, in the person of a king, the light of a not new radiance shines brilliantly. The start of its glory coincided with the nativity of our Redeemer. Thus in fitting fashion the regenerating waters brought you forth to salvation on the day when the world received the Lord of heaven, who was born for its redemption. The day renowned as the Lord's birthday is also yours — when you were born to Christ and when Christ was born to the world. On this day you have consecrated your soul to God, your life to the present generation, and your fame to posterity.

What is to be said now about the glorious ceremony itself celebrating your rebirth? Though I did not take part in person in the services, still I did not fail to participate in the rejoicing; for God laid upon your territories the duty to give thanks, and news of the lofty humility with which you were professing to be a catechumen reached us before your baptism. For that reason, the sacred night [of Christmas] found us, after waiting for it, already sure of what you were to do.

Indeed, I pondered and contemplated the nature of that event, when the numerous band of bishops, joined together in the energetic pursuit of holy service, supported the royal limbs in the life-giving waters; when the head, feared by the nations, bowed itself to the servants of God; when the hair, fostered beneath the helmet, put on the saving helm of sacred oil; when the covering of armor was taken off and purified limbs shone with the same kind of glow as the baptismal robes. The softness of that baptismal covering shall do just what you believe it will, most flourishing of kings, it shall, I say, cause in turn the hardness of your war harness to be more effective for you; and whatever good fortune has furnished to this point, let sanctity now augment it.

Now I would like to append to the congratulations you receive some encouragement, in case anything escapes your knowledge or religious practice. Shall I preach to someone who is righteous the faith that you have seen without a preacher before you achieved righteousness? Or shall I perhaps preach humbleness, which some time ago you already displayed towards us out of reverence, and which you now for the first time owe as a part of your profession of faith? Or shall I preach mercy, which a people, freed by you and until recently still captive, made known to the world with its joy and to God with its tears? There is one matter I would have improved. Since God through you makes your people completely His own, I would have you extend from the good treasury of your heart the seed of faith to more remote peoples whom none of the sprouts of perverse dogma has corrupted, because they are still situated in a state of natural ignorance. Be not ashamed or reluctant to send embassies on the matter and to add to the realm of God, who has raised up yours to such an extent...

*The letter breaks off at this point with an incomlete sentence alluding to Clovis's designs on pagan peoples outside Gaul.*

# 40. LETTER OF BISHOP REMIGIUS TO CLOVIS ON THE DEATH OF THE KING'S SISTER

*Gregory of Tours, who quotes the opening of the letter, says Clovis's sister was baptized at the same time as her brother (46, c. 31, below). On Remigius, see above, 38.*

*Emendations have not solved all the textual problems of this letter. In the opening passage I have followed variants in Gregory's* Histories. *Gregory gives the sister's name as Albofledis; the MS of the* Epistolae Austrasicae *has Albochledis.*

Source: *Epistolae Austrasicae*, no. 1; see **38**, above.

Bishop Remigius to Lord Clovis, illustrious in merit, king.

I am sorry, deeply sorry, for the cause of your sadness, the death of your sister of good memory, Albofledis. But we can take comfort that, when a person such as her departs from the light of this world, she should be held in high regard rather than mourned. For her life was such that, chosen by God and, it may be believed, received by the Lord, she has passed on to heaven. She lived for your faith, and...Christ fulfilled her desire to receive the blessing of virginity. Consecrated, she must not be mourned, she who blazes in the sight of God with a maidenly blossom, whereby she is protected by the crown which she took up on behalf of virginity. May she not be mourned by the faithful, she who deserved to be Christ's sweet perfume; for through Him, to whom she is pleasing, she can give help to those who make a request.

My lord, drive grief from your heart. With a spirit suitably composed, govern the kingdom more wisely, taking up loftier counsels by cultivating tranquillity. With happy heart, strengthen the other parts. Shake off the listlessness of mourning and you shall more ardently pay attention to salvation. You still have to administer the kingdom, and, with God's favor, to direct its course.

You are the head of peoples and preserve the political order. They are accustomed to seeing in you auspicious signs — may they not see you in mourning afflicted with moroseness. Be yourself the solace of your heart; preserve in your mind the power of that innate foresight, so that sadness does not remove clarity of thought. With regard to the present passage of her who, we must believe, has been joined to a virgin choir, the King rejoices in heaven.

I salute your glory and I introduce to you my attendant, the priest Maccolus, whom I have sent. I have to beg you to overlook the fact that I have presumed to send words of encouragement, though I should have met with you. If, however, you order me through the bearer of this message to come, I shall take to the road, despising the bitterness of winter and ignoring the cold, and strive to come to you, with God's help.

## 41. THREE LETTERS OF THEODERIC THE GREAT FROM THE *VARIAE* OF CASSIODORUS, a. 506/07

*Cassiodorus held a number of important positions under the Ostrogothic regime in Italy, including that of* quaestor *of the palace (ca. 506-ca. 511), master of the offices (a. 523-527), and praetorian prefect (a. 533-37); he also held the consulate and patriciate. In 537 he compiled a collection of his official correspondence to provide models of letter writing and to display his literary talents to his admirers. This collection, called the* Variae, *contains specimens of a number of letters written on behalf of the Ostrogothic king Theoderic the Great concerning Gallic affairs in the period before Vouillé.*

*Three of these letters are translated here: one is addressed to Clovis and concerns a recent Frankish victory over the Alamanni; two others, attempting to stave off hostilities between Clovis and Alaric, are addressed to Clovis's northern neighbours and to Clovis himself. The last two letters were part of a series of appeals made to the interested parties, including Alaric, king of the Visigoths, and Gundobad, king of the Burgundians.*

*Theoderic, who was married to Clovis's sister Audefleda, had married one of his daughters to Alaric and another to Sigismund, Gundobad's son. Around this time Theoderic also married his niece to Hermanfred, king of the Thuringians. Cf.* **47** *III 4, 5; and* **20**, Marius, *s.a. 522.*

Source: Cassiodorus Senator, *Variae* II 41, III 3, 4, ed. Theodore Mommsen, MGH AA 12 (1892). Translation by A.C. Murray.

### a. To Clovis on his Victory over the Alamanni, ca. 506

*This letter has been used to argue that Gregory of Tours incorrectly dated Clovis's defeat of the Alamanni, and hence his baptism (below, no.* **46**, *cc. 30, 31). The letter probably dates to the years prior to 508, as in that year a panegyric of Ennodius of Pavia mentions Theoderic's reception of Alamannian refugees. This conflict is hardly likely to have been the only one between Clovis and the Alamanni.*

We give thanks for the relationship we have with your valour, for the Frankish people, idle in ancient times, you have successfully roused to new battles and, with your victorious right hand, have put down the Alamanni, who have given way to stronger claims. But since the perpetrators of treachery deserve to have such excess checked, and not all should be punished for the fault of the chief culprits, moderate your actions against the tired remnants. You see that they have fled for protection to your own relations; the courtesy you owe them requires that the fugitives be allowed to get away. Do not be hard on those who hide in terror in our regions. It is a memorable triumph that the fierce Alamannian is so afraid that you can force him to beg you for the gift of his life. It is enough that king fell, along with the pride of his people. It is enough that a populous nation has been subdued, some of it by the sword and some of it by enslavement. For if you clash with the rest, you shall think that you have still not conquered all of them. Listen to someone repeatedly tested in these kinds of matters. The wars that turned out well for me were those brought to a moderate conclusion. For the man who knows restraint in all matters conquers continually, and the pleasure of good fortune tends to favor him who does not become unbending and excessively harsh. And so give in graciously to our way of thinking, for as a rule the prerogatives of kinship usually prevail....

I have also sent an experienced cithara player as you requested. May his singing and playing divert your glorious majesty with fine music. We think he will be welcome, since you had a special concern that he be sent to you.

### b. To Clovis's Northern Neighbors on the Eve of the Visigothic War: A Common Letter to the Kings of the Heruli, Warni, and Thuringians

*Despite the reference in this letter to Gundobad's support of Theoderic's position, the Burgundian king ended up aiding Clovis in the Visigothic war.*

There is general agreement that measures should be taken against pride, a quality always hateful to the divinity. For whoever tries with deliberate unfairness to overthrow a renowned nation does not decide to treat others with justice. The worst habit is to disdain truth. If an arrogant man happens to conquer in a detestable war, he believes that all things will yield to him.

You are ennobled by a sense of virtue but angered when you contemplate abominable presumption: send your envoys, along with mine and those of our brother King Gundobad to Clovis, king of the Franks, to tell him to halt the war with the Visigoths out of a regard for justice and to have recourse to the law of nations; otherwise, he will suffer the invasion of all for holding the judgment of so many in contempt. What more does he want than to be granted complete justice? Let me state my opinion plainly: whoever tries to do without law is someone whose plan is to shatter the kingdoms of all. It is better if a dangerous enterprise is stopped in its early stages; in that way, what would be a struggle for each may be won without hardship for any. Recall now the good will of the elder Euric [a. 466-484] and the many gifts with which he gave you assistance and how often on your behalf he warded off threats of war by neighboring peoples. Repay the favor to his son, recognizing that it also contributes to your own well-being. For whoever gets the better of so great a kingdom will dare to attack you without hesitation....

### c. To Clovis regarding his Dispute with Alaric

The god-given ties of affinity try to take root among kings to this end, that their pacifying spirit may bring forth the peace that peoples desire. This is sacred and must not be breached by any disturbance. What pledges guarantee good faith, if it lacks the affective ties of nature? Rulers are linked by kinship so that separate peoples should glory in the same desire, and, as if through certain channels, the longing of nations for harmony can be united and joined together.

In these circumstances, I am astonished that your feelings are so roused by petty reasons of complaint that you want to sustain a serious collision with our son Alaric, just when many who fear you will find joy in your dispute. Both of you are the kings of great peoples, both of you are in the prime of life. You will not shake your kingdoms lightly, if you are both allowed to come into conflict. Let your bravery not be the unexpected destruction of a homeland, for the mighty fall of peoples attends the serious ill-will of kings in small disputes.

Let me state my opinion freely, let me state it in the spirit of friendship. To immediately assemble troops at the first embassy shows a lack of self control. What is being sought from kinsmen may be attained once adjudicators have been chosen. They are even agreeable to including among such mediators men you choose. What would you yourself think of me if you learned that I neglected your complaints? Avoid a clash where one of you will mourn your defeat. Put down the sword if you wish to contradict my reproach.

By the right of a father and a friend I threaten you. He who thinks such warnings are to be despised —and I do not imagine this — will have myself and my friends as enemies.

For this reason I have taken special care to send so-and-so and so-and-so to you as envoys, through whom I have also sent letters to your brother and our son, King Alaric, so that no foreign maliciousness can sow dissension between you. But by staying at peace, you should bring to an amicable conclusion matters that belong among friends. I have authorized the envoys to speak with you on certain issues so that the peoples who have long flourished in peace under your kinsmen should not be brought to ruin by sudden disturbance. For you should believe him whom you know to be kindly disposed toward your well-being, since whoever tries to place another in a dangerous situation, assuredly gives him dishonest advice.

## 42. LETTER OF CLOVIS TO AQUITANIAN BISHOPS ON THE KING'S PEACE AND APOSTOLIC LETTERS, a. 507/08

*This interesting letter is probably the closest we will ever come to the 'real' Clovis. It should not be read as a personal letter, however, but rather as an official expression of royal policy at a particular moment, when an invasion of Visigothic territory was underway. It is usually dated to 507, and the campaign that brought about the defeat of the Visigoths at the battle of Vouillé. The bishops addressed in the letter are presumably those in the districts in which campaigns were being mounted. Cf.* **46**, *c. 37, below.*

Source: *Chlodowici regis ad episopos epistola*, ed. A. Boretius, MGH Capitularia regum Francorum 1 (1883), pp. 1–2. Translation by A.C. Murray.

Clovis, king, to holy lords and bishops worthy of an apostolic see.

Since report divulges the declaration and command issued to our entire army before we invaded the homeland of the Goths, we could not overlook [informing] your blessed selves [of it].

In the first place, we have commanded with respect to the rights of all churches, that no one is to try to seize any kind of property, neither from religious women nor from widows who can be shown to be dedicated to the service of the Lord; likewise, from clerics and the children of both clerics and widows staying in the homes of their parents. So too, with regard to slaves of the churches, who are established by the oaths of bishops to have been taken from the churches, the command has been given that none of them are to suffer any violence or injury.

Moreover, so that their former condition is respected, we have commanded that, if any of the above are forced into captivity, they be restored without any delay at all, whether [they reside] within or outside a church.

Regarding other lay captives who are proven to have been taken into captivity outside the peace, there is no question that you may send apostolic letters [of intercession] to anyone you wish.

Obviously as far as those people, lay or clerical, who are seized within our peace are concerned, let apostolic letters by all means be sent to me, provided you truly authenticate your letters, sealed at the bottom with your ring. You should be aware that a directive obtained from our court must be validated.

There is this stipulation. Our forces ask that on whomever's behalf you see fit to furnish your letters, you are not to delay declaring by an oath in God's name, and with your own blessing, that what you ask for is true: for the capriciousness and lies of many have been discovered, so that one perceives the truth of the scriptural phrase, "The righteous perishes with the unrighteous [cf. Gen. 18:23]."

Pray for me, holy lords and fathers worthy of an apostolic see.

## 43. LETTER OF THE BISHOPS OF THE COUNCIL OF ORLEANS TO CLOVIS, a. 511

*In 511 Clovis summoned the first general council of the Gallic church held under the Frankish kings. About half the bishops of the kingdom, some thirty-two, attended the council and subscribed to its decrees. Within this number, northern bishops were few and the newly conquered territories were well represented. The record of the council opens with a letter addressed to Clovis.*

Source: *Concilia aevi Merovingici*, ed. Friedrich Maasen, MGH Concilia 1 (1893). Translation by A.C. Murray.

To their lord the most glorious king Clovis, son of the Catholic church, greetings from all the bishops whom you have ordered to attend the council.

Concern for the glorious faith so impels you to improve the Catholic religion that you have ordered the bishops to assemble together in order to discuss the state of episcopal opinion as to what needs to be done. In accordance with the instructions and the agenda (*tituli*) that you supplied, we are reporting precisely what we think is the best action to take. If in your judgment what we have decided seems correct, may the agreement of so great a king and lord sanction with even greater authority the implementation of the decision of so many bishops.

*Thirty one canons of the Council follow. For some of these, see* **74a**.

## 44. LETTER OF BISHOP REMIGIUS REGARDING THE ORDINATION OF A CERTAIN CLAUDIUS, ca. 512

*On Remigius, see above, **38**. There are a number of obscurities in the letter and the passage on Celsus is corrupt. Nothing else is known of Claudius.*

Source: *Epistolae Austrasicae*, no. 3; see **38**, above.

Bishop Remigius to lords truly holy and in merits most blessed, brothers in Christ, Heraclius [bishop of Paris or Sens], Leo, and Theodosius [bishop of Auxerre].

Paul the apostle says in his letter [I Cor. 13:18], "charity never fails." Charity is something that has no place in your feelings when you send me such a message. On behalf of Claudius, who, you write, is no priest, I have issued a simple request that you relate to me the displeasure you feel. I do not deny he committed a serious offense. But you might have respected my age, even if not my merits, for, with God's favor, it may be said: I have had care of an episcopal see for fifty three years and no one has addressed me so impudently. You say, "It would have been better had you never been born." It would have suited me not to hear myself reproached as a transgressor. I made Claudius a priest, not corrupted by bribery, but on the recommendation of the most distinguished king, who was not only a propagator of the Catholic faith but its protector. You write, "What he ordered was not canonical. You perform the highest function of the priesthood." It was the protector of the regions, guardian of our homeland, conqueror of nations, who gave the command. Your outburst against me was so motivated by bile that you failed to give respect to the author of your own episcopacy.

I have asked that Claudius, the perpetrator of sacrilege, be reserved for penance.

*Scriptural justifications of penance follow.*

...From your holiness' angry speech, I understand that you offer no pity to the lapsed after their downfall; but I see that you prefer that he not repent and live, although God says, "I do not want the death of the dying but that they repent and live [cf. Ez. 18:23; 33:11]." It is useful for us to follow this precept, not overlooking the will of God but abiding by it, for He appointed us not to exercise wrath but to provide for people and to serve pious duty rather than rage.

You mention in your letter the removal of a certain Celsus, who put his faith in Claudius, and you are unaware whether he is alive or dead; you admonish me to be his hunter, not knowing if he should be sought in this world or in hell, and you wish me to restore his property, which I did not know was taken away. You admonish impossibilities, as you relate impieties.

You write that I am in my jubilee years, ridiculing, rather than celebrating out of affection, someone whom you neither spare nor respect, having dishonestly broken the bond of love.

## 45. LETTER OF NICETIUS, BISHOP OF TRIER, TO CHLODOSWINTHA, QUEEN OF THE LOMBARDS, ca. 564

*Chlodoswintha was the daughter of Chlothar I and granddaughter of Clovis. This letter, sent to her by Nicetius, bishop of Trier (a. 525/6-post 561), was an exhortation for her to win over her husband Alboin to Catholicism; Alboin was king of the Lombards in Pannonia and an Arian Christian. The first part of the letter, omitted here, gives doctrinal arguments for the superiority of orthodoxy over Arianism and then emphasizes the miraculous power of Gallic, Catholic saints, especially that of Saint Martin of Tours. The letter is, among other things, evidence for traditions about Clovis's conversion and baptism before Gregory of Tours wrote his* Histories.

Source: *Epistolae Austrasicae*, no. 8; see **38**, above.

Nicetius, sinner, to the lady Chlodoswintha, most merciful daughter in Christ, queen.

...You have heard how your grandmother, the lady Chlothild of good memory, came into Francia, how she led Lord Clovis to the Catholic faith; and, since he was a most shrewd man, he did not wish to give his agreement before he knew the truth. When he recognized that what I have mentioned above had been proven, he prostrated himself on the threshold of Lord Martin [of Tours] and promised to be baptized without delay. When he was baptized, you have heard all he accomplished against the heretic kings Alaric [II] and Gundobad; you are not unaware of what he and his sons were given to possess in this world.

As splendid a figure as Alboin is said to be, and as preeminent as is his reputation throughout the world, why has he not converted and why does he appear to be slow to demand the road of salvation? Good God, You who are the glory of the saints and the salvation of all, enter that man! And you, Lady Chlodoswintha, when you send word, grant the comfort of us all being able to please God by rejoicing at such a star, at such jewel. I send such greetings as I can. I beg you not to be indolent: incessantly proclaim, incessantly sing. You have heard the saying, "The husband without faith shall be saved by the wife with faith [cf. 1 Cor. 7:14]." For you should know that she first receives salvation and forgiveness who causes the sinner to be converted from his error. Keep watch, keep watch, for you have a kind God. I ask that you so act as both to make the Lombard people strong against its enemies and to allow us to rejoice over your salvation and that of your husband.

## 46. THE CAREER OF CLOVIS ACCORDING TO GREGORY BISHOP OF TOURS (†594)

*On Gregory's* Histories, *see* **X**, *Introduction. The account of Clovis appears in Book II 27-43; the book closes with the king's death. The headings in boldface are Gregory's.*

Source: Two editions were used for this translation: (1) *Historiarum libri X*, ed. Bruno Krusch and Wilhelm Levison, MGH SRM I/1, 2nd. ed. (1937-1951) (2) *Zehn Bücher Geschichten*, ed. Rudolf Buchner, vol. 1 (Berlin, 1955). Translation by A.C. Murray.

### 27. Clovis Becomes King

On Childeric's death [a. 481/82, at Tournai], his son Clovis reigned in his place.

In the fifth year of Clovis's reign [a. 486/87], Syagrius, king of the Romans and son of Aegidius, had his headquarters in the city of Soissons, which the late Aegidius had held. Clovis, along with his kinsman Ragnachar, who himself also held royal power, marched against Syagrius and challenged him to make ready a field of battle. Syagrius wasted no time, nor was he afraid to stand his ground. And so both sides joined battle, and Syagrius, when he saw his forces crushed, turned tail and slipped off at great speed to King Alaric [II, a. 484-507] at Toulouse. But Clovis sent Alaric an ultimatum to hand Syagrius over or to expect an attack for harboring him. Alaric was afraid to run afoul of the anger of the Franks for Syagrius's sake — it is the habit of the Goths to tremble with fear — and handed him over bound to the envoys. Clovis ordered his prisoner held in custody, but, when he had taken possession of Syagrius's kingdom, he had him put to the sword in secret.

In this period, many churches were plundered by the army of Clovis, because he was still enveloped in the errors of paganism. It happened that his forces took from a certain church a ewer of marvelous size and beauty, along with other items used in religious services. The bishop of that church sent messengers to the king, asking that, if his church could get back no other sacred vessel, might it at least obtain the ewer.

When the king heard this, he said to the messenger, "Follow us to Soissons, for there all the spoils are to be divided. When I get the vessel during the sharing of the spoils, I will grant what the bishop wants."

They came to Soissons and, when all the plunder was laid out in the open, the king said, "I ask you, most valiant fighting men, do not refuse to grant me that vessel" — he meant by this the above mentioned ewer — "over and above my share."

"All we see before us is yours, glorious king," said the more sensible ones when they heard the king's words. "Even we ourselves have been brought under your lordship. Go ahead and take what you desire, for no one can stand up to your power."

When they had spoken like this, one unthinking, envious, fool raised his ax and drove it into the ewer.

"You shall get nothing from here but what a regular division awards to you," he cried in a loud voice.

All were astounded at this act. The king covered his sense of outrage with a show of gentle forbearance. He took the ewer and restored it to the church messenger, keeping the wrong he felt buried in his breast.

A year passed. He commanded every unit to assemble with full equipment in order to exhibit on the March field the good condition of their arms. The king's intention was to inspect everyone, and he came to the man who had struck the ewer.

"No one carries weapons as poorly maintained as you," said the king. "Neither your spear, your sword, nor your ax are any good."

The king grabbed the man's ax and threw it to the ground. As the man started to lean over to pick it up, the king raised his own ax in both hands and planted it in the fellow's head.

"This is what you did to that ewer in Soissons," said the king.

With the fellow lying dead, the king dismissed the rest, having gained a considerable amount of fearful respect by his act.

Clovis waged many wars and won many victories. For instance, in the tenth year of his reign [a. 491], he made war on the Thuringians and subjected them to his rule.

## 28. Clovis Marries Chlothild

Another king at the time was Gundioc, king of the Burgundians [a. 455–473/74?], from the lineage of that [Gothic] persecutor [of Christians] Athanaric [† 381]. He had four sons: Gundobad, Godigisel, Chilperic, and Godomar. Gundobad put his brother Chilperic to the sword, tied a stone around the neck of Chilperic's wife, and drowned her. He sentenced her two daughters to exile. The elder of the daughters was called Crona; she put on the habit of a religious. The name of the younger was Chlothild.

Clovis often used to send delegations into Burgundy where his envoys discovered the young Chlothild. They reported to King Clovis how they had observed that she was refined and intelligent and had learned that she was of royal descent. The king lost no time in sending an embassy to Gundobad, asking to marry her. Gundobad was afraid to refuse and handed her over to the envoys, who took the girl and quickly brought her before the king. He was quite delighted when he saw her and took her for his wife. He already had by a concubine a son called Theuderic.

### 29. Baptism of their First Born Who Dies in his White Robes

The king had by Queen Chlothild a firstborn son. The mother wanted the boy baptized and constantly gave instruction to her husband.

"The gods you worship are nothing," she would say. "They could help neither themselves nor others, since they were fashioned of wood, stone, or metal. As for the names that you have given them, these were the names of men, not gods. Saturn, for example, was a man who, so it is said, fled from his son to avoid being deprived of royal power. And Jove also, the filthiest practitioner of every indecency, defiler of men, mocker of kinswomen, was someone who couldn't even keep himself from sex with his own sister, as she herself said, 'both sister and wife of Jove' [Aeneid I 46 f.]. What were Mars and Mercury capable of? They were endowed with magical arts rather than in possession of power of the divine kind.

"Who should be worshipped is He who at a word created out of nothing heaven and earth, the sea and everything within it; who caused the sun to shine and adorned the heaven with stars; who filled the waters with reptiles, the earth with animals, the air with birds; He, at the nod of whose head the lands are adorned with fruits, the trees with apples, the vines with grapes; He, by whose hand the human race was created and by whose largesse every creature was made to render service and support to the human whom He created."

Although the queen would say this, the king's spirit was brought no nearer to believing.

"By the command of our gods," he would say, "all things are created and come forth. And as for your God, he plainly can do nothing, and what's more, he turns out not to be descended from the gods."

In the meantime, the faithful queen presented her son for baptism and had the church adorned with hangings and drapery, so that he who could not be prevailed upon by instruction might more readily be brought to believe by this mystery. The boy was baptized and called Ingomer, but he died, still wearing the white robes of his baptism.

The king as a result became bitter and was not slow to reproach the queen.

"If the boy had been dedicated in the name of my gods, he would surely have lived; after baptism in the name of your God, he was utterly incapable of living."

"To almighty God, creator of all things," replied the queen, "I give thanks. He has judged me not at all unworthy and seen fit to admit to His kingdom a child born of my womb. My heart is untouched by grief at this event, because I know that those called from this world in their white baptismal robes will be cherished in the sight of God."

Afterwards she bore another son, who was baptized and whom she called Chlodomer.

When he too began to grow ill, the king would say, "There can only be the same outcome for him as for his brother — having been baptized in the name of this Christ of yours, he will die right away."

But the mother prayed, and, by the will of God, the child recovered.

### 30. War Against the Alamanni

Now the queen never ceased instructing the king to recognize the true God, and to abandon his idols. But in no way could she bring him to believe, until at last, when waging war upon the Alamanni, he was forced by necessity to confess what of his free will he had denied. It happened that, when the two hosts joined battle, the slaughter was fierce and the army of Clovis was in danger of annihilation.

When he saw this, the king raised his eyes to heaven, and, with a change of heart, began to weep.

"Jesus Christ," he said, "You who are proclaimed by Chlothild to be the Son of the living God, who are said to give aid to those in distress and to grant victory to those that put their hopes in You, I humbly implore Your glory for help. If You grant me victory over these enemies, and if I experience the power that people dedicated to Your name claim to have proven is Yours, then I shall believe in You and be baptized in Your name. For I have called upon my own gods, but as I am finding out, they have stopped helping me; so I don't think they have any power, if they don't come to help their servants. I now call upon you and wish to believe in you, provided I am rescued from my enemies."

As he said this, the Alamanni turned tail and started to run away. And when they saw that their king was killed, they yielded themselves to Clovis.

"We beg you," they cried, "stop the destruction of our people, now that we are yours."

The king put an end to the conflict, and, having admonished the people and returned home in peace, he recounted to the queen how he had been found worthy of victory by calling on the name of Christ. This happened in the fifteenth year of his reign [a. 496/7].

### 31. The Baptism of Clovis

At that point, the queen gave orders for the holy Remigius, bishop of the city of Rheims, to be summoned in secret and persuaded him to impart the word of salvation to the king. The king was brought to a private meeting and the bishop began to teach him to put his faith in the true God, maker of heaven and earth, and to abandon idols, which were of no use to either himself or others.

"Most holy father," said the king, "I myself have willingly listened to you; but there is still a problem. The people who follow me will not accept abandoning their gods; still, I will go and speak with them as you have taught me."

He met with his followers. Before he could speak, God's powers having preceded him, all the people shouted out together, "Dutiful king, we shall drive away our mortal gods, and we are ready to follow that immortal God preached by Remigius."

The news was brought to the bishop, who, filled with great joy, ordered the font to be prepared. The streets were canopied with colored hangings, the churches adorned with white drapery, the baptistery was set in order, the smell of incense spread, fragrant candles sparkled, and the whole baptismal church was filled with the divine fragrance. God granted such grace to those present there that they thought they had been transported amidst the fragrances of paradise.

To begin, the king asked to be baptized by the bishop. The new Constantine advanced to the font to wipe out the disease of the old leprosy, to wipe away in new waters the filthy stains borne from ancient times.

As the king entered the water, the saint of God eloquently addressed him with the words, "Gently bow your head, Sicamber; worship that which you have burned; burn that which you have worshipped."

Now holy Remigius the bishop was extraordinarily learned and especially proficient in rhetoric; in addition, he was so outstanding in holiness that he was the equal of holy Silvester in performing miracles. There is now a book of his life that tells how he raised a man from the dead.

Then the king, acknowledging almighty God in the Trinity, was baptized in the name of the Father, the Son, and the holy Spirit, and anointed with holy chrism under the sign of the cross of Christ.

As for his army, more than three thousand men were baptized.

His sister Albofledis, who not long after passed on to the Lord, was also baptized. When the king was depressed over her death, holy Remigius sent him a letter of consolation, which began like this: "I am sorry, deeply sorry for the cause of your sadness, the death of your sister of good memory, Albofledis. But we can take comfort that, when a such a person departs from this world, she should be held in high regard rather than mourned."

Another sister of the king was also converted. Her name was Lantechildis, and, though she had fallen into the heresy of the Arians, she acknowledged the Son and the holy Spirit as equal to the Father and received the holy chrism.

### 32. The Destruction of Godigisel

At this time the two brothers Gundobad and Godigisel were in possession of a kingdom in the area of the Rhône and Saône, including the province of Marseilles. Both they and their people were followers of the Arian sect.

Since the brothers were at odds with each other, Godigisel, who had heard of the victories of King Clovis, secretly sent envoys to him to say, "If you give me help to go after my brother, so I can either kill him in battle or drive him from the kingdom, I will pay you each year such tribute as you may wish to impose."

Clovis gladly took the offer and promised him aid whenever it was required. At the appointed time, he brought his army against Gundobad.

On hearing the news, Gundobad, unaware of his brother's treachery, sent him a message: "Come to my assistance, for the Franks have mustered against us and are approaching our territory to take it. Let us be of one mind against a people who are our enemies to avoid suffering separately what other peoples have gone through."

"I shall come with my army," said Godigisel, "and give you aid."

The three kings put their forces in the field at the same time — Clovis marching against Gundobad and Godigisel — and came to the fortress of Dijon with all the accoutrements of war. Battle was joined on the banks of the Ouche [a. 500]. Godigisel joined Clovis, and their united forces crushed the army of Gundobad. Observing his brother's treachery, which he had not suspected, Gundobad turned his back and, fleeing along the bank of the Rhône, entered the city of Avignon.

As for Godigisel, with victory achieved, he promised Clovis a part of his kingdom and went away in peace, entering Vienne in triumph, as if he were already master of the entire kingdom. Clovis reinforced his troops and went in pursuit of Gundobad, intending to drag him from Avignon and kill him.

When Gundobad heard about this, he was terrified, fearing the sudden approach of death. He had in his company, however, Aridius, a man of illustrious rank, energetic and intelligent, whom he summoned to a meeting.

"I'm hemmed in on all sides and don't know what to do," said the king. "These barbarians have attacked me with the intention of killing me and bringing ruin to the whole country."

"You have to soothe the wildness of this man, if you're to avoid destruction," answered Aridius. "So, providing this plan meets your approval, I shall now pretend to desert you and go over to his side. Once I am in his confidence, I shall make sure that they bring ruin neither on you nor on this country. For your part, you must ensure that whatever demands he makes of you on my advice are carefully fulfilled, until such time as the Lord sees fit, in his goodness, to have your cause succeed."

"I shall do whatever you tell me," said the king.

After this discussion with the king, Aridius said farewell and, taking his leave, went off to King Clovis.

"See, most dutiful king," he said to Clovis, "I come into your power as a humble servant, abandoning that most wretched man Gundobad. If your goodness will see fit to receive me, you and your offspring will find in me an honest and faithful servant."

Clovis accepted him quite readily and kept him by his side. Aridius was a delightful story-teller, full of advice, fair in judgment, and faithful in his duties.

Then, while Clovis was investing the walls of the city with his army, Aridius said to him, "King, if your majesty would kindly listen to a few humble words of mine, I would like to furnish advice and, though you have little need of it, it is completely in your interest; it would also suit both you and the cities through which you decide to pass.

"Why," asked Aridius, "do you keep this army in the field, when your enemy is protected by stout fortifications? You lay the fields waste, consume the meadows, pull apart the vines, cut down the olive trees, and destroy all the products of this region; still, you can do nothing to hurt him. Instead, send emissaries to him and impose tribute that he will pay to you every year. In this way the country can be saved, and you will be lord over a tribute-payer forever. If he refuses that, then you may do what you want."

The king took the advice and gave orders for his army to return home. At that time he sent envoys to Gundobad, imposed tribute on him and ordered him to pay it every year. Gundobad paid it immediately and promised to pay it hereafter.

### 33. The Destruction of Godigisel

After these events, Gundobad restored his forces. Then disdaining to pay the promised tribute to King Clovis, he brought an army against his brother Godigisel, shut him up in the city of Vienne and besieged the city.

When provisions began to run out among the lesser folk, Godigisel became afraid that the shortage might reach all the way to himself and so he ordered them driven from the city. When this was done, among those driven out was the artisan who looked after the aqueduct. Resentful at being driven out with the others, he went in a fury to Gundobad and pointed out how the king could break into the city and take vengeance on his brother.

The artisan led a force along the aqueduct, preceded by a good number of men carrying iron crowbars. The aqueduct had a vent covered by a great stone. Under the direction of the artisan, this was heaved aside by use of the crowbars, and so they entered the city, surprising from the rear those who were firing arrows from the walls. At the sound of a trumpet from the midst of the city, the besiegers seized the gates, opened them up, and crowded in. While the people of the city were caught between two forces and were being cut down on both sides, Godigisel took refuge in the cathedral of the heretics and there he was killed along with the Arian bishop. Next the Franks who had been with Godigisel gathered together in a tower. Gundobad, however, gave orders that none of them should suffer any harm; he had them seized and sent them to King Alaric to be exiled at Toulouse. He killed the senators and Burgundians who had accepted Godigisel.

Gundobad brought back under his authority the whole country now known as Burgundy. He established milder laws among the Burgundians to prevent them dominating the Romans.

### 34. Gundobad's Desire to be Converted

When Gundobad recognized that there was nothing to the claims of the heretics, he acknowledged that Christ, the Son of God, and the holy Ghost were both equal to the Father and asked Avitus, the holy bishop of Vienne, to grant him the chrism in secret.

"If you really believe what you say," answered the bishop, "you should fol-low the teaching of our Lord himself. For He said, 'If anyone acknowledges Me before the world, I will also acknowledge him before my Father, who is in heaven; but whoever denies Me before the world, him I will also deny before my Father, who is in heaven' [Cf. Matt. 10: 32, 33]. When He was teaching His holy and beloved blessed apostles about the temptations of future persecutions, He urged them, 'Beware of people; for they will deliver you up to councils and will scourge you in their synagogues, and you shall stand before kings and governors for My sake as a witness to them and to the nations' [Cf. Matt. 10: 17, 18]. You are a king and have no fear of anyone lay-ing hands on you, but you are frightened of an insurrection among the peo-ple and dare not acknowledge in public the Creator of all. Stop being so foolish, and that which you say you believe in your heart, utter with your lips before the people. For as the blessed apostle said, 'With the heart one believes for the sake of righteousness, but with the lips one makes confession for the sake of salvation' [Cf. Rom. 10: 10.]."

*More scriptural references on the same subject follow.*

...This argument confounded Gundobad, but he persisted in this madness to his dying day and would not acknowledge in public the equality of the Trinity.

This was a period in which the blessed Avitus was full of eloquence. For at the request of King Gundobad, he wrote against heresy that was arising in Constantinople, both the teaching of Eutyches [ca. 440] and of Sabellius [ca. 250] that there was nothing divine about our lord Jesus Christ. His splendid letters are extant: once they put down heresy, now they edify the church of God. He wrote one book of homilies, six books in verse on the creation of the world and various other subjects, and nine books of letters, including the ones just mentioned.

He relates in a homily he wrote on the Rogations that these particular services, which we celebrate before the triumph of the Lord's ascension, were established by Mamertus, bishop of Vienne, Avitus's own see, at a time when the city was alarmed by many portents. It was, for example, shaken by frequent earthquakes; also wild stags and wolves entered the gates and, as he says, wandered about the whole city without fear. These signs occurred throughout the course of a year and, as the services of the Easter period approached, the entire community devoutly awaited the mercy of God, so that this day of great commemoration might put an end to this fear. But during the very vigils of that glorious night, while mass was being celebrated, suddenly the royal palace within the city was set ablaze by fire from heaven. While everyone was stricken with fear and rushed from the cathedral, believing that either the whole city would be consumed by this fire or the earth would open up and swallow it, the holy bishop lay prostrate before the altar, begging God's mercy with groans and tears. Why say more? The prayer of the famous bishop reached the heights of heaven; the river of flowing tears quenched the burning palace. When these events had taken place, and, as I have said, the day of the Lord's ascension approached, he imposed a fast upon the people, and established the manner of prayer, the times when the fast could be broken, and the joyful disbursement of alms. The alarming events ceased after that; news of the deed spread through all the provinces, causing all the bishops to follow the example of his faith. Down to the present time, these services are held, in Christ's name, with repentant heart and contrite spirit, in all churches.

### 35. The Meeting of Clovis and Alaric

Then Alaric, king of the Goths, saw that King Clovis kept conquering nations, so he sent envoys to him to say, "If it pleases you, my brother, I am convinced that, by God's grace, we two should meet."

Clovis did not refuse and came to meet him. They got together on an island in the Loire near the village of Amboise in the territory of the city of Tours. They held discussions, ate and drank together, and, after swearing mutual friendship, departed in peace. At this time many people in Gaul had by now the most ardent desire to have the Franks as rulers.

### 36. Bishop Quintianus

As a result it happened that Quintianus, bishop of Rodez, was driven from the city for this offense. "For it is your desire," said his enemies, "that this land fall under the rule of the Franks."

A few days afterward, a quarrel arose between him and the citizens. The Goths who lived in the town became suspicious of him when the citizens accused him of wishing to put them under Frankish rule. They came to a decision to put him to the sword. When news of the plan reached the man of God, he arose in the middle of the night with his most faithful attendants, left Rodez and came to Clermont. There he was welcomed by holy Bishop Eufrasius, successor to the late Aprunculus of Dijon. Eufrasius maintained him, bestowing on him houses, lands, and vineyards.

"The riches of this church are sufficient to support both of us," he said, "provided brotherly love as preached by the blessed apostle persists among the priests of God."

The bishop of Lyons also bestowed upon him some of his church's properties located in the Auvergne.

The rest of the holy Quintianus's story, both the intrigues he endured, and the works the Lord saw fit to perform by his hands, is written in the book of his life [that is Gregory's own *Life of the Fathers*, 4].

### 37. War against Alaric

Then King Clovis said to his men, "I take it very badly that these Arians hold part of Gaul. With God's help, let's go and conquer them and bring the land under our authority."

Since this talk was to everyone's liking, he mustered his army and brought it to Poitiers. At the time, King Alaric was staying there. Since part of Clovis forces were crossing the territory of Tours, the Frankish king, out of respect for the blessed Martin, issued an edict that none of his troops were to avail themselves of anything from that district but grass as fodder and water.

A certain soldier, finding hay belonging to a poor man, said, "Has the king not authorized us to take grass and nothing else? Well, this is grass, and we shall certainly not be breaking his order if we take it."

He attacked the poor man, taking his hay by force, but report of his deed reached the king, who, quicker than it takes to say it, had him put to the sword.

"How shall there be hope of victory," asked the king, "if we offend the blessed Martin?"

The army was content to take nothing more from this district. As for the king, he sent a message to the blessed basilica.

"Go now," he said to the messengers, "and perhaps you shall receive a sign of victory from that holy temple."

At this time he gave gifts for them to present to the holy place.

"If you, Lord, are my help," said the king, "and have decreed that this unbelieving nation, which is always jealous of you, is to be delivered into my hands, please disclose for my sake at the entrance to the basilica of holy Martin if you will see fit to favor your servant."

His retainers hurried off and came to Tours as the king had commanded. As they were entering the basilica, the precentor who was leading the singing happened to intone this antiphon: "You have girded me, Lord, with strength for battle. You have subdued under me those rising up against me. You have caused my enemies to show me their backs, and You have destroyed those who hate me" [cf. Ps. 17: 40-1].

The messengers, hearing the singing, gave thanks to God and, vowing gifts to the blessed confessor, joyfully brought the news to the king.

Afterwards, when Clovis had reached the Vienne river with his army, he had no idea where to cross it, because the river was swollen by heavy rains. That night he begged the Lord to please show him a ford where he could cross the river. At dawn a hind of marvelous size entered the river in front of them at God's command, and, on its fording the river, the troops saw where they could cross.

When the king came to the Poitiers district and was camped some distance from the city, a fiery beacon issuing from the basilica of the holy Hilary seemed as if it reached out over the king; it showed that the king would, with the light of the blessed confessor Hilary, more readily overcome the legions of heretics against whom the saint himself had so often clashed for the sake of the faith. The king called upon the whole army not to despoil travelers or to seize anyone's property in the Poitiers district.

There was in the territory of Poitiers in those days a man praiseworthy for holiness, Abbot Maxentius, who lived as a recluse in his own monastery out of respect for God. I have given no particular name to the monastery, since to our own day the place has been known as the cell of the holy Maxentius. When the monks saw a troop of soldiers drawing near the monastery, they implored the abbot to come out of his cell to help them. When he took his time, stricken with fear they opened the cell door and brought him out. He went fearlessly to meet the soldiers to ask for peace. One of their number drew his sword to take a swing at the abbot's head, but when his hand was raised to his ear it stiffened and the sword fell backwards out of his hand. He fell at the feet of the holy man, begging his pardon. When the rest saw this, fearing they might all perish, they returned to the army terrified. As for the man's arm, the blessed confessor made it better again, applying consecrated oil to it and making the sign of the cross. By his intercession the monastery remained unharmed. He performed many other miracles; anyone who cares to look for them will find them all by reading the abbot's Life.

[This took place] in the twenty-fifth year of Clovis's reign [a. 507].

Meanwhile, King Clovis encountered Alaric, king of the Goths, on the field of Vouillé at the tenth milestone from Poitiers, the Goths engaging the enemy at a distance, the Franks fighting back at close quarters. When, as is their habit, the Goths turned in flight, King Clovis himself, by God's aid, obtained the victory. As his ally, he had Chloderic, son of Sigibert the Lame; this Sigibert limped after being wounded in the knee during fighting against the Alamanni around Zülpich. Then, when the Goths had been put to flight, and the king had killed Alaric, two of the enemy suddenly encountered him and struck at him with their spears on each side; but thanks to his body armor and a fast horse, he escaped with his life.

On this field at this time fell a very large contingent of Arvernian troops and their leaders, who were of senatorial families. This force was under the command of Apollinaris.

Amalaric, son of Alaric, fled from this battle into Spain and shrewdly took possession of his father's kingdom.

Clovis sent his own son Theuderic by way of the cities of Albi and Rodez to Clermont. Off he went and subjected to his father's authority those cities from the Gothic to the Burgundian frontiers.

Alaric's reign lasted twenty-two years.

As for Clovis, who spent the winter in Bordeaux, he carried off all Alaric's treasures from Toulouse and came to Angoulême. The Lord showed him such favour that the walls fell down by themselves before his eyes. He drove out the Goths and at that time subjected the city to his own rule.

After that, with victory achieved, he returned to Tours and gave many gifts to the holy basilica of the blessed Martin.

### 38. On the Patriciate of King Clovis

Then Clovis received from the emperor Anastasius documents conferring the consulate on him and, in the church of the blessed Martin, having been vested in the purple tunic and chlamys, he set a diadem upon his head. Mounting his horse, he dispersed gold and silver to the people lining the road that runs between the gate of the atrium [of Martin's basilica] and the cathedral church of the city, scattering it with his own hand with a most generous liberality and, from that day, was hailed as consul or Augustus.

He left Tours and came to Paris, where he established the seat of his government. There he was also joined by Theuderic.

### 39. Bishop Licinius

Then on the death of Eustochius, bishop of Tours, Licinius was consecrated as eighth bishop after Martin. In his time was waged the war which I have described above, and in his time King Clovis came to Tours. Licinius is said to have been to the East, to have visited the holy places, to have even entered Jerusalem itself, and to have often seen the sites of the passion and resurrection of our Lord, which we read about in the Gospels.

### 40. The Destruction of the Elder Sigibert and his Son

When Clovis was living at Paris, he sent a secret message to the son of Sigibert: "Look, your father has grown old, and limps on a bad leg. If he were to die, his kingdom would by right be yours, together with our friendship."

The prince, led astray by his desire for power, made arrangements to kill his father. One day his father left Cologne and, after crossing the Rhine, decided to take a walk in the forest of Buchau. He was taking a midday nap in his tent when his son, setting assassins upon him, had him killed in order to get possession of the kingdom.

But, by the judgment of God, the son fell into the pit which he had dug to trap his father.

He next sent messengers to King Clovis announcing his father's death and saying, "My father is dead, and I control his kingdom and treasures. Send some of your servants to me and I shall gladly hand over whatever might please you from his treasure."

Clovis answered, "I am grateful for your good will, and I ask that you disclose all the treasure to my messengers, but keep it for yourself."

On the arrival of the envoys, the prince opened his father's treasury.

"In this little chest my father used to keep gold pieces," he said, as they were looking at various items.

"Dip your hands to the bottom," said the messengers, "and find out how much is there."

So he did, and, when he was bent right over, one of them raised his ax and buried it in his brain, and in this way he deservedly met the same death that he had dealt his father.

When Clovis heard that Sigibert and his son were dead, he came to Cologne and called all that people together.

"Hear what has happened," he said. "While I was sailing on the river Scheldt, Chloderic, son of my kinsman, was in pursuit of his father, claiming that I wanted to kill him. When his father fled through the forest of Buchau, he delivered him over to death, setting bandits on him and killing him. He also has been killed, struck down by I don't know who, while opening his father's treasures. I am in no way a party to these deeds; for I couldn't spill the blood of my kinsmen — that would be a criminal act. But since these events have happened, I give you this advice, if it seems agreeable to you: turn to me, and come under my protection."

Those who heard this roared their approval, clashing their shields and shouting; and raising Clovis upon a shield, they made him their king.

Having acquired the kingdom of Sigibert and its treasury, he also received those people under his dominion. For daily the Lord laid his enemies low under his hand and increased his kingdom, because he walked before Him with an upright heart and did what was pleasing in His sight.

## 41. The Destruction of Chararic and his Son

After this he went against King Chararic. When Clovis had been at war with Syagrius, he had summoned Chararic to aid him, but Chararic kept his distance, helping neither side, and awaiting the outcome of events in order to ally himself with whoever emerged victorious. For this reason Clovis angrily marched against him. He captured Chararic and his son by trickery, bound them and cropped their hair, and even ordered Chararic to be ordained a priest and his son a deacon.

When Chararic lamented his humiliation and wept, it is said that his son replied, "These branches have been cut on green wood. They do not wither at all but shall sprout and grow. May he die just as quickly who did this."

Rumor reached the ears of Clovis that they were threatening to let their hair grow and kill him. He ordered both of them to be executed at the same time. After their death, he took possession of their kingdom, their treasury, and their people.

## 42. The Destruction of Ragnachar and his Brother

At that time Ragnachar was king in Cambrai, a man whose wantonness was so unbridled that he hardly spared his own near relatives. In this he had a counselor Farro, who was smeared with the same filth. It was said about him, that the king, when presented with any food or gift, or anything at all, used to say that it was sufficient for him and his Farro. On this account the Franks were bursting with anger.

For this reason it came to pass that Clovis gave gold armlets and belts to Ragnachar's *leudes* to entice them to call him in against their lord — actually the gifts only looked like gold, everything being copper, gilded to fool them. Afterwards, Clovis mustered his forces against Ragnachar, who frequently sent out scouts to gather information. When they returned with news, Ragnachar would ask them how strong the enemy was.

"For you and your Farro it is a very good supply," was their reply.

Clovis arrived and deployed his forces against him. Ragnachar, on seeing his army defeated, was ready to run for it, but was caught by the army and brought before Clovis with his arms bound behind his back, as was his brother Richar.

"Why," asked Clovis, "have you disgraced our lineage by allowing yourself to be bound? It would have been better for you to die."

Raising his ax, he drove it into Ragnachar's head. Then he turned to Ragnachar's brother.

"If you had given your brother help," he said, "surely he wouldn't have been bound."

With a blow of his ax, he killed him in the same way.

After the death of the brothers, their betrayers recognized that the gold that they had received from Clovis was false.

When they told the king this, he is said to have answered, "Someone who willfully lures his lord to his death deserves to receive gold such as this." He added that to be alive should be enough for them unless they wanted to pay for the wicked betrayal of their lords by being tortured to death.

On hearing this, they decided to earn his favor, claiming that it was enough if they could obtain their lives.

The above mentioned two kings were kinsmen of Clovis. Their brother, whose name was Rignomer, was killed at Le Mans by order of Clovis. With their deaths, Clovis acquired their entire kingdom and treasure. And he killed many other kings and his own near relatives whom he suspected might take away his kingship and, in this way, he extended his authority over all Gaul.

One day, however, when he had gathered together his followers, he is supposed to have said with respect to the kinsmen he had destroyed, "How sad it is for me to be left like a traveler among strangers and to have no kin to help me if trouble comes along."

He said this, not because he felt grief for their deaths, but as a trick, to see if he could still find someone to kill.

### 43. The Death of Clovis

After these events had taken place, Clovis died at Paris [a. 511] and was buried in the basilica of the Holy Apostles, which he himself had built along with Chlothild his queen. He passed away in the fifth year after the battle of Vouillé. His reign amounted to thirty years in all. His age was forty-five.

From the passing of the holy Martin to the passing of Clovis, which was in the eleventh year of the episcopate of Licinius, bishop of Tours, amounts to one hundred and twelve years.

Queen Chlothild came to Tours after the death of her husband and served there in the holy basilica of the blessed Martin, living there with extreme virtue and with kindness all the days of her life, only occasionally visiting Paris.

# CHAPTER TEN

## THE *HISTORIES* OF GREGORY OF TOURS: THE FRANKISH KINGDOM, A. 511-90

*Georgius Florentius, better known to posterity as Gregory, bishop of Tours, was born around 538 to a highly distinguished Gallo-Roman family in Clermont, in the region of the Auvergne. In 573 he was appointed bishop of Tours, succeeding his mother's cousin, Saint Eufronius, to the office. He died in 594, shortly after completing his Histories.*

*Gregory wrote a number of works. He lists them in the concluding chapter of the Histories (X 31): "I have written ten books of Histories, seven of Wonders, and one on the Life of the Fathers. I have composed one book of Commentaries on the Psalms. I also wrote one book on the Offices of the Church." Gregory's fame rests on the work that he placed first in his list — the Histories, which have long been prized as one of the most important sources of the early Middle Ages.*

*Despite the importance of the Histories, the perspective of their author has not been well understood. Moderns have generally viewed Gregory as a naïve and superstitious compiler, heaping up a confused medley of ecclesiastical and national history. Gregory's merit was thought to have been his attempt to write a 'History of the Franks,' a title often applied to his work, though never used by Gregory himself; and the value of the work was largely seen as an accidental consequence of its author's naïvité, a quality that was thought to help guarantee the veracity of the apparently depraved picture of Merovingian society presented in its pages. Recent appraisals suggest quite a different interpretation of the historian and his work. Gregory is no longer seen as the author of a national history of the Franks (a work conceived along these lines had to wait until much later, see 59, 80, and 96-102 ); and his intertwining of ecclesiastical and secular themes are increasingly recognized as integrated parts of a moral or theological perspective. Gregory is now regarded as a moralist, setting the vain strivings of a corrupt human nature against the continuing story of the marvels of the saints and the church of Christ, and consciously selecting his material and shaping it to present these themes.*

*Gregory's Histories begin with Creation, and with the earliest biblical and secular history in the fashion of the chronicles of Jerome and Orosius, authors with whom he was familiar. Although biblical history was undoubtedly central to Gregory's understanding of the theological significance of human history, the Histories are largely a record of his mature years as bishop of Tours. The work is composed of ten books. Book I covers 5596 years, from Creation to A.D. 397 and the death of Gregory's hero, Saint*

*Martin; Book II covers 114 years, from the death of Martin to 511 and the death of Clovis; Books III and IV between them cover 64 years, from 511 to 575, the second year of Gregory's pontificate. The remaining six books cover a mere 16 years, from 575 to 591; Book VII is the epicenter of the narrative, covering only two years.*

*The following translation is composed of selections from Books III to X, following the secular, political narrative of the* Histories *from the year of Clovis's death to the end of the work. This treatment of Gregory's text facilitates our reading of the narrative history of the sixth century and our interpretation of Gregory as the principal portrayer of sixth-century political events, but it cannot maintain Gregory's conjunction of the saints and the reprobate and, by its nature, precludes a full understanding of the moral and theological perspective informing the* Histories. *Those who wish to bring this perspective fully to bear on their interpretation of the narrative must avail themselves of the* Histories *in their entirety, as well as Gregory's other works devoted to the saints and their miracles.*

*In the meantime, the excerpts below may help readers judge how we should understand the term 'episodic' as frequently applied to the* Histories. *In the context of the work as a whole, Gregory's moral and theological purposes were clearly served by fragmenting his narrative, juxtaposing the political and topical, the secular and the religious. Whether the result was confusion or a lack of direction in his treatment of events, as is often supposed, readers may decide for themselves, by following a largely uninterrupted narrative. Scholars have also long believed that the events occurring during the years of Gregory's episcopate were recorded just as they happened and reflect the immediate perspective of the compiler. According to this understanding of the composition of the* Histories, *one can read into Gregory's account of events his attitude at particular times and chart his changing attitude towards the main characters, detecting in the process a record of the developing political consciousness of the historian. The excerpts presented below hardly bear out this view. There is little reason to see Gregory's selection of material as ad hoc; on the contrary the narrative of the years in which Gregory was bishop seems consistently shaped from a retrospective position, especially that of the great events of the years 585, 587 and 590. The structure of Gregory's political narrative as set within the larger framework of the* Histories *was episodic; the contents were not.*

*Although the following excerpts of the* Histories' *political narrative are lengthy, readers should be aware that material has had to be left out for reasons of space. I have tried to include as much of the history of Gallic events as possible, occasionally resorting to summary; some gems have been passed over, but I trust not too many. Gregory's account of events in Spain, Italy and the Empire — often lengthy and often inaccurate — have not fared nearly as well (I have, for example, completely excluded the affairs of the Empire). Gregory's treatment of these events has interesting implications for understanding his historical perspective, but given the choice of including narrative dealing with Frankish Gaul or that of its neighbors, I have chosen to stick with Gaul and aim for, if not quite manage, completeness. Readers should at least bear in mind that Gregory's political horizon was not as narrow as the excerpts below might suggest.*

Source: Two editions were used for this translation: (1) *Historiarum libri X*, ed. Bruno Krusch and Wilhelm Levison, MGH SRM I/1, 2nd. ed. (1937-51); (2) *Zehn Bücher Geschichten*, ed. Rudolf Buchner, 2 vols. (Berlin, 1955-56). Translation by A.C. Murray.

## 47. FROM THE DEATH OF CLOVIS TO THE DEATH OF CHLOTHAR I, a. 511-61 (BOOKS III-IV)

*Gregory's Histories may be largely a record of his mature years as bishop (see 49, below), but his understanding of history required him to deal with more distant subjects and to connect the events of his own times with the events of the past going back to Creation. For more recent times, we have his unique version of the career of Clovis, whose conquest created the political framework of his own day (see 46).*

*Gregory continued his account of Gallic affairs after Clovis's death with a history of the king's successors. This history is the major, if not the only source (cf. 20) for the half century following Clovis's death. Gregory's sources for this period remain largely unknown, his knowledge is very uneven, and his chronology is still extremely vague.*

*In the selections below, I have rearranged some of his chapters. This reorganization is intended only to facilitate reading, not to suggest anything about the chronology of events. For the same reason I have added headings in boldface, appended dates where these seem reasonable, and added comments or brief chapter headings in italics to help readers keep their bearings in the narrative. Though the headings in boldface and italics may sometimes resemble the chapter headings of the* Histories *itself, they are not translations and have been devised for the present selections. Book and chapter numbers of the* Histories *appear in parentheses.*

### Division of the Kingdom Among the Sons of Clovis

*(III 1)*

On the death of King Clovis [a. 511], his four sons, namely, Theuderic, Chlodomer, Childebert, and Chlothar, received his kingdom and divided it equally among themselves. At that time Theuderic already had a fine and accomplished son named Theudebert. Since the brothers were endowed with great courage and well provided with strong military forces, Amalaric [a. 511-531], son of Alaric [II, a. 484-507] king of Spain, asked to marry their sister.

They graciously granted his request and sent her into the country of Spain with a great quantity of rich treasure.

## A Danish Raid

### (III 3)

*The Danish king of this chapter appears to be the same as the Hygelac of the famous Anglo-Saxon poem* Beowulf.

Danes under their king Chlochilaich set sail and attacked Gaul from the sea. They landed, devastated one region of Theuderic's kingdom, and took prisoners. When they had loaded their ships with captives and other spoils, they were ready to return home, but their king had stayed on shore until the ships reached the open sea, intending to follow right behind.

When news was brought to Theuderic that his land had been ravaged by foreigners, he sent his son Theudebert into those parts with a strong force thoroughly outfitted for war. He killed the Danish king, defeated the enemy in a sea battle, and brought the plunder back to shore.

## The Death of Chlodomer and the Conquest of Burgundy

### Sigismund of Burgundy Kills His Son (III 5)

On Gundobad's death [a. 516], his son Sigismund took up his kingdom and with real expertise constructed the monastery of Agaune, with its buildings and churches.

He had lost his first wife, the daughter of Theoderic, king of Italy, by whom he had a son called Sigeric, and took another wife. As stepmothers tend to do, she began to mistreat his son badly and harass him. As a result, it so happened on a ceremonial occasion that the boy recognized his mother's dress on her and became angry.

"You don't deserve to wear those clothes," he said to her. "Everyone knows they belonged to your mistress, my mother."

Inflamed with anger, she cleverly incited her husband.

"This devil wants to get his hands on your kingdom," she said. "And when he has killed you, he plans to extend it as far as Italy. It's obvious he wants to possess the kingdom which his grandfather Theoderic [the Great] held in Italy. He knows perfectly well that while you are alive he cannot accomplish this. Unless you fall, he will not rise."

Driven by these words and others like them, Sigismund took the advice of his wicked wife and ended up an evil killer of his own flesh and blood. One afternoon he told his son, who had drunk himself into a stupor, to sleep it off, and, while the son slept, two retainers placed a kerchief under his neck, brought it around his throat and, drawing the ends together, strangled him. When it was done the father repented too late and, falling on the lifeless corpse, began to weep bitterly.

A certain old man is supposed to have said to him, "Hereafter weep on your own behalf, now that you have followed wicked advice and become a most cruel child-killer. There is no need to weep for this innocent boy who has been throttled."

Nevertheless the king went off to the monastery of Agaune and prayed for pardon, spending many days weeping and fasting. He established there a service of perpetual chant and returned to Lyons with divine vengeance on his trail.

King Theuderic married his daughter.

*Death of Chlodomer, a. 524 (III 6)*

Queen Chlothild addressed Chlodomer and her other sons.

"Dear sons," she said, "let me not regret having lovingly nursed you; I beg you, take offense at the outrage inflicted on me and put your energies into avenging the death of my father and mother [cf. **46**, II 28]."

They listened to this and went to Burgundy to attack Sigismund and his brother Godomar, whose armies were defeated. Godomar retreated. But Sigismund was captured by Chlodomer while trying to escape to the monastery of Agaune. He was taken away as a prisoner along with his wife and children and kept under guard in the territory of the city of Orleans.

When the kings were gone, Godomar recovered his strength, gathered the Burgundians together, and took back his kingdom. Chlodomer made preparations to march against Godomar once again and, at the same time, decided to kill Sigismund. The blessed abbot Avitus, a remarkable priest of that time, spoke to him.

"If, mindful of God, you change your plans and do not have these people killed," said Avitus, "God will be with you. You will go off and win victory. But if you kill them, you will be handed over into the hands of your enemies and die like them. What you do to Sigismund and his wife and children will be done to you and your wife and sons."

Contemptuous of this advice, Chlodomer said, "I think it's a stupid idea to leave enemies at home while I go against the rest of them. If this lot rises up behind me and that one in front of me, I could be caught between two armies. Victory will be achieved better and more easily if they are kept apart; when one is killed, the other can be put to death easily."

He immediately gave orders for Sigismund to be killed along with his wife and children and for them to be thrown down a well in the village of Columna, in the city of Orleans. Setting out for Burgundy, he called upon King Theuderic to help him. Theuderic, having no wish to avenge the wrong done his father-in-law, promised to go along.

When they had joined forces near Véseronce, in the district of Vienne, they clashed with Godomar. Godomar retreated with his army, and Chlodomer, in pursuit of him, became separated a considerable distance from his own men.

The Burgundians, imitating Chlodomer's battle cry, called out to him, "This way, come this way, we are your men."

Taken in by the trick, he advanced and fell into the midst of his enemies. They cut off his head, set it on a lance, and raised it aloft. The Franks saw it and realized that Chlodomer was dead. Rallying their forces, they put Godomar to flight, crushed the Burgundians, and reduced the country to their authority.

Chlothar lost no time in marrying his brother's wife, who was called Guntheuca. As for Chlodomer's sons, Queen Chlothild, took them into her keeping after the period of mourning was past. The name of the first was Theudoald, the second was called Gunthar, and the third, Chlodoald.

Godomar recovered his kingdom a second time.

*Burgundy Conquered, a.534.*
*Theuderic Prepares to Go to Clermont, a.532. (III 11)*

Chlothar and Childebert made preparations to attack Burgundy. They summoned Theuderic to their aid, but he refused to go.

The Franks who looked to his authority, however, said to him, "If you refuse to go to Burgundy with your brothers, we shall abandon you and choose instead to follow them."

But figuring that the Arvernians were disloyal to him, he said, "Follow me, and I will take you to a land where you will get as much gold and silver as your greedy hearts can desire, where you can seize herds, slaves, and raiment in abundance. Only don't follow my brothers."

Attracted by these promises, they swore to do as he wished. He arranged to make an expedition to Clermont, promising his army again and again that he would allow them to take back home all the booty to be obtained in that region, including its people.

As for Chlothar and Childebert, they marched into Burgundy, besieged Autun, and took control of all of Burgundy, once Godomar was put to flight.

*Theuderic's army ravages the Auvergne (III 12, 13).*

## War Against the Thuringians

*Kings of the Thuringians (III 4)*

At this time three brothers held royal power over the Thuringians: Baderic, Hermanfred, and Berthar. Hermanfred violently overcame his brother Berthar and killed him. At his death, he left an orphan daughter, Radegund; he left sons as well, about whom I shall write later.

Hermanfred's wife, a wicked and cruel woman named Amalaberg, sowed the seeds of civil war between the brothers. For instance, one day her lord came to dinner to find half the table unlaid. He asked his wife what she meant by this.

"Anyone who has half his kingdom taken from him," she replied, "should have half his table bare."

Egged on by this and similar provocations, he turned against his brother, sending secret messages inviting King Theuderic to attack Baderic.

"If you kill him," said Hermanfred, "we will divide his kingdom in equal parts."

Theuderic was quite happy to hear this, and came to meet Hermanfred at the head of his army. They joined forces, exchanged pledges of mutual loyalty, and set out to war. They engaged Baderic and destroyed his army, cutting his head off with the sword [ca. 525/27?].

Victory won, Theuderic returned home. Hermanfred at once forgot his pledge, regarding the fulfilment of his promise to King Theuderic as of no account. Great enmity arose between them.

*Theuderic and Chlothar Against Hermanfred, ca. 532 (III 7-8)*

Theuderic did not forget the false promise of Hermanfred, king of the Thuringians, and made arrangements to march against him, calling on his brother Chlothar to help him. He promised King Chlothar a share of the plunder if heaven should grant them the gift of victory.

Theuderic assembled the Franks and said to them, "Be angry, I beg of you, as much for my wrong as for the death of your kinfolk. Remember that the Thuringians in the past made a brutal attack upon our relations and did them great harm. Our people gave hostages and tried to make peace with them, but the Thuringians put the hostages to death in various ways and, falling upon our kinfolk, took all their property. They hung the boys by the sinews of their thighs from trees. On more than two hundred girls they inflicted a cruel death: they tied their arms to the necks of horses which they set galloping in opposite directions with sharp goads, tearing the girls to pieces. Others they staked out over ruts in the roads and had them run over by loaded wagons; and, having broken their bones, they gave them to dogs and birds for food. And now Hermanfred has broken his promise and completely ignores fulfilling it. Look, right is on our side! Let's take them on, with God's help."

When they heard this, they were angry at such wrongs and, with one heart and mind, set out for Thuringia. Off went Theuderic with the army, taking his brother Chlothar and his son Theudebert to help him. But the Thuringians prepared traps for the Franks' coming. In the plain where the fight was to take place, they dug trenches and covered the openings with thick turfs to look as if the plain were still level. So, when the fight began, many of the Frankish cavalry fell into these pits, and the stratagem seriously hindered them, though after it was discovered, they were on the lookout for it. When finally the Thuringians saw that they were taking severe losses and their king Hermanfred had taken to flight, they retreated to the river Unstrut. There such a slaughter of the Thuringians took place that the bed of the stream was filled with heaps of corpses, and the Franks crossed over them to the further bank as if on a bridge.

Victory won, they took possession of that country and reduced it to their authority. As for Chlothar, he went home, taking with him as a captive Radegund, daughter of king Berthar, and married her. Afterwards he wrongfully killed her brother through the agency of evil men. Radagund, however, turned to God and, changing her garments, built a monastery for herself in the city of Poitiers. By her prayers, fasting, and almsgiving, she attained such fame that people considered her a remarkable woman.

When the above mentioned kings were still in Thuringia, Theuderic tried to kill his own brother Chlothar. He called him to his side on the pretext that he wished to discuss something with him privately, but he had secretly put in place armed men ahead of time. In one part of the house, a tent-cloth had been stretched from one wall to the other, and he ordered the men to stand behind it. Since the cloth was too short, their feet were exposed to view. Learning of this, Chlothar came into the house with his own men armed. Theuderic, realizing that Chlothar had learned of his preparations, made up a story and talked about this or that matter. Finally, not knowing how to put a good appearance on his trap, he gave him as a favor a great silver platter. And Chlothar said his farewells, thanked him for the gift, and returned to his quarters. But Theuderic complained to his men that he had lost his dish for no good reason.

"Go to your uncle," he said to his son Theudebert, "and ask him if he will give you the gift I gave him."

Theudebert went away and got what he asked for. In this kind of deceit Theuderic was very skilled.

Theuderic returned to his own country and told Hermanfred to come to him, giving him a promise that he would be safe. Theuderic honored him with rich gifts. One day, however, it so happened that they were talking on the walls of the city of Zülpich and Hermanfred was pushed — I do not know by whom — and fell from the top of the wall to the ground, where he breathed his last. We do not know who threw him down from there; still, many claim that the deceit of Theuderic was plainly revealed in the deed.

## Childebert's War Against the Visigoths, a. 531

### (III 10)

Childebert went to Spain for the sake of his sister Chlothild. She had to endure a lot of miserable treatment from her husband, Amalaric, on account of her Catholic faith. Often, for example, as she made her way to holy church, he ordered shit and all kinds of stinking stuff thrown on her. In the end he is said to have beaten her so cruelly that she sent her brother a kerchief stained with her own blood. Childebert was extremely upset by this and set out for Spain.

When Amalaric heard, he got ships ready so he could flee. Then as Childebert drew near, Amalaric, when he should have been boarding ship, suddenly remembered that he had left behind in his treasury a great many precious stones. He returned to the city to get them but was cut off from the harbor by the army. Seeing that he could not get away, he tried to take refuge in the church of the Christians. But before he could set foot on the holy threshold, someone threw a spear that gave him a mortal wound, and, collapsing there, he died.

Childebert then received his sister and was anxious to take her with him along with the great treasure. She died upon the journey, from what cause I know not, and her body was afterwards taken to Paris and buried near her father Clovis. Among other treasures, Childebert carried off very valuable services of church plate. For instance he took sixty chalices, fifteen patens, and twenty Gospel covers, all of pure gold and adorned with precious stones. But he did not allow them to be broken up, for he presented all of them to cathedral churches and basilicas of the saints.

## A Treaty Between Theuderic and Childebert: Attalus the Hostage

### (III 15)

*The Gregory of this story, who was bishop of Langres († ca. 539), was Gregory of Tours's great grandfather. Cf. 37.20*

Theuderic and Childebert made a treaty and swore to each other that neither would attack the other. They exchanged hostages to better secure the terms of the agreement. At that time, many sons of senators were given as hostages, but they were reduced to public servitude when a quarrel arose again between the kings, and those who had taken the hostages to guard now made them their slaves. Though many hostages managed to slip away and escape, returning to their homelands, a good number were kept in servitude. Among these was Attalus, nephew of the blessed Gregory, bishop of Langres. He was subjected to public servitude and set to guarding horses. He was in service to a certain barbarian in the territory of Trier.

The blessed Gregory then sent servants to find him. Find him they did and offered his master remuneration, but he rejected it.

"A fellow of such good birth," he said, "should be bought back for ten pounds of gold."

When they had returned home, a certain Leo, one of the bishop's kitchen staff, said, "If you would give me permission, perhaps I might be able to bring him back from captivity."

His master was pleased with the suggestion. Leo came straight to the place and tried to steal away the boy in secret but could not.

Then he hired a certain man and said to him, "Come with me and sell me into the house of that barbarian. Take my purchase price as your profit. All I want is a better opportunity of carrying out what I have resolved to do."

After taking an oath, the man went and sold Leo for twelve gold pieces and then left.

The purchaser inquired of the new slave what work he could do.

"I'm especially skilled in preparing all kinds of dishes suitable for the tables of lords," he answered, "and I've no worry that my equal can be found in this art. To tell you the truth, should you even to want a feast readied for a king, I'm able to prepare royal dishes. No one is better at it than I am."

"It's almost Sunday," — for this is what the barbarians usually call the Lord's day — "on this day my neighbors and relations will be invited to my house. I ask you to make me a feast that will astonish them and make them say 'we haven't seen better in the king's palace.'"

"Let my master get together a large number of pullets and I shall do what you command."

What the slave had asked for was made ready, and, when the Lord's day dawned, he prepared a great feast crammed with delightful dishes. When they had all feasted and praised the meal, the master's relations went away. The master rewarded his slave and he received authority over all his master's stores. His master cherished him very much, and the slave used to distribute the bread and meat to all the household.

After the course of a year, when his master was now certain of him, Leo went out to the meadow near the house with the boy Attalus, the keeper of the horses. They reclined on the ground but a distance apart and with their backs turned to each other so no one could see them talking together.

"The time has come to think of home," said Leo to the boy. "Listen to me. Tonight, when you fence in the horses, don't fall asleep, come as soon as I call, and off we go."

Now the barbarian had invited many of his relations to a feast, including his daughter's husband. At midnight they rose from the table to retire, and Leo accompanied his master's son-in-law to his quarters, giving him a drink.

"Tell me, if you can, my father-in-law's trusted servant, when do you think you'll decide to take his horses and return to your own country?" The fellow said this to make a joke.

In the same way, Leo jokingly replied with the truth. "Tonight, I think — if it's God's will."

"Well I hope my slaves make sure you take nothing of mine."

They parted laughing.

When all were asleep, Leo called Attalus and, when the horses were saddled, asked him if he had a sword.

"No, I have only a small spear," he said.

Leo entered his master's quarters and grabbed his shield and sword.

When his master asked who it was and what he wanted, Leo answered, "It's me, Leo, your slave. I am waking Attalus so he can get up right away and pasture the horses; he's fast asleep as if he were drunk."

"Do what you want." And saying this, his master fell asleep.

Leo went out and armed the boy and, by divine help, found the gates of the courtyard unbarred (at nightfall Attalus had barred them by driving in wedges with a hammer to keep the horses safe). Giving thanks to God, they took the rest of the horses with them and went off, carrying a single bundle of clothing.

When they came to cross the river Moselle and were prevented from doing so by certain people, they abandoned the horses and clothing and swam the river, supported by their shields. Climbing the further bank, they hid themselves in the woods amid the darkness of the night. This was the third night they had traveled without tasting food. It was then, by God's will, that they found a tree full of the fruit commonly called plums; eating them, they were strengthened somewhat and began the journey through Champagne.

As they were going along, they heard the hoofbeats of galloping horses and said, "Let's get down on the ground so the people coming can't see us."

Look what happened next! Quite unexpectedly, there was a great bramble bush growing nearby. They got behind it and threw themselves on the ground, with their swords drawn; had they been noticed, they would have immediately defended themselves with weapons as if attacked by outlaws. In fact, when the party of horsemen reached the spot, it halted in front of the thorn bush.

And while the horses were pissing, one of the riders said, "It really bothers me that these accursed wretches take off and can't be found; I swear by my own salvation, if they are found, I will have one condemned to the gallows, and the other cut to bits by the sword."

The barbarian who was speaking was their master, coming from the city of Rheims in search of them, and he would certainly have found them on the road if night had not prevented it. The riders then galloped off.

The fugitives reached the city that very night, and going in, they found a man and asked him where the house of the priest Paulellus was. He pointed it out to them. While they were going along the street, the bell was rung for matins — for it was the Lord's day — and knocking at the priest's door they went in. Leo told him who his master was.

"My vision was true then," responded the priest. "For this night I saw two doves fly toward me and settle on my hand. One of them was white, and the other black."

"May the Lord forgive our request on this holy day," said Leo to the priest. "We ask you to give us some food; for the fourth day is dawning since we have tasted bread and meat."

The priest hid the slaves, gave them a meal with bread and wine, and went away to matins.

The barbarian, too, came along behind them, looking for the slaves a second time, but made a fool of by the priest, he went home; for the priest had an old friendship with the blessed Gregory. Then, their strength restored by a good meal, the youths stayed two days in the home of the priest before departing. And so they were brought to the holy Gregory.

The bishop rejoiced at seeing them and wept on the shoulder of Attalus his nephew. He set Leo free from the yoke of slavery with all his family and gave him land of his own, on which he lived a free man with his wife and children all the days of his life.

## Death of Chlodomer's Sons:
## Childebert and Theuderic Divide Chlodomer's Kingdom

### (III 18)

While Queen Chlothild was staying at Paris, Childebert saw that his mother had special love for the sons of Chlodomer, whom I mentioned above [III 6].

Prompted by jealously and fearful that they would get a share in the kingdom because of the favor of the queen, Childebert sent a secret message to his brother King Chlothar saying, "Our mother keeps our brother's sons with her and wants them to be given royal powers. You should come quickly to Paris. We must have a meeting to discuss what ought to be done about them, whether they should have their long hair cut and be made the same as the rest of the common people, or whether they should be killed and our brother's kingdom divided equally between ourselves."

Chlothar was very pleased with these words and came to Paris. Childebert had spread a rumor among the populace that the reason the kings were meeting was to raise the small boys to the throne.

The queen was then staying in the city, and, when the kings met, they sent her a message saying, "Send the little fellows to us, so they may be raised up to the kingship."

She was pleased with that, unaware of their treacherous plan. Giving the boys food and drink, she sent them along.

"I shall not consider that I have lost a son," she said, "if I see you take over his kingdom."

Off they went and were immediately seized. They were taken away from their retainers and governors, who were put under separate guard in one place, while the little boys were kept in another. Then Childebert and Chlothar sent Arcadius to the queen with a pair of scissors and a naked sword. Arcadius came and showed both to the queen.

"Most glorious queen," he said, "your sons, our masters, wish to know your desire. What do you think ought to be done with the boys? Would you have them live with their hair shorn, or would you have them both killed?"

She was terrified by the message and anguish quite unsettled her, especially when she saw the naked sword and the scissors. Overcome by bitterness, she was unaware of what she was saying in her troubled state of mind.

"If they are not raised to the kingship," she said simply, "I would rather see them dead than shorn."

But Arcadius paid no attention to her depressed condition and returned swiftly with the news without giving her time for fuller reflection.

"You have the queen's approval to finish what you have begun," he said; "she wants you to bring your plans to completion."

There was no delay. Chlothar grabbed the older boy by the arm and pushed him to the ground and cruelly put him to death, stabbing him under the armpit with his knife. While the boy was screaming, his brother fell at Childebert's feet and clasped his knees.

"Help me, most dutiful father," he said crying. "I don't want to die like my brother."

Then Childebert, tears running down his cheeks, said, "I ask you, dear brother, let your generosity grant me the life of this boy. I will pay for his life whatever you say — only don't kill him."

But heaping abuse on his brother, Chlothar said, "Push him away from you, or you will surely die in his place. It is you that is the instigator of this deed. Do you go back on your word this quickly?"

Childebert listened to this and, shoving the boy away, pushed him toward Chlothar, who grabbed him and thrust his knife into his side, killing him in the same way as he had his brother. Then they put the servants and the governors to death.

When they were killed, Chlothar mounted his horse and went away, viewing the killing of his nephews as of little consequence. Childebert retired to the outskirts of the city. As for the queen, she placed their small bodies on a bier and accompanied it to the basilica of Saint Peter amid much psalm singing and endless grieving. She buried them side by side. One of them was ten years old, the other seven. But the third, Chlodoald, they were unable to get hold of, since he was saved by the help of his fighting men. He put aside his earthly kingdom and passed over into the Lord's service; cutting his hair with his own hands, he became a cleric, performing good works, and passed away from this life as a priest.

The two kings divided the kingdom of Chlodomer equally between them. Queen Chlothild acted in such a way as to gain the respect of everyone; she continually gave alms, attended holy vigils the whole night through, and remained pure, living a life of chastity and decency. She was generous and readily handed out estates to churches, monasteries, and other holy places where she saw a need, so that it was thought at the time that a real handmaid of God, not a queen, was busy in His service. Neither the royal power of her sons, nor worldly ambition, nor wealth, carried her off to destruction, but humility carried her forward to grace.

## The Young Theudebert and the Death of Theuderic I, a. 533

### (III 20-24)

Theuderic betrothed his son Theudebert to Wisigard, daughter of a certain [Lombard] king.

After the death of Clovis, the Goths had overrun much of what Theuderic had acquired. To get it back, Theuderic now sent Theudebert, and Chlothar sent his eldest son Gunthecar. Gunthecar got as far as Rodez but returned, I know not for what reason. But Theudebert went on to the city of Béziers, took the fortress of Dio and sacked it. He then sent envoys to another fortress named Cabrières with a message that the whole place would be burned to the ground and its inhabitants taken captive unless they surrendered to him.

At the time there was a matron there called Deuteria, a very capable and clever woman, whose husband had withdrawn to Béziers.

She sent a message to the king saying, "Most dutiful lord, no one can resist you. We know you are our lord. Come and do what is pleasing in your eyes."

Theudebert came to the fortress, but when he peacefully entered it and saw that the people were subdued, he did no harm there. Deuteria came out to meet him. He saw that she was beautiful, and captivated by love of her, took her to his bed.

In those days Theuderic put his kinsman Sigivald [Duke of Auvergne] to the sword and sent a message in secret to Theudebert for him to execute Sigivald's son, [also called] Sigivald, whom he had by his side. But because he had taken him from the sacred font, Theudebert refused to destroy him. In fact, he had him read the letter sent by his father.

"Get away from here," Theudebert said. "I have received my father's order to kill you. After his death when you hear that I am ruling, then return to me in safety."

Sigivald thanked him for the warning, said farewell, and departed. At the time the Goths had occupied of the city of Arles, from which Theudebert still had hostages, so Sigivald fled to the city. But seeing that he would get little protection there, he went to Italy and took refuge there.

While these events were taking place, word came to Theudebert that his father was seriously ill, and that, unless he came quickly enough to find his father alive, he himself would be disinherited by his uncles and would never be able to return. At this news, Theudebert put everything else aside and returned home, leaving Deuteria with her daughter at Clermont. Not many days after his departure, Theuderic died, in the twenty-third year of his reign [a. 533]. Childebert and Chlothar turned on Theudebert, trying to take the kingdom from him, but he appeased his *leudes* with gifts, won their support, and was established in his kingdom.

Later he summoned Deuteria from Clermont and married her.

When Childebert saw that he could not overcome Theudebert, he sent an embassy to him, bidding him come on a visit.

"I do not have sons," he said, "and I want to have you for a son."

Theudebert came and was enriched with so many gifts as to astonish everyone. Childebert gave him three pair of the various costly items appropriate to a king's rank, whether weapons, clothing, or jewels, as well as horses and bowls.

When Sigivald heard that Theudebert had acquired his father's kingdom, he returned from Italy to the king. Rejoicing with his friend and kissing him, Theudebert conferred upon him a third of the gifts that he had received from his uncle; and everything from the property of the elder Sigivald that Theuderic had assigned to his fisc, Theudebert restored to the son.

## The Reign of Theudebert I, a. 534-548

*The Goodness of Theudebert (III 25)*

When established in his kingdom, Theudebert proved to be a great king and thoroughly distinguished for good qualities. For he ruled his kingdom with justice, respected bishops, endowed churches, relieved the poor, and bestowed favors on many with a pious good will. He mercifully remitted all the taxes that were owed to his treasury from churches situated in Auvergne.

*Deuteria and Wisigard (III 26-27)*

Deuteria saw that her daughter was quite grown up and was afraid that the king would want her and take her. So Deuteria placed her in a wagon hitched to untamed oxen, and sent her off a bridge; the daughter lost her life in the river. This happened in the city of Verdun.

It was now the seventh year since Theudebert had betrothed Wisigard [cf. III 20] and refused to marry her on account of Deuteria. The Franks assembled and were thoroughly outraged with him for leaving his betrothed in the lurch. This time he was stirred into abandoning Deuteria, by whom he had a little son named Theudebald, and marrying Wisigard. He had not married her for long before she died, and he took another wife. But he no longer had anything to do with Deuteria.

*Childebert and Theudebert against Chlothar (III 28)*

Childebert and Theudebert mustered their armies and made arrangements to march against Chlothar. On hearing about this, and figuring he could not withstand their forces, Chlothar took refuge in a forest, where he made great barricades in the woods, putting all his hope in God's mercy. Queen Chlothild also heard about it. She went to the tomb of the holy Martin and there prostrated herself in prayer; keeping vigil all night long, she prayed that no civil war should arise between her sons.

Childebert and Theudebert came with their armies and besieged their brother, planing to kill him on the following day. But at dawn a storm arose where they had camped. Their tents were blown down, their gear was scattered, and everything thrown into confusion. Lightning mixed with thunder and hailstones descended on them. They threw themselves on their faces on the hail-strewn ground and were severely pounded by the falling hailstones — for they had no covering left but their shields. Their chief fear was being struck by the lightning from the heavens. Their horses, too, were scattered so far that they could scarcely be recovered several miles away, and many were never found at all.

Then the kings — lashed by hailstones, as I have said, and stretched out on the ground — did penance and begged God for forgiveness for having tried to attack their own flesh and blood. On Chlothar not a single drop of rain fell; and in his camp no sound of thunder was heard, and no one felt even a breath of wind. The two kings sent envoys to him seeking peace and good relations. When their request was granted, they returned home. Let no one doubt that this miracle was the blessed Martin's, brought about through the intercession of the queen.

### Theudebert in Italy, a. 539 (III 32)

*Buccelin's expeditions actually took place in 553-4 under Theudebald I.*

Theudebert went to Italy and acquired a great deal of plunder there. But, as we are told, those areas are disease-ridden, and his army suffered losses, falling victim to fevers of various kinds; many troops died in those regions. Seeing the situation, Theudebert returned, he and his men carrying away much spoil.

It is said that at that time he went as far as the city of Pavia, against which he later sent Buccelin. Buccelin captured Lesser Italy, reduced it to the authority of the aforesaid the king, and then attacked Greater Italy. Here he fought Belisarius many times and won the victory. When the emperor saw that Belisarius was being beaten more and more, he removed him and replaced him with Narses. To humiliate him, he made Belisarius count of the stable, a post he had held before. Buccelin, for his part, fought great campaigns against Narses. Capturing all Italy, he extended his conquests to the sea, sending much treasure from Italy to Theudebert. When Narses informed the emperor of this, the emperor hired foreign forces to aid Narses. In a later engagement, Narses was defeated and then departed. Then Buccelin seized Sicily, from which he exacted tribute, which he sent to the king. He enjoyed great success in these circumstances [cf. IV 9].

### Theudebert's Gift to the Citizens of Verdun (III 34)

Desideratus, bishop of Verdun, to whom king Theuderic had done many wrongs, received his freedom again at the Lord's command, after many injuries, losses, and hardships. He took up the office of bishop in the city of Verdun, as I said, and felt sorry for its inhabitants since he saw that they were forsaken and very poor. He had been stripped of his own property by Theuderic and had nothing of his own with which to relieve them, and so, perceiving the goodness of King Theudebert and his kindness towards all, he sent a delegation to the king with a message.

"Your reputation for goodness," said the bishop, "is known over the whole world, since your generosity is such that you help even those who do not seek it. I beg you, kind lord, lend us money, if you can spare it, so that we may be able to relieve our citizens; and when those involved in trade increase business in our city to what it is in other cities, we will repay your money with lawful interest."

Then Theudebert was moved by compassion and furnished seven thousand gold pieces, which the bishop took and disbursed among his citizens. Those doing business were made rich by this and are considered to be important people to the present day.

When the Bishop Desideratus offered the king the money that was owed, the king answered, "I've no need to take this sum; it's enough for me if, by your management, the poor who were suffering want have been relieved, thanks to your request and my generosity."

Demanding nothing, the aforesaid king made the citizens rich.

### Deaths of Theudebert and Parthenius, a. 548 (III 36, 37)

Theudebert began to grow ill. The physicians lavished a great deal of attention on him, but nothing worked, for the Lord was now calling him. And so when he had grown ill for quite a while, growing weak with the sickness, he gave up the ghost.

Now the Franks went in pursuit of Parthenius, since they hated him profoundly for subjecting them to taxation in the time of the aforesaid king. Parthenius saw the danger he was in and fled the city. He humbly begged two bishops to be his escort to the city of Trier and to quell by their preaching the revolt of the raging populace. One night while they were traveling, as he lay in his bed, he suddenly let loose a loud shout in his sleep.

"Help!" he cried. "Whoever is there come help. Bring assistance to a dying man."

The shouting awakened those nearby, and they asked him what was the matter.

He replied, "Ausanius, my friend, and my wife Papianilla, both of whom I killed long ago, were summoning me to judgment. 'Come and defend yourself,' they were saying, 'for you are going to plead your case along with us in the presence of the Lord.'"

Jealousy had led him to kill his innocent wife and his friend some years before.

Coming to Trier, the bishops were unable to handle the riot of shouting people and they tried to hide Parthenius in the cathedral. What they did was place him in a chest and spread over him vestments that were used in the church. People came in and, after searching every nook and cranny of the church, went out in a rage when they found nothing.

Then one said suspiciously, "Look, there's a chest we haven't looked in for our enemy."

The guards said that it contained nothing but church furnishings, but the crowd demanded the key.

"Unless you are quick about unlocking it," they said, "we will break it open ourselves."

In the end the chest was opened and the linens removed. They found Parthenius and dragged him out.

"God has delivered our enemy into our hands," they shouted, clapping their hands.

Then they beat him with their fists and spat on him. Tying his hands behind his back, they stoned him to death against a column.

He was a great glutton and quickly digested what he ate, taking aloes to feel hungry again quickly. Moreover he use to let loose farts in public, without any consideration for those who could hear him. This is how his life ended.

...Thirty-seven years passed between the death of Clovis and the death of Theudebert, who died in the fourteenth year of his reign. His son Theudebald reigned in his place.

*This computation ends Book III.*

## The Death of Queen Chlothild, a. 544

### *(IV 1)*

Queen Chlothild died at Tours, full of days and rich in good works, in the time of Bishop Injuriosus [ca. 530-546]. She was taken to Paris with much singing of psalms and buried by her sons kings Childebert and Chlothar at the side of King Clovis in the sanctuary of the basilica of Saint Peter. She herself had erected this basilica in which the most blessed Genovefa is also interred.

## King Chlothar and the Income of the Churches

### *(IV 2)*

King Chlothar had proclaimed that all the churches of his kingdom were to pay a third of their income to the fisc. When all the bishops had unwillingly agreed to this and signed their names, the blessed Injuriosus [bishop of Tours, ca. 530-546], manfully rejected doing so and refused to sign.

"If you try to take the things of God," he said, "the Lord will quickly take away your kingdom, for it is wrong for the poor to have to fill your granary, when you should be feeding them from it."

He was angry with the king and left without saying farewell.

The king was unsettled by this and, being afraid also of the power of the blessed Martin, sent after the bishop with gifts, begging pardon, condemning his own actions, and asking also that the bishop intercede with the power of the blessed Martin on his behalf.

## Chlothar's Wives and Children

### (IV 3)

Now the king had seven sons by various wives; by Ingund he had Gunthecar, Childeric, Charibert, Guntram, and Sigibert, as well as a daughter Chlodoswintha; by Aregund, sister of Ingund, he had Chilperic; and by Chunsina he had Chramn.

I will tell why it was he married his wife's sister. When he had already married Ingund and loved her with special affection, he received a request from her.

She said, "My Lord has done with his servant as he pleased and has admitted me to his bed. Now, to complete the favor you have granted, let my lord king listen to what his servant proposes. I beg you, please provide a rich and accomplished husband for my sister, your slave. That way I shall not be humbled, but rather, by being raised higher, I shall be able to serve you more faithfully."

Hearing this, and being licentious in the extreme, he fell in love with Aregund, went to the villa on which she was living, and married her himself. After the marriage, he returned to Ingund.

"I have taken care of the favor your sweet self asked of me," he said. "Looking for a man rich and shrewd with whom to hook up your sister, I could find no one better than myself. And so you should know that I have married her, which I don't think will make you unhappy."

"Let my lord do whatever seems pleasing in his eyes," she replied. "Just let your servant live in favor with the king."

Now Gunthecar, Chramn and Childeric died during their father's lifetime. Of the death of Chramn I shall write later. Alboin, king of the Lombards, married the king's daughter Chlodoswintha [cf. 45].

## Reign of Theudebert's Son, Theudebald, a. 548-555

*(IV 9)*

Now that he had grown, Theudebald married Wuldetrada. This Theudebald, they say, had a bad nature. Once when he grew angry with someone he suspected of taking his property, he recounted a fable.

"A snake," he said, "found a jar full of wine. He went in by its neck and greedily drank what was inside. Enlarged by the wine, he could not get out the way he got in. As the snake was trying to get out, without success, the owner of the wine came along and said to him, 'First spew out what you have swallowed, and then you will be able to get away free.'"

This fable made him greatly feared and hated.

Under him, Buccelin, after reducing all Italy to the rule of the Franks, was slain by Narses [a. 554]; Italy was captured on behalf of the emperor and there was no one to recover it later.

In his time, we saw grapes grow on the tree we call elder, with no connection to a vine, and the blossoms of the same trees, which as you know usually produce black seeds, yielded the seeds of grapes. Then a star coming from the opposite direction was seen to enter the circle of the fifth moon. I believe these signs proclaimed the death of the king.

He became very weak and could not control himself from the waist down. He gradually grew worse and died in the seventh year of his reign. King Chlothar obtained his kingdom and took his wife Wuldetrada to his bed. But Chlothar was criticized by the bishops and left her, giving her to Duke Garivald [of Bavaria]. He sent his son Chramn to Clermont.

## Later Years of Chlothar I, a. 555-561

*Chlothar's Second Expedition against the Saxons (IV 14)*

*Chlothar's first expedition, in which Thuringia was also ravaged, occurred in the year of Theudebald's death (IV 10). Cf. 20, s.a. 555, 556.*

When Chlothar had taken up the kingship of Francia after Theudebald's death [a. 555] and was making a progress through it, he heard from his people that a second bout of madness had burst out among the Saxons. They were rebelling against him and disdaining to pay the tribute which they were accustomed to pay every year. Aroused by the news, he marched against them. When he was near their territory, the Saxons then sent envoys to him.

"We mean you no disrespect," they said, "nor do we refuse to make the payments we have customarily rendered to your brothers and nephews. We'll give even more if you ask for it. We ask only one thing — that there be peace and your army and our people not come into conflict."

King Chlothar said to his followers when he heard this, "These men speak well. Let's not attack them in case we sin against God."

"We know they're liars," said his men, "and will never keep their promise. Let's get at them."

The Saxons again offered half their chattels in return for peace.

Chlothar said to his men, "Leave these people alone, I beg of you, so we don't arouse God's anger."

But they would not give in. Again the Saxons made offers of garments, cattle and all their chattels.

"Take all this together with half of our land," they said, "only let our wives and little children remain free, and let no war come between us."

The Franks would not even agree to this.

King Chlothar said to them, "Give up this idea, I beg of you. Our position is not right. Don't wage a war in which you will be destroyed. If you decide to go off on your own, I will not follow."

At that the Franks became angry with King Chlothar and rushed upon him, tearing his tent in pieces. Heaping abuse on him, they dragged him away by force and were going to kill him unless he would go with them. When Chlothar realized this, he went with them against his will.

The battle began, and they suffered an immense slaughter at the hands of their enemies, and such a host perished on both sides that it was impossible to estimate or count their number. Then Chlothar, greatly confounded, asked for peace, saying that it was not of his own free will that he had come against them. He was granted peace and returned home.

### Chlothar and his Son Chramn (IV 13, 16, 17, 20, 21)

In these days, Chramn lived at Clermont [cf. IV 9]. He committed many mad acts and for this reason his departure from the world came quickly. He was roundly cursed by people. He loved no one from whom he could get good and useful advice. Instead, he gathered round himself low characters in a youthful and restless stage of their lives. He only had affection for them and listened to their advice, even issuing orders allowing them to carry off daughters of senators by force. He seriously wronged Firminus and drove him from the office of count of the city, replacing him with Salustius son of Euvodius...

Chramn, as I said, was committing evil deeds at Clermont and still holding a grudge against [Bishop] Cautinus. In this period, he became so seriously ill that his hair fell out because of a high fever. He had with him at the time a citizen of Clermont, Ascovindus, a great noble and manifestly a man of good character, who did all in his power to turn the prince from his wickedness but could not. For Chramn also had with him Leo of Poitiers, a man like the lion of his name, most savage in fulfilling all his desires, who viciously spurred him on to every kind of evil deed...

Chramn left Clermont and came to the city of Poitiers. There he stayed, exercising great power, but, led astray by the advice of evil men, he became intent on going over to his uncle Childebert and made arrangements to betray his father. Childebert promised, even though quite deceitfully, to receive Chramn, someone he should have admonished with religious arguments against becoming the enemy of his father. At that time they took oaths to each other through secret emissaries and plotted quite happily together against Chlothar. Yet Childebert forgot that whenever he had acted against his brother, he always went away the worse for it.

After entering into this treaty, Chramn went back to Limoges and subjected to his own rule all the parts of his father's kingdom through which he had earlier passed...King Chlothar now sent his two sons, Charibert and Guntram, to Chramn. They passed through Auvergne and, on hearing that Chramn was in the territory of Limoges, came to the hill called the black mountain, where they found him...Chramn cunningly sent a stranger to his brothers to announce the death of their father. The war against the Saxons, of which I have spoken above, was being waged at this time. In alarm they returned as fast as they could to Burgundy. Chramn followed behind them with his army and, coming as far as Chalon, took the town after a siege. From there he pushed on to the fortress of Dijon...

At the time King Chlothar was fighting bravely against the Saxons. Incited by Childebert, so they say, and angry with the Franks for the previous year, they had advanced from their territory into Francia, taking plunder as far as the city Deutz and inflicting serious damage.

At this point, Chramn, who had now married the daughter of Wilichar, came to Paris to establish bonds of loyalty and friendship with Childebert and swore that he was a most determined enemy of his father. While Chlothar was fighting the Saxons, King Childebert entered the champaign of Rheims and pushed on quickly to the city itself, laying everything waste by pillage and fire. For he had heard that his brother had been killed by the Saxons and, figuring that everything was now to be subjected to his authority, seized every part he could reach...

King Childebert grew ill. After being confined for some time to his bed, he died at Paris [a. 558] and was buried in the basilica of the blessed Vincent, which he had built. King Chlothar took his kingdom and treasures; Ultrogotha and her two daughters he sent into exile. Chramn was brought before his father but later proved to be disloyal. When he saw there was no other choice, he went to Brittany and there with his wife and daughters hid out with Chanao count of the Bretons.

Wilichar, Chramn's father-in-law, fled to the basilica of Saint Martin. It was then that the holy basilica was burned because of the sins of the people and the mockeries that were done in it by Wilichar and his wife. We mention this not without a heavy sigh. Moreover, the city of Tours had already been burned the year before, and all the churches built in it were left abandoned. Immediately, by order of King Chlothar, the basilica of the blessed Martin was roofed with tin and restored to its former beauty. Then two swarms of locusts appeared which, crossing through Auvergne and Limousin, so they say, came to the plain of Romagnac, where a battle broke out between them, and there was a great clash of forces.

Chlothar was in a rage against Chramn and brought his army into Brittany against him [a. 560]. Nor was Chramn afraid of coming out against his father. The armies gathered together on a plain, but both sides hung back. Just when Chramn in company with the Bretons had drawn up his forces facing his father, night fell, and they refrained from fighting.

During the night Chanao, count of the Bretons, said to Chramn, "I don't think it's right for you to go out against your father. Let me fall on him through the night and destroy him with all his army."

Chramn would not allow this to be done, prevented, I believe, by the power of God.

In the morning, both sides got under way and rushed into battle. King Chlothar went like a new David to fight against Absalom his son, loudly lamenting.

"Look down from heaven, Lord, and judge my cause," he shouted, "for I suffer wrongs wickedly inflicted by a son. Look down, Lord, and judge justly, and impose that judgment that you once passed on Absalom and his father David."

When both sides engaged, the count of the Bretons retreated and then was killed. Finally Chramn took to flight. He had ships standing by at sea, but since he tried to save his wife and daughters, he was overpowered by his father's forces, taken captive, and bound. News of this was told to King Chlothar, and he gave orders to burn Chramn together with his wife and daughters. They were shut up in the hut of a poor man; Chramn was stretched on a bench and strangled with a towel, and then the hut was burned over them. This is how he perished with his wife and daughters.

*Chlothar's Death, a. 561 (IV 21)*

In the fifty-first year of his reign, King Chlothar came to the threshold of the blessed Martin with many gifts. He visited the tomb of the aforesaid bishop at Tours, going over all the actions that he might have taken without due consideration. He prayed with loud sighs for the blessed confessor of God to obtain forgiveness for his faults, and, by his intercession with God, to blot out the irrational acts he had committed. He then went home and, in the fifty-first year of his reign, while hunting in the forest of Cuise, was seized with a fever and returned to the villa of Compiègne.

There, when the fever grew worse, he would cry out in agony, "What do you think? What kind of king of heaven is this who kills off such great kings in this way?"

Suffering in this fashion, he breathed his last. His four sons carried him with great honor to Soissons and buried him in the basilica of Saint Medard.

He died one day after the anniversary of the death of Chramn.

## 48. FROM THE DIVISION OF CHLOTHAR'S KINGDOM TO THE DEATH OF SIGIBERT I, a. 561-75 (BOOK IV)

*Gregory was a subject of the kings of the Austrasian Franks, Clermont, Gregory's home town, and Tours, the city of his episcopate, being two of the many cities these kings controlled south of the Loire. His political allegiance has an important bearing on a number of aspects of the* Histories, *including its organization. Book II ends with the death of Clovis, the founder of a unified Frankish kingdom in northern, central, and southern Gaul. Book III ends with the death of Theudebert I, the greatest of Clovis's successors and ruler of the north-eastern (or Austrasian) Franks; and Book IV, as will be seen below, ends with the death in 575 of Sigibert I, ruler of this north-eastern kingdom, called Austrasia by the time Gregory was writing. Thereafter (**49**, below), Gregory adopted a dating system tied to the regnal years of the Austrasian king Childebert II. In this scheme, the death of Chlothar I, which looms large in subsequent accounts of Merovingian history, falls, as the reader may already have noticed, in the middle of Book IV. Modern historiography, with a different set of conventions in mind than Gregory's, tends to see the death of Chlothar and the partition of the unified kingdom among his quarrelsome sons as a new, or at least distinct, stage in the history of the Frankish kingdom. I have followed this practice in arranging the present set of excerpts.*

*With the succession of Chlothar's sons in 561, Gregory's* Histories *also begin dealing with kings whose reigns coincide with Gregory's own adult years, if not yet his politically important years as bishop. It needs to be said that this circumstance does not mean that Gregory's history was composed concurrently with the events he describes. Far from it. There is sufficient indication in his text to show that Gregory wrote of the years recounted below with ample knowledge of what these events, or better yet, the persons driving them, would eventually bring upon Gaul. It does not mean, either, that Gregory's account was necessarily first-hand. He continued to use sources, some of which — like the treatment of the Lombard invasion of Italy and Mummolus's wars with Lombard dukes — are detectable, though not identifiable. (The lengthy treatment of Mummolus's campaigns is not likely to be a digression, but is background for the general's importance in political events of later books). Gregory's chronology also remains vague for the decade and a half following Chlothar's death — I have added dates where they seem reasonable and, as in 47, headings to facilitate reading.*

*Of the sons of Chlothar who inherited their father's kingdom, two in particular dominate much of the later Histories: Chilperic, who ruled a north-western kingdom later known as Neustria, and Guntram, who ruled the kingdom of Burgundy. The early death of another son, Charibert, in 567, was significant for later quarrels among his brothers over the inheritance of his kingdom. Sigibert, whose checkered career is cut short at the end of Book IV, and his wife Brunhild, approved Gregory's appointment as Bishop of Tours in the year 573.*

## The First Two Years

*Partition of the Kingdom, a. 561 (IV 22)*

After the funeral of his father, Chilperic took possession of the treasures that were stored in the royal villa of Berny. He then looked around for the most powerful Franks, softened them up with gifts, and brought them under his authority. He soon entered Paris and took over the residence of King Childebert, but he was not allowed to hold it for long. His brothers joined forces and drove him from there. That is how the four kings, that is, Charibert, Guntram, Chilperic, and Sigibert, came to make a lawful division among themselves.

The partition conferred on Charibert the kingdom of Childebert, with Paris as his capital; on Guntram, the kingdom of Chlodomer, with his capital being Orleans; on Chilperic, the kingdom of his father Chlothar, with his throne at Soissons; on Sigibert, the kingdom of Theuderic, with Rheims for his capital.

*Invasion of the Avars. Civil War between Sigibert and Chilperic (IV 23)*

*Gregory uses the old term Huns to refer to the Avars, an eastern nomadic people new to the West. At this time the Avars began to occupy the Hungarian plain and became a major military power in central Europe.*

After the death of King Chlothar, the Huns attacked Gaul [a. 562]. Sigibert led his forces against them, and in the campaign, defeated them and put them to flight. Afterwards, their king sent envoys and gained friendly relations with him. But while Sigibert was having his troubles with the Huns, his brother

Chilperic overran Rheims and took away other cities that belonged to him. What is worse, for this reason civil war broke out between them.

Returning as victor over the Huns, Sigibert took Soissons, where he discovered Theudebert, King Chilperic's son. He took him into custody and sent him into exile. He brought his forces against Chilperic, whom he defeated and put to flight, and re-established his authority over his cities. He ordered Chilperic's son Theudebert to be kept for a whole year under guard at the villa of Ponthion; but as he was merciful, he afterwards loaded him with gifts and sent him back safe and sound to his father. He did this on condition that Theudebert swear never again to act against him. The oath was afterwards broken, due to sin.

### The Kings and Their Wives

*Guntram's Wives (IV 25)*

Guntram, who was a good king, at first took to bed as a concubine Veneranda, a slave of one of his followers; by her he had a son Gundobad. Afterwards he married Marcatrude, daughter of Magnachar. He sent his son Gundobad to Orleans. After Marcatrude had a son, she jealously set out to bring about Gundobad's death, poisoning him with a doctored drink, so they say. Following his death, by the judgment of God, she lost the son she had and incurred the hatred of the king. Sent away by him, she died not long after. After her Guntram took Austrechild, also named Bobilla. By her he again had two sons; the older of them was called Chlothar and the younger Chlodomer.

*Charibert's Wives and His Death (IV 26)*

Next King Charibert married Ingoberga, by whom he had a daughter (she afterwards married a husband in Kent and was taken there). Ingoberga had in her service at the time two girls, the daughters of a poor man. The first of them was called Marcovefa, who wore the religious habit, and the other was Merofled. The king was very much in love with them. They were, as I said, the daughters of a wool worker.

Jealous that they were loved by the king, Ingoberga privately made sure that the father was put to work, supposing that when the king saw this he would take a dislike to the daughters. While the father was working, she called the king, who expected to see something special, but only saw this man at a distance sorting the royal wool. The sight made him angry, so he left Ingoberga and married Merofled.

He also had another girl named Theudogild, the daughter of a shepherd. By her he is said to have had a son, who, as soon as he came forth from the womb, was carried to the grave ...

Afterward Charibert married Marcovefa, Merofled's sister. For this reason, they were both excommunicated by the holy bishop Germanus [of Paris]. But since the king would not leave her, she was struck by God's judgment and died. In no time at all the king himself followed her to the grave [a. 567].

After his death, Theudogild, one of his queens, took it upon herself to send messengers to King Guntram, offering to marry him.

The king gave them this response, "Let her have no worry about coming to me with her treasure. For I will marry her and make her a great woman in everyone's eyes. Rest assured she will have greater honor with me than with my brother who has just died."

Very pleased, she gathered up everything and set out to him.

When the king saw what she brought, he said, "It's better for this treasure to be in my hands than under the control of this woman who was unworthy to lie in my brother's bed."

Then, having taken away much and left little, he sent her to a monastery at Arles. Theudogild took it ill to be put to fasts and vigils and so she contacted a Goth by secret messengers, promising that she would leave the monastery with her treasure and follow him willingly if he would take her to Spain and marry her. He agreed without hesitation. But when she had gathered her things and bundled them up and was ready to leave the convent, the enterprise of the abbess frustrated her desires. The abbess detected the deceit and had her severely beaten and put under guard. There she remained to the end of her life in this world, worn down by no slight suffering.

### Sigibert Marries Brunhild (IV 27)

Next, when King Sigibert saw that his brothers were marrying unworthy wives, and were themselves so worthless as to even marry slaves, he sent an embassy to Spain with many gifts to ask for Brunhild, daughter of King Athanagild [a. 551-568]. She was a well-mannered, good-looking girl, decent and well-behaved, with good judgment and a persuasive manner. Her father did not reject the request for her hand and sent her to Sigibert with great treasure. The king assembled his leading followers, prepared a feast and took her as his wife with immense rejoicing and celebration. She had been a follower of the Arian creed but was converted by the preaching of the bishops and the admonition of the king himself. Having confessed the blessed Trinity in unity, she believed and received the chrism. She continues to be a Catholic, in Christ's name.

*Chilperic's Wives (IV 28)*

*The statement in the text, as we have it, that after the death of Galswinth Chilperic's brothers "drove him from the kingdom" is difficult to accept at face value. Whatever the brothers may have done fell short of actual deposition.*

When Chilperic saw this, he asked for Brunhild's sister Galswinth, although he already had several wives, promising through his envoys that he would abandon the others, if only he could win a bride worthy of himself and the offspring of a king. With these assurances, her father sent his daughter, as he had the first, along with a great deal of wealth. Galswinth was older than Brunhild.

When she came to King Chilperic, she was received with great honor and made his wife. Moreover his love for her was considerable, for she had brought great treasure. But because of his love for Fredegund, whom he had before, a disgraceful conflict arose to divide them. Galswinth had already been converted to the Catholic creed and received the chrism. She complained to the king of the wrongs she constantly had to endure and told him that he had no respect for her. Finally she asked him to give her freedom to return to her native land if she left the treasures that she had brought with her. But he made up various excuses and mollified her with sweet words. In the end, he had her strangled by a slave, and he himself found the corpse on the bed.

After her death God revealed a great sign of his power. A lamp burned before her tomb, suspended by a cord. Without anyone touching it, the cord broke, and the lamp fell to the pavement. The hard pavement gave way before it, and the lamp, as if it had landed in some kind of soft substance, was buried to the middle and was not at all broken. To those who saw it, this did not happen without a great miracle.

The king wept over the body and then, after a few days, took Fredegund back again as his wife. When he did this, his brothers attributed Galswinth's killing to his orders and drove him from the kingdom.

At the time, Chilperic had three sons by his first wife Audovera, namely Theudebert, whom I mentioned above, Merovech, and Clovis.

But let me return to my task.

## War, Plague, and New Neighbors

*Sigibert's Second War with the Avars, a. 566 (IV 29)*

The Huns tried to get into Gaul a second time. Sigibert brought his army against them, leading a great host of good fighting men. Just when they were about to engage, the Huns, who were well-versed in the magic arts, exposed them to apparitions of various kinds and defeated them decisively.

Sigibert's army fled, and he himself was surrounded by the Huns. Sigibert was a cultivated and shrewd man, and he would have been kept a prisoner if he had not overpowered by the art of giving those whom he could not overpower by the art of war. He gave gifts and entered into an agreement with the king of the Huns that all the days of their lives they would not start wars with each other. This incident is thought to be more to his credit than otherwise, and justifiably so. Moreover, the king of the Huns gave many gifts to King Sigibert. He was called Gaganus [Khan]. All the kings of that people are called by this name.

### Sigibert Orders the Arvernians to take Arles (IV 30)

King Sigibert wanted to take the city of Arles and so he ordered the Arvernians to muster their forces. Firminus was count of the city at the time and marched off at the head of the forces. Moreover Audovar approached with an army from the other direction. They both entered the city and exacted oaths on behalf of King Sigibert. As soon as King Guntram found out, he dispatched an army under the patrician Celsus. On the march, Celsus took the city of Avignon. When he reached Arles, he surrounded the city and began hostilities against the forces of Sigibert within the walls.

At that point Bishop Sabaudus [a. 552-86] said to these forces, "Go out and join battle, for you cannot defend us, nor the territory subject to this city, if you remain penned up within the walls. If God is well disposed to you, and you defeat the enemy, we will stand by the pledge of loyalty that we made. But if they beat you, have no fear, you will find the gates open. Come back in and save your lives."

Taken in by the trick, out they went ready for battle. But they were defeated by the army of Celsus, and retreating they returned to the city where they found the gates barred. The army was stung by javelins from the rear and showered with stones by the townsmen, so the troops made for the river Rhône. There, supporting themselves on their shields, they tried to reach the farther bank. The strength of the current swept many of them away to their deaths, and the Rhône now did to the Arvernians what the Simois is said to have once done to the Trojans:

> It turned over beneath its waves the shields and helmets of men and their strong bodies. Here and there a man appeared, swimming in that vast torrent. [cf. Aeneid, I. 104 f., 118]

Swimming with difficulty, as I said, and supported by their shields, they were able to reach the flat ground on the other bank.

They regained their country not without considerable insult, having been stripped of their equipment and deprived of their horses. Firminus and Audovar, though, were allowed to withdraw. In this battle, notable Arvernians of the time were not only swept away by the force of the current but also cut down by the blows of their enemies' swords.

And so King Guntram, having recovered Arles, with his usual good will, restored Avignon to his brother's authority.

*Plague (IV 31)*

*For Cato and Cautinus, see* **51–2**.

...With the coming of the plague, people died in such numbers through the whole district [of the Auvergne] that the legions that fell could not be counted. For when the supply of coffins and planks ran out, ten or more people would be buried in a single trench. One Sunday, three hundred dead bodies were counted in the basilica of the blessed Peter alone. Death was sudden. There would appear on the groin or in the armpit a sore in the shape of a serpent and people would be killed by the poison so quickly that they took their last breath the second or third day after infection. Moreover the power of the poison robbed them of their senses.

It was at this time that the priest Cato died. When many had fled the epidemic, he stayed where he was, courageously burying people and saying mass. He was a priest of considerable humanity and a great lover of the poor. And if he could be proud, these virtues, I believe, made up for it. Bishop Cautinus [of Clermont], after running around from place to place in fear of the plague, returned to the city. He caught it and died on the Friday before Easter Sunday. At the very same hour, Tetradius his cousin also died. At that time the populations of Lyons, Bourges, Cahors, and Dijon were seriously depleted by the plague.

*Alboin and the Lombards Invade Italy, a. 568 (IV 41)*

Alboin, king of the Lombards, who had married Chlodoswintha, the daughter of King Chlothar, left his country and set out for Italy with all the Lombard people. They mustered their forces and set off with their wives and children, with the intention of settling there. They entered the country and brought the land under their control, spending almost seven years roving about despoiling churches and killing priests.

When his wife Chlodoswintha died, Alboin married another wife, whose father he had killed a short time before. For this reason the woman always hated her husband and waited for a chance to avenge the wrong done her father. And so it happened that she poisoned her husband, after acquiring a passion for one of the household slaves. When Alboin died, she went off with the slave, but they were both captured and put to death.

The Lombards then set another king over themselves [a. 574].

## Mummolus The Patrician

*His Career and Campaigns against the Saxons and Lombards (IV 42, 44)*

Eunius, also called Mummolus, was promoted to the post of patrician by King Guntram. It is necessary, I think, to recollect at greater length certain details about the beginning of his service.

He was a native of the city of Auxerre. His father was Peonius, who held the post of count of this city. Peonius sent his son with gifts to the king to secure reappointment to the office. The son delivered his father's presents, but secured his father's comital office for himself, and displaced a father whose interests he should have furthered. Advancing step by step from this start, Mummolus rose to great prominence.

When the Lombards broke into Gaul [a. 570/71], the patrician Amatus, who had lately succeeded Celsus, went against them, but after joining battle, retreated and was killed. The Lombards were said to have wreaked such havoc on the Burgundians that the dead could not be counted. Loaded with plunder, the Lombards withdrew to Italy. On their departure, Eunius, also named Mummolus, was summoned by the king and won the high office of the patriciate.

The Lombards made a second inroad into Gaul and reached as far as Mustiae Calmes near the city of Embrun. Mummolus mustered his forces and marched there with the Burgundians. He surrounded the Lombards with his army and also made an abattis. Attacking them in the remoteness of the forest, he killed a good number and captured some, sending them to the king. The king had them kept under guard in various places through the country. A few somehow escaped and brought the news back to their homeland. Present in this battle were Salonius and Sagittarius, brothers and bishops, whose protection was not the heavenly cross; instead they were armed with the helmet and mailcoat of the world, and, what is worse, are reported to have killed many with their own hands. This was Mummolus's first victory.

After this, the Saxons who had accompanied the Lombards into Italy again burst into Gaul [a. 571/74], and pitched camp in the territory of Riez, that is, near the villa of Estoublon. Dispersing through the villas of the neighboring

towns, they plundered, took captives, and laid everything waste. When Mummolus learned of this, he mustered his forces. Attacking them, he killed many
thousands, not stopping the slaughter until evening, when night put an end
to it. For he had found men with their guard down, with no thought of what
was about to happen.

In the morning, the Saxons drew up their forces and got ready for battle,
but messengers passed from one army to the other and they made peace.
Giving presents to Mummolus and abandoning all the plunder of the region
and the captives, they withdrew, first swearing an oath that they would come
back to Gaul so as to be subjects of the Frankish kings and allies of the
Franks.

The Saxons returned to Italy and, collecting their wives and children and
all their movable goods, made preparations to return to Gaul, in expectation
that Sigibert would assemble them and establish them in the district from
which they had set out. They formed two columns, as they say, and one came
by way of Nice and the other by Embrun, in fact taking the road they had
traveled the previous year. They joined up in the territory of Avignon.

This was harvest time. For the most part the crops of the district lay out in
the open; the inhabitants had not yet started to store any of them at home.
The Saxons arrived and divided the crops among themselves. They gathered
the grain up, ground it, and ate it, leaving nothing to those who had done the
work. But afterwards, when they had used up the harvest and had arrived on
the bank of the Rhône — they had to cross the river to enter the kingdom
of King Sigibert — Mummolus met them.

"You will not cross this river," he said. "Look, you have laid waste the land
of my lord king. You have gathered crops, plundered herds, put houses to the
torch, and cut down the olive groves and vineyards. You will go no further
unless you first compensate those you have left poor. Otherwise you will not
escape my hands. I shall put you, your wives, and your children to the sword
and avenge the wrong done to my lord king Guntram."

Then they were very much afraid, and, giving many thousand pieces of
gold to save themselves, they were allowed to cross. And so they came to
Clermont.

It was then springtime. There they brought out bronze bars stamped as if
they were gold. Anyone seeing them would have no doubt that they were
anything but gold proved and tested; for it was colored, by what means I
know not. For this reason, some people were deceived by the trick and, giving gold but receiving bronze, were made poor.

The Saxons went on to King Sigibert and were settled in the land from
which they had first come.

After this, three Lombard dukes, Amo, Zaban, and Rodan, burst into Gaul
[a. 574]. Amo took the route by Embrun and pushed as far as the villa called

Macho in the territory of Avignon, which villa Mummolus had obtained as a gift from the king. Here he pitched his tents. Zaban, coming down by the town of Die, reached Valence, where he set up his camp. Rodan advanced to Grenoble, where he pitched his tents. Amo subdued the province of Arles and the towns in its vicinity and, marching as far as the stony plain near Marseilles, stripped it of its herds and inhabitants. He made preparations to besiege Aix, but withdrew when he received twenty-two pounds of silver. Rodan and Zaban did much the same in the towns they came across.

As soon as this was reported to Mummolus, he mustered an army and intercepted Rodan, who had subdued the city of Grenoble. Although Mummolus' forces had difficulty crossing the Isère river, by the will of God, an animal entered the river, revealing a ford, and so the troops readily reached the farther bank. Seeing this, the Lombards without delay drew their swords and attacked them. Battle was joined and the Lombards were cut down so badly that Rodan, wounded by a spear, took refuge high in the mountains. With the five hundred men he had left, Rodan pushed through remote forests and managed to reach Zaban, then besieging Valence. He told him all that had happened. They then gave up all their plunder, and both returned to Embrun. There Mummolus confronted them with a countless host. The Lombard forces were cut down almost to the point of annihilation in the battle, and the dukes returned to Italy with a few men.

When they reached Susa, there was no warm welcome from the inhabitants, especially as Sisinnius, the emperor's master of the soldiers, had his headquarters there. Then someone pretending to be a servant of Mummolus presented a letter to Sisinnius in the presence of Zaban, greeting him in the name of Mummolus.

"Mummolus himself," proclaimed the messenger, "is close at hand!"

At these words, Zaban departed at great speed, passing the city by. When Amo heard the news, he gathered all his booty and headed off down the road. But held up by the snow, he had to abandon his spoil and barely broke clear with a few companions.

They were terrified by the power of Mummolus.

### Mummolus goes to Tours (IV 45)

Mummolus conducted many campaigns from which he emerged victorious. When, after the death of Charibert [a. 567], Chilperic had overrun Tours and Poitiers, which by agreement had been allotted to King Sigibert, this king joined up with his brother Guntram, and they chose Mummolus to restore these cities to their rightful authority. Mummolus came to Tours, drove out Clovis, Chilperic's son, exacted from the people oaths of loyalty to King

Sigibert, and proceeded to Poitiers. Basilius and Sigar, two citizens of the city, gathered people together and tried to resist; but Mummolus surrounded them from all sides and overpowered, crushed, and destroyed them. This is how he came to Poitiers and exacted oaths of loyalty to Sigibert.

This account of Mummolus is enough for a while. The rest must be told in its proper place at a later point.

## Civil War Takes a Serious Turn

*Theudebert, Chilperic's Son, Takes the Cities of Sigibert (IV 47-48)*

When Clovis, son of Chilperic, was driven from Tours [cf. IV 45], he went to Bordeaux [a. 573]. He was staying in this city, with no one particularly bothering him, when one of Sigibert's supporters, a certain Sigulf, attacked him. Clovis fled, and Sigulf pursued him with trumpets and horns, as if driving a running deer. Clovis had difficulty finding a clear way back to his father. He managed to get back to him, though, going by way of Angers.

When a dispute arose between King Guntram and King Sigibert, King Guntram assembled all the bishops of his kingdom at Paris for them to pronounce which of the two was in the right. But so that civil war should grow in intensity, the sinfulness of the kings caused them to pay no attention.

In anger Chilperic sent his eldest son Theudebert to overrun Sigibert's cities, Tours, Poitiers, and other places lying on this side of the Loire. Theudebert had once been captured by Sigibert and taken an oath to be loyal to him [cf. IV 23]. Theudebert came to Poitiers and fought against Duke Gundovald. His forces retreated and Theudebert slaughtered a great many people there. He also burned most of the district of Tours and would have destroyed all of it, had not the inhabitants surrendered in time. Gathering his forces, he overran, laid waste, and demolished the territories of Limoges, Cahors, and other regions round about them. He burned the churches, took away the sacred vessels, killed clerics, drove monks from the monasteries and treated the nuns shamefully, and laid everything waste. At that time, the sorrow in the churches was greater than in the time of Diocletian's persecution.

And to this day we are astonished and wonder why such disasters fell upon them. But let us recall what their predecessors did and what they do. After the preaching of the bishops, their ancestors gave up temples for churches; they daily take plunder from the churches. Their ancestors respected with their whole hearts the bishops of the Lord and listened to them; they not only refuse to listen to them, but even persecute them. Their ancestors enriched the monasteries and churches; they demolish and ruin them....

### Sigibert Goes to Paris (IV 49)

While these events were taking place, King Sigibert mustered the peoples who live on the other side of the Rhine and, initiating civil war, made preparations to march against his brother Chilperic [a. 574]. When Chilperic heard, he sent envoys to his brother Guntram. Together the two of them made a treaty that neither brother would allow the other to be destroyed.

Sigibert advanced at the head of those peoples, but Chilperic on his side hung back with his army. When Sigibert could find no way of crossing the Seine to attack his brother, he sent an ultimatum to Guntram.

"Unless you allow me to cross this river through your kingdom," he said, "I shall come against you with all my forces."

Fearing attack, Guntram made a treaty with him and allowed him to cross. Chilperic obviously got the impression that Guntram had abandoned him and had gone over to Sigibert, and so he moved his camp to Havelu, a place not far from Chartres. Sigibert followed trying to get him to make ready a field of battle. Chilperic was afraid that, if their two armies fought, their rule would collapse. So he sought terms of peace and restored Sigibert's cities that Theudebert had wrongfully occupied. He asked on behalf of the inhabitants of the cities that they in no way be held guilty, for Theudebert by fire and sword had unjustly forced them to change sides.

At this time most of the communities around Paris were destroyed by fire; houses and other properties were plundered by the enemy and even captives led away. King Sigibert tried to protest their doing this, but he could not control the raging madness of the peoples who had come from over the Rhine and calmly endured it all until he could return home. At this time some of them even criticized him for having pulled them back from battle. But Sigibert was a fearless man, and mounting his horse, rode towards them, calming them down with gentle words; many of them he later had stoned to death.

There is no doubt that it was not without the power of blessed Martin that the kings made peace without recourse to arms; on the very day they made peace, the limbs of three paralytics were straightened in the basilica of the saint. I recorded this miracle, with God's aid, in books I later wrote [*The Miracles of Saint Martin*, II 5-7].

### Treaty between Guntram and Chilperic. Death of Theudebert, a. 574/5 (IV 50)

It makes one heart-sick to record these civil wars.

A year later, Chilperic once more sent envoys to his brother Guntram with a message saying, "Let my brother come and we can have a meeting.

And when we have made peace, let us march against Sigibert, our common enemy."

When this was done, and they had met and honored one another with gifts, Chilperic mustered his forces and advanced as far as Rheims, burning and devastating everything in his path.

Sigibert heard the news and a second time summoned the peoples whom I mentioned. He came to Paris and made preparations to march against his brother, while sending orders to the people of Châteaudun and Tours for them to march against Theudebert. When they made up excuses, the king sent Dukes Godigisel and Guntram [Boso] to take command. They levied an army and set out against Theudebert. Abandoned by his forces, Theudebert was left with a few men, but he did not hesitate to come out to fight. The two sides met and Theudebert was defeated and cut down on the field; and his lifeless body, sad to say, was despoiled by the enemy. After being taken up by a certain Aunulf, it was washed, clothed in appropriate garments, and then buried in the city of Angoulême.

Chilperic, learning that Guntram and Sigibert had once more come to terms, fortified himself within the walls of Tournai with his wife and his sons.

### Death of King Sigibert, a. 575 (IV 51)

In that year a bright light was seen crossing the sky, just as we saw earlier before the death of Chlothar.

Sigibert, having taken the cities around Paris, marched as far as Rouen, intending to turn the cities over to the forces [from across the Rhine]. He was stopped from doing this by his own followers. On his return, he entered Paris, and there Brunhild came to him with her children. Then the Franks who had once followed the elder Childebert [I], sent a delegation to Sigibert to say that, when he reached them, they would abandon Chilperic and make him king over them. Hearing this, he sent troops ahead to besiege his brother in Tournai, intending to go there himself soon.

The holy bishop Germanus said to him, "If you leave without the intention of killing your brother, you will return alive and victorious. But if you have something else in mind, you will die. This is what the Lord spoke through Solomon, 'If you prepare a pit for your brother, you will fall into it [cf. Prov. 26:27].'"

But because of his sins, the king paid no attention.

He came to the villa called Vitry. The entire the army gathered about him, placed him on a shield, and made him king over them. At this time two slaves bewitched by Queen Fredegund, carrying sturdy knives, commonly called scramasaxes, smeared with poison, pretended to bring forward a request and stabbed him from both sides. He shouted out and collapsed. He gave up his spirit not long afterwards.

There too fell Charigisel, his chamberlain. And Sigila, who had once come from Gothia, was badly cut up. He was apprehended afterwards by King Chilperic and came to a cruel end: his every joint was burned with hot irons and he was torn limb from limb. Charigisel's character was as weak as his desires were strong. He had risen from mean circumstances and became a great man at the king's court through flattery. He was a seeker after other people's property and a breaker of testaments. The circumstances of his departure from life were such that, with death approaching, he who had so often invalidated the wills of others was not granted the time to finish a will of his own.

Chilperic was caught in a perilous situation, uncertain whether he could escape or would be destroyed, until messengers arrived to inform him of his brother's death. Then he left Tournai with his wife and children, prepared Sigibert's body and buried it in the villa of Lambres. It was later transferred to Soissons to the basilica of Saint Medard, which Sigibert himself had built, and was buried there by the side of his father Chlothar.

Sigibert died in the fourteenth year of his reign, at the age of forty. From the death of Theudebert [I] the elder to that of Sigibert there were twenty-nine years. Eighteen days passed between his death and that of his nephew Theudebert.

Upon the death of Sigibert, his son Childebert reigned in his place.

## A Summary of the Years

From the creation to the flood there were 2242 years. From the flood to Abraham, 942 years. From Abraham to the departure of the children of Israel from Egypt, 462 years. From the departure of the children of Israel from Egypt to the building of the temple of Solomon, 480 years. From the building of the temple to its desolation and the exile to Babylon, 390 years. From the exile to the passion of the Lord, 668 years. From the passion of the Lord to the death of Saint Martin, 412 years. From the death of Saint Martin to the death of King Clovis, 112 years. From the death of King Clovis to the death of Theudebert, 37 years. From the death of Theudebert to the death of Sigibert, 29 years. Which make a total of 5774 years.

*This computation of years ends Book IV.*

# 49. THE REIGN OF CHILDEBERT II, a. 575–90
## (BOOKS V–X)

*From Book V onward Gregory's narrative proceeds year by year, dated according to the regnal years of King Childebert II, the son of Sigibert and, in Gregory's view, the rightful ruler of Tours. Childebert's reign, as Gregory tells us, began on 25 December, Christmas day. From now on, I give the regnal year of Childebert and its anno domini equivalent as a heading. An increasingly important figure in Gregory's narrative from now on is Egidius, bishop of Rheims. Egidius, incidentally, consecrated Gregory as bishop of Tours in 573.*

## I. TO THE DEATH OF CHILPERIC, a. 575-84 (OCTOBER) (BOOKS V–VI)

*Gregory's Prologue to Book V*

It is unpleasant for me to record the various civil wars that severely damage the Frankish people and kingdom; worse still, here we now see that time the Lord foretold would be the beginning of sorrows: "Father shall rise against son, son against father, brother against brother, kinsman against kinsman [cf. Matth. 10:12]." They should have been terrified by the examples of former kings: as soon as they were divided, they were destroyed by their enemies. How often has the very city of cities, the head of the whole earth, fallen as a result of its civil wars; when they ceased, it has risen again as if from the ground! Would that you too, kings, were engaged in battles like those in which your fathers sweated, so that foreigners, terrified by the peace you keep amongst yourselves, might be crushed by your strength! Remember what Clovis, the author of your victories, did, he who killed opposing kings, crushed hostile foreigners, subdued their lands, and left to you complete and unimpaired rule over them! And when he did this he had neither silver nor gold such as you now have in your treasuries.

What are you doing? What are you after? What do you not have in abundance? In your residences luxuries are plentiful, in your storehouses wine, grain, and oil abound, in your treasuries gold and silver are piled up. One thing is missing: because you do not maintain peace, you lack the grace of God. Why does one take what belongs to another? Why does each lust after what is not his own? I beg of you, beware this saying of the apostle: "If you bite and devour one another, watch out that you are not both eaten [cf. Gal. 5:15]."

Study carefully the books of the ancients and you shall see what civil wars produce. Look for what Orosius writes about the Carthaginians. When he says that their city and country were destroyed after seven hundred years, he adds: "What preserved this state so long? Concord. What destroyed this state after such a long period of time? Discord." Beware discord, beware civil wars, which destroy you and your people. What else is to be expected but that, when your forces have collapsed, left without help, you shall fall immediately, overwhelmed by enemy nations? And, king, if you take pleasure in civil war, then engage in the one waged, according to the apostle, within the person, so that the spirit may struggle against the flesh and vices fall before virtues. Then you may serve your chief, that is to say Christ, as a free man, you who in shackles once served the root of evil.

## Year I of Childebert II, a. 576

### Succession of Childebert and Banishment of Brunhild (V 1)

King Sigibert was killed at Vitry while Queen Brunhild was staying with her children in Paris. When she was given the news and, in the distress of her grief and sorrow, did not know what she was doing, Duke Gundovald grabbed Childebert, her little son, and spirited him away, saving him from imminent death. Then he assembled the peoples over which Childebert's father had reigned and proclaimed him king. Childebert was barely five years old. He began his reign on the day of the Lord's birth.

In the first year of Childebert's reign, King Chilperic came to Paris, seized Brunhild and sent her to Rouen in exile. He took away the treasures that she had brought to Paris and ordered her daughters detained at Meaux.

At this time Roccolen came to Tours with troops from Le Mans, took plunder, and committed many crimes. Subsequently I shall tell how he was struck down and killed by the power of the holy Martin for all the evil he did.

### Merovech, Chilperic's Son, Marries Brunhild (V 2)

Chilperic sent his son Merovech to Poitiers with an army. But Merovech ignored his father's orders and came instead to Tours, where he spent the holy days of Easter [5 April]. His army did a great deal of damage to the district. Merovech himself made for Rouen, pretending he was going to see his mother, and there met up with Queen Brunhild and married her.

When Chilperic heard that Merovech had married his uncle's widow contrary to divine law and the canons, he became very ill-tempered, and quicker than the time it takes to tell of it he was off to Rouen. When Merovech and Brunhild realized that he was determined to separate them, they took refuge in the basilica of Saint Martin that had been built of wooden planks on the wall of the city. The king arrived, and tried many a ruse to get them out, but they refused to trust him, thinking that he was tricking them. Finally he swore an oath to them, declaring that, if it should be God's will, he would not attempt to separate them.

They accepted this oath and came out of the basilica. Chilperic kissed them, received them honorably, and took a meal with them. A few days later he returned to Soissons, taking Merovech with him.

*Chilperic's Suspicions of Merovech. Deserters. Duke Rauching (V 3)*

While they were in Rouen, there was a gathering of certain men of Champagne who marched on the city of Soissons, drove out Queen Fredegund and Chilperic's son Clovis, and tried to get the city under their control. When Chilperic found out, he brought his army there, sending messages in advance warning them that, if they did no wrong to him, both armies would escape destruction. They paid no heed to the warning and got ready to fight. Chilperic's side won the battle, driving back the other side and killing many good and experienced fighting men. With the remainder put to flight, he entered the city of Soissons.

After these events occurred, the king began to suspect his son Merovech on account of his marriage with Brunhild, saying that this battle was caused by his villainy. Chilperic took Merovech's weapons from him and had him put under guard, though not a close one, all the while pondering what he would do with him in the future.

Godin, who had transferred himself from Sigibert's kingdom to Chilperic and been generously rewarded by him, was the real originator of that fight, though, when defeated in the field, he was the first to run away. Chilperic took away the villas he had granted him from the fisc in the territory of Soissons and conferred them now on the church of Saint Medard. Sudden death caught up with Godin himself not long afterwards.

His widow married Rauching, a man full of every conceit, swollen with pride and shamelessly arrogant. He acted toward those under his control like someone without any awareness of human feelings, committing in his fury unspeakable wrongs against his own people beyond the limits of mere human wickedness and stupidity. For example, when he gave a feast, and a servant, as is customary, stood before him holding a candle, he would have the servant's legs bared and make him hold the candle between his shins until the light went out; when the candle was relit, he would do the same again until the legs of the slave holding the candle were all burned. And if the slave uttered a sound or tried to move from that place to another, he was threatened with a drawn sword so that Rauching could delight in the pleasure of the slave weeping.

Some people said that at this time two of his slaves, a man and a girl, were in love with each other, something that often happens. And when this love had lasted for two years or more, they mated, and both sought the refuge of the church. When Rauching found out, he went to the local bishop; he asked that his slaves be restored to him at once, saying that he had pardoned them.

At the time the bishop said to him, "Make sure you know what respect should be paid to the churches of God; you cannot take these two slaves, unless you promise to acknowledge that their union is lasting and pledge that they shall be spared any physical punishment."

Rauching remained silent for a while, not knowing quite what to think, but at last, turning to the bishop, he placed his hand upon the altar and swore an oath.

"They will never be parted by me," he said, "but I shall see to it that they remain in this union, because, although I am annoyed that this was connived at without my consent, still I am happy with the fact that neither of them has married the slave of another master."

The bishop believed in a simple-hearted fashion the crafty man's promise and restored the slaves, thinking they had been pardoned. Rauching took them, thanked the bishop, and went home. He at once ordered a tree to be felled and limbed, the trunk split with wedges driven in to its ends and hollowed out. He had the hollowed trunk placed in a trench dug in the ground to a depth of three or four feet. He laid the girl out in it as if she were dead and had the male slave thrown in on top. Putting the lid on the tree trunk, he filled in the trench.

"I have not broken my oath that they should never be separated," he said, burying them alive.

When the news reached the bishop, he came quickly and, rebuking Rauching, had trouble getting the slaves uncovered. However he only got the male slave out alive; he found the girl suffocated.

Rauching was utterly depraved in committing deeds like this, having no other talents than derisive laughter, treachery, and every manner of perversity. His departure from life consequently was fitting for the likes of someone who did such deeds when he had the benefits of this life. I intend to relate the events of his death at a later point [IX 9].

Siggo the referendary, who had been the keeper of King Sigibert's signet-ring and had been called upon by King Chilperic to hold the same office he held in the time of his brother, now deserted Chilperic and went over to Childebert, son of Sigibert. The property he had held in Soissons was obtained by Ansovald. Many more of those who transferred themselves from the rule of King Sigibert to Chilperic now came back. The wife of Siggo died not long afterwards; but he married another one.

### Roccolen Comes to Tours (V 4)

In these days, Roccolen, who had been sent by Chilperic [cf.V 1], arrived in Tours with great boasting and pitched his camp beyond the Loire. He sent me a message telling me to drag from the holy basilica [Duke] Guntram [Boso], who was at that time accused in the death of Theudebert. If I would not do so, he would have the city and all its suburbs burned. I listened and sent a delegation to him to say that what he wanted done had not been done since ancient times. Violation of a holy basilica could not at all be permitted. If it should happen, the outcome would be beneficial neither to him nor to the king who authorized the order. He should stand in greater fear of the holiness of the bishop [Martin] whose power only the day before had straightened paralytic limbs.

This did not frighten him at all. While staying in an establishment belonging to the church on the other side of the river Loire, he tore apart the house itself, which was held together with nails. The troops of Le Mans, who at the time had come with him, carried off the nails by the bagful, destroyed the grain, and laid everything waste.

But as Roccolen did this, he was struck by God, and, becoming saffron-colored with the royal disease [jaundice], he sent harsh commands, saying, "If you do not eject Duke Guntram from the basilica today, I will destroy every growing thing around the city, so that the place will be ready for the plow."

Meanwhile the holy day of epiphany came, and he became more and more tormented, at which point, taking the advice of his men, he crossed the river and approached the city. When the clergy came out of the cathedral and headed towards the holy basilica [of Saint Martin] singing psalms, he rode on horseback behind the cross, preceded by standards. When he entered the holy basilica, in fact, his wild threats abated, and, when he went back to the cathedral, he could take no food on that day.

Although he was very short of breath, he went off to Poitiers. It was now holy Lent, during which period he often ate baby rabbits. Proceedings in which he would penalize and condemn the citizens of Poitiers were set for the Kalends of March, but he rendered up his life on the day before. And in this way his pride and arrogance were finally stilled.

### Clovis Campaigns from Tours. Mummolus Attacks Duke Desiderius (V 13)

King Chilperic sent his son Clovis to Tours. Clovis gathered an army, crossed the regions of Tours and Angers, advancing as far as Saintes, and took the city.

Mummolus, patrician of King Guntram, passed with a great army into the territory of Limoges, and engaged Desiderius, Chilperic's duke, in battle. He lost five thousand men in this engagement, but Desiderius lost twenty-four thousand. Desiderius himself barely escaped by flight. The patrician Mummolus then returned through Auvergne, which his army laid waste in places. In this fashion he made his way to Burgundy.

*Merovech is Tonsured and Flees to Saint Martin's Basilica at Tours (V 14)*

After this, Merovech was tonsured while being kept in custody by his father; changing his clothing for the customary garb of the clergy, he was ordained a priest and sent to the monastery at Le Mans called Aninsola [Saint Calais] to be instructed in the duties of priests. Guntram Boso who, as I said, was living at the time in the basilica of Saint Martin, heard about this and sent the subdeacon Rigulf to advise Merovech to try secretly to make it to the basilica of Saint Martin. When Merovech was on his way, Gailen his slave came along from another direction. And since the force escorting Merovech was small, he was rescued by Gailen on the road, and, covering his head and putting on secular clothes, Merovech reached the shrine of the blessed Martin.

I was celebrating mass when, finding the door open, he entered the basilica. After mass, he asked me to give him some blessed bread. With me at that time was Ragnemod, bishop of the see of Paris, who had succeeded the holy Germanus. When I refused the request, Merovech began to shout that I had no right to suspend him from communion without the consent of our brother bishops. When he said this, with the consent of the brother bishop who was present, and without our transgressing canon law, he received the blessed bread from me. My fear was that, by suspending one person from communion, I would end up the killer of many more. For he kept threatening to put to death some of my people if he did not get communion from me. Still, the harm the district of Tours suffered on this account was considerable.

Around this time, Nicetius, the husband of my niece, went on business of his own to King Chilperic, accompanied by my deacon, who told the king of Merovech's flight.

When Queen Fredegund saw them, she said, "They are spies come to find out what the king is doing and to report it to Merovech."

She immediately had them despoiled and sent into exile, from which they were released in the seventh month.

Then Chilperic sent me a message to say, "Drive that apostate from the basilica. If you don't, I'll put the whole region to the torch."

I wrote back that it was impossible that what had not happened in the time of the heretics should be done now in Christian times, but he mustered a force and ordered it to march to Tours.

## Year II of Childebert, a. 577

In the second year of King Childebert, when Merovech saw that his father was set in this purpose, he thought about going to Brunhild, taking with him Duke Guntram Boso.

"Far be it from me," said Merovech, "to be the cause of the basilica of lord Martin suffering violence or his country being subjugated."

He entered the basilica during vigils and made an offering of his possessions to the tomb of the blessed Martin. He prayed for the saint to help him and to grant him his favor as he attempted to gain the kingship.

Leudast, who was then count [of Tours] and had set many snares for him out of devotion to Fredegund, at last trapped his servants who had gone out into the country and put them to the sword. He longed to kill Merovech himself if he could find the right spot.

But Merovech followed Guntram Boso's advice. Wanting to avenge himself, he gave orders for Marileif the chief physician to be seized as he was returning from the king's court. After beating him severely, he took away the gold and silver and other things he had on him and left him naked, and actually would have killed him if the man had not slipped out the hands of those who were beating him and made his way to the cathedral. I clothed him and later, having managed to get his life spared, sent him back to Poitiers.

Merovech talked about the many crimes of his father and stepmother. Although the crimes were partly true, it was not acceptable to God, I believe, for word of them to be spread by a son, as I learned from subsequent events. One day I happened to dine with him, and, while we were sitting together, he humbly asked for something to be read for the instruction of his soul. So I opened the book of Solomon and chose the first verse I came upon. This is what it said: "The eye of him who looks askance at his father, the ravens of the valleys shall pick it out [Prov. 30:17]." He did not understand it, but I regarded this verse as having been revealed by the Lord.

Then Guntram Boso sent a servant to a woman whom he had known from the days of King Charibert; she possessed the spirit of prophecy, and he wanted her to tell him what was about to happen. He used to claim, moreover, that she had made known to him before the event, not only the year, but even the day and hour in which king Charibert died.

This is what she told Guntram's servants to tell him: "It will happen that King Chilperic will die this year. And Merovech will exclude his brothers and take the whole kingdom. You will hold the ducal authority over all his kingdom for five years. But in the sixth year, in one of the cities on the river Loire, on its right bank, you will obtain the honor of the episcopal office with the approval of the people, and you will pass from this world old and full of days."

The servants returned and reported this to their master, and he, puffed up with vanity as if he were already sitting on the throne of the cathedral of Tours, immediately related the words to me.

"These question must be put to God," I said, laughing at his foolishness. "What the devil promises is not to be believed. 'He is a liar from the start and never truthful' [cf. John 8: 44]."

He left confounded, and I had a good laugh at a man who thought such things believable.

Then one night, after vigils had been celebrated in the basilica of the holy bishop [Martin], I had gone to bed and fallen asleep when I saw an angel flying through the air.

As it passed by the holy basilica, it cried out woefully in a loud voice, "God has struck down Chilperic and all his sons. No issue of his loins has survived who will rule his kingdom forever." He had at this time four sons by different wives, not to speak of daughters.

When these words were later on fulfilled, I then understood clearly that the promises of soothsayers were false.

Then, while these men were staying in the basilica of Saint Martin, Queen Fredegund, who was already secretly giving Guntram Boso protection for his part in the death of Theudebert, sent him a message saying, "If you can get Merovech out of the basilica so that he can be killed, you shall receive a great reward from me."

Guntram thought the assassins were nearby.

"Why do we hang back like slackers and cowards and skulk around the basilica like half-wits," he said to Merovech. "Have the horses brought round. Let's take our hawks and dogs, go hunting, and enjoy the open countryside."

This was cunning on his part to get Merovech away from the holy basilica. As for Guntram, in other respects he was really a good man, but he was too ready to perjure himself, and truth be told, he never took an oath to any of his friends without disregarding it right away.

And so they went out of the basilica and went as far as Jocundiacus, an establishment quite near the city. But Merovech was harmed by no one.

Guntram was accused at the time of killing Theudebert, as I have said. King Chilperic therefore wrote a letter addressed to the tomb of Saint Martin asking the blessed Martin to write back to him whether it was permissible for Guntram to be dragged from his basilica or not. The deacon Baudegisil, who delivered the letter, put a clean sheet of paper on the holy tomb alongside the one he had brought. After waiting three days, and getting no answer, he returned to Chilperic, who then sent others to exact an oath from Guntram not to leave the church without Chilperic's knowledge. Guntram eagerly took the oath and gave an altarcloth as pledge that he would not leave there without the king's permission.

As for Merovech, he did not believe the prophetess, but placed three books on the saint's tomb, namely, Psalms, Kings, and the Gospels, and kept a vigil through the whole night, asking the blessed confessor to reveal to him what was going to happen and to let him know by a sign from God whether or not he would obtain royal power. After this, he spent three days in fasts, vigils, and prayer. Going to the blessed tomb a second time, he opened one of the books.

It was the book of Kings, and this was the first verse on the page he opened: "Because you have forsaken the Lord your God and have gone after other gods and have not done right in his sight, therefore the Lord your God has delivered you into the hands of your enemies [cf. I Kings 9:9]."

This was the verse found in the Psalms: "But you have set evils upon them because of their deceitfulness; you have cast them down while they were raised up. How have they been reduced to desolation? They have suddenly failed and perished because of their iniquities [Ps. 73:18, 19]."

And in the Gospels, this was found: "You know that in two days it is the passover and the son of man will be handed over to crucifixion [cf. Matt. 26:2]."

These answers troubled him, and he wept for a long time at the tomb of the blessed bishop. Then, taking Duke Guntram with him, he left with five hundred men or more.

When Merovech had left the holy basilica and was making his way through the territory of Auxerre, he was captured by Erpo, a duke of King Guntram. Although under his custody, he escaped, I do not know how, and entered the basilica of Saint Germanus. When King Guntram heard this, he got angry, fined Erpo seven hundred gold pieces, and removed him from office.

"You held someone who my brother says is his enemy," said Guntram. "Now if you were of a mind to do this, you should first have brought him to me; but otherwise, you should not have touched someone you were not prepared to hold."

King Chilperic's army approached Tours, plundering, burning, and laying the district waste, and it did not spare Saint Martin's property; whatever it touched it stole, neither respecting nor fearing God.

Merovech remained nearly two months in the basilica of Saint Germanus and then fled, going to Queen Brunhild, but he was not accepted by the

Austrasians. His father put an army in the field against the people of Champagne, believing that he was hiding there. But it caused no harm, nor could it find Merovech.

### King Guntram Loses His Sons and Allies himself with Childebert (V 17)

King Guntram put to the sword two sons of the late Magnachar for making hateful and accursed charges against Queen Austrechild and her children; the king had his fisc confiscate their property. He himself lost two sons, who were suddenly overcome by disease; he was deeply saddened by their death, for he was left bereaved without children...

Afterwards King Guntram sent envoys to his nephew Childebert, seeking peace and asking a meeting. It was then that Childebert with his chief officials came to see him. They met at what is called Stone Bridge, greeting one another and exchanging kisses.

King Guntram said, "It has happened that through my sins I have been left without children, and so I ask that this nephew of mine be my son."

And setting him upon his own seat, Guntram handed over to him his whole kingdom.

"Let a single shield protect us," he said, "and a single spear defend us. Should I have sons, I will nevertheless regard you as one of them, so that, God as my witness, you will keep the love I promise you today, sharing it with them."

The chief officials of Childebert likewise made a promise on his behalf.

Eating and drinking together, they honored one another with suitable gifts and departed in peace. They also sent a delegation to King Chilperic, demanding that he restore what he had taken from their kingdom; and if he would not do so, he was to make ready a field of battle.

Chilperic, disdainful of the threat, had circuses put up at Soissons and at Paris as a show for the people.

### The Trial of Bishop Praetextatus. Merovech's Death (V 18)

After these events, Chilperic heard that Praetextatus, bishop of Rouen, was giving people gifts contrary to the king's interests and had him summoned to his presence. He examined him and discovered that the bishop was in possession of property entrusted to him by Queen Brunhild. This was confiscated, and the king ordered him kept in exile until the bishops could convene a hearing.

The council met, and Bishop Praetextatus was brought before it. The bishops who attended convened in the basilica of the holy apostle Peter in Paris.

"Bishop," said the king to Praetextatus, "why did you think to join in marriage my enemy Merovech, who ought to have acted as a son, with his aunt, that is, his uncle's wife? Or were you unacquainted with what the canons have established for such a case? Also, not only did you demonstrably go too far in this matter, but you even acted in conjunction with Merovech to give gifts to bring about my assassination. You have made a son an enemy of his father, you have led the people astray with money, so that none of them would maintain the loyalty they had for me, and you have tried to hand my kingdom into the hands of another."

When he said this, the crowd of Franks let out a roar and tried to break open the church doors, intending to drag the bishop out and stone him, but the king stopped this happening.

When Bishop Praetextatus denied having done what the king charged, false witnesses came forward who showed various valuable articles.

"These and these you gave us," they said, "on condition we pledge our loyalty to Merovech."

"You're right that you have often received gifts from me," he said in response to these charges, "but it was not for the purpose of driving the king from the kingdom. Since you furnished me with excellent horses and other things, what else could I do but pay you back at the same value?"

The king returned to his quarters, but we remained seated as a group in the sacristy of the basilica of the blessed Peter. As we were talking together, suddenly Aetius, archdeacon of the bishopric of Paris, came in and greeted us.

"Hear me, bishops of God, gathered here together," he said. "In this hour you shall either exalt your name and show that you deserve a glowing reputation, or instead, if you don't have the sense to stand up for yourselves or if you allow your brother to be destroyed, hereafter no one will take you for bishops of God."

When he said this, none of the bishops said anything in reply. For they feared the savage anger of the queen, at whose instigation these proceedings were being conducted.

As they considered these words, with their fingers on their lips, I said, "Please listen to what I have to say, most holy bishops, especially you who seem to be on quite friendly terms with the king; furnish him with advice as befits holy men and priests, so that he is not destroyed by God's anger, losing his kingdom and reputation in an outburst against a servant of God."

When I said this, all were silent.

Since no one spoke, I added, "My lord bishops, remember the word of the prophet: 'If the watchman sees the iniquity of a person and does not speak, he shall be guilty for a lost soul.' Therefore do not remain silent, but speak out, and set this king's sins before his own eyes, in case some evil comes upon him, and you are held responsible for his soul. Surely you can't be unaware of what has happened in modern times? How Chlodomer captured Sigismund and threw him in prison, and Avitus, God's priest, said to him: 'Do not lay hands on him and when you go to Burgundy you will win the victory.' But he disregarded what was said to him by the priest and went ahead and killed him with his wife and sons. And Chlodomer went to Burgundy and was overcome by the enemy and killed. What about the emperor Maximus? When he forced the blessed Martin to associate with a certain bishop who was a homicide, and Martin gave in to the impious king in order to help free those condemned to death, Maximus was pursued by the judgment of the eternal king and, driven from the imperial throne, was condemned to the vilest death."

When I said this, no one said anything in reply, but all stared in astonishment.

However, two flatterers among them — it is sad to have to say that of bishops — gave a report to the king, telling him that he had no greater opponent of his interests than me. Promptly a court attendant was sent to bring me before him.

When I arrived, the king was standing beside a bower made of branches; on his right stood Bishop Bertram and on his left Ragnemod. There was a table covered with bread and various dishes in front of them.

On seeing me, the king said, "Bishop, you are supposed to confer justice freely on all. But look now, I don't get justice from you. As I see it, you are giving in to iniquity: your actions are an example of the proverb that the crow does not tear out the eye of another crow."

"If any one of us, king, tries to leave the path of justice," I replied, "he can be corrected by you. But if you abandon it, who shall take you to task? We speak to you, but you pay attention only if you wish. And if you refuse to listen, who will pass sentence on you if it is not He who has proclaimed that He is justice?"

He had been inflamed against me by his flatterers and replied, "I have found justice with everyone, but with you I cannot find it. I know what I shall do to disgrace you before the people and reveal to all that you are unjust. I shall assemble the people of Tours and tell them, 'You may cry out against Gregory that he is an unjust man and renders justice to no one.' And to those who cry this out, I will reply, 'I who am king cannot get justice from him. Shall you who are less than I find it?'"

"You do not know whether I am unjust." I said. "He to whom the secrets of the heart are revealed knows my conscience. What people falsely cry out when you revile me means nothing, for everyone knows it is your doing. This is why not I but you will be the one disgraced by the outcries. But why go on with this? You have the law and the canons; search them carefully and then you will know that the judgment of God hangs over you if you do not follow their commands."

Thinking that I did not understand his artfulness, he turned to the broth that was set in front of him, as if this would soothe me.

"I had this broth prepared for you," he said. "There is nothing else in it but fowl and a few chickpeas."

Recognizing his flattery, I replied, "My food is doing the will of God, without at all overlooking whatever he commands, not partaking of the pleasures of these delicacies. As for you who find fault with others in matters of justice, promise first that you will not neglect the law and the canons. Then I shall believe that you follow justice."

Then he stretched out his right hand and swore by almighty God that he would in no way overlook the teaching of the law and the canons. After that I took bread and wine and departed.

That night, when the hymns for the night had been sung, I heard heavy knocking on the door of my lodging. From the servant I sent to answer it, I learned that messengers from Queen Fredegund were there. They were brought in, and I received greetings from the queen. Then her servants asked me not to take a position contrary to her interests and, at the same time, promised two hundred pounds of silver if I attacked Praetextatus, and he was convicted.

"We already have the word of all the bishops," they said. "Don't be the only one in opposition."

"Even if you were to give me a thousand pounds of silver and gold," I said to them, "what else can I do but what the Lord tells me to do? I will promise one thing only, that I will follow what the others agree to in accordance with the canons."

Not understanding what I was saying, they thanked me and went away. In the morning some of the bishops came to me bearing a similar message; to them I gave the same answer.

We met in the morning in Saint Peter's basilica, and the king was present.

"The authority of the canons provides that a bishop detected in theft should be removed from the office of bishop," he said.

We asked who the bishop might be against whom the charge of theft was made.

"You saw the articles of value which he stole from me," the king answered.

Three days before the king had shown us two bundles full of costly articles and treasures of different sorts, valued at more than three thousand solidi, as well as a bag of coined gold, the weight of which suggested about two thousand pieces. The king said this had been stolen from him by the bishop.

The bishop answered, "I believe you remember that I came to you when Queen Brunhild left Rouen and told you that I was holding her property in trust, namely, five parcels, and that her servants came to me quite frequently to retrieve them but I would not release them without your advice. And king, you said to me, 'Rid yourself of this stuff and let the woman have her property back, in case hostility arises between me and my nephew Childebert over these goods.' I went back to the city and gave one roll to the servants, as they could carry no more. They returned a second time and asked for the others. I again sought the advice of your magnificence. And you gave me orders, 'Get rid of this stuff, bishop, get rid of it, so it won't be the cause of a quarrel.' I again gave them two bundles and two more remained in my possession. Why now do you make a false charge and accuse me of theft, when this case should be considered one not of theft but of custody?"

"If this property was considered as being in your possession for safekeeping," responded the king, "why did you open one of these bundles, cut in pieces a belt woven of gold thread and distribute it to men who were to drive me from the kingdom."

"I told you before," answered Praetextatus, "that I had received their gifts, and, as I had nothing at hand to give, I therefore presumed to take this and give it in return for their gifts. It seemed to be my property because it belonged to my son Merovech, whom I received from the baptismal font."

King Chilperic saw that he could not convict him with false charges, and, being thoroughly confounded and disturbed by his conscience, he left us and summoned certain of his flatterers.

"I confess," he said to them, "I've been beaten by the bishop's replies and I know that what he says is true. What can I do now if the queen's will is to be done with regards to him?"

Then he said, "Go, approach him and say, as if giving your own advice, 'You know that king Chilperic is pious and tender-hearted and readily moved to mercy; humble yourself before him and say that you are guilty of the charges he laid. Then we will all throw ourselves at his feet and prevail on him to pardon you.'"

Bishop Praetextatus was deceived by them and promised he would do as they suggested.

In the morning we met at the usual place. The king approached the bishop.

"If you conferred gifts on these men in return for gifts," he said, "why did you ask them for oaths that they stay loyal to Merovech?"

"I confess," replied the bishop, "I did seek to gain their friendship for him; and I would have summoned to his aid not just a mere mortal but an angel from heaven, had it been right; for he was my spiritual son from the baptismal font, as I have often said."

When the dispute had gone on for a while, Bishop Praetextatus threw himself on the ground.

"I have sinned against heaven and against you, most merciful king," he said. "I am an unspeakable homicide; I wanted to kill you and raise your son to the throne."

When Praetextatus said this, the king fell at the feet of the bishops and said, "Most holy bishops, listen to the guilty confess his accursed crime."

In tears we raised the king from the ground, and he ordered Praetextatus to leave the basilica.

Chilperic himself went to his quarters and sent a book of canons, into which a new quaternion had been added containing the so-called apostolic canons. The following was among them: "A bishop found to have committed homicide, adultery, or perjury shall be removed from office."

This was read, and, while Praetextatus stood there in shock, bishop Bertram said, "Pay heed, brother and fellow-bishop, that you do not have the king's favor. For that reason you cannot benefit from our friendship until you win the king's pardon."

After these events, the king asked that Praetextatus's robe should be torn off him, or that Psalm 108, which contains the curses against Iscariot, be read over his head, or at least that judgment be entered against him, excommunicating him forever. These proposals I opposed on grounds that the king had promised that nothing would be done unauthorized by the canons. Then Praetextatus was taken from our sight and placed under guard. He was beaten severely trying to escape custody one night and was sent into exile on an island in the sea off the coast of the city of Coutances.

After this there was news that Merovech was trying to reach the basilica of Saint Martin [in Tours] for the second time. But Chilperic gave orders to guard the church and close every access. The guards left open one door for a few of the clergy to enter for services but kept all the rest closed. This was a cause of considerable inconvenience to people.

When I was staying in Paris signs appeared in the sky, that is twenty rays in the north part, rising in the east and moving to the west; one of these was more extended and rose above the rest and, when it reached a great height, soon faded away, and, in the same way, the rest that followed disappeared. I believe they announced Merovech's death.

As for Merovech, he was lurking in the champaign country near Rheims, fearing to entrust himself to the Austrasians openly, and was tricked by the people of Thérouanne, who said they would desert his father Chilperic and submit to him if he would come to them. He took his best fighting men and went quickly to them. They sprung the trap they had prepared: shutting him up in a certain villa, they surrounded him with armed men and sent messengers to his father. On hearing the news, Chilperic got ready to hurry there. But while Merovech was being forced to wait in some lodging-house, he began to fear that he would have to suffer many penalties to satisfy the vengeance of his enemies. He summoned Gailen his confidential servant.

"Up to now," said Merovech, "we have shared the same heart and mind. I ask you not to allow me to fall into the hands of my enemies. Take a sword and run me through."

Without hesitating, Gailen stabbed him with his blade. When the king came, he found his son dead.

There were some at the time who claimed that Merovech's words, which we have just given, were an invention of the queen, and that Merovech had been secretly killed on her orders. As for Gailen, he was seized, his hands, feet, ears, and the end of his nose were cut off, and, subjected to many other tortures, he met a very unpleasant death. Grindio they broke on a wheel, which they then raised aloft, and Ciucilo, once count of king Sigibert's palace, they killed by beheading. They also cruelly put to death in various ways many others who had come with Merovech. People even said at the time that Bishop Egidius and Guntram Boso were the chief figures behind the betrayal, because Guntram secretly enjoyed good relations with Fredegund for the killing of Theudebert, and Egidius had been her dear friend for a long time.

### Death of Samson, Chilperic's Son (V 22)

Afterwards, Samson, younger son of King Chilperic, came down with dysentery and fever and departed the mortal world. He was born when Chilperic was being besieged by his brother in Tournai; his mother, in fear of death, shoved him away and wanted him destroyed. The king's reproaches prevented her letting this happen, and she gave orders for the child to be baptized. He was baptized, and the bishop himself received him from the water, but the boy died before completing even the first stage of life. His mother Fredegund was grievously ill at the same time, but she recovered.

### Guntram Boso Rescues his Daughters and Chilperic Attacks Poitiers (V 24)

Guntram Boso came to Tours with a few armed men and carried off by force his daughters, whom he had left in the holy basilica. He took them to the city of Poitiers, which belonged to King Childebert.

King Chilperic attacked Poitiers and his troops put those of his nephew to flight. They removed Ennodius from the comital office and brought him before the king. He was sentenced to exile and his property confiscated by the fisc, though a year later he was restored to his homeland and property.

Guntram Boso left his daughters in the basilica of the blessed Hilary and joined King Childebert.

### Year III of Childebert II, a. 578

*Death of Dacco and Dragolen (V 25)*

In the third year of King Childebert, which was the seventeenth of Chilperic and Guntram, Dacco, son of the late Dagaric, deserted King Chilperic, and, while wandering from place to place, was treacherously seized by Duke Dragolen, who was known as 'the Zealous.' Dragolen bound him and, having given him an oath that he would obtain his life for him before the king, brought him to King Chilperic at Berny. But forgetting his oath, Dragolen charged him with abominable crimes and along with the king brought about his death. When Dacco was being kept in bonds and saw that he had no chance of escape, he asked absolution from a priest without the king's knowledge. After receiving it, he was put to death.

At the time that Dragolen was hastening home, Guntram Boso was attempting to remove his daughters from Poitiers. As soon as Dragolen heard, he attacked him. But Guntram's men, who were prepared for this, fought back, constantly taking measures to defend themselves. Guntram sent one of his friends to Dragolen.

"Go and give him this message," he said to his friend. "Since you know that an agreement exists between us, I ask you to stop ambushing my men. I won't stop you taking what you want of my possessions. Just let me go where I want with my daughters, though I be stripped of everything I have."

Dragolen, who was boastful and silly, answered, "Look at the rope with which I have led other culprits bound before the king. With this same rope, Guntram shall today be tied up and taken bound to the same king."

When he had said this, he spurred his horse forward and charged Guntram at a swift gallop. The blow he struck was to no effect because his lance shaft broke, and he dropped his sword. Guntram, when he saw death staring him in the face, called upon the name of the Lord and the great power of the blessed Martin and, raising his lance, struck Dragolen in the throat. As Dragolen was hanging from his horse, one of Guntram's friends thrust a spear into his side and finished him off. Dragolen's party was put to flight, and his body despoiled; Guntram got away scot-free with his daughters.

Some time afterwards, his father-in-law, Severus, had a grave charge brought against him by his sons before the king. When Severus heard about it, he went to see the king, bearing great gifts. He was seized on the road, despoiled and exiled; his life ended with a very miserable death. His two sons, Burgolen and Dodo, were condemned to death on a charge of treason; one of them died in a fight with troops; the other was caught attempting to flee and died when his hands and feet were cut off. All their property, like that of their father, was confiscated by the fisc; they had possessed great riches.

*Campaign against the Bretons. A Fine Levied on Tours (V 26)*

Forces of Tours, Poitiers, Bayeux, Le Mans, and Angers, with many others, went off to Brittany at the orders of Chilperic and took up a position on the banks of the Vilaine, threatening Waroch, the son of the late Macliav [brother of Chonoober]. But the enemy made a surprise attack at night upon the Saxons of Bayeux and slew the greater part of them. Three days later Waroch made peace with the leaders of King Chilperic's forces, gave his son as a hostage, and bound himself by oath to be loyal to King Chilperic. He also restored the city of Vannes on the condition that he would be entitled to rule it at the king's command and would pay each year the tribute and everything owed from there without a demand having to be made. When this agreement was reached, the army withdrew from that region.

Afterward Chilperic ordered that the ban be extracted from the poor and servants of the cathedral [of Tours] and basilica [of Saint Martin] because they had not served in the army. But it was not the custom for them to carry out any public service.

After these events, Waroch, forgetting about his promise and wishing to break his agreement, sent Eunius, bishop of Vannes, to King Chilperic. But the king became angry and, after scolding the bishop, ordered him to be exiled.

## Year IV of Childebert II, a. 579

*New Tax Assessments by Chilperic (V 28)*

Chilperic ordered new and heavy tax assessments to be made throughout his kingdom. For this reason, many left their cities and personal possessions and went to other kingdoms, thinking it better to emigrate than to run such a danger. For it was decreed that a landlord [*possessor*] render from his own [demesne] land one amphora of wine per arpent [of vineyard]. Also many other obligations that could not be fulfilled were imposed on the other lands and dependents.

When the people of Limoges saw they were laden with such a burden, they gathered on the Kalends of March and tried to kill Marcus the referendary, who had been ordered to institute this; and would have done so if Bishop Ferreolus had not delivered him from immediate danger. The mob that assembled also seized the assessment registers and burned them.

The king was very vexed at this and sent people from the court to impose penalties on the populace, to terrify them with tortures, and to inflict the death penalty. They say, too, that at that time abbots and priests were strung up on posts and subjected to various tortures, the royal agents accusing them falsely of having been accomplices in burning the registers during the insurrection of the people. And then they imposed even severer taxes.

## Year V of Childebert II, a. 580

*Gregory begins the year with a list of natural (and some very unnatural) events and disasters (V 33).*

### *Dysentery and the Death of Chilperic's Sons (V 34)*

A very serious epidemic followed these portents. For while the kings were quarreling and again making ready for civil war, dysentery affected nearly all of Gaul. Those who suffered it had a high fever with vomiting, extreme pain in the kidneys, and headaches and neck-pains. Their vomit was saffron colored or even green. It was claimed by many that it was a secret poison. Country folk called it internal boils; this is not incredible, because when cupping glasses were placed on the shoulders or legs, tumors formed and broke, the corrupt matter ran out, and many were cured. Also herbs that cure poisons could be taken and brought help to a good many.

This sickness began in the month of August and first affected the little children, carrying them off to their deaths. We lost children, so sweet and dear to us, whom we sat on our laps or carried in our arms and nourished with such care, feeding them with our own hand. But wiping away our tears, we say with the blessed Job: "The Lord has given; the Lord has taken away; what pleases the Lord has been done. Blessed be his name through the ages [cf. Job 1:21]."

In these days, king Chilperic became seriously ill. As he grew better, his younger son, who was not yet reborn in water and the holy spirit, became sick. When they saw that the end was near, they baptized him. He was doing a little better when his older brother named Chlodobert was stricken by the same disease. Their mother Fredegund saw that they were in danger of death and too late became repentant.

"For a long time the divine goodness has endured our evil doing," she said to the king. "Often it has rebuked us with fevers and other afflictions, and repentance did not follow. Look, now we are losing our sons! The tears of the poor, the laments of widows, and the sighs of orphans are killing them. We are left without a reason for gathering up anything. We pile up riches and do not know for whom we gather it. Our treasury will be left without an owner, full of plunder and curses. Were not our storehouses overflowing with wine? Were our barns not full of grain? Were our treasuries not laden with gold, silver, precious stones, necklaces, and the rest of the trappings of emperors. Look, we are losing what we hold to be even more beautiful! Now please come, let us burn all the unjust registers, and let what was sufficient for your father King Clothar, be sufficient for our fisc."

When the queen had said this, beating her breast with her fists, she ordered brought forward the registers that Marcus had delivered from her cities. She had them thrown in the fire and then turned to the king.

"Why do you delay," she said. "Do what you see me do, so that even if we lose our dear children, we may at least escape eternal punishment."

Then the king, deeply moved, handed all the tax registers over to the fire, and when they were burned, he sent word to stop future assessments.

After this, the younger child wasted away in severe pain until he died. They carried him with immense mourning from the villa of Berny to Paris and had him buried in the basilica of Saint Dionysius [Denis]. As for Chlodobert, they placed him on a litter and took him to the basilica of Saint Medard in Soissons. They threw themselves down at the holy tomb and made vows on his behalf, but he was already short of breath and weak, and he died in the middle of the night. They buried him in the holy basilica of the martyrs Crispin and Crispinian. There was loud lamentation among the entire population; for men, weeping, and women, wearing mourning clothes, followed his funeral cortege in the fashion of the processions that occur when a spouse dies.

After this, King Chilperic was generous to cathedrals, basilicas, and the poor.

### Queen Austrechild (V 35)

In these days, Austrechild, wife of King Guntram, fell prey to this disease. Before she took her last wicked breath, sighing deeply and realizing she could not survive, she decided that others should share in her demise and arranged for the lamentations of their deaths to accompany her own funeral. She is supposed to have made a request of the king in the fashion of Herod.

"I would still have a chance to live," she said, "if I had not fallen into the hands of wicked physicians. The medicines I have received have robbed me of my life and have caused me to lose strength rapidly. And so, I beg you, don't let my death go unavenged. I want you to take an oath that you will have them put to the sword as soon as I depart from this life. Just as I cannot live longer, they too shall not promote themselves after my death, and our friends and theirs shall share the same grief."

With these words she gave up her unhappy soul. When the usual period of mourning was over, the king, forced by the oath to his wicked wife, complied with her evil instructions. He ordered the two physicians who had attended her to be executed. In the considered opinion of many, this was not done without sin.

### Death of Clovis, Chilperic's Son (V 39)

In the month of October, after the death of his sons, King Chilperic was staying with his wife in the forest of Cuise, still grief stricken. At that time, he sent his son Clovis to Berny at the queen's suggestion; the intention was clearly that Clovis should suffer the same fate as his brothers. The disease that had killed them was raging there in force in this period. But Clovis suffered no ill effects from his stay.

The king himself went to the villa of Chelles in the territory of Paris. A few days later he ordered Clovis to come to him. I have no qualms recounting the manner of his death.

While staying with his father at this villa, he began to boast prematurely, "Look, my brothers are dead. The whole kingdom has been left to me. All Gaul is at my command; the fates have granted me rule over everything. When my enemies have fallen into my hands, I shall do to them whatever I please."

He also disparaged the unseemly qualities of his step-mother Fredegund. When she heard, she became very afraid. A few days later she had a visitor.

The visitor said to the queen, "That you are sitting bereft of your children is the work of Clovis's treachery. He has a passion for the daughter of one of your female slaves and has killed your sons by the magic arts of the girl's mother. So I warn you, you can hope for no better yourself, now that the hope by which you would have ruled has been taken from you."

The queen, overwhelmed now with fear, inflamed with rage and grief-stricken by her recent loss, ordered the arrest of the girl on whom Clovis had cast his eye. She had her severely beaten and her hair shorn and gave orders for her to be fastened to a cleft stake and set up before Clovis's quarters. The girl's mother was bound and subjected to torture for some time until Fredegund drew from her a confession confirming that the charges were true. These she brought before the king along with other matters of this kind and asked for vengeance on Clovis.

At the time the king had gone hunting and ordered his son to be brought before him in secret. When Clovis arrived, at the king's command, he was manacled by Dukes Desiderius and Bobo, his weapons and clothing were stripped from him, and he was taken bound and contemptibly dressed to the queen. She ordered him held in custody. She wanted to find out from him whether matters were really as she had heard; whose plan he had followed or by whose prompting he had acted; and especially what friendships he had contracted. He revealed a number of friendships, denying everything else. Three days later the queen had him taken in bonds across the Marne and put under guard in the villa called Noisy. While in custody there, he was stabbed to death, and his body was buried on the spot.

In the meantime, messengers reached the king, saying the prince had stabbed himself with his own hand; they declared that the knife that struck the blow was still sticking in the wound. Deceived by this account, King Chilperic never shed a tear for the son whom, as I would say, he himself handed over to death at the urging of the queen.

Clovis's servants were dispersed to various places. His mother [Audovera] was put to a cruel death. His sister was tricked and placed in a monastery by the queen's servants, where she assumed the religious habit and where she now remains. All their wealth was handed over to the queen. The woman who informed against Clovis was sentenced to be burned. As she was being led to her death, the wretched woman tried to cry out in protest that she had uttered lies, but her words availed her nothing; she was bound to the stake, and consumed alive in the flames. The treasurer of Clovis was brought back from Bourges by Chuppa, count of the stables, and handed over bound to the queen to undergo various kinds of torture. But, on my intercession, the queen ordered him released from his punishment and from his bonds and allowed him to go free.

### Envoys (V 40, 41, 43)

Elafius, bishop of Châlons, was sent to Spain on an embassy to deal with the interests of Queen Brunhild. He came down with a fever and breathed his last....

Mir, king of Galicia, sent envoys to King Guntram. As they were passing through the territory of Poitiers, King Chilperic, then in possession of that region, was informed. He had them brought before him under guard and kept in custody in Paris.... After a year the envoys of the Sueves were released and returned to their own country...

King Leovigild sent as an envoy to Chilperic Agilan, a man of no brains, whose training in logical argument took the form of malevolence against the Catholic faith. His route brought him through Tours, and he tried to challenge my belief and attack the doctrines of the church.

*A long debate on the Trinity follows between the Arian Agilan and Gregory.*

Afterwards on his return to Spain, weakened by sickness, he was converted to our faith out of necessity.

### Chilperic's Writings (V 44)

At the same time king Chilperic issued a circular to the effect that the holy Trinity was to refer not to distinct persons but only God, claiming that it was unseemly for God to be called a person like a mortal of flesh and blood; he also declared that the Father is the same as the Son, and that the Holy Spirit is the same as the Father and the Son.

"This is how it appeared to the prophets and patriarchs," he said, "And this is how the law itself proclaimed Him."

Having had this read out to me, he said, "This is the view I want you and the other teachers of the church to believe."

"Dutiful king," I responded, "Give up this false belief. You must observe the doctrines passed on to us by other teachers of the church who followed in the footsteps of the apostles, the teachings furnished by Hilary and Eusebius, and the confession you yourself made at baptism."

The king grew angry at this point.

"It's quite obvious," he said, "that I regard Hilary and Eusebius as my bitterest opponents in this issue."

To which I responded, "It would suit you better to watch out that you do not make God or his saints angry. For you should know that the Father, Son, and Holy Spirit are all distinct in person. It was not the Father who took on a body of flesh and blood, nor the Holy Spirit, but the Son, so that he who was the Son of God would, for the redemption of humankind, be considered the son of a virgin. It was not the Father who suffered, nor the Holy Spirit, but the Son, so that he who had taken on the body of this world was himself made an offering on behalf of this world. As far as persons are concerned, what you say must be understood not in a corporeal but in a spiritual sense. In these three persons there is one glory, one eternity, one power."

Agitated, he said, "I will expound these matters to wiser men than you, and they will agree with me."

"He will be no wise man, but an idiot, who would want to follow what you propose," I replied.

Grinding his teeth at this response, he said no more.

A few days later Bishop Salvius of Albi visited him. Chilperic had his views read out to him, begging him to be in agreement. On hearing them, Salvius rejected them with such disgust that if he could have laid hands on the paper on which they were written, he would have torn it to shreds. And so the king gave up the project.

The king also wrote other books in verse in imitation of Sedulius. But those poor verses follow no acceptable form of metre at all. He also added letters to our alphabet, namely *w* as in Greek, *ae*, *the*, and *wi*, which are written by the following characters: ω, ψ, Z, and Δ. And he sent letters to all the cities of his kingdom, telling them that boys should be taught these letters and that books written in ancient times should be erased with pumice and rewritten.

### Eunomius becomes Count of Tours (V 47)

Chilperic heard all about the harm that Leudast [count of Tours] was doing to the churches of Tours and the entire population, and so the king sent Ansovald there. He came on the festival of Saint Martin, and, as the choice of count was granted to me on behalf of the people, Eunomius was raised to the comital office.

Leudast, seeing himself set aside, went to Chilperic.

"Most dutiful king," he said, "up to now I have guarded the city of Tours. But now that I have been removed from office, look how it will be guarded. You should know that Bishop Gregory is preparing to surrender it to the son of Sigibert."

"Not at all," said the king on hearing this, "you bring this up only because you have been removed."

"The bishop speaks of even greater matters that concern you," said Leudast; "for he says that your queen is committing adultery with Bishop Bertram."

At that point the king became angry. He punched and kicked Leudast, ordering him thrown into prison, loaded with chains.

### The Career of Leudast (V 48)

Although this book should come to an end, I would like to tell something of Leudast's career. It seems best to begin with his birth, his homeland, and his character.

Gracina is the name of an island off Poitou, where Leudast was born to Leuchadius, a slave of a vine-dresser of the fisc. From there Leudast was summoned to service and assigned to the royal kitchen. But as his eyes were poor when he was young, and the bitter smoke did not agree with them, he was removed from the pestle and promoted to the baker's basket. Although he pretended to be happy among the fermented dough, he soon ran away and abandoned his service. And when he had been brought back two or three times, and could not be prevented from attempting to escape, he was punished by having one of his ears clipped. Then, since there was no way for him to conceal the mark imprinted on his body, he fled to Queen Marcovefa, whom King Charibert loved very much and had admitted to his bed in the place of her sister [cf. IV 26]. She received him willingly, promoted him, and appointed him keeper of her best horses. On this account, now overcome with self-importance and full of arrogance, he canvassed for the office of count of the stables. When he got it, he looked down his nose at everyone, holding them of no account. He was swollen with conceit and undone by the pleasures of the senses; he burned with greed, and, as a favorite of his patroness, went here and there on her affairs. After her death, being well-provided with plunder, he tried to maintain with King Charibert his former position by giving gifts.

After this, due to the sinfulness of the people, he was sent as count to Tours, and there the prestige of the high office allowed him to be even more arrogant. He showed himself to be a greedy plunderer, a loud-mouthed brawler, and a filthy adulterer. By sowing dissension and bringing false charges, he there amassed no small fortune.

After Charibert's death, when the city became part of Sigibert's share [cf. IV 45], he went over to Chilperic, and everything that he had unjustly amassed was seized by the adherents of Sigibert. Then king Chilperic, through his son Theudebert, overran Tours [cf. IV 47]. Since by this time I had arrived in Tours, Theudebert strongly recommended to me that Leudast should hold the office of count, which he had held before. Leudast acted very humbly toward me and was subservient, repeatedly swearing on the tomb of the holy bishop Martin that he would never act unreasonably and that he would be loyal to me in matters affecting my own person as well as in all the needs of the church. For he was afraid that King Sigibert would bring the city back under his authority, as later happened [cf. IV 50]. On Sigibert's death, Chilperic succeeded to his rule and Leudast again became count. When Merovech came to Tours [cf. V 14], he plundered all Leudast's property. During the two years that Sigibert held Tours, Leudast took refuge among the Bretons.

When he assumed the office of count, as we have said, his capriciousness reached the point of his entering the cathedral manse wearing body armor and mail, with a bow case slung from a belt, a lance in his hand and a helmet on his head, a man safe from no one because he was the enemy of everyone. If he presided over a trial along with leading members of the clergy and laity and saw someone pursuing justice, he would now immediately go into a rage and belch forth abuse on the citizens; he used to order priests dragged away in fetters and soldiers beaten with staves, and he showed such cruelty as to beggar description.

When Merovech, who had plundered his property, went away, Leudast came forward with false charges against me, claiming that Merovech had followed my advice in taking away his property. But after the injury had been done, he again repeated his oath and offered a covering from the tomb of the blessed Martin as a pledge that he would never be my enemy.

## The Trial of Gregory and the Fall of Leudast (V 49)

*There are two clerics called Riculf in this narrative: the priest Riculf, and the subdeacon Riculf. The Synod of Berny, before which Gregory was tried, and the subsequent confession of the subdeacon Riculf, took place before the deaths of Fredegund's sons and the death of Clovis (V 34, 39; and cf. V 50).*

But as it is a long story to follow step by step Leudast's perjuries and other crimes, let me come to his attempt to overthrow me by unjust and execrable calumnies and the divine vengeance wreaked upon him, fulfilling the saying, "Everyone who overthrows shall be overthrown [cf. Jerem. 9:14]," and again; "Whoever digs a pit shall fall therein [cf. Prov. 26:27]."

After the many wrongs he inflicted on me and mine, and after the many seizures of ecclesiastical property, he joined forces with the priest Riculf, a man as twisted as himself, and blurted out the charge that I had accused Queen Fredegund of a criminal act; he claimed that, should my archdeacon Plato or my friend Galien be put to torture, they would certainly convict me of having spoken in this way. It was then, as I have said above [V 47], that the king had become angry and, after punching and kicking him and loading him with chains, had him thrown into prison.

Now Leudast said that he had the support of the cleric Riculf, on whose testimony he made these charges. This Riculf was a subdeacon, just as unstable as Leudast. The year before, he had plotted with Leudast on this matter and looked for grounds for going over to him due to my anger. At last he found them and went to him. After preparing all their tricks for four months and having laid their traps, Riculf then came back to me with Leudast and begged me to take him back without penalty. I did it, I confess, and publicly received a secret enemy into my household.

On Leudast's departure, Riculf threw himself at my feet.

"Unless you help me quickly, I am lost," he said. "At the instigation of Leudast, I have said what I should not have said. Send me now to another kingdom; if you do not, I shall be arrested by the king's men and suffer tortures that will kill me."

"If you have said anything that does not correspond to the truth, your words shall be on your own head," I said. "I will not send you to another kingdom in case I fall under suspicion of the king."

After this Leudast came forward as Riculf's accuser, claiming that he had heard the previously mentioned testimony from the subdeacon. Riculf was bound and put under guard, while Leudast in turn was released. Riculf claimed that Galien and the archdeacon Plato were present on the very day the bishop had uttered his charge.

The priest Riculf, who by this time had been promised the episcopal office by Leudast, was so carried away with himself that his pride was the equal to that of Simon Magus. On the sixth day after Easter [April 26], he who had taken an oath to me three or more times on the tomb of Saint Martin spewed out such abuse that he could scarcely keep his hands off me, confident, of course, in the trap that he had laid.

On the next day, that is, the Sabbath after Easter, Leudast came to the city of Tours pretending to have some business to attend to. He arrested Plato the archdeacon and Galien, tied them up, and ordered them taken to the queen, loaded with chains and stripped of their robes. I heard of this while in my quarters in the cathedral manse, and, saddened and disturbed, I entered the oratory and took up the Psalms of David so that some consoling verse might be revealed when I opened them. This is what was found: "He led them away in hope and they were not afraid, and the sea covered their enemies [cf. Ps. 78:53]."

Meanwhile, as they began crossing the river on a ferry whose deck rested on two skiffs, the boat that was supporting Leudast sank, and, if he had not escaped by swimming, he might have perished with his comrades. As for the other boat, which was connected to the first and carried the bound prisoners, it was kept above water by God's help.

Then the prisoners were taken to the king and charges that carried a death sentence were immediately laid against them. But the king, on reflection, freed them from their bonds and kept them under guard, unharmed and unshackled.

At Tours, in the meantime, Duke Berulf and Count Eunomius concocted a tale that King Guntram wanted to take the city, and, for that reason, to prevent anything going wrong, they said, the city must be provided with a guard. They pretended to set watches at the gates to protect the city, but they were really guarding me. They also sent people to advise me to take valuables from the church and make off secretly to Clermont. But I would not take their advice.

Next the king summoned the bishops of his kingdom and ordered the case carefully investigated.

When the cleric Riculf was repeatedly being examined in secret, and, as he often did, was uttering many lies against me and my associates, Modestus, a certain carpenter, said to him, "Unlucky man, who so stubbornly has these designs against his bishop, it would be better for you to be quiet, beg pardon from the bishop, and procure his favor."

At this Riculf began to shout out in a loud voice, "Look at this man who bids me be silent and not pursue the truth. He is an enemy of the queen and will not allow the reasons for the charge against her to be investigated."

These words were immediately reported to the queen. Modestus was arrested, tortured, whipped, put in chains, and kept under guard. He was bound to a post by chains between two guards, but in the middle of the night, when the guards fell asleep, he prayed for the Lord to be so kind as to exert his power on behalf of a wretched man and to let an innocent prisoner in bonds be freed by the visitation of the bishops Martin and Medard. The bonds were broken, the post shattered, the door opened, and soon he entered the basilica of Saint Medard [in Soissons], where I was keeping vigils.

The bishops then assembled at the villa of Berny and were ordered to meet in one building. Next the king arrived and took his seat, after greeting everyone and receiving their blessing. At that point Bertram, bishop of Bordeaux, against whom, along with the queen, this charge had been brought, explained the case and addressed me, saying that the charge had been brought against him and the queen by me. I denied in truth having uttered these things, saying, I heard others say them, but I had not devised them.

Outside the building there was a lot of talk among people, who said, "Why are these charges made against a bishop of God? Why does the king prosecute such charges? How could a bishop have said such things, even about a slave. Lord God, help your servant."

The king said, "The charge against my wife dishonors me. If therefore it is your judgment that witnesses should be presented against the bishop, here they are. But if it seems that this should not be done, and that the matter should be left to the honor of the bishop, speak up. I will gladly pay heed to your command."

All were amazed at the king's wisdom and forbearance.

At that point, when all the bishops said, "The testimony of an inferior cannot be admitted against a bishop," the case came down to this, that I should say three masses at three altars and clear myself of the alleged charges by taking an oath. And though these conditions were contrary to the canons, still they were fulfilled for the sake of the king. Also I cannot be silent about the fact that [the king's daughter] Queen Rigunth, out of sympathy for my suffering, fasted with all her household until a slave reported that I had fulfilled all that had been required of me.

Then the bishops returned to the king.

"All that was imposed upon the bishop has been carried out," they said. "What remains to be done now, king, if not the excommunication of you and Bertram, the accuser of a brother?"

"O no," said the king, "I only reported what I had heard."

They asked who had said this, and he answered that he had heard these things from Leudast. He had already fled owing to the weakness of his plan or his resolution. All the bishops then decided that this sower of discord, traducer of the queen, and accuser of a bishop, should be shut out of all churches, because he had withdrawn from the hearing. To the bishops who were not present, they sent a letter to this effect, bearing their signatures. After this, each of them returned to his own see.

When Leudast heard, he took refuge in the church of Saint Peter in Paris. But on hearing the royal edict prohibiting anyone in Chilperic's kingdom from receiving him, and especially since the son whom he had left at home had died, he came to Tours in secret and carried away his more valuable possessions to Bourges. The king's retainers pursued him, but he escaped by flight. They captured his wife, and she was sent into exile in the district of Tournai.

The subdeacon Riculf was sentenced to death. I managed to obtain his life but I could not free him from torture. Nothing, not even metal, could have endured such beating as was given this wretch. With his hands tied behind his back, he was suspended from a tree from the third hour of the day; at the ninth hour, he was taken down, wracked on pulleys, beaten with staves, rods, and doubled thongs, and not by one or two assailants, but by as many as could reach his wretched limbs. Only at the critical point in the torture did he then reveal the truth and make known the secrets of the plot. This was the explanation he gave for the charge being made against the queen: when she was driven from power, Clovis would obtain the kingdom, once his brothers and father had been killed; Leudast would get a ducal office. As for the priest Riculf, who had been a friend of Clovis from the times of the blessed Bishop Eufronius, he would win appointment to the bishopric of Tours. The subdeacon Riculf was promised the archdiaconate.

I returned to Tours by God's grace and found the church thrown into a turmoil by the priest Riculf. Now this man had been picked out from among the poor under bishop Eufronius and appointed archdeacon. Later he was raised to the priesthood and withdrew to his own property. He was always self-important, arrogant, and impudent. For example, while I was still with the king, he brazenly entered the cathedral manse as if he were already bishop, inventoried the church silver, and brought the rest of the property under his control. He enriched the more important clergy with gifts, granted vineyards, and parceled out meadows; to the lesser clergy, he administered beatings and many blows, even raising his own hand against them.

"Acknowledge your master," he said. "He has gained victory over his enemies, and it is by his devices that Tours has been purged of that crew from Clermont."

The wretched man did not know that, with the exception of five bishops, all the others who have held the bishopric of Tours were descendants of my ancestors. He was accustomed to repeating to his intimates the proverb that no one can expect to trick a wise man without using perjury.

Upon my return, when he continued to hold me in disdain and did not come to greet me as did the other citizens, but rather threatened to kill me, I ordered him taken away to a monastery on the advice of the bishops of my province. While he was closely confined, representatives of bishop Felix [of Nantes], who had supported the charge against me, intervened. The abbot was taken in by their perjuries; Riculf slipped away and went to Bishop Felix, who received him warmly, though he should have cursed him.

Leudast meanwhile went to Bourges, taking with him all the treasure that he had plundered from the poor. Not long after, forces from Bourges under their count attacked him and carried off all his gold and silver and whatever else he had brought with him, leaving him nothing but what he had on his person; and they would have taken his very life if he had not fled. He regained his strength and in turn led some men from Tours in an attack against his plunderers; killing one of them, he recovered some of his property and returned to the territory of Tours. Duke Berulf heard about this and sent his own retainers outfitted for war to seize him. Leudast realized that he would now be captured, and so he abandoned his property and fled to the church of Saint Hilary in Poitiers. Duke Berulf meanwhile sent the property that he seized to the king.

Leudast would leave the basilica and attack the houses of various people, taking plunder without trying to disguise the fact. He was also repeatedly caught in adultery in the holy confines of the very porch of the basilica. For these reasons, the queen, disturbed that a place consecrated to God was being defiled in such a fashion, ordered him to be expelled from the holy basilica. On being expelled, he went again to his supporters in Bourges, begging them to hide him.

### Prediction of the Blessed Salvius about Chilperic (V 50)

I should have mentioned my conversation with the blessed Bishop Salvius earlier, but, as it slipped my mind, I do not consider it unwarranted if it is written later.

When I had said farewell to the king after the council that I mentioned [V 49], and was anxious to return home, I did not want to go without taking leave of Salvius with a kiss. I looked for him and found him in the courtyard of the domain of Berny. I told him that I was about to return home.

We had moved off a little and were speaking of one thing and another when he said to me, "Do you see what I see upon this roof?"

"Why, I see the roof-covering that the king lately had installed," said I.

"Don't you see anything else?"

"I see nothing else." I suspected that he was making some kind of a joke. "Tell me what more do you see?" I added.

Drawing a deep breath, he said, "I see the sword of divine wrath, unsheathed and hanging over this house."

Indeed, the bishop's words were not wrong; for twenty days later died the two sons of the king, whose deaths I have already described [V 34].

*This chapter concludes Book V.*

## Year VI of Childebert II, a. 581

*Alliance of Childebert and Chilperic. Flight of Mummolus (VI 1)*

In the sixth year of his reign, King Childebert repudiated the peace with King Guntram and allied himself with King Chilperic. Not long afterwards Gogo [governor of King Childebert] died; Wandelen was appointed in his place.

Mummolus fled from Guntram's kingdom and shut himself within the walls of Avignon.

A synod of bishops assembled at Lyons to decide various matters in dispute and to pass judgment against persons failing in their responsibilities. The king then presided over the council to deal with many matters arising from the flight of Duke Mummolus and some arising from the quarreling [of the kings].

*Chilperic's Envoys return from Byzantium (VI 2)*

Meanwhile king Chilperic's envoys, who had gone three years before to the emperor Tiberius, returned, but not without severe loss and hardship. Since they dared not enter the harbor of Marseilles because of the quarreling of the kings, they sailed to Agde, located in the kingdom of the Goths. Before they could land, however, the ship was driven by the wind, dashed on the shore, and broken into pieces. The envoys and their servants saw that they were in danger and, seizing planks, barely managed to reach the shore; many of the men were lost, but most escaped. The locals took the goods that the waves carried ashore, but the envoys did get back the more valuable items and brought them to King Chilperic. The people of Agde, nevertheless, held on to a great deal.

At that time I had gone to the villa of Nogent to meet the king, and there he showed me a great salver, weighing fifty pounds, which he had had fashioned of gold and gems.

"I had this made to honor and ennoble the Frankish people," he said.

"Moreover, I shall make many more if things go well."

He also showed me gold pieces, each of a pound's weight, sent by the emperor, having on one side the likeness of the emperor and the inscription in a circle, *Of Tiberius Constantinus, Forever Augustus* and on the other side a four-horse chariot and charioteer with the inscription, *Glory of the Romans.* He showed me many other treasures brought by the envoys.

### Childebert's Envoys to Chilperic (VI 3)

Then, while Chilperic was residing at Nogent, Egidius, bishop of Rheims, came to him on an embassy with the leading officials of Childebert. They discussed depriving King Guntram of his kingdom and establishing peace between themselves.

"My sins have grown so great that I have no sons left," said King Chilperic, "and I have no other heir but King Childebert, my brother Sigibert's son. Therefore let him be heir to all that my efforts may win; just let me keep the whole without trouble or dispute for as long as I live."

They thanked him, signed agreements to confirm the terms discussed, and returned to Childebert with expensive gifts. After their departure, King Chilperic sent Bishop Leudovald with the leading men of his kingdom. They gave and received oaths of peace, signed agreements, and came back well rewarded.

### Lupus, Brunhild's Supporter, Driven from the Kingdom (VI 4)

For some time now, Lupus, duke of Champagne, had been constantly harassed and plundered by various enemies, especially by Ursio and Berthefred. Finally they made an agreement to kill him and raised a force against him. Queen Brunhild found out about it, and distressed at the unjust attacks on her loyal supporter, girded herself like a man and rushed in between the opposing battle lines.

"Men, don't do this evil," she cried. "Don't persecute the innocent; for the sake of one man, don't engage in a battle that will destroy the forces of the region."

This brought a response from Ursio.

"Get back, woman," said he. "It's enough for you to have held power under your husband. Now your son rules. We preserve his kingdom as its guardians, not you. Get back, or our horses' hooves will trample you into the ground."

After many more exchanges of this kind, the queen's determination that they should not fight prevailed.

On leaving the area, however, they burst into dwellings belonging to Lupus, seized all the furnishings and took them home, pretending that they were going to place them in the king's treasury and uttering threats against Lupus.

"He will never escape alive from our hands," they said.

Lupus saw that he was in danger and, placing his wife within the walls of the city of Laon for safety, fled to King Guntram, who welcomed him. He remained with the king in hiding, waiting for Childebert to come of age.

*Priscus the Jew. Chilperic Goes to Paris (VI 5)*

Then Chilperic, while still at the villa of Nogent, had his belongings sent ahead and made preparations to go to Paris. When I went to see him to say farewell, a Jew by the name of Priscus arrived. He was the personal agent charged with making purchases for the king.

Taking Priscus gently by the hair, the king said to me, "Come, bishop of God, and lay your hands on him."

When Priscus struggled, the king said, "O obstinate spirit and ever unbelieving people which does not recognize the Son of God promised to it by the voices of its prophets and the mysteries of the church prefigured in its own sacrifices."

The Jew replied to these words, "God never married, was never blessed with offspring, nor did He ever allow anyone to share his kingdom, for He said by the mouth of Moses, 'Behold, behold, for I am the Lord and without me there is no God. I shall kill and I shall make alive. I shall strike and I shall heal [cf. Deut. 32:39].'"

*Arguments of Chilperic and Priscus, and a long discourse by Gregory follow.*

Although I said this and more, the wretched man's conscience showed no signs of believing. When Priscus was silent, and the king saw that my words had had no effect, Chilperic then turned to me and asked to receive my blessing before he departed.

"To you, bishop," he said, "I will say what Jacob said to the angel that was speaking with him, 'I will not let you go unless you bless me [Gen. 32:36].'"

And saying that, he ordered water brought for our hands. After washing and saying a prayer, I received the bread and, giving thanks to God, partook of the bread myself and offered some to the king; taking a draught of wine, I said farewell and left. As for the king, he mounted his horse and returned to Paris with his wife and daughter and all his household.

*Trouble for Theodore, Bishop of Marseilles (VI 11)*

At Marseilles, Dynamius, governor of Provence, began to plot heavily against Bishop Theodore. While preparing to make a journey to see King Childebert, the bishop was arrested by the governor and kept prisoner in the middle of the city; he was finally released after enduring severe abuse. The clergy of Marseilles were in on Dynamius's scheme to throw Theodore out of his bishopric.

As Theodore was on his way to King Childebert, he was arrested together with the former prefect Jovinus on the orders of King Guntram. The clergy of Marseilles were filled with great joy on hearing the news, supposing that, now the bishop was in custody, he would be exiled, and that things had now reached a point that he would never return. So they seized the properties of the church, made inventories of the sacred vessels, opened the strong boxes, and pillaged the store-rooms, rummaging through all the property of the church as if the bishop were already dead. All the while, they uttered various criminal charges against him, which, with Christ's help, were afterwards discovered to be false.

As for Childebert, after making a peace agreement with Chilperic, he sent envoys to King Guntram to demand restoration of the half portion of Marseilles that Childebert had given to him after the death of his father Sigibert; should he refuse, the envoys said, he should know that the holding of this portion would cost him dear. But Guntram would not restore it and ordered the roads closed, so that the right to cross through his kingdom would not be made available to everyone.

When Childebert saw this, he sent to Marseilles Gundulf, a former *domesticus*, who was of senatorial birth and had been appointed duke. Since he did not dare travel through Guntram's territory, Gundulf came to Tours. I welcomed him warmly and discovered that he was my mother's uncle. I made him stay with me for five days, and, after providing him with all that he needed, let him go off. When he reached Marseilles, he was unable to enter the city in face of the opposition offered by Dynamius. Bishop Theodore, who at this point had now joined Gundulf, was also not welcomed back to his church. Dynamius and the clergy barred the city gates, together taunting and heaping abuse on both of them, the bishop and Gundulf.

Finally, Dynamius was invited to a meeting with the duke and came to the basilica of the blessed Stephen, next to the city. The doorkeepers guarding the entrance to the church stood ready to close the doors the moment Dynamius passed in. When they did this, the crowds of armed men following Dynamius were locked out and could not get in. Dynamius himself was unaware of what was happening. As soon as they discussed various matters at the altar, they moved away from it and passed into the sacristy. Dynamius entered with them, and they assailed him with terrifying accusations, now that he was deprived of the support of his men. His followers were driven off — on his removal they began crowding around noisily with weapons in their hands — and then Gundulf assembled the principal citizens in order to enter the city with the bishop. Seeing all that had happened, Dynamius now sought pardon. He presented numerous gifts to the duke, and, when he swore an oath that in future he would be loyal to both the bishop and the king, his equipment was restored to him. The gates of the town and the doors of the churches were then opened, and the duke and the bishop both entered the city, with the ringing of bells, acclamations, and various flags waving in their honor.

Then the clergy involved in this shameful crime — the ringleaders were the abbot Anastasius and the priest Proculus — fled to the protection of Dynamius's residence, asking refuge of the man who had set them up to it. Many of them were released on finding satisfactory sureties and were ordered to proceed to the king's court. Meanwhile, Gundulf returned to the king, having brought the city under the authority of King Childebert and restored the bishop to his see.

But Dynamius paid no attention to the loyalty that he had promised to the king and sent messengers to King Guntram telling him that he would lose the half portion of the city owed to him on account of the bishop, and that he would never hold Marseilles in his power until this fellow was driven from the city. King Guntram became angry and, contrary to divine law, gave orders for the priest of the most high God to be brought before him in bonds.

"Let the enemy of my kingdom be driven into exile," he said, "so he can't do us any more harm."

*Theodore was again seized and carried off to Guntram.*

The bishop was taken before the king but found not guilty; he was allowed to return to his city, where he was welcomed with great honor by the citizens.

Out of this affair bitter enmity arose between King Guntram and his nephew Childebert. They broke the treaty and began to lie in wait for each other.

## Chilperic Attacks the Cities of Guntram
### (VI 12)

King Chilperic saw the dissension arising between his brother and his nephew. He summoned Duke Desiderius and ordered him to inflict some harm on his brother. Desiderius raised a force, drove off Duke Ragnovald and occupied Périgueux. After exacting oaths, he then went on to Agen. When Ragnovald's wife heard that her husband had fled and that these cities were being brought under King Chilperic's authority, she took refuge in the basilica of the holy martyr Caprasius [in Agen]. But she was brought out, despoiled of her property and the support of her servants, and then, when she had given sureties, sent to Toulouse; there she took up quarters in the basilica of the holy Saturninus. Desiderius took all the cities belonging to King Guntram in the region [of Aquitaine], and subjected them to the authority of King Chilperic.

Duke Berulf, hearing that the people of Bourges were quietly talking about invading the territory of Tours, raised a force and took up a position on their borders. At this time the districts of Yzeures and Barrous in the region of Tours were seriously devastated. Those who were unable to join in this blockade [of Bourges] were later sentenced without mercy.

Duke Bladast went to Gascony where he lost the greater part of his army.

### Year VII of Childebert II, a. 582

*Gregory begins the seventh year of Childebert's reign again with a list of portents, and an account of the plague (VI 14).*

#### Conversion of Jews by Chilperic (VI 17)

King Chilperic ordered many Jews to be baptized that year and received a number of them from the sacred font [as godfather]. Some of them, however, were purified in body only, not in heart, and, lying to God, returned to their former perfidy and could be seen observing the Sabbath as well as honoring the Lord's day.

Priscus [cf. VI 5] could not be influenced by any argument to recognize the truth. The king became angry with him for that and ordered him put in prison, thinking that, if he could not get him to believe of his own accord, he would make him listen and believe even against his will. But Priscus offered gifts and asked for time until his son could marry a Hebrew girl at Marseilles; he promised falsely that he would then do what the king demanded.

Meanwhile, a quarrel arose between Priscus and Phatyr, one of the Jewish converts, who was now a godson of the king. And when on the Sabbath Priscus was retiring to a secret place to fulfill the law of Moses, wearing a kerchief and not carrying a weapon, Phatyr suddenly appeared and put him to the sword, together with the companions who were with him. When they were killed, Phatyr fled with his men to the church of Saint Julian [in Paris], on a neighboring street. While there, they heard that the king had granted the master his life but ordered his men to be dragged like criminals from the church and put to death. Their master had already been driven away at this point, so one of them drew his sword and killed his comrades. He then left the church armed with his sword, but people attacked him and he was cruelly killed. Phatyr obtained permission to return to Guntram's kingdom from where he had come, but he was killed by Priscus's kinsmen not long after his return.

### Chilperic's Envoys Return from Spain Where They were Arranging the Marriage of Chilperic's Daughter (VI 18)

Then Ansovald and Domigisel, King Chilperic's envoys who had been sent to Spain to examine the bridal endowment [promised to Rigunth, Chilperic's daughter], returned home. At this time King Leovigild was accompanying the army sent against his son Hermenigild, from whom he took the city of Merida. I have already explained how the prince had allied himself with the generals of Emperor Tiberius [*omitted here*]. This matter had delayed the return of the envoys. When I saw them, I was anxious to learn whether faith in Christ still burned among the few [true] Christians remaining in that land.

Ansovald gave me this reply: "The Christians now living in Spain preserve the Catholic faith unimpaired. But the king is trying to disturb it with a new scheme, for he pretends to pray at the tombs of the martyrs and in the churches of our faith. And he says, 'Of course I know that Christ is the Son of God and equal to the Father. But I can't believe at all that the Holy Spirit is God, because this isn't written in any of the scriptures.'"...

Ansovald went to Chilperic, followed by an embassy from Spain, which went on from Chilperic to Childebert and then returned home.

### Chilperic Loses Men at the River Orge (VI 19)

King Chilperic had placed guards at the bridge over the Orge in the territory of Paris to prevent infiltrators from his brother's kingdom doing any harm. The former duke Asclepius got advance knowledge of this arrangement. In a night attack he killed all the guards and devastated the district near the bridge. When Chilperic got the news, he sent messengers to the counts, dukes, and other officials, ordering them to muster an army and invade his brother's kingdom. But he was dissuaded from so doing by the counsel of good men.

"They have acted wrongly," they told him, "but you should act wisely. Send envoys to your brother; if he will redress the outrage, you will do nothing harmful, but if he refuses, then is the time to consider what course to pursue."

The king accepted their argument, halted the army, and dispatched an embassy to his brother. Guntram made complete amends and sought full reconciliation with his brother.

*New Counts Appointed. Intercepted Letters of Bishop Charterius (VI 22)*

Since King Chilperic had overrun cities belonging to his brother, he appointed new counts and ordered that all taxes of the cities be paid to him. We know this was done as directed.

In these days, two men were arrested by Nonnichius, count of Limoges. They were carrying a letter in the name of Charterius, bishop of Périgueux, that contained many insulting things about the king. In it, in the midst of other matters, was a passage in which the bishop seemed to be complaining that he had fallen from paradise into hell, meaning that he had been transferred from the kingdom of Guntram to the dominion of Chilperic. The count just named sent the letter and the two men under heavy guard to the king. The king calmly had the bishop brought before him to say whether the charges against him were true or not.

The bishop came and the king produced the men and the letter. He asked the bishop if it had been sent by him. He said it had not. The men then were asked from whom they had received that letter. They said from Frontonius the deacon. The bishop was asked about the deacon. He replied that he was his chief enemy and there could be no doubt that this wickedness was his doing since he had often instigated evil accusations against him. The deacon was brought at once and questioned by the king. He testified against the bishop.

"It was I who wrote this letter," he said, "at the bishop's order."

The bishop cried out that this man had often devised clever tricks to cast him out of office. The king took pity, and, commending his cause to God, let them both go, interceding with the bishop for the deacon and begging the bishop to pray for the king.

In this way the bishop was sent back to his city with honor. In two months count Nonnichius, who was the cause of this outrage, died from a stroke. As he was without children, his property was granted to several people by the king.

*Son Born to Chilperic (VI 23)*

Afterwards a son was born to Chilperic, who had buried so many sons. In honor of the event, the king commanded the gates of the prisons to be opened and those in bonds to be set free and issued instructions not to exact delinquent penalties due to the fisc. But later this infant was the cause of great evil.

*Bishop Theodore Again and the Arrival of Gundovald in Gaul (VI 24)*

Fresh attacks were now made against Bishop Theodore. For Gundovald, who said he was the son of King Chlothar, returned from Constantinople and landed at Marseilles. I would like to record briefly certain facts about his origin.

He was born in Gaul and brought up very carefully. He wore his hair long down his back, as is the fashion of its kings, and was instructed in letters. His mother presented him to King Childebert [I].

"Here is your nephew, the son of King Chlothar," she told him; "as his father hates him, take him up, for he is your flesh."

Childebert received the child because he had no sons and kept him with him.

This was reported to King Chlothar, who sent messengers to his brother saying, "Let the boy go, so he may come to me."

Without delay Childebert sent the boy to Chlothar, who, when he looked at him, ordered his hair to be shorn.

"I did not produce this son," he said.

Then after the death of King Chlothar, Gundovald was taken in by King Charibert. Sigibert summoned him, once more cut his hair, and sent him to the city of Agrippina, which is now called Cologne. He escaped from there, let his hair grow long again, and made his way to Narses, who governed Italy at the time. There he took a wife, produced sons, and went to Constantinople.

After a long time, he landed at Marseilles, invited by a certain person to return to Gaul, so they say, and was received by Bishop Theodore. He got horses from the bishop and joined Duke Mummolus, who was then at Avignon, as I have said earlier [VI 1].

Duke Guntram Boso arrested Bishop Theodore and imprisoned him on account of this affair, charging him with introducing a foreigner into Gaul and wanting to subject the Frankish kingdom to imperial rule by this means. It is said that the bishop produced a letter signed by the great men of Childebert's kingdom.

"I did nothing on my own," he said, "but only what our lords and chief officials commanded me."

The bishop was kept under guard in a cell and not allowed to go near a church. One night, while he was earnestly praying to the Lord, the cell shone with a bright light so that the count who was guarding him was thoroughly terror stricken; an immense ball of light was seen above the bishop for a period of two hours. In the morning, the count related this event to the others who were with him. After this, Theodore was taken before King Guntram along with Bishop Epiphanius, who had fled from the Lombards and was living at Marseilles, because he was thought naturally enough to be an accessory in this affair. The king examined them, but they were found to have committed no offense. However, he did order them to be kept in confinement, in which Epiphanius died after a great deal of suffering.

As for Gundovald, he withdrew to an island in the sea to await the outcome of events. Duke Guntram Boso divided the property of Gundovald with King Guntram's duke, and carried off with him to Auvergne, so they say, an immense weight of silver and gold and other goods.

## Year VIII of Childebert II, a. 583

*Guntram Boso and Mummolus (VI 26)*

Duke Guntram Boso first returned to Auvergne with the previously mentioned treasures and then went to King Childebert. On his way back, he was arrested along with his wife and sons by King Guntram and detained.

"The invitation that brought Gundovald to Gaul came from you," said the king; "this is why you went to Constantinople a few years ago."

"It was your own duke Mummolus who welcomed him and kept him by his side at Avignon," replied the duke. "Allow me to bring him to you, then I shall be free of the charges brought against me."

"I'm not letting you go anywhere until you pay the penalties that fit the crimes you've committed," replied the king.

Seeing death near, the duke said, "Here is my son. Take him as a hostage for what I promise my lord the king, and, if I can't bring Mummolus back to you, let me lose my little boy."

That was when the king allowed him to go, but he kept the child with him.

Duke Guntram Boso took with him troops from Clermont and Velay and went off to Avignon. But Mummolus saw to it with one of his tricks that unsafe boats were readied for them at the Rhône. They boarded them without suspicion, and, when they reached the middle of the river, the boats filled and sank. In danger of drowning, some swam to safety and a number tore planks from the boats and reached the shore, but a good many who had less presence of mind were drowned in the river. Duke Guntram Boso, nevertheless, reached Avignon.

Before Mummolus's arrival at Avignon, only a small part of the city remained unguarded by the Rhône. Mummolus on entering the city had made sure that the whole place was protected by a channel into which he led water from the river. He had trenches of great depth dug and the flowing water concealed the traps he had made.

On Guntram Boso's approach, Mummolus cried out from the wall, "If good faith still exists between us, let Guntram come to one bank and I to the other, and let him say what he wants."

When they met, the new channel of the river separated them.

"If it's all right with you," Guntram Boso said from his side, "I'll cross, because we have some things to discuss in greater privacy."

"Come, don't be afraid," said Mummolus.

Guntram Boso entered the water with one of his friends. As the friend was weighed down with a mailcoat, he sank under the water immediately on reaching a trap in the river and did not reappear. But when Guntram Boso sank and was being carried along by the swift current, one of his men nearby reached out a spear to his hand and brought him ashore. After Guntram and Mummolus had hurled insults at one another, they both departed.

As Guntram Boso lay siege to the city with King Guntram's army, news of this was brought to Childebert. He became angry because Guntram Boso was doing this without his orders and dispatched Gundulf, whom I have mentioned before, to Avignon. Gunulf put an end to the siege and took Mummolus to Clermont. But a few days later Mummolus returned to Avignon.

*Chilperic Enters Paris at Easter. Baptism of Theuderic (VI 27)*

Chilperic went to Paris the day before Easter was celebrated. To avoid the curses contained in the agreement between him and his brothers [made following the death of Charibert, a. 567] that none of them should enter Paris without the consent of the others, the relics of many saints were carried before him as he entered the city. He spent Easter with a great deal of revelry and had his son baptized [cf. VI 23]. Ragnemod, bishop of the city, received the child from the holy font. Chilperic gave the boy the name Theuderic.

*War Between Chilperic and Guntram. Mutiny of Childebert's Army (VI 31)*

Next King Chilperic received envoys from his nephew Childebert. Their leader was Egidius, bishop of Rheims.

Brought before the king and given an audience, they said, "Our master, your nephew, asks you to keep with special care the peace you have made with him, for he cannot have peace with your brother, who took away half of Marseilles after his father's death and retains fugitives whom he is unwilling to send back. Therefore your nephew Childebert wishes to preserve unbroken the good relations which he now has with you."

"My brother has proven to be guilty of many things," said Chilperic. "If my son Childebert would look for reasonable explanations, he will see at once that his father Sigibert was killed with my brother's connivance."

"If you would join with your nephew, and he with you, and muster an army, speedy vengeance could be inflicted on Guntram as he deserves," responded Bishop Egidius.

When an oath was sworn to that effect and hostages were exchanged, the envoys departed.

Relying on their promises, Chilperic then mustered the army of his kingdom and came to Paris. When residing there, he was the cause of great expense to the inhabitants.

Duke Berulf advanced with the forces of Tours, Poitiers, Angers, and Nantes to the territory of Bourges. Desiderius and Bladast with all the army of the province entrusted to them [that is, southern Aquitaine] hemmed in Bourges from the other side, greatly devastating the country through which they came. Chilperic ordered the army that had gathered at his command to come by way of the territory of Paris. As they passed through, he joined them and advanced to the town of Melun, burning and laying everything waste. Although his nephew's army did not join him, Chilperic was accompanied nevertheless by Childebert's dukes and envoys.

At this point, Chilperic sent messengers to Dukes Berulf, Desiderius and Bladast, saying, "Enter the territory of Bourges, advance to the city and extract oaths of loyalty in my name."

The forces of Bourges, however, gathered at the town of Châteaumeillant to the number of fifteen thousand and fought against Duke Desiderius there; great slaughter was done, so that more than seven thousand men from both armies fell. The dukes advanced to the city with the men that were left, plundering and laying everything waste. The devastation inflicted was such as has never been heard of since ancient times, so that no house nor vineyard nor tree was left; but they cut down, burned, and overthrew everything. They even carried off sacred vessels from the churches, which they then set on fire.

King Guntram advanced with an army against his brother [Chilperic], placing all his hope in the judgment of God. One day, towards evening, he loosed his forces and destroyed a greater part of his brother's army. In the morning envoys met and the kings made peace. They promised one another that the party that had exceeded the limits of the law would compensate the other party with whatever the bishops and leaders of the people decided. And in this way they parted peaceably.

When King Chilperic could not keep his army from plundering, he put the count of Rouen to the sword. And so he returned to Paris, leaving all the booty and releasing the captives. The besiegers of Bourges, on getting orders to return home, took with them so much plunder that the entire district they left behind was believed to be emptied of man and beast alike. The army of Desiderius and Bladast entered the territory of Tours, burning, plundering, and killing in the manner usually inflicted on enemies; for they even took captives, most of whom they despoiled and afterwards let go. This disaster was followed by disease among the herds, so that scarcely enough livestock remained to make a new start, and it was strange for anyone to see a bullock or catch sight of a heifer.

During the time these events were happening, King Childebert and his army remained in the same spot. Then one night, when the troops had been assembled, the lesser ranks raised loud complaints against Bishop Egidius and the king's dukes.

They began to shout aloud and openly yelled out, "Get rid of those around the king who sell his kingdom, subject his cities to the dominion of another, and hand over his people to the rule of another prince."

While they continued to shout complaints like this, the morning came. They rushed to the king's tent, weapons in hand; their hope was to get a hold of the bishop and chief officials, overpower them, give them a beating, and cut them up with their swords. When the bishop found out about this, he took flight, mounting a horse and heading for his own city. The troops pursued him in an uproar, hurling stones and spewing forth abuse. The reason he was saved at this time was the fact that they had no horses ready. When the horses of his companions flagged, the bishop continued on alone, so terrified that he did not even bother to collect a boot that slipped off his foot. And this is how he reached his city and shut himself within the walls of Rheims.

### The Death of Leudast (VI 32)

A few months earlier, Leudast [cf. V 47-49] had come to Tours with a royal directive enabling him to get back his wife and to take up residence in the city. He also brought me a letter signed by bishops recommending that he be readmitted to communion. But since I saw no letter from Queen Fredegund, on whose account in particular he had been excommunicated, I refused to admit him.

"When I receive the queen's authorization," I said, "at that time I will not delay admitting him."

In the meantime, I sent her a message, and she wrote back saying, "I was urged by many and had no choice but to let him go. I ask you not to extend peace to him or allow him to receive the holy bread from your hand until I consider more fully what should be done."

When I read the letter, I was afraid he would be killed. I sent for his father-in-law, informed him of the letter, and implored him to tell Leudast to be wary until the queen's animosity was assuaged. But the advice that I gave honestly in the sight of God was received by Leudast with suspicion, and, since he was my enemy, he refused to heed any warning that came from me. And so was fulfilled the proverb that I once heard an old man say: "Always give good advice to friend and foe alike because the friend will take it and the foe reject it."

Having spurned this advice, Leudast went to the king, who was staying in the district of Melun with his army, and implored the troops to ask the king to grant him an audience. When all the troops interceded, the king gave him a hearing. Leudast threw himself at his feet and begged for pardon.

"Be careful for a little while yet," said the king, "until I see the queen and arrange how you are to return to her favor, for you still have much to answer for with regard to her."

But Leudast was reckless and foolish and put his confidence in having received an audience with the king. So on the Sunday, when the king returned to Paris, Leudast prostrated himself at the queen's feet in the holy cathedral and asked for pardon. Furious and cursing the sight of him, she drove him away.

"I have no sons left to prosecute wrongs done against me," she said, weeping. "I leave it to you, Lord Jesus, to defend my interests." And throwing herself at the king's feet, she added, "I am heartsick when I see my enemy and can do nothing to overpower him."

At that point Leudast was driven from the holy place, and mass was celebrated.

Then the king and queen came out of the holy church, and Leudast followed them along the street, having no idea what was about to happen to him. He went around the shops of the merchants, grubbing through their costly wares, testing the weight of silver articles, and examining various pieces.

"I'll buy this one and that one," he said, "for I still have lots of gold and silver."

Just as he said this, the queen's retainers arrived suddenly and tried to put him in chains. But he grabbed his sword and struck one of them. This angered them and, grasping their swords and shields, they rushed him. One of them got in a blow that took hair and skin off a great part of his head. When he fled across the bridge of the city, his foot slipped between the planks with which the bridge is made and he broke his leg. He was overpowered and, with his hands tied behind his back, placed in custody.

The king ordered physicians to attend him, so that, once cured of his wounds, he could be put to death with prolonged torture. He was taken to one of the villas of the fisc, but, when he had reached death's door because his wounds were putrefying, he was stretched out on his back by order of the queen; then a great bar of iron was placed under his neck and they struck his throat with another bar. And in this way a faithless life came to a just end.

## Year IX of Childebert II, a. 584

*Restoration of Marseilles (VI 33)*

In the ninth year of King Childebert, King Guntram himself restored half of Marseilles to his nephew.
*News from Spain and reports of disease and portents follow.*

*Marriage Plans and the Death of Chilperic's Son Theuderic (VI 34)*

A legation came again from Spain. It brought gifts and received King Chilperic's agreement to the marriage of his daughter to the son of King Leovigild, in keeping with the previous understanding. The agreement made, and all points considered, the envoy started back home.

A new sorrow now afflicted King Chilperic when he left Paris to go to the territory of Soissons. His son, whom the water of holy baptism had cleansed the year before, came down with dysentery and breathed his last. This was the meaning of the bright light descending from the cloud that I recorded above [VI 33].

Utterly grief-stricken, they then returned to Paris and buried the boy. They sent for the envoy to return, hoping that the time the king had set for the wedding might be postponed.

"Look, I have to preserve a period of mourning in my household, so how can I celebrate the nuptials of my daughter?" said Chilperic.

At this point he wanted to send to Spain another daughter, whom he had by Audovera and had placed in the monastery of Poitiers. But she declined and the blessed Radegund especially opposed the project.

"It is unseemly," she said, "that a girl dedicated to Christ should return once again to the pleasures of the world."

*Allegations about Theuderic's Death (VI 35)*

*Mummolus the prefect of this chapter is a different person from Duke Mummolus.*

While these events were taking place, the queen was informed that the boy who had died had been taken away by evil arts and spells and that Mummolus the prefect, whom the queen already hated for some time now, was an accessory to this.

It turned out that Mummolus had been having a feast at home when someone from the king's court complained that a boy dear to him had been stricken with dysentery.

"I have an herb all ready," replied the prefect, "so that if a sufferer from dysentery, no matter how hopeless the case, drinks some of it, he will soon be cured."

This was reported to the queen and she was consumed by even greater rage.

Meanwhile women were arrested in the city of Paris. The queen applied torture to them, forcing them with beatings to confess what they knew. They admitted that they were witches and testified that they had caused many to die, adding something I cannot believe for any reason.

"Queen, we offered your son in exchange for the life of Mummolus the prefect," they said.

Thereupon the queen, after inflicting more severe torments on the women, killed some off by torture, had some burned, and attached others to wheels, breaking their bones over the spokes. And so she retired with the king to the villa of Compiègne and there disclosed to him what she had heard about the prefect.

The king sent his men with orders to fetch the prefect. After interrogating him, they loaded him with chains and subjected him to torture. He was suspended from a beam with his hands tied behind his back and then asked what he knew of evil arts, but he confessed nothing of what we have recorded above. Yet he did admit to one thing: that he had often received ointments and potions from those women to secure for himself the favor of the king and queen.

When he was taken down from the punishment, he called the executioner to him.

"Tell my master the king," he said, "that I feel no ill effect of the tortures inflicted on me."

When the king was told, he said, "Is it not true that he is a sorcerer, if he has not been harmed by these tortures?"

Mummolus was then racked by rope and pulley and beaten with triple thongs until his torturers were tired out. Then they drove splinters under the nails of his fingers and toes. When matters had reached the point that the sword was poised to cut his head off, the queen obtained his life; but the disgrace that followed was not less than death. All his property was taken from him, and he was put on a cart and sent to his birthplace, the city of Bordeaux. On the way he had a stroke and barely managed to reach his destination. Not long after he breathed his last.

After this, the queen took all the boy's effects, both garments and costly articles, either in silk or whatever she could find in fleece, and burned them. They say there were four wagon-loads. She had the items of gold and silver melted down in a furnace and stored so that nothing might remain intact to recall the grief she felt for her son.

*An Envoy from Spain (VI 40)*

Ingund, sister of Childebert and daughter of Brunhild, had been married to Leovigild's son Hermenigild, who rebelled against his father. An envoy, named Oppila, came from Spain, bringing many gifts to King Chilperic. Leovigild, king of Spain, was afraid that King Childebert might muster forces against him to avenge the wrong done to his sister. When Leovigild had arrested and imprisoned his own son Hermenigild, who had married King Childebert's sister, Hermenigild's wife had been left with the Greeks.

*A theological debate follows between Gregory and Oppila.*

*Chilperic Retreats to Cambrai. Birth of Chlothar II (VI 41)*

When King Chilperic found out that his brother Guntram and his nephew Childebert had made peace [cf. VI 33] and were planning to take away from him the cities he had seized by force, he withdrew with all his treasure to Cambrai, taking with him everything he could easily move. He sent messengers to the dukes and counts of the cities telling them to repair the walls of their cities and to bring their property, wives, and children within the protection of the walls; if the need arose, they themselves were to offer stout resistance to prevent the enemy doing any harm to the cities.

"And if," he added, "you suffer any loss, you shall get more than was taken from you when we take revenge upon our enemies."

He said this not knowing that achieving victory lies in the hand of the Lord.

Thereafter he several times called up his army, but on each occasion ordered it to stay within his own territory.

At this time, a son was born to him, whom he ordered to be brought up in the villa of Vitry, "in case," he said, "the child suffers harm while being seen in public and dies."

*Childebert Invades Italy (VI 42)*

King Childebert, however, went to Italy. On news of this, the Lombards submitted to his authority out of fear that they would be slaughtered by his army; they gave him many gifts, promising him loyalty and submission. Having achieved all that he wished with them, the king returned to Gaul and had an army assembled, which he ordered sent to Spain, but he abandoned the plan.

Some years before Childebert had received fifty thousand solidi from the emperor Maurice to get rid of the Lombards from Italy. Now the emperor, hearing of the peace just concluded with that people, asked for his money back. But Childebert, sure of his strength, would not even answer.

*The concluding chapters of Book VI are preceded in VI 44 by a survey of the year's portents and natural afflictions, including locusts, frosts, storms, and drought.*

### Departure of Rigunth, Daughter of Chilperic (VI 45)

The Kalends of September came round and a great embassy of Goths visited King Chilperic [to convey Rigunth to Spain].

Chilperic himself had now returned to Paris and ordered many households to be taken from fiscal properties and placed on the wagons; and many people who wept and refused to go he ordered imprisoned, to make it easier to send them off with his daughter. They say that a good number in their anguish hanged themselves, dreading being separated from their relations. Son was taken from father, mother from daughter, and they departed with loud groans and curses. There was such lamentation in the city of Paris that it might be compared with the lamentation of Egypt. Many of the better born who were forced to go made wills and left their property to churches, requesting that, when the girl had entered Spain, the wills should be opened at once as if they were already buried.

Meanwhile envoys arrived in Paris from King Childebert, warning King Chilperic not to take anything from the cities he held belonging to the realm of Childebert's father Sigibert, not to endow his daughter with anything from the late king's treasury, and not to dare touch the dependents or horses or yokes of oxen or anything of that kind belonging to him. One of these envoys, they say, was secretly killed, but it is not known by whom; suspicion, however, fell on the king.

King Chilperic promised that he would touch nothing from these cities. Summoning the more important Franks and others who were loyal to him, he celebrated his daughter's marriage. He handed her over to the envoys of the Goths and presented her with a great treasure. Her mother also brought forth a huge quantity of gold and silver and garments, so that when the king saw it he thought he was left with nothing. The queen noticed that he was disturbed and turned to address the Franks.

"Don't think, men, that I have anything here from the treasuries of previous kings," she said. "All that you see has been brought from my own property, for the most glorious king has given me much; and I have gathered a good deal by my own efforts, and have procured most of it from enterprises granted to me, from both revenues and taxes. You also have often enriched me with your gifts, from which come those things you now see before you. But there is nothing here from the public treasury."

And so the concerns of the king were falsely put to rest.

There was so much stuff that it took fifty wagons to carry the gold and silver and other ornaments. The Franks offered many gifts, some giving gold, some silver, many giving horses, and most garments; each as he was able gave a gift.

After tears and kisses, the girl said farewell and was going out the gate when an axle on the carriage broke.

"Evil hour [cf. Fr. *malheur*]," everyone said. Some took it as an omen.

She made her way from Paris and ordered the tents pitched at the eighth milestone from the city. Fifty men rose in the night, took a hundred of the best horses with the same number of golden bridles and two great serving bowls, slipped away, and went to King Childebert. Moreover, along the whole route, when any one could slip away, he took off, carrying whatever he could lay his hands on.

Abundant supplies were gathered largely from the cities along the route. The king ordered that nothing should be supplied from his own fisc but all from the contributions of the poor. And as the king was suspicious that his brother or nephew might prepare an ambush for the girl on the road, he directed that she travel surrounded by an army. Very distinguished officials were with her: Duke Bobo, Mummolen's son, with his wife as attendant to the bride; Domigisel and Ansovald; and the mayor of the palace, Waddo, who had once held the comital office of Saintes; the rest of the crowd numbered over four thousand. Other dukes and chamberlains who had traveled with her turned back at Poitiers, but those continuing the trip went on as best they could. Such spoils and plunder were taken on this journey as can scarcely be described. For they robbed the huts of the poor and ruined the vineyards by cutting off vine-stems with their grapes and carrying them away. Lifting cattle and whatever they could find, they left nothing along the road they traveled. The words that were spoken by Joel the prophet were fulfilled: "What the locust has left, the cankerworm has eaten; and what the cankerworm has left, the caterpillar has eaten; and what the caterpillar has left, the blight has eaten [cf. Joel 1:4]."

That is what happened at this time. What was left by frost the storm leveled, what was left by the storm the drought burned up, and what was left by the drought this host carried away.

### The Death of King Chilperic (VI 46)

While they continued on their way with this plunder, Chilperic, the Nero and Herod of our time, went to his villa of Chelles about one hundred stades [11-12 miles] distant from Paris and there went hunting. One day, returning from the hunt after dusk, he was being helped down from his horse and had one hand on a retainer's shoulder, when a man came up and stabbed him with a knife under the armpit and with a second stroke pieced his stomach.

As a flood of blood poured from the king's mouth and the open wound, his wicked life at once came to an end.

The text above shows the evil that he did. For he frequently laid waste and burned many districts; and he had no feeling of anguish in doing this but rather joy, like Nero before him, when he recited tragedies as the palace burned. He often punished men unjustly to get their wealth. In his time few clerics were promoted to episcopal office. He was a glutton and his god was his belly. He used to claim that no one was wiser than he. He wrote two books on the model of Sedulius, but their feeble little verses cannot stand on their feet at all, for in his ignorance he put short syllables for long, and long syllables for short. He wrote small pieces also, hymns and masses, which cannot reasonably be used. He hated the interests of the poor. He was constantly blaspheming the priests of the Lord, and, when he was in private, he derided and ridiculed no one more than the bishops of churches. He called this one a lightweight, that one arrogant, another was a spendthrift, and this one a lecher. He would claim that this or that bishop was proud or haughty, because he hated nothing more than churches.

"Look! our fisc has been left poor," he often used to say, "and our wealth has been transferred to the churches. No one rules at all except the bishops; our office will perish and has been ceded to the bishops of the cities."

This being his view, he would constantly invalidate wills made in favor of churches, and he trampled under foot the dispositions of his own father, thinking that no one was left to preserve his wishes. As to lust and debauchery, nothing can be thought of that he did not realize in deed. He was always looking for new means to injure people; at this time, if he found any one guilty, he would order his eyes torn out. In the directions he sent to his judges on matters touching his interests, he would add, "if anyone disregards our orders, let his eyes be torn out as punishment."

He never loved anyone sincerely and was loved by no one, with the result that, when he breathed his last, all his followers abandoned him. Mallulf, bishop of Senlis, who had been sitting in his tent for three days, unable to see him, came when he heard of his death. He washed him and clothed him in better garments. After spending the night singing hymns, he took him by boat to Paris and buried him in the basilica of Saint Vincent. Queen Fredegund was left in the cathedral church.

## II. THE AFTERMATH OF CHILPERIC'S DEATH AND THE REVOLT OF GUNDOVALD, a. 584 (OCTOBER)-586 (BOOKS VII—VIII)

### Year IX of Childebert II, a. 584 (cont'd)

*Orleans and Blois against Châteaudun and Chartres (VII 2)*

After Chilperic died and found the death he had long been looking for, troops of Orleans joined those of Blois and attacked the people of Châteaudun, taking them off guard and defeating them. Houses, stores of grain, and whatever they could not readily move they put to the torch; they took herds and carried off anything they could lift. Upon their departure, the forces of Châteaudun with others from Chartres followed their trail and gave as good as they got, leaving nothing in their houses, outside their houses, or belonging to their houses. While they were still raging and inciting quarrels among themselves, and the people of Orleans were marshaling their forces to fight back, the counts intervened and established peace until there could be a hearing and judgment given, at which time the side that had unlawfully ignited the conflict could pay compensation according to the provisions of the law. And in this way the war was brought to an end.

*Fredegund Takes Refuge. Treasure Taken to Childebert (VII 4)*

Now that Fredegund was a widow, she came to Paris and took refuge in the cathedral with treasure which she had earlier deposited within the city walls. She was given support by Bishop Ragnemod. The remaining treasure had been left at Chelles and included the large gold salver that Chilperic had recently had made [cf. VI 4]; it was now removed by officials of the treasury, who at once went off to King Childebert, then staying in Meaux.

*Guntram and Childebert Come to Paris (VII 5)*

Queen Fredegund took advice and sent envoys to King Guntram with this message: "Let my lord come and take the kingdom of his brother. I have a small infant, whom I wish to place in his arms; as for myself, I bow to his authority."

When Guntram learned of his brother's passing, he wept quite bitterly, but when his grief subsided, he mustered an army and marched to Paris. He had already been received within the walls when his nephew King Childebert arrived from another direction.

### Guntram Tells Off Childebert's Envoys and Takes the Kingdom of Charibert (VII 6)

When the people of Paris refused to admit Childebert, he sent envoys to King Guntram with a message saying, "I know, most dutiful father, that it has not escaped your attention how up to the present time a hostile party has prevented both of us finding the justice that is our due. Therefore I humbly beg you now to keep the agreements that were reached between us after my father's death [cf. V 17]."

At this point, King Guntram said to the envoys, "You wretches, ever false, you haven't a speck of truth in you and don't stick to your promises; look, you abandoned every pledge you made to me and wrote a new agreement with King Chilperic to drive me from my kingdom and divide my cities between you [cf. VI 3]. Here are your very agreements. Here are your signatures by which you confirmed your conniving. Now you have the nerve to ask me to receive my nephew Childebert, whom you tried to make my enemy by your depravity?"

"If you're so overcome with anger that you will not grant your nephew what you have promised," replied the envoys, "at least stop taking what is due to him from Charibert's kingdom."

"Here are the agreements made between us," said the king. "Whoever entered Paris without his brother's consent was to lose his portion, and Polioctus the martyr, along with Hilary and Martin the confessors, were to judge him and take retribution. After this my brother Sigibert entered; he died by the judgment of God and lost his portion [cf. IV 49, 51]. So did Chilperic [cf. VI 5, 27]. Because of these violations, they lost their portions. For this reason, since my brothers have been taken away according to God's judgment and by the curses in the agreement, I will subject all Charibert's kingdom with its treasury to my rule by right of law, and I will not grant anything from it to anyone, except of my own free will. Be off with you, then, you everlasting liars and perjurers, and tell this to your king."

### Guntram, Fredegund, and Chlothar II (VII 7)

They departed, but envoys came again to King Guntram with a message from Childebert demanding Queen Fredegund: "Give up that killer who strangled my aunt [cf. IV 28], killed my father [cf. IV 51] and uncle [cf. VI 46], and put my cousins to the sword [cf. V 18, 39]."

"We shall have a meeting," said Guntram, "and consider what ought to be done and decide all matters there."

For he was supporting Fredegund with his patronage, often inviting her to dinner and promising he would become her strongest advocate. One day, when they were dining at the table together, the queen tried to rise to take her leave but was halted by the king.

"Eat something more," he said.

"Please pardon me, my lord," she replied, "As is the way with women, I happen to be getting up because I am pregnant."

When he heard this, he was astonished, knowing that it was the fourth month since she had borne a son, but he permitted her to rise.

The leading figures of Chilperic's kingdom, such as Ansovald and others, gathered about Chilperic's son, who, as I have said, was four months old and whom they called Chlothar. In the cities that had formerly looked to Chilperic, they exacted oaths of loyalty to King Guntram and his nephew Chlothar.

Guntram, after proper judicial process, restored everything that King Chilperic's followers had wrongfully taken from various sources, and he himself conferred much upon churches. The wills of those who established churches as their heirs when they had died, which Chilperic had suppressed, he restored. He was gracious to many and gave much to the poor.

### Guntram and the Parisians (VII 8)

But as Guntram had no trust in the people among whom he had come, he surrounded himself with armed men and never went to church or to the other places he liked to visit without a strong guard. And so it happened one Sunday, when the deacon had called for silence among the congregation so attention might be paid to the mass, that the king turned and addressed the people.

"Men and women present here," he said, "I charge you, please maintain your loyalty to me unbroken and do not kill me as you lately did my brothers. Allow me three years at least to raise my nephews, who have become my adopted sons. For it could happen — and may the eternal Deity not allow it — that if I die while they are infants, you will perish at the same time, for there will be no strong member of our line to protect you."

When he said this, all the congregation readily said a prayer to the Lord on behalf of the king.

### News of Chilperic's Death Reaches Rigunth's Party (VII 9)

While these events were going on, Rigunth, King Chilperic's daughter, reached Toulouse with the treasures described above [VI 45]. And seeing she was now near Gothic territory, she began to make up excuses for delay. Moreover her own people told her that she ought to remain there for a time, since they were exhausted from the journey, their clothing was shabby, their shoes torn, and the accoutrements for the horses and carriages were not yet assembled, having been transported on the wagons. All these preparations, they said, must be carefully made first, before setting out on the journey and being received in an elegant state by her betrothed; otherwise they might be laughed at by the Goths by appearing among them shabbily outfitted.

While they were delaying for these reasons, news of Chilperic's death reached the ears of Duke Desiderius. He gathered his best men, entered Toulouse, found the treasures, and took them from the queen's control. He put them in a certain house, affixed seals, and posted a guard of capable men. He allowed the queen a scanty living allowance until such time as he should return to the city.

### Gundovald Raised to the Kingship. Rigunth at Toulouse (VII 10)

Desiderius hurried off to Mummolus, with whom he had entered into an alliance two years before. Mummolus was at this time staying in the town of Avignon with Gundovald, whom I have mentioned in an earlier book [VI 24, 26]. Gundovald now went in the company of the two dukes to the territory of Limoges and arrived at Brives-la-Gaillarde, where a holy man named Martin, a disciple, as they say, of our own Martin, lies buried. There, placed on a shield, Gundovald was raised up as king. But when they went around with him for the third time, it is said that he fell, so that he was only barely held up by the hands of those standing about him. Then he made a circuit of the neighboring cities.

Rigunth was staying in the basilica of the blessed Mary at Toulouse, where Ragnovald's wife, whom I mentioned previously, had taken refuge out of fear of Chilperic [VI 12]. Ragnovald now returned from Spain, where he had been sent on an embassy by King Guntram, and recovered his wife and property.

At this time the basilica of the abovenamed Martin at Brives was burned by a threatening enemy so that the altar as well as the columns, made of different kinds of marble, were split by the flames. Later this shrine was so well restored by Bishop Ferreolus that it seemed never to have suffered any damage. The inhabitants devoutly venerate and revere this holy Martin, for they have often proved his miraculous power.

### Portents (VII 11)

It was the tenth month of the year [December] when these events took place. At this time fresh shoots with misshapen grapes appeared on the vinestocks, and blossoms were seen on the trees. A great beacon crossed the heavens, illuminating the earth far and wide before day dawned. Rays also appeared in the sky. In the north a fiery column was seen for the space of two hours, hanging as it were from the heavens, and above it was a great star. There was an earthquake in Angers, and many other portents appeared, announcing, I believe, the death of Gundovald.

### *Guntram's Counts Take Cities of Sigibert. Tours Surrenders (VII 12)*

Then King Guntram sent his counts to take the cities that the late Sigibert had received from the kingdom of his brother Charibert, with orders to exact an oath of loyalty and subject all to his authority.

The people of Tours and Poitiers wanted to go over to Childebert, Sigibert's son, but the forces of Bourges were mustered, made preparations to march against them, and began setting fires in the territory of Tours. At this time they burned down the church of Mareuil in Tours's territory, where relics of the holy Martin were preserved. But the power of the saint was present; for even in so fierce a fire, the altarcloths were not consumed by the flames; and not only these, but even herbs, gathered long ago and placed upon the altar, were not burned at all.

Seeing these fires, the people of Tours sent an embassy to say that it was better for them for the present to submit to King Guntram than for everything to be laid waste by fire and sword.

### *Poitiers (VII 13)*

Immediately on the death of Chilperic, Duke Gararic had come to Limoges and received oaths in the name of Childebert. From there he went to Poitiers, where he was received and where he remained.

When he heard what the people of Tours were suffering, he sent an embassy charging us, if we wished to look after our interests, not to go over to Guntram's side, but rather to remember Sigibert, the late father of Childebert. We, however, sent back this advice to the bishop and citizens of Poitiers, that unless for the time being they submitted to Guntram, they would suffer as we did. We maintained that Guntram now stood in the place of a father over two sons, meaning Sigibert's and Chilperic's, whom he had adopted, and so held the leadership of the kingdom, as his father Chlothar had done before him.

They did not agree with this, and Gararic came out of the town intending to bring forward an army, leaving behind him Ebero, chamberlain of Childebert. Sichar, with the count of Orleans, Willachar, who at that time had received Tours, mustered an army against the people of Poitiers, figuring that forces from Tours and Bourges could lay the whole territory waste from two directions.

When they had approached the territory and had begun to burn houses, the people of Poitiers sent envoys with a message saying, "We ask you to hold off until Kings Guntram and Childebert hold the conference they have arranged. If it is agreed that King Guntram should receive these districts, we shall not resist; if not, we will recognize our lord, to whom we should render service to the full."

"None of this business is our concern, except fulfilling the commands of our prince," was the reply. "If you refuse, we shall finish what we started and lay everything waste."

Since the alternative was complete destruction by fire, pillage, or captivity, the Poitevins drove Childebert's men from the city and swore oaths to King Guntram, though they did not keep them long.

### Childebert's Envoys before Guntram (VII 14)

As the day of the meeting approached, King Childebert sent Bishop Egidius, Guntram Boso, Sigivald, and many others to see King Guntram.

"We give thanks to almighty God," said the bishop, on entering the king's presence; "He has restored you, most dutiful king, to your regions and kingdom after much trouble."

"Due thanks must be given to him who is King of kings and Lord of lords, who in his mercy thought it right to accomplish these things," said the king. "But no thanks are due to you, by whose deceiving counsel and perjuries districts of mine were burned last year [cf. VI 31]. You've never kept faith with any man; your deceit is spread everywhere; you've show yourself, not a priest, but an enemy of my kingdom."

At these words the bishop, though angered, was silent.

But one of the envoys spoke up, "Your nephew Childebert begs you to have the cities that his father held given back to him."

"I have already told you before," said the king in reply to this, "that our agreements confer them on me, and so I refuse to restore them."

Another of the envoys said, "Your nephew asks you to order the witch Fredegund, through whom many kings have been killed, to be turned over so vengeance can be taken for the death of his father, uncle and cousins [cf. VII 7]."

"She cannot be given into his power," said King Guntram, "because she has a son who is king. Besides, I don't believe what you say against her is true."

Then Guntram Boso approached the king, intending to say something. Since it had been reported that Gundovald had been publicly raised up as king, the king broke in before he could speak.

"Enemy of my country and kingdom, you went a few years ago to the East with the purpose of bringing into my kingdom a certain Ballomer" — that is what the king used to call Gundovald. "You are a perpetual liar and never keep your promises."

"You are lord and king and sit on a royal throne," said Guntram Boso, "and no one dares answer the charges you make. But I declare that I am innocent of this charge. And if there is someone of my rank who pins this crime on me in secret, let him come forward openly and speak. Then, most righteous king, we can put the matter to the judgment of God so He can decide it, when he sees us fighting on the level field of single combat."

At this all were silent.

"This matter [of Gundovald]," added the king, "ought to make everyone eager to drive from our territories an adventurer whose father ran a mill; to tell the truth, his father sat at the loom and wove wool."

And although it is possible for one man to be trained in the two trades, still, one of the envoys answered the king with a rebuke.

"Thus, according to you," he said, "this man had two fathers at the same time, one a woolworker, the other a miller. To speak so poorly, king, hardly becomes you. For it is an unheard of thing that one man should have two fathers at the same time, except in a spiritual sense."

Many of them burst out laughing at this, and another envoy spoke up.

"We say farewell to you, king," he said. "Since you have refused to restore your nephew's cities, we know that the ax is still safe that was driven into the heads of your brothers. Soon it will be driven into your brain."

Thus they went off in anger.

As they left, the king, inflamed at their insults, ordered horseshit, rotten shavings, putrefying chaff and hay, and even the stinking muck of the city to be thrown on their heads. Covered with this filth, they went away, not without immeasurable offense and insult.

### *Fredegund Misbehaves in the Cathedral (VII 15)*

While Queen Fredegund was residing in the cathedral at Paris, Leonard, a former *domesticus*, who had just then arrived from Toulouse, went to see her and began to tell her the instances of abuse and the insults inflicted on her daughter.

"As you commanded, I went with Queen Rigunth," he said, "and I saw her humiliation and how she was despoiled of treasure and all her property [cf. VII 9]. I slipped away and have come to report to my mistress what happened."

On hearing this report, Fredegund became enraged and ordered him despoiled in the very church; she had him stripped of his garments and the belt that he had as a gift from King Chilperic and ordered him out of her presence. Cooks and bakers, and whoever else she learned had returned from this journey, she left beaten, plundered, and maimed.

She tried to ruin Nectar, brother of bishop Baudegisil, by means of unspeakable charges before the king, claiming he had taken a great deal from the treasury of the dead king. In an effort to have him bound and thrown into a dark prison, she also used to say that he had taken hides and large quantities of wine from the storehouses. But the king's forbearance and help from Nectar's brother Baudegisil prevented this from happening.

She did many foolish things and showed no fear of God in whose church she was seeking help. She had with her at the time a judge, Audo, who had been her accomplice in many misdeeds in the time of the king. For together with Mummolus the prefect, he subjected to public taxation many Franks who in the time of the elder King Childebert were freeborn. After the king's death Audo was despoiled by those he had taxed and stripped, so that he had nothing left except what he had on his person. They burned his house and would surely have taken his very life if he had not fled to the cathedral with the queen.

### Bishop Praetextatus Returns from Exile (VII 16)

She received Bishop Praetextatus unwillingly. The citizens of Rouen had recalled the bishop from exile after the king's death and restored him to the city amid loud acclamation [cf. V 18]. After his return he came to Paris and presented himself to King Guntram, entreating him to make a thorough investigation of his case. The queen maintained that he should not be taken back, since he had been removed from his episcopal office at Rouen by the sentence of forty-five bishops. When the king was going to summon a council to deal with the matter, Ragnemod, bishop of Paris, gave an answer on behalf of all bishops.

"You should know," he said, "that the bishops sentenced him to do penance, but he was by no means removed from his episcopal office."

And so he was received by the king, welcomed to his table, and then returned to his own city.

### King Guntram Hears of a Plot against His Life (VII 18)

When the king was staying in Paris, a certain poor man came to him.

"Listen, king, to what I have to say," he said. "You should know that Faraulf, chamberlain of your late brother, is seeking to kill you. I have heard his plan to attack you with a knife or run you through with a spear when you go to church for matins."

The king was astounded, and sent for Faraulf. He made a denial, but the king, fearful of what he had heard, surrounded himself with a strong guard. He never went to the holy places, or anywhere else, except in the company of armed men and guards. Not long afterwards Faraulf died.

*Fredegund Sent into Retirement. Chlothar II Taken by the Magnates (VII 19)*

A great outcry was raised against those who had been powerful officials under King Chilperic; they were of course accused of having taken villas and other possessions from other people's property. All that had been unjustly taken the king now ordered restored, as I have previously pointed out [VII 7].

He also ordered Queen Fredegund to go off to the villa of Rueil in the territory of Rouen. All the better born of Chilperic's kingdom attended her and left her there with Bishop Melantius, who had been removed from the see of Rouen. They then went over to her son, promising her that they would bring him up with the very greatest care.

*Attempt to Assassinate Brunhild (VII 20)*

After Queen Fredegund had gone away to the villa of Rueil, she was very dejected because her power had now partly been taken from her. Considering herself better than Brunhild, she secretly sent a cleric of her household to deceive that queen and kill her. The plan was that he would insinuate himself into her household, obtain her trust, and stab her to death in secret. The cleric came and gained the Queen Brunhild's favor by various deceptions.

"I am running from Queen Fredegund," he said, "and ask your help."

He tried to pretend to everyone that he was humble, valuable and obedient, and devoted to the queen. But it was not long before they realized that he had been sent under false pretenses. He was bound and beaten and, once he had confessed the secret mission, was permitted to return to his patroness. When he disclosed to her what had happened and told how he could not carry out her orders, he was punished by having his hands and feet cut off.

*Eberulf Condemned for Chilperic's Death (VII 21, 22)*

After these events, King Guntram, who had now returned to Chalon, was attempting to investigate his brother's death. Fredegund had put the blame on the chamberlain Eberulf. For she had asked him to stay with her after the king's death but could not get her way. As this was a cause of bad feeling, the queen said that the king had been killed by Eberulf and that he had taken a great deal from the treasury and, for this reason, had gone off to Tours; and so, if the king wished to avenge his brother's death, he should know that Eberulf was the leader in this affair.

At that point the king swore to all his magnates that he would destroy not only Eberulf himself but also his family to the ninth generation, so that by their deaths the wicked custom of killing kings might be done away with before more kings were killed.

When Eberulf found out about this, he headed for the basilica of Saint Martin, whose property he had often seized. At this time, troops of Orleans and Blois were given the chance to guard him and used to come in turn to keep watch; at the end of each fifteen-day stint, they would return home with lots of plunder, leading draught animals, cattle, and whatever else they could take away.

The ones who led off the blessed Martin's draught animals started quarreling, however, and stabbed one another with their spears. Two, who were taking mules, went to a neighboring house and asked for a drink. When the householder said he did not have one, they raised their spears to strike him, but he drew his sword and ran them both through; they both fell down dead. Saint Martin's draught animals were returned. So many offenses were committed at the time by the men of Orleans as to beggar description.

While this was going on, Eberulf's property was being granted to various people; his gold and silver and other valuable items that he had with him were offered for sale. Property he had been granted was confiscated by the state. Herds of horses, swine, and draught animals were also taken. His townhouse, which he had taken from the possession of the church, and which was full of grain, wine, hides, and many other things, was completely cleaned out and nothing left but the bare walls. Because of this he was particularly suspicious of me, although I was running around on his behalf in good faith, and he kept promising that if he ever regained the king's favor he would take vengeance on me for what he had gone through. God, to whom the secrets of the heart are revealed, knows that I helped him honestly as much as I could. And although in former times he had often played me false in order to get Saint Martin's property, still there was a reason why I should forget that — I had taken his son from the holy font.

But I believe that the greatest stumbling block for the unlucky man was that he showed no respect for the holy bishop [Martin]. Continually engaged in excessive drinking and foolishness, Eberulf often resorted to violence within the very atrium, which was close to the saint's feet. When a priest refused to bring him wine, since he was plainly drunk already, Eberulf forced him onto a bench and beat him with his fists and with other blows, so that he looked as if he were about to die; and perhaps he would have died if the cupping-glasses of the physicians had not helped him.

Because of his fear of the king, he had his lodging in the reception chamber of the holy basilica. When the priest who kept the door keys had closed the other doors and gone, Eberulf's female servants, going in with the rest of his attendants by the door of the reception chamber, would look up at the paintings on the walls and grub through the ornaments on the holy tomb, which was quite outrageous in the eyes of the religious. When the priest learned of this he drove nails in the door and fitted bars on the inside. After dinner, when he was drunk, Eberulf noticed this; we were singing in the basilica at the service held at nightfall and he entered in a rage and began to attack me with abuse and curses, accusing me, among other charges, of wanting to keep him away from the holy bishop's tomb cover. I was amazed that such madness possessed the man and tried to calm him with soothing words. But as I could not overcome his rage by gentle words, I decided to keep silent. Finding that I would say nothing, he turned to the priest and spewed out abuse at him. For he assailed both him and me with shameless language and assorted insults. When we saw that he was driven by a demon, so to speak, we left the holy basilica and ended the disgraceful scene and the vigils. We were especially distressed that he had instigated this altercation before the very tomb, without respect for the holy bishop.

In these days I had a dream and told him about it in the holy basilica.

"I thought that I was celebrating mass in this holy basilica," I said. "When the altar with the offerings was already covered with a silk cloth, I suddenly caught sight of King Guntram entering. He shouted in a loud voice, 'Drag out the enemy of my family, tear this killer away from God's sacred altar.'

"When I heard him, I turned to you and said, 'Take hold of the altarcloth with which the holy gifts are covered, you poor wretch, so you won't be thrown out of here.'

"Although you laid hold of it, your hand was not closed, and you did not hold on tightly. But I stretched out my arms and pressed my chest against the king's chest, saying, 'Don't cast this man out of the holy basilica. You risk your life by being struck down by the power of the holy bishop. Don't kill yourself with your own weapon. If you do this, you will lose your life, for now and eternity.'

"When the king opposed me, you let go of the cloth and came behind me. I was very angry with you. And when you returned to the altar, you took hold of the cloth, but again let go. While you held it feebly and I stoutly resisted the king, I woke up terrified, not knowing what the dream meant.'"

When I had told him these things, he said, "The dream you saw is true, because it very much agrees with my own intention."

"And what was your intention?" I asked.

"I've decided," he said, "that, should the king order me dragged from this place, I will hold the altarcloth with one hand and a drawn sword in the other. I will first kill you and then lay out as many clerics as I can get at. After this, having to die would not be an injustice, as long as I first took vengeance on the clerics of this saint."

I was amazed to hear this and wondered how it was that the devil spoke through his mouth. He never had any fear of God. While he was at liberty his horses and herds were loosed among the crops and vines of the poor. But if those whose labor was being destroyed drove the animals away, they were at once beaten by his men. Even in his present straits, he used to recall repeatedly how he had unjustly taken the property of the blessed bishop. Finally, the year before, he had urged on a certain foolish citizen and had him bring a suit against stewards of church property. At this time, with no regard for the provisions of the law, he took away property once in the possession of the church under the pretense of purchasing it, giving the man a gold portion of his belt. He also acted depraved in many other matters to the end of his life, which I shall recount later.

## Year X of Childebert II, a. 585

### Poitiers Plundered (VII 24, 25)

In the tenth year of Childebert's reign, King Guntram mustered the peoples of his kingdom and put together a great army. The larger part of it, with the forces of Orleans and Bourges, marched on Poitiers. The people there had broken the pledge they had made to the king [cf. VII 13]. The army sent a delegation before them to discover whether it would be received or not; but Maroveus, bishop of Poitiers, gave the envoys a harsh reception. The troops entered the territory of the city, pillaging, burning, and killing. On their way home with their plunder, they crossed the territory of Tours and, though oaths had already been given, did the same there, even setting the very churches on fire and carrying off everything they could seize. The invasion was repeated until the Poitevins at last were forced to recognize the king. When the army was drawing nearer the city, and the Poitevins realized that the greater part of their territory had already been ravaged, only then did they send messengers declaring their loyalty to King Guntram.

As soon as the troops were admitted within the walls of the town, they rushed upon the bishop, accusing him of disloyalty. But he, seeing himself hard pressed by them, broke up one of the gold chalices used in the service of the altar, had it made into tokens, and so ransomed the people and himself.

The troops eagerly surrounded Marileif, who had been considered the chief physician in King Chilperic's household. He had already been well plundered by Duke Gararic, but he was stripped bare by them a second time, so that he had no property left. They took away his horses, gold, and silver, as well as the more valuable items he had, and reduced him to a dependent of the church. For his father had been obligated to service in the mills of the church, and his brothers and cousins and other relatives were attached to the royal kitchens and bakehouse.

### Gundovald in the South (VII 26-28)

*Gregory mentions a Sigulf in IV 47, but tells us nothing about the earlier revolt of the Sigulf mentioned here.*

Gundovald wanted to come to Poitiers, but was afraid, for he had heard that an army had been mustered against him. In cities that had belonged to King Sigibert, he received oaths sworn in the name of King Childebert; in the others, which had belonged to Guntram or Chilperic, the oath to remain loyal was taken in his own name. After this he went to Angoulême. When he had received oaths there and rewarded the leading citizens, he proceeded to Périgueux. The bishop at the time [Charterius], suffered severely at his hands for not having welcomed him with due honor.

From there he moved on to Toulouse. He sent a message telling Magnulf, bishop of the city, to receive him. But the bishop was mindful of wrongs he once had to endure from Sigulf, who had tried to raise himself to the kingship. He addressed his fellow citizens.

"We know that Guntram and his nephew Childebert are kings," said the bishop, "but as to this man, we don't know where he comes from. Therefore make preparations, and, if Duke Desiderius tries to bring this disaster upon us, let him be destroyed in the same way as Sigulf, and let him be an example to all that no outsider should dare to profane the kingship of the Franks."

Though the citizens had no intention of giving in and were preparing to fight, Gundovald arrived with a large army; when they saw that they could not withstand it, they received him into the town.

Later, when seated with Gundovald at the table in the church manse, the bishop said to him, "You claim to be the son of King Chlothar, but we don't know whether that is true or not. And as to your carrying out your enterprise, to our thinking that is unbelievable."

"I am the son of King Chlothar," said Gundovald, "and I am now about to take possession of part of the kingdom; I shall go quickly to Paris and establish the capital of the kingdom."

"Is it true then," asked the bishop, "that no one from the line of Frankish kings is left, if you can do what you say?"

Mummolus, hearing the dispute, raised his hand and slapped the bishop around, saying to him, "Isn't it shameful for such a base idiot to answer a great king in this way?"

In fact, when Desiderius found out from the bishop about his comments, he too became enraged and grabbed him. They both hit the bishop with their spears, punched him with their fists, and kicked him. They then bound him with a rope and condemned him to exile and took all his property from him, both personal and that belonging to the church.

Waddo, former mayor of the palace to Queen Rigunth, joined Gundovald's party, but the others who had left Paris with him [cf. VI 45] slipped away and fled.

Later, the army [cf. VII 24-25], which had now been moved out of Poitiers, advanced in pursuit of Gundovald. Many people from Tours accompanied it in hope of profit, but the forces of Poitiers fell upon them; some of them were killed, and the greater part returned home despoiled. The troops from Tours who had earlier joined the army now also left. And so the host moved forward to the river Dordogne and waited for news of Gundovald. As I said above, he had been joined by Duke Desiderius and Bladast, as well as by Waddo, mayor of the palace to Queen Rigunth. His chief commanders were Bishop Sagittarius and Mummolus. Sagittarius had already been promised the see of Toulouse.

## Death of Eberulf (VII 29)

While these events were taking place, King Guntram entrusted a certain Claudius with a mission.

"If you go and drive Eberulf from the basilica [cf. VII 22]," said the king, "and put him to the sword or bind him in chains, I will enrich you with great gifts. But above all, I warn you, do no injury to the holy basilica."

Claudius, a foolish and greedy fellow, quickly ran off to Paris, for his wife was a native of Meaux. He began to wonder if he should see Queen Fredegund.

"If I see her," he thought, "I may be able get a reward from her, for I know that she is the enemy of the man against whom I am sent."

He did go to see her and was well rewarded right away. Much was promised him, provided he could get Eberulf out the basilica and kill him, or trap him and bind him in chains, or just cut him down in the atrium itself.

Returning now to Châteaudun, he called upon the count to furnish him with three hundred men to guard the gates of Tours, but actually intending on his arrival there to overpower Eberulf with their assistance. While the count was mustering the men, Claudius himself went to Tours. En route he began to pay attention to auspices, as barbarians have a habit of doing, and to find them unfavorable. At the same time, he made many inquiries whether the power of the holy Martin had shown itself of late against oath-breakers and, especially, whether vengeance had been taken immediately on anyone doing wrong to those who placed their hope in the saint.

Disregarding the men who, as I said, were to have come to help him, he went in person to the basilica. There he at once joined up with the hapless Eberulf, gave him his oath, and swore by everything sacred, by the power of the holy bishop [Saint Martin] there present, that no one who could present his case before the king was more loyal to his interests than himself.

For the wretched man Claudius had said to himself, "Unless I can deceive him by false oaths, I shall not have the better of him."

Indeed, when Eberulf heard him make such promises upon oath within the basilica and in the porticoes and other venerated parts of the atrium, the scoundrel believed the perjurer.

The next day, while I was staying at a villa some thirty miles from the city, Eberulf was invited to a dinner at the holy basilica with Claudius and some other citizens. Claudius would have struck him down with his sword on the spot, if only Eberulf's retainers had been standing further away. But Eberulf in his vanity noticed nothing. When the meal was over, he and Claudius strolled together through the atrium of the manse of the basilica, promising each other loyalty and friendship by exchanging oaths.

While talking in this way, Claudius said to Eberulf, "It would please me to drain a cup at your quarters, if the wine were mixed with spices, or if your lordship could get drink with more kick to it."

Eberulf was delighted with the suggestion and answered that he had wine.

"You shall find at my lodging everything you want," he said, "if only my lord will see fit to enter the hovel I am staying in."

He sent his servants, one after the other, to get stronger wines, those of Latium and of Gaza. As soon as Claudius saw that the servants had gone and left their master alone, he lifted up his hand towards the basilica.

"Most blessed Martin," he said, "help me to see my wife and relations soon." For the unhappy man was now at the critical juncture: he was planning to kill Eberulf in the atrium and was fearful of the power of the holy bishop.

At that point one of the Claudius's servants who was very strong seized Eberulf from behind, clasped him between his powerful arms, and bent his chest back to receive a fatal blow. Claudius drew his sword from his belt and went for him. But Eberulf, held tight though he was, pulled a dagger from his belt and got ready to strike. As Claudius raised his arm high and thrust his blade into Eberulf's breast, Eberulf quickly drove his dagger under his adversary's armpit, withdrew it, and with a second stroke cut off Claudius's thumb. Then the servants of Claudius gathered round with their swords and wounded Eberulf in several places. He slipped out of their hands, and, as he drew his sword and tried to get away, though already near death, they inflicted a deep wound on his head. He fell down dead with his brains spilled out. He did not deserve to be saved by him to whom he never knew how to make an appeal out of faith.

Claudius, filled with terror, made for the abbot's cell, seeking protection from one whose patron he had not had enough sense to respect.

"A great crime has been committed" he said to the abbot, who was in the cell. "Without your help, we'll be destroyed."

As he was saying this, in rushed the servants of Eberulf with swords and spears. Finding the door barred, they broke the glass panes of the cell and threw their spears through the windows in the wall, piercing Claudius, who was already half dead. His followers hid behind doors and under beds. Two of the clergy grabbed the abbot and barely managed to get him out alive through the swarm of drawn swords. The doors were now open, and the crowd of armed men entered. Even some of the registered recipients of alms, along with other poorfolk, angered at the crime, tried to pull off the roof of the cell. Moreover, those possessed and various indigents came with stones and clubs to avenge the outrage to the basilica, distressed that it should be the scene of the kind of deeds never done there before. What need is there to say more? The fugitives were dragged from their hiding-places and cruelly cut down; the floor of the cell was stained with gore. Once they were killed, their bodies were then dragged outside and left naked on the cold ground. Their killers took the spoils and slipped away the following night.

God's vengeance was immediate on those who had defiled the blessed atrium with human blood. But the offense of that man cannot be reckoned slight whom the holy bishop [Saint Martin] permitted to endure such things.

The king was very angry at what happened, but when he learned the reason, he calmed down. The property of the hapless Eberulf, movable and real, which he had inherited from his ancestors, the king distributed among his loyal followers. The dead man's wife was left in the holy basilica thoroughly despoiled. The bodies of Claudius and the others were taken away by their next of kin to their own part of the country and buried there.

### Gundovald at Bordeaux (VII 30, 31)

Two envoys, in fact clerics, were sent by Gundovald to his friends. One of the envoys, the abbot of Cahors, hid the message he received under the wax in the hollowed out boards of writing tablets. He was arrested by King Guntram's men and, when the message was discovered, brought before the king.

He was severely beaten and thrown into prison.

Gundovald was in Bordeaux at this time and highly esteemed by Bishop Bertram. Gundovald was looking for whatever might help his cause, and someone told him that a certain king in the east had taken the thumb of Saint Sergius the martyr and attached it to his own right arm. Whenever the need arose to drive away his enemies, the king would rely on it for help; when he raised his right arm, the enemy host would immediately run away, as though overcome by the power of the martyr. Hearing this, Gundovald began to make careful inquiries whether there might be someone in Bordeaux who had managed to get relics of Sergius the martyr. Bishop Bertram suggested Eufronius, a merchant against whom he bore a grudge. Bertram, craving the man's property, had once had him tonsured against his will, but Eufronius in disdain moved to another city and returned when his hair had grown again.

And so the bishop said, "There is a Syrian here called Eufronius. He has made his house a church and placed relics of this saint in it, and he has observed them work numerous wonders, helped by the power of the martyr. Once when the city of Bordeaux was being consumed by a great fire, his house, though surrounded by flames, was not harmed at all."

At these words, Mummolus at once rushed off to the Syrian's house, accompanied by Bishop Bertram. They stood round the man, and Mummolus ordered him to show the sacred relics. He refused.

But thinking that this was a trap being laid for him out of malice, he added, "Do not trouble an old man or do wrong to the saint, but take a hundred gold pieces from me and go away."

When Mummolus still insisted on seeing the relics, Eufronius offered two hundred pieces, but he could not get Mummolus to leave without the relics being seen. Mummolus then ordered a ladder to be put up against the wall — for the relics were hidden in a casket in the top of the wall facing the altar — and told his deacon to climb it. The deacon went up the ladder step by step and grasped the casket, but was shaken with such trembling that no one thought he would get back down to the ground alive. But, as I have said, having gotten hold of the casket, which was hanging from the wall, he brought it down. The casket was searched and Mummolus found a bone from the saint's finger, which he had no fear of striking with a knife. He struck it first on the upper side, then on the lower. When after many blows he managed to break it with some difficulty, it split into three parts, which vanished in different directions. I think it was unacceptable to the martyr to be treated in this way. Eufronius now started to sob, and all prostrated themselves in prayer, begging God to see fit to reveal what had been removed from mortal sight. After the prayer, the fragments were found. Mummolus took one of them and departed, but not, I believe, with the favor of the martyr, as was made plain in subsequent events.

While Gundovald's party were at Bordeaux, orders were given for the priest Faustian to be consecrated bishop of Dax. The bishop of the city had recently died and Nicetius, count of Dax and brother of Rusticus, bishop of Aire, had obtained a directive from Chilperic for him to be appointed bishop of the town, once he had been tonsured. Gundovald, intent on annulling Chilperic's decrees, convoked the bishops and ordered them to give Faustian the blessing. Bishop Bertram was metropolitan but, wary of the future, charged Palladius of Saintes with giving the blessing. It is true that Bertram's eyes were troubling him at the time. Orestes, bishop of Bazas, was also present at the consecration; he afterwards denied this before the king.

### Gundovald's Envoys Before Kings Guntram and Childebert (VII 32, 33)

After these events, Gundovald again sent two envoys to the king. They carried consecrated rods according to the custom of the Franks, believing naturally that their persons would not be touched by anyone and that they could return safely with an answer after relating the nature of their mission. But they carelessly revealed to many people what they were after before they entered the king's presence. Word of this reached the king in no time at all, and so they ended up being brought before him in chains.

In no position to deny who sent them, whom they were to see, and what they were to accomplish, they said, "Gundovald, who recently has come from the East, says that he is the son of your father King Chlothar. He sends us to receive the portion of the kingdom that is his due. If you do not restore it, know that he will come into these regions with an army. For all the best fighting men in the part of Gaul beyond the Dordogne have joined him. These are his words: 'When we have joined on the level field of single combat, God will then judge whether I am Chlothar's son or not.'"

The king was furious at this and ordered them racked by rope and pulley and severely beaten, so that they might give clearer proof that they were telling the truth, or, if they were still concealing any information in the secrets of their hearts, the force of the torture might wrench it from them against their will. As the torments were increased, they said that the king's niece, King Chilperic's daughter, had been exiled with Magnulf, bishop of Toulouse; that all her treasure had been taken by Gundovald; and that all King Childebert's well-born followers wanted Gundovald to be king. In particular, they said that Guntram Boso, when he had gone to Constantinople a few years before, had invited Gundovald to come to Gaul [cf. VI 24, VII 14].

After the envoys had been beaten and cast into prison, the king had his nephew Childebert sent for, thinking that both of them together should hear these men. The two kings met and questioned the prisoners, who repeated in the presence of the two kings what previously King Guntram had heard alone. They also remained firm in their statements that the matter, as I have said above, was known to all the chief men in Childebert's kingdom. For this reason some of King Childebert's leading officials at the time who were suspected of being parties to the affair were afraid to attend the present conference.

After this, King Guntram placed a spear in the hand of King Childebert.

"This is a sign," said Guntram, "that I have transferred all my kingdom to you. By virtue of this, go now and subject to the dominion of your authority all my cities as if they were your own. Because of my sins, none of my line remains, except only you who are my brother's son. Succeed as my heir to the entire kingdom, for I have disinherited the others."

Leaving the gathering and taking the boy aside, he spoke with him privately at this time, first earnestly charging him not to reveal the secrets of their conversation to anyone. He now indicated to him the men whose advice he should consider and those whom he should remove from his counsel; those whom he might trust, and those whom he should avoid; those whom he should distinguish by rewards, and those whom he should remove from their offices: all the while enjoining him on no account to trust or have about him Egidius, the bishop [of Rheims], who had always been his enemy and had often sworn falsely both to him and his father.

When they assembled for a banquet, King Guntram then exhorted the entire army.

"Look, men, how my son Childebert has now become a big man," he said. "Look and beware that you do not take him for a child. Now is the time to abandon your disloyalty and the high-handed practices you engage in; for he is a king whom you should now serve."

When Guntram had spoken these words and others like them, the kings feasted and celebrated together for three days. They separated in peace, exchanging many valuable gifts. It was on this occasion that King Guntram restored to his nephew all that had belonged to Sigibert his father, calling upon him not to visit his mother in case this gave her an opportunity to write to Gundovald or to receive letters from him in return.

*Siege of Saint Bertrand-de-Comminges and the Death of Gundovald (VII 34-38)*

Gundovald, on hearing that an army was approaching, crossed the Garonne with Bishop Sagittarius, Dukes Mummolus and Bladast, and Waddo and made for Saint Bertrand-de-Comminges (Convenae). Duke Desiderius had abandoned him.

*Guntram wrote a false letter in the name of Brunhild intended to persuade Gun-*
*dovald to abandon the army and go to Bordeaux. But Gundovald shut out many of*

*the inhabitants of Saint Bertrand-de-Comminges and prepared for a siege. The army under Leudegisel, Guntram's master of the stables, besieged the city using battering rams.*

*During the siege Gundovald answered the taunts of the besiegers with a defense of his cause:*

"Everyone knows that my father Chlothar hated me; that my hair was cut short, first by him and later by my brothers, is apparent to all. This was why I joined Narses, prefect of Italy, in which country I took a wife and had two sons. On her death, I went to Constantinople, taking my sons with me. I was kindly received by the emperors and lived there down to the present time. Some years ago, Guntram Boso came to Constantinople, and with some concern I carefully inquired how matters stood with my brothers. I learned that our family was seriously diminished and that of our line there remained only Kings Guntram and Childebert, a brother and a brother's son. The sons of King Chilperic had died with him, and only one small child was left. My brother Guntram had no sons; my nephew Childebert was not at all strong.

"At this time, Guntram Boso, after carefully laying out these circumstances, gave me an invitation. 'Come,' he said, 'for all the leaders of King Childebert's realm invite you, and no one has dared mutter a word against you. We all know you are Chlothar's son, and there is no one left in Gaul to rule that kingdom if you do not come.'

"I gave him many gifts, and he assured me under oath in twelve holy places that I might enter this kingdom in safety. I came to Marseilles, where the bishop graciously welcomed me; he possessed letters written by important officials of my nephew's kingdom. Then I went to Avignon, according to the wishes of Mummolus the patrician. Guntram Boso, ignoring his oath and promises, took my treasures and appropriated them as his own [cf. VI 24].

"Can't you see now, I am a king just like my brother Guntram. But if your hearts are filled with too great a hatred, take me to your king, and if he recognizes me as his brother, he can do what he wants with me. If you will not do this, at least let me return to the place from where I first set out. I will go away and do no harm to anyone. If you want to know the truth of what I say, ask Radegund [widow of Chlothar I] at Poitiers and Ingitrude [mother of Bishop Bertram and kinswoman of King Guntram] at Tours, for they will confirm what I say is right."

While he made this speech, many of the besiegers accompanied his words with abuse and derision.

*Bladast, fearing the city would be taken, deserted Gundovald. Mummolus, whose wife and children had fallen into the hands of King Guntram, as well as Sagittarius, Chariulf, and Waddo, agreed to betray Gundovald in exchange for their lives. Gundovald was persuaded to leave the city and was put to death outside the walls. Com-*

*minges was then sacked, and its inhabitants put to the sword, "so not one was left to piss against a wall" (cf. I Kings 25:34).*

### The End of Mummolus and Sagittarius. Rigunth (VII 39, 40, 43)

Leudegisel, on his return to camp with Mummolus, Sagittarius, Chariulf and Waddo, sent messengers secretly to King Guntram to ask what he wanted done with these men. The king ordered the death penalty for them. By that time Waddo and Chariulf had left their children as hostages and departed. The message regarding their death sentence came, and when Mummolus learned of it, he armed himself and went to Leudegisel's hut.

"Why do you come as if you are on the run?" said Leudegisel when he saw him come in.

"Nothing of the promise that was made is to be kept, I see," said Mummolus, "for I know that I'm close to death."

"I shall go outside and settle everything," said Leudegisel.

He went out and immediately ordered the house surrounded so that Mummolus could be killed. Mummolus held out against his attackers for quite some time, but when he came to the door and stepped out two men struck him with spears on each side. That is how he fell and died.

Bishop Sagittarius saw what was happening, and, while he was overwhelmed with fear, someone standing by said to him, "Look with your own eyes, bishop, at what is being done. Cover your head so you won't be recognized, make for the woods and hide for a while. When their anger passes you can get away."

He took the advice, but while he was trying to get away with his head covered, a certain man drew his sword and cut off his head, hood and all.

Then everyone returned home, taking much plunder and committing homicides along the way.

In these days Fredegund sent Chuppa to Toulouse to bring out her daughter from there any way he could. Many said he was really sent to entice Gundovald with many promises, in the event he could be found alive, and to bring him to Fredegund. But when Chuppa had been unable to do this, he took Rigunth and brought her back from Toulouse, not without great humiliation and abuse....

Duke Leudegisel came to the king with all the treasure [taken from Gundovald's party]. The king later dispersed it to the poor and the churches. He arrested the wife of Mummolus and tried to determine what had become of the treasures that she and her husband had amassed. When she learned that her husband had been killed and that all their arrogance was humbled in the dust, she revealed all, and said that there was still much gold and silver in Avignon that had not come to the king's attention. Immediately the king sent men to get it with a servant whom Mummolus had greatly trusted and into whose charge it had been committed. They went and took possession of everything that had been left in that city. It is said that there were two hundred and fifty talents of silver and more than thirty of gold. All this, so they say, Mummolus took from an ancient treasure that had been found. The king divided the amount with his nephew Childebert and gave away his own share to the poor for the most part. Guntram left the widow with nothing more than what she had inherited from her relations....

Desiderius looked to secure his person and his possessions behind the walls of fortresses. Waddo, former mayor of the palace to Rigunth, went over to Queen Brunhild; she welcomed him, gave him gifts and sent him away with her favor. Chariulf headed for the basilica of the holy Martin.

### Guntram at Orleans, July 585 (VIII 1-7)

Then King Guntram, in the twenty-fourth year of his reign, went from Chalon to the city of Nevers. He had been invited to go to Paris to receive from the holy font of regeneration Chilperic's son, whom they were already calling Chlothar. From Nevers he came to the city of Orleans and at that time made his presence conspicuous to its citizens. For on receiving invitations he went to their homes and ate of the meals that were offered to him. They gave him many gifts, and he bestowed many gifts on them with lavish generosity.

The day on which he came to the city of Orleans was the [summer] festival of the blessed Martin, namely the fourth before the Nones of the fifth month [4 July]. A huge throng of people came to meet him, singing his praises and carrying standards and banners. The acclamations reverberated with the diverse sounds of different languages, here that of the Syrians, there that of the Latins, and even that of the Jews.

"Long live the king," was the shout. "May his reign over the peoples last countless years."

The Jews, who could be seen taking part in the cheering, were calling out, "May all peoples honor you, kneel before you, and be subject to you."

And so it happened, when mass had been said and the king was seated at dinner, that he commented, "Woe to the Jewish people, wicked, without faith, always living a life on the edge of deceit. Today they shouted out their flattering praises that all the peoples should honor me as master for this reason: their synagogue was torn down some time ago by Christians; they want me to order it rebuilt at public expense. By God's command, that I shall never do."

King famous for wonderful wisdom! He understood the craft of the heretics so well that he later flatly turned down their petition.

When the meal was already half way over, the king said to the bishops present, "I hope I may obtain your blessing to-morrow in my house; let me receive the spiritual benefit of your coming, so I may be saved from sin when you pour forth upon my low self your words of blessing."

When he said this, all thanked him, and, as dinner was finished, we rose.

In the morning, while the king was visiting the holy places to pray, he came to my quarters. These were in the basilica of Saint Avitus the abbot, whom I mention in my book of wonders. I was delighted to get up to meet him, I admit, and after saying a prayer, asked if he would see fit to accept the blessed bread of Saint Martin in my lodging. He did not refuse, and graciously came in, drank a cup, invited me to the dinner and went away in good humor.

At that time Bertram, bishop of Bordeaux, as well as Palladius of Saintes, were very much in the king's disfavor for having received Gundovald, an event I referred to above [VII 31]. Bishop Palladius, in addition, had particularly offended the king by too often deceiving him. They had been examined a short time before by the other bishops and the magnates as to why they had welcomed Gundovald, and why they had consecrated Faustian bishop of Dax because of an inconsequential order of Gundovald. But Bishop Palladius removed the blame for the consecration from his metropolitan Bertram and shouldered it himself.

"My metropolitan's eyes were shut with severe pain," he said, "and I was robbed, treated with contempt, and dragged to the place against my will. I could do nothing else than obey one who claimed he had received complete authority over Gaul."

When this was told to the king, he was greatly irritated. Only with difficulty could he be prevailed upon to invite to the dinner those bishops whom he had not previously received.

And so when Bertram came in the king asked, "Who is this one?" The king had not seen the bishop for a long time.

"This is Bertram, bishop of Bordeaux," they said.

"We thank you for keeping faith with your own kindred," said the king. "You ought to have known, beloved father, that you are my kinsman on my mother's side, and you should not have brought a plague from abroad on your own people."

When Bertram had listened to this and more, the king turned to Palladius.

"Not many thanks are due you either, Bishop Palladius," he said. "You perjured yourself to me three times — an evil thing to say of a bishop — sending me messages full of deceit. With one letter you were giving me excuses and with another you were calling in my brother.

"God will judge my cause, since I have always tried to treat you as fathers of the church, and you have always been treacherous to me."

He said to the bishops Nicasius [of Angoulême] and Antidius [of Agen], "Most holy fathers, tell me what you have done for the good of your region or the benefit of our kingdom."

They made no reply, and the king, after washing his hands and receiving a blessing from the bishops, sat down at the table with a smiling face and a cheerful appearance, as if he had said nothing about the poor way he had been treated.

The dinner had reached the half-way point when the king had me tell my deacon to sing; he had sung the responsorium at the mass the day before. As the deacon sang, the king again told me to instruct each of the bishops present to appoint a cleric from his church and to have him sing before the king. And so I made the request at the king's command, and each sang the responsorium before the king to the best of his ability.

When the courses were being served, the king said, "All the silver you see belonged to that perjurer Mummolus, but now, by the help of God's grace, I own it all. I have already had fifteen of his dishes, like the larger one you see there, broken up, and I have kept only this one and one other of a hundred and seventy pounds. Why keep more for daily use? It's too bad I have no other son but Childebert. He has enough treasure from what his father left him and from what I had sent to him from this wretched man's property found at Avignon. The rest will have to be distributed to the needs of the poor and the churches.

"There is only one thing that I ask of you, priests of the Lord. Pray for the Lord's mercy for my son Childebert. He is a man of sense and ability. It would be hard over a period of many years to find someone as circumspect and energetic as he is. If God sees fit to grant him to Gaul, perhaps there will be hope that by him our lineage, which has almost been consumed, can rise again. This will happen through His mercy, I don't doubt, because this is what the birth of the boy indicated. It was the holy day of Easter and my brother Sigibert was standing in the church while the deacon was reading from the holy book of the Gospels. A messenger came to the king, and the words of the gospel and the message were uttered at the same time: 'A son has been born to you.' So it happened that at both announcements everyone cried out at the same time, 'Glory to almighty God.' Besides, the boy was baptized on the holy day of Pentecost and raised up as king on the holy day of the Lord's birth no less. And so if your prayers attend him, God willing, he will be able to rule."

When the king had spoken, all said a prayer to the Lord in His mercy to keep both kings safe.

"It's true," the king added, "that his mother Brunhild threatens to kill me, but I have no fear on that account. For the Lord who snatched me from the hands of my enemies will save me from her plots."

At this time he had much to say against Bishop Theodore [of Marseilles, cf. VI 11, 24], declaring that, if the bishop came to the synod, he would exile him again.

"I know it was for the sake of these people [i.e. Gundovald's party]," said the king, "that he had my brother Chilperic killed. And I shouldn't be considered a man, if I cannot avenge his death this year."

"And who killed Chilperic," I responded, "if not his own evil actions and your prayers? He laid many traps against you contrary to justice; these brought about his death. I would say this was the meaning of a dream I had: in it, when I saw him he had previously been tonsured and was being ordained bishop; then I saw him placed on a plain chair covered only in black and being carried along with shining lamps and tapers going before him."

On my recounting this, the king said, "I also had a dream that foretold his death. He was brought into my presence loaded with chains by three bishops. One of them was Tetricus [of Langres], the second was Agricola [of Chalon], and the third was Nicetius of Lyons.

"Two of them were saying: 'Release him, we entreat you, beat him and let him go.'

"Bishop Tetricus on the contrary was bitterly answering them, saying, 'May it not be so; he shall be burned in a fire for his crimes.'

"And while they argued long and hard, as if quarreling, I saw at a distance a cauldron placed on a fire and boiling furiously. Then as I wept, they seized unhappy Chilperic, broke his limbs, and threw him into the cauldron. Without delay he dissolved and melted in the steam from the water so that no trace of him at all remained."

When the king told this story, we were amazed, and, the banquet being over, we rose from the table.

The next day [6 July 585] the king went hunting. On his return I brought before him Garachar, count of Bordeaux, and Bladast, for, as I said earlier [cf. VII 37], they had taken refuge in the basilica of Saint Martin because they had been allied with Gundovald.

Since I had previously interceded on their behalf to no avail, I now spoke as follows, "Powerful king, listen to my words. You see, I have been sent to you on an embassy by my master. What shall I tell him who sent me, if you will not give me any answer?"

In astonishment, he said, "And who is the master who sent you?"

"The blessed Martin sent me, " I said, smiling.

Then he ordered the men brought forward. When they entered his presence, he reproached them for their many acts of disloyalty and perjury, repeatedly calling them tricky foxes, but he restored them to his favor, giving back what he had taken from them.

When Sunday came [8 July 585], the king went to church to attend the celebration of mass. The brethren and fellow-bishops who were there gave Bishop Palladius the honor of conducting it. When he began to read the Prophetia [Luke 1:68-79], the king inquired who he was. When they told him that it was Bishop Palladius who had begun the service, the king immediately became angry.

"Will someone who has always been disloyal and faithless to me now preach to me sacred words," he said. "I will leave this church immediately. I will not listen to my enemy preaching."

With these words, he started to leave the church.

The bishops, now upset by the humiliation of their brother, said to the king, "We saw him attend the banquet you gave and we saw you receive a blessing at his hand. Why does the king reject him now? Had we known he was hateful to you, we would certainly have turned to another to conduct the service. Now, with your permission, let him continue the service he began; if you bring any charge against him tomorrow, the strictures of the holy canons can settle it."

By this time Bishop Palladius had retired to the sacristy greatly humiliated. The king now had him recalled and he finished the service he had begun.

Now when Palladius and Bertram were again summoned to the king's table, they became angry and accused each other of numerous adulteries and fornications, and not a few perjuries as well. Many laughed at these matters, but a number who had a quicker understanding found it deplorable that the weeds of the devil should so flourish among the bishops of the Lord. And so Palladius and Bertram left the king's presence but gave pledges and sureties to ensure their appearance at the synod on the tenth day before the Kalends of the ninth month [23 October].

### Guntram at Paris (VIII 9)

After these events, the king came to Paris and addressed everyone.

"My brother Chilperic on his death is said to have left a son," he said. "The child's governors, at the mother's request, asked me to receive him from the holy font at the feast of the Lord's Nativity; but they never came. They next requested that the infant be baptized at the holy Paschal feast; but the child was not brought at this time either. A third time they asked if he might be presented on Saint John's day [29 June], but they didn't come then. And so now they have had me move from my home in the hot season. I've come, and look! the boy is hidden away and not shown to me. This leads me to think that nothing is as promised and to believe that one of our *leudes* is the real father of the boy; if the child had been of our line, surely they would have brought him to me. You had better know, then, that I shall not acknowledge him unless I get clear proof of his birth."

When Queen Fredegund heard this, she assembled the principal leaders of her kingdom, three bishops and three hundred of the best men, and they all took oaths that the boy's father was Chilperic. In this way suspicion was removed from the mind of the king.

### (VIII 10)

*Guntram recovered the bodies of Chilperic's sons, Clovis and Merovech, and buried them side by side at Saint Vincent's basilica, later Saint Germain-des-Près, Paris.*

### Theodore of Marseilles Arrested Again (VIII 12)

Then, since King Guntram was trying with all his might to bring charges against Bishop Theodore [of Marseilles] again [cf. VI 11, 24; VIII 5] and, since Marseilles had already been restored to King Childebert's rule, Ratharius was sent there as duke by King Childebert to carry out an investigation. Setting aside the duty with which the king had charged him, however, Ratharius surrounded the bishop, demanded sureties, and sent him to King Guntram. The intention was to present him for condemnation before the bishops who were to meet in the synod at Mâcon.

*Divine vengeance was taken on Ratharius's household, including his son, who died of disease. Gregory tells a story confirming Theodore's sanctity.*

### Gregory, the Envoy Felix, and King Childebert (VIII 13)

Then King Guntram sent envoys to his nephew Childebert, who was staying at the time at the fortress of Coblenz [*castrum Confluentis*] — the place was so called because the Moselle and the Rhine rivers flow together at this spot and are joined. There had been an agreement for an assembly of bishops of both kingdoms to be held at Troyes in Champagne, but the meeting was not suitable to the bishops of Childebert's kingdom. Arrival of the embassy from Guntram was announced, and credentials delivered by the envoy Felix.

"King," said Felix, "your uncle earnestly asks who is it that causes you to withdraw from this promise, so that the bishops of your kingdom refuse to come to the council that you and he had decided upon. Perhaps there are wrongdoers who cause the root of discord to sprout between you two?"

I responded at this point, because the king was silent, "It's hardly surprising if tares are sown among subjects; but none that take root can readily be found between these two kings. As everyone knows, King Childebert has no other father than his uncle, and his uncle wants no other son than Childebert, to go by what I heard him say this year [cf. VII 33, VIII 4]. Heaven forbid that the root of discord should grow, since they both should love and protect each other."

Childebert called Felix to a private conference and at that time made a request.

"I beg my lord and father to do no harm to Bishop Theodore. There shall be an immediate quarrel between us if he does so. Hampered by dissension, we whose duty it is to maintain the bonds of love and remain at peace shall be disunited."

The envoy received an answer on some other matters and departed.

### Acts of the Synod at Mâcon, October 585 (VIII 20)

The day of the assembly came round, and by command of King Guntram the bishops gathered in the city of Mâcon. Faustian, who had been consecrated bishop of Dax at the command of Gundovald [cf. VII 31], was removed from office on condition that Bertram, Orestes, and Palladius, who had given him the blessing, would support him in turn, furnishing him with a hundred pieces of gold a year. Nicetius, a former layman, who had earlier obtained a directive from King Chilperic, now took over the episcopal office in Dax. Ursicinus, bishop of Cahors, was excommunicated because he openly confessed to having received Gundovald. This was the sentence passed on him: that he do penance for three years, not cut his hair or beard, and abstain from meat and wine; he must never presume to celebrate Mass, ordain clergy, bless churches and the holy chrism, or offer blessed bread. The administration of the business of the church was to be conducted entirely under his direction in the usual manner.

At this council there was a certain bishop who was saying that women could not be included in the term 'man' [homo], but he accepted the reasoning of his brethren, and said no more...

In those days also, King Guntram fell gravely ill, so that some believed he could not recover. I believe this was an act of God's providence. For the king was thinking about driving a number of bishops into exile.

And so Bishop Theodore returned to his city and was welcomed with cheers and the applause of all the people.

### Childebert's Assembly, October 585. Guntram Boso Defaults (VIII 21)

While this synod was being held, King Childebert met with his men at his villa of Beslingen, which lies in the midst of the forest of the Ardennes. There Queen Brunhild lodged a complaint before all the leading men on behalf of Ingund her daughter, who was still detained in Africa [cf. VI 40], but she received little sympathy.

A case against Guntram Boso was brought forward. A few days before, a female relative of his wife died without children and was buried in a basilica at Metz with fine jewelry and a great deal of gold. It so happened that a few days later the festival of the blessed Remigius took place. This is celebrated at the beginning of the eighth month [October]. Many inhabitants accompanied the bishop out of the city, and especially the chief personages and the duke. Servants of Guntram Boso then came to the basilica where this woman was buried. Going inside, they closed the doors behind them, and, opening the tomb, removed all the jewelry they could find on the body. The monks serving the basilica heard them and came to the doors, but Guntram's men would not let them in. For this reason, the monks sent messages to the bishop and the duke. Meanwhile the servants had taken the stuff, mounted their horses, and were trying to get away. But fearing that they might be arrested on the road and subjected to various penalties, they returned to the basilica. They laid the stolen jewels on the altar, but did not dare go outside.

"Guntram Boso sent us," they cried out.

When Childebert and his leading officials held their assembly at the villa I mentioned, proceedings were begun against Guntram Boso on this matter. But he gave no reply and quietly fled. All the property that he had held in the Auvergne as a grant from the fisc was later taken from him. In the haste of his departure, he also left behind many things which he had unjustly taken from a number of people.

*Important Deaths. Brunhild Asserts Control over her Son (VIII 22)*

Laban, bishop of Eauze, died in this year. Desiderius, a former layman, succeeded him. The king had promised under oath never to appoint a bishop from the laity, but 'is there anything to which the sacred thirst for gold will not compel human hearts' [cf. Aeneid III 56].

Bertram [bishop of Bordeaux] came down with a fever when he returned from the synod. He summoned Waldo the deacon...and entrusted him with executing all the terms of his will and his charitable bequests. When Waldo left, the bishop died...

At this time, Wandelen, governor of King Childebert, died [cf. VI 1], but no one was appointed in his place because the queen-mother wanted to have the charge of her son herself. Whatever Wandelen had received from the fisc was now returned to the fisc's administration...

*Desiderius Forgiven (VIII 27)*

Duke Desiderius [cf. VII 43] came to see King Guntram along with certain bishops, the abbot Aredius, and Antestius. The king had no inclination to receive him but was overcome by the entreaties of the bishops and took him back into favor. Eulalius was there at the time intending to bring a suit on account of his wife, who had left him and taken up with Desiderius; but he was reduced to silence by laughter and humiliation. Desiderius was rewarded by the king and went home with the king's favor.

### Death of Ingund and Hermenigild and a Failed Attempt to Conquer Septimania (VIII 28-30)

Ingund, who, as I have written above [cf. VIII 21], had been left by her husband with the imperial army, died and was buried in Africa while being conducted to the emperor with her little son. Leovigild put to death his own son, her husband, Hermenigild. King Guntram was distressed at these events and decided to send an army into Spain; it was first supposed to conquer Septimania, which is still considered a part of Gaul, and then go on from there...

*During the mobilization of forces, a letter was discovered, purportedly between Leovigild and Fredegund, referring to a plot against Childebert and Brunhild. Fredegund went through with the plot (c. 29), but the clerics she sent to carry out the assassination were picked up and tortured into confessing the details.*

The whole army of Guntram's kingdom was mustered and sent to Septimania. The peoples dwelling beyond the Saône, Rhône, and Seine joined the Burgundians, seriously despoiling the banks of the Saône and Rhône of produce and herds. They were guilty in their own territory of murder, arson, and rapine, stripping bare the churches, killing clerics, priests and others, even in front of altars consecrated to God. In this fashion they advance to Nîmes. The forces of Bourges, Saintes, Périgueux, and Angoulême, and other cities that at the time were under Guntram's authority, committed similar acts all the way to Carcassonne.

*The campaigns of the two armies of Guntram were complete and humiliating disasters.*

On their return, King Guntram was thoroughly heartsick. The leaders of the army took refuge in the basilica of the holy martyr Symphorian [in Autun]. When the king attended services for the saint's feast-day, they were brought before him on condition that a hearing would later be held. Four days later he assembled the bishops and well-born laity and began to investigate the commanders.

"How are we to gain victory in these times," he said, "if we don't preserve the practices of our fathers? They built churches, placing all their hope in God; they honored the martyrs, and respected priests; and so they gained victories, and with God's help subdued hostile peoples with sword and shield. As for us, not only do we not fear God, but we plunder his holy places, kill his servants, and even lay waste and scatter in contempt the very relics of the saints. We cannot win victory when such deeds are done. So our hands are weak, our sword grows soft, our shield no longer defends and protects us as once it did. If therefore this is my fault, let God put the blame on me. But if it is you who scorn the king's orders and fail to carry out my commands, it is time that the ax were buried in your heads. It will be a lesson to the whole army if one of its leaders is executed. Now is the time to determine what is to be done. If anyone is prepared to follow justice, now is the time to do it. If anyone holds it in contempt, let the vengeance of the community hang over his head. It is better that a few obstinate people be destroyed than that the anger of God should be visited upon the whole innocent country."

To this speech, the leaders of the army replied, "It is no easy matter, most excellent king, to describe your generous goodness. You fear God, love the churches, reverence bishops, take pity on the poor, and provide for the needy. But although everything your glorious self utters is judged to be right and true, what can we do when the forces are sunk in vice and love to do harm to their fellow man? No one fears the king, no one respects duke or count; and, if a commander thinks this isn't right and tries to correct it in order to further the length of your life, immediately there is mutiny in the ranks and a riot ensues. They all become savagely hostile to their superior to such an extent that he believes that to shut up is the way to escape with his life."

"The man who acts according to law shall live," replied Guntram; "but if anyone rejects the law and our orders, let him henceforth be executed so that this sacrilege will no longer hound us."

When he had spoken, a messenger arrived.

"Reccared, son of Leovigild, has come out of Spain," he said. "He has taken the fortress of Cabaret, ravaged the greater part of the territory of Toulouse, and led off captives. He has stormed the fortress of Beaucaire in the district of Arles, carrying off its people and possessions, and from there has shut himself up within the walls of Nîmes."

On hearing the news, the king appointed Leudegisel duke in place of Calumniosus, called Egilan, putting him in charge of the whole province of Arles and posting over four thousand men as guards along the frontier. In addition, Nicetius, duke of Auvergne, also brought guards and patrolled the border.

### The Assassination of Bishop Praetextatus (VIII 31)

While these events were going on and Fredegund was living at Rouen, she had bitter words with Bishop Praetextatus, telling him that the time would come when he would be back in the exile in which he had once been kept.

"Whether in exile or out of exile," he said, "I was, am now, and always shall be a bishop; but as for you, you won't enjoy royal power forever. By God's grace I have been brought from exile back to the world; but you shall be taken from this kingdom and plunged into the abyss. It would be better for you now to give up your stupid, wicked behavior and turn to better things. Stop this boasting, which always makes you excitable. Even you may strive to attain eternal life and can lead the infant you have borne to his age of majority."

When he had said this, she left his presence seething with anger. The woman took his remarks badly.

On the day of our Lord's Resurrection [that is, Sunday], the bishop went early to the cathedral to conduct the church services and, as is the practice, began the singing of the antiphons in their proper order. As he was resting on the bench during the chanting, a bloody-minded assassin appeared. Drawing a blade from his belt, he stabbed the bishop under the armpit. The bishop called out for help to the clergy who were present, but, of all those standing near, no one came to his aid. As he held out his blood-covered hands over the altar, praying and giving thanks to God, he was carried by his followers to his chamber and laid upon his bed.

Fredegund appeared immediately, along with Duke Beppolen and Ansovald.

"Holy bishop," she said, "that such a thing should have happened as you were conducting services ill becomes me and the rest of your flock. Let's hope the person who dared do this can be pointed out so he can receive the punishments that suit his crime."

"Who did this," he answered, knowing she was lying, "if not the person who has killed kings, repeatedly shed innocent blood, and committed many crimes in this kingdom?"

"I have skilled doctors in my service who can heal this wound. Let them visit you," said the queen.

"God has now had me called from this world," said the bishop. "But you, who have been found out to be the person behind these crimes, shall be accursed down through the ages, and God shall take vengeance on you for my death."

When she left, the bishop put his house in order and breathed his last.

Romachar, bishop of Coutances, came to bury him. Great grief now overcame all the citizens of Rouen, especially the chief Franks of the city. One of their leaders came to Fredegund.

"You have committed a great deal of evil in this world," he said, "but nothing has been worse than having a bishop of the Lord killed. May God swiftly avenge the innocent blood. We shall all investigate this deed, so you won't be allowed to carry on your bloody work much longer."

When he had said this and left the queen's presence, she sent a messenger after him to invite him to dine. He refused, and she asked that, if he would not dine with her, would he at least drink a cup and not go from the royal residence thirsty. He waited for a cup, and when he received it, drank its mixture of absinthe, wine, and honey, as is the custom of the barbarians. The drink contained poison.

As soon as he drank it, he felt a severe pain in his chest, as if his insides were being cut up, and called out to his companions, "Run, you poor devils, run from this evil or you will be destroyed with me."

Refusing the drink, they lost no time getting away. He immediately became blind, collapsed, and died after riding a distance of three stadia [about a third of a mile].

After this, Leudovald, bishop [of Bayeux], sent letters to all the bishops and, on their advice, closed the churches of Rouen, so that the people should expect no more religious services in them until the author of this crime was found through a general investigation. He arrested some people and wrung from them by torture the truth that these things were done as part of a plot devised by Fredegund. She offered a defense against the charge, and the bishop was unable to take vengeance. It was said that assassins approached Bishop Leudovald because he was resolved to investigate this matter keenly; but he was surrounded by his bodyguard, and the assassins were unable to do him any harm.

When the news was told to King Guntram, and accusations were made against Fredegund, the king sent to the alleged son of Chilperic (who as I have written above [VII 7, VIII 1] was called Chlothar) three bishops, namely Artemius of Sens, Veranus of Cavaillon, and Agricius of Troyes. The bishops, along with the child's governors, were supposed to search out the author of the crime and deliver that person before the king.

When the bishops told their orders to Chlothar's senior officials, the latter replied, "These deeds are thoroughly distressing to us and we are increasingly anxious to take vengeance for them. But we reject the idea that, if someone among us is found guilty, that person should be brought before your king, since we are capable of putting down the crimes of our own people using royal authority."

At this point the bishops said, "You should know that, if the person who committed this crime is not brought before us, our king will come here with an army and lay waste the entire country with fire and sword; for it is plain that she who had the Frank [of Rouen] killed by witchcraft also had the bishop put to the sword."

With these words, they left without getting a reasonable answer. They nevertheless lodged a protest that Melantius [cf. VII 19], who had already been appointed to succeed Praetextatus, should never perform in that cathedral the duties of the episcopal office.

A son was born to King Childebert. He was taken up from the sacred font by Magneric, bishop of Trier, and called Theudebert.

Guntram was so pleased that he sent an envoy with many gifts for the boy and with a message saying, "Through this child God will see fit to raise up the kingdom of the Franks by the love of His divine majesty, provided the father lives for the child and the child for the father."

## Year XI of Childebert II, a. 586

*Childebert's eleventh year receives very little attention from Gregory, taking up a scant five chapters VIII 38-42.*

*Further Investigation of Praetextatus's Murder (VIII 41)*

When word that Praetextatus had been killed by Fredegund spread through the whole country, the queen ordered a slave arrested and beaten in an effort to clear herself of the charge.

"You have pinned this slander on me by attacking Praetextatus, bishop of Rouen, with a sword," she said.

She handed him over to the bishop's nephew, who had him tortured. The slave clearly disclosed the whole matter.

"From Queen Fredegund I got a hundred pieces of gold to do this," he said, "from Bishop Melantius, fifty, and from the archdeacon of the city, another fifty. I also received a promise that I would be freed along with my wife."

On the slave's saying this, Praetextatus's nephew drew his sword and cut the accused to pieces.

As for Fredegund, she established Melantius in the cathedral church. It was Fredegund who had earlier placed him in the bishopric.

## III. REVOLT IN AUSTRASIA AND THE FALL OF EGIDIUS, a. 587-90 (BOOKS IX—X)

### Year XII of Childebert II, a. 587

*Childebert's twelfth year begins near the end of Book VIII (cc. 43-45). Among other matters these chapters recount another attempt by Fredegund to assassinate Guntram and the death of Duke Desiderius fighting the Goths. The book ends with the succession of Reccared to the kingship of the Goths.*

*Book IX opens with an account of improved relations between Reccared and his father Leovigild's widow, Goiswinth (IX 1). She was also the widow of the former king Athanagild and the mother of Brunhild. Gothic envoys were received warmly by Childebert and not at all by Guntram.*

#### Death of Radegund (IX 2)

In this year the most blessed Radegund passed away from this world. In the monastery that she had founded she left behind great grief. I myself was present at her burial. She died on the thirteenth day of the sixth month [August], and was buried three days later. In my book of wonders I have endeavored to write more fully about the miracles that happened on that day and of the circumstances of her funeral.

#### Birth of Theuderic (IX 4)

In this year another son was born to King Childebert. Veranus, bishop of Cavaillon, received him from the baptismal font and gave him the name Theuderic. At the time he was a bishop endowed with great power of miracle, so that when he made the sign of the cross over the sick they were often immediately restored to health by God's grace.

#### Death of Guntram Boso and Revolt against Childebert (IX 8-12)

Since the queen hated Guntram Boso, he began to canvass the bishops and leading men, begging rather late in the day for the pardon that to this point he had scorned to ask. During the minority of King Childebert, he had often provoked Queen Brunhild with reproaches and taunts; he had also been in favor of the injustices that her enemies had inflicted on her. To revenge the wrong done to his mother, King Childebert ordered him to be hunted down and killed.

When Guntram Boso saw that the critical point was at hand, he made for the cathedral church of Verdun, believing he could obtain a pardon through the mediation of Bishop Ageric, the king's godfather. The bishop now hurried to the king to intercede for him. The king was unable to refuse the petition.

"Let him come before us," said the king, "and then, when he's given sureties, let him go before my uncle; we'll follow whatever judgment our uncle comes to."

Guntram Boso was then conducted to the place where the king was staying. Stripped of his arms and manacled, he was presented to the king by Bishop Ageric.

"I have done you and your mother wrong by not obeying your commands and by acting contrary to your will and to the public good," he said falling at the king's feet. "Now I ask you to forgive the evil that I have committed against you."

The king told him to rise from the ground and put him into the hands of the bishop.

"Let him remain in your charge, holy bishop," said the king, "until he appears before King Guntram."

He then told him to withdraw.

After these events, Rauching [one of Childebert's dukes, cf. V 3] allied himself with the leading officials in the kingdom of Chlothar, son of Chilperic. He pretended that he was carrying on discussions with them about maintaining the peace and preventing attacks and raids being carried out between the territories of the two kingdoms. They planned in fact to kill Childebert; Rauching would then control a kingdom of Champagne with Theudebert, the king's elder son; Ursio and Berthefred were to take charge of Theuderic, the younger son recently born, and control the rest of the kingdom, shutting out King Guntram. They also muttered many times that they would humiliate Queen Brunhild, as they had earlier done during her widowhood. Rauching, carried away by his great power and, as I would say, vaunting the glory of the regal sceptre itself, made preparations to travel to King Childebert to carry out the plot he had entered into.

But the goodness of God brought word of these plans beforehand to the ears of King Guntram, who sent messengers in secret to King Childebert, bringing the entire affair to his attention, and saying, "Quickly, let us have a meeting, for there are issues to be discussed."

Childebert carefully investigated what had been told to him and, finding it to be true, sent for Rauching. As soon as Rauching arrived, but before the king had him admitted to his presence, the king issued letters and dispatched his servants with a warrant for use of the public post to take possession of Rauching's property in its various locations; then he ordered the duke to be admitted to his chamber. He talked with him about one thing or another and dismissed him. As Rauching was coming out, two doorkeepers grabbed him by the legs, and he fell on the steps of the entranceway, one part of his body lying inside it, the other outside. Those who had been ordered to finish the job fell upon him with swords and beat his head into so many bits that it looked entirely like brain. He died immediately. The body was stripped, flung from a window, and committed to the grave.

Rauching lacked character and, greedy beyond human measure, was envious of the property of others. He was arrogant in the extreme because of his wealth, so much so that at the time of his death he was claiming to be the son of King Chlothar. Much gold was found on him.

As soon as he was killed, one of his servants dashed away at full speed and told his wife what had happened. She was on a street in Soissons at the time, on horseback, decked out with large pieces of jewelry and precious stones and covered with flashing gold, with an escort of servants before and behind; she was riding to the basilica of Saints Crispin and Crispinian to hear Mass, for it was the day of the passion of these blessed martyrs [25 October]. After meeting with the messenger, she turned back by another street, threw her jewels to the ground, and took refuge in the basilica of the holy Bishop Medard, thinking to find safety there under the protection of that blessed confessor. The servants sent by the king to claim the property of Rauching discovered more among his treasures than they could find even in the coffers of the public treasury; all of it was brought before the king for him to look at.

On the day of Rauching's death there were many citizens of Tours and Poitiers with the king. The plan was that, should the plotters have been able to carry out their crime, they would have subjected these people to torture, saying, "It was one of you who caused the death of our king." Then having put them to death with various punishments, the plotters would have boasted of being the avengers of the king's murder. But Almighty God confounded their plans, for these were wicked, and fulfilled that which is written: "The pit which you prepare for your brother, into it you yourself will fall [cf. Prov. 26:27]."

Magnovald was sent as duke in place of Rauching.

Ursio and Berthefred, sure that Rauching would be able to carry out what they had discussed, had collected an army and were already coming. Hearing how he had died, they reinforced the host of followers that was still with them and, with guilty consciences, fortified themselves with all their property in a fortress in the Woëvre near the villa of Ursio. If King Childebert tried to take measures against them, they intended to defend themselves against his forces from a position of strength. Ursio was their chief and the cause of the evil.

Queen Brunhild sent a message to Berthefred.

"Separate yourself from my enemy," she said, "and you'll have your life;

otherwise you'll die with him." For the queen had received Berthefred's daughter from the baptismal font and for this reason wanted to have mercy on him.

"I'll never abandon him," said Berthefred, "unless death tears me away."

While these events were taking place, King Guntram again sent a message to his nephew Childebert, saying, "Enough delay, come so I may see you. There is a reason for us to see one another; it concerns both your own life as well as the public welfare."

When Childebert heard, he took his mother, sister, and wife and hurried to meet his uncle.

Bishop Magneric of the city of Trier was also present at the meeting, and Guntram Boso, whom Bishop Ageric of Verdun had taken into his charge, came as well. But the bishop, who had promised to stand surety for him, was not present, for there had been an agreement that Guntram Boso should appear before the king without an advocate. The point of the agreement was that, if the king decided that he must die, he would not be pardoned due to the bishop's intervention; and if the king granted him life, he would go free.

The kings met and Guntram Boso was judged guilty on various grounds. The order was given for him to be killed. He found out and rushed to Magneric's lodging, closing the doors and shutting out the clerics and servants.

"Most blessed bishop," he said, "I know that the kings have great respect for you. And now I take refuge with you to escape death. Look, the executioners are at the door. Clearly understand from this that, if you don't rescue me, I'll kill you and then go outside to meet my own death. Know plainly that either we both live or we die as one. Holy bishop, I know that you share with the king the place of father to his son [cf. VIII 37]. Since you get whatever you ask of him, I know he'll not be able to deny at all whatever your holiness requests. Therefore obtain a pardon or we shall die together."

He said this with his sword unsheathed.

Alarmed at what he heard, the bishop said, "What can I do if I am kept here by you. Let me go beg the king's mercy, and perhaps he will take pity on you."

"Forget that," Guntram Boso replied. "Send abbots and men you trust to report what I am saying."

The king was not told, however, how matters really stood. The messengers said that Guntram Boso was being protected by the bishop. This made the king angry.

"If the bishop will not come out," he said " let him be destroyed along with that traitor."

When the bishop heard of his reply, he sent messengers to the king. Although they recounted what was happening, King Guntram said, "Set fire to the building, and if the bishop cannot come out, they can both be burned together."

Hearing this, the clergy forced open the door and dragged the bishop outside.

The wretched Guntram Boso then saw that he was hemmed in by raging flames on every side and went to the door armed with his sword. As soon he crossed the threshold of the house and stepped outside, a soldier threw a spear and struck him in the forehead. He was thrown into confusion by the blow and, as if out of his mind, tried to thrust with his sword. Those standing around wounded him with so many spears that the heads sticking in his body and the shafts supporting him prevented him from falling to the ground. The few who were with him were also killed and exposed on the field at the same time. Permission to bury them was obtained from the princes only with difficulty.

Guntram Boso acted without consideration and was avaricious, desiring other men's property beyond measure. He swore oaths to all and kept his promises to none. His wife and children were sent into exile and his property confiscated by the fisc. A great quantity of gold, silver, and valuable items of various kinds was found in his coffers. Also what he had concealed underground out of consciousness of his wrongdoing did not remain hidden. He often made use of soothsayers and lots and, in his desire to learn the future, was always deceived by them.

King Guntram concluded peace with his nephew and the queens [Treaty of Andelot, 28 November 587, cf. IX 20]. Having exchanged gifts and set affairs of state on a firm footing, they sat down together at a banquet. King Guntram began to praise the Lord.

"I give you most hearty thanks, Almighty God," he said. "You have allowed me to see the sons of my son Childebert. For this reason I don't think I have been completely forsaken by your majesty, for you have allowed me to see the sons of my son."

Then Childebert received Dynamius [cf. VI 11] and Duke Lupus [cf. VI 4], who had been restored to him, and gave back Cahors to Queen Brunhild. And so, having signed the agreements, the kings gave each other presents, exchanged kisses, and went off each to his own city in peace and rejoicing, rendering thanks again and again to God.

King Childebert mustered an army and ordered it to march to the place where Ursio and Berthefred were waiting behind fortifications. In the district of the Woëvre there was a villa commanded by a steep hill. On the summit, a basilica had been built in honor of the holy and blessed Martin. They say that in antiquity there was a fortress there, but these days it had been fortified, not by art, but by nature. The two men had shut themselves up in this basilica, with their property, wives, and servants. The army having been assembled, as we said, Childebert, ordered it to proceed there. Even before the force that had been mustered reached Ursio and Berthefred, it burned and looted everything wherever it could find their villas and property. Reaching the spot, the troops climbed the hill and surrounded the basilica with armed men. The commander of the force was Godegisel, son-in-law of Duke Lupus.

When the troops were unable to get the besieged out of the basilica, they tried setting the building on fire. Seeing what they were doing, Ursio came out armed with a sword and created such havoc among the besiegers that no one he caught sight of could get away alive. Trudulf, count of the royal palace, fell there, and many soldiers were laid out. But when Ursio was seen to be out of breath from the slaughter, someone wounded him in the thigh, and he fell crippled to the ground; others rushed on him, and he was killed.

Godegisel saw this and began to shout out, "Let there be peace now. Look, the chief enemy of our lords has fallen. Let Berthefred have his life."

At these words, and since all the troops were longing to plunder the property amassed in the basilica, Berthefred mounted his horse and rode to Verdun. He thought he would be protected in the oratory, located in the church manse, especially as Bishop Ageric was living in the manse.

When King Childebert was told that Berthefred had escaped, he was heart-sick.

"If he gets away alive," said the king, "Godegisel shall not escape my grasp."

But the king did not know that Berthefred had entered the church manse, thinking instead that he had fled to some other region.

Godegisel was now afraid. Once more mustering his force, he surrounded the church manse with armed men. Since the bishop could not surrender Berthefred, and even tried to protect him, the attackers climbed the roof and killed him by hitting him with the tiles and materials covering the oratory; he died with three of his servants. The bishop was greatly pained by this, not only because he could not give him protection, but also because he had seen the place where he was accustomed to pray, and where relics of the saints were gathered together, polluted with human blood. King Childebert sent him gifts to cheer him up, but he would not be comforted.

In these days many withdrew to other regions out of fear of the king. Not a few were deprived of the dignity of the ducal office, and others were promoted in their place.

### Reconciliation between Bishop Egidius and Duke Lupus (IX 14)

Egidius, bishop of Rheims, was considered a suspect in the crime of high treason for which the above mentioned men [Rauching, Ursio, and Berthe-

fred] had lost their lives. He came to Childebert with rich gifts to plead for
mercy, having first received assurances on oath in the basilica of the holy
Remigius that he would suffer no harm on the way. He was received by the
king and departed in peace.

He also obtained peace with Duke Lupus, who, as I recorded above [VI
4], had been driven from the ducal office of Champagne at his instigation. As
a result King Guntram became very bitter: Lupus had promised him never to
make peace with Egidius, a known enemy of the king.

### Year XIII of Childebert II, a. 588

*Gregory as an Envoy to Guntram. The Goodness of Guntram (IX 20-21)*

*Although Guntram and Childebert were supposed to be reconciled and Guntram had
adopted his nephew, relations between the two remained tense. Instances of trouble
between the two kingdoms appear from time to time in Gregory's narration of events in
Books IX and X. Among the issues dividing the kings was the old problem of relations
with the Visigothic monarchy of Spain. In 587, as Gregory reports (IX 15, 16), the
new Visigothic king, Reccared, became a Catholic and asked to marry Childebert's sister Chlodosind; Guntram remained hostile to the Visigoths, ostensibly over Septimania
and the treatment of Ingund. The question of the control of cities was not satisfactorily
settled either. Joint assemblies of the bishops of the two kingdoms, which Guntram
dearly wanted, were resisted by Childebert. And last but not least, the status of
Chlothar II, Fredegund's son, remained a trouble spot. Would Guntram recognize him
and make him an heir?*

*These problems came up in the following conversation between the envoys of
Childebert — namely Gregory himself and an unknown bishop Felix (likely of
Châlons-sur-Marne) — and King Guntram. Although the Treaty of Andelot was
signed in November of 587, Gregory refrained from giving the text until his account of
the following interview with Guntram. Immediately afterwards (IX 21) is a description
of what Gregory calls Guntram's goodness.*

In that year, the thirteenth of King Childebert, when I had gone to meet the
king in the city of Metz, I was ordered to go on an embassy to King Guntram.

I found him at Chalon.

"Famous king," I said, "your glorious nephew Childebert sends you bountiful greetings and renders thanks beyond measure for your dutiful goodness.
You remind him continually to do what is pleasing to God, acceptable to
you, and beneficial to the interests of the people. With respect to the matters
you discussed together, he promises to fulfill everything and pledges to break
no item of the agreements drawn up between you [cf. IX 11]."

To this the king replied, "I don't offer him the same thanks, because he has broken the promises that were made to me. My part of the city of Senlis has not been relinquished; they have not discharged the people whom in my interests I wanted moved, since they are my enemies. How can you say that my dearest nephew does not wish to break any of his written agreements?"

"He wishes to do nothing contrary to those agreements," I replied, "but promises to fulfill all of them. So if you wish to send representatives to divide Senlis, do not delay for a moment; you shall immediately receive what's yours. And as to the people you mention, give me a list of their names and all that is promised shall be fulfilled."

When we had discussed these matters, the king ordered the agreement itself to be read over again before those who were present.

### Copy of the Agreement

In the name of Christ, the most excellent lords Kings Guntram and Childebert and the most glorious lady Queen Brunhild met out of regard for each other at Andelot to settle in a broader forum all matters that might in any way cause quarrels between them. With the mediation of bishops and leading officials and the help of God, it was settled, resolved, and agreed between them, out of regard for each other, that they would be loyal to each other and maintain a mutual affection pure and sincere as long as almighty God preserved their lives in the present world.

§ Likewise, since Lord Guntram claimed, in accordance with the agreement he had made with Lord Sigibert of good memory, that the entire share that Sigibert had acquired from Charibert's kingdom belonged completely to him, and since Lord Childebert wanted to recover everything his father had possessed, they have, after deliberation, agreed to the following: that the third portion of the city of Paris, with its territory and people, that had come to Lord Sigibert from Charibert's kingdom by written agreement, with the fortresses of Châteaudun and Vendôme, and whatever the said king received of the districts of Étampes and Chartres for right of passage, with their lands and people, were to remain perpetually under the jurisdiction of Lord Guntram, along with whatever Guntram previously held from Charibert's kingdom during Lord Sigibert's lifetime.

Equally, however, King Childebert from this day forward has the right to Meaux, two-thirds of Senlis, Tours, Poitiers, Avranches, Aire, Saint Lizier, Bayonne, and Albi, with their territories.

The above terms are conditional on the following: whichever of these kings the Lord should allow to survive, shall vindicate fully and forever the kingdom of the one that passes on from the light of the present world without children and shall, with God's help, leave it to his successors.

§ The following special agreement is to be faithfully observed in all its details. Whatever the lord king Guntram has bestowed, or yet by God's favor shall bestow, upon his daughter Chlothild in all kinds of property and persons, in cities, lands, and revenues, shall remain under her ownership and control. And if she wishes of her own free will to dispose of properties of the fisc, valuable articles, or movables, or to bestow them on any one, let that gift, with God's help, be protected forever and not be taken by anyone at any time. Let her possess with full honor and respect under the defense and protection of Lord Childebert everything of which he finds her in possession at her father's death.

Equally, the lord king Guntram promises that, if during his lifetime, owing to the uncertainty of human life, Lord Childebert should happen to pass from the light — may the divine goodness not allow such a thing and Guntram has no desire to see it — Guntram will receive under his care and protection, like a good father, Childebert's sons Theudebert and Theuderic and any others that God wishes to give him, so that they shall possess their father's kingdom in its entirety. And he will receive under his care and protection with a spiritual love Lord Childebert's mother, Queen Brunhild, and her daughter Chlodosind, sister of King Childebert, as long as she might be in the country of the Franks, and his queen Faileuba, like a good sister and daughters, and they shall possess with full honor and respect, secure and without disturbance, all their property, namely, cities, properties, revenues, and all rights and powers of that property, both what they possess at the present time and what they may justly add in the future by Christ's aid. If they wish to dispose of any fiscal properties, or precious articles, or movables, of their own free will or to bestow them on anyone, let the gift be permanent and perpetual, and let their will in this respect not be upset by anyone at any time.

As to the cities, namely, Bordeaux, Limoges, Cahors, Béarn, and Cieutat, which Galswinth, Lady Brunhild's sister, acquired as a marriage portion and as *morganegyba*, that is, as morning gift, when she came to Francia, and which Lady Brunhild acquired by the judgment of the most glorious lord King Guntram and of the Franks in the lifetime of Chilperic and King Sigibert, it is agreed that from this day forward

Lady Brunhild shall take possession of the city of Cahors with its lands and all its people. As for the other cities named above, Lord Guntram shall possess these as long as he lives, on condition that, after his death, they shall by God's grace be restored in their entirety to the control of Lady Brunhild and her heirs. During Lord Guntram's lifetime, however, they shall not at any time, or under any pretext, be claimed by Lady Brunhild or her son King Childebert or his children.

§ Likewise, it is agreed that lord Childebert shall hold Senlis in its entirety; and as far as the one third share due from there to Lord Guntram is concerned, the latter shall be compensated by the third share belonging to Lord Childebert in Ressons.

§ Likewise, in accordance with the agreements made between Lord Guntram and Lord Sigibert of blessed memory, with respect to the *leudes* who originally took oaths to Lord Guntram after the death of Lord Chlothar, if they are proven to have afterwards gone over to Sigibert, it is agreed that they shall be removed from the places where they live. Likewise, those who are proven to have first sworn allegiance to lord Sigibert after the death of King Chlothar, and then to have passed over to Guntram, shall also be removed.

§ Likewise, whatever the aforesaid kings have bestowed on churches, or on their followers, or, in the future, shall bestow by God's grace in accordance with the law, shall be held permanently.

As regards whatever is owed justly and according to law to any of their followers in either kingdom, let the matter not be treated prejudicially, but let their followers be permitted to possess and to obtain the property that is their due; and if anything is taken from anyone who is without fault on account of divisions of the kingdom, a hearing shall be held and the property shall be restored.

As regards what each follower possessed through the generosity of previous kings down to the death of the lord king Chlothar of glorious memory [a. 561], let each have secure possession. And as regards whatever has been taken from followers since then, let each immediately get it back.

§ And since the friendship binding the aforementioned kings together is pure and honest, it is agreed that neither kingdom will deny passage to the followers of the other king who wish to travel on public or private business.

§ It is likewise agreed that neither king shall entice away the other's *leudes* or receive them when they come. And if it happens because of some transgression that a follower thinks he has to flee to the other kingdom, let him be absolved according to the nature of the offense and sent back.

§ It has been decided also to add this to the agreement. If either party shall at any time violate the present provisions on some artful pretext, he shall lose all the benefits conferred, both prospective and present, and let the advantage be his who faithfully maintains all the terms written above, and let him be absolved in all matters from the obligations of his oath.

All these matters having been decided, the parties swear by the name of almighty God, the inseparable Trinity, all that is divine, and the fearful day of judgment, that they will faithfully observe all that is written above without any fraud or deceit.

This treaty was made four days before the Kalends of December [28 November] in the twenty-sixth year of the reign of Lord King Guntram and in the twelfth year of Lord Childebert [a. 587].

When the agreements were read over the king said, "May I be struck by God's judgment if I violate any one of the terms contained here."

And he turned to Felix, who had come with us as an envoy.

"Tell me, Felix," he said, "have you finished creating ties of friendship yet between my sister Brunhild and that enemy of God and man, Fredegund?"

When he denied this, I said, "Let the king have no doubt that the friendship that was made many years ago is being kept up between them. Surely you know that the hatred once established between them still grows; it is not withering. Most glorious king, would that you yourself had less friendly dealings with Fredegund. For, as we have learned repeatedly, you give her embassies greater consideration than ours."

"You should know, bishop of God," he said, "that I receive her embassies in such a way as not to neglect the affection I have for my nephew King Childebert. For I cannot have friendly ties with someone from whom regularly come assassins looking to take my life."

When he had said this, Felix said, "I believe the news has reached you, glorious king, that Reccared has sent an embassy to your nephew to ask for your niece Chlodosind, your brother's daughter, in marriage. But your nephew would not promise anything without your advice."

The king said, "It's hardly the best idea for my niece to go to the same place where her sister was killed [cf. VIII 28]. It seems inconceivable to me that the death of my niece Ingund is not avenged."

"They want very much to clear themselves of her death either by oath or by any other means you demand," answered Felix. "Only give your consent for Chlodosind to be betrothed to Reccared as he asks."

"If my nephew fulfills the terms that he wished inserted in the agreements," said the king, " then I will do what he wants in this matter."

We promised that he would fulfill everything, and then Felix added, "He begs your goodness to help him against the Lombards. If they can be driven from Italy, the part which his father claimed possession of during his lifetime can be restored to him, and the other part can be returned by your help and his to the dominion of the emperor."

"I can't send my forces to Italy. That would be consigning them to death. A devastating plague is now wasting the country."

I said, "You have indicated to your nephew that all the bishops of his kingdom should meet together, since many matters need investigation. However, your glorious nephew thinks in accordance with the canons that each metropolitan should meet with the bishops of his province, and whatever wrongs were being done in each district could then be set right by the authority of the bishops. What is the reason for so great a number assembling together? The faith of the church is not rocked by any danger; no new heresy is arising. Why is there need for so many bishops meeting together?"

"Many wrongs have been done that should be investigated, both incestuous relations as well as matters in dispute between us," answered the king. "In particular, there is an issue greater than all others, that of God. You must investigate why Bishop Praetextatus was put to the sword in his church. Also there should be an investigation of those who are accused of licentiousness, so that, if they are found guilty, they can be corrected by the sentence of the bishops, and, if they are found to be innocent, the false charge can be publicly removed."

He gave orders at that time for the synod to be delayed until the Kalends of the fourth month [1 June].

After this conversation we went to church; it was the day celebrating the Lord's resurrection [Sunday]. After mass he invited us to a dinner that was no less laden with food as it was rich in cheer. For the king talked constantly of God, of building churches, and of protection for the poor. Now and then he would laugh and make a pious joke, even throwing in a suitable quip so we might enjoy some of the merriment.

And he said this: "If only my nephew will keep his promises! Everything I have is his. Still, if it disturbs him that I receive my nephew Chlothar's envoys, am I so far gone that I am unable to mediate between them and stop the quarreling going further? I know it's better to cut strife short than to have it spread. If I acknowledge that Chlothar is my nephew, I will give him two or three cities somewhere so that he shall not seem to be disinherited. Leaving him this will not disturb Childebert."

He said this, and other things, and, treating us warmly and loading us with gifts, told us to depart, charging us always to give King Childebert advice that would benefit him.

King Guntram, as we have frequently said, was generous in almsgiving and disposed to vigils and fasting. At the time, there were reports that Marseilles was suffering greatly from a plague affecting the groin and that the disease had spread swiftly as far as the village of Saint-Symphorien d'Ozon in the Lyons district. The king, like a good bishop providing remedies that cure the wounds of a sinful people, commanded all to assemble in the cathedral and celebrate rogations with the utmost piety. He ordered that no food should be eaten but barley bread and clean water, and that all should continually attend vigils. And all was done as he said. For three days he gave alms with more than his usual generosity, and he showed such concern on behalf of all the people that he was at this time already regarded as not only a king but also as a bishop of God. Placing all his hope in the mercy of God, he directed the thoughts that came to him towards God from whom he believed with perfect faith they could be given effect. A common story was told at the time among the faithful about a woman whose son was suffering from a four-day fever and was lying sick in bed. Slipping behind the king in a throng of people, she secretly tore off a fringe from the king's garments, put it in water, and gave it to her son to drink. Immediately the fever died down, and he was cured. I do not doubt this story, since I myself have heard the demons of those possessed being compelled by the wonderful power of this man to call out his name and confess their own crimes.

## Year XIV of Childebert II, a. 589

*Quarrels between Fredegund and Her Daughter (IX 34)*

Rigunth, Chilperic's daughter, kept insulting her mother, saying that she herself was the mistress and would return her mother to servitude, and repeatedly provoking her with heaps of abuse. Sometimes they punched and hit each other.

"Why do you annoy me so, daughter?" said her mother. "Here, take the things of your father that I have in my possession and do with them as you please."

She went into the storeroom and opened a chest full of necklaces and costly jewelry.

When for some time she had taken various items from the chest and handed them to her daughter, who was standing by, she said, "I am tired now. You put in your hand and take out what you find."

As Rigunth thrust her arm in and was taking things from the chest, her mother seized hold of the lid and slammed it down on her daughter's neck. She forced it down and the chest's lower edge pressed against Rigunth's throat so that even her eyes were ready to burst.

One of the female servants who was in the storeroom shouted out, "Please come quickly, come quickly. My mistress is being throttled to death by her mother."

Those waiting for them to come out burst into the room, rescued the girl from imminent death, and took her outside.

After this affair the hostility between mother and daughter increased in intensity. There were continual quarrels, and blows were exchanged between them. The main reason for the trouble was Rigunth's fondness for adulterous relationships.

### Childebert Sends his Son Theudebert to Soissons (IX 36)

Childebert was staying with his wife and his mother in the territory of the town called Strasbourg. At this time some of the better fighting men who lived in Soissons and Meaux came to him.

"Give us one of your sons," they said, "so that we may serve him. That way if we have among us one of the offspring of your line, we shall the better resist the enemy and diligently defend the territory of your city."

The king was pleased with the request and decided to send them his elder son Theudebert, to whom he assigned counts, *domestici*, mayors, governors, and all the persons required for serving a king. In the sixth month [August] of this year, he dispatched Theudebert in accordance with the wishes of those who had asked the king to send a son. The people received Theudebert with joy and with prayers that the divine goodness might grant him and his father a long life.

### A Plot against Faileuba, Brunhild, and Childebert (IX 38)

While Faileuba, King Childebert's queen, was weak from giving birth to a child that soon died, she got word that certain people were plotting against herself and Queen Brunhild. As soon as she had regained her strength, she went before the king and revealed to him and to his mother all that she had heard.

This is roughly what she had been told. Septimina, her children's nurse, would advise the king to drive out his mother, leave his wife, and take another spouse; the conspirators would then do with him as they liked or obtain from him whatever they wanted. If the king would not agree to what she suggested, they would kill him by witchcraft, raise his sons to the throne, and rule the kingdom themselves, while the children's mother and grandmother would be driven out just the same. Associates in this plot, declared Faileuba, were Sunnegisil, count of the stables, Gallomagnus the referendary, and Droctulf, who had been appointed to aid Septimina in raising the king's children.

Next, these two, Septimina and Droctulf, were seized. Without delay they were spread between posts and beaten severely. Septimina confessed that she had killed her husband Jovius by witchcraft out of love for Droctulf, with whom she played the whore. They both confessed to all the matters which I have related above and denounced the people I have mentioned as involved in the plot.

A search was made at once for them also, but guilty consciences caused them to seek refuge in the enclosures of the churches. The king himself went to them.

"Come out," he said, "and stand before a tribunal so we may examine whether the charges brought against you are true or false. I am of the belief that you never would have fled to this church, if a bad conscience had not terrified you. Nevertheless, you may have a promise that your lives shall be spared, even if you are found guilty. For we are Christians, and it is wrong even for criminals to be punished [with death] if they have been taken out of a church."

They were then led outside and came with the king before the court. When they were examined, they protested innocence.

"Septimina and Droctulf revealed this plot to us," they said. "But we, cursing and shunning it, would never consent to this crime."

"If you hadn't just winked at this," said the king, "surely you would have brought the matter to our attention. Is it not so, therefore, that you gave consent in this matter, when you decided to conceal this from my knowledge?"

Immediately they were driven outside and once more they made for the church.

Septimina was severely flogged, together with Droctulf, and her face was branded with hot irons. Everything she had was taken from her. She was led away to the villa of Marlenheim to turn the mill and to prepare each day flour for the food of the women in the gynaeceum. Droctulf's hair and ears were cut off, and he was assigned to work in the vineyards; but after a few days he slipped off and fled. Search was made by the steward, and he was again brought before the king. He was severely beaten and sent back to the vineyard that he had left.

Sunnegisil and Gallomagnus were stripped of all the property which they had received from the fisc and sent into exile. But envoys, among whom were bishops, came from King Guntram to intercede for them, and they were recalled from exile, though they were left nothing but their private property.

## Year XV of Childebert II, a. 590

*Attempt to Assassinate Childebert (X 18)*

As the king entered the oratory of his house at Marlenheim, his servants saw a man unknown to them standing at a distance.

They said to him, "Who are you and where do you come from? What's your business? We don't know you."

"I am one of you," he answered.

He had no sooner said this than he was thrown out of the oratory and interrogated. It was not long before he confessed, saying that he had been sent by Fredegund to kill the king.

"Twelve of us have been sent here by her," he said. "Six have arrived, while the other six have stayed behind at Soissons to snare the king's son. As for me, while I was waiting my chance to strike down King Childebert in the oratory, fear came over me, and I decided not to carry out my purpose."

When he said this, he was immediately subjected to savage tortures and named his accomplices. Search was made for them in various quarters. Some were consigned to prison, some were left with their hands cut off; some were released, shorn of their ears and noses, to be laughed at. Many of those who were confined, fearing various kinds of torture, stabbed themselves with their own weapons. Not a few also succumbed under torture so that the king could get vengeance.

*Removal of Egidius, Bishop of Rheims (X 19)*

*Sunnigisil's confession regarding Chilperic's death is puzzling and may be due to an error in the text, as the context seems to require a reference to the assassination attempt on Childebert.*

Sunnegisil [cf. IX 38] was once more subjected to torture and was flogged daily with rods and whips. His wounds festered, but, as soon as the pus cleared up and the wounds began to close, he was put to the torture again. Under these torments he confessed not only to the assassination of Chilperic but also of having committed various crimes. In these confessions he also added that Egidius, bishop of Rheims, had been an accomplice in the plot of Rauching, Ursio, and Berthefred to kill King Childebert.

The bishop was instantly arrested and taken to Metz, though he was at the time quite worn out by a prolonged illness. There he was kept in custody while the king ordered the bishops to be summoned to examine him; they were to meet at Verdun at the beginning of October. The king was blamed at the time by the other bishops for having ordered this man to be carried off from his city and kept in custody without a hearing. For this reason he allowed Egidius to return to his city, but issued letters, as I have said, to all the bishops of his kingdom, requiring them to be present in the aforesaid city in the middle of November to investigate the matter. There were heavy rains and immeasurable torrents, the cold was unbearable, the roads were awash in muck, and the rivers overflowed their banks; but the bishops could not disobey the king's command. Finally, they met and were obliged to continue to Metz, where the aforesaid Egidius also appeared.

The king at that time declared him his enemy and a traitor to the country. He directed Ennodius, the former duke, to conduct the prosecution.

Ennodius's first question was this: "Tell me, bishop, why was it that you did forsake the king in whose city you enjoyed the episcopal dignity to place yourself among the friends of King Chilperic, who has always proven himself to be the enemy of our lord king, who killed our lord king's father, sentenced his mother to exile, and overran his kingdom? And in these cities which, as we have said, he subjected to his authority by unjust invasion, why was it that you received from him farms from the property of the fisc?"

To these points Egidius responded: "That I was the friend of King Chilperic, I cannot deny, but this friendship never grew to prejudice the interests of King Childebert. The villas that you mention I received through written authorizations of King Childebert."

At this he produced them before the court, but the king denied having granted them. Otto was summoned. He had been the referendary at the time and a likeness of his signature was on the documents. He appeared and denied that it was his signature. For his hand had been forged in the writing of this document. On this charge the bishop was for the first time found guilty of deception.

After this were produced letters of his to Chilperic that contained many criticisms of Queen Brunhild; likewise letters of Chilperic sent to the bishop, in which, among other things, was this passage: "If the root of anything is not cut, the stalk that grows from the earth will not wither." Here it was quite clear that this was written with the meaning that, when Brunhild was overthrown, her son could be destroyed.

The bishop denied sending these letters in his own name or receiving them as an answer from Chilperic. But a confidential servant of the bishop was present with shorthand copies for the records of correspondence. There remained no doubt to those sitting there that they were sent by the accused.

Next, agreements were produced in the names of Kings Childebert and Chilperic containing a clause that the two kings, after expelling King Guntram, would divide his kingdom and his cities between themselves [cf. VI 3, 31; VII 6]. The king denied that he had been a party to this.

"You set my uncles against each other, stirring up civil war," he said. "As a result an army was mustered that devastated and laid waste the city of Bourges, the district of Étampes, and the town of Châteaumeillant. In this war many were killed. God's judgment, I believe, shall hold you responsible for their deaths."

This charge the bishop could not deny. For these documents were found together in one of the letter-cases in the vault of King Chilperic and had passed into King Childebert's possession at the time he took delivery of the treasure removed from Chelles, the royal villa in the territory of Paris, following Chilperic's death [cf. VII 4].

The discussion of matters of this kind dragged on for some time when Epiphanius, the abbot of the basilica of the holy Remigius, appeared and said that Egidius had received two thousand pieces of gold and many valuable items to preserve his friendship with King Chilperic. Envoys who had accompanied the bishop to the aforesaid King Chilperic also testified.

"He left us and conferred for a long time alone with the king," they said. "We knew nothing of what they said, until later we learned that the above-mentioned devastation had been carried out."

The bishop denied these charges, but the abbot, who had always been a party to his secret plans, named the place where the gold pieces were delivered and the person who brought them. He recounted how it happened, step by step, that an agreement was reached to devastate the region and kill King Guntram.

Convicted, Egidius now confessed to the charges.

On hearing this and seeing that a priest of the Lord had been an abettor of such great evil, the bishops who had been summoned sighed deeply and begged a space of three days to consider what they had heard, thinking that Egidius might recover himself and find some means of clearing himself of the charges brought against him. At dawn on the third day, they gathered in the church and asked the bishop, if he had any excuse, to declare it.

"Do not delay passing sentence on a guilty man," he said, confounded. "For I know that I deserve death on the charge of high treason. I have always opposed the interests of the king and his mother, and on my advice many campaigns were conducted in which not a few parts of Gaul were devastated."

When the bishops heard this and mourned the disgrace of a brother, they obtained his life but removed him from the priesthood after reading the sanctions prescribed by the canons. He was immediately taken to Argentoratum, now called Strasbourg, and placed in exile. Romulf, son of Duke Lupus, already in priest's orders, succeeded to his position as bishop. Epiphanius, who presided over the basilica of the holy Remigius, was removed from his post as abbot. Many pounds of gold and silver were found in the vault of Egidius. The proceeds from his actions in the service of evil were handed over to the royal treasury. The proceeds from taxes or other business of the church were left there.

### The Baptism of Chlothar (X 28)

Fredegund sent envoys to King Guntram with a message saying, "Let my lord king come to Paris. Summon my son, his nephew, and have the boy consecrated with the grace of baptism. Let him take the child from the sacred font and be so kind as to treat him as his own foster son."

When he heard this the king gathered bishops, namely, Aetherius of Lyons, Syagrius of Autun, Flavius of Chalon, and others he wanted, and told them go to Paris, saying that he would follow later on. Also present at this assembly were many officials from his kingdom, *domestici* as well as counts, involved in making the necessary preparations for the king's expenses. Though the decision to go to the assembly had already been made, the king was held up by a foot ailment. Upon his recovery, he came to Paris and from there quickly went off to the villa of Rueil in the territory of that city; summoning the boy, he ordered a place of baptism made ready in the village of Nanterre.

While this was going on, envoys came to see him from King Childebert.

"Your recent promise to your nephew Childebert hardly included establishing ties of friendship with his enemies," they said. "As far as we can tell, you are keeping no part of your word. Rather, ignoring your promise you are making this boy king with his throne in the city of Paris. God shall judge you for not recalling what you promised of your own accord."

"I don't disregard the promise that I made to my nephew Childebert," replied the king. "There is no need for him to take offense if I receive his cousin, my own brother's son, from the sacred font; no Christian should refuse the request to do so. And God knows very well that I undertake the duty without ulterior motives and in the simplicity of a pure heart, for I fear angering God. Our line suffers no disparagement if I accept this child. For if masters take up their servants at the sacred font, why can't I receive a near relation and make him a son by the spiritual grace of baptism? Be off and tell your lord that I am anxious to preserve intact the agreement I made with him, and, if your side does it no harm, it shall certainly not be set aside by me."

After these words, the envoys withdrew, and the king approached the sacred font, presenting the boy for baptism. On receiving him from the font, he said he wanted him to be called Chlothar.

"Let the boy grow and fulfill the meaning of this name," he said. "And may he enjoy such power as the former Chlothar whose name he has received."

At the end of the ceremony he invited the boy to his table and honored him with many gifts. When in turn, he had been invited by his nephew and loaded with numerous presents, he departed, deciding to return to Chalon.

*The above chapter is the last political event of Gregory's narrative. King Guntram died in March 592. Gregory mentions the king's death in his* Wonders, *but does not record it in his* Histories, *which he finished writing in 594 (cf. X 31), just before his own death in the same year.*

*Chlothar II went on in 613 to become the sole ruler of the Frankish kingdom in the fashion of his grandfather Chlothar I. See* **58**.

# CHAPTER ELEVEN

# THE WORLD OF GREGORY OF TOURS

*This chapter is intended to shed additional light on the milieu in which Gregory of Tours lived and to supplement the political narrative drawn from his Histories and collected in the previous chapter. It relies once again on Gregory's own account of his times and on the poetry of his friend Venantius Fortunatus.*

## A. ANTIQUE POETRY AND THE MEROVINGIAN COURT

## 50. VENANTIUS FORTUNATUS BEFORE THE SYNOD OF BERNY, a. 580: ON THE VIRTUES OF CHILPERIC

*Venantius Fortunatus (ca. 530-ca. 610) was a native of Treviso, near Venice. In 565, shortly before the Lombard invasion of Italy, he came to Gaul on a pilgrimage to the tomb of Saint Martin. Welcomed at the royal courts of the Merovingian kings and in the churches of the ecclesiastical elites, he settled in Gaul and eventually became bishop of Poitiers. His warm reception in Gaul was due in no small measure to his literary talents. He was a writer of poems of various kinds, a composer of hymns, and an author of saints' vitae. As a poet, he was an able practitioner of the late antique genre of verse panegyric, and wrote pieces praising Sigibert and Brunhild, Charibert, Chilperic, and Childebert II and Brunhild, among others. The piece below is notable because of the favorable picture it gives of Chilperic and Fredegund, so different, it would seem, from the depiction of these monarchs in the histories of his friend, Gregory of Tours. We also know some of the circumstances surrounding the delivery of the panegyric. It was given before the synod that met at the villa of Berny in 580 to try Gregory for treasonous remarks about Fredegund (cf. 49, V 49).*

Source: *Venantius Fortunatus: Personal and Political Poems*, trans. Judith George (Liverpool, 1995), pp. 73-80.

O company of priests, Christ's revered champions, you whom bountiful faith has made our fathers in our religion, I humbly beg to speak forth the praises of our noble king. May your love compensate for my lowly verses.

O king, renowned in war and sprung from a noble line of kings, foremost of those of old, commanding the foremost heights, as leader you inherited honor by birth, but increased it by your wise rule. Sprung as a vigorous shoot from your father's line, in turn you each have ennobled the other; you have been an ornament to your forefathers' line, as they likewise are to you. You have received glory from your lineage, but through you lustrous distinction has been added to your ancestors. When you were born to your father, another light was created for the world; you cast the new rays of your fame in every direction; the East, the South, the West, and the North exalt you; by your honour and renown you reach even places where your foot does not tread. Through your fame, O king, you have traversed every sector of the world, you speed on the track the sun's wheel traces; you are known even by the Red Sea and the Indian Sea, your dazzling reputation for wisdom has crossed even the Ocean. Neither wind nor wave prevent your name from being proclaimed abroad; thus do all things, heaven and earth, favor you. O king, of admirable virtue, of lofty fame and noble ancestry, in whom so many exalted leaders find their leader; defender of our country, our hope and protection in time of war, of steadfast courage for your people, of renowned vigor, O powerful Chilperic; if a barbarian interpreter were at hand, your name would be rendered also as 'valiant defender.' It was not for nothing that your parents named you thus; this indeed was a complete presage, an omen of your repute. Even then, events gave a sign for the newborn, yet later blessings bring to fruition earlier promises. On you, dear one, rested all your father's hopes, among so many brothers you alone thus were his love. For he realized even then that you were worthy of greater things; just as your father nurtured you more, so he gave you preference; the sire set on high the child he loved best; no one can set aside the king's judgment.

You grew up under auspicious signs, greatest prince, abiding in the love of both the people and your father But suddenly life's fortune, jealous of such qualities, seeking to disrupt the peace of your reign, and disturbing the disposition of the people and the agreements of your brothers, favored you with success in its attempt to bring you down. But then, as danger menaced your valiant head, the hour which could have struck you down instead drove death away from you. When you were held encompassed around by the weapons of destruction, fate rescued you from the sword by God's intervention. Brought to life's extremity, you returned from the point of destruction; the day which had been your last became your first. When enemies were seeking to raise destructive war against you, faith, strong against arms, fought for you. Your cause successfully reached a judgment without you, and the lofty seat returned to its rightful place.

Good king, do not weep. The fate which wearied you with troubles, now for the same reason has given you better fortune. Through your enduring such hardship for so long, happier times have now come, and you reap the joy which is sown of such sorrow. Having endured many threats, you take up your royal power again; for it is by great labors that great achievements usually grow. Harsh fortune has not harmed you; in its harshness it has proved you; you emerge the more exalted from what bore you down. You rise all the higher with constant trials of arms. You are not broken by them; the effort itself makes you a master of war-craft. Through the multitude of your dangers, you become a stronger ruler; through your sweated toil you gain the benefits of peace. Whilst you live on as king, the world does not grieve for any loss; the lands due to you have stood firm. The Creator decreed that for the sake of your house, your country, and your people, you live, a hero, whom the nations fear. You are here hailed as victor and give protection far and wide to prevent the armed rebel rampaging through the countryside of Gaul. You inspire fear in the Goths [*Getae*], the Basques [*Vascones*], the Danes [*Dani*], the Jutes [*Euthiones*], the Saxons and the Britons [that is Bretons]. With your father, as men know, you vanquished them in battle. You are a terror to the furthest Frisians and the Suebi, who seek your rule rather than prepare to fight you. To all these peoples you were given as a terror on the battlefield through His judgment; by this new threat you have been transformed into an object of deep love. In you, our governor, the land has a wall of defense cast around it, and an iron portal raises its lofty head. You shine forth, an adamantine tower for your country from the south, and you shelter the people's hopes under a steadfast shield. Lest any should oppress these, you set out your protective defenses and cherish the wealth of the land with your strong boundaries.

What shall I say of your administration of justice, O prince? No-one fares badly with you if he truly seeks justice, for in your honest speech are held the scales of just measure and the course of justice runs straight. Truth is not hindered, falsehood and error settle nothing, deceit flees before your judgment, and order returns. What more? by your superior learning and eloquence you master even those you hold sway over already by the authority of your power, understanding different languages without the aid of an interpreter; a single tongue echoes back the languages of the nations. Your generosity raises up all the needy; you consider to be yours what you give your servants. Thus your praises spread forth, and this wave of approbation strikes the heavens with its clamor.

At one and the same time war looks upon you with favor, and learning grants you her abiding affection; you delight by your valiant courage in the former, by your learning in the latter. In both spheres you are wise; tested in arms and in law, you are glorious as a warrior and resplendent in your law-giving. Your courage recalls your father, your eloquence your uncle, but you surpass your whole family in your enthusiasm for learning. Among the kings, your equals, you are given higher esteem for your verse, no forefather was your equal in learning. Warlike qualities make you like your family, but your literary pursuits single you out as exceptional. Thus you are at once the equal and the superior of the kings of old. O king, whom I greatly admire, your strength wages war nobly, your polishing perfects your verses. You rule warfare by law, and enforce law by strength of arms; so the paths of the different arts converge. If everyone, my lord, could learn of each and every virtue of yours, more would praise the good which you alone do.

Yet may your good fortune remain and increase, and may it be granted that you enjoy your spreading domain with your rightful consort. She adorns the king's domains with her virtues, and shares the rule on high; wise in counsel, clever, shrewd, a good mistress of your palace, intelligent, of pleasing generosity. The noble Fredegund excels in all virtues, the glorious light of day shines forth from her countenance; she carries the oppressive weight of the cares of state, she cherishes you with her goodness, she helps you by her service. With her guidance at your side, your palace grows, by her help your house gains greater honor. Seeking to double the prayers for the safety of her husband, she seeks benefit from Radegund for you. She shines resplendent through her own merits, a glory to a king, and, made queen, a crowning glory for her own husband. In the fullness of time, may she honor you with offspring, so that a grandson will be born to make you a grandfather, giving you fresh life. Therefore may thanks duly be given to the Creator. Worship, O king, the King who gives you His aid, so that He may preserve and increase your good fortune. For the Prince on high Who alone possesses all is He Who has given you so much.

Forgive me, victorious lord, that your praises have overwhelmed me; the very fact that I am so overcome is to your greater honour. Humble though I am, yet I wish that these hopes may be realized, and that those blessed gifts are given from heaven to earth. May the skies prosper you with gentle breezes, may the seasons bless you with peace, may the fields glow with harvests, and may treaties hold the kingdoms fast. May you vanquish your enemies, may you protect the faithful with love, may you be the pinnacle of faith for all true Christians, most noble king, through whom honor is given, with whom may long life and bountiful faith abide.

Let others bring their rulers gold and gifts of jewels; from Fortunatus, a poor man, accept these words.

# B. EPISCOPAL APPOINTMENTS IN GREGORY OF TOURS'S *HISTORIES*

*When bishops emerged as leaders of local Christian communities in the early church, the episcopal office became and remained a flash point of contention among competing interests. The importance of the office transcended its spiritual significance. By the late empire it became in effect an organ of local government as secular communities were forced to yield power to appointees of the central authority and the growing influence of the Christian church. By the Merovingian period, the church probably controlled resources comparable in importance to those of municipal government in its heyday. Canon law provided for the participation of various sectors of the community in the selection of the bishop, but these norms, which had developed in political circumstances increasingly distant from that of Gallic communities and kingdoms, were imprecise or variously interpreted. Divergent and genuine interests intersected, not always harmoniously, when a new bishop needed to be appointed. Such circumstances, combined with many of the less wholesome characteristics of human society, made the process of episcopal appointment a disruptive feature of political life in the Gallic cities. Yet for all the discord, episcopal appointment was still a process marked with very distinct institutional regularities. Cf. for the fifth century, 37.18 (on Chalon); 37.22-24 (on Bourges); for the seventh century, 63, and 73-4 for secular and canon law.*

*The following selections from Gregory's* Histories *cover about twenty years, from 551 to about 571, and concern Clermont, Tours, and Saintes. As usual, Gregory's own perspective is as germane to the subject as the events he recounts.*

Source: for editions of the *Histories*, see **X**, Introduction. Translation by A.C. Murray.

# 51. THE RIVALRY OF CATO AND CAUTINUS IN CLERMONT

*From Book IV 5, 6, 7. Clermont was Gregory's hometown before he came to Tours.*

... When Saint Gall [bishop of Clermont] had passed from this life [a. 551], and his body had been washed and taken into the church, the priest Cato immediately gained the nomination of the clergy for the post of bishop. He took control of all church property as if he were already bishop, dismissing its superintendents and discharging its officials, arranging everything on his own.

The bishops who came to Saint Gall's funeral said to the priest Cato after the interment, "We see that you are by far the most popular choice for bishop; come then, agree with us, and we will bless and consecrate you as bishop. As for the king, he is still a boy, and, if any blame falls on you, we will take you under our protection, deal with the leaders and chief officials of Theudebald's kingdom, and see to it that no wrong is done to you. You can put your confidence in us because we promise that, should you suffer loss, we will make it all up to you from our own resources."

Cato from the high horse of vanity replied, "You know from what people say that from the very beginning I have always lived a religious life. I have fasted, I have been happy to give alms, I have often kept long vigils. I have even stayed at my post continually singing psalms all night. My Lord God, to whom I have given such service, will not allow me to be deprived of this office. Also I have always attained the various grades of the clergy according to the rules of the canons. I was reader for ten years. I tended to the duties of the subdiaconate for five years. For fifteen years I was assigned to the diaconate. I have held the dignity of the priesthood now for twenty years. What else is there for me but to attain the office of bishop, which my faithful service deserves? You should return to your cities and do whatever is in your interest. As for me, I intend to get this office in the manner prescribed by the canons."

Hearing this, the bishops left, cursing his pointless vanity.

When the clergy had agreed to elect Cato as bishop and he had taken charge of everything, though he was not yet ordained, he then began to make threats against the archdeacon Cautinus.

"I will discharge you," he said, "I will humble you, I will have death prepared for you in many ways."

"I desire your favor, pious lord," replied Cautinus. "If I am worthy of that, there is one kindness I can do for you. Without your troubling yourself, and without deception, I will go to the king and get the office of bishop for you. I ask nothing for myself but to earn your favor."

Cato suspected Cautinus was trying to trick him and quite scornfully rejected the offer.

When Cautinus saw that he was being humiliated and subjected to false charges, he pretended to be sick and, leaving the city in the middle of the night, went to King Theudebald and reported the death of Saint Gall. When the king and his court heard this, they assembled bishops at the city of Metz, and Cautinus the archdeacon was ordained bishop. By the time the messengers of the priest Cato arrived, Cautinus was already bishop. Then, by command of the king, these clerics and everything they brought with them from church property were handed over to Cautinus, and bishops and chamberlains were appointed to accompany him on his journey back to Clermont. Cautinus was readily accepted by the citizens and clergy and Clermont was provided with a bishop.

Later intense hostility arose between Cautinus and the priest Cato because no one could ever persuade Cato that he was subject to his bishop. A split among the clergy developed, some following Bishop Cautinus and some the priest Cato, a situation that was completely disastrous for Cato's party. Cautinus saw that there was no way to make Cato obey him, and so he took away all church property from Cato and his friends, or whoever agreed with him, leaving them penniless and destitute. However, any of them who came over to his side received back what he had lost.

## 52. CATO AND TOURS

*From Book IV 11, 15. Cato got a second chance at an episcopal appointment after the death of Theudebald in 555, when Chlothar I assumed the kingdom. The following events took place around the time Chramn was misbehaving in Clermont.*

Bishop Gunthar died at Tours, and the priest Cato was asked to assume direction of the church of Tours, at the suggestion, it is said, of bishop Cautinus. And so it happened that the clergy assembled and, accompanied by Leubastes, *martyrarius* and abbot, made a great show of going to Clermont. When they had made known the king's will to Cato, he kept them hanging around for a few days waiting for an answer.

Anxious to go home, they said, "Tell us your decision so we know what we're doing; otherwise we're going back home. It wasn't our idea to approach you; the king commanded it."

Cato, in his pointless desire for glory, got together a crowd of poor folk and had them cry out, "Good father, why do you abandon us, your children, whom you have raised up to now? Who will give us food and drink if you go away? We, whom you are accustomed to nourish, ask you not to leave us."

At that point, turning to the clergy of Tours, he said, "Now you see, dear brothers, how this multitude of poor people loves me. I can't leave them and go with you."

With this answer, they returned to Tours.

Now Cato had made friends with Chramn and got a promise from him that the moment King Chlothar died Cautinus would be tossed out of the bishop's office and Cato given control of the church. But he who scorned the throne of the blessed Martin did not get what he wanted, and in this was fulfilled the song of David, "He refused the blessing and it shall be taken far from him [Ps. 109:17]."

Cato struck vain poses, thinking that no one was his superior in holiness. For example, he once hired a woman to cry out in church as if possessed and say that he was a great holy man, beloved of God, and that Bishop Cautinus was guilty of every sort of crime and unworthy of attaining episcopal rank.

*Gregory recounts the excesses of Bishop Cautinus (IV 12), before returning to the story of Cato.*

*The family of Eufronius, mentioned below, was also that of Gregory of Tours. The petition drawn up on Eufronius's behalf was called a* consensus; *a model of such a document is preserved in the formulary of Marculf, dating from the following century.*

The people of Tours on hearing that King Chlothar had returned from slaughtering Saxons [a. 555] drew up a petition nominating Eufronius and went to the king.

When they delivered their request, the king answered, "I have given instructions for the priest Cato to be ordained at Tours; why has my order been rejected?"

"We asked him," they replied, "but he wouldn't come."

As they were saying this, the priest Cato suddenly turned up asking the king to have Cautinus expelled from Clermont and him appointed instead. The king laughed at that suggestion, and Cato made a second request, that he be ordained to the bishopric of Tours, which he had earlier scorned.

"My first instructions were for them to consecrate you bishop of Tours, but, from what I hear, you disdained that church. So you shall be kept well away from control of it."

And so Cato went off confounded.

When the king asked about the holy Eufronius, they told him that he was a grandson of the blessed Gregory [bishop of Langres], whom I have mentioned before [III 15].

"This is a great and prominent family," said the king. "May the will of God and the blessed Martin be done; let the selection process be brought to an end."

He issued a directive and the holy Eufronius was ordained bishop, the eighteenth after the blessed Martin.

## 53. DOING IT THE WRONG WAY:
## A BISHOP FOR SAINTES

*From Book IV 26. The petition in favor of Heraclius is also a* consensus.

... In the times of King Charibert [a. 561-567], Leontius [metropolitan bishop of Bordeaux] gathered the bishops of his province at the city of Saintes and deposed Emerius from the bishopric, claiming that Emerius had not being appointed to this position in accordance with the canons. Emerius had received a directive issued by King Chlothar allowing him to be consecrated without the consent of the metropolitan, since the metropolitan was not present. They expelled Emerius from office and drew up a petition in favor of Heraclius, then a priest of the church of Bordeaux, signed it with their own hands, and sent Heraclius with the document to King Charibert. Heraclius came to Tours and informed the blessed Eufronius what had been done, requesting him to sign the document. The man of God flatly refused to do so.

After the priest Heraclius entered the gates of the city of Paris and came before the court, this is how he addressed the king, "Greetings, glorious king. An apostolic see sends your eminence best wishes."

"Have you been to Rome, then, that you bring us greetings from its pope?" asked the king.

"It is your father Leontius who, together with the bishops of his province, sends you greetings," said Heraclius. "He is announcing that Cymulus" — this was what Emerius used to be called as a child — "has been expelled from office because he attained the episcopacy of the city of Saintes by ignoring the stipulations of the canons. And so they have sent you a petition nominating another in his place. Thereby violators of the canons may be censured according to its rules and the power of your reign may be known in ages to come."

When Heraclius said this, the king in a rage ordered him dragged from his sight, placed in a wagon full of thorns, and taken off into exile.

"What do you think —" said Charibert, "no son of King Chlothar is around to uphold the actions of his father just because these people have, without my consent, cast out a bishop whom my father chose?"

Immediately he sent men of religion to restore Bishop Emerius to his post and also dispatched some of his chamberlains to exact a thousand gold pieces from Bishop Leontius and to fine the other bishops as much as was feasible. And so the insult to the prince was avenged.

## 54. DOING IT THE RIGHT WAY: AVITUS, BISHOP OF CLERMONT

*From Book IV 35. These events took place after both Cautinus and Cato died in the plague (cf. 48, IV 31, and 20, s.a. 571). The king in question was Sigibert. He and Brunhild also approved Gregory's consecration.*

When, as I have said, Bishop Cautinus had died at Clermont, many candidates contended for the bishopric, offering much and promising more. The priest Eufrasius, son of the late senator Evodius, for instance, acquired from the Jews many a costly item, which he sent to the king by means of his kinsman Beregisil, with the hope of obtaining by bribery what he could not get by merit. His manners were agreeable but his actions were indecent and, while he would often make the barbarians drunk, he seldom refreshed the poor. I think the stumbling block in the way of his success was that he tried to attain this dignity not through God but through men. But what the Lord said through the mouth of holy Quintianus cannot be changed, "The line of Hortensius will never produce anyone to govern the church of God."

When the clergy assembled in the church of Clermont, the archdeacon Avitus made no promises to them, but he still received the nomination and went off to see the king. Firminus, who had received the office of count of Clermont, then tried to block Avitus's appointment. But he did not go in person to the king; instead, friends of his whom he had sent on this mission asked the king to postpone Avitus's consecration for at least one Lord's Day; if this delay were announced, they would give the king a thousand pieces of gold. But the king would not listen to them.

So it happened that the citizens of Clermont assembled together and the blessed Avitus, at the time, as I said, archdeacon, was elected by the clergy and people and received the episcopal throne. The king held him in such high esteem that he bypassed for a moment the strictness of the canons, and ordered Avitus's consecration to take place in his own presence.

"May I deserve to receive the blessed bread from his hands," said the king.

Avitus was consecrated at Metz by royal favor.

When Avitus had received the bishopric, he showed himself a great man in every respect, providing people with justice, the poor with support, the widow with assistance, and the orphan with all the help he could give.

# C. FEUDS IN GREGORY OF
## TOURS'S *HISTORIES*

*Feud should be understood not as a synonym for vengeance but as a state of hostility existing between two parties as the result of a legal wrong inflicted by one upon the other. It certainly could lead to vengeance and bloodshed, as these excerpts show, but in social and institutional conditions like those of Frankish Gaul it was regularly resolved by settlement and litigation. Feud is not an adjunct of lawlessness but a recurrent feature of compensation-based legal systems, such as that which operated among the elites, both Roman and Frankish, of the Merovingian kingdom. For Gregory's account of a feud among Gallic Jews, see,* **49** *VI 17. It is worth noting that the principal participants in the hostilities described by Gregory were all important people. Many features of feud as found in Gregory's pages are illuminated by excerpts from* Lex Salica *(**64**, **65**, **68**), but also show correspondences with the norms of Roman and canon law and the ancient legal practices of Roman provincials. Gregory does not use the Germanic* *term 'feud' (which did have Latinized analogues in the period), but a series of conventional Latin terms for 'dispute,' 'quarrel,' and 'conflict.'*

Source: for editions of the *Histories*, see **X**, Introduction. Translation by A.C. Murray

## 55. FEUD IN THE FAMILY: SILVESTER'S SON AND GREGORY'S BROTHER PETER, a. 576

*From Book V 5. Gregory places this account ostensibly under the year 576, when he got Felix's letter, but the narrative recounts events of the previous number of years and is written from a perspective of at least the middle part of the 580s. Peter was Gregory's elder brother.*

At this time [a. 576] Felix, bishop of Nantes [a. 549-582], wrote me a letter full of insults, even saying that my brother [Peter, deacon in Langres] had been killed because he had killed his bishop out of a greedy desire for the bishopric. The reason Felix would write such a thing is that he coveted a villa belonging to the church; when I refused to give it up, full of anger, he vomited up a thousand insults against me, as I said.

I finally replied to him, "Remember the saying of the prophet: 'Woe unto those who join house to house and unite field to field! Are they alone going to inhabit the earth?' [Cf. Isaiah 5: 8] If only you were bishop of Marseilles! Ships would never bring oil or other goods there, only papyrus, so you could have all the more opportunity of writing disgraceful accusations against honest men. Only a lack of papyrus puts an end to your wordiness."

He was a man of incredible greed and boastfulness.

I shall put aside these matters, however, not to appear like him, and just relate my brother's passing from this world and the swift vengeance the Lord took upon his killer.

At a time when the blessed Tetricus, bishop of the church of Langres, was getting on in years, he dismissed the deacon Lampadius, whom he had employed in a position of trust. My brother, wanting to aid the poor whom Lampadius had wickedly despoiled, agreed with the humbling of Lampadius and for this reason incurred his hatred. Meanwhile the blessed Tetricus had a stroke. Nothing the doctors could give him did any good. The clergy were alarmed, and, since they were deprived of a pastor, they asked for Munderic. The king granted their request and Munderic was tonsured and ordained bishop, with the stipulation that as long as blessed Tetricus survived, Munderic would govern the stronghold of Tonnerre as archpriest and have his residence there; when his predecessor died, however, then he would succeed him.

While Munderic was living in Tonnerre, he incurred the king's anger. He was charged with furnishing King Sigibert with supplies and assistance when the king was marching against his brother Guntram [cf. IV 47]. Munderic was dragged from the stronghold and exiled to a cramped roofless tower on the bank of the Rhône. Here he lived for nearly two years in considerable hardship; then through the intercession of the blessed bishop Nicetius, he returned to Lyons and lived with the bishop for two months. But since he could not persuade the king to restore him to the position from which he had been expelled, he fled in the night and went over to Sigibert's realm. He was made bishop of the town of Alais with fifteen parishes more or less under him. It was the Goths who first held these, but now were under the authority of Dalmatius, bishop of Rodez.

Now that Munderic was gone, the people of Langres again asked for a bishop in the person of Silvester, a kinsman of mine and of the blessed Tetricus. Their asking for Silvester was the doing of my brother. Meanwhile the blessed Tetricus passed away [a. 571] and Silvester was tonsured, ordained a priest, and given control of the property of the church. He made preparations to go and receive episcopal consecration at Lyons. In the midst of the preparations, he was seized by an attack of epilepsy, a disease he had long been susceptible to, and, quite bereft of his senses and bellowing constantly for two days, died finally on the third day.

After these events, Lampadius, who, as I said above, had been deprived of his post and his means, joined with Silvester's son in hatred of Peter the deacon, contriving an allegation that Peter had killed Silvester by witchcraft. Silvester's son, who was young and not too bright, was incited into accusing Peter in public of parricide. When Peter heard this, a date was set for a hearing before Saint Nicetius, bishop [of Lyons], my mother's uncle; Peter made his way to Lyons. There in the presence of Bishop Siagrius [of Autun] and many other bishops and leaders of the laity he cleared himself by oath of ever having been involved in Silvester's death.

Two years later [a. 574], again goaded by Lampadius, Silvester's son pursued the deacon Peter along the road and stabbed him with a spear, killing him. Peter's body was then carried from there and taken to the town of Dijon and buried beside Saint Gregory, our great-grandfather. As for Silvester's son, he fled and went over to King Chilperic, leaving his property to the treasury of King Guntram.

Silvester's son traveled through a number of districts, but on account of the crime he had committed there was no safe place for him to settle down. At last, as I believe, innocent blood cried out to the divine power against him [cf. Gen. 4:10], and, as Silvester's son was travelling somewhere, he drew his sword and killed a man who had done nothing to him. The man's relatives, in a terrible state at the death of their kinsman, raised a commotion, and, drawing their swords, cut Silvester's son to pieces, scattering bits of his body around. This is the kind of end this wretched man met by the just judgment of God, so that he who slew an innocent kinsman, such a criminal did not himself survive for long, for this happened to Silvester's son in the third year [after the killing of Peter].

*Langres finally got a bishop, by the name of Pappolus. Gregory passes over his misdeeds, which he has heard by report, "in case I appear to be a disparager of my fellow bishops," though he does linger on the details of Pappolus' death.*

Following Pappolus, the abbot Mummolus, surnamed the Good, was made bishop. Many praise him highly, saying that he is chaste, abstemious, and temperate, always ready to do a good deed, a friend of justice and lover of charity with all his heart.

When he took the bishopric, he was aware that Lampadius had taken a lot of church property by fraud, and had piled up fields, vineyards, and slaves from the spoil of the poor. He ordered him stripped of everything and driven from his presence. Lampadius now lives in the worst poverty and makes his living by manual labor.

I have said enough on these matters.

## 56. THE FEUDS OF SICHAR, a. 585 and 588

*From Books VII 47 and IX 19. Apart from his account of Clovis, Gregory's story of the feud between Sichar and Chramnesind is probably the most famous passage in his* Histories *and has often been taken as an exemplar of both Gregory's primitive prose style and the crude legal institutions of his day. A different reading of Gregory's prose and the events he narrates is possible.*

*The* iudex, *or judge, acting in concert with Gregory, was the count. The 'judges' determining the sums owed by Chramnesind and Sichar were assessors and citizen-members of the court, often called 'rachineburgs' or 'good men,' who advised tribunals on the law and assisted in its administration (cf.* **65, 75 d, e, f**).

*The beginning of Sichar's story appears among the events of 585. Sichar, by the way, is a Latin name.*

At this point a serious internal conflict arose among the citizens of Tours.

While Sichar, son of the late John, was holding Christmas celebrations in the village of Manthelan [near Tours], with Austrighysel and other people of the district, the local priest sent round a servant to invite some people to have a drink at his place. So the servant arrived and one of the men he was inviting thought nothing of drawing a sword and striking him with it. The servant fell down dead on the spot. Sichar was connected to the priest by friendship, and as soon as he heard that the servant had been killed, he grabbed his weapons and went to the church to wait for Austrighysel. When Austrighysel heard about this, he grabbed his arms and went after Sichar. In the general commotion of the fighting that ensued when the two sides came together, Sichar was saved by some clerics and escaped to his villa, leaving behind in the priest's house money, garments, and four wounded servants. After Sichar had fled, Austrighysel attacked again, killing the servants and carrying off the gold and silver and other property.

After this the parties appeared before a tribunal of citizens. It found that Austrighysel was subject to legal penalty because he had committed homicide, killed servants, and seized property without obtaining judgment. An agreement was reached [for Austrighysel to pay compensation] and a few days later Sichar heard that the stolen property was being held by Auno, his son, and his brother Eberulf. Setting the agreement aside, Sichar, accompanied by Audinus, created a public disturbance by attacking them at night with an armed force. Sichar broke apart the quarters where they were sleeping, did in the father, brother, and son, killed slaves, and took off with property and cattle.

I was very upset when I heard news of the attack and, acting in conjunction with the count (iudex), sent a delegation with a message for the parties to come before us so that a reasonable settlement could be made and they could depart in peace without the dispute going any further.

When they arrived, and the citizens had assembled, I said, "Men, stop this criminal behavior and prevent the evil spreading further. We have already lost sons of the church; now I fear we shall be deprived of even more of them by this quarrel. Be peacemakers, I beg of you; let whoever did wrong pay compensation out of brotherly love, so that you may be peaceable children and worthy, by God's gift, to occupy His kingdom. For He Himself said, 'Blessed are the peacemakers, for they shall be called the children of God [Matt. 5:9].' Listen carefully! if anyone who is liable to a penalty has insufficient resources, church money will be paid out on his behalf. In the meantime, let no man's soul perish."

In saying this, I offered money of the church, but the party of Chramnesind, who had a claim for the death of his father [Auno], his brother, and his uncle, refused to accept it.

When they went away, Sichar made preparations for a journey to visit the king; with this in mind he first went to see his wife in Poitiers. While admonishing a slave at his labors, Sichar beat him with a rod. The fellow drew a sword from its baldric and without hesitation wounded his master with it. Sichar fell to the ground, but his friends ran up and caught the slave. They beat him viciously, cut off his hands and feet, and hung him up on a gibbet.

Meanwhile rumor reached Tours that Sichar was dead. When Chramnesind heard, he mustered his kinsmen and friends, and rushed to Sichar's home. He plundered it, killing some slaves and burning down all the buildings, not only Sichar's, but those of other landlords in the villa, and took off with the herds and anything he could move.

At this point the parties were brought into the city by the count and pleaded their own causes. The judges found that the side that had earlier refused compensation and then put houses to the torch should forfeit half the sum formerly awarded to it — this was done contrary to law only to ensure that they would be peaceable; as for the other side, Sichar was to pay the other half of the compensation. He paid it, the church providing the sum that the judges had determined, and he received a notice [from Chramnesind] discharging him from future claims. Both sides took oaths to each other that neither would ever so much as mutter a word against the other.

And so the dispute came to an end.

*The conclusion of the story comes three years later, under the year 588.*

The conflict among the citizens of Tours that I said above had ended arose again with renewed madness.

Sichar had struck up a great friendship with Chramnesind after having killed his relatives. They had such affection for each other that they often ate together and slept together in the same bed. One day Chramnesind had an evening dinner prepared and invited Sichar to the feast. He came and they sat down at the meal together.

Sichar got stinking drunk on wine and bragged a lot at Chramnesind's expense, until at last, so we are told, he said, "Dear brother, you owe me a great debt of gratitude for doing in your kinsmen. There's certainly no lack of gold and silver around here since you got compensation for them. If this business hadn't given you a bit of a boost, you'd now be naked and poor."

Chramnesind took Sichar's words badly and said to himself, "If I don't avenge my kinsmen's death, I should lose the name man and be called a weak woman."

He immediately extinguished the lights and split open Sichar's head with his dagger. Emitting a little cry at the end of his life, Sichar fell down dead. The servants who had come with him scattered. Chramnesind stripped the lifeless body of its clothes, hung it on a fence post and, mounting his horse, rode off to see the king [Childebert].

He entered the church and threw himself at the king's feet.

"Glorious king," said Chramnesind, "I ask for my life because I have killed men who slew my kinsmen in secret and stole their property."

When the details of the matter were brought to light, Brunhild took it badly that Sichar, who was under her protection, had been killed in this way, and the queen became angry at Chramnesind. When he saw that she was against him, he went to the Vosagus district in the territory of Bourges where his kinfolk lived, because it was considered part of Guntram's kingdom.

Sichar's wife Tranquilla left her sons and her husband's property in Tours and Poitiers and went to her family in the village of Mauriopes, and there she got married again.

Sichar was about twenty years old when he died. In his life he was a foolish, drunken killer, who inflicted harm on not a few people when he was drunk.

As for Chramnesind, he came back to the king, and the judgment he received was that he prove his killing of Sichar was unavoidable. This he did. But since Queen Brunhild had placed Sichar under her protection, as I have said, she ordered Chramnesind's property confiscated, but it was later restored by the *domesticus* Flavian. Chramnesind also went quickly to [Duke] Agino and got a letter from him protecting his person. Chramnesind's property had been granted to Agino by the queen.

*The translation of the last two sentences is uncertain.*


## 57. FREDEGUND BURIES THE HATCHET, a. 591

*From Book X 27.*

A not insignificant dispute arose among the Franks of Tournai because the son of one of them kept angrily criticizing the son of another, who had married his sister, for leaving his wife and going to a whore. When accusations failed to mend the behavior, the anger of the boy reached the point that he and his men rushed upon his brother-in-law and killed him. The boy himself was struck down by his brother-in-law's followers and there was only one man left from both parties without an adversary to do him in.

Relatives on both sides were in fury at each other as a result, but Fredegund kept telling them to give up their enmity and make peace because persistence in the quarrel would only lead to a greater public disgrace. But when she was unable to pacify these people with soft words she suppressed both sides with the ax.

She invited many guests to a feast and had three of these people sit on the same bench. When the dinner had gone on beyond nightfall, the table was taken away, as is the custom of the Franks, and the guests remained sitting on the benches in the places they had been assigned. A lot of wine had been consumed, and they were so far gone that their retainers were drunkenly sleeping wherever they had fallen down in the corners of the room. At that point, as the woman had arranged, three of her men with axes stepped up behind the three occupying the same bench. They were talking together as the hands of the queen's retainers swung their axes, in one movement, as I would say, striking the three men down and ending the banquet. The names of the dead were Charivald, Leodovald, and Valeden.

When this was told to their relatives, they began to watch Fredegund closely and sent messengers to king Childebert asking him to arrest her and put her to death. The forces of Champagne were mustered over this matter, but time was wasted, and Fredegund, saved by the help of her men, went somewhere else.

# CHAPTER TWELVE

# FREDEGAR ON FRANKISH HISTORY, A. 584-642

The Chronicle *of Fredegar is a compilation of historical materials intended to provide an outline of history from Adam down to the author's own time. The work is anonymous; it is now traditional to call the author 'Fredegar,' though the name was first used only in the sixteenth century and is not likely to be a sound attribution.*

*Authorship of the chronicle has been controversial, but for another reason than the name. Many scholars have thought that there was more than one Fredegar, that is that the chronicle, as it now exists, was gradually compiled over time by multiple authors. This view is now difficult to maintain. In the comments here, and in* **XVI**, *which also deals with Fredegarian excerpts, I treat the work as the product of a single author.*

*Fredegar represented himself as undertaking two different historiographical tasks in compiling the chronicle. The first was the excerpting of previous written historical material. Among the works he treated in this fashion were the chronicles of Jerome and Hydatius, and the histories of Gregory of Tours. As far as Gregory is concerned, Fredegar used an early abridgment in six books that ended with the death of Chilperic. We know that Fredegar did more than simply excerpt, however; sometimes he abridged, but more importantly he also added material to his excerpts. These interpolations are of considerable interest; those of any length are given below in* **79, 81-95**.

*Fredegar also composed an original chronicle for the period from 584 to his own day. In accordance with the organization of the standard edition, this original section is commonly known as Book IV of the chronicle, though Fredegar conceived of his work as being composed of chronicles not of books. In this final, original chronicle, Fredegar certainly drew on written sources; the one that we know of is Jonas'* Life of Saint Columbanus, *which Fredegar abridged without acknowledgment. Fredegar's so-called Book IV is translated below. Picking up from the death of Chilperic as described by Gregory of Tours, it gives a narrative of Frankish history down to 642. It is our chief source for the events of this period.*

*The chronicle as we have it ends in 642, but this was certainly not Fredegar's intention. The author mentions events of 659 that he meant to treat later, and the entry for 642 ends the chronicle abruptly. The chronicle as we have it, therefore, is either fragmentary or uncompleted; given its use by later Carolingian redactors and its manuscript history, the last supposition is the likelier explanation. The simplest assumption is that the author died before he could finish it. The author's incidental mention of events of the late 650s is the main indication we have of the date of the chronicle's composition, which must be ca. 660 or later, though I think not much later.*

*Evaluations of the authority of Fredegar's account of the period from 584-642 vary widely. Some have thought they detected the immediacy of the eyewitness and contemporary (an assumption made easier when multiple authorship has been accepted). Others have spotted rather Fredegar's penchant for a good story told without much regard for veracity or probability.*

*There is also much in the chronicle to suggest the author's views on political, human, and divine affairs. But efforts to tie these to a particular clerical, religious, or lay status are inevitably confounded by reliance on stereotypical views of the orders of Gallic society.*

*In the following translation I have abandoned the organization of the chronicle in chapters, which has no claim to being original. Instead I have laid it out it out according to regnal dates. Chapter numbers of the standard edition of Bruno Krusch have been placed in the margin. The system of regnal dating seems to me to show clearly that the work is a product of the Burgundian kingdom, and this view is reflected in my assignment of subheadings.*

*A note on chronology: no claim of authority on the rat's nest of Merovingian chronology is made for this translation. In assigning dates to the chronicle, I have attempted wherever possible to assign one anno domini date to Fredegar's system of regnal dating; these dates are placed in the text in boldface. Other generally accepted dates are given in a plain font.*

Source: three editions of the chronicle have been used for this translation: (1) *Chronicarum quae dicuntur Fredegarii scholastici libri IV,* ed. Bruno Krusch, MGH SRM 2 (1888), pp. 118-168; (2) *The Fourth Book of the Chronicle of Fredegar,* ed. and trans. J. M. Wallace-Hadrill (London, 1960); (3) "Die Vier Bücher der Chroniken des sogenannten Fredegar," ed. and trans. Andreas Kusternig, in *Quellen zur Geschichte des 7. und 8. Jahrhunderts,* ed. Herwig Wolfram (Darmstadt, 1982), pp. 160-271. Translation by A.C. Murray.

# 58. THE SIXTH CHRONICLE OF FREDEGAR (BOOK IV)

## The Prologue

*Fredegar recapitulates how he has previously excerpted the work of five chroniclers and explains the origin of his own, new, sixth chronicle, which begins in the year 584.*

*The first sentence, which combines false humility, ambiguous grammar, and obscure logic, is fraught with translation problems. The only explanation I can offer for it is that*

*Fredegar knew that Jerome translated Eusebius's chronicle from Greek, and so has played with the word 'translate' as a term for his own efforts in epitomizing and adding to his sources. The first sentence has strong verbal correspondences with Jerome's introduction to his chronicle, where he discusses the problems of translation.*

While I cannot express anthing with a single, appropriate word, unless God provides me with it, and, when I try to complete a sentence, I can barely handle a short expression with a lengthly circumlocution, still, the word 'translate' sounds ridiculous in ordinary speech. Were I compelled to change the order of the words to any extent, it would seem as if I were failing to meet the standards of a translator. What I have done is very carefully go over the chronicles of blessed Jerome, of Hydatius, of a certain wise man [Hippolytus of Porto], of Isidore [of Seville], as well as of Gregory [of Tours] from the origin of the world to the declining years of Guntram's reign. In an appropriate format, I have placed into the five chronicles of this little book, one after the other, whatever these most expert men faultlessly recorded, omitting very little. In these circumstances, I have felt it necessary to pursue the truth with some care, and for this reason I even noted down for myself in prior versions of these chronicles, for some future work as it were, the dates of all the kings. I placed those dates in the format before you and quite carefully put the deeds of the various peoples into order, drawing on what those most wise men whom I mentioned above wrote. They composed weighty chronicles (this is a Greek word which in Latin is translated 'the deeds of the times'), generously pouring forth floods of eloquence like the purest spring. My hope had been that such eloquence might have fallen to my lot, even if the resemblance were only slight, but it is harder to draw water where the flow is not constant. The world now grows old. And so our mental abilities lose their edge, and there is no one to match or even challenge the orators of past times. As far as my rustic habits and limited understanding would permit, I have dared to compose to the best of my ability a most careful summary from these very books. Let no reader of this work doubt anything. The name of each book is identified, and should he return to the original author, the reader shall find everything corresponds to the truth.

Having finished with the pages of Gregory's book, I did not stop writing in the pages of this little book the events of the times from every quarter, as I found them in writings, and as I learned about them at a later date, and the deeds of kings and the wars that peoples waged, everything I knew to be true from both reading and listening and even seeing. I made a careful effort to add as much of this as I could and began to write at the very point where the events treated by Gregory came to an end and he fell silent, that is where he described the death of Chilperic. So ends the Prologue.

IN THE NAME OF OUR LORD JESUS CHRIST,
THE SIXTH CHRONICLE BEGINS

## The Last Years of Guntram, a. 584-593

[1] By the 23rd year of his reign, Guntram, king of the Franks, was ruling the kingdom of Burgundy with success and full of goodness. Indeed to the bishops, he presented himself in the fashion of a bishop; to his *leudes,* he was completely satisfactory; and he gave generously to the poor. He ruled a kingdom in such a healthy state that all the neighboring peoples sang his praises to the full.

IN THE 24TH YEAR OF HIS REIGN **[a. 584],** for the love of God, the king had the admirable church of the blessed Marcellus built with care, and there this precious man rests in the body; the church is in the suburban region of Chalon, although the territory is that of the Seine. There the king gathered monks, founded a monastery and endowed the church with many possessions.

Guntram ordered a synod of 40 bishops to convene [Synod of Valence, a. 584], and he saw to it that the meeting of the synod confirmed the foundation of the monastery of Saint Marcellus, following the model of the monastery dedicated to the saints of Agaune; the foundation of Agaune had been confirmed in the times of King Sigismund by Avitus and by other bishops on the orders of the prince.

[2] In this year, in the month of November, Gundovald with the assistance of Mummolus and Desiderius dared to invade part of Guntram's kingdom and to overthrow cities. Guntram sent against him an army under Leudegisl, count of the stable, and Aegyla, the patrician. Gundovald retreated and took refuge in Saint Bertrand-de-Comminges. Thereafter, Gundovald was thrown from a cliff by Duke Boso and died.

[3] When Guntram was informed that his brother Chilperic had been killed, he hurried to Paris and there he ordered Fredegund and Chilperic's son Chlothar to come to him. He ordered Chlothar to be baptized at the villa of Rueil and, lifting him from the holy baptismal font, established the child's right to the kingdom of his father.

[4] IN THE 25TH YEAR OF GUNTRAM'S REIGN **[a. 585]**, Mummolus was killed at Senuvia at the king's command. The *domesticus* Domnolus and the chamberlain Wandalmar delivered Mummolus's wife Sidonia and all Mummolus's treasure to Guntram.

[5] IN THE 26TH YEAR OF GUNTRAM'S REIGN, his army invaded Spain but, overcome by a sickness of the region, quickly returned home.

IN THE 27TH YEAR OF GUNTRAM'S REIGN, Leudegisl was appointed patrician for the region of Provence. There was news of the birth of Theudebert [II, a. 596-612], the son of King Childebert.

In this year, the rivers were in full flood in Burgundy and easily overran their banks.

In the same year, Count Syagrius went to Constantinople on Guntram's orders as an envoy and was there deceitfully appointed patrician. This criminal fraud, though conceived, was never able to hatch.

In this year, a sign appeared in the sky — a ball of fire fell sparkling and glowing to earth.

[6]     In the same year, Leuvigild, king of Spain, died, and his son Reccared succeeded him [a. 586].

IN THE 28TH YEAR OF LORD GUNTRAM'S REIGN [a. 587], there was news of another son being born to King Childebert; the child's name was Theuderic [II, a. 596-613].

[7]     Guntram met Childebert to establish peace at Andelot. There the mother, sister, and wife of King Childebert were all present. And there a special agreement was reached between Lord Guntram and Childebert that Childebert would obtain Guntram's kingdom on his death.

[8]     At the same time, Rauching and Guntram Boso, Ursio and Berthefred, magnates of King Childebert, were killed at the command of the king, because they had planned to kill him. Leudefred, duke of the Alamanni, also incurred the disfavor of the said king and went into hiding. Uncelen was appointed duke in his place.

In this year, Reccared, king of the Goths, embracing the love of God, was first baptized in private. Afterwards he had all Gothic adherents of the Arian sect gather at Toledo and had all Arian books handed over. When the books had been deposited together in one building, he ordered them burned. He saw to it that all the Goths were baptized into the Christian faith.

[9]     In this year, Caesara, the wife of Anaulf, the emperor of the Persians, left her husband and, along with four male and as many female attendants, came to the blessed John, bishop of Constantinople. She said she was a commoner and sought out the aforesaid blessed John in order to be baptized. When she was baptized by the bishop, the Augusta, [wife] of the emperor Maurice, received her from the holy baptismal font. Caesara's husband, the emperor of the Persians, often sent envoys to demand her return; Emperor Maurice did not know Caesara was his wife.

But then the Augusta, seeing that Caesara was very beautiful, and suspecting that it was she whom the envoys were seeking, said to the envoys, "A certain woman came here from Persia. She said she was a commoner. Look at her; perhaps she is the woman you are looking for."

When the emissaries saw Caesara, they sank to the ground to venerate her, saying that she was the mistress whom they were seeking.

The Augusta said to her, "Give them an answer."

"I shall not speak with them," responded the Caesara. "Their way of life is that of a dog. If they can be converted to Christianity, as I was, then I shall answer them."

The envoys willingly received the grace of baptism.

Afterwards Caesara said to them, "If my husband wishes to become a Christian and receive the grace of baptism, I shall be happy to go back to him, but otherwise there is no chance I will return."

When the emissaries reported to the emperor of the Persians, he immediately sent an embassy to the emperor Maurice to say that, if holy John came to Antioch, he would receive baptism from John's hands.

Then the emperor Maurice ordered endless preparations to be made at Antioch, where the emperor of the Persians was baptized with sixty thousand of his people; Persians were baptized for two weeks by John and other bishops before the above number was reached. Gregorius, the bishop of Antioch, received the Persian emperor from the baptismal font. Emperor Anaulf asked Emperor Maurice to give him bishops and clergy whom he could establish in Persia in sufficient numbers to administer the grace of baptism to all Persia. Maurice was happy to furnish them, and with remarkable speed all Persia was baptized in the worship of Christ.

[10] IN THE 29TH YEAR OF GUNTRAM'S REIGN [a. 589], an army was sent to Spain on the king's orders, but it was badly cut to pieces by the Goths owing to the negligence of its commander, Boso.

[11] IN THE 30TH YEAR OF THE AFORESAID PRINCE [a. 590], the tunic of our lord, Jesus Christ was discovered due to the confession of Simon, the son of Jacob. The tunic had been taken from Christ during his passion and lots drawn for it by the soldiers who guarded him, as the prophet David had said: "And lots were cast on my clothing." As a result of various tortures inflicted over a period of two weeks, Simon finally confessed that the tunic was located in a marble coffer in the city of Joppa near Jerusalem. Bishops Gregory of Antioch, Thomas of Jerusalem, John of Constantinople, along with many other bishops, fasted for three days. Then they were worthy of leading a procession on foot that brought the tunic and the marble coffer (now become as light as wood) to Jerusalem with the utmost piety. They placed the tunic in a triumphal manner in the place where the cross of the Lord was venerated.

In this year, there was an eclipse of the moon.

In this year, war broke out between the Franks and the Bretons on the

[12] Vilaine river. Beppolen, a duke of the Franks, was killed by the Bretons due to the intrigues of Ebrachar, also a duke. On account of this, Ebrachar was later stripped of his property and reduced to utter poverty.

[13] IN THE 31ST YEAR OF THE REIGN OF GUNTRAM **[a. 591]**, Theudefred, duke of the territory beyond the Jura, died. Wandalmar succeeded him to the honor of the ducal office.

In the same year, Duke Ago [i.e. Agilulf] was raised to the kingship over the Lombards in Italy.

IN THE 32ND YEAR OF THE REIGN OF GUNTRAM **[a. 592]**, the sun was in eclipse from dawn to midday until barely a third of it was visible [March 19].

[14] IN THE 33RD YEAR OF THE REIGN OF GUNTRAM **[a. 593]**, on the fifth day before the Kalends of April [28 March], the king died. He was buried in the church of Saint Marcellus in the monastery which he himself constructed. Childebert obtained his kingdom.

In the same year Wintrio, duke of Champagne, led an army in an invasion of Chlothar's kingdom. Chlothar came to meet him with his forces and put Wintrio to flight, but both armies were badly cut up.

## The Last Years of Childebert II, a. 593–596

[15] IN THE 2ND YEAR AFTER CHILDEBERT RECEIVED THE KINGDOM OF BUR-GUNDY **[a. 594]**, Frankish and Breton armies fought each other, and both were severely cut up in the fighting.

IN THE 3RD YEAR OF CHILDEBERT'S RULE IN BURGUNDY **[a. 595]**, many signs were revealed in the sky. A comet appeared [in January].

In this year, the army of Childebert fought fiercely with the Warni [Thuringians], who had attempted to rebel, and the Warni were cut up and defeated so badly that very few of them were left.

[16] IN THE 4TH YEAR AFTER CHILDEBERT RECEIVED THE KINGDOM OF BURGUNDY **[a. 596]**, he died, and his sons Theudebert and Theuderic obtained his kingdom. Theudebert got Austrasia as his share, with Metz as his capital. Theuderic received the kingdom of Guntram in Burgundy with his capital in Orleans.

## The Reign of Theuderic II, a. 596–613

[17] In this year, Fredegund with her son King Chlothar took possession of Paris and other cities like barbarians and positioned an army in a place called

Laffaux against King Childebert's sons, Theudebert and Theuderic. The camps were situated facing one another. Chlothar with his forces rushed upon Theudebert and Theuderic and cut their army up severely.

IN THE SECOND YEAR OF THE REIGN OF THEUDERIC[a. 597], Fredegund died.

[18] IN THE 3RD YEAR OF THE REIGN OF THEUDEBERT [a. 598], Wintrio was killed at the instigation of Brunhild.

IN THE 4TH YEAR OF THE REIGN OF THEUDERIC [a. 599], Quolen, a Frank by birth, was appointed patrician.

In this year, the plague severely ravaged Marseilles and other cities in Provence.

In this year, in the Thunersee, into which the Aar river flows, warm water boiled so vigorously that it cooked a great many fish.

In this year, Warnachar, Theuderic's mayor of the palace, died. He distributed all his property as alms to the poor.

[19] In this year Brunhild was expelled from Austrasia and was discovered on her own in the countryside of Arcis by a certain poor man. At her request, he took her to Theuderic. Theuderic was glad to welcome his grandmother and did her honor in a grand style. As a reward for the service the poor man had rendered her, Brunhild saw to it that he obtained the episcopacy of Auxerre.

*The poor man was Saint Desiderius, bishop of Auxerre (a. 603-623).*

IN THE 5TH YEAR OF THE REIGN OF THEUDERIC [a. 600], the signs that were seen in the year recorded above — balls of fire coursing through the sky resembling a multitude of fiery spears — were again visible in the west.

[20] And in the same year, Kings Theudebert and Theuderic sent their army against King Chlothar, and the opposing forces met in battle on the river Orvanne, not far from the village of Dormelles. There the army of Chlothar suffered the worse losses. After Chlothar had fled with his remaining forces, Theudebert and Theuderic plundered and ravaged the districts and cities along the Seine that had submitted to Chlothar. Once the cities were forced open, great numbers of captives were taken from them by the army of Theudebert and Theuderic. Overcome, Chlothar had no choice but to acknowledge in agreements that Theuderic's share of the kingdom included the region between the Seine and the Loire all the way to the Ocean sea and the frontier with the Bretons, and that beyond the Seine and the Oise, Theudebert would have the entire duchy of Dentelin to the Ocean. Twelve districts only, between the Oise, the Seine, and the shores of the Ocean sea, remained to Chlothar.

IN THE 6TH YEAR OF THE REIGN OF THEUDERIC [a. 601], Cautinus, one of Theudebert's dukes, was killed.

[21] IN THE 7TH YEAR OF THE REIGN OF THEUDERIC [a. 602], a son was born from a concubine and called Sigibert [II, †613]. Aegyla the patrician was bound and killed at the instigation of Brunhild, not because he had committed an offense but only out of a greedy desire for the fisc to obtain his property.

In this year, Theudebert and Theuderic sent an army against the Gascons and, with the aid of God, overthrew the Gascons, subjected them to their rule and made them tributaries. The kings appointed a duke over them by the name of Genialis, who successfully ruled them.

[22] In this year, the body of Saint Victor, who suffered martyrdom at Solothurn with Saint Ursius, was found by blessed Aeconius, the bishop of Saint-Jean-de-Maurienne. One night, in his own city, the bishop received a revelation in a dream to get up and go immediately to the church that Queen Sideleuba built in the suburb of Geneva: the body of the saint would appear in the middle of the church at a spot that would be pointed out. When the bishop had hurried to Geneva and, along with the blessed Bishops Rusticius and Patricius, held a fast for three days, a light appeared through the night where that glorious and magnificent body was. Without speaking, the three bishops, in tears and praying, lifted a paving stone and discovered the body of the saint buried in a silver coffer, his face ruddy, as if they found him alive. King Theuderic was present at the time and, granting a great deal of property to this church, confirmed on the spot its possession of the greater part of Warnachar's property [cf. c. 18]. From the day of the body's discovery, wonderful miracles were constantly being revealed by the power of God at the tomb of that saint.

In this year Aetherius, bishop of Lyons, died. Bishop Secundinus was ordained in his place.

[23] In this year, Phocas, duke and patrician of the empire, returned victorious from Persia and killed emperor Maurice [in December]. Phocas replaced Maurice as emperor.

[24] IN THE 8TH YEAR OF THE REIGN OF THEUDERIC [a. 603], a son by the name of Childebert was born to the king by a concubine, and a synod gathered at Chalon. The synod deposed Desiderius, bishop of Vienne, at the instigation of Aridius, bishop of Lyons, and Brunhild. Domnolus was chosen for the episcopal office in his place, and Desiderius was exiled to an island.

In this year, there was an eclipse of the sun [12 August].

In this period also, Bertoald, a Frank by birth, was mayor of the palace of

Theuderic. He was moderate in his habits, wise and careful, bold in battle, and kept faith with everyone.

IN THE 9TH YEAR OF THE REIGN OF THEUDERIC [a. 604], a son called Corbus was born to the king by a concubine. Protadius, a Roman by birth, was by now ardently revered by all in the palace. Since Brunhild wanted to exalt him with honors in return for his sexual attentions, she arranged, on the death of Duke Wandalmar, for Protadius to be appointed patrician for the region beyond the Jura and of the Scotingi.

They sent Bertoald to examine fiscal properties in the cities and districts along the banks of the Seine up to the Ocean sea, where there was a better [25] chance he would be killed. On the orders of Theuderic, Bertoald hurried off to the region with only three hundred men. He came to the villa of Arèle and went hunting there. When Chlothar found out, he sent his son Merovech and the mayor of the palace Landeric with an army to crush Bertoald and, in violation of the treaty, had the presumption to invade most of the districts and cities between the Seine and the Loire belonging to Theuderic's kingdom. Bertoald heard about this, and since he was not strong enough to hold his ground, he retreated to Orleans where he was received by the blessed Bishop Austrenus.

Landeric and his army surrounded Orleans and called on Bertoald to come out and fight.

Bertoald answered from the walls, "If you will consider waiting for me and keeping the rest of your army in check some distance away, the two of us may meet in single combat to be judged by God."

But Landeric refused to do so.

"Since you dare not fight," added Bertoald, "the next time our lords join in battle because of what your forces are doing, let you and I both wear red clothing and be out in front where the battle lines come together. There your skill and mine will be plainly seen. Let us promise each other before God to be true to our word."

[26] This exchange took place on the day of the feast of Saint Martin the bishop [11 November].

When Theuderic found out part of his kingdom had been overrun by Chlothar contrary to the treaty, he came without delay at Christmas with an army to Étampes on the river Louet. There Merovech, the son of Chlothar, came to meet him along with Landeric and a large force. The ford across the river Louet was narrow and scarcely a third of Theuderic's army had crossed over when the battle started. Wherever Bertoald made an attack, he called on Landeric in accordance with the agreement, but Landeric refused to get as involved in the actual fighting as he had promised. In this battle, Bertoald was killed along with his followers by Chlothar's forces because he got too far ahead of the other troops. Bertoald did not try to get away, since he figured he was to be removed from office by Protadius. Merovech, the son of Chlothar, was taken prisoner. Landeric fled. A great part of Chlothar's army was cut down in the fight.

Theuderic entered Paris as victor. Theudebert made peace with Chlothar at Compiègne and both armies returned home without losses.

[27] IN THE 10TH YEAR OF THE REIGN OF THEUDERIC [**a. 605**], Protadius was appointed, at Theuderic's command but at Brunhild's instigation, to replace the mayor of the palace. Protadius was very bright and energetic in all matters, but cruelly unfair to people. He acted too strictly on behalf of the fisc, trying cleverly to fill it and to enrich himself with the property of individuals. He tried to humble each and every person he discovered of noble lineage, so that there would be no one around to take the office he had procured. Too smart for his own good in these and other matters, he gained the enmity of almost everyone in Burgundy.

Brunhild never stopped admonishing her grandson Theuderic to move his forces against Theudebert, saying that Theudebert was not the son of Childebert but of a certain gardener; Protadius supported this advice. Eventually Theuderic commanded the army to get under way.

When Theuderic and the army laid out their camp at a place called Quierzy, Theuderic was urged by his *leudes* to make peace with Theudebert. Only Protadius urged that battle be joined. Theudebert was located not far from there with his army. The opportunity now presented itself for the whole army of Theuderic to rush upon Protadius, saying that it was better for one man to die than for the whole army to be put in danger. Protadius was sitting in King Theuderic's tent with Peter, the chief physician, playing a board-game. As the army completely surrounded Protadius, Theuderic's *leudes* prevented the king from approaching the scene. Theuderic sent Uncelen to issue his order to the army to desist from waylaying Protadius.

Uncelen immediately announced to the army, "Lord Theuderic orders that Protadius be killed."

Falling upon Protadius, the troops cut through the tent everywhere with their swords and killed him.

Theuderic, in confusion and under compulsion, made peace with his brother, Theudebert, and both armies returned home without losses.

[28] IN THE 11TH YEAR OF THE REIGN OF THEUDERIC [**a. 606**], after the death of Protadius, Claudius, a Roman by birth, was chosen to replace him as mayor of the palace. He was a wise man, a delightful teller of stories, and

energetic in all matters. He practiced forbearance, was full of good advice and was well educated in letters. Completely reliable, he sought friendship with everyone, and, as he was anxious to avoid the sorry example of his predecessors, he showed himself gentle and forbearing when he had risen to power. He suffered this one defect — he was too fat.

IN THE 12TH YEAR OF THE REIGN OF THEUDERIC [a. 607], Uncelen who had deceitfully called for the death of Protadius, had his foot cut off at the instigation of Brunhild. Despoiled of his property, he was reduced to the meanest circumstances.

[29]     Brunhild also arranged by order of Theuderic for the patrician Wulf to be killed at the villa of Faverney; Wulf had agreed to the death of Protadius. Ricomer, a Roman by birth, was chosen to replace him in the office of patrician.

In the same year, a son by the name of Merovech was born to Theuderic by a concubine. Chlothar received him from the holy baptismal font.

[30]     In the same year, Theuderic sent Aridius, bishop of Lyons, Rocco, and the constable Eborinus to Wetteric, king of Spain. Their mission was to bring back Ermenberga, the king of Spain's daughter, so she might be married to Theuderic. When in Spain, they gave oaths that Ermenberga would never be removed as queen by Theuderic. They received her and delivered her at Chalon to Theuderic, who was delighted to give her a warm welcome. It was his grandmother Brunhild's doing once again that he did not have intercourse with his bride. His grandmother Brunhild and his sister Theudila told him things that made Ermenberga odious to him. After a year, Theuderic sent Ermenberga back to Spain, deprived of her property.

[31]     Furious at these events, Wetteric sent an embassy to Chlothar. An envoy from Chlothar along with Wetteric's envoy went to Theudebert. Likewise, Theudebert's envoys along with those of Chlothar and Wetteric approached Ago [Agilulf], king of Italy. All four kings arranged to attack Theuderic with armies from all sides, take away his kingdom, and condemn him to death, because they stood in such fearful awe of him. As for the envoy of the Goths, he set sail and returned to Spain by sea from Italy. But it was God's will that this plan not be realized. When Theuderic found out about it, he held it in utter contempt.

[32]     In this year, Theuderic, following the faithless advice of Aridius, bishop of Lyons, and the recommendation of his grandmother Brunhild, had Desiderius, who had returned from exile, stoned to death. From the day of his death, God saw fit to reveal continually wonderful miracles at his tomb — which makes one believe that the kingdom of Theuderic and his sons was destroyed because of this evil deed.

[33]    In this year, Wetteric died [a. 610] and Sisebut succeeded to the kingdom of Spain [a. 612-21]. He was a wise man and greatly praised throughout Spain, being very pious. For he had fought boldly against the empire and subjected the province of Cantabria, once held by the Franks, to the kingdom of the Goths. A duke by the name of Francio had governed Cantabria in the time of the Franks and for a long time had paid tribute to the Frankish kings. But after Cantabria had been brought back to the imperial side, the Goths took possession of it first, as mentioned above, and Sisebut took many cities on the coast away from the empire and razed them to the ground.

When Romans were cut down by his forces, Sisebut used to say with genuine piety, "It makes me sad that the blood of so many people should be shed in my time."

He spared the life of anyone he could reach.

The kingdom of the Goths in Spain was established from the coast to the Pyrenees mountains.

[34]    Ago [Agilulf], king of the Lombards, married the sister of Grimoald and Gundoald. Her name was Theudelinda and she was a Frank by birth. Childebert had been betrothed to her. When he had put her aside on the advice of Brunhild, Gundoald moved with his property to Italy and took along his sister, Theudelinda, whom he gave in marriage to Ago. Gundoald took a wife from a noble Lombard family, by whom had two sons by the names of Gundebert and Charibert. King Ago, son of King Authari, had a son by Theudelinda by the name of Adaloald and a daughter by the name of Gundeberga. Because Gundoald was too popular with the Lombards, King Ago and Theudelinda, who by now were jealous of him, saw to it that he died; he was struck by an arrow when sitting on a stool defecating.

[35]    IN THE 13TH YEAR OF THE REIGN OF THEUDERIC **[a. 608]**. At this time Theudebert was married to Bilichild, whom Brunhild had purchased from merchants. Bilichild was accomplished and esteemed highly by all the Austrasians. She bore Theudebert's simpleness with dignity. She certainly did not regard herself as inferior to Brunhild, and indeed her envoys often conveyed her contempt for Brunhild. At the same time, Brunhild was always going on about Bilichild having been her slave. Finally, when they had angered one another by having envoys running about bearing messages of this kind, a meeting was arranged on the boundary between the Colroy district and the Santois so that the two queens could meet to discuss making peace between Theuderic and Theudebert. But Bilichild refused to come to it on the advice of the Austrasians.

*The following account of Saint Columbanus is derived quite closely from the saint's vita written by Jonas of Bobbio ca. 640. Fredegar preferred his miracles of the saints post mortem, and so some of Jonas's more extraordinary incidents have been excised.*

[36] IN THE 14TH YEAR OF THE REIGN OF THEUDERIC **[a. 609]**. The renown of the blessed Columbanus [† 615] had by now increased everywhere in regions throughout all the provinces of Gaul and Germany. He was praised and venerated by everyone to such a degree that King Theuderic often came to him at Luxeuil and begged in all humility to be recommended in his prayers. As the king came quite often, the man of God began to reproach him for being mixed up in adulterous relations with concubines rather than enjoying the solace of legitimate marriage; the royal stock should issue from an honorable queen and not be sprung from whores.

The king said he would submit to the direction of the man of God and promised to refrain from all illicit relations. Thereupon, the old serpent entered the mind of the king's grandmother Brunhild (as she was a second Jezebel) and, when she had been goaded by the sting of pride, roused her against the man of God, for she perceived that Theuderic obeyed him. In fact she feared that if Theuderic had the concubines ejected and set a queen over the court, he would deprive her of the dignities and honors that were her due.

One day the blessed Columbanus happened to come to Brunhild, for at the time she was staying at the villa of Brocaria. When she saw him come into the court, she brought to the man of God the sons whom Theuderic had from adulterous relationships. When he saw them, he asked what they wanted from him.

"They are the sons of the king," Brunhild replied. "Give them the strength of your blessing."

"Know this," he said. " They'll never take up the scepters of kings: they are sprung from whores."

Furious, she ordered the children away. As the man of God was crossing the threshold on his way out of the court, there was a terrifying clap of thunder, but it did not check the fury of the wretched woman.

She next contrived to make difficulties. She sent orders to the neighbors of the monastery for them to deny any of the monks passage out of the monastery's lands and to withhold from the monks refuge or any aid.

Seeing the anger of the royal family roused against him, the blessed Columbanus hurried to them to warn them to curb the effects of their wretched obstinacy. At the time, the king was at the royal villa of Époisses. The man of God arrived when the sun was setting. Attendants informed the king that he had arrived and did not wish to enter the king's quarters. At that point Theuderic said that it was better to pay honor to the man of God with appropriate refreshment than to provoke God's anger by offending one of his servants. He ordered suitable items prepared in royal style and sent to the servant of God. And so attendants brought offerings and presented them to Columbanus as the king had ordered.

When he saw the food and drink served up in royal style, Columbanus asked what they were trying do.

"These are for you," said the attendants, "sent to you from the king."

Treating the food as accursed, Columbanus said, "It is written, 'the Almighty rejects the gifts of the impious.' It is not fitting that the lips of the servants of God be polluted by the food of one who denies the servants of God access not only to their own dwellings but those of others."

When he had spoken these words, the vessels were broken into pieces, the wine and drink spilt on the floor and everything else scattered about.

Terrified, the servants related to the king what had happened. Struck with the same terror, Theuderic rushed to see the man of God at daybreak, accompanied by his grandmother. They begged forgiveness for their offense and promised to do better in the future. Columbanus returned to his monastery, placated by these promises.

But they did not feel bound by their word for very long and broke their promises; their wretched behavior grew worse and the king went back to his adultery. When the blessed Columbanus heard, he sent the king a letter full of reproach and threatened excommunication if the king tried to put off mending his ways. Brunhild became infuriated again and aroused the king against Columbanus. She made every effort to agitate the king. Pleas were made to the leading men, courtiers, and all the magnates to stir up the king against Columbanus. She tried to inveigle the bishops into disparaging his faith and dishonoring the rule which he made his monks observe. The palace officials, complying with the promptings of the wretched queen, stirred up the king against the man of God, forcing him to go investigate the religious observance of the monastery.

And so driven to it, the king came to the man of God at Luxeuil. The king demanded to know why he deviated from the practices of the Gauls and why access to the inner precinct of the monastery was not given to all Christians. Blessed Columbanus, as he was a bold and spirited man, replied to the king's reproach that it was not the custom of the monks to allow lay persons and strangers to his rule to enter the residences of God's servants but that they had also prepared here fit and suitable quarters for welcoming all sorts of guests.

"If you want us out of generosity to grant gifts and fill your needs," the king replied, "the whole monastery must be opened up to all."

"If you try to violate what up to now has been held together by the restrictions of our rule," answered the man of God, "I shall not suffer your gifts or assistance of any kind. And if the reason you come to this place is to destroy the communal life of God's servants and to pollute the discipline of the rule, your kingdom will soon fall to ruin and disappear, along with the royal offspring."

Later events showed this to be true.

By this point, the king had rashly entered the refectory. As a consequence of these alarming words, he quickly stepped back outside.

Then the man of God heaped dreadful reproaches upon the king, and Theuderic said to him in return, "You are hoping I will give you the martyr's crown."

The king said he was not so mad as to commit such a crime, but had a better idea: he had the means of ensuring that someone who deviated from the customs of the whole world would go back to where he came from. With one voice the courtiers shouted out their desire not to have in these quarters someone who refused to associate with all. In reply, blessed Columbanus said he would not leave the precincts of the community unless he were dragged out by force.

The king then left, leaving one of his magnates by the name of Baudulf. When the king was gone, Baudulf drove the man of God from the monastery and led him into exile to the town of Besançon, until such time as the king should tell him what he wanted done with him.

Columbanus afterward saw that he was not restricted by guards nor bothered in any way — for all saw that the power of God burned in him, and for that reason stood clear of the treatment he was receiving to avoid being associated in the offense. So on a Sunday he climbed to the summit of a precipitous section of the hill. Now the site of the town is such that there were no pathways to this spot. For there are dense thickets on the broad side of the hill's slope, and high, steep banks rise up, everywhere cut sheer and surrounded by the course of the river Doubs. There he waited until midday to see if anyone might block his path back to his monastery. Since there was no one to stop him, he marched back through the middle of the town with his companions to his monastery.

When Brunhild and Theuderic heard of his return from exile, they were goaded even more fiercely to anger.

They gave orders to Count Berthar to diligently hunt him down with a troop of soldiers, and they also sent Baudulf (whom they had employed above). When these two arrived, they found the blessed Columbanus in the church, singing psalms and praying with the entire congregation of brethren.

They addressed him in this way, "We beg you to obey the king's commands as well as our own and to leave by the same route you took when you first came here."

"Surely," said Columbanus, "I can't believe that the Creator would be pleased if I returned to my native land when I left it for the sake of Christ."

When Berthar saw that the man of God would by no means obey him, he departed, leaving certain men who were of a more savage disposition. Those who remained behind, however, urged the man of God to take pity on them. They were unfortunate, so they said, to have been left to do such a job; he should help them in their danger, for if they did not drag him away by force, they would be subject to the penalty of death. But Columbanus said that he had already borne witness a number of times that he would not leave unless dragged out by force. Impelled by fear from all sides, the dangerous dilemma that faced them gave some the courage to lay hands on the vestments that Columbanus wore. Others flung themselves at his knees, begging him in tears to forgive their great offense of complying, not with his wishes, but with the commands of the king.

Now that the man of God saw that there would be danger for others if he maintained his own strict standards, he left, thoroughly stricken with grief and sadness. Guards were set who were not to leave his side until such time as he was driven from the jurisdiction of the kingdom. Their leader was Ragumundus, who led him to Nantes.

And so expelled from Theuderic's kingdom, Columbanus was inclined to return to Ireland. But as no one at all has the power of choosing the road he will travel without the permission of the Most High, in fact the holy man sought out Italy, and built a monastery in a place called Bobbio. Full of days, he departed from his holy life and went to Christ.

[37] IN THE 15TH YEAR OF THE REIGN OF THEUDERIC [a. 610], Alsace, where Theuderic had been brought up and which he held by a written directive of his father Childebert, was overrun in a barbarous fashion by Theudebert. As a result, a meeting was arranged between the two kings at the fortress of Seltz so that the issue could settled by a judgment of the Franks. Theuderic came there with two divisions of ten thousand men, but Theudebert arrived with a great army of Austrasians eager to fight a battle. Surrounded on all sides by Theudebert's army, Theuderic was terrified and against his will had to agree to the terms of a treaty recognizing Alsace as part of Theudebert's kingdom. At the same time, he even lost the Santois, the Thurgau and Campanensis, regions he had often claimed. Both parties returned home.

In those days, also, the Alamanni invaded the region of Avenches beyond the Jura. As they were plundering the district, Counts Abbelen and Herpin, along with other counts of the region, led an army to intercept them. Battle was joined at Wangen. The Alamanni defeated the Transjurans and cut down a large number of them. They set much of the district of Avenches on fire, led away great numbers of people as captives, and headed back home with their plunder. Following these outrages, Theuderic gave his constant attention to planning how he could crush Theudebert.

In this year, Bilichild was killed by Theudebert. He took as his wife a girl by the name of Theudechild.

IN THE 16TH YEAR OF THE REIGN OF THEUDERIC [a. 611], the king sent an embassy to Chlothar to inform him of his intention of marching against Theudebert, because Theudebert was not his brother [cf. c. 27]. If Chlothar would agree not to help Theudebert, Chlothar would, in the event of Theuderic's victory, receive jurisdiction over the Duchy of Dentelin, which he had renounced in favor of Theudebert [cf. c. 20]. After envoys were exchanged and an agreement to this effect was approved by Theuderic and Chlothar, Theuderic mustered an army.

[38] IN THE 17TH YEAR OF THE REIGN OF THEUDERIC [a. 612], in the month of May, an army gathered at Langres drawn from all the provinces of his kingdom. Marching by way of Andelot, it took the fortress of Naix, before advancing to Toul and capturing the city. Theudebert with an army of Austrasians arrived and the armies clashed in the countryside around Toul. Theuderic defeated Theudebert and laid his army low. A great host of brave men in his forces were slaughtered in the battle. Theudebert retreated through the territory of Metz, crossed the Vosges, and fled to Cologne.

As Theuderic with his army followed in pursuit, the blessed and apostolic Leudegesius, bishop of the city of Mainz, who admired Theuderic's ability and hated Theudebert's folly, came to Theuderic and said, "Finish what you started. You must get right to the root of this matter to benefit from it. There is a country story in which a wolf went up into a mountain and, when its cubs had begun to hunt, the wolf summoned them to the mountain and said, 'In every direction as far as the eye can see, you have no friends, save the few who are of your own stock.' Finish what you started."

Theuderic and his army went through the Ardennes and reached Zülpich where Theudebert came against him, along with Saxons, Thuringians, and other peoples he could gather from across the Rhine or anywhere else. There a battle was fought once again. It is said that the Franks and other peoples had never seen such a battle perhaps since ancient times. The slaughter by both armies was such that in the thick of the battle, where fighting units contended with each other, the corpses of those killed had no room to fall, but the dead stood upright side by side with other corpses, as if they were all alive. But with God leading the way, Theuderic again defeated Theudebert, and from Zülpich to Cologne Theudebert's army everywhere littered the ground, cut down by the sword. The same day, Theuderic reached Cologne and took possession of Theudebert's entire treasure there.

Theuderic sent Berthar the chamberlain across the Rhine after Theudebert. Assiduously pursuing Theudebert, who by now was fleeing with a few men, Berthar captured him and delivered him for display before Theuderic at Cologne. Theudebert was stripped of his royal vestments. His horse with the royal harness and all its trappings was granted to Berthar by Theuderic. Theudebert was sent in chains to Chalon. Theudebert's son, a little boy by the name of Merovech, took his last breath. At Theuderic's command, someone took the boy by the foot and smashed his brains out against a rock.

Chlothar brought the duchy of Dentelin completely under his jurisdiction according to the agreement with Theuderic.

IN THE 18TH YEAR OF HIS REIGN [a. 613], Theuderic, now that he controlled all Austrasia, became very displeased with Chlothar's possession of the duchy of Dentelin and ordered an army to be mustered from Austrasia and Burgundy to oppose him. First he sent an embassy demanding Chlothar fully withdraw from the said duchy; otherwise, Chlothar should know that Theuderic would have his forces completely overrun Chlothar's kingdom. Events bore out the words of his envoys.

[39] In the same year also, when his army was marching against Chlothar, Theuderic died from dysentery at Metz. The army immediately returned home.

## The Reign of Chlothar II, a. 613-29

Brunhild was staying at Metz with the four sons of Theuderic — Sigibert, Childebert, Corbus, and Merovech — trying to establish Sigibert [II, a. 613] in the kingdom of his father, when Chlothar entered Austrasia, at the invitation of Arnulf [of Metz], Pippin [I of Landen], and other leading men.

[40] As Chlothar approached Andernach, Brunhild was staying at Worms with the sons of Theuderic and sent envoys by the names of Chadoin and Erpo to Chlothar, warning him to withdraw from Theuderic's kingdom, which had been left to his sons. Chlothar responded by telling Brunhild through envoys that he would promise to abide by whatever the Franks, under God's leadership, decided amongst themselves — their decision being determined by those chosen to make this judgment.

Brunhild dispatched Theuderic's eldest son Sigibert to Thuringia. She sent with him Warnachar, mayor of the palace, Alboin, and other leading men to recruit the peoples across the Rhine, so that resistance could be offered to Chlothar.

After their departure, she sent an order for Alboin and the others to kill Warnachar, because he wanted to go over to Chlothar's side. After Alboin read the order, he tore it up and threw it on the ground. It was discovered by a retainer of Warnachar and restored on a wax tablet. When Warnachar read the order and saw that his life was at stake, he began to think seriously about the overthrow of Theuderic's sons and about giving his allegiance to Chlothar. He gave the peoples who were already recruited secret advice causing them to withdraw their help from Brunhild and Theuderic's sons.

The envoys returned and accompanied Brunhild and the sons of Theuderic to Burgundy. They sent officials all around Austrasia and attempted to [41] muster an army. As for the Burgundaefarones, both bishops and other *leudes*, they feared and hated Brunhild. Conferring with Warnachar, they decided that none of the sons of Theuderic should escape; they would overthrow all of them, kill Brunhild, and seek out the rule of Chlothar. Events bear this out.

At the command of Brunhild and Sigibert, the son of Theuderic, an army [42] from Burgundy and Austrasia marched against Chlothar. When Sigibert reached the territory of Châlons-sur-Marne and the plains on the river Aisne, Chlothar and his forces intercepted him. By now Chlothar was accompanied by many Austrasians, due to the efforts of the mayor of the palace Warnachar. For some time he had made such arrangements with the agreement of Aletheus, the patrician, and Dukes Rocco, Sigoald and Eudila. Before the battle began, just at the point when the forces should have engaged the enemy, a signal was given, and Sigibert's army retreated and returned home. As was agreed, Chlothar followed slowly with his army until he reached the Saône river. He captured three of Theuderic's sons — Sigibert, Corbus and Merovech, whom he had received from the baptismal font. Childebert mounted a horse and fled, never to return. The army of the Austrasians returned home without losses.

Warnachar, mayor of the palace, with almost all the rest of the leading men of Burgundy, saw to it that Brunhild and Theuderic's sister Theudila were brought from the villa Orba in the Transjuran territory and delivered by the constable Erpo to Chlothar at the village of Renève on the river Vingeanne. Sigibert [II] and Corbus, the sons of Theuderic, were killed at the command of Chlothar. Because he had received Merovech from the holy baptismal font, Chlothar had great affection for him. Chlothar in secret had Merovech taken to Neustria and placed in the care of the *grafio* Ingobad. Merovech lived there for many years.

Brunhild was brought into Chlothar's presence. He harbored the deepest hatred toward her and accused her of being responsible for the death of ten kings of the Franks — that is Sigibert [I]; Merovech and his father Chilperic [I]; Theudebert [II] and his son Chlothar; Merovech, the son of Chlothar [II]; and Theuderic [II] and his three sons, who had just been eliminated. Chlothar had Brunhild tortured in various ways for three days. First of all, he had her led through the whole army mounted on a camel. After this, he had her tied to the tail of a vicious horse by her hair, one foot, and one arm. She was then torn to pieces by the hooves and the pace of the galloping horse.

Warnachar was appointed mayor of the palace for the kingdom of Burgundy. He received an oath from Chlothar that he would never be dismissed during his lifetime. In Austrasia, likewise, Rado obtained the equivalent office.

The entire kingdom of the Franks was secured just as during the reign of the first Chlothar [a. 558-561]. All the treasuries were put under the authority of the second Chlothar. He exercised that authority successfully for sixteen years, maintaining peace with all the neighboring peoples. Chlothar was habitually forbearing, well-read, god-fearing, and a generous donor to churches and priests. He gave alms to the poor, showing himself to be liberal to all and full of piety. His constant hunting was excessive and at the end he paid too much attention to the suggestions of women and girls, for which reason his *leudes* spoke badly of him.

[43] When, in the 30th year of his reign [i.e. a. 613], he had taken hold of the kingship of Burgundy and Austrasia, he appointed Erpo, a Frank by birth, as duke in the place of Eudila in the district across the Jura. Erpo was very quick to take measures for keeping the peace in the district, curbing the foolishness of evil doers. As a result, he was killed by the locals who had the audacity to rise against him, at the instigation of his enemies and with the advice of the patrician Aletheus, Bishop Leudemund, and Count Herpin. When Chlothar arrived with Queen Berthetrude at the villa of Marlenheim in Alsace, he took measures to keep the peace and cut down many of those law-breakers.

[44] The same Leudemund, bishop of Sion, came to Queen Berthetrude and, on the advice of Aletheus, made her this disgraceful proposal in secret: Chlothar, he said, was bound to pass away this very year, so she should transfer in secret as much treasure as she could to his city of Sion, because it was a very safe place. Aletheus would be prepared to leave his wife and marry Queen Berthetrude. Because Aletheus was of the royal stock of the Burgundians, he could take the kingdom after Chlothar. When she had heard the suggestion, Queen Berthetrude, fearing there might be truth here, burst into tears and went away to her chamber. Leudemund realized that he had endangered himself with this kind of talk and fled in the night to Sion. From there he sought refuge in Luxeuil with lord Eustasius, the abbot. Afterwards the abbot got Chlothar to pardon Leudemund for his offenses, and the bishop returned to his city. While Chlothar was staying at the villa of Mâlay-le-Roi

[near Sens] with his leading officials, he ordered Aletheus to come to him. His wicked plan was disclosed. Chlothar ordered him to be cut down by the sword.

IN THE 33RD YEAR OF THE REIGN OF CHLOTHAR [a. 616], the king ordered the mayor of the palace Warnachar to come with all the bishops of Burgundy and Burgundaefarones to the villa of Bonneuil [near Paris]. There he gave assent to all their just petitions and issued directives to confirm them.

[45]    I shall relate how the nation of the Lombards came to render tribute of 12,000 solidi to the power of the Franks every year, and I shall not make a secret of how they ceded the two cities of Aosta and Susa, along with their territories, to the Franks.

On the death of their prince Cleph [a. 574], the twelve dukes of the Lombards went twelve years without kings. At that time, as may be found written above [Bk III 68, *omitted in this translation*], they overran districts within the kingdom of the Franks. To compensate for this presumption, they ceded the cities of Aosta and Susa with all their territories and people to the kingdom of Guntram. Thereafter, they dispatched an embassy to the emperor Maurice: the twelve dukes each sent a representative to seek peace and patronage (*patrocinium*) from the empire. Likewise the twelve sent other representatives to Guntram and Childebert, with an offer that, if the Lombards could have the patronage and protection of the Franks, they would pay 12,000 solidi every year to the two kings as tribute, and likewise cede to Guntram's kingdom the valley of Lanzo [north-west of Turin]. The dukes were prepared to agree to the patronage through their envoys wherever was most convenient. Thereafter they chose to give their full allegiance to the patronage of the Franks. With the permission of Guntram and Childebert, the Lombards soon raised Duke Authari to the kingship over them [a. 584-590]. Another Authari, likewise a duke, subjected himself and his entire duchy to the authority of the empire, and remained in that relationship. And every year King Authari paid over the tribute that the Lombards had promised to the kingdom of the Franks. After his death, his son Ago [Agilulf, a. 590-616] was raised to the kingship; he also paid the tribute.

IN THE 34TH YEAR OF THE REIGN OF CHLOTHAR [a. 617], three envoys, nobles from the nation of the Lombards by the names of Agilulf, Pompeius and Gauto, were sent by King Ago to Chlothar. They were trying to claim that the 12,000 solidi they paid every year to the treasury of the Franks should be canceled. Cleverly they delivered in private three thousand solidi, of which Warnachar took a thousand, Gundeland [mayor of Neustria] a thousand and Chuc [mayor of Austrasia?] a thousand. At the same time, they paid thirty-six thousand solidi to Chlothar. On the advice of the above mentioned officials, who had secretly received gifts, Chlothar canceled the obligation on the part of the Lombards to pay tribute and established with oaths and agreements eternal friendship with them.

[46] IN THE 35TH YEAR OF THE REIGN OF CHLOTHAR [a. 618], Queen Berthetrude died. Chlothar loved her with special affection, and all the *leudes*, recognizing her goodness, held her in high esteem.

[47] IN THE 39TH YEAR OF THE REIGN OF CHLOTHAR [a. 622], the king shared the kingship with his son Dagobert and appointed him king over the Austrasians, keeping for himself [Austrasian] territories facing Neustria and Burgundy bounded by the Ardennes and Vosges.

[48] IN THE 40TH YEAR OF THE REIGN OF CHLOTHAR [a. 623], a man by the name of Samo, in origin a Frank from the territory of Senonagus, recruited a number of merchants to go and do business among the Slavs called Wends. The Slavs were in the process of rebelling against the Avars, called Huns, and their king, Khagan.

Since ancient times, the Wends had been *befulci* of the Huns, so that when the Huns conducted a military expedition against some other people, the Huns would mobilize their forces and take up a position in front of the camp, but the Wends would do the fighting. If the Wends were able to win, then the Huns would advance to take booty, but if the Wends were beaten, they would get the support of the Huns, and the Wends would be able to recover their strength. Thus they were called *befulci* by the Huns because they drew up their battle line and advanced before the Huns into the thick of the fighting twice.

Every year in winter the Huns used to come among the Slavs and take their wives and daughters to bed. Over and above other humiliating burdens they endured, the Slavs paid tribute. The sons of the Huns who were born of the wives and daughters of the Wends, finally unable to bear the wickedness and humiliation, rejected the rule of the Huns and, as I said above, began a revolt.

When the Wends set out on an expedition against the Huns, Samo the merchant, whom I mentioned above, went on the expedition with them. The ability he showed against the Huns was such as to excite wonder, and the Wends cut down a great multitude of the Huns. The Wends, recognizing Samo's ability, chose him to be king over them. He reigned successfully for thirty-five years. Under his leadership they engaged in a number of battles against the Huns: the Wends always won through his planning and ability.

Samo had twelve wives of Wendish stock and by them he had twenty two sons and fifteen daughters.

[49]     In this same 40th year of the reign of Chlothar, Adaloald, king of the Lombards [a. 616-626], and son of King Ago, on succeeding his father to the kingship, kindly received an envoy of the emperor Maurice [†602]. The envoy's name was Eusebius and he came to trick the king.

Adaloald was persuaded by Eusebius to be anointed in a bath with I know not what ointment and, after the anointing, could do nothing unless urged to do it by Eusebius. The king was convinced by Eusebius to arrange to have all the chief men and great nobles in the kingdom of the Lombards killed; when they were eliminated, the king and all the Lombard people were to surrender to the empire.

Now by the time the king had cut down twelve of them — and they quite innocent of any offense — the other nobles saw that their lives were in
[50] danger. As a result, all the most noble lords of the Lombard people unanimously chose to raise to the kingship Arioald [a. 626-36], Duke of Turin and the husband of Adaloald's sister, Gundeberga. Adaloald died, swollen up by poison. Arioald immediately seized the throne.

Taso, one of the dukes of the Lombards, puffed up with pride because he governed the province of Tuscany, started a rebellion against King Arioald.

[51]     Queen Gundeberga was handsome in appearance, kindly in all matters, full of Christian piety, generous in giving alms, and unsurpassed for her goodness. For all these reasons she was beloved by all. There was a certain man of Lombard birth by the name of Adalulf engaged in constant service to the king in the palace. One day when he came to the queen and stood in her presence, Queen Gundeberga, holding him in the same esteem as everyone else, said that Adalulf was blessed with a fine build.

Hearing this remark, he said to Gundeberga in private, "You saw fit to praise my build, order me to your bed."

She adamantly refused, and contemptuously spat in his face.

Adalulf, recognizing that his life was in jeopardy, immediately ran to King Arioald requesting greater privacy to disclose what he had to tell him.

He was granted the opportunity, and said to king, "My mistress, your queen, Gundeberga, for three days has been discussing with Duke Taso how she might kill you with poison, marry Taso, and raise him to the kingship."

King Arioald believed the lies he heard and exiled Gundeberga to a single tower in the fortress of Lomello.

Chlothar sent envoys to King Arioald to ask why he had humiliated Gundeberga, a kinswoman of the Franks [cf. c. 34], by exiling her. Arioald answered, believing the lies he told were true.

At that point, one of the envoys by the name of Ansoald said to Arioald, not as if he had been charged to do so, but on his own, "You can be rid of any criticism in this matter. Order the man who told you tales of this kind to arm himself. Let another represent the side of the queen and each come forward armed for single combat. Through these two combatants one may learn God's judgment, whether Gundeberga is innocent of the charge or — it may turn out — guilty."

Since this suggestion pleased King Arioald and all the chief men of his palace, he ordered Adalulf to arm himself and come forward to fight. Meanwhile, on Gundeberga's side, she and her cousin Aripert arranged for a man by the name of Pitto to come forward armed for battle against Adalulf. When the fighters engaged, Adalulf was killed by Pitto. Gundeberga returned from her three year exile and was immediately raised to the queenship.

[52] In the 41st year of the reign of king Chlothar [a. 624], when Dagobert was already ruling capably in Austrasia, Chrodoald, one of the leading men from the noble house of the Agilolfings, fell into disfavor with Dagobert. The disfavor was brought on by the blessed Bishop Arnulf, the mayor of the palace Pippin, and other prominent magnates in Austrasia, who said that, though endowed with vast properties, Chrodoald greedily overran the property of others; pride and self-importance were his distinguishing features, and nothing good could be found in him. Since Dagobert already wanted him killed for his crimes, Chrodoald turned to Chlothar in hopes that Chlothar might see fit to intervene with his son to spare his life. Chlothar and Dagobert met, and, during the discussion of other matters, Chlothar asked for Chrodoald's life. Dagobert promised that, if Chrodoald made emends for the criminal deeds he had committed, his life would not be in jeopardy. But Dagobert did not bother to wait. Chrodoald was killed at the king's command while accompanying Dagobert to Trier. Berthar, a man from Scarponne, drew his sword and cut off Chrodoald's head at the door to his chamber.

[53] In the 42nd year of the reign of Chlothar [a. 625], Dagobert, at the command of his father, came honorably and in royal state with his *leudes* to Clichy near Paris. There he married Gomatrude, the sister of Queen Sichild [Chlothar's wife].

On the third day after the nuptials had been concluded a serious dispute arose between Chlothar and his son Dagobert. The latter claimed that he wished to take under his jurisdiction all the lands which belonged to the kingdom of the Austrasians. Chlothar stoutly rejected the claim and said he would concede nothing. Twelve Franks were chosen by the two kings to bring an end to the dispute by their decision. Lord Arnulf, bishop of Metz, with other bishops was chosen to be among them, and most affably, as became his holiness, he spoke in favor of peace and harmony between father and son. Finally the father was reconciled to the son by the bishops and the wisest of the leading officials. And Chlothar restored to him in its entirety the territory that had belonged to the kingdom of the Austrasians. Of this, he retained under his own jurisdiction only the regions located on this side of the Loire and in parts of Provence.

[54] IN THE 43RD YEAR OF THE REIGN OF CHLOTHAR [a. 626], Warnachar, mayor of the palace, died. His son Godin, who was not of a serious disposition, married his step-mother, Bertha, the same year. On account of this, Chlothar's attitude toward Godin changed to one of extreme anger. He ordered Duke Arnebert, who had married Godin's sister, to take his troops and kill him. Godin, realizing his life was in danger, retreated and with his wife went to King Dagobert in Austrasia, taking refuge in the church of Saint Epvre-lès-Toul, in utter fear of the king. Through envoys Dagobert kept interceding with King Chlothar to spare his life. Finally, Chlothar promised to grant Godin his life provided he left Bertha, whom he had married against the rules of canon law.

Now when Godin had left her and returned to the kingdom of Burgundy, Bertha went without delay to Chlothar and said that Godin would try to kill the king should he be brought before him. At Chlothar's command Godin was conducted to the chief holy places — the churches of Saint Medard at Soissons and Lord Dionysius [Saint Denis] at Paris — ostensibly to swear that he would always be faithful to Chlothar but actually until a suitable opportunity could be found of separating him from his men and killing him. Chramnulf, one of the leading officials, and the *domesticus* Waldebert said to Godin that he still had to go to the church of Saint Anianus in Orleans and to the threshold of Saint Martin in Tours to fulfill his oath. When Godin came at the dinner hour to a certain small villa on the outskirts of Chartres, guided there by Chramnulf who had pointed the place out, Chramnulf and Waldebert attacked him with their forces and killed him. As for those who stood by him to this point, some they killed and others they despoiled and let escape by flight.

In this year Palladius and his son Sidoc, bishops of Eauze, charged Aighyna, duke [of Aquitaine], with being implicated in a Gascon rebellion and were exiled.

Boso from the district of Étampes, the son of Audelenus, was killed by Duke Arnebert on the orders of Chlothar, who accused him of adultery with Queen Sichild.

In this year Chlothar met with the leading officials and *leudes* of Burgundy at Troyes. He was interested in whether they wanted to raise up another to the post held by Warnachar, now that he was dead. But they all unanimously decided that it would be fruitless to chose a mayor of the palace and fervently asked the king's gracious permission to deal directly with him.

[55] IN THE 44TH YEAR OF THE REIGN OF CHLOTHAR [a. 627], the bishops and all the leading men of his kingdom, both from Neustria and Burgundy, assembled with Chlothar at Clichy for the well-being of the king's affairs and the good of the country. While they were assembled, a man by the name of Ermarius, who was curator of the palace to Charibert, Chlothar's son, was killed by the retainers of Aighyna, a magnate of Saxon stock. The slaughter of a great many men would have come of this, but was curbed in the nick of time due to the intervention and forbearance of Chlothar. At Chlothar's command, Aighyna retired to the mount of Mercury [Montmartre] with a good-sized body of fighting men. Brodulf, Charibert's maternal uncle, gathered an army from all around, intending along with Charibert to attack Aighyna. Chlothar gave a special commission to the Burgundaefarones to crush promptly and forcefully whichever party tried to ignore his judgment. The fear this inspired caused both sides to quieten down at the king's command.

## The Reign of Dagobert, a. 629–39

[56] IN THE 46TH YEAR OF HIS REIGN [a. 629], Chlothar died and was buried in the church of Saint Vincent on the outskirts of Paris. When Dagobert learned that his father was dead, he ordered an army mobilized from all the *leudes* he ruled in Austrasia. He sent officials to Burgundy and Neustria to see to it that those regions chose his rule. When he came to Rheims on the way to Soissons, all the bishops and *leudes* of the kingdom of Burgundy submitted to him there. Moreover the bishops of Neustria and the greater part of its leading men sought Dagobert's rule. Charibert, his brother, was striving to take the kingdom if he could, but his simple-mindedness ensured that this desire had little effect. Intending to put his nephew in power, Brodulf started to lay traps against Dagobert but the outcome demonstrated the reward he got for his pains.

[57]     Now that the kingdom of Chlothar, both Neustria and Burgundy, had been taken over by Dagobert and the treasuries had been seized and subjected to his authority, he was finally moved by mercy. Taking the advice of wise men, Dagobert ceded districts and cities between the Loire and the Spanish frontier, which is located in regions of Gascony and the Pyrenees mountains. This area was sufficient for his brother Charibert to handle in the manner of a private person for as long as he lived: it comprised the districts of Toulouse, Cahors, Agen, Périgueux, Saintes, and what is bounded by them

facing the Pyrenees mountains. This is all he ceded for Charibert to rule and even tied to the concession agreements that would prevent Charibert ever daring to claim more of his father's kingdom from Dagobert.

Charibert chose Toulouse as his capital and ruled part of the province of Aquitaine. In the third year after he began to reign, he conquered all of Gascony with an army, reducing it to his authority and making his kingdom somewhat more extensive.

[58]    Dagobert, while now in the seventh year of his reign [cf. c. 47], took most of his father's kingdom, as I have said, and entered Burgundy. His arrival struck such fear in the bishops and leading officials dwelling in the kingdom of Burgundy, and in his other *leudes*, as to be a source of wonder to all. To the poor with judicial complaints, it inspired ardent joy. When Dagobert came to the city of Langres, he passed judgment among all the *leudes*, lofty and poor ones alike, with a fairness that was believed to be completely pleasing to God. No bribe intervened nor a regard for persons; all that ruled was justice, which the Most High loves. Next he went to Dijon and even spent a few days in Saint-Jean-de-Losne, such was the importance he attached to rendering justice to all the people of his kingdom. He was full of a desire to dispense his goodness and neither slept nor ate, seriously thinking all could leave his presence having received justice.

On the same day that he was making preparations to leave Saint-Jean-de-Losne for Chalon, just before dawn, he gave an order as he was entering his bath for the killing of Brodulf, the uncle of his brother Charibert. Brodulf was killed by Dukes Amalgar and Arnebert and the patrician Willebad.

Then from Chalon, where he directed his attention to finishing the judicial work he had begun, Dagobert next went to Auxerre by way Autun, and came to Paris by way of Sens. There, leaving Gomatrude at the villa of Reuilly where he had married her, he married Nantechild one of his servant girls and raised her up to the queenship.

From the beginning of his reign up to this time, Dagobert placed the highest value on the advice of the blessed Arnulf, bishop of Metz, and Pippin, mayor of the palace, and as a consequence the king's rule over Austrasia prospered to such an extent that he was the subject of boundless praise from all peoples. Indeed, as it happened, such fear was raised by his ability that they were now quick to submit obediently to his authority. Even the peoples dwelling on the border of the Avars and the Slavs readily came to him to ask him to back them up; they promised confidently that if he did so he would subject to his authority the Avars, Slavs, and other groups of peoples as far as the empire. After the departure of the blessed Arnulf, he still made use of the advice of the mayor of the palace Pippin and Chunibert, bishop of Cologne. Being vigorously counseled by them, he ruled all the peoples subject to him with such a deep understanding of the requirements of justice and successful rulership that no previous king of the Franks earned more praise — until, as I said above, he came to Paris.

[59] IN THE 8TH YEAR OF HIS REIGN [a. 630], as the king traveled around Austrasia in royal state, he admitted to his bed a girl by the name of Ragnetrude, by whom he had a son that year by the name of Sigibert [III].

[60] Returning to Neustria, he chose his father's capital and was determined to stay there all the time. Since he had forgotten all about the justice he had once loved, greed drove him to covet the property of churches and of his *leudes*, and he wished with a shrewd longing to fill new treasuries with all the spoil he had amassed from everywhere. He surrendered himself to boundless sensuality. Three of his women were special and acted as queens and a great many more were concubines. These were the queens: Nantechild, Wulfegund, and Berchild. To have included the names of the concubines would have increased the size of this chronicle, because there were so many of them.

Now while he had a change of heart, as I said above, and his thoughts turned away from God, nevertheless, afterwards — and would that he had profited from this in obtaining the true reward — he generously disbursed limitless alms to the poor, and it is believed that he would have merited the eternal kingdom, if his keen sense of the value of almsgiving had not been hampered by his acquisitive impulses.

[61] Pippin perceived that Dagobert's *leudes* were groaning about the king's behavior. Pippin was the most circumspect of them all, very prudent, completely faithful, beloved by all for the love of justice that he had wisely taught to Dagobert when the latter had been following his advice. Therefore, though he was not in the least unmindful of justice nor averse to the path of goodness, when he came before Dagobert, he treated all matters with prudence and in every way showed himself to be circumspect. The Austrasians grew very angry with him and even tried to make him hateful to Dagobert, the better to bring about his death. But the love of justice and the fear of God, which he had devoutly embraced, saved him from evil.

[62] Indeed that very year he went to king Charibert along with Dagobert's son, Sigibert. Charibert came to Orleans and received Sigibert from the holy baptismal font.

Among the Neustrians, Aega was Dagobert's constant adviser.

This year the envoys that Dagobert had sent to Emperor Heraclius [610-641] returned home. Their names were Servatus and Paternus. They brought news that they had concluded an everlasting peace with Heraclius. As to the astounding deeds performed by Heraclius, I shall not pass them over.

[63] Heraclius had been patrician of all the provinces of Africa at the time

when Phocas, who, as is the way with tyrants, had killed the emperor Maurice [a. 582-602] and was ruling the empire he had seized in the worst way [a. 602-610]. Like a madman, Phocas threw his treasure into the sea, saying that he was giving gifts to Neptune. The senators saw that he would destroy the empire through foolishness, and, at the instigation of Heraclius, the senate seized Phocas, cut off his hands and feet, put a stone around his neck, and threw him into the sea. Heraclius with the agreement of the senate was raised up to the emperorship.

[64]     In the days of the emperors Maurice and Phocas, many provinces had been ravaged by Persian attacks. The emperor of the Persians in the usual way again attacked Heraclius with an army. Ravaging the provinces of the empire, the Persians came to the town of Chalcedon, took it by storm, and set it on fire. Next they approached Constantinople, the imperial capital, trying to destroy it [a. 626].

Heraclius came out to meet them with an army. He sent envoys to the emperor of the Persians, Chosroes [II, a. 590-628], and proposed that the two emperors should station their forces some distance away and meet in single combat by themselves. He to whom victory was given by the Most High should receive the empire of the loser as well as his people, without it suffering losses.

The emperor of the Persians agreed to the terms and promised that he would come out to fight in single combat. Heraclius took up his arms, leaving behind in readiness his men drawn up in battle array, and came forth like a new David to fight in single combat. Chosroes, the emperor of the Persians, had a certain patrician among his men whom he could see was a powerful fighter. The Persian emperor sent him to fight in his place against Heraclius, as if this were part of the agreement.

As the two men neared one another on horseback to begin the fight, Heraclius said to the patrician, whom he took for Chosroes, emperor of the Persians, "It was agreed that we should fight in single combat, why are others following behind you?"

As the patrician turned his head to have a look at who might be coming up behind him, Heraclius spurred his horse forward sharply with his heels and, drawing his sword, cut off the head of the patrician of the Persians.

Chosroes was defeated along with the Persians and thrown into confusion. He was killed during the retreat by his own people as if he were a tyrant. The Persians retreated and returned to their own homes.

Heraclius set sail and invaded Persia with his army. He reduced all of Persia to his authority, having captured treasures and seven sets of war harness. Persia was subjected to his authority for about three years after being ravaged. Thereafter, the Persians established an emperor over themselves again.

[65]     Heraclius was a fine-looking man, with a handsome face and a well-

proportioned body. He was stronger than anyone else and a distinguished fighter: he even killed a good many lions single-handedly in the arena and in the wild. Being quite well educated in letters, he became an astrologer. Through astrology he learned that, according to divine will, the empire was to be ravaged by circumcised peoples. Therefore he sent a legation to king Dagobert asking the king to order all Jews of his kingdom to be baptized in the Catholic faith. Right away Dagobert fulfilled his request. Heraclius decreed that the same be done through all the provinces of the empire. He did not know from where this disaster to the empire would come.

[66]    The descendants of Hagar, or Saracens, are, as a book of Orosius attests, a circumcised people who lived at one time on the side of the Caucasus mountains by the Caspian sea in a land called Ercolia. Their numbers increased greatly to the point where they took up arms and invaded the provinces of the emperor Heraclius to plunder them. Heraclius sent troops to stop the invasion. In the battle that resulted, the Saracens were victorious and cut down the forces of Heraclius in large numbers. It is said that in this battle 150,000 men were killed by the Saracens. The Saracens sent envoys offering to let Heraclius receive the spoils of battle.

Heraclius, wanting revenge on the Saracens, not spoils, refused the offer. When he had assembled a great host of soldiers from all the provinces of the empire, Heraclius sent an embassy to the Caspian gates. The Macedonian Alexander the Great had ordered the gates to be built of bronze on the shore of the Caspian sea and to be barred on account of the flood of extremely violent peoples who dwelt on the other side of the Caucasus mountains. Heraclius ordered the gates to be opened. Through them he admitted 150,000 fighters, hired with gold to help him in the war against the Saracens. The Saracens numbered almost 200,000, under two princes.

When the armies had pitched their camps not far from each other so that they could join battle the next day, that very night the army of Heraclius was struck by the sword of God: 52,000 of the soldiers in his camp died in their beds [Battle of Yarmuk, a. 636]. The next day when his men should have gone to battle, they saw that a major part of their troops had been killed by divine judgment and dared not join battle with the Saracens. All of Heraclius' army returned home, and the Saracens continued, as they had begun, to pillage the provinces of the emperor Heraclius.

By the time they were approaching Jerusalem, Heraclius saw that he could not stop their fury and, in the grip of a despondent bitterness, was already a follower of the heresy of Eutyches. Having left the Christian religion and having married the daughter of his sister, he was cruelly afflicted with fever and died [a. 641]. His successor to the imperial office was his son Constantine, in whose time the empire was severely ravaged.

[67] IN THE NINTH YEAR OF THE REIGN OF DAGOBERT [a. 631], King Charibert died, leaving a small son by the name of Chilperic, who soon after died. It is said that Dagobert was behind his being killed. Charibert's entire kingdom, along with Gascony, Dagobert immediately made subject to his authority. He arranged for Duke Barontus to take Charibert's treasure and deliver it to him. Barontus was responsible for the severe losses it suffered, for, in league with the treasurers, he misappropriated a good amount of the treasure.

[68] In this year, the Slavs called Wends killed Frankish merchants in Samo's kingdom, along with a host of others, and despoiled them of their property. This was the beginning of a quarrel between Dagobert and Samo, king of the Slavs.

Dagobert sent Sichar as an envoy to Samo, asking Samo to compensate fairly for the merchants his people had killed and the property they had wrongly seized. Samo did not want to see Sichar and did not allow him to come to him. Sichar dressed himself up like a Slav and along with his men got into the presence of Samo. He conveyed all of his instructions to Samo. But, as is the way with the heathen and those deformed by pride, Samo made no amends for the deeds committed by his people. He wanted only to fix a day in which justice could be rendered by both sides in regard to this dispute and others that had arisen between the parties.

Sichar, like a foolish envoy, used unsuitable language, which he had not been instructed to use, and threatened Samo. He said that Samo and the people of his kingdom owed service to Dagobert.

Now insulted, Samo replied, "The land we have is Dagobert's and we ourselves are too, provided he is determined to maintain friendship with us."

"It is not possible," said Sichar, "for Christians and servants of God to establish friendship with dogs."

Samo said in rebuttal, "If you are God's servants and we are his dogs, as long as you continue to act against him, we have received permission to bite you."

Sichar was ejected from Samo's presence.

When Sichar reported this to Dagobert, the king arrogantly ordered an army to be mobilized from all the kingdom of the Austrasians against Samo and the Wends. The army moved against the Wends in three mounted divisions. At the same time, the Lombards, in the pay of Dagobert, likewise attacked the Slavs.

The Slavs in various regions made preparations to resist. An army of Alamanni under Duke Chrodobert was victorious in the region it invaded. The Lombards too were victorious, and the Alamanni and Lombards took from the Slavs a good number of captives. But the Austrasians surrounded the fortress of Wogastisburg, fortified by a huge force of warlike Wends. In a three-day battle many men from Dagobert's army were cut down there. The Austrasians fled the field, leaving all their tents and property, and returned home.

Many times afterwards the Wends invaded Thuringia to pillage it and other districts in the kingdom of the Franks. Dervan, duke of the Sorbs, a people of Slavic descent, had long been dependent on the kingdom of the Franks, but even he yielded himself and his people to the kingdom of Samo. That victory won by the Wends against the Franks was due not so much to the courage of the Slavs as to the Austrasians' being out of their minds at seeing themselves hated by Dagobert and constantly despoiled.

[69]   In this year, Arioald, king of the Lombards [a. 626-636], quietly sent an envoy to Isaac the patrician [Exarch of Ravenna, a. 625-643] to ask him to kill Taso, duke of the province of Tuscany, by any means he could. In return for this favor, Arioald would immediately cede to the empire one hundred weight of gold from the three hundred weight the Lombards received from the Roman state as annual tribute.

When he heard the offer, Isaac the patrician pondered what tricks he could use to fulfill the request. He cunningly sent Taso a message suggesting that, as long as Taso was in disfavor with King Arioald, he could establish friendly ties with him; indeed he would help him against King Arioald. Taken in by such deceit, Taso went to Ravenna. Isaac sent him a message on the road saying that he dared not, out of fear of the emperor, receive Taso and his men within the walls of the city of Ravenna armed. Taso believed this message and had his men leave their arms outside the city. When he entered Ravenna, immediately those who had been made ready rushed Taso and killed him and all the men who had come with him.

King Arioald ceded one hundred weight of gold to Isaac and the empire, as he had promised. Thereafter only two hundred weight of gold were paid every year to the Lombards by the patrician of the Romans. A hundred-weight contains one hundred pounds. Right afterwards king Arioald died [a. 636].

[70]   All the Lombards had sworn to be faithful to Queen Gundeberga. Therefore she ordered a certain Rothari, one of the dukes from the territory of Brescia, to come to her and, forcing him to leave his wife, had him marry her; through her, all the Lombards, she said, would raise him to the kingship. Rothari was happy to agree and confirmed by oaths at the holy places that he would never set Gundeberga aside nor diminish at all her official position; loving her with a singular affection, in all respects he would give her the honor she deserved.

Induced by Gundeberga, all the chief men of the Lombards raised Rothari to the kingship [a. 636-52]. When Rothari began to rule, he killed many

Lombard nobles whom he felt were not obedient to him. In pursuit of peace Rothari imposed iron discipline and fear on the entire kingdom of the Lombards. Rothari forgot the oaths he had sworn to Gundeberga and put her away in a single chamber within the perimeter of the palace at Pavia and had her lead a private life. For five years he kept her in seclusion. Rothari never ceased wantonly reveling in his concubines. Because she was a Christian, Gundeberga blessed Almighty God in this tribulation, and constantly devoted herself to fasting and praying.

[71]   When God so pleased, the envoy Aubedo was sent on a delegation by Clovis [II, a. 639-57] to Rothari, King of the Lombards. He arrived in the Italian city of Pavia, also called Ticinum, and saw that the queen, whom he was used to seeing when he came on an embassy and who always welcomed him kindly, had been displaced. Among other matters, he brought it to Rothari's attention, as if instructed to do so, that the king ought not to humiliate his queen, a kinswoman of the Franks responsible for his obtaining the kingship; the kings of the Franks and the Franks, he suggested, were extremely displeased with the situation.

Rothari out of deference for the Franks immediately had Gundeberga come forth. After almost five years, Gundeberga at last visited the holy places in royal state throughout the city and beyond to pray. Rothari ordered her villas and fiscal properties restored to her. She afterwards happily held these and her official rank until the day of her death, enriched by great wealth and in royal splendor. Aubedo, to be sure, was richly rewarded by Queen Gundeberga.

Rothari with his army took away from the empire the coastal cities of Genoa, Albenga, Varigotti, Savona, Oderzo, and Luni. He pillaged them, took them by storm, and set them on fire. He seized the people, despoiled them, and condemned them to captivity. The walls of the said cities he destroyed to their foundations and ordered the cities to be called villages.

[72]   In this year, in the kingdom of the Avars, also called Huns, in Pannonia, a serious dispute arose. The matter at issue concerned who should succeed to the kingdom. The parties in the dispute were, on one side, an Avar and, on the other side, a Bulgar. Both sides gathered their forces and attacked one another. In the end, the Avars beat the Bulgars.

The defeated Bulgars, amounting to nine thousand men along with women and children, were driven out. They sought out Dagobert, asking him to allow them to live in the land of the Franks. Dagobert ordered the Bavarians to take them in for the winter, while he discussed with the Franks what was to be done with them. When they had been dispersed among the holdings of the Bavarians for the winter, Dagobert, with the advice of the Franks, ordered all the Bavarians with Bulgars on their holdings to kill them on a given night, including wives and children. The order was immediately carried out by the Bavarians. Nor did any of the Bulgars survive except Alcioc who was saved in the Wendish March along with seven hundred husbands, wives, and children. Afterwards he lived along with his people for many years with Walluc, duke of the Wends.

[73]    I shall not pass over what happened in this year to the regions of Spain and her kings. Suinthila had succeeded to the kingdom within about a year of the death of Sisebut, a most gentle king. Suinthila [a. 621-631] had been very hostile to his people and had incurred the hatred of all the chief men of his kingdom. Therefore Sisenand, on the advice of the other leading men, sought out Dagobert to ask him to support them with an army in order to depose Suinthila.

To repay the favor, Sisenand promised to give Dagobert a most noble gold platter from the Gothic treasury weighing five-hundred pounds; King Thorismund had received it from the patrician Aetius [cf. **81**]. Dagobert was greedy and, on hearing this promise, ordered the mobilization of an army from all Burgundy to help Sisenand. When word spread in Spain that the army of the Franks was advancing in support of Sisenand, the entire army of the Goths yielded to his authority. Abundantius and Venerandus with an army from Toulouse only got as far as the city of Saragossa with Sisenand, and there all the Goths from the kingdom of Spain raised Sisenand to the kingship [a. 631]. Abundantius and Venerandus were honored with gifts and returned home with the army from Toulouse.

Dagobert sent an embassy consisting of Duke Amalgar and Venerandus to Sisenand, asking him to send Dagobert the platter he had promised. When the platter was given by Sisenand to the envoys, it was taken away by the Goths by force, and they would not allow it to be removed. After envoys went back and forth, Dagobert received as the value of this platter 200,000 solidi. He weighed the amount carefully.

[74]  IN THE 10TH YEAR OF DAGOBERT'S REIGN [a. 632], the king was informed that an army of Wends had invaded Thuringia. He advanced from the city of Metz with an army drawn from the kingdom of the Austrasians, crossed the Ardennes, and came to Mainz, determined to cross the Rhine. He was accompanied by a corps (*scara*) of able men selected from Neustria and Burgundy under dukes and *grafiones*.

The Saxons sent messengers to Dagobert asking him to concede to them the tribute they paid to the authorities of the fisc. The Saxons for their part pledged to apply their energies and abilities to opposing the Wends and promised to guard the frontier of the Franks in their direction. Dagobert, having gotten the advice of the Neustrians, granted the request. The Saxons who had come to make these proposals took oaths on behalf of all their people, swearing the oaths, as was their custom, on weapons clashed together. But this promise produced little of consequence. The tribute, however, which the Saxons were accustomed to render, was granted to them by the command of Dagobert. What Dagobert gave up was the five hundred cows of *inferenda,* which had been assessed by Chlothar I, and which the Saxons used to render each year.

[75]  IN THE IITH YEAR OF THE REIGN OF DAGOBERT **[a. 633]**, at Samo's command, the Wends, having repeatedly crossed their frontier, invaded Thuringia and other districts in a furious rage to pillage the kingdom of the Franks.

Dagobert came to the city of Metz, and there on the advice of the bishops and leading men, and with the consent of all the chief men of the kingdom, he raised up Sigibert his son to be king of Austrasia and allowed him to have Metz as his capital. He appointed Chunibert, bishop of the city of Cologne, and Duke Adalgisel to direct the affairs of the palace and the kingdom. He gave his son a sufficient-sized treasury, conferring on him, as was fitting, the lofty rank he deserved. Dagobert issued separate charters to validate the various grants to his son. Thereafter the zealous Austrasians ably defended the frontier and the kingdom of the Franks.

[76]  IN THE 12TH YEAR OF THE REIGN OF DAGOBERT **[a. 634],** a son by the name of Clovis was born to the king from Queen Nantechild. On the advice and urging of the Neustrians, Dagobert made an agreement with Sigibert, his son. All the chief men of the Austrasians, bishops, and other *leudes* of Sigibert, raised their hands and swore oaths to confirm their acceptance of its terms. According to the agreement, Neustria and Burgundy would remain undiminished and belong to the kingdom of Clovis on Dagobert's death. Austrasia likewise would remain undiminished and, because it equaled Neustria in population and size, it would belong in its entirety to the kingdom of Sigibert. And whatever formerly had pertained to the Austrasian kingdom Sigibert would recover for his own jurisdiction and rule and would hold it in perpetual dominion, except the duchy of Dentelin, which had been wrongly taken by the Austrasians. Again it was joined to Neustria and subjected to Clovis's rule. The Austrasians, however, were compelled by fear of Dagobert to confirm these agreements, whether they liked them or not. Later in the times of Kings Sigibert [a. 633- ca. 56] and Clovis [a. 639-57], they were preserved.

[77]  The son of Chamar, Duke Radulf, whom Dagobert appointed duke of Thuringia, fought against the Wends many times, defeated them and put them to flight. Exalted by pride in so doing, Radulf showed hostility toward Duke Adalgisel on a number of occasions. Gradually by this point he had begun to rebel against Sigibert. He acted like this because, as the saying goes, "he who loves to fight, thinks about dissension."

[78] IN THE 14TH YEAR OF THE REIGN OF DAGOBERT **[a. 636]**, the king ordered an army mobilized from all of the Burgundian kingdom, since the Gascons had raised a serious revolt and had taken a lot of plunder in the kingdom of the Franks that Charibert had ruled. Dagobert appointed as general of the army Chadoind, the referendary, who in the times of Theuderic, the late king, had shown himself effective in many a battle. The army came to Gascony with the forces of ten dukes, namely Arnebert, Amalgar, Leudebert, Wandalmar, Walderic, Ermeno, Barontus, Chairaard, Franks by birth; Chramnelen, a Roman by birth; Willebad the patrician, a Burgundian by birth; Aighyna, a Saxon by birth; as well as many counts who had no duke as a superior.

The whole land of Gascony was filled by the army of Burgundy. The Gascons emerged from among the rocks of the mountains and quickly prepared for battle. But when the battle had begun, they retreated when they saw they would be beaten, as is their custom, and took refuge in the narrow passes of the Pyrenees mountains, concealing themselves in very secure positions among the rocks. The army under its dukes followed behind them, defeated the Gascons, and took large numbers of prisoners; of these the army killed a good number. It set fire to all their homes and despoiled them of their cattle and property. Finally, the Gascons, overpowered and subdued, asked the abovementioned dukes for mercy and peace. They promised to deliver themselves before the glorious presence of King Dagobert, to surrender to his authority, and to fulfill every one of his instructions.

This army would have returned home successfully without injury, if Duke Arnebert in particular had not been killed by the Gascons along with the lords and nobles of his army in the valley of the Soule, due to negligence. Still, the army of the Franks, which had gone from Burgundy to Gascony, returned home, having gained victory.

While staying at Clichy, Dagobert sent a message to Brittany for the Bretons to quickly make amends for the harm they had done and to surrender to Dagobert's authority; if not, the Burgundian army that had been in Gascony would have to invade Brittany right away. When Judicael, king of the Bretons, heard the message, he went quickly to Dagobert at Clichy with many gifts, and there asked for mercy. He pledged to make amends for all the wrongs committed against the *leudes* of the Franks by those belonging to his kingdom of Brittany and promised that he and the kingdom of Brittany over which he ruled would always be subject to the authority of Dagobert and the kings of the Franks. Nevertheless, he would not join Dagobert at the table nor eat, because Judicael was very religious and had a great fear of God. When Dagobert sat down to eat, Judicael left the palace and went to eat at the house of Dado [*also called Audoenus, Saint Ouen*], whom he knew to be a follower of holy religion. The next day Judicael, king of the Bretons, bade farewell to Dagobert and returned home to Brittany. However, he was honored with gifts from Dagobert and deservedly so.

IN THE 15TH YEAR OF THE REIGN OF DAGOBERT [a. 637], all the Gascon lords came from the land of Gascony with duke Aighyna to Dagobert at Clichy. There, stricken by fear of the king, they took refuge in the church of Lord Dionysius [Saint Denis]. They were granted their lives by the mercy of Dagobert. The Gascons made a promise, strengthening it at the same time with oaths, that they would be faithful for all time to Dagobert, his sons, and the kingdom of the Franks: afterwards events showed that in their accustomed fashion they kept the promise as well as they usually did. With Dagobert's leave, the Gascons returned to the land of Gascony.

[79] IN THE 16TH YEAR OF HIS REIGN [a. 638/39], Dagobert began to suffer from dysentery at the villa of Épinay-sur-Seine, near Paris. He was taken from there by his men to the basilica of Saint Dionysius. A few days later, when he felt his life was in danger, he ordered Aega to come quickly. Dagobert entrusted Queen Nantechild and his son Clovis into Aega's hands and, already sensing that he was about to die, went over a plan with Aega by which the kingdom would be well directed by his steady hand. These matters completed, a few days later Dagobert breathed his last [19 January 639]. He was buried in the church of Saint Dionysius.

Seeking the precious patronage of the saint, he had earlier decorated the church appropriately with gold and gems and many valuable items which he ordered put up all around it, as was fitting. Such wealth was conferred on the church by Dagobert, and so many villas and possessions in various places, as to be a source of wonder to many people. He had instituted there the chanting of psalms on the model of the monastery of the saints of Agaune. But Abbot Aigulf was easy-going and opposed this institution.

## The Reign of Clovis II, a. 639-42

After Dagobert's death, his son Clovis, though of a tender age, assumed the kingdom of his father. All the *leudes* of Neustria and Burgundy raised him to the kingship at the villa of Mâlay-le-roi.

[80] IN THE 1ST, 2ND, AND THE BEGINNING OF THE 3RD YEAR OF CLOVIS' REIGN [a. 639-41], Aega, with Queen Nantechild, Dagobert's widow, fittingly directed the affairs of the palace and the kingdom. Among the chief officials of Neustria, Aega was indeed superior to all the others, for he acted with more prudence and was filled with an abundance of forbearance. He was of noble birth, very wealthy, a devotee of justice, cultivated in speech, and

ready with an answer. However, he was reproached by many for having surrendered to avarice. The property that had been unjustly seized at the orders
of Dagobert from many people in the kingdom of Burgundy and Neustria,
and unjustly subjected to the powers of the fisc, was restored to its owners on
the advice of Aega.

[81]    In this year, the Emperor Constantine died [a. 641]. His son Constans [II,
a. 641-668], though of a tender age, was raised to the emperorship on the
advice of the senate.

In his times, the empire was ravaged severely by the Saracens. Jerusalem
was captured by the Saracens [a. 638] and other cities reduced to ruins. The
Saracens spread through upper and lower Egypt [a. 641/2]. Alexandria was
captured and sacked. All of Africa was ravaged, and little by little the Saracens
took possession of it. Gregory the patrician was killed there by them [ca.
648]. Only Constantinople, the province of Thrace, a few islands, and the
province of Rome were left under imperial authority. For almost the whole
empire was rubbed out by the Saracens. And at last, even the emperor Constans had no choice but to become a tributary of the Saracens so that he
could preserve his authority over Constantinople and a few islands and
provinces. For about three years, and even more, it is said, Constans paid
every day 1,000 solidi in gold to the treasury of the Saracens. Finally, when
Constans had regained his powers, he recovered the empire to some extent
and refused to pay tribute [a. 659]. How this result came about I shall tell in
proper order under the year in which it was brought to completion, and I
shall not stop writing until, God willing, I carry out my wishes regarding this
and other matters, and put in this book everything known to me to be true.

[82]    In this year, the king of Spain Chintila, who succeeded Sisenand to the
kingship, died [a. 639]. His son, by the name of Tulga, though of a tender age,
was raised to the kingship of Spain [a. 639-42], because he was his father's
candidate. The Gothic people are restless unless they are made to bear a heavy
yoke. During Tulga's youth, all Spain in its usual way was infected by every
kind of mad behavior.

Finally, many of the senators of the Goths and other people assembled and
raised one of their chief men by the name of Chindaswinth to the kingship
[a. 642-53]. He deposed Tulga and had him tonsured as a cleric. He secured
all Spain under his authority. He was aware of the disease the Goths had of
deposing kings, because he had often been involved with them in conspiracies. From among those liable to this vice, he ordered all those he knew to
have been implicated in driving kings from the kingship to be killed one at a
time. Others he condemned to exile and gave their wives, daughters, and
property to his followers. It is said that of the chief men of the Goths, two
hundred were killed in repressing this vice; of the middle-level Goths, he had
five hundred killed. Until Chindaswinth knew that this disease of the Goths

was overcome, he never ceased from having those he suspected killed. The Goths in fact were subdued by Chindaswinth and dared not enter into conspiracies against him, as they were accustomed to do with their kings.

When Chindaswinth was full of days, he established his son, whose name was Recceswinth, over the whole kingdom of Spain [a. 649-72]. Chindaswinth, doing penance and generously distributing alms from his own property, died at a great age — ninety, so it is said.

[83]   IN THE 3RD YEAR OF THE REIGN OF CLOVIS [a. 641], Aega died, afflicted by fever.

A few days before, Ermenfred, who had married Aega's daughter, killed count Chainulf in the village of Augers during a judicial hearing. For this offense, Chainulf's relations, and many other people, were given leave by Nantechild to destroy Ermenfred's property. Ermenfred took refuge in Austrasia at the church of Saint Remigius in Rheims, and stayed there for many days out of the way of this attack and the royal anger.

[84]   After the death of Aega, the mayor of the palace Erchinoald, who was a blood relation of Dagobert's mother, was made mayor of the palace [a. 641-657] to Clovis. He was a forbearing man, full of goodness, combining forbearance and circumspection. He displayed humility and good will towards priests, answered everyone with patience and kindness, and was not swollen with arrogance nor crazy with greed. In his day, the pursuit of peace was such as to be pleasing to God. He was wise, but almost always in an uncomplicated fashion. He enriched himself moderately and was beloved by all.

Now I should not overlook how after the death of King Dagobert his treasure was divided among his sons, but shall take care to include a plain account of it in this book.

[85]   After the death of Dagobert, the mayor of the palace Pippin and the other Austrasian dukes who had been kept under Dagobert's authority up until his passing all agreed to seek out Sigibert. Pippin and Chunibert had earlier taken pains to cultivate each other's friendship. As they had at that time, now again of late they both undertook to keep their friendship intact forever. With prudence and charm the two of them drew all the *leudes* of the Austrasians to their side and, gently directing their affairs, compelled them always to preserve friendship among themselves.

Through envoys Sigibert then demanded from Queen Nantechild and King Clovis the part of Dagobert's treasure that was owed to him, and a meeting was set for the restoration of the treasure. Chunibert, the bishop of the city of Cologne, the mayor of the palace Pippin, and some of the chief men of Austrasia were sent by Sigibert and came to the villa of Compiègne, and there, at the command of Nantechild and Clovis and at the direction of the mayor of the palace Aega, the treasure of Dagobert was delivered and divided equally. However, Nantechild took a third part of Dagobert's acquests. Chunibert and Pippin had Sigibert's part of the treasure taken to Metz. It was delivered to Sigibert and inventoried.

A year later, it is said, Pippin died [a. 640]. His passing was the source of not a little grief among everyone in Austrasia, because he was beloved by them for his cultivation of justice and his goodness.

[86]    His son, Grimoald, since he was a vigorous man, was loved like his father by a great many people. A certain Otto, the son of the *domesticus* Uro, had been a tutor to Sigibert from youth. He grew arrogant towards Grimoald, whom he hated, and ventured to hold him in contempt. Grimoald, allying himself with Chunibert through ties of friendship, began to think how he could have Otto removed from the palace and how he himself could obtain the office of his father.

[87]    When Sigibert was reigning in his 8th year [a. 641], Radulf, duke of Thuringia, raised a violent revolt against Sigibert [cf. c. 77]. All the *leudes* of the Austrasians were summoned at Sigibert's command to join the army. Sigibert crossed the Rhine with his army, and the peoples from all the districts of his kingdom across the Rhine joined together under him.

In the first encounter, the army of Sigibert cut its way through to Fara, Chrodoald's son [cf. c. 52], who had made common cause with Radulf, and killed him. All Fara's people that escaped the sword were assigned to captivity. All Sigibert's commanders and the rank and file gave one another their right hand as a pledge that no one would grant Radulf his life. But this promise came to nothing.

Next Sigibert brought the army through the Buchenwald and proceeded quickly to Thuringia. Seeing Sigibert's advance, Radulf built a fortress of wood on a certain hill on the Unstrut river in Thuringia, gathered an army as large as he could from all around, and with his wife and children prepared to defend himself in the fortress. Sigibert came there with the army of his kingdom, and his forces completely surrounded the fortress, while Radulf sat inside ready to put up a good fight.

But the battle began unplanned. This was the doing of King Sigibert's youthfulness. There was no agreement on a plan, for the king and some others wanted to start the battle on the same day, while others wanted to wait until the next day. Seeing the situation, Grimoald and Duke Adalgisel had grave concerns about Sigibert's safety and guarded the king constantly. Bobo, duke of Auvergne, with part of the forces of Adalgisel, and Innowales, count of the Saintois, with his compatriots and a great many other forces of the army, reached the gate of the fortress and immediately began fighting against Radulf. He had an understanding with certain dukes of Sigibert's army that they would not attack him with their forces. He burst out through the gate of the fortress with his men and played such havoc on Sigibert's army as was a wonder to behold. The troops from Mainz were unfaithful in the battle. It is said that many thousands of men were cut down there.

Radulf, having gained the victory, went inside the fortress again. Sigibert and his followers were overcome with bitterness. Sitting on his horse, the king burst into tears in sorrow for the men he had lost. For both Duke Bobo and Count Innowales, as well as other fine noble fighting men and a good number of the army of King Sigibert who entered the thick of the fight with them, were cut down in this battle before the eyes of the king. Even the *domesticus* Fredulf, who was said to be a friend of Radulf, fell in this battle. Not far from the fortress, Sigibert and his army passed the night in their tents.

The next day, they saw that there was no way to prevail against Radulf. Delegations arranged terms for recrossing the Rhine in peace and made an agreement with Radulf for Sigibert and his army to return home.

Radulf got carried away with pride and deemed himself a king in Thuringia. He concluded agreements of friendship with the Wends and obliged other neighboring peoples by cultivating ties of friendship. However he never rejected Sigibert's authority in so many words, though in deeds he stoutly resisted the rule of the king.

[88] IN THE 10TH YEAR OF THE REIGN OF SIGIBERT [a. 642], Otto, who was bursting with hostility towards Grimoald out of pride, was killed by Leuthar, duke of the Alamanni, at the instigation of Grimoald. The office of mayor of the palace in the court of Sigibert and all the kingdom of the Austrasians were firmly established in the hands of Grimoald.

[89] IN THE 4TH YEAR OF THE REIGN OF CLOVIS [a. 642], after the death of Aega, Queen Nantechild came to Orleans in the kingdom of Burgundy with her son Clovis. She ordered all the leading men, bishops, dukes, and chief officials of the kingdom of Burgundy to come to her there. And one by one she won them over: Flaochad, a Frank by birth, was elected mayor of the palace in Burgundy by the bishops and all the dukes and installed in this office by Nantechild. She betrothed her niece, by the name of Ragneberta, to Flaochad.

I do not know who instigated this betrothal. At any rate, Flaochad and the queen certainly devised in secret another plan, which is believed not to have been pleasing to God and therefore was not granted success. Since the mayors of the palace Erchinoald and Flaochad both followed, as it were, one and the same policy, they were prepared by mutual agreement to exercise their offices by giving each other support.

Flaochad confirmed in writing and by oaths to all the dukes of the kingdom of Burgundy and its bishops that he would always preserve the office and dignity of each one of them and his friendship with them. Once he had been raised up to the dignity of his office, he traveled about the kingdom of Burgundy. Mindful of an earlier hatred that he had long concealed in the secrets of his heart, he busied himself with a plan to kill the patrician Willebad.

[90] Willebad was very rich, and, by robbing a great many people of their property by various devices, he had made himself fabulously wealthy. Moreover his office of patrician and the conceit of great wealth had caused him to give in to pride. And so his opposition to Flaochad grew and he ventured to hold him in contempt.

Flaochad summoned the bishops and dukes of the kingdom of Burgundy to Chalon to consider matters bearing on the well-being of their homeland and fixed the meeting for the month of May. Willebad arrived for the meeting leading a multitude of followers. At that very moment Flaochad was making preparations to kill him. Seeing the situation, Willebad refused to enter the palace. Flaochad came out to do battle with Willebad. Flaochad's brother, Amalbert, however, interposed himself between the combatants to make peace just as the fighting was about to start. Willebad escaped from the danger by seizing Amalbert and keeping him by his side. When others intervened, both sides parted without losses. Flaochad now furiously plotted the killing of Willebad.

In this year, Queen Nantechild died.

In the same year, in the month of September, Flaochad, along with Clovis and Erchinoald, likewise mayor of the palace, and some of the chief men of Neustria, left Paris and came by way of Sens and Auxerre to Autun, where Clovis ordered Willebad the patrician to come to him. Discerning that a deadly plot had been hatched against his life by Flaochad, his brother Amalbert, and Dukes Amalgar and Chramnelen, Willebad gathered as large a force as he could from the region he ruled as patrician, including bishops and nobles and fighting men, and took the road to Autun. Willebad was wavering between proceeding or retreating to avoid danger, for which reason King Clovis, the mayor of the palace Erchinoald, and Flaochad, sent the *domesticus* Ermenric to meet him and make him promises that would ensure he continued to Autun. Willebad believed Ermenric and honored him with appropriate gifts. Willebad reached Autun just behind Ermenric and he and his men set up their tents not far from the city. On the same day of his arrival, Willebad sent Ailulf, bishop of the town of Valence and Count Gyso into Autun to see what was going on. They were detained in the town by Flaochad.

The next day, Flaochad, Amalgar, and Chramnelen, who had been of one mind in devising the plot against the life of Willebad, moved out of the town of Autun early, and other dukes from the kingdom of Burgundy joined forces with them. Erchinoald, along with the Neustrians who accompanied him, likewise armed themselves and advanced to this battle. Willebad, on the other side, drew up whoever he could gather together into a battle formation. Both forces joined battle and began to fight. In the engagement, Flaochad, Amalgar, Dukes Chramnelen and Wandelbert, with their men, took part in the fighting against Willebad, but the other dukes and Neustrians, who were supposed to surround him on all sides, held back. They looked on, awaiting the outcome and preferring not to attack Willebad. Willebad was killed there and a great many with him were cut down.

In the fighting, the count of the palace Berthar, a Frank from the Transjuran district, was the first one into the engagement against Willebad. The Burgundian Manaulf, gnashing his teeth, left the ranks and led his men forward to fight Berthar.

Because Berthar had once been his friend, Berthar said to Manaulf, "Come under my shield, I shall save you from this danger."

When Berthar lifted his shield to save him, Manaulf struck him in the chest with his spear.

The others who had come with Manaulf surrounded Berthar, who had advanced beyond the rest of his men. Berthar was wounded seriously. At that point, Aubedo [cf. c. 71], Berthar's son, seeing his father's life in danger, raced to help him. He struck Manaulf with his spear and laid him out on the ground and killed all the others who had struck his father. And so, like a faithful son, he saved his father Berthar from death, with the help of God.

The dukes who had preferred not to attack Willebad with their forces, plundered the tents of Willebad and the bishops and those who had come with him. A good amount of gold and silver was taken, and other property and horses were seized by those who preferred not to fight.

When these deeds were done, the next day Flaochad left Autun and went to Chalon. He entered the town and the next day almost the whole town was burnt down, I know not by what cause. Flaochad was struck by the judgment of God. He was afflicted with a fever and placed on ship, which was to take him to Saint-Jean-de-Losne by way of the river Arar, also called the Saône. He breathed his last during the journey, on the eleventh day after the death of Willebad, and is buried in the church of Saint Bénigne, on the outskirts of Dijon. Many believe that because these two — Flaochad and Willebad — gave many oaths to one another in the places of the saints to establish ties of mutual friendship and because both, driven by greed, wickedly pressed hard on the people subject to them and, at the same time, stripped them of their property, that the judgment of God had freed a great multitude from their oppression and had caused both of them to be killed for their faithlessness and lies.

# CHAPTER THIRTEEN

# KINGS AND MAYORS: THE ANONYMOUS *HISTORY OF THE FRANKS (LHF)* AND THE FRANKISH KINGDOM, A. 639-727

*The History of the Franks (Liber Historiae Francorum, abbreviated LHF) was written in 726/27 in the western kingdom of Neustria by an anonymous author: recent candidates for its provenance are the monastery of Saint Medard and the nunnery of Notre Dame, both in Soissons. Though regarding the Austrasians as Franks, the author tended to reserve use of the term 'Franks' (Franci) to the Neustrians. Francia is Neustria and the Neustrian Franks are the real subject of the history.*

*The LHF begins with the origins of the Franks and for most of its early chapters is dependent on Gregory of Tours's Histories. Selections from the early chapters are given in **80, 96–102**.*

*Despite the brevity of its later chapters (43-53), the LHF is the chief historical source for Merovingian politics in its broad outlines after the death of Dagobert in 639. It should be read in conjunction with saints' lives for the period of Queen Balthild and her sons (see **61–63**), which are dated closer to the events they describe than the corresponding sections of the LHF. The LHF is also frequently supplemented by accounts of Carolingian historiography, which are questionable and even more retrospective. The chronology of the LHF's author is vague and, where it is more precise and can be checked, often found to be faulty, especially in the earlier chapters of the following selection.*

*The LHF is written with a Neustrian bias, but the attitude the author takes to Merovingian rulers, the Neustrian aristocracy, and the powerful house of the Pippinids (that is Carolingians) is complicated and, like the work's value for evaluating the eventual eclipse of Merovingian power, interpreted in a variety of ways by historians.*

*To facilitate reading and reference, I have placed the names of the Neustrian kings in the text as subheadings; the names of important figures, mainly, but not exclusively mayors of the palace, have been placed in the margin in italics.*

Source: *Liber historiae Francorum*, ed. Bruno Krusch, in *Fredegarii et aliorum chronica*, MGH SRM 2 (1888), pp. 215-328. Translation by A.C. Murray.

## 59. CHAPTERS 43-53 OF THE
## *HISTORY OF THE FRANKS (LHF)*

### Dagobert I, a. 629-39

42. As time passed, old King Chlothar [II] died. He reigned 44 years. His son King Dagobert quickly took over sole rule of all three kingdoms. Dagobert was very strong, a guardian of the Franks, quite hard in his judicial decisions, and a benefactor of churches. He was the first to disperse abundant alms to the churches of the saints in the form of dues (*census*) drawn from the revenues of the palace. He established peace in the entire kingdom. His fame resounded among many peoples. He struck fear and dread into all the surrounding kingdoms. Peaceable, like Solomon, he held the kingdom of the Franks with restraint.

*Audoin*      At that time also the blessed Audoin was famous when he rose to be bishop [a. 641].

*Erchinoald*      In this period King Dagobert appointed Erchinoald as mayor of the palace on the death of Gundoland [but cf. **58**, c. 83, 84]. The aforesaid king had two sons, Sigibert and Clovis, by his queen Nantechild, who was of [Anglo-]Saxon birth. He established a kingdom in Austrasia for Sigibert, his *Pippin I* elder son, and sent him there with Duke Pippin [a. 633]. Clovis he kept by his side.

43. Afterwards King Dagobert was seized with a raging fever, grew sick and died at the villa of Épinay-sur-Seine in the district of Paris; he was buried in the basilica of the blessed Dionysius the martyr [Saint Denis]. The Franks mourned him for many days. He reigned for 44 years.

### Clovis II, a. 639-57

*Balthild*      The Franks set his son Clovis [II] over them as king. He took a wife of [Anglo-]Saxon birth by the name of Balthild, a fine looking woman, artful and enterprising.

*Grimoald*      Afterward, on the death of Pippin, Sigibert, king of Austrasia, appointed Grimoald, Pippin's son, as mayor of the palace [cf. **58**, c. 88]. Time passed, and on the death of Sigibert, Grimoald tonsured the king's son, a small boy by the *Dagobert II* name of Dagobert, and had Dido, bishop of Poitiers, take the boy on a pilgrimage to Ireland. Grimold placed his own son upon the throne. The Franks were quite angry at this and hatched plots against Grimoald. They removed him and delivered him to Clovis, king of the Franks, to be condemned. He was confined in prison in the city of Paris, and, tormented by being kept in bonds, ended his life in great suffering, for he deserved death for what he had done to his lord.

44. At that time, Clovis cut off the arm of holy Dionysius the martyr at the prompting of the devil. Throughout that period, the king brought the kingdom of the Franks to ruin with disastrous calamities.

Clovis himself was given over to every kind of obscenity; bent upon gluttony and drunkenness, he was a fornicator and a violator of women. Of his death and final days, history records nothing of value. In fact writers condemn his end in many ways, but not knowing how his wickedness came to a close, they dubiously report one thing or another about it. From Balthild, his queen, they say he had three children: Chlothar, Childeric, and Theuderic.

And so in the end the aforesaid King Clovis passed away. He reigned for 16 years.

## Chlothar III, a. 657-73

The Franks established Chlothar [III], the elder of the three boys, as their king to rule with the queen, his mother.

*Ebroin*    45. At this time, when the mayor of the palace Erchinoald died, the Franks had no clear successor in mind, but they held a council and established Ebroin to the lofty dignity of mayor of the palace in the court of the king. In these days, Chlothar, the boy king, died. He reigned 4 years.

## Theuderic III, a. 673, 675-91, Childeric II, ca. 662-75

His brother Theuderic [III] was raised up as king of the Franks. And as for *Wulfoald*  Childeric [II], his other brother, they sent him to Austrasia with Duke Wulfoald to assume the kingship there.

At this time, the Franks plotted against Ebroin. They rose up against Theuderic and ejected him from the kingship. They removed both of them by force, cutting their hair. Ebroin they tonsured and sent to the monastery of Luxeuil in Burgundy. Messengers were sent to Austrasia to make arrangements with Childeric. He came with Duke Wulfoald and was raised to the kingship of the Franks.

Now Childeric had very little sense. He conducted all his affairs without paying the slightest heed, till at length, employing a heavy hand on the Franks, he was the cause of violent hatred and outrage among them. He had one of them called Bodilo tied to a stake and beaten without due process. When the Franks saw this, they were roused to great anger, so that Ingobert and Amalbert and other well-born Franks stirred up a rebellion against Childeric himself. Bodilo, along with others, rose up against him with the intention of trapping the king. Bodilo killed the king and his queen, who was pregnant, which is a distressing event to report. As for Wulfoald, he barely escaped by flight and returned to Austrasia.

*Leudesius*    The Franks chose Leudesius, Erchinoald's son, as mayor of the palace. In agreement with this plan was the blessed Leudegar, bishop of Autun, and his brother Gaerin, from Burgundy.

*Ebroin again*    Ebroin let his hair grow. Gathering together his associates to help him, he came forth from the monastery of Luxeuil looking for trouble and returned to Francia outfitted for war. He sent to the blessed Audoin to ask for advice. Audoin sent back by messengers a letter containing just this reply: "Recall the advice of Fredegund [cf. **100**]." And Ebroin, as he was very clever, understood. He raised a force, and marching by night, came to the Oise river, where he killed the guards and crossed over the river at Pont-Sainte-Maxence. There he killed any of the conspirators he found.

Leudesius escaped by flight along with King Theuderic and as many comrades as were able to get away. Ebroin pursued them. When he came to the villa of Baisieux he seized the royal treasury. Afterwards when he came from there to Crécy-en-Ponthieu, he recovered the king. He sent word to Leudesius to trick him with a promise that he could come to him [in safety]. When Leudesius came, Ebroin killed him and quickly recovered control of the state. He inflicted various punishments on the holy Leudegar and then ordered him put to the sword. Gaerin, Leudegar's brother, he condemned to harsh penalties. As for the other Franks who were their allies, they barely escaped by flight. Some roamed in exile and were deprived of their own property.

*Martin*    46. At this time also, when Wulfoald of Austrasia had died, Martin and the
*Pippin II*    younger Pippin, son of the late Ansegisel, ruled in Austrasia on the death of the kings. Now at last these dukes came to hate Ebroin and raising a huge army of Austrasians they sent an expedition against King Theuderic and Ebroin.

Theuderic and Ebroin came to meet them with an army. The forces engaged at a place called Bois-du-Fay (Lucofao) and laid each other out with great slaughter. Countless numbers of men fell there. The Austrasians, beaten, turned their backs and fled. Ebroin pursued them, inflicting the most heartless slaughter. Most of the district was laid waste. Martin fled to Laon and shut himself up there. Pippin, on the other side of the battlefield, got away.

With victory achieved, Ebroin returned. When he came to the villa of Asfeld, he sent messengers to Martin swearing that Martin could come to Theuderic with assurance. Their oaths to him were fraudulent, falsely sworn on empty relic boxes, but Martin believed them and came to Asfeld, where he was killed with his companions.

47. And so Ebroin more and more subdued the Franks unmercifully, until finally he made covert preparations to trap the Frank Ermenfred. But Ermen-

fred attacked the aforesaid Ebroin by surprise in the middle of the night, cruelly killing him, and escaped by flight to Pippin in Austrasia.

*Waratto* The Franks deliberated together and made Waratto, a man of illustrious rank, mayor of the palace in Ebroin's place by order of the king. Meanwhile Waratto himself received hostages from the aforesaid Pippin and made peace with him.

*hislemar* At that time Waratto had a son, powerful and diligent, with a wild temperament, and coarse in his habits, a plotter against his father, whom he removed from high office. His name was Ghislemar. The blessed Bishop Audoin forbade the son from inflicting this villainy upon his father, but he would not listen. There were civil wars and much dispute between Ghislemar and Pippin. Ghislemar was struck down by God because of the harm he inflicted on his father and other depraved sins and took his last wicked breath just as holy Audoin told him he would. When he was dead, Waratto obtained his former position once again.

In these days, the blessed Audoin, bishop of Rouen, passed on to the Lord, full of days and famous for his miracles, at the royal villa of Clichy, in the suburban district of the city of Paris. He received a glorious burial in the basilica of Saint Peter the apostle, in the city of Rouen.

*Berchar* 48. In the course of time the aforesaid Waratto died; his wife was a noble and clever woman by the name of Ansefled. The Franks, clearly, were split along various lines and could not decide who should succeed him. In the meantime, still divided among themselves, the Franks blundered into appointing as mayor of the palace the late Berchar, a man short in stature, undistinguished for his wisdom, and inadequate in devising plans.

In Austrasia, Pippin rose up, gathering the largest army he could, and launched an expedition against King Theuderic and Berchar. The forces came together at a place called Tertry [a. 687], and when they fought, King Theuderic retreated along with Berchar, mayor of the palace. Pippin emerged the victor.

*ippin II* And so time passed, and the same Berchar was killed by his sycophants. Afterwards at the instigation of Ansefled, Pippin, as mayor of the palace, began to be the chief guide of King Theuderic. He took control of the treasury, left one of his men, the late Nordebert, with the king, and himself returned to Austrasia.

Prince (*princeps*) Pippin had a most noble and wise wife by the name of Plectrude. He had two sons by her: the name of the elder was Drogo and the name of the younger was Grimoald. Drogo received the duchy of Champagne.

49. King Theuderic died [a. 691]. He reigned 19 years.

## Clovis III, a. 691-694?

Theuderic's son assumed the royal throne, the boy Clovis [III], born from a queen by the name of Chrodechild. Not long after, Clovis the boy king died. He reigned 2 years.

## Childebert III, a. 694-711

*Grimoald*  His brother Childebert [III], a celebrated man, was placed in the kingship. Nordebert also died. Grimoald, the younger son of prince Pippin was made mayor of the palace in the court of King Childebert.

Pippin waged many campaigns against the pagan Radbod [ruler of the Frisians] and other princes, and against the Suevi and as many peoples as he could. Grimoald fathered a son by the name of Theudoald by a concubine. Almost at the same time, Pippin's son Drogo died, though the aforesaid prince Pippin still had by another wife a son called Charles [Martel], a cultivated man, distinguished and accomplished in war.

50. Then the most glorious lord Childebert, a just king of good memory, passed on to God. He reigned 17 years and is buried in the basilica of holy Stephen the protomartyr at the monastery of Choisy-au-Bac.

## Dagobert III, a. 711-15

Dagobert [III], Childebert's son, ruled in his place.

Then Grimoald took a wife named Theudesind, the daughter of the pagan duke Radbod. Grimoald as mayor of the palace was pious, moderate, gentle and just. Time passed and his father, prince Pippin, grew ill. As soon as he came to visit his father, Grimoald was killed by the pagan Rantgar, a son of Belial, in the basilica of the holy Lambert the martyr at Liège. They *Theudoald*  appointed Theudoald on the orders of his grandfather to the lofty dignity of his father's office in the palace of the king.

51. At that time, Pippin was seized by a raging fever and died [a. 714]. He held the position of prince [*principatus*] under the above mentioned kings for 27 and a half years. Plectrude with her grandchildren and the king continued to direct all affairs under a separate regime.

In those days, at the instigation of the devil, the Franks again fell upon one another in the forest of Compiègne and laid one another low in a fearful slaughter. Theudoald took to flight and was taken out of harm's way; at the time there was a fierce persecution.

*Ragamfred*  As Theudoald had been put to flight, they chose Ragamfred for the prince's position of mayor of the palace. Along with the king, they gathered an army and crossed the Ardennes forest, wasting and burning those lands as far as the Meuse river; they struck an alliance with the pagan duke Radbod.

*Charles Martel*   In those days Charles was held prisoner and kept under guard by the lady Plectrude, but, with the help of God, he managed to get away.

52. After a time Dagobert grew sick and died. He reigned 5 years.

## Chilperic II, a. 715–721

The Franks of course put into the kingship Daniel, a former cleric who let his hair grow, and called him Chilperic [II]; and indeed at this time they gathered an army once more and sent it to the Meuse against Charles. On the other flank, the Frisians rose up under Duke Radbod. Charles fell upon the Frisians; in the fighting he suffered quite severe casualties among his followers and withdrew in flight.

Time passed, and again Chilperic and Ragamfred raised a force, entered the Ardennes forest and advanced to the Rhine river and Cologne, laying the country waste. They received a vast treasure from the matron Plectrude and turned back. But in a place called Amblève, they suffered severe casualties when Charles fell upon them.

53. Likewise at this time, the aforesaid Charles marshaled his forces and again rose up against Chilperic and Ragamfred. They gathered their army and rushed to prepare for war against him. But Charles asked for peace to be made. Rejecting his offer, they came out to fight at a place called Vinchy, at first light on Sunday, 12 days before the Kalends of April [21 March 717], during Lent. They did fight bravely, but Chilperic and Ragamfred retreated. Charles emerged the victor.

He laid the districts waste, took captives, and so returned to Austrasia. When he came to the city of Cologne, he started an insurrection. In a dispute with the matron Plectrude, he quickly took possession of his father's treasury and set up a king of his own called Chlothar [IV, a. 717-19].

And so Chilperic and Ragamfred sought aid from Duke Eudo [Duke of Aquitaine], who brought forward an army against Charles. Undaunted Charles calmly came to meet him. But Eudo fled back to the city of Paris and, taking up Chilperic and the royal treasure, retired beyond the Loire. Charles pursued him but could not catch him.

Chlothar [IV], the above mentioned king, died that year and the next year Charles sent a delegation to Eudo and made an alliance with him. Eudo handed over King Chilperic along with many gifts, but the latter did not occupy the kingship for long. For he died after this and is buried in the city of Noyon. He reigned 5 and a half years.

## Theuderic IV, a. 721-37

And as for the Franks, they set up a king over them, Theuderic [IV], a son of the younger Dagobert [III], raised in the monastery of Chelles, and he is now in the sixth year of his reign [a. 726/27].

# CHAPTER FOURTEEN

# SANCTITY AND POLITICS IN THE TIMES
# OF BALTHILD AND HER SONS

*Fortunately our understanding of Frankish political life in the period after Fredegar's sixth chronicle breaks off (see, 58) does not depend solely on the often slim pickings of the* LHF *(see, 59). A remarkable series of saints' lives survive which provide distinctive, even detailed, perspectives on events and personalities in the four decades following the death of Dagobert I. Modern readers, however, are likely to find the conventions of these works peculiar or frustrating. Though the term Life, as a generic description for compositions of this type, might suggest biography, those inclined to read them uncritically in this light are doomed to disappointment. The saints' lives excerpted here, like all the sources in this book, have to be handled with circumspection and with attention to audience, authorial purpose, and the genre in which they were composed. Their connection to real human beings and real events, however, is indisputable; they offer valuable insights into the politics, ideology, and personalities of the seventh century.*

## A. QUEENSHIP, RELIGION, AND POLITICS

### 60. THE *LIFE OF LADY BALTHILD, QUEEN*

*The* Life of Lady Balthild *was written by an anonymous contemporary of the queen sometime after her death, which probably occurred around 680. Balthild was the queen of Clovis II (a. 639-57), king of Neustria, and regent for her son Chlothar III (a. 657-73). As regent, she ruled in conjunction with her former master (and, one presumes, mentor) Erchinoald, mayor of the palace; his successor in the post, Ebroin; and other magnates. Balthild's removal from power and her entry into the monastery of Chelles took place sometime around 665 under circumstances that the discreet style of the* Life *renders with baffling obscurity. By the time of her removal Chlothar had reached the age of majority.*

*The* Life *is important for the biographical details it gives of Balthild's early life as a slave brought from England and for its account of her religious program as wife of Clovis and then as regent. The author is silent about the political dimension of her career, which can be reconstructed from this and other sources of the period in a variety of ways. The following excerpt contains the account of her life up to her entry into Chelles.*

Source: *Vita Sanctae Balthildis*, ed. Bruno Krusch, in *Fredegarii et aliorum Chronica. Vitae Sanctorum*, MGH SRM 2 (1888), pp. 473-508. Translation by A.C. Murray.

[2]...Divine providence summoned Lady Balthild, the queen, from across the sea, and this precious and best pearl of God arrived here, having been sold at a low price.

She was acquired by the late Erchinoald, the prince of the Franks and a man of illustrious rank, in whose service she grew up and lived a decent life. Her pious and admirable company was pleasing to the prince and all his servants. For she was kind hearted, moderate in all her habits, sensible and circumspect, never meaning harm to anyone. Her conversation was not trivial nor did her speech presume too much, but everything she did was quite proper. And as she was a Saxon by birth, the shape of her body was pleasing and very delicate. Her appearance was elegant, her face cheerful, and her walk dignified. Given these qualities, she was quite cherished by the prince and found favor in his eyes. He appointed her to serve him drink in his private quarters, and she was often in his presence serving him as a most virtuous cup-bearer. This favorable position did not make her proud; rather, humble to the core, she was obedient and amiable to all her fellow servants, tending to the senior ones with the honor they deserved, so that she removed the shoes from their feet, which she wiped and washed. She also brought them water for washing and speedily made ready their garments. And she performed these services for them with a good and pious heart without complaint.

[3] Her noble behavior gave rise among her peers to the greatest praise and affection. She was so deserving of her favorable reputation that, when the wife of the abovesaid prince Erchinoald died, he wanted to take to the marriage bed the most virtuous virgin Balthild. When she learned of this, she secretly and carefully removed herself from his sight. And when he called her to the chamber of the prince, she hid in a corner under worthless rags where no one would think a person would hide. Wise and shrewd virgin that she was, even then fleeing empty distinctions and loving humility, she tried as best she could to avoid the mortal bed so that she might deserve to come to the spiritual and heavenly bridegroom. It was brought to pass, no doubt by divine providence, that when the prince could not at all find her whom he was seeking, he married another. And then at last the girl Balthild was discovered, but by the will of God, so that she who had avoided the nuptials of the prince might later receive in marriage Clovis [II, a. 639-657], son of the late King Dagobert, and he might raise her up to a higher station due to the virtue of her humility. To honor her in that station, a divine plan had determined that, though she had spurned the servant of the king, she would join

herself to the king, and a royal progeny should proceed from her. This has now come to pass, as is clear to all, for the royal progeny that now rules is hers.

*Her children were Chlothar III, king of Neustria/Burgundy a. 657-73; Childeric II, king of Austrasia ca. 662-75, and then Neustria/Burgundy a. 673-75; and Theuderic III, king of Neustria/Burgundy a. 673, 675-91, and king of Austrasia a. 687-91.*

[4] As the gift of prudence was granted to her by God, with attentive devotion she gave obedience to the king as to a master and showed herself to the princes as a mother, to the bishops as a daughter, to the young and immature as the finest of governesses. She was amiable to all, loving priests deeply as fathers, monks as brothers, and the poor as a pious provider. She dispensed generous alms to all of them, preserved the honor of the princes, abided by the fitting advice they gave, always urged religious endeavors on the young, and humbly but constantly brought to the attention of the king the interests of the churches and poor. Since she already wanted to serve Christ, though still in secular garb, she prayed daily, commending herself with tears to Christ the king of heaven.

The pious king Clovis had regard for her in accordance with his faith and devoutness and gave to her as a help his faithful servant Abbot Genesius. Ministering to the bishops and the poor through his hands, she fed the needy, clothed the naked, and assiduously saw to it that the dead were buried, sending generous gifts of gold and silver through Genesius to monastic communities of men and virgins. Afterwards this servant of Christ, at Christ's command, was ordained bishop of Lyons in Gaul. For at the time the abbot was constantly working in the palace of the Franks. Through him, as we said, the Lady Balthild, with authority from King Clovis and with the advice of that servant of God, provided generous alms of the king to all the poor in many places.

[5] What more is to be said? At God's command, King Clovis her husband passed from his body. His sons were left with their mother, and immediately his son, the late Chlothar [III, a. 657-73], took up the kingdom of the Franks after his father. At the time there were distinguished princes, Chrodobert, bishop of Paris; Lord Audoin; Ebroin, mayor of the palace, and the rest of the senior officials (*seniores*); and a great many others. Moreover, the kingdom of the Franks was at peace. In fact, at the time, even the Austrasians had just received in a peaceful fashion Clovis's son Childeric [II, ca. 662-75] as king, thanks to arrangements made by Balthild, and on the advice of senior officials to be sure. As for the Burgundians and Franks, they were made one. And we believe that, under God's guidance, those three kingdoms preserved the harmony of peace among themselves at that time as a consequence of the great faith of Lady Balthild.

[6] At the time, the Simoniac heresy [i.e. simony], whereby bishops

received their episcopal offices by paying recompense for them against ecclesiastical law, polluted the church of God through perverted practice. By the will of God, at the urging of good bishops, it came to pass through Balthild's agency that this sacrilegious abomination was forbidden. For the aforesaid lady prohibited any reward at all changing hands when sacred offices were acquired. She — or rather, through her, God — ordained that another, even worse, impious custom should stop. On account of it a great many people were more eager to kill their offspring than to raise them, for they feared that, by accepting civil obligations that were imposed upon them by custom, they would thereby place upon their children the most grievous encumbrance of their property. To gain divine reward, the lady forbade anyone to presume to do this. A very rich reward for this deed awaits her.

[7] Who can tell how numerous and exceedingly great were the benefits she granted to the communities of religious for building cells and monasteries, giving them entire estates and large forests; how even she herself built, as God's own and special quarters, a great monastery for virgins with girls dedicated to God, that is Chelles in the Paris district, where she appointed the servant of God, the very devout maid Berthila, as mother superior? The venerable Lady Balthild had determined that there she herself would later live under its unspoiled monastic rule and would rest in peace, and in truth she devoutly did so willingly.

Whatever God miraculously works among his saints and elect must not be passed over, since it pertains to praising God, for as the scriptures say, "among his saints God is wondrous," and his spirit, the Paraclete, works within through a good will, as is written, "to everyone willing what is good, God is a helper." It is well known that this was truly the case with this great lady. As we said before, neither our tongue, nor, I believe, that of anyone else however learned, can recount all her good deeds. How many comforts and supports and how many advantages and benefits did she confer on the houses of God and his poor for the love of Christ, and what of the monastery called Corbie that she built with her own resources in the diocese of Amiens? There the venerable Lord Theudofred, now bishop but then abbot, guided his large flock of brothers, which the aforesaid Lady Balthild sought from the late most reverend Lord Waldebert, abbot of the monastery of Luxeuil, and miraculously sent to that monastery of brothers, a deed acknowledged to be praiseworthy even know.

[8] What shall I say now? For the construction of a monastery, she granted to the monk Lord Filibert at Jumièges a great wood from the fisc where that monastery of brothers is located as well as many gifts and pasture from the royal fisc. And how many gifts to Lord Laigobert at the monastery of Corbion [Saint-Laumer-de-Mer] by way of a large villa and many talents of silver and gold? Also the royal belt which she wore, she devoutly removed from her

sacred loins and sent it to the brothers as alms. And all this she dispersed with a cheerful and kindly heart; as the scripture says: "God loves the cheerful giver." Likewise she granted many revenues to Saint Wandrille and Logium. How many entire villas did she grant to Luxeuil and to other monasteries in Burgundy and how many countless sums of money did she send? What did she grant to the monastery of Jouarre, from where she summoned those holy virgins with the aforesaid abbess Berthila to her own monastery of Chelles? How many gifts in fields and great sums of money did she confer? Likewise she often sent generous gifts to the monastery of holy Fara [Faremoutier]. To the city of Paris, to the basilicas and monasteries of the saints, she granted large and numerous villas and enriched them with a great many gifts. What more is there to say? As we said, we cannot recount each and every good deed, not even a half of them, and for us to recount all of them is utterly impossible.

[9] We must not pass over how she gave orders to the bishops and abbots throughout the senior basilicas of the saints — those of Lord Dionysius [Saint Denis], of Lord Germanus, of Saint Peter, of Lord Anianus, and of Saint Martin — or of any place that came to her attention, encouraging an ardent love of God and sent letters to them to this end, that the brothers dwelling within those places must live under the order of a holy rule. And so that they might willingly acquiesce to this, she had a privilege approved for them and also granted immunities the better to entice them into entreating the mercy of Christ, the highest king, on behalf of the king and peace.

And it must be remembered — for it has a bearing on the magnitude of her divine reward — how she prohibited Christian persons from being treated as captives and issued edicts to each region completely forbidding anyone from transporting a Christian as a captive within the kingdom of the Franks. But more than that, she ordered a great many captives purchased and set free, and some of them she introduced into monasteries, especially captives taken from her own people [i.e. Anglo-Saxons], men and large numbers of girls whom she had raised as her own. As many as she could acquire she entrusted to the holy monasteries and she commanded them to pray for her. Also she often sent many generous gifts to the churches of blessed Peter and Paul at Rome and to the Roman poor.

[10] It was indeed her sacred vow that she dwell in the monastery of female religious that we mentioned previously, that is Chelles, which she her-self built. But the Franks delayed this as long as possible out of love for her and would not allow it to happen, until there was trouble due to the wretched Bishop Sigobrand, who deserved death for his pride towards the Franks. And a dispute developed as a result, for they killed him against her will, and fearing that the lady would be ill-disposed toward them and would take up the matter, they suddenly allowed her to proceed to the monastery.

There is perhaps no doubt that at the time those princes were not well inten-
tioned in allowing her departure, but the lady perceived in it the will of God
whereby this was not so much their plan as it was the design of God for her
holy vow to be fulfilled, with Christ's guidance, through some pretext or
another. Escorted by some senior officials, she came to her aforesaid
monastery of Chelles, and there she was honorably and quite lovingly
received into the holy congregation by those holy maids. At the time she had
a not insignificant complaint against those whom she had sweetly fostered,
because they had falsely been suspicious of her and even paid her back bad
for good. But quickly consulting with bishops on the matter, she mercifully
yielded everything to them and begged them to yield to her that disturbance
of the heart. And so peace was fully restored among them, by God's gift.

*The Life concludes with examples of Balthild's humble works in the monastery and
a description of her death. Only one miracle is attributed to her, and that minor and
post mortem.*

# B. A VIEW FROM ABROAD

## 61. BALTHILD, EBROIN, AND DAGOBERT II IN STEPHEN'S *LIFE OF WILFRID*

*The* Life of Wilfrid *was written around 720. Its subject, the English saint Wilfrid
(ca. 634-709), bishop of York, was a controversial figure in the political life of the
Northumbrian church. The author of the* Life *in a partisan fashion presents the bishop
as the leading opponent of Irish/Scottish schismatics and the principal champion of
Roman practices in the Northumbrian church; moderns have often seen him, not quite
rightly, as representing a Gallic model of episcopal authority. Wilfrid came into conflict
with two Northumbrian kings and two archbishops of Canterbury, and spent many
years in exile. There is no doubt that his ambitions were lofty, as were his connections
in the British Isles and the continent.*

*The extent of the author's personal knowledge of his subject is a matter of dispute.
His name was Stephen, and some have identified him with Eddius Stephanus, brought
to Ripon in the late 660s by Wilfrid himself, though this attribution is weak. Stephen
also employs the first person plural in his narrative; scholars are divided on whether
this attests to Stephen's participation in events by about 679, or whether the author
speaks in a collective sense (he and his audience were Wilfridian loyalists).*

*In two instances Stephen's narrative brings his hero into the midst of Frankish pol-
itics: (1) on Wilfrid's first journey to Rome in the middle and late 650s as a young
man, when he spent some time in Lyons and is supposed to have witnessed the killing
of its bishop, executed on the orders of Balthild; (2) on the occasion of Wilfrid's second*

*journey to Rome in 678, when he was escaping the clutches of Ebroin and renewing his acquaintanceship with Dagobert II, king of Austrasia; at this point Stephen tells us about the special service that Wilfrid had performed for the Austrasian king.*

Source: *The Life of Bishop Wilfrid by Eddius Stephanus*, ed. and trans. Bertram Colgrave (Cambridge, 1927). Translation by A.C. Murray.

## (1) The Dalfinus/Aunemund Episode

*There are considerable onomastic and chronological problems with Stephen's version of this episode. The identification of the bishop of Lyons at this time as Dalfinus is incorrect. His name was Aunemund. Much later stories that attribute the name Dalfinus to Aunemund or his brother, the ruler of Lyons, probably go back indirectly to the* Life of Wilfrid, *via the famous eighth-century English historian Bede, who drew on Stephen's account.*

*The major chronological difficulty concerns the date of Dalfinus/Aunemund's execution: according to the usually accepted chronology of Wilfrid's life, Dalfinus would have been put to death in 658; but Aunemund's name is attested in charters, generally held to be genuine, as late as 660. In view of the date of Stephen's writing and the broad strokes of his chronology, the gap is probably not insurmountable, but this circumstance in itself is no guarantee of the reliability of the narrative. Wilfrid was back in Northumbria for a substantial, if indefinite, period of time before the Synod of Whitby in 664.*

*Aunemund's successor in Lyons was Genesius, Balthild's helpmate (see **60**, c. 4, above).*

*Wilfrid's journey to Rome started in 653 or 654. On reaching Lyons, Wilfrid and his traveling companion Benedict Biscop parted company, Benedict pushing on to Rome and Wilfrid and his party remaining behind in Lyons "for a period of time."*

[4]...In the city of Lyons was the archbishop Dalfinus [Aunemund], in whose eyes Wilfrid the most gentle servant of God found favor. The archbishop generously gave him and his companions hospitality, seeing in his peaceful countenance the reflection of a blessed mind. He lavished on them everything they needed as if they were his own and wanted to adopt Wilfrid as his son.

"If you promise to stay," he said, " I shall give you a good part of Gaul to rule permanently and shall marry you to the virgin daughter of my brother; you yourself I shall adopt as a son and you will have me as a father to help you loyally in all endeavors."

Holy Wilfrid, servant of God, wisely responded, as he had been taught, "My vows are to God and I shall fulfill them. Leaving my kin and my father's house, as did Abraham, I shall visit the apostolic see to learn the rules of ecclesiastical discipline so that our nation may grow in the service of God..."

*Wilfrid visited Rome for "many months," studying under the archdeacon Boniface, who presented him to the pope.*

*The emphasis below on the tonsure of Saint Peter is meant to contrast continental practice with the Celtic tonsure found in the English church as a result of the conversion by Scots from Iona.*

[5]...The servant of God with the help of the holy relics he found in Rome set out in the peace of Christ and returned as was appropriate to his father, the archbishop of the Gallic city of Lyons.

[6] Dalfinus the archbishop being found safe and sound, the thankful son went to see the father and the man of God Wilfrid recounted in detail all the blessings of his journey. The bishop gave thanks to God that He had kept his son safe on the journey there and back.

Now Wilfrid stayed with him for three years and learned much from very expert teachers; the love of father and son for each other grew more and more. Wilfrid, the servant of God ardently desired the form of the tonsure of the apostle Peter shaped like the crown of thorns encircling Christ's head and gladly received it from the holy archbishop Dalfinus. Placing his hands on Wilfrid's head Dalfinus intended in his heart to make him his heir if God so willed it, but God had something better in mind for our nation.

For at that time a spiteful queen by the name of Balthild was persecuting the church; just like the most evil Jezebel who once killed the prophets of God, she had nine bishops killed, not counting deacons and priests. One of the bishops was Bishop Dalfinus whom malicious dukes had ordered to appear before them. He went fearlessly to the place of suffering knowing what the future had in store for him.

The holy bishop Wilfrid was with him and, when the bishop forbade him to come, rejoicing Wilfrid said, "There is nothing better for us than that father and son die together and be with Christ."

Now the holy bishop received the crown of martyrdom. But when the holy Wilfrid was fearlessly standing stripped and readied for the palm of martyrdom, the dukes said, "Who is that handsome youth who is ready to die?"

"A foreigner from the nation of the Angles from across the sea in Britain," they were told.

"Spare him, don't touch him," said the dukes.

See how our holy Wilfrid was already now made a confessor, just as John the apostle and evangelist sat unharmed in a cauldron of boiling oil and drank deadly poison with no ill effect...

## (2) The Ebroin-Dagobert Episode

*The following events are dated to 678 and 679. At the time, Wilfrid's diocese had been divided among other bishops without his consent, and he decided to take his complaint before the pope.*

[25] Bishop Wilfrid of blessed memory prepared to board ship with his companions and clergy, leaving many thousands of monks lamenting and weeping under the authority of newly ordained bishops and praying continually to God to direct Wilfrid's journey as He willed it. But the enemies of our leader, mindful of their misdeeds, thinking that he would be sailing south to Étaples and thereby taking the direct route to the holy see, sent their agents ahead. They brought gifts to Theoderic [III], king of the Franks and to Ebroin, the wicked duke, to persuade them to condemn Wilfrid to greater exile or to kill his companions and despoil him of all his property.

The Lord however freed Wilfrid from the hands of his enemies as though from the hands of Herod. For at that time the holy Bishop Winfrid had been driven from Lichfield and was taking that road. He fell into the hands of the above mentioned enemies as into the jaws of a lion. He was immediately taken prisoner and despoiled of his money. They killed many of his companions and left the holy bishop naked and in the worst kind of misery. They mistakenly thought he was the holy bishop Wilfrid and fortunately confounded the first syllables of their names.

[26] Our holy bishop decided on the contrary to turn the prows of his ships to the east and, with a moderate breeze blowing from the west, landed in Frisia with all his company as he intended. There he found pagans in great number and was warmly welcomed by their king Aldgisl. Then our holy bishop immediately got permission from the king to preach daily the word of God to the peoples, telling them of the true God, almighty father, and Jesus Christ, his only son, and the holy spirit, coeternal with them; and he taught them clearly that there was one baptism for the remission of sins, and eternal life after death in the resurrection of the body. In the view of the pagans, all his teaching was greatly helped by the fact that, at the time his company arrived, the year was better than usual in the fishery and fruitful in other respects and they attributed this to the glory of God about whom the holy man of God was preaching.

So in that year they accepted his preaching, and he baptized in the name of God all the chief men, with a few exceptions, and many thousands of the common people. And like the apostle he first laid the foundation of the faith there upon which his son, who was raised at Ripon, Willibrord, bishop by the grace of God, is still building, toiling laboriously; his reward awaits him in heaven.

[27] Also at that time, Ebroin, duke of Theuderic, king of the Franks, sent his agents with a letter to Aldgisl, king of the Frisians, greeting him in peace, and promising under oath to give him a bushel basket of gold solidi, if he

would deliver up Bishop Wilfrid alive or would kill him and send his head. Immediately the king had the letter read out for all to hear during a feast in the palace with the emissaries and his people while we were present.

And after the letter was read, King Aldgisl took it in his hands, tearing it up for all to see, and threw it in pieces in the fire in front of him.

"Tell your lord that this is my response," said the king to the letter-bearers. 'In this way may the creator of things tear up, destroy, and reduce to ashes the kingdom and the life of anyone who perjures himself before his god and does not keep the agreement into which he has entered.'"

Then the emissaries, confounded, left a king who would not consent to a crime and returned to their own lord.

[28] After our bishop, beloved of God, had spent the winter among the Frisians, converting many people to the Lord, when spring came, with God's help he resumed his journey to the Holy See along with his companions.

He came to the king of the [Austrasian] Franks called Dagobert [II, a. 676–79], who welcomed him kindly, honoring him for the service the bishop had previously rendered the king. For the aforesaid king in his youth had been condemned to exile by his enemies, who were ruling, and had sailed to the island of Ireland with God's help. In the course of the years, his friends and relations heard from travelers that he was alive and flourishing in the prime of life. They sent their agents to the blessed Bishop Wilfrid, asking him to invite Dagobert from Scotland and Ireland and to send him to them as a king. Our holy bishop did this; welcoming Dagobert when he came from Ireland, Bishop Wilfrid sent him forth to his own country in fine style, having furnished him with arms and supported him with a force of companions. And now the king, mindful of these kindnesses, earnestly asked him to assume the greatest bishopric of his kingdom, that of Strasbourg; but when Wilfrid declined the offer, the king sent him to the holy see with gifts and lavish presents and with the king's bishop Deodatus [of Toul] to guide him...

*Strasbourg was vacant in 679; Deodatus was bishop of Toul in 679-80.*

# C. THE POLITICS OF MARTYRDOM IN SEVENTH-CENTURY SAINTS' LIVES

## 62. THE *PASSION OF LEUDEGAR*

*The reigns of Theuderic III and Childeric II are dealt with very briefly in LHF 45-9. They are illuminated by the accounts of two martyrdoms connected with the political events of the period. A narrative account of a martyrdom was called a* passio, *or passion, which means suffering. The term derives from descriptions of the last days of Christian martyrs during the Roman persecutions. Like all genres, the* passio *often employed stock motifs and interpreted events according to its own conventions and the expectations of its audience. The two examples of the genre below are distinguished by being written shortly after the deaths of their subjects and by the attempt to set their subjects within the political events of the day. Taken together, their value is enhanced by the different perspective each* passio *takes of the leading characters in those events.*

*Saint Leudegar —Saint Léger in French — was Bishop of Autun from about 662 to 676. According to the LHF 45, he supported the appointment of Leudesius as mayor of the palace in 675. Leudegar was executed around 678/79 on the orders of the mayor Ebroin. The* Passion of Leudegar *was written in the 680s and dedicated to Hermenar, Leudegar's successor to the see of Autun and a participant in the events surrounding Leudegar's removal and death.*

*Leudegar's uncle Dido, bishop of Poitiers (ca. 628-67), mentioned in chapter 1 of the* Passio, *was involved in taking the young Dagobert II to Ireland (LHF 43). In chapters 9-12, the principal events surrounding Leudegar and Hector's flight from Autun at Easter of 675 take place over only a few days: Thursday, the day of the last supper; Easter Friday, the day of Christ's passion; Saturday, on which vigils were held in the evening; and Sunday, the day of the resurrection. This period, with a different set of details, also figures in the account of the* Passion of Praejectus *(below,* **63**, *cc. 23-27). Readers attempting to reconstruct the chronological sequence of events in Leudegar's career, should be aware of the author's habit of bringing the reader to a certain point in the narrative and then backtracking to recapitulate previously unmentioned events.*

*The following translation includes most of the* Passio, *but I have omitted the prologue and postumous miracles.*

Source: *Passio Leudegarii* I, ed. Bruno Krusch, in *Passiones vitaeque sanctorum aevi Merovingici*, MGH SRM 5 (1910), pp. 282-332. Translation by A.C. Murray.

[1] Glorious and renowned Leudegar, bishop of the city Autun, has been created a new martyr in Christian times. Just as he was nobly born according to earthly descent, so, accompanied by divine grace and growing in manly

strength from an early age, he stood out prominently ahead of others no matter what the office or order in life to which he was promoted. His uncle Dido, bishop of Poitiers, who was provided with a notable abundance of prudence and wealth beyond that of his neighbours, took great pains to raise him; and so, thoroughly polished in all respects by the file of instruction in the various studies that the powerful of the world are accustomed to undertake, Leudegar was chosen to assume the burden of the archdiaconate of the same city.

His courage and wisdom became so conspicuous that he appeared to have no equal among his predecessors. Especially because he was not unacquainted with the penalties of the temporal law, he was a terrifying judge of secular matters. And since he was filled with the doctrines of the church canons, he emerged as a distinguished teacher of clerics. He was also spirited in the punishment of offenders and never tried to be lenient with excesses of the flesh. He was vigilant, keenly concerned with the duties of church personnel, energetic in keeping accounts, prudent in giving advice, and glowing with eloquence.

[2] Meanwhile it became necessary to ordain him bishop of the city of Autun. For lately a dispute between two candidates for the episcopal office of that city had erupted and had reached the point of bloodshed. When one of the candidates lay dead on the spot and the other had been exiled for committing the crime, Balthild, who with her son Chlothar [III] was in charge of the palace of the Franks, at that point, inspired, I believe, by divine counsel, sent this energetic man to that city to be its bishop. The church which, as if widowed, had already been left to the uncertainties of the world for almost two years, would now be protected by his direction and strength and defended against those who were attacking it.

How much more should be said? All the enemies of the church and the town, as well as those who endlessly disputed among themselves with hateful acts and killings, were so afraid on his arrival that they did not want to hear the outrage that had taken place recalled. Those whom his preaching could not persuade to accept peace, the terror of justice forced to do so.

Now that he was in office by God's will, he lavished such concern on giving alms to the poor that it would take too long to recount it in detail. But if we are silent, his works are a witness: the station for poor relief (*matricula*) that he established stands at the doors of the church; the beauty of the precious objects which glow with the flash of gold in the service of the church; and also the decorations of the baptistry made with marvellous workmanship. The tomb of Saint Symphorian and the translation of his body reveals to those who remain silent the extent to which he was devoted to the love of the martyrs. Moreover the pavement and the golden awning of the church, the construction of a new atrium, the repair of the town walls, the restoration of buildings and his reconstruction of whatever had deteriorated through great age, suggest as visible reminders to onlookers the extent of his energy.

Let these few special examples among many suffice. We turn in our account to the time the champion of Christ first took up the fight against the devil...

[4] In those days Ebroin was, as we say, mayor of the palace. He ran the palace at that time under King Chlothar [III, a. 657-73], for the queen whom we mentioned above was now living in the monastery which she had previously prepared for herself. Moreover, envious men came to Ebroin and roused his anger against Leudegar the man of God, and whereas they found no charge to lay that was true, they made up a false one that, while everyone obeyed Ebroin's commands, only Bishop Leudegar defied his orders.

The aforesaid Ebroin was so inflamed by the torch of gain and so captive to the desire for money that only those who brought more money had their cause judged to be just by him. As some out of fear, and others to purchase justice, lavished immense sums of gold and silver on him, for this reason the hearts of certain people were roused against him, distressed at being robbed but especially because he not only trafficked in plunder but even shed the innocent blood of many nobles for a minor offense. And so Ebroin continued to be suspicious of Bishop Leudegar; for Ebroin could not conquer him by words, and Leudegar, unlike others, did not pay court to him with flattery. Ebroin recognized that Leudegar always remained firm in the face of all his threats.

At the time Ebroin had issued a tyrant's edict that no one should presume to come to the palace from Burgundy without receiving his authorization. Out of fear, all the leading men were now suspicious that he was contemplating adding to his crime by condemning certain people to lose their heads or by inflicting losses of property on them.

[5] While the matter remained unresolved, King Chlothar, called by God, passed away [a. 673]. But although Ebroin ought to have called the magnates together and, as is customary, solemnly raised to the kingship the king's brother, Theuderic [III, a. 673, 675-91] by name, he was puffed up with pride and decided not call them from this time onwards. They became more afraid because as long as he kept control of the king, whom he should have raised up in public for the glory of the homeland, he would be able fearlessly to inflict evil on anyone he desired in the king's name. A host of nobles were hastening to meet the new king when Ebroin sent a command for them to give up their journey. They took counsel among themselves, abandoned the king, and all sought out Childeric [II], the king's younger brother who had been allotted the kingship in Austrasia. Whoever did not want to accept this decision either escaped by flight or agreed against his will under threat of death by burning.

[6] When, out of fear of the tyrant Ebroin, they had all brought Childeric into the kingdom of Neustria as well as that of Burgundy, the tyrant recognized that it was his own villainy that brought this about and took refuge at the altar of the church; his treasure was at once broken into many pieces and what the wicked man had gathered together wrongly for so long was immediately well dispersed. They did not kill him because certain bishops stepped in between them, and especially because the bishop Leudegar intervened; but they sent him to the monastery of Luxeuil in exile so that, through penance, he might escape the consequences of the crimes he had committed. But since the eyes of his heart were blinded by the dust of earthly desire, spiritual wisdom did not prevail in his spiteful soul.

Childeric ordered his brother, against whom he had been asked to come, brought into his presence so he could speak with him. That is when certain leaders in the kingdom who wanted to dissuade Childeric from bloodshed through flattery had the audacity to order the hair of their lord cut and took pains to deliver him before his brother in this condition. But when Theuderic was asked by his brother what he wished done to him, he declared only that he was awaiting the swift judgment of God because he had been unjustly degraded from his position as king. Then orders were given that Theuderic live in the monastery of the holy martyr Dionysius; and he was kept safe there until such time as he grew back the hair they cut off. And the God of heaven, whom he had declared as his judge, happily allowed him to reign afterwards.

[7] Meanwhile everyone asked King Childeric to issue throughout the three kingdoms he had acquired edicts to the following effect. Judges must, as in antiquity, preserve the law and custom of each of the homelands. Officials (*rectores*) must not pass from one province into another. And one person must not be allowed to usurp power in the fashion of Ebroin, and then, like him, hold his peers in disdain; as long as it was recognized that advancement to the top offices would take place by turns, no one would dare set himself before another. Although the king granted the requests freely, he was corrupted by foolish, almost heathen, counselors — for the superficiality of youth got the better of him — and immediately opposed what he had authorized with the advice of wise men.

[8] The king kept holy Leudegar constantly by his side in the palace because he had seen that the bishop outshone everyone in wisdom. For this reason the envy of evil men revived and grew. Again they looked for grounds for making accusations against him, so that whatever the king did, whatever just or unjust decision he made, they accused Leudegar of doing it. Had the king complied with Leudegar's advice, he would have acted with divine authority. But by now the sentence laid down by heaven had overtaken him, so that his heart could not comprehend the teachings of justice; instead he

deserved that a swift sentence carry out the judgment that Theuderic declared he was awaiting from God.

When the man of God saw the envy of the devil heat up once more against him, following the apostle, he took up the armor of faith, the helmet of salvation and the sword of the Spirit, which is the word of God, and went into single combat with the ancient enemy. And since priestly integrity knows not how to fear the threats of a king, Leudegar censured him for suddenly altering the customs of the kingdoms after he had ordered them to be preserved; and likewise, it is said, he told him that the queen [Bilichild], his wife, was the daughter of his uncle [Sigibert III]; and, if he did not emend these deeds as well as other transgressions, he should know truly that divine vengeance would immediately be at hand.

Indeed, at first the king began to listen willingly, but the advice of his followers got the better of him. At the same time as he should have been using Leudegar's words to reform himself, the king began to look for pretexts for bringing about the bishop's death. This was on the advice of those who wanted to overturn justice and, disorderly themselves, were in favor of the king acting in an immature fashion, as well as of those who enticed the king into breaking his own decree. All of them, and others like them living amidst the desires of the world, feared their works would be destroyed by the man of God, for by now they knew that he marched a straight course along the path of justice. The old world, weighed down by vices, could not withstand the manly power of the heavenly citizen.

[9] There was in those days a certain nobleman called Hector, who had taken up the fasces of office over the patriciate of Marseilles. He was endowed beyond others with nobility of birth and wordly wisdom, being descended from a famous lineage. He had come to see King Childeric about a certain legal case and hoped to gain what he was seeking through the intercession of the man of God. The holy man of God had welcomed Hector to his city and provided him with lodging, waiting for the time when he could recommend Hector to the king and speak on his behalf, as Hector had requested. For Leudegar had asked Childeric to come to the church of his city during the celebration of Easter. The envious ones found this the pretext by which they might fill the king's heart to the full with the vileness they had lately been pouring into it. They brought the then mayor of the palace, who was called Wulfoald, into their subterfuge and made up a lying story that Leudegar and Hector had joined together to overthrow royal authority and usurp for themselves the reins of power.

[10] There was also at the time in the monastery of Saint Symphorian a certain man in the garb of a religious by the name of Marcolinus, a recluse in body but not in mind and, as was publicly revealed afterwards, rather too eager to seek human praise and honors through the false appearance of reli-

gion. Of his way of life I think it better to be silent than to speak, especially since it was revealed to everyone. The king, therefore, mistook this fellow for a prophet of God in all matters because Marcolinus flattered his desire to be favored above all else with accusations against the man of God.

And so on the night when the holy vigils of Easter were celebrated in the city, the king, by now suspicious, refused to come there, but with a few flatterers sought the advice of the aforesaid hypocrite; and since the king bore ill feelings towards the servant of God, he had no qualms about receiving the Easter sacrifice at the right time where he was.

But afterwards, shamefully drunk on wine, he entered the church while others, fasting, were awaiting the holy services. He looked for Leudegar, shouting out his name, trying to put him to flight; all the while he terrified those who now relayed messages, threatening to strike them with the sword. Frequently calling for Leudegar, the king learned that he was in the baptistery, and when he entered it, stood amazed at the brightness of the light and the aroma of the chrism that was used by those conducting baptisms there to give blessings. But although Leudegar answered the shouting by saying, "I am here," the king completely failed to see him. He crossed the baptistry and took up quarters in the manse of the church, which had been made ready.

The other bishops who were celebrating the vigils with the man of God returned to their quarters. But when Leudegar finished the holy office, showing no sign of fear, he approached the angry king and gently asked him why he had not come before the vigils and why he stayed so angry through the celebrations of such a holy night. Disturbed, the king could only answer the ineffable wisdom of Leudegar by saying that he had suspicions about him concerning a certain matter.

[11] Leudegar the man of God saw that the king had not changed his mind. The king, at the urging of his followers, would inflict death on him and Hector, just as he had resolved; or Hector, with no place to turn, would rise up against the despised king, just as the king's men feared. Leudegar was not concerned for his own life but for those who had come to him for protection, and looking for safety, chose for the time being to find refuge in flight rather than offer a pretext for the church to be bloodied by his martyrdom or to be ravaged during the celebrations of Christ's resurrection, or for those who had turned to him to lose their lives without any consideration. For surely there is no one who thinks that he was afraid even of martyrdom?

In fact, when earlier he got word of his own destruction through a monk by the name of Berthar on the day of the Lord's supper, the next day, that of the passion of the Lord, he went to the king's palace, and, bursting in uninvited, tried to offer his blood to Christ on the very day that Christ poured forth his own blood for the salvation of the world. On the same day the king even tried to strike him with his own hand, but, because of the respect due the day, was prevented from doing so by the wise advice of certain magnates. One must believe without doubt that he was saved at that moment by heaven so that the furnace of lengthy persecution would purify any impurity he might have acquired from living a human life, which cannot be led without fault. And placed like pure gold in the crown of his own king, he would afterward shine like gleaming jewels by the power of miracle.

Those who were waiting to exploit this opportunity thereupon mounted a swift pursuit of him. Hector was killed on the spot; and since he manfully tried to defend himself, as was God's will, it took large numbers to overcome him and some of those accompanying him. And it is believed to be not impossible that indulgence can be obtained from God through the merits of the holy martyr for those souls who along with him tried innocently to ward off the storm of persecution.

[12] As soon as Leudegar, the servant of God, had been taken into custody by certain of his pursuers, they immediately sent word to Childeric that the deed was done; he who had successfully arrested Leudegar thought that he would enjoy the utmost favor of the king. On the advice of the magnates and bishops, orders were given for Leudegar to be taken to the monastery of Luxeuil until such time as they could deliberate together as to what to do with a man of such rank.

In the meantime, Childeric inquired of all the chief officials of the palace together what judgment they would determine for this saint of God, and they answered unanimously that, if the king granted him his life, he should order Leudegar to remain in perpetual exile in Luxeuil. The king immediately authorized the judgment decreed against him. Some bishops and priests, for their part, agreed to it to free Leudegar for the moment from the anger of the king.

For, led astray by the advice of the wicked, the king had given orders for him to be taken from Luxeuil and placed at the disposal of his accusers as an object of mockery for them to have killed as they wished, as formerly Herod had intended the Jews to do to Peter. Now there was present a venerable abbot of the church of Saint Symphorian by the name of Hermenar — it was to him that the king assigned the city at the request of the people after the death of the man of God — and he repeatedly threw himself at the feet of the king begging him over and over again to allow Leudegar to remain in Luxeuil and not to have him led into the waiting arms of cruel men whose anger the devil had inflamed against him. Because of entreaties of this kind, Leudegar was at that time at last saved from death. But some were of the false belief that Hermenar often visited the lodging of the king to be first among Leudegar's accusers and thereby more readily get permission to hold the bishopric. At length the truth emerged, and because the eye of the flesh does not see spiritual love, the deeds of that man afterwards bore witness, for as long as

Leudegar was still alive he tended to his needs with devout charity as best he could.

[13] In those days Ebroin was still lodged as an exile in Luxeuil, tonsured and in a monk's garb, pretending to act with the peaceable intention that as long as both he and Leudegar were serving the same but separate sentences of exile they would lead their lives in harmony.

In the meantime, after these events had taken place, divine vengeance did not refrain long from imposing its judgment on Childeric. For his loose behavior among the palace magnates grew worse. Then one of them, who found this more troubling than the others, gave him his death wound as he was hunting in safety in the forest.

[14] But before that happened, while a certain two dukes to whom the orders had been given to remove Leudegar from Luxeuil were waiting to do that, one of their servants agreed to put Leudegar to the sword if he saw him outside Luxeuil. When the time came to do it, an unbearable trembling so engulfed the man's heart that he not only said in a public confession that he was contemplating such a momentous deed but also told why. Trembling, he threw himself at Leudegar's feet begging to be forgiven by him for this wickedness.

[15] As soon as Childeric's death was suddenly announced, certain of those who had been sentenced to exile at his command returned without fear, like poisonous snakes after wintertime that come forth from their caves in the spring. Their wild rage caused a huge disturbance in the homeland, so that it was openly believed that the approach of the Antichrist was at hand. As for those who should have been in charge of the regions, they rose against each other, and those who should have kept the bonds of peace together began to provoke each other with hateful deeds. And as long as the king was not established on top, each one did what seemed right according to his own desires, without fear of punishment. Indeed we recognized at that time that the anger of God became manifest, so that even a star that the astrologers call a comet was seen in the sky [August 676]: on its rising, they say, the land is thrown into confusion by famine, by the succession of kings, and by disturbance among the nations, and destruction by the sword is imminent. It is certain that all these events plainly happened after that. But as it is written that the foolish cannot be corrected by words, much less by portents, they returned from exile with evil intent. They made the claim that whatever they had suffered for their crimes was the fault of Leudegar's supporters.

[16] In these days the man of God was held in custody by the aforementioned dukes for safety's sake and had by now recently been taken by them from Luxeuil. At that very moment divine grace had granted its servant a venerable honor whereby those same dukes, their wives, all their servants and their households, and also the common people in those districts, were joined

together in such love of him that, if the need had arisen, they would not have hesitated to sacrifice themselves on his behalf. When those who were holding the servant of God in their custody informed the other authorities round about that they could see that divine grace was upon the servant of God, they now came together in pious Christian love to support him. Reaching an agreement among themselves, they affirmed that, as long as the disorderly confusion that had arisen prevailed in those districts, holy Leudegar would be protected with their help should anyone try to do harm to him before they had also raised Theuderic to the kingship.

In those days Ebroin also came forth from Luxeuil, like Julian [the Apostate] who pretended to live the life of a monk. And since he was immediately mobbed by a swarm of friends as well as servants, the aforesaid exiles, who were seeking to serve him — and an evil service it was, tacked together from their own claim of injustice — made him leader. This way they could use Ebroin's help and advice to take vengeance on the man of God all together. Ebroin himself raised his venomous head, and like a viper restoring its poison, he pretended to be a follower of Theuderic, hurrying to his side for that reason as quickly as possible.

[17] As the man of God was traveling quickly along the same road with his above-mentioned allies, it happened that, when they were less than a day's journey from the city of Autun, Ebroin, forgetting the pledge of friendship he had once made and at the urging of his associates, would have seized him at that point, had he not been prevented by the advice of Genesius, metropolitan of Lyons or been frightened by the strong band accompanying Leudegar. Again Ebroin feigned friendship; and joining forces they reached the city together.

The church rejoiced at the restored presence of its shepherd, the streets were strewn with fresh boughs, the deacons prepared candles, the clergy celebrated with singing, the whole city rejoiced at the advent of its bishop after the storm of persecution. And not undeservedly was the display of praise offered to him, for in the presence of God he rushed toward the crown of martyrdom, and there, as part of the advent of their pastor, they made ready pleasures for his enemies.

The next day Leudegar and Ebroin moved on together so that they might arrive at a meeting with Theuderic united.

[18] The journey begun, they went to meet the king, but in the meantime, almost in the middle of the trip, the tyrant Ebroin abandoned their company and pressed straight on to his own people, tossing aside his clerical status and returning to his wife [now a nun] behind the holy veil, as a dog returns to its vomit. He who could not serve in the camp of Christ took up the weapons of the world with his enemies. And whereas he had now abandoned faith and God, he showed himself an open enemy of his earthly lord.

Now Theuderic had already recovered the kingdom and was staying safely at the time at the villa of Nogent-les-Vierges when Ebroin attacked swiftly with Austrasians. Who can recount fully the plundering that then took place of the royal treasury and of the vessels of the church that previous Catholic princes had devoutly conferred on the Lord's sanctuary out of Christian love; and who can recount the killing of Theuderic's mayor of the palace?

[19] The reason Ebroin committed this evil was that he was furnished with advice by diabolical and envious men. Their complaint was that they had been brought down by the punishment they deserved. Since they saw that the whole realm had faithfully taken Theuderic's side, that he was now established in the kingship, and that Leudegar the servant of God was living in his own city with the king's favor, envious, they began to be tormented by spite again. For as long as the just were standing tall, the wicked would be unable to make a comeback. Under the influence of the devil, who stripped them of faith, and now blinded, they could devise no truthful strategy for bringing about the ruin of the man of God; and so they resorted to greater destruction by inventing a lie: with this they introduced into the kingdom great evil and devastating slaughter in persecuting many people.

What they did was take a certain young lad and pretend that he was the son of Chlothar [III], raising him up to the kingship in Austrasian territory. By this means they gathered many people together for war because everyone thought he was genuine. And since they subdued the homeland by devastation and now issued directives to the judges in the name of their king, whom they had falsely created, anyone at that time who would not willingly acquiesce to them either lost the right to exercise authority or, if he did not flee into hiding, perished by the sword. Because of this deliberate fiction how great a number of people believed at the time that Theuderic was dead and Clovis was the son of Chlothar [III]?

[20] The leaders in this lie, acting as palace officials, were Desideratus, called Diddo, who had formerly held authority (*principatus*) in Chalon as well as his colleague Bobo, who once had the city of Valence under his control (*dominium*). They did not deserve to be called bishops. They were more anxious to pile up money for earthly desires and worldly profits than to look after the souls committed to their charge, for whom they would render an accounting to a severe judge. It was priests the likes of these and magnates of the same sort whose advice Ebroin followed, so that he was exalted in this world and blinded by it, until such time as he was hurled impenitent into hell.

Let us return to the task we have undertaken.

[21] In those days, after Childeric was killed, and after the bishops and patricians returned with the magnates to Burgundian territory from Neustria and the court of Theuderic, events transpired in each kingdom now that

Theuderic was established in the kingship in such a way that they lived securely in their own lands. In the meantime the envious ones got their forces under way to inflict on Leudegar the malice Ebroin had first conceived against him under King Childeric.

Their forces wasted no time in reaching the city.

As the man of God Leudegar had taken up residence in his city in order to restore his people, he entertained no thought of taking another step to get away when he heard of the enemy attack aimed against him. But without fear he awaited God's judgment on himself. Members of his household as well as clergy and followers were eager for him to remove the treasure that he had gathered there and to depart so that the enemy, when they heard of this, would hold off from destroying the city and pursuing him; but he would not agree to this at all.

Instead Leudegar immediately summoned them to the treasury and, pointing to everything he had added to it, spoke words like these, "Brothers, all these things you see, I have faithfully collected here as well as I could, as long as God's grace wished that I have them for the general embellishment of those on earth. Perhaps they are now angry with me because God sees fit to call us to the grace of heaven. Why should I take from here that which I cannot take with me to heaven? If you are agreed, therefore, I adopt the plan of giving these things away for the benefit of the poor rather than wandering the world here and there with this unseemly baggage. Let us imitate the blessed Laurence; because of what he dispersed and handed over to the poor, his justice remains forever and his power is exalted in glory."

Immediately he commanded the guards to throw out of the treasury as many silver plates and other objects as they could and the silver smiths to come with their hammers to break everything into bits, which he ordered paid out to he poor through the hands of his followers. What was suitable from it for use in churches, he added to the vessels of the church. As for the monasteries of men as well as women in the city and countryside, there he relieved the poverty of many from the same silver. What widow or orphan or general member of the poor who was there at the time did not receive support from his generosity?

[22] As the man of god was full of the spirit of wisdom, he said this to the clergy: "I have decided, brothers, to think no more at all about this world but to fear wickedness of the spirit rather than an earthly enemy. If those on earth receive the power from God, they may pursue, seize, plunder, burn and kill: we cannot escape by turning away from this. And if at this time the transitory course of events means that we are to be delivered over to punishment, we shall not despair but rather shall rejoice in the pardon to come. Let us fortify the soul with virtue and the guarding of the city with valor to prevent the enemy gaining access to either of them and putting us in peril."

He mobilized the people of the town and, after fasting for three days, made a circuit of the walls with the relics of the saints, making the sign of the cross. At each of the gateways he prostrated himself on the ground and entreated God with tears not to allow the people entrusted to him to be taken captive should God call upon him to endure suffering. And events turned out just as he prayed they would.

[23] And so, out of fear of the enemy, people from all over eagerly took refuge in the city, barricaded the gates with strong bars and set offensive works in place overlooking everything. Then the man of god ordered everyone to enter the church and begged the pardon of everyone together, asking that they forgive him if he made accusations against anyone in his eager desire for correctness, as happens, or hurt one of them with words. Walking the path of suffering, the man of God knew that martyrdom would be of no benefit unless it was illuminated by the light of charity and the heart was first purified by being cleansed of spite. There was no one there at the time so hard of heart as not to relinquish devoutly all the malice in their hearts, even if they had been seriously hurt.

Not long afterwards the city was surrounded by the army, and on the same day there was stiff fighting on both sides until evening. But when the forces of the enemy had surrounded the city with a strong blockade and day and night went around the city howling like dogs, the man of God, taking a careful look at the danger threatening the city, stopped all the fighting from the walls.

He set about encouraging his people as follows, "I beg of you to stop engaging these people in battle. If they have come here only on my account, I'm ready to satisfy their desires with regard to me and to calm their anger. However, so that we don't go out without a chance to plead our case, let one of the brothers be sent to ask them why they are besieging this city."

Immediately they prepared a way down through the defensive works of the wall for abbot Meroald, who went to Diddo and said: "If our crimes have incurred this attack, I ask you to recall the passage of the Gospels where God said: 'If you do not forgive people their sins, your heavenly father will not forgive you your sins'; and 'In whatever matter you give judgment, you shall be judged.'" At the same time he begged Diddo to stop his forces and accept what ransom he wished.

But as Diddo's heart had now hardened with the hardness of a stone, as once did that of the king of Egypt [Ex. 10:1], Diddo could not at all be softened by divine words; he threatened to keep attacking the city until such time as he could get his hands on Leudegar and satisfy the mad desire of his anger, unless Leudegar pledged loyalty to Clovis, whom they had falsely created king. This cause was feigned because everyone was asserting by oath that Theuderic was dead.

[24] When the man of God heard what was said, he gave them this answer, "All of you take note, friends and brothers as well as foes and enemies. As long as it is God's will that I live, I shall not be budged from the loyalty to Theuderic that I have promised before God to maintain. I have decided to give my body over to death rather than shamefully to strip bare my soul by disloyalty."

The enemy, when they heard this reply, lost no time in attempting to storm the city with fire from all sides and under a hail of missiles. As for Leudegar, he bade farewell to all the clergy, sharing bread and wine and strengthening their doubtful hearts, entrusting the recollection of his suffering to them, like Christ to his disciples. He reached the gates unshaken by fear, and when the gates were opened, he offered himself of his own free will to his enemies on behalf of the city.

Like wolves taking up a harmless sheep, his enemies rejoiced in their prey and thought up a most wicked type of punishment. For they blinded him, tearing his eyes out of his head. The stamina he displayed when the blade was inserted was beyond human endurance. Many men of illustrious rank who were present at the scene are witnesses that he suffered no restraints being placed on his hands nor did a cry escape his lips as his eyes were pulled from his head, but glorifying God he continually tried to chant psalms.

[25] There was among others a certain duke of Champagne by the name of Waimar, who had come with Diddo from Austrasian territory to perpetrate this crime. These two gave power over Autun — the power of laying the city waste would be the way to phrase it — to a certain Bobo, who had recently been thrown out of the episcopacy of the city of Valence with anathema. The citizens of Autun, crushed, received the enemy, for now they had lost their shepherd. Under Bobo's direction almost all the chattels of the church were carried off. For a pretext was found for putting the city to ransom and the silver of the church was taken away to the sum of 5000 solidi, apart from loot from the citizens. And though the church made up the amount from its transitory possessions, God permitted no one to be taken from there as a captive.

[26] The enemy joyfully divided the spoils and gave the man of God into the custody of the above-mentioned Waimar, who returned quickly to his homeland with him and all the army. Desideratus, called Diddo, with Bobo and Duke Chaldaric, whom they wanted to be patrician of Provence, marched to Lyons to subdue the homeland. They would have taken Genesius from there, as a short time before they had driven Leudegar from Autun, but a strong force of people gathered from all over and under God's leadership prevented them from storming this very great city.

[27] As for those who conducted the man of God Leudegar, when they sent news to Ebroin of what had been done, he ordered Leudegar to be taken

to the depths of the forest and slowly starved to death. In the meantime a lying tale about his death was to be concocted according to which he died by drowning and even his grave mound was to be made. Whoever was able to hear or see this evidence believed it to be true.

But he who fed Elijah in the desert by means of a raven [3 Kings 17:4] did not abandon his servant. After a long starvation, which God's martyr endured, Waimar could not conceive that the human nature in Leudegar could hold out to this extent, unless the grace of Christ sustained him, and so he had him brought into his house: Waimar's hard feelings had now begun to soften with piety. When Waimar became accustomed to speaking familiarly with him, in a short period of time Leudegar so tamed his ferociousness — and converted him and his wife to the fear of God — that Waimar devoutly offered the silver of the church, which he had lately taken for the ransom of the city of Autun, to Leudegar for him to do with as he wanted. The man of God accepted the silver and sent it by means of a certain loyal abbot called Berto to the aforesaid city; and dividing the silver, according to the apostle, among the members of the faith, Berto faithfully fulfilled Leudegar's wish in a charitable act.

[28] As was said, Ebroin could not hide his crime any longer, so, in order to return to the palace of Theuderic, he dropped from his plans the false king whom he created. The interests of certain people were served and he was suddenly made mayor of the palace again.

When they raised him up to the top post, some rejoicing and others fearful, he immediately issued an edict to the effect that no legal actions were permitted regarding losses or plundering suffered during the previous troubles. This was an excuse not to return the loot which his servants brought to him from their spoliation of many people. As he began to swell with restored pride, he became at the same time sorry for himself and fearful that an enemy might have survived on whose relatives he had inflicted injury. Now that he had seized the reins of power, he doubled his malice with spite. He began right away to persecute the more powerful magnates: he either put to the sword the ones he could catch or caused them to flee and took away their property. He even destroyed the monasteries of noble women, sending their abbesses into exile. As he had received the power to trample upon pearls, without pity, like a pig, he had no fear of breaking into the treasury of Christ. And since he could have no regard for heaven, in his heart he was stuck beyond measure in the mud of earthly desire.

[29] Since Ebroin had sated his fury in the above-mentioned matters, he began again to look for a pretext whereby he might remove from human sight his blasphemous cruelty. Now he pretended that he was distressed about the death of Childeric, although no one wanted the king to die more than he did. But without this excuse he did not dare persecute in public those whom

he hated. He now brought holy Leudegar back from his exile into the open and claimed that Leudegar and his brother Gaerin were leaders in the killing of Childeric. For that reason he cruelly ordered Leudegar's lips and cheeks slit through and also the end of his tongue cut out with a knife. As for Gaerin, he ordered him to be crushed by stones. Gaerin, encouraged by his holy brother, breathed his last giving thanks to God.

[30] And so they kept the holy Leudegar alive longer out of vengeance. They ordered him shamefully stripped and led along the swampy roads naked, and they handed him over for vengeance to Waning, as if he had been disgraced, to breath out his last breath crucified under Waning's harsher authority. Since where he was to stay was some distance away, they placed the holy Leudegar on a contemptible mule. And he uncovered the meaning of this verse of the Psalm when he saw that it was thereby fulfilled: "I have been made like a beast of burden before You, and I shall always be with You [Ps. 73:22-23]." And although he now had no lips or tongue, his devout mind could not hold back praises of God which he sounded from the depths of his heart with what voice he could manage.

Everyone who saw him in this condition, severely bloodied, believed that he would breath his last because of it. One of our brothers, the abbot called Winobert, followed him at a distance to the aforesaid lodging, begging the guards in secret not to deny him access; when he got it at last, he found Leudegar lying in straw covered with an old tent cloth, panting weakly. And though he believed he would die right in front of him, he found an unexpected miracle. Amidst the bloody spittle, without lips, Leudegar's tongue, which had been cut short, began to be given back its accustomed speech. The cutting away of his lips had bared the rows of teeth; however, they rendered the sound of words when struck by the breath within.

Then he who had come to prepare his corpse for its passage began to weep with joy and excitedly brought the news to Bishop Hermenar. The bishop approached Waning and asked him to give him access to Leudegar the martyr of God. When the request was granted with trepidation — everyone feared the tyrant, savage as an angry lion — he tried to care for his wounds attentively, to use whatever skill he had to restore him with drink and food, and to clothe his body with a better garment than he had. He respectfully paid him honor, not as a man of this earth, but as one removed from it by martyrdom. For which reason he obtained from him not only forgiveness for what had been done in the past but also a blessing for the future.

[31] After Waning took him to his residence, by God's grace Leudegar's lips as well as his tongue began quite quickly to regenerate contrary to nature; also I saw a stream of words flow from his mouth even beyond what had been usual. When Waning learned of this miracle, he did not harden his heart to inflict his wickedness as the tyrant had commanded. Quite the contrary.

Instructed by God, Waning had previously built a monastery of virgins. Now understanding that his prisoner was a martyr of God, he no sooner had that monastery prepare lodging for Leudegar than there, out of deference for the faith, Waning as well as his wife and everyone in the monastery reverently rendered him service as though they had gotten to see Christ the lord himself. Because of Leudegar's frequent preaching, Waning set aside all his fierce pride and with the help of his prayers was made, along with his followers, so devout in the fear of God that it was as if he had been changed from a beast into a lamb. Since Leudegar there regained the use of his face and tongue within the short space of hours, he tried to make daily sacrifice, for he himself had been offered to God. And although the light of the spirit filled him from within, there was no bodily cure for his eyes.

[32] When faithful people reverently rendered him service after so much scourging, as befits a martyr, the Almighty clearly revealed to all that a light cannot be hidden under a bushel basket: it was then that He began to take revenge on Leudegar's enemies. For while Leudegar stayed there praising God for almost two years, he heard news that his enemies had either been killed or put to flight to other regions for the offense of disloyalty; he did not rejoice in vengeance, but he wept sorely for them in case death's destruction overtook them before they could repent.

[33] One of his enemies was left — Ebroin, the cunning artisan for making the crown of the blessed martyr complete: he would do what was still needed to fulfill the glory of Leudegar's passion. Again the ancient serpent, the envious one, taking it ill that he had been driven from the same place by Leudegar's prayers, began to stir up Ebroin again. He ordered Leudegar brought back to the palace so that he might rend apart his priestly robe in a council of bishops; thereby Leudegar would be prohibited from daring to offer further sacrifice.

When Leudegar had been brought forward into the midst of the assembly, they tried to get from him a confession that he had been privy to the killing of Childeric. Then realizing that again conflict threatened him because of a diabolical fiction, Leudegar said that, just as he did not absolve himself from human wrongdoing, so too he had never advised this deed, but declared that God knew this rather than man. They interrogated him for some time but could not get anything else out of him. So they tore apart his tunic from top to bottom, and the impious tyrant gave orders for him to be handed over to a certain Chrodobert, who was count of the palace at the time, and for his life in this world to be taken from him by a stroke of the sword.

The martyr of God found joy in all his suffering, for he could sense the approach of the martyr's crown that was due to him as a reward from God. Now Chrodobert took him to his own residence. And he obtained such a heavenly blessing on his arrival that, when all those living there saw this plainly, they abandoned their own sins by confessing and eagerly took refuge in the healing medicine of penance. God had adorned his servant with this gift so that whenever he was handed over as an exile to be treated badly, those who received him, on the contrary, all paid him the reverence due from servants.

[34] At last arrived the day of death on which his persecution came to an end. At that time the results of a judicial decision were issued by the palace that Leudegar must live no longer. The impious Ebroin, fearing that faithful Christians would pay Leudegar the respect of a martyr, gave orders for a well to be found deep in the woods and his mutilated corpse to be sunk in it so that, once the mouth of the well was filled in with earth and stones, people would not know where he was buried.

Meanwhile Leudegar, by his preaching to Chrodobert, had already begun to some extent to bring about the latter's conversion. Because Chrodobert could not bear to look at the death of the man of God, he charged two of his servants to carry out the orders he had been given. When this news reached his house, his wife began to weep in bitter distress because such a cruel and shameful act had become the duty of her husband.

[35] When the man of God saw that his end was now at hand, he began to comfort the weeping woman, saying, "Please do not weep over my passing. No demand for vengeance will ever be made against you for my death, but rather a blessing will be given by God from heaven if you devoutly bury my body in its grave."

And when he had spoken these words, he said goodbye at the urging of the servants and was taken to the woods for them to carry out the sentence of the order.

Now they had previously found a well where they could hide his body as they had been told; but they never found it again. While looking for the well, they wandered hopelessly about and on this account put off killing him. In the meantime the martyr of God was allowed to prostrate himself in prayer and to entrust his passing to God. To both of his killers, who were looming over him, he began to predict the future through the spirit of prophecy. One of them, sparked by the ancient enemy, was quite anxious to carry out the deed. But the other, who was a gentle man, tremblingly begged him not to take vengeance on Leudegar.

Leudegar addressed the two of them.

"You, who follow orders against your will," he said, "confess your previous sins immediately to a priest and by doing penance you shall also escape the consequences of this deed."

To the other he said, "And as for you, if you do not do the same, you shall have to be delivered up immediately to God for swift vengeance."

Again, prostrating himself in prayer, he confidently entrusted his soul to

Christ the lord. And getting up, he extended his neck and bade the executioner do what he had been ordered to do. And when the man we mentioned above suddenly cut off his head, a chorus of angels, rejoicing, conducted the spirit of the blessed martyr to heaven to be presented to the Lord so he might reign in heaven with all the saints. There in joyful company of the saints is our lord Jesus Christ, who with the Father and holy Spirit lives and reigns through the course of the ages...

*The* Passio Leudegarii *concludes with post-mortem events and miracles. Leudegar's executioner died horribly four days later. Chrodobert's wife found the body and placed it in an oratorium. The fame of Leudegar's healing power spread despite efforts by Ebroin to suppress the truth.*

*The final event was Ebroin's death.*

And so Ebroin should not escape unpunished for having committed such crime, he sought the moment of death like a madman. For he found a pretext to despoil a certain magnate, who was in charge of fiscal obligations, even to the point of confiscating all his chattels as a penalty; moreover he was also threatening him with death. The man seeing that, now he had suffered confiscation, death too was at hand, found help by stiffening his resolve and keeping watch just before light in the morning for the departure of his enemies; for it was Sunday, so Ebroin was going to morning services. When he put a foot over his threshold, it happened — the man burst forward unexpectedly and struck him in the head with a sword. Ebroin fell down dead from two of the man's sword strokes. And so his wicked rule was removed from the kingdom, as previously David removed a disgrace from the children of Israel when he brought Goliath the Philistine to the ground.

## 63. FROM THE *PASSION OF PRAEJECTUS*

*The events in Autun during Easter of 675, when Leudegar and Hector fled from King Childeric II, are told from quite a different perspective in the* Passion of Praejectus. *According to the* Passio, *Praejectus was bishop of Clermont during the reign of King Childeric II (ca. 662-75). His martyrdom, which can be dated to January 676, came in the wake of the assassination of Childeric and his queen. Though its text is not without complications, the* Passio *appears to have been written not long after the saint's death.*

*The* Passio *contains many interesting details about seventh-century life; the following excerpts emphasize Praejectus's dealings with the Austrasian court and the events leading to his martyrdom. Clermont, and with it the Auvergne, was subject to the kings of Austrasia, as it had been in the days of Gregory of Tours and before. Among the many sidelights the* Passio *casts on contemporary life is the continued control exercised by Merovingian kings south of the Loire.*

Source: *Passio Praejecti episcopi et martyris Arverni*, ed. Bruno Krusch, in *Passiones vitaeque sanctorum aevi Merovingici*, MGH SRM 5 (1910), pp. 225-248. Translation by A.C. Murray.

...[1] Holy Praejectus was born in the province of Auvergne and his light shone forth from a lineage of Roman origin. His father was called Gundolen, his mother Eligia. They traced their descent from a long line of Catholic men, most worthy of their Christian faith, through whom God also revealed miracles.

But we must not fail to mention that when his mother was about to bring him into the world in the fashion of earthly creatures, it is said that, a few days before the time, she saw in amazement how her son came forth from her side followed immediately by a flood of blood that drenched him. Shaken and trembling at the vision, she then began to wail over it and was eager to determine what such things held in store for her. While she was thinking about this, it happened that the most holy archpriest Peladius arrived and, being her brother, began to inquire in detail as to why she was shaking in an unaccustomed manner. She then told him the vision. The holy man of God revealed everything to her: that she would give birth to such a son as would be a great man among his contemporaries in this world and would end his career in martyrdom...

[2] The boy was born, he cried in his cradle, and he was nourished with milk. What more is there to say? He grew as a human does, and, when the time came for him to learn the finer points of letters, he was handed over to a teacher to be taught in the parish of Issoire. Oh truly the Lord filled out his boy in every way! So quickly was he replenished with God's secret that to all that were there he appeared no youngster and, in truth, led the way for his age mates in the sounds of the grammarians and church chant...

[4]...At the time the archdeacon [of Clermont] was Genesius, who not long afterward was raised to the post of bishop. Praejectus's parents had the boy assigned to Genesius's office. Genesius took him in, raised him with the affection of a father, taught him carefully, and, when the archdeacon was made bishop, took him as his personal advisor, making him the distributor of the money set aside for the poor...

*While miraculously mollifying vicious dogs, confounding envious rivals, and rescuing injured construction laborers, Praejectus rose to become one of the leading clerics of the diocese of Clermont.*

*His first attempt to become bishop of Clermont, following the death of Bishop Felix, was not a success. In the selection below, the claim of his rival Garivald to the bishopric of Clermont was based on a right sanctioned by customary practice, not the law of ecclesiastical or secular courts.*

[13] In the time of Bishop Felix, who had just died, Garivald, who had held a diaconal office, had acquired the post of archdeacon. It came to pass that five of the senior clergy came together, that is the aforesaid Garivald of

holy memory; the aforesaid Praejectus; also Arivald, a leader of great faith in the priesthood; and Aginus, priest; the fifth was also a deacon, Stephanus. They had all agreed to the drawing up of a letter [of understanding] because they held the chief positions over the clergy in the aforesaid town. It said that those five were in agreement that Garivald should, God willing, take up the episcopal office after the death of the abovesaid Felix. And this agreement, or compact, had been made to assist the archdeacon's claim, for he believed that he was the successor to the episcopal office because it had been the practice there of earlier generations that whoever served in the diaconal post [of archdeacon] used to acquire episcopal office if the situation presented itself.

When Garivald learned that the blessed Praejectus was recounting the vision which he had learned from his parents, the archdeacon showed the letter openly before the whole church in opposition to him. Furthermore, the aforesaid men who had put their signatures to that letter were helping to elect the blessed Praejectus. Since Garivald saw that he had been hedged in on all sides, and was suffering defeat on account of putting his trust in a pledge on the part of the clergy, he put these men aside, abandoned his association with the other clergy, and sought the assistance of the laity, plying them with gold and silver. They took the money, used force to put down all the clergy, and raised the aforesaid Garivald to the episcopal dignity.

After not much time — forty days elapsed — Garivald fulfilled the debt of nature and left the throne he had unworthily seized to someone better...

*The second time around as an episcopal candidate Praejectus was more fortunate. Count Genesius was a different person than the bishop of the same name in chapter 4.*

[14] In the reign of King Childeric [II, ca. 662-75] of divine memory, who ruled Germania, the church of Auvergne was almost bereft of episcopal authority. At the time Genesius, a very energetic and generous man, rich in resources, held the civic office [of count] of the aforesaid town... The views of various parties regarding the episcopal succession were examined, as is done in such matters: some were trying to promote one candidate and some another, and they were debating among themselves. The largest group arranged with great effort for Genesius to be raised to the episcopal office by royal edicts, but he was struck with fear in case he acted against the decrees of the canons. He spoke publicly, maintaining that he would be unworthy of the priestly office, and the citizens advocated the election of Praejectus, who in those days exercised the office of the priestly order in the aforesaid town. When word of this consensus reached the ears of the common folk, the voice of all clerics and laymen united in declaring that Praejectus deserved the episcopacy. What more is there to say? By God's doing he was ordained bishop...

*Praejectus then saw to the construction of monasteries and is said to be responsible for some less than miraculous miracles.*

[20] At that time it happened that the man of God went to the palace of King Childeric [II] on the business of the church. During his journey, when he was traveling the road through the huge waste called the Vosges, after traversing mountains and valleys and climbing a steep hill, he came with difficulty at last to a place which the barbarians call Doroangus in the gentile language. Near there the venerable Amarinus of blessed memory had quite laboriously built a cell with the leave and permission of the magnate Warnachar [mayor of the palace, a.613-26/7]...

*After curing Amarinus of a fever with the sign of the cross, Praejectus continued his journey.*

[22] ...With the blessing of the brothers he took the road he had begun and reached the prince in peace. God conferred on him such favor before the mayor of the palace [Wulfoald] that he attained with great honor what he asked for. The king was pleased, as were his courtiers, leading officials, and magnates, and he was warmly welcomed by the bishops of the Lord. With Christ's help, he returned home with the privilege of the church approved by the authorization of the prince.

*His next trip to see Childeric II in 675 brought Praejectus into the events surrounding the king's quarrel with Leudegar.*

*In the selection below, Queen Chimnechild is the mother-in-law of Childeric. She had been the wife of Sigibert III, and it was her son Dagobert II who had been sent to Ireland by Grimoald (59.43; 61.28). She married her daughter Queen Bilichild to Childeric II (cf. 60.5 and 59.45) when he assumed the throne in Austrasia.*

[23] There was at that time in the abovesaid territory of Auvergne a certain woman consecrated to God called Claudia. She used to come diligently to hear Praejectus preach and donated part of her property to the aforesaid bishop and the poor over whom he had authority. Not long after, she fulfilled the debt of nature. She was buried with great honor by Praejectus.

And so these events had come to a conclusion. But there was a certain notorious man called Hector, who had attained the office of patrician of Marseilles. He had abducted the daughter of Claudia and illicitly lived with her. Next, though responsible for creating the wretched condition of concubinage, he went to prince Childeric [II], who was reigning at the time, having taken control of both kingdoms. There was another man, called Leudegar, who was associated in Hector's wickedness. This association afterwards set off the violent dispute that ended in Leudegar's martyrdom. Hector charged Bishop Praejectus with claiming properties of Claudia for himself, explained his charges to the king, and had the prince despatch agents to send Praejectus to the king's court and make sure he was delivered by means of sureties.

[24] When the suit was explained to Praejectus and he came to give his answer, he felt grief for now the day of Easter was at hand [a. 675], and he would not be able to hold services on that most holy Easter night in his own city; but, as the proverb truly says, the integrity of priests does not fear the attack of a king, so armed with faith and putting on the helmet of salvation, as Paul the famous preacher says [Eph. 6:16], he hurried to the palace. As is the custom at the king's court, he entered the place where claims are presented to have an accounting with Hector concerning the matter mentioned above.

He himself began by refusing to answer the charges and by giving a valid excuse according to canon law and the law that is called Roman [Theodosian Code 2.8.19]: since it was the great day of the sabbath [Saturday] on which the vigils of the holy easter are conducted, in no way could he respond. But as is the way with contentious people, they all tried to force him not to delay replying for such a reason. When the man of God saw that he was hemmed in on all sides, forced by necessity, his response was to testify that he had assigned the church's legal business to Queen Chimnechild. When they heard this declaration, the matter was left unfinished. Finally the blessed Praejectus explained the hardship of his task and how he came to be presented by sureties. The king and queen were struck with fear and in front of everyone begged the bishop's pardon and were saddened by his distress.

[25] At that time Bishop Leudegar was on the side of Hector. The sun had already passed the midday zone of the heavens and was beginning to set and the customary hour was seen to be at hand when it would be permissible to hold the solemn vigils of Easter. Then, with the leave of the king and of the well-born, the elder bishops and priests who had gathered in Autun because the royal majesty was there zealously asked the blessed Praejectus with suppliant voices — or rather they begged him — to conduct the sacrifice to God on that holy night on behalf of the well-being of the king and the peace of the church. When Hector learned of this deep respect, and especially because he had abused the trust of Wulfoald the senior official in the palace, both Hector and Leudegar fled in the middle of the night after a wicked sentence had been passed against holy Leudegar. With appropriate changes, the epitaph that is given in the *Acts of Holy Sylvester* for Perpenna Tarquinius can be applied to Hector. There it is written that, on the same hour that had been set for the blessed Sylvester to stand before his tribunal, he was 'cast from his house and taken to the grave on a litter.'

[26] But when the day dawned and sunlight had illuminated the earth, and after the king learned through his leading officials that Hector had fled, they could not do enough to honor Bishop Praejectus. As for Hector, he was captured and executed on the instructions of the king. And as for Leudegar, he was taken away to perform penance by being sent to Luxeuil in exile. Later,

below the walls of his own city, Leudegar suffered at the hands of a certain Waimar who had the bishop's eyes torn out; Waimar was a faithless and wicked man who later seized control of the city of Troyes. And not long after that, Leudegar was executed quite sacrilegiously by Ebroin, count of the palace — in other matters a dynamic man but too savage in killing priests — and attained the palm of martyrdom. Now Leudegar is renowned for holy miracles.

[27] And so, regarding the properties that the aforesaid Hector claimed, thanks to royal edicts and the generous gift of the king, blessed Praejectus acquired a judgment to his satisfaction that the church possessed these by perpetual right. Saying farewell to the king and magnates, he returned home, having been honored magnificently.

*Praejectus returned to Clermont, taking with him Amarinus, the holy man he had met earlier in the Vosges.*

*Both were killed, very likely nine months after the events in Autun, in January 676; by this time Childeric II had also been assassinated. The author offers no explanation for the death of Praejectus other than the hostility of the devil. Praejectus's involvement in the downfall of Hector provides a possible motive. Volvic, where he was killed, lies just to the north of Clermont.*

[29] ...The enemy of human kind...approached a certain wicked man and son of Belial, and then through a certain Agricius hurried on to important men of the Auvergne to goad them into killing the man of God by every device he could. At that time Agricius obtained the advice of wicked people, and, like a wild animal, such as the age-old snake hiding in the grass, lost no time in attacking the man of God at the villa of Volvic with a host of followers.

A mile from the villa, they sounded a horn from the woods, like rapacious wolves howling at a sheepfold. Blessed Praejectus and Amarinus heard the sound of horns and both began to pray, waiting to receive the unfading crown from the Lord. All the staff in the service of the bishop were struck with fear when they heard the braying of war trumpets. Stripped of their clothing and despoiled of their weapons, they retreated through thornbushes and thick groves of trees. When the evil men approached the door of the house and were trying to get in, then, it is said, one of the man of God's officials, the doorkeeper named Gundolen, fought in defense of him, preferring to die by the sword than to have to announce to the world a halt in the fighting before the man of God was dead.

[30] But when a band of twenty armed followers of the evil men had gotten in to the house, then we are told that the venerable Amarinus spoke to the man of God Praejectus.

"My Lord," he said, "If your plan for us had been to retreat before the voices of these howling and evil men, perhaps the boundless goodness of God may see fit to snatch us from the snares of the wicked."

To this the man of God Praejectus replied: "Be quiet, brother, be quiet, for if you cheat yourself of this crown now, you shall never find it again."

Amarinus stopped talking like this. But the blessed Praejectus poured forth even more prayers to God and entrusted his holy spirit to Him.

The wicked men entered when the prayers were finished and, at first taking the servant of God Amarinus for blessed Praejectus, cut his throat in a corner of the house. And while the man of God lay upon his couch and soaked it with tears, the executioners returned from where they had come and left the blessed Praejectus unharmed.

Seeing that he was cheated of his crown by this, Praejectus took on the task of offering himself to the searchers.

"I am the man you are looking for," he said; "follow your orders."

When he said this, one of those charged with killing him, Radbert by name and a Saxon by birth, who was a bolder criminal than the rest, pulled out a knife and stabbed the blessed Praejectus in the chest. The man of God, drenched by a tide of holy blood, could not bear to see the sword edge and covered his eyes with his hands. And after this the executioner jammed his sword into his head and spilled out his brains. And so that holy spirit, freed from the bonds of the flesh, journeyed to God.

[31] From among the senators who had agreed to resort to martyrdom, Bodo and Placidus, since they were standing not far away, saw three stars rising to heaven over that house in which the holy men of God lay killed; and one of those stars gave off a brighter glow. The aforesaid men affirm even today that they saw this sight. This miracle also, we believe reveals the glory of the slain and the summons of those senators to penance. For no one in this life must despair of pardon if he wishes to be converted...

# CHAPTER FIFTEEN


# FRANKISH LAW


*The Frankish period is rich in legal sources, though these are frequently beset with major problems of interpretation. A number of law codes were in use in one way or another in the Merovingian kingdom: the Breviary of Alaric (a version of the Theodosian Code, cf. 32), the Burgundian Code (first issued by King Gundobad), the Salic Law, the Ribvarian Law; and beyond the Rhine, in the seventh and eighth centuries, Alamannian and Bavarian codes. Unfortunately, the relation of these codes to the law-in-practice and the administration of justice is often poorly understood. For the sixth and early seventh centuries a small number of edicts of the Merovingian kings survive, and an extensive series of canons of church councils. As this record of legislation comes to an end, we are fortunate that the documentary record begins, though haltingly. Genuine and even original charters from the Merovingian period are extant but their range and distribution are limited, a circumstance that is offset to some extent by the survival of an extensive selection of formulae, that is to say, exemplars used by notaries to draw up legal documents.*

*The modest selection of excerpts given here must be read in light of this ample but somewhat intractable and uneven record of the legal dimensions of life under the Merovingian kings.*


## A. THE SALIC LAW (*LEX SALICA*)

Lex Salica *is the most celebrated of the law codes of the early medieval kingdoms and probably the least understood. Its fame is of course a reflection of the importance of the Franks themselves and their influence on European institutions.* Lex Salica *is a central document in the history of European law and provides us with a unique window on the society of the Franks who settled in northwest Gaul. For all its importance, the code would be far more useful if we knew the precise date and circumstances of its compilation and its relationship to the Frankish monarchy. Although modern scholarship seems happy with the idea that Clovis issued* Lex Salica, *there is in fact no evidence that he did so, nor does the codification as we have it come provided with the bureaucratic apparatus that would connect it with royal legislative activity. If* Lex Salica *was issued as an official codification by a king, Clovis is a good candidate, but this is hardly sufficient reason to attribute the code to him. A date of at least the early sixth-*

*century seems assured for the earliest redaction, but the code's contents are best read first without supposing a particular political or institutional context for its compilation. The contents should also be read without presupposing (as has commonly been done in the past) that the laws reflect archaic 'tribal' or 'Germanic' custom. The sources of the law are undoubtedly diverse and reflect the various long-standing institutional and cultural influences affecting the peoples of the Rhine mouth.*

*Lex Salica has been transmitted in a number of versions, or redactions, which also complicate our understanding of the codification. These versions come from various periods and their value in relation to the earliest redaction (A) is a contentious issue; later redactions are undoubtedly the result of complicated textual development and can by no means be read simply as later law-in-practice. As a consequence, Lex Salica must be read and interpreted as a series of redactions, not as one unified, composite codification.*

*In the following translation, I have stuck for the most part to the A redaction, which is generally acknowledged to be the earliest version of the codification. (This means on occasion abandoning the numbering system, and sometimes the readings, of the standard edition, which gives a composite and reconstructed text.) The A redaction is composed of four manuscripts, and includes the earliest Lex Salica MS, dating from the late eighth century. I have also sometimes noted later versions (usually the still Merovingian, C redaction), and some early laws that are associated with the earliest version of the codification where they have a direct bearing on the contents of Lex Salica. For the same reason, I have included laws from Lex Ribvaria, a seventh-century adaptation of Lex Salica made for the Austrasian Franks, and selections from the early formularies.*

*Though Lex Salica occasionally employs Franko-Latin words, the code was written in Latin. In some versions, including the earliest, many of the laws are provided with so-called 'malberg glosses' containing legal terms in Frankish. (The name 'malberg' comes from a Franko-Latin word for 'court'). The Frankish terms are much deteriorated in the surviving MSS, often hopelessly so, and were affixed to the code at some unknown point. Following the standard literature, I have treated the passages in which the terms appear as glosses. I have made no effort to translate the terms nor to standardize their case; in a translation such as this, some of the terms can only be regarded as flavoring. With the exception of the well attested Franko-Latin word leodis, I give the terms in the form reconstructed by the editor of the standard edition or in the form that they have in the text; I endorse neither form. They are introduced in the translation by the phrase 'the forensic term for this is.'*

*Finally, it should be noted, I have grouped the excerpts together thematically.*

Sources: *Pactus legis Salicae*, ed. Karl August Eckhardt, MGH LL Leges Nationum Germanicarum 4/1 (1962); *Edictum Chilperici*, ed. J.H. Hessels, *Lex Salica: The Ten Texts with Glosses and the Lex Emendata* (London, 1880); *Lex Ribvaria*, ed. F. Beyerle, MGH LL Leges Nationum Germanicarum 3/2 (1954); *Formulae Merowingici et Karolini aevi*, ed. K. Zeumer, MGH LL Formulae (1882–86). Translations by A.C. Murray.

# 64. WERGELDS AND COMPENSATION

*Legal sources are valued by historians not just because they treat some of the finer points of institutions and procedure but because they seem to hold out the promise of telling us about the broader divisions of society. Historians have long used the graduated wergelds of the early medieval law codes as a template for contemporary social structure. Lex Salica has not been exempted from this practice; the lack of a wergeld for nobles in its provisions has been the subject of much controversy. The following excerpts largely concern the free class, the focal point of Lex Salica regulations, but as you read on you will notice other legal classes, slaves (servi) and the half-free (leti).*

*The Franko-Latin word* leodis *means wergeld.*

### Homicides of Children and Women (Title 24)

1 If someone is convicted of killing a free boy under 12 years of age, let the offender be judged liable for 24000 denarii, which amounts to 600 solidi. The forensic term for this is *leodis*.

*MS A1 sets the age at 10. The Carolingian D redaction describes the boy as "without his hair cut."*

2 If someone kills a long-haired boy, let the offender be judged liable for 24000 denarii, which amounts to 600 solidi. The forensic term for this is *leodis*.

3 If someone beats a freewoman who is pregnant, should she die, let the offender be judged liable for 28000 denarii, which amounts to 700 solidi. The forensic terms are *anouaddo* and *anouaddo leodis*.

4 Should someone be convicted of killing a child in the womb of its mother or before it receives a name [within 9 nights, *according to the C redaction*], let the offender be judged liable for 4000 denarii, which amounts to 100 solidi.

6 If someone kills a free woman after she has begun to have children, let the offender be judged liable for 24000 denarii, which amounts to 600 solidi.

7 Should the woman be past the age of child-bearing, let the offender be judged liable for 8000 denarii, which amounts to 200 solidi. The forensic term for this is *leodinia*.

### Homicides of Freemen (Title 41)

1 If someone is proven to have killed a free Frank or barbarian who is living by Salic law, let the offender be judged liable for 8000 denarii, which amounts to 200 solidi. The forensic term for this is *leodis*.

2 Should he put the body in a well or under water or cover it over with branches or bark or any material whatever in order to conceal it, let the

offender be judged liable for 24000 denarii, which amounts to 600 solidi. The forensic term for this is *matteleodis*.

3  Should he kill a member of the king's retinue (*trustis dominica*), let the offender be judged liable for 24000 denarii, which amounts to 600 solidi. The forensic term for this is *leodis*.

4  Should he put the body under water or in a well or cover it with branches or bark or any material whatever, let him be judged liable for 72000 denarii, which amounts to 1800 solidi. The forensic term for this is *matteleodis*.

5  If someone is proven to have killed a Roman, who is a companion (*conviva*) of the king, let the offender be judged liable for 12000 denarii, which amounts to 300 solidi.

6  Should it be a Roman landlord (*possessor*) that he killed, not a royal companion, let the offender be judged liable for 4000 denarii, which amounts to 100 solidi. The forensic term for this is *uualaleodis*.

7  Should he have killed a Roman tributary, let the offender be judged liable for 63 solidi [45 solidi *in the C redaction*]. The forensic term for this is *uualaleodis*.

8  If a person finds someone left without hands and feet at a crossroads by his enemies, and it is proven that he finished the man off, let the offender be judged liable for 4000 denarii, which amounts to 100 solidi. The forensic term for this is *friofalto*.

9  If someone throws a free man in a well and the man gets out of there alive, let the offender be judged liable for 4000 denarii, which amounts to 100 solidi.

*Various redactions contain more offenses connected with homicide.*

## A Freeman Killed Serving in the Army (Title 63)

1  If someone kills a freeman serving in the army, let him be judged liable for 24000 denarii, which amounts to 600 solidi. The forensic term for this is *leodis*.

2  Should the person who was killed have been a member of the royal retinue (*trustis dominica*), let the offender be judged liable for 1800 solidi. The forensic term for this is *mother*.

*C version of article 1:* If someone kills a fellow companion while they are serving in the army, let the offender make a three-fold compensation according to the rate he would pay had he killed him in civilian life.

*The following title treats regional royal officials. The* grafio *was a northern equivalent to the southern count (*comes*). The* sacebaro *had a role in collecting payments connected with lawsuits (see below,* **65***).*

## Killing a *Grafio* (Title 54)

1 If someone kills a *grafio*, let the offender be judged liable for 24000 denarii, which amounts to 600 solidi. The forensic terms are *leodis saccemitem*.

2 If someone kills a *sacebaro* [or, *in MS A1*, a subordinate of the *grafio*] who is an unfree dependent of the king (*puer regius*), let the offender be judged liable for 12000 denarii, which amounts to 300 solidi.

3 If someone kills a *sacebaro* who is free, let him be judged liable for 24000 denarii, which amounts to 600 solidi

*The categories of kin involved in the paying and receiving of wergeld are regulated by a number of titles the versions of which sometimes vary widely from redaction to redaction due to contamination from neighboring titles; the versions below stick closely to MSS A1 and A2.*

## Compensation for Homicide (Title 62)

1 If someone's father is killed, let the sons collect half the compensation, and let the next of kin on both the father's and mother's side divide the other half between them.

2 Should there be no relative on one side, whether the paternal or maternal, let the fisc take that portion.

*The following addition to* Lex Salica *is found in MSS A1 and A2 and appears to modify title 62.*

## Killing a Free Person (Title 68)

If anyone kills a free person, and he who did the killing is convicted, he must compensate the relatives according to law. The son must have one half the compensation. Half the remainder is owed to [the son's mother, that is the widow of the deceased] so that she takes possession of one quarter of the wergeld (*leodis*). The other quarter is owed to the near relatives, that is three [categories] from the paternal and maternal kin [of the deceased]. If the mother [of the son, that is the deceased's widow] is not alive, let the aforesaid relatives, that is the three [categories] of next of kin from the paternal and maternal side divide the half portion of the wergeld between them. Provision must be made that those who are nearer in degree take according to previously established conditions [namely that the first category takes two thirds] and leave three parts to be divided between the [remaining] two; and also he who is nearer among those two takes two thirds of that third part and leaves a third part to his kinsman.

*The obligation of relations to participate in the paying of wergeld is dealt with only in the title below,* De Chrenecruda. *The meaning of 'chrenecruda' is obscure. The Carolingian D redaction comments on the law that "it was followed in pagan times," and the later E redaction adds "thereafter it was never in force, for because of it the wealth* (potestas) *of many was destroyed."*

## On *Chrenecruda* (Title 58)

1  If anyone kills a person and, having given all his property, still does not have enough to pay fully the amount owed according to law, he must produce 12 oathtakers [to swear] that neither above the ground nor below does he have any more property than that which he has already given.

2  Then he must enter his house and gather in his hand dirt from the four corners; and then he must stand in the doorway, that is on the threshold, looking into the house, and with his left hand throw dirt over his shoulders upon his next of kin.

3  Should his father and brothers have already paid, he must throw the dirt upon his relatives, that is upon three [categories of] next of kin from the family of his mother and upon three from the family of his father.

4  And then, in his shirt, without belt or shoes, and with a rod in his hand, he must vault the hedge so that the former three [categories, that is the maternal kin] pay half the amount of compensation that is lacking or that the law awards; and the latter three, who come from the paternal kin, must do the same.

5  Should there be any near relation among them who does not have enough to allow the homicide to pay the whole debt, let the poorer relation again throw *chrenecruda* upon whoever among them is richer so that the homicide may pay the whole legal amount.

6  Should the homicide still not have enough to pay the whole amount, at that point those who have been his sureties must deliver him before the court and act as his sureties for four meetings of the court. And if no one will stand surety for him in respect to the compensation, that is to redeem the debt that he has not discharged, at that point let him compensate with his life.

*A law unique to early medieval legal codifications, but with analogies to much later practices, permitted a person to dissolve the legal consequences of kinship with particular relatives. The* thunginus *presided at the court but his role is controversial. He was likely not a royal official.*

## On a Person Who Wishes to Dissociate Himself from a Blood Relationship (*parentilla*) (Title 60)

He must go into court before the *thunginus* and there must break four alder rods over his head. And he must throw them to the four corners of the court, and there he must say that he dissociates himself from oath[helping], inheritance and all the affairs of those persons. Thereafter if any of his kinsmen are either killed or die, neither inheritance nor compensation may pertain to him.

*An addition (here from C) adds:* If he dies or is killed, the claim for compensation or inheritance does not pertain to his relations but shall pertain to the fisc or to whom the fisc wishes to give it.

# 65. ORDINARY PROCEDURE

*Ancient and early medieval law codes never deal with the entirety of the law nor do they attempt a systematic exposition of its working. In the case of* Lex Salica, *individual laws and incidental references nevertheless do tell us something about how a defendant might be brought before the court, the process by which judgment was obtained and executed, and the role of those adjudicating the administration of justice.*

## Summoning (Title 1)

1 If someone is summoned to court according to the royal laws and does not come, and if a legitimate excuse does not hold him back, let him be judged liable for 600 denarii, which amounts to 15 solidi. The forensic term for this is *reapten.*

2 Should the person who summons another party not come himself, and a legitimate excuse does not detain him, let him be judged liable to him whom he summoned for 600 denarii, which amounts to 15 solidi. The forensic term for this is *reapten.*

3 He who summons another must go with witnesses to the home of that person. And if the person is not present, let him call upon the wife or another member of the household to inform him of the summons.

4 Should the person be involved in royal service, however, the summons cannot be carried out.

5 Should the person be within the district on his own business, the summons can be carried out as we said above.

## Binding Freemen (Title 32)

1 If someone binds a freeman without cause, let him be judged liable for 1200 denarii, which amounts to 30 solidi. The forensic term for this is *andrepus*.

2 Should someone take the person who has been bound to some place, let him be judged liable for 1800 denarii, which amounts to 45 solidi.

*The following articles appear in the C redaction:*

3 Should a Roman bind a Frank without cause, let him be judged liable for 1200 denarii, which amounts to 30 solidi.

4 Should a Frank bind a Roman without cause, let him be judged liable for 600 denarii, which amounts to 15 solidi.

5 Should anyone take a bound man from a *grafio* out of arrogance and by force, let him pay with his life. The forensic term for this is *mithiofrastatitho*.

## He who Lays a Charge before the King against an Innocent Person (Title 18)

If someone lays a charge before the king against an innocent person who is not present, let him be judged liable for 2500 denarii, which equals 62½ solidi. The forensic term for this is *seolandouefa*.

## On *Rachineburgii* (Lawspeakers) (Title 57)

1 If any *rachineburgii* sitting in court refuse to speak the law while they are examining a case between two parties, the person who brings the case must say, "Here I press upon you to speak the law according to Salic law." But if they will not speak the law, let seven of those *rachineburgii* (each, *according to C*) be held liable for 120 denarii, which amounts to 3 solidi, before the sun sets. The forensic term for this is *schodo*.

2 Should they refuse to speak the law or to pledge to pay the 3 solidi, let them be held liable for 600 denarii, which amounts to 15 solidi, after they have been given until sunset (again, *according to C*).

3 Should those *rachineburgii* speak but do not make their determinations according to law, let the person against whom they gave their decision prosecute his own suit, and if he can prove that they did not make their determinations according to law, let them each be held liable for 600 denarii, which amounts to 15 solidi.

## *Grafio* and *Sacebaro*

Lex Salica *mentions other personnel involved in the adjudication of legal matters: the* grafio, sacebaro *(pl.* sacebarones)*,* centenarius, *and* thunginus. *Their roles are* *much contested. The* grafio *and* sacebaro *were royal appointees, the* centenarius *was the subordinate of the* grafio; *the* thunginus *was likely unconnected with royal administration. The following provision mentioning the* grafio *and the* sacebaro *belongs with Title 54 on the wergelds of royal officials, above. Nothing apart from what appears in this title is known about* sacebarones.

54 § 4    There must not be more than 3 *sacebarones* in each court, and if they say that a payment made to them with respect to a lawsuit has been discharged, this payment, on account of which they issue a notice of discharge (*securitas*), cannot be the subject of a claim before the *grafio*.

*The following complicated, and obscurely worded, law may suppose two hearings before the king's court. In the first hearing, 9 witnesses swear in 3 successive groups of 3 regarding the following: (1) the session of the regional court in which the original judgment was given against the defendant; (2) the session of the regional court in which the judgment was supposed to be performed 40 days later; and (3) the summons to the king's court issued 14 days after that. Three more witnesses are present, making up the 12 referred to in article 2; these three testify at a second hearing as to the failure of the defendant to appear at the first session of the royal court.*

## On Disdaining to Come to Court (Title 56)

1    When someone disdains to come to court or delays fulfilling what was judged against him by the *rachineburgii* and will not make a promise with regard to the compensation, the cauldron ordeal, or any judgment, the complainant at this time is to summon him before the king.

2    And 12 witnesses are to be present there. Let three of them each swear that they were present when the *rachineburgii* determined that the defendant should go to the cauldron or should make a promise regarding compensation and that he refused.

3    Again another three must swear that they were present on the day set by the *rachineburgii* for the defendant to exonerate himself by cauldron ordeal or by compensation, that is 40 nights later when the complainant again waited at the court and gave the defendant until sunset but the defendant would not at all fulfill the judgment.

4    This is the time for the complainant to summon the defendant before the king, that is in 14 nights, and three witnesses shall swear that they were there when he summoned the defendant and gave him until sunset. If the defendant does not come this time, let 9 witnesses swear as we said above.

5    Likewise, on that day, should the defendant fail to come [before the king], let the complainant wait for the defendant until sunset, along with three witnesses to testify to that fact. At that time, if he who summons the defendant

fulfills all those requirements, and he who is summoned will not come to any session that has been set, let the king before whom he has been summoned then declare the defendant an outlaw (*extra sermonem [regis]*).

6 Then the defendant and all his property shall be held liable. And whoever either feeds him or gives him lodging, even if his own wife [*a phrase, or female next of kin, may also belong here*], shall be held liable for 600 denarii which amounts to 15 solidi, until he compensates for all those matters of which he is convicted. The forensic term for this is *lampicii*.

*The following law, with different details than title 56 above, deals with a litigant who has accepted the judgment of the court and made a solemn promise to fulfill the judgment.*

## When A Promise is Made (*Fides Facta*) (Title 50)

1 If a free or a half-free person (*litus*) makes a promise to another, then he to whom the promise is made must come in forty nights, or in whatever period of time was established when the promise was made, to the house of the person who made the promise, bringing with him witnesses or those who shall appraise the payment. And if he will not fulfill the promise he made, let him be judged liable for 600 denarii, which amounts to 15 solidi, in addition to the debt that he promised to pay. The forensic term for this is *thalasciasco*.

*The words 'intervention' and 'intervene' in the following article stand for the sense of corrupt and poorly understood Frankish phrases.*

2 If he still will not satisfy the debt, the creditor must summon him to court and in the following fashion must claim the court's intervention: "I request, *thunginus*, that you intervene against my adversary who gave me his promise and owes me a debt." And he must declare what kind of debt the debtor owes on account of which he made his promise. Then the *thunginus* shall say: "I intervene and hold him to the requirements of Salic law." Then the creditor shall demand that the debtor neither pay nor give a pledge of payment to another person without first discharging what he owes him.

And with witnesses the creditor must go quickly to the house of the person who gave him his promise and request that he pay his debt. If the debtor will not pay, let the creditor give him until sunset. If he gives him until sunset, let him add 120 denarii, which amounts to 3 solidi, to the above debt. The creditor must do this on three occasions for three market periods [*nundinae, or perhaps just three weeks*] and if by the third time all these procedures have been carried out and the debtor still will not pay compensation, let the debt increase by 360 denarii, that is 9 solidi, that is so that for each summoning and day's grace 3 solidi are added to the debt.

3 If anyone will not discharge a promise he has made within the legally prescribed period of time, then let the creditor go before the *grafio* of the district
in whose territory he resides, and grasping a rod (*festuca*) let him say: "*Grafio*,
such and such a person has made a promise to me. According to law I have
put him in default and have summoned him as Salic law provides. I pledge by
my person and property that you may lay hands on his property with security." And let him say for what reason and for how much the debtor had
made the promise to him.

Then let the *grafio* collect seven suitable *rachineburgii* and accordingly let
him go with them to the residence of the person who made the promise
and, if he who made the promise is present, let him say: "You who are present, pay this man what you promised him of your own free will, and choose
two suitable men as you wish to appraise along with the *rachineburgii* what
you ought to pay, and satisfy this debt of yours according to a just evaluation." But if he is present and will not listen, or he is absent, let the *rachineburgii* then take from his property an amount appraised for as much as the debt
which he owes is worth. And from that amount he owes as determined by
law, let him whose suit it is claim two thirds and the *grafio* take for himself a
third part as a peace-fine (*fredus*), provided the peace payment was not already
paid for in this case.

4 If the *grafio* is asked and a legitimate excuse does not prevent him or specific
royal business, and if he refuses to go and does not put on the case someone
who by law can enforce justice for him, he ought to be liable for his life or
redeem himself for as much as his life is worth.

## Redeeming a Hand from the Cauldron (Title 53)

1 If a person is summoned to the cauldron, it may turn out that an agreement
is reached whereby he who is summoned may redeem his hand and give
oathtakers; if the suit is the kind in which, on conviction, he must pay by law
600 denarii, which amounts to 15 solidi, let him redeem his hand with 120
denarii, that is 3 solidi.

2 If he gives more than that to redeem his hand, let as much peace-fine (*fredus*)
be paid to the *grafio* as the accused would pay if convicted.

3 Should the suit be one in which the accused could be judged liable for 35
solidi on conviction, and if there is agreement that he may redeem his hand,
let him redeem his hand for 240 denarii, which amounts to 6 solidi.

4 But if he gives more than that, let as much peace-fine (*fredus*) be paid to the
*grafio* as the accused would pay if convicted with regard to this suit.

Let that payment for the redemption of his hand serve accordingly up to
suits that require payment of wergeld (*leodis*).

*The C redaction recognizes the category of suits valued at 62½ solidi.*

5 Should someone make a charge against another involving wergeld (*leodis*), however, and summon the accused to the cauldron, and there is agreement that the accused may give oathtakers and redeem his hand, let him redeem his hand with 1200 denarii, which make 30 solidi.

6 But if he gives any more than that, let the peace-fine (*fredus*) appropriate to a suit requiring wergeld (*leodis*) be paid to the *grafio*.

### Young Offenders

*This article referring to the liability of children is found among the list of wergelds in Title 24.*

24 § 5 If a boy under 12 years of age commits an offense, the peace-fine (*fredus*) shall not be demanded of him.

## 66. SPECIAL PROCEDURE I: TRACKING AND THIRD-HAND PROCEDURE

*Special procedures were available in Frankish law for tracking down and recovering stolen property. 'Third-hand procedure,' called 'Anefang' in some legal histories, was the process for reclaiming property found in another's possession; it resembles what English legal history calls 'vouching to warranty.' The general character of third-hand procedure should be clear from the following translations, but the details are controversial. In particular, opinion is divided on the question, to whom does the 'third hand' refer? A third-party trustee of the property? The person from whom the defendant claims he received the property, usually through purchase (called the warrantor in the translations below)? Or the plaintiff or defendant in the role of trustees of the property prior to the judicial hearing? There is no third-party trustee of the property in my opinion.*

### On Following A Trail (Title 37)

1 If anyone loses a cow, a horse, or any animal through theft and overtakes it within three nights in the course of following its tracks, and the person who leads it states and declares that he acquired it by purchase or exchange, the person who follows the tracks shall promise [to bring forward] his property [for procedure] by the third hand.

2 Should three nights have elapsed by the time the person who seeks his property finds it, let the person in possession of the property when it was found be allowed to make the promise, if he says that the property was acquired by sale or exchange.

3 Should the person who follows the trail refuse [to promise] to bring forward the property he identifies as his own [for procedure] by the third hand when the other party makes his counterclaim, or refuses to wait until sunset [to permit a reply] according to law, let him be sentenced to a payment of 30 solidi if he is convicted of taking from the other party by force the property he claims is his.

*The meaning of the Frankish word* filtortus *in the following law is uncertain.*

### On *filtort(us)* (Title 47)

1 If someone identifies a male or female slave, a horse, or cow, or any property at all, in the possession of another as his property, let him put it to the third-hand [procedure]. And the person in whose possession the property was identified must make the promise.

And if both claimant and defendant live on this side of the Loire and the Ardennes, let the person who identifies his property and the person in whose possession the property is identified set a day for a judicial hearing within 40 nights. And as many people as there are who sold the horse in question, exchanged it, or perhaps gave it as a payment, let them all be summoned within this period to attend the hearing, that is let each summon the person who supplied him with the property.

2 Should someone be summoned, and, though legitimate cause does not hold him back, he refuses to come to the hearing, let the person who engaged in a transaction with him present 3 witnesses to testify how he summoned him to the hearing and another 3 to testify that he conducted business with him in public and in a proper manner. If he does this, he clears himself of the charge of theft. The person who did not come, concerning whom the witnesses testified on oath, shall be a thief with respect to the person who identified his property. Let the thief restore the purchase-price to the person with whom he conducted business and compensate according to law the person who identified his property.

All this must be done in the judicial forum to which belongs the person who was in possession of the property when it was first identified and put to third-hand [procedure].

3 Should those who had possession of the property live across the Loire or Ardennes, the requirements of this procedure shall be followed within 80 nights.

*Title 66, found in two MSS, is appended to the earliest version of* Lex Salica, *which contains sixty-five titles.*

## On Property in a Father's Inheritance (Title 66)

If someone claims third-hand procedure with respect to property that another person acquired from the inheritance of his father, the person upon whom the claim for third-hand procedure is made shall produce 3 witnesses to testify that he acquired this property from the inheritance of his father and another 3 witnesses to testify how his father acquired the selfsame property. If he can does this, he establishes legal title to the property put to third-hand procedure.

If he cannot do this, let him produce 3 oathtakers *(iuratores)* [to support his assertion] that he acquired the property from the inheritance of his father. If he can do this, he frees himself from the penalty of the suit. If he does not do this, let the person who instituted the third-hand procedure on the property ...[*the rest of the sentence is defective, containing a variant of the* filtortus *of Title 47; but the claimant now clearly vindicates the property*]. Then, as the law provides in this matter, let the person in whose possession the property was discovered be held liable for a penalty of 35 solidi.

*Lex Ribvaria is a seventh-century code intended for the Franks in the Cologne area. It is in part a revised version of* Lex Salica *and contains versions of* Lex Salica *Titles 37 and 47, as well as new rules on tracking and third-hand procedure.*

## On Tracking (*Lex Ribvaria*, Title 49)

1 If a person tracks one of his animals and within three days finds it at some-one else's place, or anywhere at all, he is permitted to take it back without third-hand procedure.
2 Should the animal be in a residence and the master of the residence forbids him to conduct a search, let the master of the residence be considered a thief.
3 Should the pursuer enter the place by force, let him be fined 15 solidi, or let him take an oath with 6 co-swearers.

*Dilatura in the next two titles was compensation connected with the temporary removal of property (usually stolen property) from its owner. It was paid in addition to the penalty for theft.*

## On Third-hand Procedure (*Lex Ribvaria*, Title 37)

1 If someone identifies his property, let him put a hand upon it; and as a conse-

quence, let the person upon whom the claim is made for third-hand procedure seek out the third hand. At this time both parties shall immediately take
an oath with weapons in their right hands while they hold onto the property
with their left hands. Let one swear that he is placing his hand upon his own
property, and let the other swear that he vouches the hand that gave him the
property.

And let the defendant deliver his warrantor within 14 nights, if he is
within the duchy; within 40 nights, if he is outside the duchy. But let the
defendant present his warrantor before the king's column or at the place
where the court to which the defendant belongs is located within 80 nights,
if he is outside the kingdom.

2  Should the defendant be unable to deliver the warrantor, let him take an oath
with six co-swearers *in haraho* [on the gospels or on relics?], affirming that he
had summoned the warrantor there according to law and that the property in
question had not been transferred to him by another person. Accordingly, let
the defendant be given a period of time within 14, 40, or 80 nights for him
to recover the replacement price of the property before witnesses and to
show it as proof to the person who had his property put to third-hand procedure. At that time the defendant may be safe from an accusation of theft. Let
the person who claimed third-hand procedure demand the penalty for theft
and *dilatura* from the person who undertook to pay [back the replacement, or
purchase price].

3  Should the warrantor come but refuse to receive back the property put to
the third hand-procedure, let the person upon whom the claim of third-hand
procedure was made then apply himself to paying the value of the property,
*dilatura*, and the penalty for theft.

4  Should the defendant answer at the time when the property is claimed by
third-hand procedure that he does not know the previous possessor, let him
immediately promise an oath with six co-swearers. And within 14 nights let
him make sure that he swears that he does not know the warrantor or his
warrantor's place or doorposts, and let him restore the property in question
without suffering a penalty [for theft].

## On the Death of a Human or Animal Put to Third-Hand Procedure (*Lex Ribvaria*, Title 75)

1  If someone put a human to third-hand procedure and the human dies before
the day set for a hearing, let the deceased be buried at a crossroads with a
rope of osier branches attached to his feet, and let [the party charged with his
custody] go there with witnesses on the day of the hearing, and, with six of
them who saw him carry out the burial, let him swear *in haraho* [on the
gospels or relics?] that he who was claimed by third-hand procedure lies

buried there and died in the usual way, not having been killed by man or beast or anything else, and has the rope of osier branches attached to his feet. Then he must always go from hand to hand over the grave with the rope of osier branches until he comes to the hand that sold the deceased illegally or stole him. And if he fails to proceed in this fashion, let him be judged liable for the value of the property and *dilatura*, as well as the penalty provided by law or the payment for theft.

2 Should [the human put to third-hand procedure] have taken off and fled, let [the party charged with his custody] be granted a period of 14 nights if [the fugitive is] within the duchy, 40 if outside, and 80 if outside the kingdom. But if he cannot deliver the fugitive within that period of time, let him be judged liable for the value of the property and *dilatura* and the payment for theft or the penalty of the law.

3 Should someone kill [the human put to third-hand procedure], and should the deceased not be buried at a crossroads with the rope of osiers, let [the party charged with his custody] be judged liable for the value of the property and *dilatura*, as well as the payment for theft or the replacement cost or the penalty of the law.

4 Should a human commit an offense while he has been put to third-hand procedure, let him who kept him in his custody at the time [of the offense] be judged liable for this.

5 If a human who has been placed in trust or has taken to flight dies, likewise let him be buried at a crossroads with a rope of osier branches attached to his feet. Let him who kept him in his custody, if he fails to proceed in this fashion, be judged liable for the price of the property along with the penalty of the law.

6 If an animal that has been put to third hand-procedure dies before the day set for a hearing, the plaintiff with witnesses shall then state the value that had been set upon it, and the person upon whom the claim for third-hand procedure was made must show the hide and skinned head to his warrantor in the presence of the judge. And if the warrantor accepts it, let him pay only 1 solidi replacement price for the hide.

7 Should the animal be alive, but is injured or emaciated, let the warrantor restore as a replacement price the value of the animal at that time. If, however, the animal is returned in a healthy and uninjured state, let the purchaser then receive the full price he paid.

8 Should the animal have been stolen, then let the person upon whom the claim for third-hand procedure was made be judged liable for the value of the property and *dilatura*, along with the penalty for theft.

9 We prohibit clothing or suchlike that lack reliable markings from being claimed by third-hand procedure.

## 67. SPECIAL PROCEDURE II: CHARGING AND INTERROGATING SLAVES

### If a Slave is Charged with Theft (Title 40)

1 In the case of a lawsuit of the kind in which a free person would have had to pay 600 denarii, that is, 15 solidi, as compensation, let a slave be stretched on a rack and let him receive 120 strokes with the rod.

2 Should the slave confess before he is tortured, he may, if the master of the slave agrees, pay 120 denarii, which amounts to 3 solidi, to save his back. Let the master restore the value of the [stolen] property in place of the slave.

3 If the offense is a greater one, however, in which a free person would pay 1400 denarii, which amounts to 35 solidi, again let the slave receive 120 blows.

4 Should the slave not confess, let him who puts the slave to torture, if he still wants to torture the slave against his master's will, give the slave's master a pledge. And so let the slave then be subjected to greater torture, and, if he confesses, let no weight be given to what he says with respect to his master; for he who is subjecting the slave to torture is about to have the slave in his authority. Let the master of the slave, regarding whom he has already received a pledge, receive the price of his slave.

Should the slave confess during the earlier torments, that is before completion of the 120 strokes, either let him be castrated, or let him pay 240 denarii, which amounts to 6 solidi. Let the master of the slave, however, restore the value of the [stolen] property to the plaintiff.

5 If a slave is charged with a greater crime, that is one in which a free person could be judged liable for 1800 denarii, which amounts to 45 solidi, and during the application of torture the slave confesses, let him suffer a sentence of death.

6 When a slave is charged with any kind of crime, the plaintiff shall call upon the master of the slave in question, provided the slave is present, to give his slave over to torture at a place where the plaintiff shall have rods prepared as thick as the little finger and have ready a rack on which to stretch the slave out.

7 Should the master refuse to give his slave over to torture and should the slave be present, the plaintiff must immediately give the master of the slave until sunset [to comply]. And he must set a date for a hearing in 7 nights for the master to hand his slave over to torture.

8 Should the master refuse to hand over his slave in 7 nights, let the claimant again give him until sunset, and let him set a day for a hearing in another 7

nights, that is, 14 nights are to pass from the time the master was first called upon [to hand over the slave].

9 Should the master not be willing to give up his slave to torture after the completion of 14 nights, let the master of the slave bear the suit in its entirety and be responsible for the compensation, that is if it was a suit of the kind in which a free person could pay in compensation 600 denarii, which amounts to 15 solidi, let the master pay that amount. If it is a greater offense, on account of which a free person could pay 1400 denarii, which amounts to 35 solidi, likewise let the master pay that. If it is a still greater offense, in which likewise a free person could pay 1800 denarii, which amounts to 45 solidi, and the master does not deliver over his slave, let the master render that amount and the value of the [stolen] property. And should an even greater offense be imputed to the slave, let the master of the slave pay not as if a slave committed the offense but let him accept the obligation to pay the entire amount as if a free person was responsible.

10 Should the slave against whom the charge is made be absent, then, the plaintiff shall, in private and in the presence of three witnesses, call upon the master of the slave to deliver the slave within a period of 7 nights. If the master fails to do this, let the plaintiff in the presence of witnesses give him until sunset and then set another day for a hearing in 7 nights. And if he does not deliver the slave in question in another 7 nights, for a third time the plaintiff must give him a period of 7 nights, that is, so that the entire number of nights amounts to 21. If, after dates have been set three times, the master will not deliver his slave bound and give him over to torture, and if the plaintiff gave him until sunset on each scheduled appearance, then let the master of the slave assume the whole claim, as we said above, restoring such compensation to the claimant as would a free person if he committed the offense, not a slave.

11 In the case of a female slave being found out in the type of crime on account of which a male slave would be castrated, either let her master pay 240 denarii, which amounts to 6 solidi, provided he agrees to do so, or let her receive 240 [or 144, or 300] strokes of the rod.

## 68. MISCELLANEOUS OFFENSES

*Lex Salica lists a host of offenses, along with the compensation for committing each one; the offenses include what we would regard as civil and criminal law. Many offenses touch upon the daily concerns of agricultural societies, and incidentally have much to tell us about the complex activities of rural life. Those are not the offenses translated here. The following are somewhat more lurid, or peculiar examples, and while they cast an interesting light on Frankish values, the suits in which they appear should not all be regarded as typical components of daily life.*

## Witchcraft (*Maleficia*) (Title 19)

1 If someone gives another person a herbal potion to drink so that the person dies, let the offender be judged liable for 8000 denarii, which amounts to 200 solidi [*and in MS A2:* or of course let the offender be given over to fire]. The forensic term for this is *touuerfo*.

2 Should someone practice witchcraft on another person, but the person on whom the witchcraft was practiced escapes, let the perpetrator proven to have committed this crime be judged liable for 2500 denarii, which amounts to 62½ solidi.

*The Merovingian C redaction adds the following articles 3 and 4.*

3 If someone casts an evil spell (*maleficium*) upon another, no matter where it is put, let the offender be judged liable for 62½ solidi.

*In the Carolingian K redaction, the passage is construed as follows:*

If someone casts some kind of evil spell upon another or puts it in any spot at all by applying bunches of herbs, let the offender be judged liable for 2500 denarii, which amounts to 62½ solidi.

4 If a woman practices witchcraft upon another woman with the result that she cannot have children, let her be judged liable for 62½ solidi.

## On a *Herburgius* (Witch's Apprentice) (Title 64)

1 If someone declares another person to be a *herburgius*, that is a witch's porter, or the one who is said to carry the cauldron in which witches (*strigae*) do their cooking, and the charge cannot be proven, let the offender be judged liable for 2500 denarii, which amounts to 62½ solidi. The forensic term for this is *humnisfith*.

2 If someone declares that a free woman is a witch and cannot prove it, let the offender be judged liable for 2500 denarii, which amounts to 187½ solidi at a threefold rate.

*An addition in C:*

3 If a witch eats a man and the case is proven against her, let her be judged liable for 8000 denarii, which amounts to 200 solidi. The forensic term for this is *granderba*.

## Insults (Title 30)

1  If someone calls another a queer, let the offender be judged liable for 15 solidi.

2  If someone declares another to be full of shit, let the offender be judged liable for 120 denarii, which amounts to 3 solidi.

3  If someone, man or woman, declares another free woman to be a whore and cannot prove it, let the offender be judged liable for 1800 denarii, which amounts to 45 solidi.

4  If someone declares another to be a fox, let the offender be judged liable for 3 solidi.

5  If someone declares another to be a hare, let the offender be judged liable for 120 denarii, which amounts to 3 solidi.

6  If someone charges another with throwing away his shield and cannot prove it, let the offender be judged liable for 120 denarii, which amounts to 3 solidi.

7  If someone declares another to be an informer or calumniator and cannot prove it, let the offender be judged liable for 600 denarii, which amounts to 15 solidi.

## Despoiling Corpses (Title 55)

1  If someone despoils the body of a dead person in secret before it is put in the ground, let the offender be judged liable for 2500 denarii, which amounts to 62 ½ solidi. The forensic term for this *muther.*

2  If the corpse has already been buried when he despoils it, and the charge is proven, let the offender be an outlaw (*wargus*) until the day he comes to an agreement with the kinfolk of the deceased and they ask on his behalf that he be allowed to associate with people [again]. And whoever gives him food or lodging, even if his own wife [*the phrase,* or female next of kin, *may also belong here*], let them be judged liable for 600 denarii, which amounts to 15 solidi. As for the convicted perpetrator of this crime, let him be judged liable for 8000 denarii, which amounts to 200 solidi. The forensic term for this is *tornechale.*

3  If someone lays a dead person on top of another in a wooden or stone sarcophagus and the charge is proven, let the offender be judged liable for 1800 denarii, which amounts to 45 solidi. The forensic term for this is *chaminis.*

## Sexual Offenses

*The following list of sexual offenses is drawn from titles 15 and 25, where their placement and order varies in the MSS. Acts, like abduction, which might accompany some of these offenses, were calculated separately, and raised the penalties considerably.*

15 § 1    If someone takes away another man's wife while her husband is alive, let the offender be judged liable for 8000 denarii, which amounts to 200 solidi. The forensic term for this is *affaltheca*

15 § 2    If someone has sexual relations with a free girl by force, let the offender be judged liable for 2500 denarii, which amounts to 62½ solidi. The forensic term for this is *uueruanathe.*

15 § 3    If someone has sexual relations with a free girl and they both agree of their own free will, let the offender be judged liable for 1800 denarii, which amounts to 45 solidi. The forensic term for this is *firilasia.*

25 § 1    If a freeman has sexual relations with another's female slave and is convicted, let the offender be judged liable to the master of the slave for 600 denarii, which amounts to 15 solidi. The forensic term for this is *theualasina.*

25 § 2    If someone has sex with a female slave of the king, let the offender be judged liable for 1200 denarii, which amounts to 30 solidi. The forensic term for this is *theualasina.*

25 § 3,4    If a freeman openly cohabits with another's female slave, let him remain in servitude with her. Likewise, if a free woman takes another's male slave in marriage, let her remain in servitude.

## 69. INHERITANCE

*Title 59 is one of the most famous passages in* Lex Salica *and central to understanding female succession rights and the proprietal distinctions of Frankish inheritance law. There is general agreement that the chapter deals only with the matrilateral side of inheritance. The law also seems to be specifying which near female heirs will succeed and may be encapsulating the distinguishing features of Frankish inheritance in comparison with contemporary Roman-law practice. Variations in the inheritance sequence found in later redactions (not translated here) should be regarded as resulting from textual transmission, not the law-in-practice of subsequent ages.*

### On Inheritances (*De alodis*) (Title 59)

1    If someone dies leaving no children, should his mother survive, let her succeed to the inheritance.

2 Should there be no mother, but the deceased leaves a brother and sister, let them succeed to the inheritance.

3 Should there be no brother and sister, at that point let the sister of the mother succeed to the inheritance.

4 And thereafter whoever is more closely related in degree to them, he shall succeed to the inheritance.

5 With regard to land, no inheritance shall pertain to the woman, but the land in its entirety shall pertain to the male sex who are brothers [*of the sister and mother's sister?*].

*The C redaction defines the 'land' (terra) of article 5 as terra salica, a phrase unlikely to mean 'Salic land'; it refers rather to land connected to the home farm, or sala.*

*The next law on new settlers does not concern inheritance directly, but its treatment of 'neighbors' (vicini), that is, neighboring landholders in a villa, is relevant to the rules of inheritance as they appear in the regulations of the Edict of Chilperic, which follow.*

*The term villa could embrace various configurations of rural settlement, including villages and estates, which often were held by a number of landholders. The rights mentioned here suggest that the villa as a whole was treated as a fiscal unit by the state. Rights of vicini analogous to those mentioned in the next two laws can be found in the Theodosian Code.*

## On New Settlers (*De Migrantibus*) (Title 45)

1 If someone wishes to settle upon another's property in a villa, and although one or any number of those who dwell in the villa wish to accept him, he shall not be allowed to settle there if there is even one person who objects.

2 [*The procedure for expelling the new settler, with the help of the* grafio *if necessary, is described. The new settler refusing to leave is fined.*] And since he would not listen to the law, let him lose the fruit of his labor and be judged liable for 30 solidi.

3 Should someone have settled, and no one opposes him for 12 months, let him remain as secure as the other neighbors.

## The Edict of Chilperic

*From legislation of King Chilperic (a. 561-584). The mention of 'Salic law' in this article does not necessarily refer to the codification.*

[3] (108) It is resolved and agreed that if a person with neighbors dies and is survived by sons and daughters, the sons shall have the land as long as they live, as is

Salic law, and, if they die suddenly, the daughter likewise shall receive those lands just like the sons if they had been alive. And [failing surviving children] if the person is survived by a brother, let the brother receive the lands, not the neighbors, and if the person dies suddenly without leaving a surviving brother, at that time let his sister accede to the possession of the land.

### *Lex Ribvaria* (Title 57)

*The seventh-century, east Frankish* Lex Ribvaria *also contained an inheritance regulation (c. 57), using* Lex Salica *as a model. It dealt with both matrilateral and patrilateral heirs.*

1 When someone dies without children, should the father and the mother be alive, let them succeed to the inheritance.

2 Should there be no father and mother, let the brother and sister succeed together.

3 Should none of them be alive, then at that point let the sister of the mother and sister of the father succeed. And thereafter let he who is next of kin succeed to the fifth degree.

4 But when there is a member of the male sex, let the female not succeed to the ancestral inheritance (*hereditas aviatica*).

### The Formulae

*The Salic law postponement of daughters by sons (or to look at the sibling pair from a slightly different angle — the postponement of sisters by their brothers) was still the rule in the seventh and eighth century as shown by these two formulae. The first one is from the formulary of Marculf (2.12), dating probably from the latter part of the seventh century. Formularies were collections of specimen charters (*formulae*) for notaries to use when drawing up actual documents. In the translation, N. stands for the place where the names of the parties would be inserted.*

[1] Document for the Succession of a Daughter to the Paternal Inheritance alongside her Brothers

To my dearest daughter, N. A longstanding but impious custom exists among us whereby sisters may not have a share of the paternal land with their brothers, but I have carefully considered this impiety and believe that just as you children are equally gifts from God, so you are equally to be loved by me and you are equally to be favored with my property after my death. Therefore by this document, my dearest daughter, I name you with respect to your brothers, my sons, N., as an equal and legitimate heir to all my inheritance. You shall divide and share equally the paternal inheritance as well as the acquests, dependents, and our chattels, and whatever we leave on our death, and you shall receive a share in no respect less than they, but all of you shall divide and share equally each and every thing among you...

*The second formula is from the Sens formulary (no.45) dating from 768-775.*

[2]   A Testamentary Disposition

I, N., a man of great standing, to N., my dearest and in all respects most beloved daughter. It is not unknown to everyone that, as is contained in the Salic Law, you could not at all succeed along with your brothers, my sons, to the inheritance of my property that came to me from the inheritance of my parents. For this reason, my request that this testamentary document be drawn up for you and confirmed accords fully and completely with my wishes, whereby, if you survive me in this world, you may succeed along with your brothers, my sons, to the inheritance of all my property, from the inheritance of my parents as well as what I myself acquired..., and all of you shall divide and share this equally among yourselves. You [daughter] may freely and without challenge exercise your right of doing whatever you wish with what you receive...

# B. LEGISLATION OF THE MEROVINGIAN KINGS

## 70. THE AGREEMENT OF CHILDEBERT I AND CHLOTHAR I FOR KEEPING THE PEACE, a. 511-58

*These are arrangements made by Clovis's sons, Childebert and Chlothar, sometime between 511 and 558, for dealing, in the main, with thieves. The procedures of the Agreement should be compared with the procedures of* Lex Salica. *Part of the arrangements of the kings involved the reorganization of local watches and the establishment of* centenae *(or 'hundreds,' a term with a long institutional history ahead of it) for handling the pursuit of rustlers. These measures have clear precedents in Roman administrative practice. The Agreement is also notable for its treatment of rights of sanctuary for runaway slaves, elsewhere found in the canons of the church (below,* **74 a**).

*The text of the Agreement, though contained in a good number of MSS, is poorly preserved. It seems to consist of three parts. A) Regulations of King Childebert (art. 1-8). B) Regulations of Chlothar (art. 9-15). These two sections contain some parallel provisions, which differ, however, in details (cf. 1, 2 with 10; 3 with 13; 4 with 10; 5 with 11, 12). C) A joint statement of both kings (art. 16-18).*

Source: three editions were used as the basis of the translation: (1) *Lex Salica: The Ten Texts with Glosses and the Lex Emendata*, ed. J. H. Hessels (London, 1880), pp. 415-19; (2) *Capitularia regum Francorum*, ed. Alfred Boretius, MGH LL Capitularia (1896), 1: 3-7; (3) *Pactus legis Salicae II.2: Kapitulieren und 70 Titel Text*, ed. K. A. Eckhardt, Germanenrechte, N. F. (Göttingen, 1956), pp. 394-408. The numeration of the articles follows Hessels and Boretius. Translation by A.C. Murray.

### AGREEMENT OF KINGS CHILDEBERT AND CHLOTHAR FOR KEEPING THE PEACE

#### [A] The Decree of King Childebert

[1] Since the madness of many people has grown strong, those evil doers must be given what they deserve for the savagery of their crimes. For that reason, it is decreed that whoever is proven to be a thief (*latro*) after the present proclamation shall incur the peril of death.

*The opening phrase of the next article is difficult to construe but should be understood as referring to the capture of a thief in possession of stolen property; cf. art. 4 and 10.*

[2] If someone binds a freeman because of theft and a denial is made, [the plaintiff] must offer 12 oathtakers, one half chosen [by the accused], [to support

the plaintiff's claim] that his accusation of theft is true. Then let the thief redeem himself if he has the means. If the means are lacking, let him be presented to three court sessions by his kinfolk, and if he is not redeemed, let him lose his life.

[3] If someone on his own locates stolen property, and, secretly without [bringing the suit before] a judge, takes compensation, he is similar to a thief.

[4] If any freeman is accused of theft and, summoned to the cauldron, scalds his hand, let him compensate for as much as he was accused.

[5] If a slave is accused of theft, let his master be called upon to deliver him before the court within 20 nights, and, if there is doubt, let him be put to the ordeal of the lot. But if a legitimate excuse delays the time set for the hearing, let another period of 20 nights be set. And the plaintiff shall present three from among his peers (*consimiles*) and another three from those chosen in order to support by oath that Salic law procedure was followed with regard to the court appointments. And if the lord does not deliver his slave, let him pay as compensation the amount established by law for this kind of suit and surrender the slave.

[6] If a slave steals less than a third of a solidus (*tremissis*) and pulls a bad lot, let the lord of the slave pay 3 solidi, and let the slave receive 300 strokes.

[7] If anyone unjustly holds another's slaves (*mancipia*) and does not return them within 40 days, let him be held liable as a thief of slaves (*mancipia*).

[8] If a half-free person (*letus*) goes to the ordeal of the lot on account of an accusation and pulls a bad lot, let him compensate half the legal amount of a freeman, and he must give 6 oathtakers, one half chosen.

## [B] The Decree of King Chlothar

*In the following laws* centena *(pl.* centenae*), or hundred, is not yet the common medieval term for the sub-district of the county; this meaning appears only in the eighth century. Here it means the command, unit, or jurisdiction of a* centenarius, *a subordinate of the count or* grafio; *by extension, however, it could refer to the district under the* centenarius's *authority and the watches (*vigiliae*) or posse (*trustis*) under his command. Posse includes the band that pursues thieves as well as those with the duty to join it when summoned. Article 9, which means that local watches were put under the command of* centenarii, *should be read in conjunction with articles 16-18, and the Decree of King Childebert II, below,* **78**, *III 2, 4, 5.*

[9] Because the night watches do not catch thieves but exercise their watch in various districts in collusion with the thieves or while overlooking their crimes, it has been decreed that those deployed as night watches should be organized as *centenae*.

Whoever loses property [to theft] should receive its value in the *centena* of the *centenarius* where the property was lost, and let the thief be pursued and let him be arrested even if he appears in the *centena* of another; and if anyone summoned to this pursuit is negligent when summoned, let him be condemned to pay 5 solidi. However [if the pursuit extends outside the *centena* where the property was originally stolen] let the person who lost the property receive its value without question from that *centena* [into which the thief fled] that is from the second or third. If the trail of the thief is confirmed, however, he must be punished either now or in the future.

And if the person who lost property catches the thief by himself, let him receive the entire compensation. But if the thief is found by the posse, let the posse acquire one-half the compensation and exact the value of the stolen property from the thief.

[10] If someone finds stolen property at another's domicile under lock and key, let the master of the house compensate with his life.

If someone is taken with stolen property, let him be subject to the preceding law. And if he is accused out of suspicion, let him go to the ordeal of the lot. And if he takes a bad lot, he is a thief; however, let three of the persons [taking oaths] for both parties in the dispute be chosen [by the other side], so that there can be no collusion.

[11] Concerning slaves of the church and the fisc or anyone else, if one of them is accused by someone, let the slave be put to the ordeal of the lot [*from hereon the meaning is uncertain*] or to the 'pledge' (*plebium*), or let his value be restored to his lord. For those who have been tested shall undergo peril.

[12] If the slave of any of the powerful (*potentes*) who have possessions in diverse places is considered a suspect in a crime, let his master be summoned secretly before witnesses to deliver him within 20 nights before a judge. But if within the established time, he does not do so because of collusion, let the lord render account in his own status [as a freeman], including the payments for peace (*fredus*) and feud (*faidus*), according to the degree of the offense. If the slave has left his lord before the summons, let the lord restore the value of the property in question and yield his claim to the slave, so that when the slave is found he may be given over to punishment.

[13] If someone secretly accepts compensation from any sort of thief with regard to property stolen from him, let both be subject to the charge of theft. [*And in one MS:*] Moreover let thieves be delivered to judges. Let no one presume to hide thieves or any guilty person. Who does so shall be subject to the same charge.

[14] As agreed upon by the bishops, let no one presume to drag any thief or guilty person from the atrium of a church. But if there are churches whose atriums are not enclosed, let an area of 120 feet (*aripennis*) of ground be rec-

ognized as an atrium on both sides of the walls. Let no fugitive take himself outside the aforesaid places through a desire for work. If he does, however, and is captured, let him be condemned to the punishment he deserves.

[15] Should someone's slave desert his master and flee to a church, when his master comes the first time, let the slave be returned immediately once his lord has excused him, though nothing prevents an agreement being reached on the sale-price of the slave. However, if the slave is not given over to his lord who seeks him, but flees, let him who did not wish to give him up give over the slave's price; afterwards, if the slave is found, and there is agreement, let him be restored to his lord and his price returned. We decree this with regard to slaves of the fisc as of all lords.

### [C. Joint Statement of the Kings]

[16] For the preservation of the peace, we order that *centenarii*, through whose loyalty and attention the aforesaid peace may be observed, are to be selected and placed in the posse. And since, by God's grace, brotherly love maintains an unbroken bond between us, *centenarii* are to have the right to pursue thieves and follow the tracks they leave within our adjoining provinces; and, as was said, let the suit against the thief remain the responsibility of the posse that fails, so that — provided it searches diligently for the thief — it may hasten to restore immediately to the person who lost it the value of the stolen property. If the posse manages to catch the thief, let it claim one-half the compensation, and let the damages accruing from the thief's removal of the property (*dilatura*), if any are due, be paid from his property to the person who suffered loss. And should the person who lost property have pursued and taken the thief, he shall claim for himself full compensation, both the payment for the offense (*solutio*) and whatever expenses (*dispendium*) there are; let the peace-fine (*fredus*), however, be reserved for the judge of the thief's province.

[17] If anyone summoned to follow a thief's trail chooses not to come, let him be condemned by the judge to pay five solidi.

[18] And what we have established in the name of God for the maintenance of the peace, we wish to preserve forever. Thus any judge who presumes to violate this decree should be aware that he does so at the risk of his life.

## 71. THE DECREE OF CHILDEBERT II, a. 596

The Decree (Decretus *or* Decretio) *of Childebert II introduces the Roman-law notions of representation in the direct line (I 1) and ten-year prescription to accompany the old rule of thirty years (II 1). Church law is also influential in the injunctions against incestuous marriage and working on Sunday (I 2, III 7).*

*The Decree is notable also for the hard measures it takes against homicides and abductors, and (continuing a theme of earlier legislation) its continued efforts to deal with thieves and to regulate the operations of posses under the command of* centenarii. *Chlothar II in his legislation would later recognize some of these types of measures as abuses.*

*Childebert died in 596, after reigning for twenty-one years. The decree's regnal year numbers, which vary in the MSS, must be incorrect if, as seems likely, the decree records deliberations conducted over three years.*

Source: the present translation is based on two editions: (1) *Pactus legis Salicae II 2, Kapitulieren und 70 Titel-Text*, ed. K. A. Eckhardt, Germanenrechte N. F. (Göttingen, 1956), pp. 440-449, and (2) *Capitularia regum Francorum*, ed. Alfred Boretius, MGH LL Capitularia (1896) 1: 15-17. The numeration follows Eckhardt, but I have not always followed his text. Translation by A.C. Murray.

## DECREE OF CHILDEBERT [II]

To men of illustrious rank. Since we have deliberated in the name of God with our magnates every Kalends of March with regard to all kinds of matters, we wish to bring this to the attention of everyone.

## [I]

Thus, with God's help, at Andernach on the Kalends of March in the 20th year of our reign:

[1] It was agreed that grandchildren through a son or daughter, in the event of the death of their father or mother, shall succeed to the property of their grandfather along with their uncles and aunts just as if their mother or father were alive. This rule should be followed with regard to children born from a son or daughter [*that is in the direct line*], not children born of a brother or sister.

[2] Next the following decision was reached with our *leudes*: We have decreed that no one enter into an incestuous marriage, that is with the wife of his brother, or with the sister of his wife, or the wife of his uncle or consanguineous kinsman. If someone takes the wife of his father, let him incur the peril of death. And with regard to past unions which are incestuous, we order that they be corrected according to the proclamation of the bishops. May he who will not listen to his bishop and is excommunicated endure that condition before God forever, and let him be an utter stranger to our palace. Let him who wishes not to undergo the cures of his bishop, yield all his property to his legitimate relations.

## [II]

At Maastricht.

[1] It was agreed that no one may have the right to put to the third-hand procedure a slave or field or any property that someone possesses without legal disturbance for 10 years, if the litigants are subject to the jurisdiction of the same duke or judge; as an exception, we have given orphans the right up to 20 years. If someone presumes to put property to the third-hand procedure, let him be judged liable for 15 solidi and let him give up the property he put to the third hand.

As far as grounds for other suits are concerned, the 30-year rule completely excludes them all, [*the meaning of the following clause is uncertain*] except what the kingdoms [fisc?] have retained down to the present.

[2] It was likewise agreed on the Kalends of March among all those assembled that from now on whoever dares to commit abduction, which has been the source of the most wicked of vices, must be struck with the peril of death, and let none of our magnates presume to intercede for him, but let everyone pursue him as an enemy of God. Should someone presume to transgress our edict, let the judge in whose district the deed was first committed gather support and kill the abductor. And let him lie slain without the benefit of the law (*forbatutus*). And if he takes refuge in a church, they must be given up to the bishop and, without any special pleading, separated and exiled. For to be sure, if the woman consents to the abduction, both equally are to be placed in exile, and if they are taken outside the church, both equally are to be killed. Their property is to be acquired by their legitimate relatives and the fisc is to take what is due to it.

[3] With regard to homicides, we have ordered the following: that someone who kills another rashly without cause is to be struck with the peril of death. For let him not ransom himself or make compensation with a redemption payment. If it turns out that the parties agree to stoop to payment, let none of the homicide's kinsmen or friends do anything to help him, unless in all such instances the person who presumes to aid him compensates with his own wergeld. For it is just that he who knows how to kill should learn to die.

*'Farfalium' in the next law may mean something like 'outrage' (modern German Frevel), but the context remains thoroughly obscure.*

[4] The following was agreed with regard to *farfalia*: that whoever presumes to bring forward *farfalia* in a court shall without doubt compensate with his own wergeld; and moreover let the *farfalium* be repressed. If perhaps, as happens, the judge gives his assent and perhaps agrees to protect (attend?) that *farfalium*, let him in all cases face the peril of death.

[5] Concerning thieves and malefactors, we have decreed the following law to be followed: that if 5 or 7 men of good faith say under oath — and not because

of personal enmity — that someone is a criminal (*criminosus*), let the criminal die without law, just as he stole without law. If any judge is convicted of freeing a captured thief, let him lose his life, and by all means let order be respected among the people.

## [III]

Again on the Kalends of March at Cologne:

[1] It was agreed and we have so ordered that if any judge hears of an incorrigible (*criminosus*) thief, the judge is to go to the thief's house and have him bound. Should the thief be a Frank (*francus*), he is to be sent to our court; should the thief be of the inconsequential classes (*leviores personae*), he is to be hanged on the spot.

*The following articles (2, 4, 5) should be read in conjunction with **70**, art. 9, 16, 17, on the establishment of* centenae, *above.*

[2] If someone refuses to help a *centenarius* or any judge pursue a malefactor, by all means let the offender be fined 60 solidi.

[3] Whoever has an incorrigible (*criminosus*) slave and refuses to deliver him when asked by the judge should in all such cases compensate with his wergeld.

[4] Again, it was agreed that, if there is a theft, let the *centena* immediately restore the value of the theft, and let the *centenarius* claim the suit along with the *centena*, and let it redound to their benefit.

[5] Likewise, it was agreed that if a *centena* engaged in a pursuit follows the trail into another *centena* or onto [property of] any of our followers (*fideles*) and [the second *centena*] cannot at all follow the trail out into another *centena*, either let it return the convicted thief or immediately restore the value of the stolen property; and let it clear itself of [suspicion of complicity in] this matter with the oaths of twelve persons.

[6] If a slave of the church or the fisc commits theft, let him sustain the same penalty as slaves of other Franks (*franci*).

[7] As regards the Lord's day, it was likewise resolved that if any free person presumes to do any work on the Lord's day, apart from what pertains to cooking and eating, the offender is to be judged liable for 15 solidi if he is a Salic [Frank]. Let a Roman compensate 7½ solidi. As for slaves, either let a slave render 3 solidi or compensate with his back.

Certified by Asclipiodus.

Given, under good auspices, on the Kalends of March in the 21st year of our reign at Cologne.

# 72. CONSTITUTION OF CHLOTHAR
## (II?, 584-629)

*Scholarship has long been divided on whether this decree of Chlothar was by the first king of that name (a. 511-561), or by his grandson Chlothar II (a. 584-629); I accept the second attribution.*

*Chlothar calls his decree a* constitutio, *a* generalis auctoritas, *and a* praeceptio. *The decree also mentions orders of the king issued in written form, granting individuals various types of rights. The name for these orders is also* auctoritates; *a common synonym in other sources is* praeceptiones. *I translate both terms, here and elsewhere, as 'directives.' Chlothar's Constitution is a* generalis auctoritas, *a general directive. Its contents have numerous analogues in Roman law texts, especially the Theodosian Code.*

Source: Capitularia regum Francorum, ed. Alfred Boretius, MGH LL Capitularia (1896), 1: 18-19. Translation by A.C. Murray.

Chlothar, king of the Franks, to all his officials. It is the practice of the princely clemency to consider with prudent care what the provincials and all people subject to him require and to draw up in a constitution arranged in titles whatever must justly be attended to for their contentment: the more justice and righteousness are expended upon them, the more readily do they evince eager devotion. Thus we command by this general directive that the rules of the ancient law are to be observed in all suits and that no judgment of any judge is to possess a validity that exceeds the due measure of law and equity.

[2] Therefore, whatever was settled by the laws in the times of my kinsmen shall be respected, but the privilege of procuring something [by request] has been abrogated for all; if a privilege has been procured or acquired by some means, it is to be considered as empty and void, if the judges refuse to accept it.

[3] If someone is accused of a crime, that person is not at all to be condemned without a hearing. Should he be accused of a crime, and after a trial is held, it turns out that he is convicted, let him be sentenced as he deserves to a punishment that fits the crime.

[4] Among Romans we order that suits be brought to a conclusion by Roman law.

[5] If someone surreptitiously elicits a directive of ours contrary to law by deceiving the prince, it shall not be valid.

[6] If a judge unjustly condemns someone contrary to the law, let him be censured in our absence by the bishops so that, conversely, he takes care to correct his false judgment when a [new] trial has been better conducted.

[7] Let no one presume to seek marriage with a widow or girl against her will

by means of a directive of ours; nor let them be abducted unjustly by means of deceitful requests [or *possibly*, intimations].

[8] Let no one dare to join himself in marriage to a woman dedicated to God (*sanctimonialis*).

[9] Directives conforming to justice and law shall remain in all respects valid, nor shall they be nullified by subsequent directives elicited contrary to law.

[10] We warrant by the present constitution that offerings of the dead assigned to churches are not to be taken away by anyone's claims.

[11] To show the depth of our faith, we resign to the church the levies on fields (*agraria*) and pasture (*pascuaria*) and the tithe on pigs, and thereby no [fiscal] agent or tithe collector may enter church property.

Let state officials demand no public charge (*functio*) from the church and clerics who earned immunity from our grandfather, or father.

[12] Let what was conferred with liberal generosity to the church or to clerics or to any persons whatever by the aforesaid princes of glorious memory remain completely valid.

[13] Let whatever property the church, clerics, or our provincials are proven to have held for 30 years without their rights being disturbed remain in their possession under their control, provided their possession began justly; nor let any action that has been buried for more than this period of time be revived contrary to law, for the possessor without doubt retains possession.

Let all judges, therefore, see to it that they comply fully with this decree.

# 73. THE EDICT OF PARIS OF CHLOTHAR II, OCTOBER 614

*Following the defeat of the regime of Brunhild, Chlothar II convoked a general council of the Gallic church at Paris in October 614, attended by seventy-eight bishops. The deliberations of the Fifth Council of Paris ended on 10 October and resulted in a body of seventeen canons. A week later, consultation with the bishops and the lay magnates resulted in an ordinance now known as the Edict of Paris. It repeats in slightly different wording some of the canons of the council and deals with other matters of secular law. With the possible exception of the Constitution of Chlothar, the Edict of Paris is the last surviving record of the legislation of the Merovingian kings.*

*The Edict survives in only one MS, attached to a collection of canon law. Unfortunately the text is damaged in critical parts and unreadable. In the translation below those parts of the text that cannot readily be translated are marked with an ellipsis.*

Source: *Chlotharii II Edictum*, ed. A. Boretius, *Capitularia regum Francorum*, MGH LL Capitularia (1896), 1: 20-23. Translation by A.C. Murray.

There is no doubt that the happiness of our kingdom grows and divine favor increasingly reveals itself, if we strive in our times to preserve inviolate whatever, with God's grace, has been well determined, resolved, and decreed in our kingdom. We have also decided, with Christ as protector, to correct generally by the contents of this edict of ours what has been determined and instituted against the order of reason, so that in the future it does not come about that God turns from us.

[1] It is our resolution therefore that the regulations of the canons be maintained in all respects, and those that were overlooked in the past hereafter at least always be maintained. And so on the death of a bishop, the person who is to be ordained in his place by the metropolitan with the provincial bishops shall be selected by the clergy and people. If he is a worthy person, he shall be ordained by order of the king. Should he be selected from the palace, of course, he is to be ordained because of the merit of his person and religious training. *Cf. the Council of Paris, below,* **74 g 2.**

[2] No bishop in his lifetime may choose his successor, but let another be substituted for him when the bishop's condition is such that he cannot rule his church or clergy. Likewise, let no one in a bishop's lifetime presume to take his place. If someone seeks it, let it not at all be given.

[3] If a cleric of any rank, scorning his bishop or ignoring him, decides to approach the prince or powerful officials (*potentiores*) or any persons and to ask for their patronage, let him not be received, unless he is seeking pardon. And if for any reason he approaches the prince and returns to his bishop with a letter of that prince, let him be accepted back excused. Let those who presume to retain him after warning by his bishop be excommunicated.

[4] No judge of whatever rank shall presume on his own to try or to condemn clerics in temporal suits (*civiles causae*), apart from criminal matters, [and] unless the cleric is manifestly convicted, priests and deacons being excepted. Those who are convicted of a capital crime are to be tried according to the canons and examined in the presence of bishops. *Cf. the Council of Paris, below,* **74 g 6.**

[5] If a suit exists between someone whose forum is the public courts (*persona publica*) and dependents of the church (*homines ecclesiae*), the chief officials of the churches (*praepositi ecclesiarum*) and the public judge together shall preside from both sides over a public hearing (*audientia publica*) and judge them.

[6] If anyone dies intestate, let his relations succeed to his property according to law without the opposition of judges.

[7] Those freed by any free persons at all must be defended by the bishops according to the terms contained in the charters of their freedom; nor must they be judged or subjected to the jurisdiction of the public courts outside the presence of the bishop or chief official of the church. *On the church and freed persons, cf. below,* **74 f 7, g 7; 75 c.**

[8] Wherever a new assessment has been impiously added and the people object, let it be corrected mercifully by inquest.

[9] On tolls: they are to be exacted in the same areas and with regard to the same goods as under preceding princes, that is up to the passing of our kinsmen and lords of good memory, Kings Guntram, Chilperic, and Sigibert.

[10] Jews must not exercise public charges giving them authority over Christians. Whoever presumes to associate... let him incur the severest penalty of canon law. *This law corresponds to a decree of the Council of Paris (can. 17) that makes baptism a condition for Jews to exercise public authority.*

[11] With Christ's help, may there always be peace and public order in our kingdom, and may the rebel and the arrogance of evil men be most severely repressed.

[12] And let no judge be appointed from outside a region or province; thus if he commits some wrong with respect to matters giving rise to litigation, he shall have to make good from his own property according to law what he wrongly took away.

[13] Let our directives be fulfilled in all respects...

[14] ... Let public judges defend with legal remedies the property of churches, of priests, and of the poor who cannot defend themselves, until such time as the case is heard, without violation of the immunity that previous kings granted to the church, to the powerful (*potentes*), or whomever, for establishing peace and preserving public order.

[15] If dependents of churches or of the powerful (*potentes*) are accused of criminal offenses, and their administrators refuse to deliver them to a public tribunal to render justice...outside their estates when asked to do so by public officials, let them also be compelled to deliver them...

[16] Whatever our kinsmen who ruled before us, or we ourselves, have granted in accordance with the law and authorized shall be confirmed in all respects.

[17] And if one of the king's men (*fideles ac leudes*) lost something while preserving his faith to his legitimate lord during a division of the kingdom, we issue a general decree that his possession of the property justly due him be reinstated without any disadvantage.

[18] On devout and holy girls and widows who have dedicated themselves to God, those dwelling in their own homes as well as those placed in nunneries. Let no one seek one by means of a directive of ours nor presume at all to carry her off or marry her. And if anyone manages to get a directive from us, let it have no force. If anyone takes her away, either by force or in any manner at all, or presumes to marry her, let him be struck down with a capital sentence. If they are married in church, and she, already abducted or about to be so, consents to this, let them be separated from each other and exiled, and let their property be shared out among their relatives.

[19] Bishops or the powerful (*potentes*) who have possessions in a number of districts may not appoint judges or itinerant representatives (*missi*) outside the region in which the appointee obtains justice and renders it to others.

[20] The officials of bishops or of the powerful (*potentes*) are not to gather posses and take away someone's property by force, and let them not presume to cause anyone harm on their own.

[21] Swineherds of the fisc are not to presume to enter the woods of churches or of private persons without the permission of the landlord.

[22] Neither a free person nor a slave must be killed by judges or anyone at all without a hearing, provided he is not caught with stolen property.

[23] And when there is no pannage for the fattening of pigs, let the provisions tax not be exacted by the fisc.

[24] If someone presumes to violate this resolution, which we have drawn up with the bishops as well as our great men and loyal followers in a synodal assembly, let a capital sentence be adjudged against him so others shall not commit the same offense.

We have certified the validity of this directive or edict for all time by signing it with our own hand. Hammingus.

I, Chlothar, have signed this decree in the name of Christ.

Given on the 15th day before the Kalends of November [18 October] in the 31st year of our reign, at Paris.

# C. ECCLESIASTICAL LEGISLATION

## 74. CLERICAL PRIVILEGE AND ECCLESIASTICAL JURISDICTION IN THE CANONS OF CHURCH COUNCILS

*Numerous episcopal councils, or synods, met during the Merovingian period to deal with matters of importance to the church and to the rulers of the Gallic kingdoms. The resolutions of the councils sometimes took the form of general legislation for the church. Over two dozen of the councils have left a record of their legislative activity.*

*The following selections constitute a very small part of the total number of decrees, or canons, promulgated by the councils. I have selected those that deal with the sensitive question of clerical privilege and ecclesiastical jurisdiction. These were issues of long-standing importance since the fourth century and would continue to be a source of friction in the Christian West long after the Merovingian period. A number were treated in the Fifth Council of Paris and the Edict of Paris of 614. (Note that the Edict is given above, **73**, in its entirety; only three of the seven corresponding canons of the Council are given below.)*

*References in the canons to a 'judge' means in most instances the count or his delegate, though the term was also applied to other royal officials such as dukes. This usage follows late imperial practice; the 'judge ordinary' of the late empire was the governor.*

Source: *Concilia aevi Merovingici*, ed. Friedrich Maassen, MGH Concilia 1 (1893). Translation by A.C. Murray.

### a. From the Council of Orleans (I), a. 511.

*The first general council of the Merovingian church. It was called by Clovis, who provided at least some of the agenda. For the introductory letter of the bishops to Clovis, see **43**.*

1  Regarding homicides, adulterers, and thieves, who take refuge in a church, we have decided that what the ecclesiastical canons decreed and the Roman law established on these matters must be followed: namely that such people may in no way be dragged from the atriums of churches, or from the manse of the church or bishop. They are not to be surrendered except on condition that oaths are taken on the gospels preserving them from death, mutilation, and every kind of [afflictive] penalty, and provided that the criminal agrees to pay compensation to the person to whom he is liable.

Should someone be convicted of violating his oath, let whoever is guilty of perjury be excommunicated not only from the church and all clerics but even from the fellowship of Catholics.

Should the person to whom the criminal is liable lay a charge and not want to receive compensation, and the criminal, driven by fear, leaves the church, let neither the church nor clerics seek him out.

2 Regarding abductors, our resolution is as follows. If the abductor takes refuge in the church with the woman he abducted, and it is established that the woman was subjected to force, let her immediately be freed from the power of the abductor. The abductor is to be granted exemption from death or afflictive penalties, but let him be reduced to slavery or let him try to redeem himself with compensation.

But if she who was abducted has a father and the girl gave her consent to the abductor either as regards the abduction itself or after she was abducted, let her be restored to the power of her father, after he has excused her. Let the abductor be held liable to the father to make amends for the above offense.

3 If a slave takes refuge in a church because of some offense, and if he receives from his master an oath with respect to the offense he committed, let him be compelled to return to the service of his master immediately.

If, as a consequence of the oaths sworn by his master, the slave has been surrendered, and it is proven that he suffered some penalty on account of the same offense for which he was excused, let the master be considered a stranger to the communion and fellowship of Catholics, as in the previous canon, on account of his disdain for the church and deviation from the faith.

If a slave, who has been accorded the protection of the church for his offense, receives oaths from his master exempting him from punishment at the insistence of clerics, his master may, should the slave prove unwilling to go, take possession of him.

4 Regarding ordinations, our resolution is as follows. No lay person may aspire to clerical office except by order of the king or with the permission of the judge. There is this condition. The sons of clerics — that is descendants of fathers, grandfathers, and great grandfathers —, who are considered to be connected to the clerical order because of the service of their ancestors, remain under the authority and jurisdiction of bishops.

5 Regarding offerings or fields which our lord king has deigned to confer on the churches as his gift, or, by the inspiration of God, will confer upon those who have not yet received any. Since the king has granted immunity, we have decided with respect to such fields or clerics that it is just that whatever God deigns to provide by way of revenues should be spent in the repair of churches, in the maintenance of bishops and the poor, and in the buying back of captives, and that clerics should be compelled to assist in the church's task.

Should there be any bishop who is not attentive and committed to this activity, let him be publicly censured by the bishops of his province.

Should such shame not cause him to mend his ways, let him be considered unworthy of the communion of his brothers until he corrects the fault.

6 If someone believes he must sue a bishop for the restoration of something possessed in his own right or as a representative of his church, the complainant must not be removed from the communion of the church on account of this single judicial proceeding, provided he hurls no abusive or false accusations.

## b. From the Council of Epaône, a. 517.

*This was a council of the Burgundian kingdom, assembled by Avitus, bishop of Vienne, during the reign of the Burgundian king Sigismund.*

11 Clerics shall not presume to go before a public tribunal or to have recourse to its forum without the sanction of their bishop. But if claims are made against them, let them not delay attending the secular court.

22 If a deacon or priest commits a capital crime, let him be removed from the dignity of his office and consigned to a monastery. There, for the rest of his life, he must only take communion.

24 We permit laymen, if they are preparing to make a criminal charge, the power of lodging a suit against a cleric of any grade, on condition the plaintiff provides true statements.

## c. From the Council of Orleans (III), a. 538.

*Attended by bishops, or their representatives, from the kingdoms of Childebert I and Theudebert I.*

35 Let no cleric of any grade whatsoever presume to drag anyone before a secular court without the permission of his bishop. Nor is it permitted for a lay person to produce a cleric in secular court without asking the cleric's bishop.

## d. From the Council of Orleans (IV), a. 541.

*This was a large council but there is no reference to royal initiative in its convocation.*

20 Let no layman on his own authority dare to distrain, examine, or pass judgment on a cleric, bypassing the bishop or head of a church; moreover, should a cleric, at someone's request, be summoned by an official of the church with

respect to a legal suit, let the cleric promise to attend the hearing and let him not in an artful fashion answer the complaint falsely.

But whenever a suit involves a cleric and lay person, the public judge may not presume to hear the matter without a priest or archdeacon, or whoever is head of that church. Of course, if the litigants, by mutual consent, want to proceed to the judgment of a secular court, the head of the church in question may give the cleric permission to do so.

28 Provided someone who willfully commits homicide dares to kill an innocent person, even if the homicide clears himself in some way with the princes or with the family, he remains in the power of the bishop to be judged with respect to the amount of penance.

### e. From the Council of Mâcon (I), a. 581/3.

*Assembled by order of Guntram.*

7 No cleric is to suffer harm or be imprisoned for any reason by a secular judge without examination by his bishop.

But if any judge presumes to do this to someone's cleric without benefit of a criminal charge, that is one regarding homicide, theft, or sorcery, let him be repulsed from the thresholds of the church for as long as the bishop of that region pleases.

8 No cleric is to presume by any means to accuse before a secular judge another brother cleric or drag him before the court to defend himself, but all legal business of clerics is to be concluded either before the bishop, or before priests or the archdeacon. But if any cleric fails to abide by this rule, let him receive thirty-nine strokes if he is a junior member of the clergy, and if he is of greater standing, let him be penalized by thirty days' incarceration.

### f. From the Council of Mâcon (II), a. 585.

*This was a large council assembled again on Guntram's initiative from his kingdom and that of the young Chlothar II. The bishops of Childebert II did not attend. Cf. Gregory,* Hist. *VIII 13, 20.*

7 ... Praetextatus [bishop of Rouen] and Pappolus [bishop of Chartres], men most blessed, said, "Let the remarkable strength of your authority make a determination concerning the wretched freedmen, who are especially harassed by judges because they are commended to the holy churches. Decree that whoever says he has claims against them is not to bring those actions before the magistrate, but only before the court of the bishop, in

whose presence the plaintiff may make his case and receive a judgment in accord with justice and truth. For it is shameful that those who have been manumitted legitimately in holy church or who enjoy the right of liberty by charter or by testament or through the long passage of time should be unjustly harassed by anyone."

The whole episcopal congregation said, "It is just that those who covet the patronage of the immortal church should be defended against the devices of all false accusers and whoever tries through pride to violate the decree on freedmen issued by us should be struck by a penalty of irreparable damnation.

"But if a bishop sees fit to summon to his side a judge ordinary or any other layman to a hearing involving freedmen, let it be so since this is the desire of the bishop, but provided that no one else dares to go into the cases of freedmen except the bishop whose business it is or him to whom the bishop delegates the hearing."

9  The canons, most respectfully, and the laws, most piously, expressed judgment on the episcopal court almost at the very inception of Christianity. However, since this judgment has been ignored and human presumption against the bishops of God flourishes to the point of dragging bishops violently from the atriums of venerable churches and putting them in public prisons, we have decreed that no one provided with the fasces of secular power, obstinately on his own authority and carrying out his duty falsely, should dare to drag a bishop from the church over which he presides. But if a powerful person has complaints against a bishop, let him proceed to the metropolitan bishop and relate to him the grounds of his complaint. The metropolitan has the authority to summon the bishop concerned in the case honorably. Let the bishop answer his accuser before the metropolitan and there take counter measures in his own defense.

But if such is the enormity of the case that the metropolitan alone cannot bring it to a conclusion, let him avail himself of one or two fellow bishops. And, if there is doubt among them, let him fix a council for a set day or time in which the entire brotherhood, duly brought together, may investigate the defense of their fellow bishop and, according to its merit, clear him or find him guilty. For it is wrong that a bishop be dragged from the church at the hands or by the order of him for whom the bishop always prays to God and on whose behalf the bishop, calling on the name of God, gives the eucharist for the salvation of his body and soul. Let whoever boldly transgresses this decree resolved upon by us, as well as all who are in accord with him, be suspended with anathema from the church until the holding of a general council.

10  What we have decreed regarding bishops applies to the clergy so that neither

priest, deacon, or sub-deacon must be dragged from the churches or suffer any harm without the knowledge of their bishops.

But whoever holds something against them must bring it to the attention of the proper bishop who shall try the case in a just fashion and satisfy the feelings of the accuser of clerics.

12 What divine scripture teaches regarding widows and orphans is not unknown to us. Thus, whereas God has especially committed to our care the cases of widows and orphans, it has reached our attention that they have been harassed by judges irreparably and with considerable cruelty, in view of the insignificance of the cases, as though they lacked a defender.

For that reason we decree that judges not summon widows and orphans without first informing the bishop under whose protection they reside — and if the bishop is absent, the archdeacon or one of his priests — so that sitting jointly in common deliberation they may terminate their cases so justly and fairly that thereafter the aforesaid persons may not be disturbed by such things.

But if the judge or plaintiff inflicts injury on them or transgresses the decree of such a great council, let him be suspended from communion.

It is unworthy of those to whom care of great things have been entrusted to esteem lightly persons of little account. Disrespect for even the smallest matters commonly becomes bit by bit a great evil.

## g. From the Council of Paris (V), October 614.

*Cf. 73, art. 2, 6, 7, above.*

2 On the death of a bishop, the person ordained in his place, by Christ's favor, shall be chosen by the metropolitan who is to carry out the ordination with his fellow provincial bishops and by the clergy and people of the city in question, without payoffs and gifts of money of any sort being involved. But if he is brought into the church in another way, due to the improper use of power or to carelessness, without the election of the metropolitan and the consent of the clergy and people, his ordination shall be considered invalid according to the canons of the fathers.

6 No judge shall take it upon himself to try or condemn a priest or deacon, cleric or minor members of the clergy without their bishop knowing. If a judge does so, let him be excommunicated from the church upon which he inflicted that wrong until he recognizes his fault and emends it.

7 Those freed by any free person at all are to be defended by bishops and in no way to be subject to the jurisdiction of the public courts. Someone so presumptuous as to try to harass them and subject them to a public tribunal shall

be excommunicated if, summoned by the bishop, the offender fails to come to a hearing or refuses to make emends for his deeds.

## h. From the Council of Clichy, a. 626/27.

*Called by Chlothar II.*

9 Anyone who tries to reduce a freeborn or freed person to servitude, or perhaps has already done so and, having been admonished by the bishop, fails to cease his harassment or will not make emendation, should be excommunicated as someone guilty of calumny.

20 Clerics of any order whatsoever must not go before a secular court on their own behalf or on behalf of suits involving the church nor dare answer complaints there unless, they receive the permission and advice of his bishop.

27 Judges who, contrary to the directive and edict of the king, disregard the provisions of the canons and violate the royal edict that was drawn up at Paris, should be deprived of communion if they refuse to make emendation after having been admonished to do so.

## i. From the Council of Losne, a. 673/5.

*Held before Childeric II, this appears to be the last major legislative council of the Merovingian kings.*

3 To prevent bishops losing their temper, angered by the friction of pleading a case, no bishops should bring forward lawsuits except through an advocate.

# D. FROM THE FORMULARIES

*Formulae are exemplars, or model charters, which notaries copied when they drew up a document, filling in details as needed; formulae often contain alternate wording and even reminders to the notary as to what might be included. Though shorn of some specifics, usually names and dates, formulae may contain particulars showing that they were copied from charters dealing with individual circumstances. A collection of* formulae *is a formulary.*

*In the translation, I have marked the place where the appropriate name was to be inserted with the abbreviation N.*

Sources: (1) *Formulae Merowingici et Karolini Aevi*, ed. K. Zeumer, MGH LL Formulae (1882–1886); (2) *Marculfi Formularum Libri Duo*, ed. and trans. A. Uddholm (Uppsala, 1962). Translation by A.C. Murray.

## 75. ANGERS FORMULARY

*This collection of* formulae *was drawn up in Angers before 678, but how much before is a matter of debate. Some would date it to the late sixth century.*

### a. Loans and Mortgages

*These two documents, called* cautiones *(sing.* cautio*), are securities. The term for 'fruits'* (blada) *in the first one is Celtic.*

[1] I, N.

It is known that I have received, and indeed I have received in view of this security, a loan from N. for a satisfactory number of solidi in silver.

As a condition of that loan, I cede to you as a pledge for a period of so many years one half a vineyard of so many measures, which is in the territory of saint N., in the villa N.; the vineyard of N. bounds it on one side. As long as I have your property in my possession, you shall have the authority of taking as your own the fruits which God provides there.

And when the term of years is completed as expected, I will restore your property, and you shall have my security restored, either you yourself or whomever you gave it to for the purpose of collection. (no. 22)

[2] To the distinguished lord, brother N.

It is known that I have received from you, and indeed I have received in view of this security, a loan worth so many ounces of silver.

In place of a pledge, I deliver to you one half my status, whereby for so many days each week I shall carry out whatever legitmate work you assign to me. When so many years have passed, I shall restore your property and you will return this security to me.

If during that stipulated period I am negligent or slow with respect to those tasks or matters or shall not have fulfilled your will, then it is known that I shall restore your property twofold, either to you yourself or to whomever you give this security to collect the debt. (no. 38)

### b. Debt Bondage

[1] I, N., to my lord N. and his wife N.

I heedlessly stole your property and cannot otherwise make a settlement without being obliged to place my entire person in your service. No authority compels me to do this, but to redeem my heedless behavior, I have decided of my own free will, and notwithstanding that I may appear unsound in doing so, to bind my entire person to your service.

I am to receive from you an agreed-upon sum of so many solidi, so that, under God's protection, you may hereafter have the power of doing whatever you wish with me in all matters, just as you do with other dependents (*mancipia* ) indebted to you.

If I myself or any of my kinfolk or some outsider tries to act against this sale which I requested of my own free will, let that person furnish you and the fisc with so many solidi; let him compensate you, let his claim fail, and let this sale and my will remain in force. (no. 2)

[2] I, N., to my own lord N.

I am responsible for the heedless commission of thefts on account of which I was tortured and confessed, and for that reason have run the risk of a death sentence; but your goodness has provided so many solidi [for my redemption] from your property.

Thus I have had this document of sale issued to you regarding my person and all my property, so that, under God's protection, in all matters you may hereafter have the power of doing whatever you wish with me, just as with other dependents (*mancipia*) born in your power... (no. 3)

*The document concludes in a fashion similar to no. 1.*

### c. Manumissions

[1] In the name of God, to our favorite N.

You know that, out of respect due to the divinity and in consideration of the health of my soul and eternal reward, we have instructed that from this day forward you are to be free, as if born from free parents; know that you will owe no service or obedience to my heirs or their heirs but rather will be able to dwell under the protection of saint N. in complete freedom.

And if there is one of my heirs or any unrelated person at all, who presumes to oppose or deny this manumission, which I asked to be drawn up of my own free will, first let that person incur the judgment of God, and let him be made a stranger to the holy places; in addition let him suffer the penalty of law, one pound of gold, a weight of so much silver; and let his claim fail and this manumission remain valid for all time. (no. 20)

[2] I, N., to our favorite, N.

You know that out of respect due to the divinity and in consideration of the health of my soul and eternal reward, we have freed you from the yoke of servitude to this extent: that as long as you live you shall not depart from my service, and after my death, with all the property that you have or acquire by labor, you shall live the life of a free person, as if you were born from free parents, and know that you owe no service or obedience whatever to my heirs or their heirs, and shall be required to offer obedience only under the protection of the holy basilica of saint N. ...(no. 23)

*This document concludes in a fashion similar to no. 1.*

## d. A Judgment and Notice of its Performance

*There are a number of pairs of documents like the following ones in the Angers formulary. The first document is a* iudicius, *a judgment against a defendant. The second is a* noticia, *the record of an act, in this case, the performance of the judgment prescribed by the court.*

[1] In the city of Angers, N. along with his brothers german came before the illustrious count N. and other *rachineburgii* who were with him, whose signatures and marks are appended below, and charged a certain person, N. The plaintiff recounted how prior to this year the defendant killed their kinsman.

The defendant was asked what response he would give in this matter, and he strongly denied the charge in its entirety.

And so, with the approval of the brothers, the judgment was given by the court that within four [?] days, by the Kalends of [the next month], the defendant should take an oath in the cathedral church of the city with 12 co-swearers, composed of neighbors of like status to himself, with himself being the 13th. The oath is to state that he never consented to the death of the abovementioned person, nor did he kill him, nor was he ever aware of, or in agreement with, the killing being done.

If he can do this, let him remain for the days of his life free of this matter; but if he cannot, let him take pains to compensate with as much as the law provides. (no. 50)

[2] Record of the oath and the appearance of N. in the cathedral church of the city of Angers on the Kalends of March, and those who were present there.

According to the conditions of his judgment, N. said under oath with 12 persons, himself being the 13th: "By this holy place and the protection of all the saints who rest here: the plaintiff and his brothers german, N., have accused me of having killed their late kinsman, N., or of having him killed, but I did not kill him, nor have him killed, nor was I conscious of, or in agreement with, his death, nor do I owe anything with respect to this matter except the appropriate oath which I have been adjudged and which I have completed according to law." (no. 50b)

*The names of the witnesses to the oath, with their confirmation, would be listed.*

### e. Warranting and Default

*The following two* noticiae, *though separated in the formulary, seem to belong together and document separate phases in the same suit. In documents of this period the 'good men' (*boni homines*), a term of Roman law origin, resemble the Salic law* rachine-burgii.

[1] Record of how the plaintiff N. came to the city of Angers before the venerable abbot N., and a great many other good men who were with him, whose signatures and marks are appended below, and charged the following persons, N. and N. The plaintiff said that the defendants illegally invaded his vineyard in the place called N.

Since the defendants responded that they had a legal warrantor named N. the elder, and that he gave them that vineyard, the members of the court instructed the defendants to present him to warrant his possession on such-and-such date in the city of Angers; if they did not do this, they were to restore the vineyard to the plaintiff with the benefit of law. (no. 47)

*The following type of* noticia *is called a* solsadius, *a Franko-Latin term meaning default.*

[2] Record of the appearance of the plaintiff N. in the city of Angers on such-and-such a month and day to keep the appointment set for him to confront the defendants N. and N. Some time before they were involved in a

lawsuit with regard to their vineyard in the place called N., and promised to deliver their warrantor N. to vouch for the vineyard on their behalf.

The plaintiff came to the hearing that had been set and attended it from morning to night according to law and established default. For the defendants N. and N. were present but could not at all fulfill what they promised.

For that reason it was necessary for him to receive a record of this at the hands of the good men. He has done so, so that he might give attention to whatever the law stipulates in the future for the two parties. (no. 53 )

## f. Notice of Discharge (*Securitas*)

I, N., who dwell in the villa N. of saint N.

I agree to express my good will toward N. with a notice of discharge, which I have done. He had in his possession certain property that made him liable for a charge of theft, and I received so much money on that account. Therefore I agreed for that reason to give the discharge to you authenticated by my hand and that of good men, so that you might reside undisturbed and secure with respect to this matter from this day forth.

And if it should happen that either I myself or another person objects to this discharge, which I gave confirmed with my own hand, that person should compensate both you and the fisc with so many solidi; let him fail to get what he seeks and let my good will remain secure. (no. 42)

## g. Divorce

I, N. to my — not the sweetest, but rather — most bitter and mocking husband, N.

It is not unknown that the intervention of God's hostility prevents us from living together; therefore we have decided before good men that we ought to release one another. And we have done so.

Let my husband have the complete power of taking a wife as he wishes; likewise it is agreed that I have complete power of receiving a husband as I wish.

And if hereafter it happens that one of us dares to oppose this document in court or make a claim, let the judge have that person compensate his counterpart so many solidi, and let the claim come to nothing, and let this document remain valid for all time. (no. 57)

## 76. THE FORMULARY OF MARCULF

*Marculf's formulary is divided into two books, the first concerned with state business and matters concerning the court, and the second concerned with everyday legal transactions. The predominant view dates the collection to the late seventh century.*

### a. Royal Appointment of a Count, Duke, or Patricius

Royal kindness is fully commended if, above all, good and attentive people are sought out everywhere; and it is improper to grant judicial honours to just anyone, unless first his loyalty and energy have been demonstrated.

Because we have learned of your loyalty and ability, we therefore grant to you the office of count — or duke or patrician — in the district N., which your predecessor N. has held up to the present, for you to administer and govern, provided you preserve inviolate your loyalty to our rule. Let everyone dwelling there, whether Franks, Romans, Burgundians, or other nations, live and be restrained under your rule and direction. Steer them along the right path according to law and their own custom. Show yourself especially to be a defender of widows and orphans. Sternly repress the crimes of brigands and evildoers so that right-living people shall rejoice to remain at peace under your rule. And whatever proceeds the jurisdiction of the fisc can expect as a consequence of your official duties, you yourself must bring each year to our treasury. (1.8)

### b. Enrolling in the King's Retinue

*The kings' military retainers were called* antrustiones.

It is right that those who promise us unbroken loyalty should get help from our protection.

By God's favor, our follower (*fidelis*) N. has come here to our palace and, bearing arms, has pledged to us under oath his support and loyalty. For that reason, through the present directive, we decree and command that hereafter the said N. be counted among the ranks of *antrustiones*. And if it happens that someone dares to kill him, let the offender know that he will be held liable for a wergeld of 600 solidi. (1.18)

### c. A License to Become a Cleric

We do not withhold permission to those who decide to enter upon the duties of the clerical estate, for we have faith God will repay us, as it is written: "Do not stop someone who is able to do a good deed from doing so; do a good deed yourself if you can [Prov. 3:27]."

N. came to into the presence of our serene highness and asked us for permission for him to remove the hair from his head for the sake of the duties of a cleric and to serve in the basilica N. — or monastery. Know that we have gladly granted him permission in the name of God.

Therefore we command that, provided the said N. is truly free in respect to his person and is not registered on a public tax roll, let him have permission to shear the hair of his head, to serve in the abovementioned basilica — or monastery — and to pray intently for God's mercy on our behalf.

### d. Grants of Immunity

*Immunity is a term of Roman and Frankish public law meaning 'exemption.' The character of exemption changed over the course of the Merovingian period; the fiscal and even judicial exemptions mentioned in earlier legislation should not be equated with the broad judicial exemptions described below.*

*Note that the following grants are addressed to local officials (who would be counts usually), not the actual beneficiaries of the king's largesse. The form is essentially negative, in part because the grants are cast as royal orders, or directives, forbidding the king's representative from exercising particular royal rights.*

*The first charter addresses the king's representative with the honorific* vestra sollertia, *a term of politeness translated below with the prosaic term 'sir.'*

[1] We believe that we afford the greatest protection for our kingdom if with kind consideration we grant advantageous benefits to churches — or to whomever you wish to insert here — and, under God's protection, sanction the durability of the benefits in a charter.

Know sir that at the request of a man of apostolic rank, lord N., bishop of the city N., we have granted in return for everlasting reward a benefit of the following kind: no public judge may enter into the villas of the church of lord (i.e. saint) N., for the purpose of hearing cases or extracting peace-fines anywhere at any time; which villas are either possessed at the present time by virtue of a grant from us or from someone, or else in the future may be added to the ownership of that holy place by the goodness of God. As a result of the grant, let the bishop and his successors be able to administer the property with the full right of immunity.

Thus we establish that neither you nor your subordinates, nor your successors, nor any public judicial authority may presume to enter the villas of that church anywhere in our kingdom, whether granted by the generosity of the king or private persons or yet to be granted in the future, to hear disputes or to collect peace-fines with respect to any cases, or to draw lodging or provisions, or to take sureties. Whatever the fisc was able to expect from there by way of peace-fines, or whatever, from the freeborn or the servile, or those of other stations, who dwell on the farms, territories, or lands of the aforesaid church, let church officials forever use for the lighting of that church through our kindness and for our future salvation.

...And that the present directive may, with God's help, remain inviolate in the present and the future, we declare that we have authorized it below by our own signature. (1.3)

*The following exemplar provides three prologues for royal grants, two of them designed to reward laymen for their service. The third prologue for a holy place seems out of place, as the body of the grant is to a layman. The address formula has two more inflated, and untranslatable titles, rendered here by 'your excellency.'*

[2] Deservedly are they raised up by the gift of our generosity who from youth served our parents or ourselves with a ready sense of duty.

Another prologue. That which, God willing, is granted with deliberation to his faithful followers is accounted chief among the benefits of serving the king.

Another prologue, for a holy place. As the apostle said (Tim. 1:6,7), "we bring nothing into this world, nor can we take with us anything from it," except what we share with the holy places as a devout offering to the Lord for the salvation of our soul.

[*Body of the grant*] Therefore may your excellency know that we have readily granted to N., a man of illustrious rank, the villa N., located in the district N., with every benefit and with its extent undiminished, as it had been possessed, or in recent times was possessed, by N., or by our fisc. For this reason, by this present charter of ours, we proclaim our order, which will endure forever, namely that, as we said, the aforesaid N. is to be ceded forever the villa N. in its entirety, with lands, houses ... appurtenances, and with whatever kind of persons live there subject to our fisc, in full immunity, exempted from judges entering it to exact peace-fines with regard to any suit. He may have, hold, and possess it by proprietary right without waiting for delivery of possession by a judge; and, with God's help, he may leave it by our generosity to the possession of his descendants, or whom he wishes, and let him, by our permission, have the power in all respects of doing with it as he wishes... (1.14)

## e. Loan and Interest

*From Book Two of the formulary, concerning ordinary legal business. A* cautio *(as in the Angers formulary,* **75 a,** *above) in the form of a bond.*

N. to his lord N.

It is known that I received so many solidi from you, as indeed I did, and that I am in your debt, as indeed I am. For those solidi I promise every year to pay you a third of a solidus per solidus for as long as I have the loan. If I refuse to do this or prove to be negligent, I promise to repay the loan twofold. When I am able repay those solidi from my own property, I shall receive back this bond. (2.26)

## f. A Mandate

*A mandate (*mandatum*) conveyed power of attorney.*

N. to [his] brother, lord N.

Whereas I have a lawsuit before the king's court — or any court —concerning inheritance — or anything matter — with a man called N., I pray and entreat your lordship to agree to conduct the suit in my place before the courts and plead the case against the said N. And you may know that whatever action you carry out or perform with respect to him in this matter I consider ratified and concluded.

Date and place of the mandate. (2.31)

# E. ROYAL CHARTERS

## 77. DISPUTE SETTLEMENT BEFORE THE KING'S COURT: A JUDGMENT OF CHILDEBERT III, a. 709 or 710

*Charters from the Merovingian period have come down to us principally in two forms: originals, some of which are on sheets of papyrus; and copies entered in the ecclesiastical registers, or cartularies, of later ages. Unfortunately a large percentage of supposedly Merovingian charters in cartularies are forgeries intended to document the privileges and landed endowment of the later churches that drew them up. As for originals, there are only fifty-odd specimens extant, which, along with the* formulae, *are the basis for studying the legal instruments of the Merovingian period and for evaluating the authenticity of cartulary copies. About three dozen of these originals are diplomas, a common modern term for charters issued by, or in the name of, Merovingian monarchs; these include grants of various types and judgments made in the royal court. Most diplomas were preserved in the monastery of Saint Denis (Dionysius) and are, as one would expect, favorable to the monastery's claims. The following document is a judgment (called a* placitum *in modern scholarship) which also happens to mention earlier royal grants.*

*The following judgment is interesting for the diplomatic form of its text and for incidental information regarding a fair on the feast of Saint Dionysius, commerce, indirect taxes, and royal administration. The legal substance of the text may not quite be what it seems. Older scholarship saw the* placitum *as recording the outcome of a genuine dispute, but recent opinion tends to the view that the dispute is a fiction, the procedure actually serving to strengthen the monastery's claim to exemption by means of a royal judgment.*

*Gaerin, count of Paris, was Saint Leudegar's brother (cf.* **62**). *The reference to Childebert's 'brother' Chlothar is puzzling. Childebert's kinsman Chlothar IV, as far as we know, only came to the throne for the first time in 717; Childebert did have an uncle, Chlothar III, and a brother Clovis III, who ruled earlier.*

Source: *Chartae Latinae Antiquiores. Facsimile Edition of the Latin Charters prior to the Ninth Century*, Part XIV, France II, ed. H. Atsma and J. Vezin (Dietikon-Zurich, 1982), no. 586. Translated by A.C. Murray.

Childebert [III], king of the Franks, to those of illustrious rank.

Representatives of the venerable Dalfinus, abbot of the basilica of our own special patron Saint Dionysius, wherein lies the precious body of this lord, came before us and our leading men in our palace at Montmacq. They claimed in opposition to the representatives of the illustrious Grimoald, mayor of our palace, that over a long period of time our grandfather the late Clovis [II], and after him our uncle Childeric [II] and our father Theuderic [III], as well as our brother (*germanus*) Chlothar [III, IV, Clovis III?], had issued directives granting to that basilica of Saint Dionysius the entire toll collected from all merchants, whether of Saxon or other nationality, who attend the fair held on the holy feast of Lord Dionysius [9 October]; as a consequence of the grant, they said, the fisc was precluded at that time [of Clovis II] and later from exacting or collecting on its own behalf tolls from those merchants either there, at the fair, or within the district of Paris or within the city of Paris; the basilica of Saint Dionysius, they said, had been granted and awarded this right in its entirety for all time.

They then produced the directives of the aforesaid princes to that effect for the court to read. Those directives were deposited and examined, and it was determined that such a grant in its entirety had been made to that house of God by those princes.

Then the representatives of Dalfinus said that the representatives of Grimoald, mayor of our palace as well as count of the district of Paris, collected half the toll from them, removing its benefits from the basilica.

The representatives of the mayor of our palace Grimoald replied on the contrary that for a long time it had been customary for the house of Saint Dionysius to receive one half the toll and the count the other on behalf of the fisc.

The representatives of Saint Dionysius contended in reply that Gaerin, the late count of Paris, introduced this custom by force and at times collected half the toll from them; but those representatives informed the palace of this and, they said, always renewed their royal directives without diminution of the grant.

Again an examination was undertaken of numerous people and of the directives that the aforesaid princes had granted originally and had subsequently confirmed without diminution of the grant.

And so, with Grimoald's agreement and that of many other loyal followers of the king, a determination was made and judgment given that the representatives of Grimoald were on behalf of our fisc to invest that toll in its entirety once again upon the agents of the abbot by means of a pledge. And so they did.

Whereas it is known that the suit has been brought forward and settled, investigated and adjudicated, in just such a fashion as the illustrious count of our palace Rigofred has reported, it is our command, now that the previous directives granted to the monastery have been examined, that for all time the aforesaid monastery of Saint Denis, wherein that most precious lord's body rests, and abbot Dalfinus and his successors have successfully sued for and laid claim to that entire toll collected at the feast of Saint Dionysius, both that which arises on the lands of the basilica and later in Paris.

In earlier times, the market was moved on account of a catastrophe from the site of Saint Dionysius and was established in the city of Paris between the basilicas of Saints Martin and Laurence. The abbey received directives from the aforesaid princes to the effect that the aforesaid basilica of Saint Dionysius should get the toll in its entirety either there or wherever it set up to conduct business and commerce on the occasion of that feast. In view of these circumstances, if it happens that on account of some catastrophe or interruption the fair should be moved somewhere else, let that aforesaid toll, because of our devotion to that holy place, in present and future times, remain granted to and bestowed upon that house of God to offset the cost of lighting. And between our fisc and the representatives of Saint Dionysius, may all dispute and contention be laid to rest.

Actulius has been ordered to certify this.

Given, under auspicious signs, in December, on the thirteenth day, in the sixteenth year of our reign at Montmacq.

# CHAPTER SIXTEEN

# HISTORY, LEGEND, AND ROMANCE

*The histories of Frankish Gaul are especially prized for what they tell us about contemporary or near contemporary events and what they preserve from earlier sources no longer extant. But the value of Gregory's* Histories *(47-49),* Fredegar's Chronicle *(58), and the LHF (59) also extends beyond their utility for the reconstruction of real events, people, and institutions. All these histories contain stories about the more or less distant past. The stories are often painfully ill informed; sometimes we have better sources that reveal the extent of the errors, and sometimes the character of the account itself betrays its origin in a narrative realm exempt from the modest checks imposed upon writing contemporary history. Modern historians have often been tempted, nevertheless, to exploit these stories in the belief that, where the account is not demonstrably wrong, it may contain nuggets of reliable oral tradition. The real interest of the stories, however, lies not in the remote possibility of recovering stray historical facts, but in what the accounts reveal about the historical and literary imagination of the period and the sense of the past shared by historians and their contemporaries. That beliefs about the past failed to correspond in large degree to what we would accept as true casts light on the nature of Merovingian historiography, the forces shaping contemporary identity, and the character of early Frankish history.*

*The emphasis in the following excerpts is on Fredegar and the author of the LHF — a circumstance that is explained in part by their incorporating and building on earlier versions of stories in Gregory's* Histories *and in part by Gregory being more addicted to ecclesiastical varieties of romance and legend than the types represented here. Gregory's most contentious contribution to the secular variety (though mixed with sources of genuine historical value) has already been given (46).*

Sources: For Gregory of Tours: (1) *Historiarum libri X*, ed. Bruno Krusch and Wilhelm Levison, MGH SRM 1/1, (1951) 2nd. ed; (2) *Zehn Bücher Geschichten*, ed. Rudolf Buchner, 2 vols. (Berlin, 1955-56). For Fredegar: (1) *Chronicarum quae dicuntur Fredegarii Scholastici libri IV*, ed. Bruno Krusch, MGH SRM 2 (1888), pp. 118-168; (2) "Die vier Bücher der Chroniken des sogennanten Fredegar," ed. Andreas Kusternig, in *Quellen zur Geschichte des 7. und 8. Jahrhunderts*, ed. Herwig Wolfram (Darmstadt, 1982), pp. 160-271. For the *LHF*: *Liber historiae Francorum*, ed. Bruno Krusch, MGH SRM 2 (1888), 215-328. Translations by A.C. Murray.

# A. THE ORIGINS OF THE FRANKS AND
# THEIR KINGS

*Gregory of Tours, Fredegar, and the author of the* LHF *all attempted to grapple with the problem of Frankish origins. Gregory, who was mainly interested in discovering the origin of kingship among the Franks, laid down the agenda to some extent, but his concentration on kingship was replaced in the later historians by a broader problem of the origin of the Franks as a people. Is this a reflection of differing personal interests or of broader changes in historical consciousness?*

*The solution to the problem of the origin of the Frankish people as we find it laid out in Fredegar and the* LHF *derived from a theme already widely used in European historiography. The Romans and some other western peoples, taking their cue from Greek historiography, had long since claimed to owe their origins to the dispersal of the Trojans after the sack of Troy, the great event of early Hellenistic history. In Fredegar and the* LHF *the motif of Trojan descent was applied to the Franks, whose origins now, and for almost a millennium hereafter, were traced to the fall of Troy. Fredegar's Chronicle is the earliest source that attests to this cliché; the* LHF *version is similar but not dependent on the Fredegarian account. Gregory's account of Frankish origins is also peculiar enough to raise the possibility that he was already aware of a version of this solution to Frankish origins, but had rejected it.*

## 78. GREGORY OF TOURS, *HIST.* II 9–10

*When Gregory reached the mid-fifth century in his narrative, he raised the question of the origins of Frankish kingship, which he treated as a problem to be solved, not as a story to be recounted.*

Many are unaware who was the first king of the Franks. For example while the history of Sulpicius Alexander tells many things, still it does not at all name their first king...

*Gregory then gives extracts from the works of Sulpicius Alexander and Renatus Profuturus Frigeridus (cf.* **25 A, C**).

This is the information that Sulpicius Alexander and Renatus Profuturus Frigeridus have left to us regarding the Franks, without naming their kings.

*In the following passage, reference to a left-bank 'Thuringia' is puzzling: it is often thought that Tongres and the Tungri are meant. Dispargum is usually identified as Duisburg. Richimer the Frank is not the great patrician Ricimer (a. 457-72), who was of Suevic and Visigothic descent.*

Now many say that the Franks left Pannonia and at first inhabited the banks of the river Rhine. From there they crossed the Rhine and traversed

Thoringia; and then they set over themselves in the territories of the Gallic towns (*pagi vel civitates*) long-haired kings, from their first, and as I would say, more noble, family. This was shown to be true later by Clovis's victories, as I shall subsequently narrate. We read in the consular annals that Theudomer, king of the Franks, the son of Richimer, and his mother Ascyla, were put to the sword. It is said also that Chlodio, skilled in war and the most noble among his people, was king of the Franks at the time; he lived in the fortress of Dispargum, which is in the region of the Thoringi. In those parts, that is toward the south, the Romans were living up to the river Loire. Beyond the Loire the Goths ruled. The Burgundians, followers of Arian doctrine, lived across the Rhône, near the city of Lyons. Chlodio sent scouts to the city of Cambrai; when they had surveyed everything, he followed, crushed the Romans, and took the city. Staying there for a short time, he extended his control to the Somme. Some say that king Merovech, whose son was Childeric, was of his line.

The Franks of that time, however, paid service to pagan religion and were entirely without knowledge of God...

*A homily against paganism follows.*

# 79. FREDEGAR, *CHRON.* II 4-6, 8-9, AND III 2,9

*Fredegar is the name modern scholars give to an anonymous writer who compiled a series of chronicles around a. 660 (for more details, see* **XII**, *Introduction). Fredegar summarized work of earlier chronicles, but in the course of doing so sometimes added material of his own.*

## a. Interpolations in the *Chronicle* of Jerome

*Fredegar's compendium includes long extracts from the chronicle of Eusebius-Jerome dealing with secular and biblical history; within this he inserted an account of the origins of the Franks (Chron. II 4-6).*

*Material from Eusebius-Jerome is in a smaller font, Fredegar's interpolations are in a larger font. (Note, for example, that Fredegar is responsible for Priam being the abductor of Helen in the second sentence.)*

Under Tautanus, king of the Assyrians, Troy was captured... At this time, Priam abducted Helen. The ten-year Trojan war arose because of the apple that was the prize of three women contending over beauty, one of them promising Helen to the shepherd who was their judge. Memnon and the Amazons brought aid to Priam. The origin of the Franks is due to these events. They had Priam as their first king.

It is written in books of history how afterwards they had Frigas as king. Later they were divided into two parts. One part went to Macedonia. They are called Macedonians after the people by whom they were received and the region of Macedonia. They had been invited to give assistance to the Macedonians, who were being overwhelmed by neighboring peoples. Afterwards when united with that people, they gave birth to a great many offspring and from that stock the Macedonians were made into the strongest of fighters. In the future, in the days of King Philip and his son Alexander, report confirms what kind of courage they possessed.

Now the other part, which advanced from Frigia [=Phrygia], had been deceived by Ulysses and, though not taken captive, had nevertheless been driven forth from there. Wandering through many regions with their wives and children they chose from amongst themselves a king by the name of Francio; from him they are called Franks. Francio, it is said, was very strong in war, and for a long time fought with a great many peoples, but in the end, after devastating part of Asia, he entered Europe and settled between the Rhine, Danube and Ocean.

There Francio died. Since only a small band of them now were left, because of the many battles Francio had fought, they established dukes from amongst themselves. Ever rejecting the authority of another king, they lived for a long time under the rule of their dukes until the time of the consul Pompey, who fought with them and with the other peoples that lived in Germania, and subjected all of them to the authority of Rome. But the Franks, immediately forming an alliance with the Saxons, resisted Pompey and rejected his power. Pompey died in Spain fighting against a great many peoples. Afterwards, no people up to the present time has been able to conquer the Franks, but the Franks have been able to subjugate them to their authority. Cast in the same mold were the Macedonians, who were of the same descent, and although they had been ground down by brutal wars, still they have always tried to live free from foreign domination.

Report confirms that a third people of the same origin were the Turks. When the Franks had experienced many battles in their travels through Asia and entered Europe, one part of them settled on the bank of the river Danube between the Ocean and Thrace. They even chose from among themselves a king, called Torquotus, from whom the Turks get their name.

The Franks in this journey made their way with their wives and children, and there was no people that could withstand them in battle. But since they fought a great many battles, when they settled on the Rhine, a small band of them arrived, for they were diminished by [the separation of] Torquotus. From the capture of Troy to the first Olympiad amounts to 406 years...

*After a brief chapter on Hebrew history, Jerome's chronicle turns to the early Romans, another occasion for a Fredegarian interpolation on Trojan origins* (Chron. II 8, 9).

In that time Tautanus reigned in Assyria. This was the period in which Troy was captured. Among the Hebrews, Lepdon was judge, and, in Egypt, Dinastia was king. The first king of the Latins arose at this time, for they had fled from Troy, and he and Frigas were from that stock. But on account of the capture of Troy and the flood of Assyrians and their persecution, they had left that city and region in two parts. For that reason, they established one kingdom of Latins and another kingdom of Frigians. Aeneas ruled the Latins, who were later called Romans, in the third year after the capture of Troy, or as some believe, in the eighth year. Aeneas and Frigas, it is said, were brothers.

Aeneas ruled the Latins for three years, and Frigas ruled Frigia [=Phrygia]. Before Aeneas and Frigas, [J]ann[us], Saturn, Picus, and Latinus after whom the Latins are named, also ruled in Italy for about one hundred and fifty years...

## b. Interpolations in the *Histories* of Gregory of Tours

*When Fredegar excerpted Gregory of Tours's* Histories, *he returned to the Trojan origins of the Franks* (Chron. III 2) *at the point where Gregory discussed the origins of Frankish kings* (Hist. II 9, above **78**). *Fredegar's interpolation at this point clarifies the sequence of bifurcating divisions underlying his interpolations in Eusebius-Jerome (see fig. 1).*

*The opening reference to Jerome is to Fredegar's interpolated version of Jerome's chronicle. The text in the smaller font is based on that of Gregory.*

Concerning the kings of the Franks, blessed Jerome has written who they were once upon a time, and before him the poet Virgil [in the Aeneid] told the story. They had Priam as their first king. When Ulysses took Troy by deceit, they departed from there. Afterward they had Frigas as king. Divided into two, part of them proceeded to Macedonia. The others under Frigas were called Frigians; they wandered about Asia and settled on the shore of the Danube and the sea of Ocean. Again there was a division into two, and one part of them under Francio their king entered Europe. Wandering about Europe, they settled along with their wives and children on the bank of the Rhine. And they sought to build a city named after Troy not far from the Rhine [Colonia Traiana=Xanten?]. This work was begun but was left uncompleted. The remaining part of them that stayed on the bank of the Danube elected from among themselves a king, Torcoth [i.e. Torquotus] by name and were then called Turks after him. The others are called Franci after Francio. For a long time afterwards under their dukes they always rejected the rule of strangers.

*Fredegar very imperfectly follows the accounts and chronology of Gregory's excerpts from earlier historians (cf. **25 A, C**). The following description of the origins of the Merovingians (Chron. III 9), apparently set ca. 450s, is interpolated into Gregory's discussion of the creation of long-haired kings (above, **78**). Text dependent on Gregory is in a smaller font.*

The Franks after diligent inquiry set over themselves a king, chosen from their midst, long-haired, as earlier had been the case, and from the stock of Priam, Frigas, and Francio. His name was Theudemar, the son of Richimer, who was killed by the Romans in the battle I mentioned above [*omitted here*]. His son Chlodio replaced him in the kingship, the most warlike man among his people; he lived in the fortress of Esbargium, which is in the territory of the Thoringi. The Burgundians lived on this side of the Alps and were also followers of Arian doctrine. Chlodio took note of everything by sending scouts to the town of Cambrai, and then followed them himself. He crushed the Romans, captured the city, and extended his control to the Somme. The Franks of that time were devoted to pagan practices.

It is said that when Chlodio was staying with his wife on the sea shore in the summer, his wife went to the water to bathe at noon, and a beast of Neptune resembling the Quinotaur [=Minotaur] sought her out. As she conceived right away, either by the beast or by her husband, she afterwards gave birth to a son called Merovech, after whom the kings of the Franks were later called Merovingians.

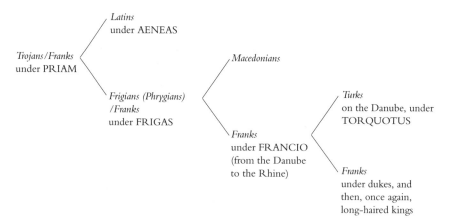

*Fig. 1. Origin of the Franks and their Kings according to Fredegar*

## 80. THE ANONYMOUS *HISTORY OF THE FRANKS (LHF)* 1-5

*Gregory of Tours did not write a history of the Franks, and even Fredegar, who attempted to document the origins and rise of Frankish power, cast the first part of his work in the form of a universal chronicle and to the end maintained a broad interest in the events of the world at large. From its opening sentence the* LHF *took as its theme the Frankish peoples and their kings, and stuck with it, though eventually narrowing the concept of Franks largely to the Neustrians.*

1. Let us present the beginning of the kings of the Franks, the origins and deeds of the kings and those peoples. In Asia [Minor] is the country of the Trojans; the city there is called Ilium and was ruled by Aeneas. The people were brave and strong, the men fighters and very unruly, waging endless wars and conquering the neighboring districts round about. The kings of the Greeks, however, rose up against Aeneas with a big army and fought him in a bloody conflict; many Trojans fell there. And so Aeneas fled, and shut himself up in the city of Ilium. The Greeks attacked the city for ten years.

When the city was conquered, Aeneas the tyrant fled to Italy to hire other peoples for the struggle. Other leaders, namely Priam and Antenor, also embarked on ships with the rest of the force of Trojans, to the number of twelve thousand, and came to the Don river. Sailing into the Maeotian marshes, they reached the regions of Pannonia adjoining the Maeotian marshes and began to build a city as a memorial. They called it Sicambria; they lived there for many years and grew into a great people.

2. In that time, the Alans, a perverse and wicked people, rebelled against Valentinian, emperor of the Romans and other peoples. He then levied a great host from Rome, marched against the Alans, engaged them in battle, overthrew and defeated them. When they were cut down on the Danube river, they fled into the Maeotian marshes.

The emperor now said, "Whoever can penetrate the marshes and drive out that perverse people, I will remit to them the tax offerings for a period of ten years."

Then the Trojans assembled and set ambushes, a practice at which they were trained and knowledgeable. They entered the Maeotian marshes with another people of the Romans, drove out the Alans, and put them to the sword. It was then that the emperor Valentinian called them, in the Attic tongue, Franks, that is *feri*, from the hardness and boldness of their hearts.

3. After a space of ten years, the aforesaid emperor sent tax collectors along with Duke Primarius from the Roman Senate to receive the usual taxes from the Frankish people.

As they were cruel and savage, they adopted a worthless plan, saying to each other, "The emperor with the Roman army could not drive the Alans, a brave and bellicose people, from their dens in the marshes; as it was us who beat them, why should we pay taxes? Let's rise up against this Primarius and those tax collectors; if we strike them down, take everything they have, and give the Romans no taxes, we shall always be free."

So they set ambushes and killed them.

4. The news ignited the emperor's rage and furious anger. He ordered an army to be assembled composed of Romans and other peoples under the general Arestarcus and sent the force against the Franks. A great slaughter then ensued on both sides. The Franks were destroyed and cut to pieces, and as they saw that they could not withstand so great an army, they fled. Priam, the strongest of them, fell there. They also left Sicambria and came to the most distant regions of the river Rhine, to the regions of the Germanies, and there they lived under their princes, Marchomir, the son of Priam, and Sunno, the son of Antenor.

When Sunno died, they were advised to establish one king for themselves like other peoples. It was Marchomir who gave them this advice. They chose Faramund, Marchomir's son, and raised him up over them as a long-haired king. Then they began to have laws, which the most prominent men by birth expounded. Their names were Wisowastus, Wisogastus, Arogastus, and Salegastus [and they lived] in villas beyond the Rhine called Bothagm, Salechagm, and Widechagm.

5. When King Faramund died, they raised up Chlodio, his son with long-hair, to the kingdom of his father. That was the time they began to have long-haired kings. They came quickly to the territory of the Thuringians, and there they settled.

And so King Chlodio lived in the fortress of Disbargum in the region of Germania. At that time the Romans lived in those districts on this side of the Rhine up to the Loire river, and also, beyond the Loire the Goths ruled. The Burgundians were quite pagan and held by the perverse Arian doctrine; they lived by the Rhône river near the city of Lyons.

King Chlodio now sent spies from the Thuringian fortress of Disbargum as far as Cambrai. He then crossed the Rhine with a great army, killed a large number of the Roman people and put them to flight. He entered the Carbonarian forest and took the city of Tournai. From there he came to Cambrai where he settled for a short period of time; he killed the Romans he found there. Chlodio took possession of the region between Cambrai and the Somme river.

When King Chlodio died, Merovech [a kinsman] of his line received his kingdom. Chlodio reigned for twenty years. It is from Merovech, an able king, that the kings of the Franks are called Merovingians.

# B. HISTORICAL TALES AND HISTORICAL ROMANCE IN FREDEGAR'S *CHRONICLE*

*Many of Fredegar's interpolations were inserted in his summary of Gregory's* Histories *and deal with the early Franks; excerpts will be found below,* **86–95**. *The following stories are Fredegar's main interpolations to the chronicles of Jerome and Hydatius and deal with non-Frankish themes; one interpolation to Gregory's* Histories *with similar subject matter has been included as well.*

*The interpolations themselves must have had sources, but determining what they might have been is an imperfect process; written sources now lost, oral storytelling, and Fredegar's own invention and elaboration may all have contributed in varying degrees to the composition of the interpolations.*

*The interpolations have real historical backgrounds, and one can, with some ingenuity, link their contents to actual events and people, but they can hardly be regarded as history. Filled with wild inaccuracies, mixing up or inventing characters, oblivious to chronology, these stories are dedicated to the pungent scene and the moralizing maxim rather than historical truth. The desire for the past to be dramatic, edifying, and entertaining is enduring, and though these tales have their own conventions, they bear a resemblance to what often passes for history in modern media and entertainment — they are certainly no worse. It may be more disconcerting to notice in these stories similarities with Fredegar's approach to history in his own chronicle of the early seventh century* (**58**).

*I have added dates but the reader should not take those as endorsements of the narrative nor expect them to be consistent with the narrative's own chronology.*

## 81. AËTIUS, THE HUNS, AND THE GOTHS (II 53)

*The following story is inserted in the* Chronicle *of Hydatius s.a. 451 (cf.* **18**). *Some of the elements appear already in* Gregory of Tours, Hist. II 7, *where Aëtius tricks the Goths and Franks into leaving the battlefield so that he can collect the booty. The first sentence is Hydatius's.*

[53] The Huns broke the peace and fell on the Gallic provinces. When Aëtius learned of their coming, he sent the holy Anianus, bishop of Orleans, as ambassador to Theoderic [I, 418-451], king of the Goths, to ask for help against the Huns; if Theoderic was successful in withstanding them, Aëtius promised he would give a half part of Gaul to the Goths. When Theoderic agreed to the request and aid was promised, Aëtius sent envoys to meet Attila, king of the Huns, and asked for help against the Goths, who were trying to seize the Gallic provinces; if the Huns were successful in protecting them from the Goths, Aëtius would allow them to take half of Gaul.

King Attila and the Huns came quickly, sparing the cities of Germania and Gaul, and joined battle with the Goths on the river Loire, not far from Orleans. Of the Goths, 200,000 were killed. King Theoderic fell in the battle. Of the Huns, 150,000 were killed. The city of Orleans was protected by the prayers of the blessed Anianus.

The Huns, retreating to Troyes, took up a position on the Mauriac plain. Thorismund, the son of Theoderic and his successor to the kingdom [a. 451-53], gathered the army of the Goths to avenge his father and joined battle with Attila and the Huns at Mauriac. There for three days the battle lines fought each other and an innumerable host of people fell.

Aëtius, who was very quick at devising a plan, came to Attila at night and said to him, "It had been my desire to be able to deliver this region from the faithless Goths by your strength, but it cannot at all be done. Up to now you have been engaging the least of their fighters, but this night Theoderic [II, a. 453-66], the brother of Thorismund, comes with a host beyond measure and with the boldest fighters of the Goths. You will not withstand them; I do hope at least you can escape."

It was then that Attila gave Aëtius 10,000 solidi so that he could retreat to Pannonia without interference.

That night Aëtius went to Thorismund and presented him with a similar tale, namely that up to now he had fought the second-rate fighters of the Huns; for a very great host and the boldest fighters had reached Attila from Pannonia that very night. And Aëtius said there was a report that Thorismund's brother, Theoderic, had taken the treasury of the Goths and wished to seize the kingdom. Unless Thorismund rapidly carried out a retreat, he was in danger of being removed.

Aëtius also received 10,000 solidi from Thorismund, so the Goths might return home free from interference and protected from pursuit by the Huns. The Goths immediately departed.

As for Aëtius, he brought up the rear of the Huns with his own forces, including Franks, following them at a distance to Thuringia. He gave orders to his men that when they stopped at night each man should build ten campfires spread out so that they resembled an immense host.

Aëtius's ruse brought a halt to the fighting. Gaul was freed from its enemies. Afterwards when king Thorismund and the Goths were informed of this trick, they demanded that Aëtius fulfill his promise [to give them half of Gaul]. Aëtius refused. For the sake of peaceful relations, a golden dish, decorated with precious stones and weighing fifty pounds, was sent by Aëtius to Thorismund as compensation and the dispute was settled. This showpiece is faithfully revered and preserved as a prize of the Gothic treasury even today [cf. 58, c. 73].

## 82. THE DEEDS OF THEODERIC THE GREAT
### (II 56, 57, 59)

*The following stories about Theoderic the Great, Ostrogothic ruler of Italy (a. 490-526), follow directly on Hydatius's chronicle (ending in a. 468) without any indication of a break in the narrative. The stories, which later circulated as a separate work based on Fredegar's Chronicle, are thought to derive from a lost anonymous work, called by scholars the* Gesta Theoderici, *"The Deeds of Theoderic."*

*Note that Fredegar is careful to distinguish the Visigothic king Theoderic II from Theoderic the ruler of Italy, who was, in his account, a Macedonian by birth. The significance for Fredegar of this particular ancestry is no doubt tied to his understanding of the Trojan origin of the Franks (above, 79), the Macedonians being regarded as offshoots of the Trojans/Franks. The notion of peoples bifurcating is used in this account as it is in Fredegar's treatment of Frankish origins. Fredegar also equates the Huns with the Avars, using the terms interchangeably. Theoderic never fought the Huns in Pannonia, as these tales claim, and the arrival of the Avars lay over a generation in the future; Theoderic did campaign there against the Gepids. The emperor Leo was dead well over a decade before Theoderic marched to Italy.*

In the times of Emperor Honorius, after the capture of Rome [a. 410], the realm of the Goths divided in two. Those who had settled in Italy surrendered to the authority of the empire. The rest chose Athaulf as king, selecting as their capital Toulouse in the province of Aquitania. Afterwards, as the above events [of Hydatius's chronicle] confirm, it was ruled by the Goths. As for the Goths who settled in Italy and continued to be subject to the Roman Empire, Theoderic, a Macedonian by birth, obtained the permission of Emperor Leo to govern them, as the deeds of this book attest. Obviously the other Theoderic [II], the son of Theoderic [I], was a Goth by birth.

[57]

The birth of the king Theoderic who was of Macedonian descent and ruled Goths and Romans in Italy took place in this fashion. Although Idacius, the patrician, and Eugenia, his wife, had no children, they did have in their service a boy by the name of Theodorus, who was their confidential servant, and a girl by the name of Lilia. When they learned that Theodorus and Lilia loved one another, they gave them permission to marry. They were both Macedonian by birth and had been removed as captives when still very young.

Eugenia gave the girl instructions: "When you have intercourse with your husband, do not fail to tell me the next morning what you see that night in your dreams while asleep. For it is believed that there is truth in what newly-weds see on the first night."

When they were united that very night, the girl had a dream that a tree

was born, springing forth from the middle of her belly so high that it penetrated the clouds. She told her husband her mistress's orders and the vision
that she had seen.

"When you see your mistress today," said her husband, "as she has no children, say this to her: 'During the night I beheld a stallion and mare with
exceedingly fine manes, both horses more beautiful than any other. Following
them was a third horse, young and very much like them, and they all entered
the house of my master and mistress.' When you tell her this, you will find
favor in her eyes."

Rising, Lilia, immediately told her mistress everything as her husband had
directed. When Eugenia heard, she told her husband, and they thought there
would be a child. Filled with joy, they ordered Theodorus and Lilia to be set
free, drew up papers of manumission, and enriched the pair with a considerable amount of property. Lilia gave birth to the child she had conceived, a son
by the name of Theoderic, who was lovingly raised and presented to Idacius
and Eugenia. They commanded that he stay with them, showering love on
him to such an extent that they adopted him as their own son. He grew up a
handsome boy, in stature a good cubit taller than others, and proved to be
wise and very courageous.

On the death of Idacius and Eugenia, Theoderic, at the command of
Emperor Leo [a. 457–474], had to become a soldier. Serving for twelve years,
he waged war with such courage and cleverness that at first he was greatly
esteemed by all the senators of the palace. Finally, the disease of acute envy
caused them to grumble with resentment against him, and to look for ways
he might be destroyed by the command of the emperor. One of the senators,
a certain Ptolemy, who quietly opposed this plan, entered into a very deep
friendship with Theoderic that he maintained up to the day of his death.

After the Goths devastated Rome [a. 410] and took possession of the land
of Italy, they transferred themselves of their own free will to the authority of
Leo. As they would have been continuously devastated by Odoacer [king of
Italy, a. 476–493], the Heruls, and other peoples who were their neighbors,
they asked Leo through ambassadors to appoint Theoderic as patrician on
their behalf so that, through him, they might withstand their enemies. Leo
mercifully agreed and, with the advice of the Senate, sent Theoderic to
Rome. He was received by the Romans and Goths into the office of the
patriciate with full honors and fought many times against the Heruls.

On one occasion, when Theoderic and the Goths had joined battle with
King Odoacer and the Heruls, Theoderic and his men fled into Ravenna.

There his mother came to meet him, reproaching him: "There is no place
to run, my son, unless I lift my skirts for you to enter the womb from which
you were born."

When he heard this, he was completely disconcerted, and preferring to die rather than live, went out to meet Odoacer and the Heruls with any men he could find. Since he came upon the Heruls unprepared and scattered about, in the end he defeated them with a few men. With renewed vigor he summoned the Goths and pursued Odoacer, defeating and killing him along with his wife and children, and obliterating the people and realm of the Heruls.

The emperor Leo was informed of this, and as he was often advised by the Senate to destroy Theoderic, he ordered him to come before him. Theoderic gathered the finest fighters of the Gothic army along with its nobles, amounting to 12,000 men in all and, as if in compliance with the order, sailed to meet the emperor Leo in Constantinople. His friend Ptolemy had no way to tell him what was happening, but in quite a skillful and simple fashion he ruined the plans of those who were opposed to Theoderic. Although the emperor Leo and the Senate had decided that Theoderic should be led aside bit by bit as soon as he entered the palace, separated from his men, and then killed, Theoderic was freed from this danger by the advice of his friend, Ptolemy.

"It does not contribute to your glory," Ptolemy said to the emperor, "to kill this man so deceitfully. Do not let it be said by his men who came with him that you were unable to kill him in public, but only by a trick, once he had been separated from his men. Instead, order him bound, and send the leading senators outside the city to the camp of the Goths who came with Theoderic, and let the senators convey to them the offense of Theoderic and your Lordship's anger, for which he deserves death. They themselves should decide whether he should be beheaded or given over to the beasts to be eaten."

Since Ptolemy's advice seemed good, five senators of the party opposing Theoderic were sent along with Ptolemy to make this announcement to the Goths.

Ptolemy sent a servant to the Goths in secret to tell them to surround and bind him and the other senators when they arrived to make the announcement. Then the Goths were to send a message to the emperor telling him this: "Unless the emperor restores our lord Theoderic to us alive and well, and promises on oath to allow us to return safely to our homeland with him, we shall kill these senators and make war on this city with every means at our command."

Ptolemy's advice was followed, and, while Theoderic was held bound in the palace, Ptolemy was bound and held in the same fashion along with his associates. As soon as that happened, the emperor Leo had no choice but to restore Theoderic safely to the Goths and to promise in addition that he might withdraw to his homeland safely with his men. Theoderic was saved by the plan of Ptolemy.

Theoderic returned to Italy and waged war on the Avars. Both sides inflicted tremendous destruction. The Huns poured into Italy, defeating Theoderic and the Goths and devastating many towns. Finally, Theoderic regained his strength and fell upon the Avars whom he overthrew and drove in flight into Pannonia.

When he followed them, he dared not enter the territory of Pannonia. He made camp and then set off on horseback from the camp with four of his retainers to determine in advance if the Avars were moving against him again. Quite some distance from the camp he crossed paths with an Avar by the name of Xerxer, the most warlike of them all, who was also coming alone to spy on Theoderic. When Xerxer was spotted at a distance, Theoderic sent three of his fighting men to take him alive or to kill him. The Avar, feigning flight, killed each of them in turn. Again, Theoderic sent another three men to capture him; they likewise were killed by the Avar. After that, Theoderic entered the fray, fighting in single combat with the Avar. Both men for some time wheeled their horses in circles, but after the Avar had been struck in the arm with a lance, he was overcome by Theoderic. Theoderic bound him and took him to the camp.

Since Theoderic recognized that the Avar was very brave in war, he tried to flatter him into taking an oath of loyalty to him, promising a rich reward in return. The Avar, Xerxer by name, strongly rejected this suggestion; he did not want to pledge loyalty but only wished to return to his own land. After this, he was forced by Theoderic to endure threats and various torments; rejecting Theoderic's authority, however, Xerxer would in no way give a promise of loyalty. As his rejection was vehement, Theoderic permitted him to return to his homeland.

After swimming the Danube river with his horse, Xerxer looked across from the other side at Theoderic and said, "I have been freed from your power; I recognize that I have a free choice. Now that your power is no longer over me, I shall return to you, and I will be the most loyal of your followers."

Theoderic enriched him with many treasures and valued him above all others. And in the many wars waged with the Vandals, Suevi, and other peoples, Theoderic saw that in the battle line Xerxer was always close at hand and was the bravest fighter of his guard. For that reason, he was valued highly by Theoderic.

When word of Theoderic's accomplishments and the wars that he waged reached the imperial palace, the emperor Leo again ordered him to come, advised by the Senate to complete the dealings they had already begun with him. He bound the senators by oath not to betray the plan and made them agree that anyone who was found to have done so must be punished by death.

It was then that Theoderic sent one of his servants in secret to Ptolemy to find out what was in his interest: should he come, or perhaps would it be best to refuse?

Ptolemy heard the inquiry in private and said to the servant, "I'm not sending back any message to Theoderic. Today is a feast day. By command of the emperor, all the senators shall recline at a meal in the imperial palace. What you will do is serve at my back as my attendant and take careful notice of the tales I tell the Senate. Return at once and report to him who sent you."

On that very day, as the senators reclined to eat, Ptolemy, attended by the servant, said: "Since this is a happy day of feasting, let's enjoy ourselves with stories:

"As the lion (leo) was the strongest of the animals, he was chosen as king by the all the other animals. They all came to meet him at the dinner hour, including a stag. When the stag did obeisance before him, the lion seized his antler so he could have the stag for dinner. Pulling back sharply, the stag lost his antler, and quickly fled into the wilderness. At the command of the lion, a fox was sent from among the animals to trick him into returning. Since it was naturally given to trickery and not afraid to swear an oath, the fox got the best of the stag by means of oaths and led him into the presence of the lion. When the stag did obeisance again to the lion, he was violently seized by him and torn to pieces. The fox stole the heart and ate it. When the lion wanted to eat the heart of the stag, he looked for it, roaring loudly. All the animals trembled with fear when they could not find the heart of the stag.

"'The fox who led him forward was closer than anyone else when he was torn apart,' they said. 'The fox stole his heart.'

"The fox was subjected to torture, and the demand was made that he restore what he stole.

"'I do not deserve these torments,' he said. 'The stag has no heart; for if he had a heart, I would not have been able to get the better of him and he would never have come here. The first time he lost his antler and in the end just managed to escape; how could he have come back here if he had a heart?'"

Listening carefully the servant remembered what he heard, and speedily recounted Ptolemy's advice to Theoderic. Again, Theoderic was saved from danger.

After this Theoderic rejected the authority of the empire and reigned with the greatest good fortune for 22 years with the Goths. In all, Theoderic held power in Italy for 32 years. His rule extended from Pannonia to the Rhône river, from the Tyrrhenian sea to the Pennine Alps and the Isère river. He paid only one full peck of dirt to the public treasury each year, so that it might be said: "Theoderic renders each year one full peck to the public treasury." An imperial decree established that no more should be sought from him. He caused all the towns that he governed to be marvellously restored with public works and to be most expertly fortified. He also had palaces built in the most distinguished city of Ravenna, as well as in Verona and Pavia, which is also called Ticinum. He later ruled a kingdom of such prosperity, maintaining peace with neighboring peoples, that it was a wonder to behold. Sigismund, king of the Burgundians, married his daughter.

*A story about Theoderic's role as mediator between Clovis and Alaric follows at this point. It seems unlikely to have originally been part of the* Gesta Theoderici; *it can be found below,* **91**.

*The conclusion of Theoderic's life that follows next also seems unlikely to have been part of the original* Gesta. *Theoderic had no brother Gaiseric; the vision of Theoderic's death is found in Gregory the Great's* Dialogues *(IV 31).*

[59]     When Theoderic condemned to death the Roman Pope John without cause and likewise caused the patrician Symmachus to be destroyed for no reason at all, he was struck by divine anger and killed by his brother Gaiseric. According to a vision by a certain priest in the *Dialogues* of Saint Gregory, Theoderic was bound by the bishop and patrician and dragged into a pot of fire in Sicily.

## 83. CHROC FOLLOWS HIS MOTHER'S ADVICE (II 60)

*The story of Chroc follows directly on Fredegar's account of Theoderic, but is intended to fit the invasions of the early fifth century. It bears a marked resemblance to Gregory of Tours's account* (Hist. I 31, 34) *of an Alamannian king called Chroc in the third century. Much later stories of a Saint Antidius have their subject martyred under a Vandal King Chroc in 411. Marius is unidentifiable, unless he is based on the third-century usurper of that name.*

Chroc, king of the Vandals, along with the Sueves and Alans, left their homes and attacked Gaul. He followed the very twisted advice of his mother.

"If you wish to do something new and acquire a name for yourself," she said, "destroy everything that others have built, and when you defeat people, kill the lot of them. For you can no longer put up a building better than those who came before you or do a greater deed by which you can make your name stand out."

Chroc cleverly crossed the Rhine by the bridge at Mainz — that was the first town and people that he devastated. Next, besieging all the towns of Germania [superior], he reached Metz where, by God's will, the wall of the town collapsed during the night, and the town was taken by the Vandals. The people of Trier, however, were delivered by means of the town's arena, which they had fortified. Thereafter, Chroc destroyed some towns by siege, others he took cleverly by force, overrunning and ravaging all the Gallic towns along with the Vandals, Sueves, and Alans. No town or fortress in the Gallic provinces was spared by them. When they besieged Arles, he was captured by a certain soldier by the name of Marius and bound with fetters. He was put to the torture throughout all the towns he had ravaged, and his impious life came to an end with the kind of death he deserved.

*Fredegar continues the history of the Vandals, using the account of Gregory of Tours (Hist. II 2, 3), down to the end of the kingdom under Gelimer (a. 530-534). The destruction of the Vandal kingdom by the east Roman general Belisarius leads to the following tales about Justinian and his circle.*

## 84. JUSTINIAN, BELISARIUS, AND THEIR WIVES (II 62)

*Justinian was emperor at Constantinople from 527 to 565. He was a figure of great historical significance, reconquering Africa from the Vandals, Italy from the Ostrogoths, and parts of Spain from the Visigoths. His general in the campaign against the Vandals and in the first part of the war against the Ostrogoths was Belisarius.*

*Justinian, Belisarius, and their wives are the subjects of the following stories, called* fabulae obscoenae *by the editor of the standard edition of Fredegar's chronicle; modern readers are unlikely to find them obscene in any sense of that word. The stories are lively and entertaining, but alas, completely unreliable, though they do reflect real characters and events — the marriages of Justinian and Belisarius, the Vandal campaign and Gelimer's capture, and the Nike revolt.*

*The wives are identified as two sisters, of Amazonian descent, called Antonia and Antonina. Justinian's real wife was Theodora, whose past was said to be as questionable as Antonia's. Antonina was the name of Belisarius's wife. The real-life women were friends, not sisters.*

[62] Before Justinian had taken power — when he was *comes cartarum* in the days of the emperor Justin [I, a. 518-27] — he and Belisarius, who was count of the stables, were bound together by deep ties of affection for each other. They both swore that, no matter how successful each of them became, they would always remain faithful one to the other.

One day, they picked out of a brothel two sisters of Amazonian descent with whom to have sex. At midday, the elder sister Antonia was lying with Justinian under some trees in an orchard and Justinian fell asleep. As the sun beat down, his head grew hot. At divine command, an eagle came and spread its wings to shade the sleeping Justinian from the heat of the sun. When Antonia, who was awake, noticed this, she hoped that this was a sign that Justinian would take the office of emperor.

When he awoke, she said to him: "If you are made emperor, will your servant be worthy to lie with you?"

"If I'm to be made emperor," he said smiling, since it was difficult for him to be worthy of this honor, "you'll be my empress."

They exchanged rings, and Justinian said to Belisarius: "You should know that Antonia and I have agreed that, if I'm made emperor, she will be my empress. We entered into this agreement by exchanging rings."

"If my sister is going to be your empress," said Antonina, "then let me be made the wife of Belisarius."

"If Antonia is made empress," said Belisarius, by divine command, "you may share my bed as a wife."

They also went off to exchange rings.

Not long afterwards, the emperor Justin made war on the Persians, but when he crossed over to Chalcedon, he died of disease. With the consent of the Senate and the soldiers, Justinian was raised up to the royal office. He overthrew the king of the Persians and, when he held him in bonds, ordered him to sit upon the throne, as if that did him honor. Justinian then demanded that the towns and provinces of the empire be restored — if that were done, he would ratify an agreement.

When the king would answer, "I shall not give them over," Justinian would say, "Yes, you will give (*daras*) them."

For this reason, in the place where these events took place, a town by the name of Daras was founded by order of Justinian and is called by this name even to this day.

After Justinian had taken back a great many provinces and towns by such means, transferring them from the rule of the king to that of his own, and all the particulars had been ratified in a treaty, he allowed the king to resume his rule of the Persians.

Justinian returned to Constantinople in great triumph and occupied the imperial throne. Antonia took five gold coins, gave two to the doorkeepers, and was granted entrance to the palace. Three she gave to those who draw the curtains [at the entrance of the consistory] so she might bring forward her case.

"Most merciful emperor," she said to Justinian, "in this city a certain youth gave me a ring as a pledge of betrothal and received one from me. He promised on oath that he would marry no other but would take me for his wife. This matter is not being attended to. What, most dutiful emperor, do you command should be done?"

"If this promise were made," said Justinian, "it cannot be altered."

Then, reaching out with the ring, Antonia said, "Let my lord recognize whose ring this was. He who gave it to me cannot hide from you."

Justinian recognized the ring he had given and, remembering his promise, gave orders for her to be conducted into his chamber and clad in splendid clothing. He shared his bed with her as his empress.

When this news was announced to the people, the Senate arranged for the rabble to clamor out, "Lord emperor, give us back our woman."

Justinian heard the shout. Carefully investigating who was responsible for it, he ordered two senators killed for what had been said. Later everyone quietened down, and no one dared utter those words after that. Belisarius even received Antonina as his wife.

Justinian loved Belisarius with a singular affection and appointed him patrician for the parts of Africa not occupied by the Vandals, constantly enriching him with many resources. This caused the Senate out of jealousy to seek some means of destroying him.

One at a time the senators approached Justinian and all said the same thing, "If we had wanted to give in to Belisarius's plans, you would already have been removed from the imperial office some time ago. He intends to take your place as emperor."

When Justinian heard this, he secretly became jealous of Belisarius and, with the advice of the Senate, ordered him to expel the Vandals from Africa. There the best soldiers and many legions had often been cut down by the Vandals. Belisarius had twelve thousand retainers of his own, bold fighters, whom he paid himself. By virtue of his office of patrician, he had eighteen thousand fighting men experienced in going to war.

After he heard his orders, Belisarius returned home, overcome with a sickening fear, for he thought it was impossible to overcome the Vandals. Antonina saw him stricken and depressed and could not understand what this affliction might be. Alarmed when none of the retainers could reveal the matter to her, since it was unknown to all of them, she then turned to her husband.

"My lord," she said, "why are you sunk in depression and not happy as you usually are when you come from the empire. Let nothing get in the way; tell me how this matter came about. Perhaps your servant shall hit on the right course of action for you to turn sadness into happiness."

"This is not an issue in which the counsel of women is useful," Belisarius told her, "and you have nothing valuable to offer in this matter."

But since she was a Christian, she said to her husband, "It is written, 'The unfaithful husband shall be saved by the faith of the wife [cf. I Cor. 7:14].' Tell me what the situation is. I believe by the power of omnipotent God that a plan will be given to you by divine inspiration and you will be able to leave behind these evil days."

Belisarius listened to this advice and told his wife about the emperor's decree that he was to go to war against the Vandals.

"Vow that you will immediately be baptized in Christ the Lord and will believe faithfully in the indivisible trinity," Antonina told him. "Then you may understand that you shall overcome the Vandals by His power and assistance, and on account of this you will be more renowned than ever."

Belisarius promised to fulfill this advice devoutly.

Antonina said to him, "Of the twelve thousand retainers that are ours, call upon four thousand for yourself; and of the eighteen thousand fighters you command as patrician, call upon twelve thousand. You will lead these troops as a land force and I will advance leading a naval force of eight thousand retainers and six thousand regular troops. If we were to set a day on which we both invested the camp of the Vandals from all sides, protected by divine assistance, we will overthrow them. My lord, if you make use of the advice of your servant, by the providence of God, you will accomplish what you desire. Do not let those in your household see you depressed. Whatever reservations you may have deep down, cover them with a cheerful face. To enable us to signal to one another when you take the land route and I the sea route, have your men light fires on the shore at night, and we shall post lanterns on the ships, so that our arrival may be coordinated. And it won't be necessary to urge anyone on, provided we invest the enemy together with both our forces."

Since Antonina's advice in this matter was valuable, they both wasted no time implementing it.

When the Vandals under their prince Gelimer learned of the army approaching by land, they laid out their camp upon the shore, completely unaware of the naval force. Having gathered their wives and children in the camp, they went forth to battle against Belisarius. When they were just about to join battle, Antonina and her forces came ashore and wiped out the wives and children of the Vandals, not sparing a living soul among them. News quickly reached Gelimer that the wives and children of the Vandals had been wiped out. He and the Vandals, the ranks of their army broken, quickly retreated to the camp. Then Belisarius and Antonina surrounded the Vandals on all sides and cut them down. They were slaughtered even to the point of annihilation.

King Gelimer with a few Vandals, a mere twelve in all, fled to a certain fortress that was very secure, but they were not spared. Gelimer, compelled by the difficult straits he found himself in, asked only that Belisarius not deliver him to the emperor bound. Belisarius promised that he would not be confined in bonds of iron, wood, leather, or bronze, and Gelimer, trusting him, was taken prisoner. Belisarius did bind him, but with royal shackles, made of silver chains. He killed Gelimer's companions and delivered him alone to Justinian. Justinian commanded that he be lodged in his palace.

Gelimer was spat upon by Justinian's people and overwhelmed with showers of abuse of various kinds. He made a request to the emperor.

"I cannot endure such abuse," he said. "The people in your palace overwhelm me, spitting on me and goading me. It is better for me to die than to live like this. Give the order for twelve of those who spit upon me and abuse me and for me alone, mounted on the horse I once possessed, to fight fully armed in the presence of your majesty. Then you will know who is the warrior and who the coward."

Now Justinian commanded twelve youths on horseback to fight with Gelimer as a spectacle. As for Gelimer, when he came against them, he pretended to flee and killed all twelve, one by one. Afterwards, at Justinian's command, Gelimer was made a eunuch, and appointed patrician in the provinces on the border with the Persians. He conducted many successful expeditions against them.

The Senate again pursued its grudge against Belisarius. They made him hateful to Justinian, on the grounds that Belisarius, puffed up with his victory over the Vandals, wanted to seize the imperial title. Although the senators were not successful in bringing about his death, he was deprived of his position as patrician.

They attempted to get rid of Justinian from the imperial office by the following expedient. One day they urged Justinian to attend the circus and distribute tokens of his consulship to the people, all the while intending to elevate to the imperial dignity the man of their choice, a certain Florianus. They put Justinian under custody by himself and took away his crown. Justinian sent a retainer to Belisarius to ask for help.

"Were I possessed of the lofty dignities that I once had," Belisarius told him, "I would be able to help. Now I cannot help him at all."

Belisarius arranged for his retainers to seize the circus, where the imperial throne was being prepared for Florianus. He himself led the way, pretending to the senatorial party that he was prepared to do reverence to Florianus.

"I see all my enemies circling the throne of the emperor," he said to his retainers. "Be prepared to follow up on whatever you see me begin."

Pretending to do reverence to Florianus, Belisarius stabbed him with his sword. His retainers surrounded his enemies and killed them all. Belisarius took the imperial crown and came to Justinian.

"Your sycophants," he said to Justinian, "removed you from the imperial office. By taking their advice, you agreed to my humiliation. As for me, I will return to you good for evil. I do so not out of consideration for your loyalty, but because I remember the promise I made and preserve my loyalty unimpaired."

He set the crown on Justinian's head and made him emperor.

Belisarius conducted many expeditions against the Persians and gloriously defeated them. He was defeated in Italy by a Frank called Buccelin. Renowned for his reputation but defeated by Buccelin in such a notable victory, Belisarius lost his reputation and his life.

## 85. THE LOMBARDS, NARSES, AND ITALY (III 65)

*Most of Fredegar's interpolations in Gregory of Tours's* Histories *concern Frankish matters. The following famous stories about the Lombards and the circumstances surrounding their invasion of Italy in 568 are exceptions. Cf.* **48**, *Gregory,* Hist. *IV 41.*

*The story of how the Langobards (the term Lombard is preferred by modern historians) got their name has analogues in Italian Lombard sources. The statement that Narses invited the Lombards into Italy has verbal parallels with the chronicle of Isidore of Seville, which makes the same claim. As usual, Fredegar uses the term 'Huns' for Avars. The text derived from Gregory is in a smaller font.*

The Langobards — before they took that name — came from Scathinavia, which is between the Danube and the sea of Ocean, and crossed the Danube with their wives and children. They were discovered crossing the Danube by the Huns, who, when they were on the point of attacking them, asked what people it was who presumed to enter their territory. The Langobards commanded their women to bind the hair of their heads to their cheeks and chins, by which they might better imitate the appearance of men — the hair of the women around their cheeks and chins looked like very long beards — and appear to be a great enemy host.

It is said that a voice declared from above both battle lines, "These are Langobards." These peoples say this was spoken by their god, whom in pagan practice they call Wodan.

The Langobards are supposed to have shouted at that point, "Whoever has given a name, grants victory."

In this battle they defeated the Huns, and invaded part of Pannonia.

Not long afterwards Narses the Patrician became terrified by the threats of Emperor Justin and his Augusta Sophia. Because Narses was a eunuch, the Augusta sent him a device, made of gold, upon which a woman could do her spinning, so that he might direct the affairs of spinners not a people.

But he answered: "I shall spin a thread of which neither the emperor Justin nor the empress will ever reach the end."

Then inviting the Langobards from Pannonia, he introduced them under their king Alboin into Italy. Alboin married Chlodoswintha, the daughter of Chlothar. When she died, he took another wife whose father he had killed.

# C. TALES OF THE EARLY
# FRANKS AND THEIR KINGS

*Though both Fredegar and the author of the* History of the Franks (LHF) *based their accounts of Frankish history in Gaul on the earlier history of Gregory of Tours, both authors also added fresh material. (On Fredegar's interpolations, see above, B, intro.) Figures, real and imagined, from earlier history had obviously been the subject of fanciful, historical fiction for some time. That these figures are pictured as tricky bold ruffians (of both sexes) rather than as upright heroes may seem curious but is an historical viewpoint with no shortage of medieval and modern analogues; it is a relief from the stupefying righteousness of contemporary hagiographic traditions. At least some of the stories came in different versions. One of the incidental benefits of Fredegar's and the LHF's coverage of similar material is that it allows us to see variant treatments of what must have been common subjects.*

## I FREDEGAR'S *CHRONICLE*

*The following stories are, with one exception, all interpolated into Fredegar's epitome of Gregory of Tour's* Histories. *The text printed in a smaller font is dependent on Gregory; the interpolations in a larger font are Fredegar's.*

## 86. OVERTHROW OF TRIER (III 7)

*The sack of Trier in Gregory's history comes from Renatus Profuturus Frigeridus and belongs to the early fifth century (see **25 C**). Fredegar's story is set in the time of Emperor Avitus (a. 455-56).*

The city of Trier was captured and burned through the intrigue of one of the senators called Lucius. This came about for these reasons. Avitus was an emperor who was a captive of his senses and Lucius had a wife prettier than all others. Avitus pretended to be confined to his bed because of illness and ordered all the wives of senators to visit him. When Lucius's wife came, Avitus took her by force.

The next day he rose from his bed and said to Lucius, "You have beautiful warm baths, too bad you bathe in the cold."

Lucius was indignant at this insult, and the city, at his connivance, was pillaged and burnt by the Franks.

# 87. CHILDERIC AND WIOMAD (III 11)

*Gregory of Tours (Hist. II 12) tells a brief tale of how Childeric was driven from his throne by the Franks for debauching their women but was eventually accepted back. In Gregory's version, Childeric's loyal retainer is not named nor are any details given as to why the Franks allowed Childeric to return.*

But when Childeric, the son of Merovech, succeeded to the rule of his father, he subjected the daughters of the Franks to debauchery, because he was excessively licentious. For this reason they became indignant and deposed him. The Frank Wiomad was more faithful than the others to Childeric; by taking to flight, he had freed him when he and his mother were taken captive by the Huns.

Perceiving that the Franks were intending to kill Childeric, Wiomad divided with him the gold coin that had resulted from this affair and said to him, "Flee to Thuringia, hide out there for a while. If I can reconcile the Franks, I will send half the coin to you as a sign; and if I cannot reconcile them, wherever you go, keep me informed of your whereabouts. Whenever I can, I will send you my part, and if the parts can be joined together to make a single coin, you may come home safely."

While living in Thuringia, Childeric took refuge at the court of King Bisinus and his wife Basina. The Franks then unanimously accepted Aegidius as king. Wiomad, the friend of Childeric, was appointed by Aegidius as sub-king over the Franks, and on his advice Aegidius imposed a tax on each of the Franks of a single gold coin. They assented and paid it.

Wiomad again spoke to Aegidius.

"This is a hard people which you have ordered me to govern. Not enough tax has been imposed on them. They are fierce and full of pride. Command that three solidi be paid."

When this was done, the Franks assented, saying, "It is better for us to give three solidi as tax than to endure a miserable existence under Childeric."

Wiomad again spoke to Aegidius.

"The Franks are becoming rebellious towards you. If you do not order their throats cut in great numbers, you will not tame their pride."

Wiomad chose one hundred non-combatants and unneeded misfits and sent them to Aegidius who, following Wiomad's advice, had them killed.

Wiomad in secret said to the Franks, "Are not the taxes you pay enough? How long will you endure the evil of your kinsmen being slaughtered like cattle?"

Then the Franks unanimously said, "If we were to accept Childeric willingly as king — supposing we can find him — perhaps through him we would be snatched from these afflictions."

Wiomad then went immediately to Aegidius and said, "Now the Frankish people have been subdued by your punitive measures."

Again Wiomad gave advice, namely that envoys be sent to the emperor Maurice [a. 582-602] to tell him that neighboring peoples could be recruited, provided the emperor send fifty thousand solidi; if they received this gift they would more readily subject themselves to the empire.

Wiomad added, "I have served as your representative, earning a small quantity of solidi. I, your slave, have too little silver. I would like to send a retainer with your envoys to avail himself of the opportunity of purchasing silver for me in Constantinople."

After he had received from Aegidius as a gift five hundred gold coins for purchasing what he needed in Constantinople, Wiomad sent a trusted retainer with half of the gold coin that he had divided with Childeric, and a sack of lead coins that the retainer carried in place of the solidi. The retainer already knew that Childeric was in Constantinople and made his approach to the city in company with the envoys, but with orders to get ahead of them. He was to inform Childeric right away, before the envoys came into the presence of the emperor, that Aegidius, who was responsible for paying taxes to the public treasury, would try to have the emperor pay tax [to him]. When Childeric informed Maurice of this, the emperor was filled with anger and indignation, and when the emissaries of Aegidius were presented to the emperor and conveyed to him a message of this kind, he ordered them thrown into prison.

Childeric also said to the emperor, "Command me, your slave, to go to Gaul; I will avenge your anger and indignation on Aegidius."

Childeric was enriched with many gifts from Maurice and returned to Gaul by ship.

After Wiomad learned of Childeric's arrival through a message brought by the retainer, he came to meet him at the fortress of Bar. Childeric was welcomed by the people of Bar, and on the advice of Wiomad, generously granted them remission of all public renders in return for their being the first to welcome him. Thereafter, he was raised once again to the kingship and fought many campaigns against Aegidius; much carnage was inflicted by him on the Romans.

## 88. BASINA, CHILDERIC, AND VISIONS IN THE NIGHT (III 12)

*Gregory of Tours's brief anecdote about the marriage of Childeric and Basina (Hist. II 12) is the basis of a much more elaborate tale in Fredegar. Fredegar's beasts seem to owe something to the biblical prophecy of Daniel (Dan. 7).*

When Basina, whose husband was King Bisinus in Thuringia, heard that Childeric had been raised to the kingship by the Franks, she quickly left Bisinus for Childeric.

When Childeric carefully questioned her as to why she came to him from so far, she is said to have answered, "I know your military ability, and that you are very strong, so I have come to live with you. If I knew of someone, somewhere, more able, I would seek him out."

Childeric was delighted by her, and smitten by her beauty, joined himself in marriage to her.

On the first night, as soon as they coupled on the bed, his wife said to him, "Let's abstain from intercourse this night. Rise unnoticed and tell your maidservant what you see before the halls of the palace."

When he arose he saw, in the likeness of animals, lions, unicorns, and leopards walking around. He returned and told his wife what he saw.

His wife said to him, "My lord, go again and tell your maidservant what you see."

When he went outside, he saw animals in the likeness of bears and wolves walking about. When he told this to his wife, she made him go a third time and tell her what he saw. When he went out a third time, he saw minor beasts in the likeness of dogs and lesser creatures, dragging one another down and tumbling about. He told all this to Basina, and they kept themselves chaste until the next day.

When they arose from bed, Basina said to Childeric, "What you saw as apparitions, have a reality. This is what these creatures mean. A son shall be born to us who, in his strength, will have the mark and the look of a lion. As for his sons, in strength they shall have the mark of the leopard and the unicorn. Thereafter will be born to them those who are like the bear and the wolf in strength and voraciousness. The third time you saw what will happen when the supports of this kingdom fall apart; they will rule it like dogs and lesser animals and they will have the strength to match. The multitude of lesser creatures which tumble about dragging one another down resembles the peoples who, without the fear of princes, ravage one another."

Basina conceived and gave birth to a son called Clovis, a great and distinguished fighter, like a lion, stronger than other kings.

# 89. CLOVIS, AURELIANUS, AND CHLOTHILD
## (III 18, 19)

*Cf. **46**, Gregory, Hist. II 28. Fredegar tells us elsewhere that Chlothild's elder sister Saedeleuba constructed a church in the suburb of Geneva (**58**, c. 22).*

Clovis often sent delegations to Burgundy. They learned of Chlothild. Since it was not permitted to see her, Clovis sent a certain Roman called Aurelianus to inspect Chlothild by any means he could devise. Unaccompanied, in the guise of a beggar dressed in rags and with a bag on his back, Aurelianus reached the Burgundian region, carrying with him Clovis's ring, by which he might the more readily be trusted. He came to the town of Geneva, where Chlothild resided with her sister Sadeleuba. Since they practiced the hospitality due strangers, they took him in for the sake of [divine] reward.

When Chlothild was washing his feet, Aurelianus leaned over toward her and said secretly, "My lady, I will inform you of a great matter if you will please provide a place where I may secretly convey the information."

She agreed and listened to the message in secret.

"Clovis, king of the Franks, has sent me," said Aurelianus. "If it is the will of God, he wishes you to marry his majesty. So you may act with assurance, he has sent this ring to you."

She received it, was greatly delighted, and said to Aurelianus, "Accept one hundred solidi for the burden of your labour and this ring of mine. Hurry back to your lord and say to him, 'If he wants me to marry him, let him ask my uncle by means of envoys right away. Let the emissaries who come immediately make sure of what has been gained and set a day [for the nuptials] without delay. If they do not hurry to carry out the arrangements, I fear the arrival from Constantinople of a certain wise man called Aridius, by whose counsel all this may be squandered, if he comes too soon."

Aurelianus returned to his own country in the same clothes in which he came. By the time he approached the region of Orleans, not far from his own home, he was traveling with a certain poor beggar as a companion. Now free from care, he fell asleep. The bag of solidi was stolen by his companion. When Aurelianus awoke, he quickly made for home full of sorrow and sent retainers to look for the beggar with his bag. They caught him and delivered him to Aurelianus, who allowed him to go, after giving him a good beating for three days. At once Aurelianus reported to Soissons giving King Clovis all the details.

As Clovis was pleased with the quality of Chlothild's character and her good advice, he sent an emissary to Gundobad asking him to give his niece Chlothild to Clovis in marriage. Fearing to refuse the request and hoping to establish friendship with Clovis, Gundobad promised that he would hand her over. Presenting a solidus and a denarius, as was the custom of the Franks, the envoys betrothed her on Clovis's behalf and asked that a date be set right away for handing over Chlothild in marriage to Clovis. Without delay they made an agreement, and preparations for the nuptials were made at Chalon. The Franks came quickly, received Chlothild from Gundobad, raised her upon a litter, and sent her on her way with many treasures to Clovis.

Since Chlothild had just learned of the arrival of Aridius, who was returning from the empire, she said to the leaders of the Franks, "If you wish to deliver me to your lord, take me down from this litter, put me up on a horse, and head for home as soon as you can. I will not make it into his presence in this litter."

The Franks put Chlothild on a horse and quickly went to Clovis.

When Aridius heard of these events, he left Marseilles and came quickly to Gundobad.

"Have you heard," said Gundobad, "that we have established friendship with the Franks and that I have handed my niece over to Clovis?"

"This will not promote friendship," answered Aridius, "but is the beginning of perpetual strife. You have to remember, my lord, that you cut down with the sword Chlothild's father, your brother, that you ordered her mother to be drowned with a stone tied to her neck, and that you had her two brothers decapitated and thrown in a well. Once she is powerful, she will be in a position to avenge her relatives. Send an army after her right away to bring her back. It is easier for you to endure a single quarrel than for you and yours to constantly suffer the outrages of the Franks."

Gundobad listened to this advice and sent an army to detain Chlothild. Her pursuers seized the entire treasure and litter.

As Chlothild neared Villery, in the region of Troyes, where Clovis was staying, but before she had crossed the border with Burgundy, she asked the courtiers who were conducting her to plunder and burn Burgundy for twelve leagues in both directions.

When this was done with Clovis's consent, Chlothild said, "I give you thanks, omnipotent God, that I see a beginning made in avenging my parents and brothers."

## 90. THE BAPTISM OF CLOVIS (III 21)

*Cf. 46, Gregory of Tours, Hist. II 31.*

When Clovis went to war against the Alamanni, he was persuaded by the queen to vow that he would become a Christian if he obtained a victory.

Both armies joined battle and Clovis said, "I call upon God, whom queen Chlothild worships. If he commands that I should conquer my enemies in this battle, I shall be his faithful follower.'

The Alamanni turned their backs and fled. When they saw that their king was killed, they were unable for nine years as exiles from their homeland to find any people to aid them against the Franks. Finally they submitted to the authority of Clovis.

When Clovis returned to Rheims from the above mentioned battle, in secret at the hands of Remigius, bishop of the city of Rheims, and also induced by Queen Chlothild, he was consecrated by the grace of baptism at Easter along with six thousand Franks.

After a reading from the gospel on the kind of suffering endured by Jesus Christ was preached to him by Saint Remigius, Clovis, clad in his baptismal robes, said, "If I had been there with my Franks, I would have avenged the wrong done to him."

Already revealing his faith by his words, he confirmed that he was a true Christian.

## 91. PATERNUS, CLOVIS'S ENVOY TO ALARIC (II 58)

*This excerpt is part of an interpolation in the chronicle of Hydatius dealing with the deeds of Theoderic the Great, the Ostrogothic ruler of Italy (a. 490-526); see above, 82.*

One time, after many conflicts with one another, Clovis, king of the Franks, and Alaric, king of the Goths [a. 484-507], who had his capital at Toulouse, exchanged envoys. They undertook to establish peace on the following terms: that Alaric touch Clovis's beard and become his godfather; that they both abide by an everlasting peace; and that the Franks and Goths arrive at the place set for the meeting completely unarmed. They set a date to assemble at a mutually agreed upon location.

There the emissary of Clovis, by the name of Paternus, approached Alaric to find out whether the Goths were in attendance in the fashion they had promised, unarmed, or whether they might in their usual manner be showing themselves to be false, which afterwards proved to be the case. While Paternus was addressing Alaric, conveying Clovis's greetings and inquiring in what way they should meet, the Goths were deceitfully carrying short swords in their hands in the place of staves. Paternus grabbed one of the weapons and unsheathed it.

"Your agreements are false, king," said Paternus, "when you try to trick my lord and the Franks."

Another agreement was made with Alaric, and Paternus promised on behalf of the Franks to let the judgment of Theoderic, king of Italy [a. 490-526], end this matter.

Then the envoy of King Alaric and Paternus, representing Clovis, hurried off to the court of Theoderic. Paternus laid out the case of Clovis and the Franks in detail, and the envoy of Alaric could not deny it; he could only ask that Theoderic's judgment resolve the dispute. Theoderic considered the consequences of this case and, keeping in mind his own needs for the future, concealed his jealousy of these two kings.

He said to the envoys, "Tomorrow, I shall not fail to commend to my brothers in complete love and with lavish affection what I, along with the chief officials of the palace, consider to be most conducive to a peace-agreement in this matter, as the order of justice demands."

Now acting upon what he had once concealed in the secrets of his heart, he was anxious that these two kings should always be in disagreement with one another. He brought down a judgment for them of a kind that made it difficult for the Goths over whom Alaric reigned to make good on the compensation for the offense. An envoy of the Franks was to come before the palace of Alaric, on horseback and holding a lance upright; Alaric and the Goths were to shower him with solidi until they covered the envoy, the horse, and the point of the lance.

The emissaries immediately carried back to Alaric the terms of Theoderic's judgment on the matter. Since it was difficult for Alaric and the Goths to fulfill it, they tried to trick Paternus, the envoy of the Franks. He was lodged on a balcony, the supports of which collapsed during the night, and in the end he barely managed to escape with a broken arm. The next day, Alaric took him to show him the treasury and swore that he possessed no more solidi than he was now revealing to him in the laden coffers.

Whereupon, Paternus took a solidus from his hand and, tossing it, said, "I shall take these solidi as a deposit for my lord Clovis and the Franks."

When Paternus returned to Clovis and recounted each event, Clovis mobilized his forces against Alaric, whom he killed on the field of Vouillé, at the tenth milestone from Poitiers, and he cut down with the sword most of the army of the Goths there. He took away his kingdom bounded by the Loire and Rhône rivers, the Tyrrhenian sea, the Pyrenees mountains and the Ocean; even today it rightly remains subject to the kingdom of the Franks.

## 92. THE EXPULSION OF MARCATRUDE BY GUNTRAM (III 56)

*Marcatrude, the daughter of Magnachar, was the wife of King Guntram. Cf. **48**, Gregory, Hist. IV 25 and V 17.*

Marcatrude had a son by Guntram and killed [her stepson] Gundobad by poison. By the judgment of God, she lost the son she had and incurred the hatred of the king because she was fat...This was Guntram's excuse for dismissing Marcatrude. Her mother, after the death of [her husband] Magnachar, took her husband from among the lowborn, a man fostered in the household (*nutritus*) of Magnachar. At the instigation of her sons Ciuccio and Wiolic, the servant (*puer*) was separated from the mother at Guntram's order and killed. The sons carelessly alleged their mother was a concocter of potions (*herbaria*) and a whore. On this occasion he expelled the daughter from the kingdom.

## 93. GOGO, BRUNHILD, AND CHRODIN (III 57-59)

*Cf. **48, 49**, Gregory, Hist. IV 27, VI 1. Gogo actually died in 581. Chrodin died the next year at the age of seventy (Hist. VI 20).*

[57]  Sigibert...sent Gogo as an emissary to king Athanagild to ask for his daughter Bruna in marriage. Athanagild sent her to Sigibert to be married along with much treasure. An addition was made to her name to embellish it, so she was called Brunhild. Sigibert received her as his wife with a great deal of happiness and celebration.

[58]  Before this marriage, during the childhood of Sigibert, the Austrasians would have chosen Chrodin as mayor of the palace, because in all matters he was brave, god-fearing, and imbued with forbearance; and no other qualities were to be found in him except those pleasing to God and man.

He rejected the honor, saying, "I'm in no position to establish peace in Austrasia, especially since all the chief men and their children are blood relations of mine. I'll not be able to impose order on them or kill any of them. Through me they'll rise up to act in an overbearing fashion. May God not allow their deeds to send me to hell. Choose from among yourselves someone else you like."

[59]  But when they could not find someone, on the advice of Chrodin they chose as mayor of the palace a person fostered in his household (*nutritus*), the above mentioned Gogo. The next day, Chrodin was the first to reach Gogo's home to acknowledged his authority, taking Gogo's baldric upon his neck.

When the rest of them saw this, they followed his example.

Conditions were favorable for Gogo to conduct affairs, until he brought Brunhild from Spain. Brunhild immediately caused Sigibert to hate him and, incited by her advice, Sigibert killed him. Brunhild's advice caused sufficient evil and bloodshed in Francia to fulfill the Sibyl's prophecy that said, "Bruna comes from the regions of Spain and before her gaze many peoples will perish." As for Brunhild, she was trampeled to pieces by the hooves of horses.

## 94. THE DEATH OF SIGIBERT AND THE RESCUE OF CHILDEBERT II (III 70-72)

*Cf. 48, Gregory, Hist. IV 47, 50-51*

[70] Chilperic occupied Poitiers and Tours in the kingdom of Sigibert, put Duke Sigulf to flight and defeated his army. Chilperic restored to Sigibert the cities he occupied. A year later Chilperic attacked Sigibert's kingdom with a great army, but they made peace after exchanging emissaries.

[71] Afterward, they both agreed to levy forces against Guntram with the intention of killing him and taking over his kingdom. Sigibert was staying at Arcis-sur-Aube and Chilperic at Pont-sur-Seine. Hearing this, Guntram quickly put his army on the march and came to Virey-sous-Bar. They exchanged emissaries and the three brothers, Sigibert, Guntram, and Chilperic, met together at Troyes. In the church of Saint Lupus, Sigibert and Chilperic swore an oath to Guntram that they would preserve peace. Guntram likewise swore to maintain peace with them.

The troops returning to camp in Austrasia raised a complaint against Sigibert.

"Just as you promised," they said, "give us the chance to get rich and to engage in battle. Otherwise we shall not return home."

Under pressure of his own troops, Sigibert was willing to go against Guntram, but those with great prudence in Austrasia said to him, "You have confirmed the peace with Guntram under oath. By what terms can we attack him?"

Shouting out in agreement that they wanted to go against Chilperic, the troops immediately set out to attack him. By now Chilperic's army, which was speedily returning home, was some distance away. When Chilperic understood what had happened, he retreated to Tournai. Sigibert in pursuit came to Paris.

There Sigibert saw the holy and blessed Germanus, bishop of the city of Paris, and heard these prophetic words from him: "In case you are thinking of pursuing your brother, determined to kill him and take his kingdom, the bible says, "The pit you prepare for your brother — into it you yourself will fall."

Unwilling to acknowledge this reproof, Sigibert thought about fulfilling his desires. When he came to Vitry, all of Neustria came to him, and placed themselves under his authority. Only Ansoald stood by Chilperic. Fredegund cunningly sent two retainers who killed Sigibert, and were themselves killed. His strength renewed, Chilperic took back his kingdom.

[72]    Brunhild and her son Childebert were kept under guard in Paris. But Duke Gundoald had Childebert placed in a sack and handed through a window to a retainer. The retainer, on his own, showed him at Metz, and there the child was raised to the kingdom of his father by Gundoald and the Austrasians. Brunhild, at Chilperic's command, was exiled to Rouen. In that year a light was seen to course across the heavens. Sigibert was interred in the church of Saint Medard, at the age of forty, in the fourteenth year of his reign.

## 95. THE DEATH OF CHILPERIC (III 93)

*Cf.* **48**, *Gregory, Hist. IV 46.*

Chilperic was killed at the villa of Chelles, not far from Paris, by a man named Falco, who had been sent by Brunhild: he put an end to the life of a most cruel man who deserved death.

## II THE ANONYMOUS
## *HISTORY OF THE FRANKS (LHF)*

*Like Fredegar's* Chronicle, *the* LHF *also bases its early history on Gregory of Tours's* Histories. *Also like Fredegar, the anonymous author of the* LHF *adds tales about some of the chief figures of Gregory's work. These tales sometimes resemble those of Fredegar, but they are independent of his versions.*

## 96. CLOVIS, AURELIANUS, AND CHLOTHILD
## (*LHF* 11-14)

*Cf.* **46**, *Gregory, Hist. II 28, and Fredegar,* **89**. *A motif incomplete as it stands in both Fredegar's and the* LHF's *version is the propensity of Aurelianus for losing his bag.*

11. ... [Hearing reports of Chlothild] Clovis sent his emissary Aurelianus to Gundobad to ask for his niece Chlothild. Chlothild was a Christian. One Sunday when Chlothild was attending the celebrations of the mass, Aure-

lianus, Clovis's representative, put on the clothes of a poor man — he left the good cloths he had been wearing with his friends in the woods — and sat among the poor folk in front of the church's station for poor relief. When mass was done, Chlothild as was the custom began to give out the usual alms to the poor. She came to Aurelianus who was pretending to be a poor man and put a gold coin in his hand. Kissing the hand of the girl, he pulled back the pallium [covering her hand]. After she entered her chamber, she sent her servant girl to summon the stranger. Holding in his hand the ring of Clovis, he put the rest of the betrothal jewelry back in the bag, which he left by the door of the room.

Chlothild said to him, "Tell me young man, why do you pretend to be a poor man and why did you pull back my pallium."

And he said, "I beg of you, may your servant speak in private with you?"

"Speak," she said.

"My lord Clovis, king of the Franks, sent me to you," he said. "He wishes to have you as his queen. Here is his ring and other betrothal jewelry."

He looked behind the door of the room. He could not find his bag, and became troubled and dejected.

She made careful inquiry and said, "Who took away the bag of this poor man?"

She found the bag and secretly retrieved the betrothal jewelry. When she received the ring that King Clovis had sent with Aurelianus, she placed that in the treasury of her uncle.

"I extend greetings to Clovis," she said. "It is not permitted for a Christian woman to marry a pagan. See to it no one knows of this matter. Whatever my lord God, whom I confess before all, commands, so let it be. Go now in peace."

Aurelianus came and reported this to his lord.

12. The next year Clovis sent his envoy Aurelianus to Gundobad on behalf of his betrothed, Chlothild.

Gundobad was frightened when he heard this and said, "As all my strongest advisers and companions among the Burgundians know, Clovis is looking for any excuse against me, for he has never been acquainted with my niece."

And he said to Aurelianus, "You have come looking for an opportunity to spy upon our palace. Report to your lord that he lies in vain when he says he is the betrothed of my niece."

"My lord authorizes me to say this to you," Aurelianus calmly replied. "Should you not wish to give him his betrothed and designate a place, of your choosing, where he may receive his betrothed Chlothild — in that case, he is prepared to come to meet you with an army of Franks."

"Let him come, whenever he likes," Gundobad said. "I'm prepared to resist him with a vast army of Burgundians so his fall may put an end to the slaughter that has been perpetrated on many peoples and be revenge for the blood of many people covering your hands."

Hearing this, the Burgundians who were his advisors were very afraid of the anger of the Franks and Clovis and gave advice to Gundobad, "Let the king have his servants and chamberlains conduct a search to see if at some point gifts were not by artifice brought by the emissaries of King Clovis, so no pretext can be found against your people and kingdom and you can be victorious over him, for Clovis's villainy is quite mad."

The Burgundians, as was customary, gave this advice to their king. They made inquiries and found in the king's treasury a ring inscribed with Clovis's name and image. Then greatly saddened King Gundobad ordered the girl to be questioned about this matter.

She said, "I know, my lord king, a few years ago small gold presents were brought to you as a gift by agents of Clovis and a small ring was placed in the hand of your servant, myself. I stored it away in your treasury."

"This was done honestly and unintentionally," said Gundobad.

He took her and handed her over angrily to Aurelianus. When he had received her, Aurelianus and his companions took her with great joy to Clovis at the city of Soissons in Francia.

King Clovis rejoiced and married her. In the evening of the day on which they were to sleep together as husband and wife, she turned in her wise fashion, having confessed God, and said, "Next, my lord king listen to your maidservant and deign to grant what I ask before I subjugate myself to your authority."

"Ask what you wish," said the king, "and I shall grant it."

"First," she said, "I ask that you believe in the God of heaven, the almighty father, who made you. Second confess Lord Jesus Christ, his son, who redeemed you, who is the king of all kings, sent from heaven by the father, and third, the Holy Spirit, which confirms and illuminates all that is just. Acknowledge the total ineffable majesty and coeternal omnipotence and believe in what you have acknowledged. Abandon empty idols, which are not gods but empty statues. Burn them and rebuild the churches you have burnt. And remember, I pray, that you must demand the share of my father and my mother, whom my uncle Gundobad wrongly killed, if God is to avenge their deaths."

"One of the things you ask is difficult," said Clovis, that I abandon my gods and worship your god. I shall do what else you ask if I can."

"Most of all I ask this," said Chlothild, "that you worship the lord, almighty God, who is in heaven."

13. Clovis again sent Aurelianus to Gundobad in Burgundy, this time on account of the treasure of his queen Chlothild.

Gundobad got angry.

"Are my kingdom and my treasures to be handed over to Clovis?" he asked. "Have I not called upon you, Aurelianus, never to come to my kingdom again to spy on my resources? On behalf of the well-being of princes, I swear, return quickly and get out of my sight or I'll kill you."

Aurelianus answered him by saying, "Long live my lord King Clovis and the Franks who are by his side, for I do not fear your threats while my lord lives. And your own son, King Clovis, authorizes me to determine where he may come for the treasure of his wife, my mistress."

Then the Burgundians, as was customary, gave advice to Gundobad their king.

"Give your niece whatever belongs to her from her treasure," they said, "for this is deemed to be just. Thereby you may have a treaty and friendship with Clovis and the people of the Franks preventing them from falling upon our land, for the people are strong and wild, without God."

Gundobad listened to their advice and gave to Clovis through Aurelianus the greater part of his treasure, gold, silver, and many precious objects.

"What else remains," said Gundobad, "but to divide all my kingdom with Clovis?"

To Aurelianus he said, "Return to your lord for you have many gifts to take to him that you haven't worked for."

"Your son is my lord Clovis," said Aurelianus; "all you have will be in common."

And the wise men of the Burgundians said, "Long live the king who has such *leudes*."

Aurelianus returned with many treasures to his lord in Francia.

Clovis had a son called Theuderic by a concubine.

14. At this time Clovis enlarged his kingdom, extending it to the Seine. Subsequently he occupied territory up to the Loire. Aurelianus received the fortress of Melun and ducal powers over that whole region...

## 97. FROM CLOVIS'S CAMPAIGN AGAINST THE GOTHS (*LHF* 17)

*When Clovis decided to attack the Arian Goths, he founded the church of Saints Peter and the Holy Apostles in Paris. Cf.* **47**, *Gregory of Tours, Hist. IV 1.*

17. ... Queen Chlothild gave the king advice.

"May the lord God put victory in the hands of my lord," she said. "Listen to your maidservant and let us build a church in honor of the blessed Peter, prince of the Apostles, so he may help you in the war."

"What you suggest is good," said the king. "Let's do it."

Then the king threw his ax, called a francisca, in front of him, and said, "Let the church of the blessed apostles be built there when, with God's help, we return."...

*Prior to engaging the Visigoths, Clovis, seeking assistance, gave gifts to Saint Martins at Tours, including a favorite horse. After Alaric's defeat the king returned to Tours.*

Clovis gave a hundred solidi to the poor servants of the church (*matricularii*) to get back the horse he had previously given to the church. When he gave the money, the horse did not move.

"Give another hundred solidi," he said.

When they gave another hundred solidi, the horse was immediately released and came forward.

Then the king cheerfully said, "Truly the blessed Martin is good in giving help and dear in transacting business."

## 98. FREDEGUND DISPLACES AUDOVERA (*LHF* 31)

*Cf. **48**, Gregory of Tours, Hist. IV 28.*

31. ... Fredegund was the lowest member of the household. When Chilperic had marched to war with his brother Sigibert against the Saxons, Audovera remained behind pregnant. She gave birth to a daughter.

Fredegund tricked her with this advice, "Mistress, my lord king is returning as a victor. How can he receive his daughter joyfully if she is not baptized?"

The queen listened to this and had preparations made for a baptism and summoned a bishop to baptize the child. When the bishop came, there was no matron there to take up the child.

Fredegund said, "No equal of yours can ever be found to receive the child. Just take up the child yourself."

The queen listened to this advice and took up the child from the holy font.

The victorious king came and Fredegund went out to meet him.

"Thanks be to God," she said, "for our lord king receives victory against his enemies, and a daughter has been born to you. With whom will my lord sleep tonight, since my mistress the queen as godmother of your daughter Childesind is related to you spiritually?"

"If I can't sleep with her," he said, "I'll sleep with you."

When the king entered his palace, the queen came to meet him with her little girl.

The king said to her, "Your lack of sense has caused you to do an unspeakable thing. Now you can no longer be my wife."

And he asked that she take the holy veil along with her daughter. He gave her many estates and villas. But he sentenced the bishop that baptized his daughter to exile. As for Fredegund, he made her queen.

## 99. FREDEGUND, LANDERIC, AND THE DEATH OF CHILPERIC (*LHF* 35)

*Cf.* **48**, *Gregory,* Hist. *VI 46; and* **58**, *Fredegar, c. 25.*

35. ... Queen Fredegund was beautiful, very cunning, and an adulteress. At the time Landeric was mayor of the palace, a clever and warlike man, whom the said queen loved a great deal, for he took pleasure in having intercourse with her. One day early in the morning the king set out to go hunting at the villa of Chelles in the Paris district. Since he loved her very much, he returned to the bed chamber of the palace from the stables while she was washing her hair in the chamber. Coming up behind her, the king slapped her on the buttocks with his riding-crop.

Thinking it was Landeric, she said, "What are you doing, Landeric?" Looking back, she saw it was the king. She became very frightened. As for the king, he was very unhappy and went on with the hunt.

And so Fredegund summoned Landeric, told him all that happened, and said, "Think what you must do, for tomorrow we shall be put to severe torture."

Landeric's spirit was broken, and, moved to tears, he said, "It was an evil hour my eyes saw you. I don't know what I shall do, for I'm hedged in on all sides."

"Don't be afraid," she said. "Listen to my advice, and let's do this without delay. When the king at the end of his day of hunting comes at night, let's send men to kill him, and let them shout that Childebert, the king of Austrasia, has ambushed him. With the king dead, we shall reign with my son Chlothar."

When night came and Chilperic was returning from the hunt, killers were sent by Fredegund, drunk with wine. The assassins stabbed the king in the stomach with two scramasaxes as the king was dismounting from his horse and the others were entering their lodgings. He let out a shout and died.

The assassins whom the queen had sent cried out, "Ambush, there is an ambush upon our lord by Childebert, king of Austrasia."

...Chilperic ruled for twenty three years. Fredegund remained in power with her small son King Chlothar and Landeric, whom they elected mayor of the palace. The Franks also set up the aforesaid small boy King Chlothar to rule over them.

## 100. FREDEGUND DEFEATS THE AUTRASIANS AT DROIZY (*LHF* 36)

*Droizy was near Soissons. The author of the* LHF *was under the misapprehension that King Guntram had died before Chilperic.*

36. When Childebert, king of Austrasia, son of Sigibert, nephew of Chilperic, heard of the death of his uncle and the wickedness of Queen Fredegund, he gathered an army. His uncle Guntram being dead, he received the kingdom of Burgundy. The Burgundians and the upper Franks of Austrasia together levied a great army; marching boldly through Champagne, it advanced under the patricians Gundoald and Wintrio to plunder the district of Soissons. Fredegund heard about this and gathered an army under Landeric and other dukes of the Franks. She came to Berny and enriched the Franks with many gifts and presents, urging them to fight against their enemies.

She gave notice to the assembled force that the enemy army was exceedingly large and offered the Franks who were on her side a plan.

"Let's go against them at night by lantern light," she said. "Some of our men, who shall precede us, will carry tree branches in their hands, with bells tied to their horses, so that the sentries of their army cannot recognize us. At first light let's fall upon them, and who knows, maybe we'll beat them."

They agreed to the plan. An agreement was announced for a day on which they should meet in battle at the place called Droizy in the district of Soissons. Fredegund set out at night, as she had planned, and, cradling the small king in her arms, reached Droizy, accompanied by a mounted force of armed men carrying branches and the other things we mentioned above.

When the sentries of the Austrasian army perceived the tree branches in the Frankish force as if they were on hillsides, and heard the tinkle of the bells, one of them said to his companion, "Weren't there fields in those places over there yesterday? Why do we see woods?"

"You've been drunk, now you're out of your mind," his companion said, laughing. "Don't you hear the bells of our horses grazing by the woods?"

When these event had transpired, at the crack of dawn, the Franks under Fredegund and the small boy Chlothar fell upon the sleeping Austrasians and Burgundians with trumpets blaring. And they killed most of that force, a very great army, from the highest to the lowest. Gundoald as well as Wintrio fled, barely getting away. Landeric pursued Wintrio, who escaped by means of a swift horse. Fredegund with the rest of the army advanced to Rheims, burning and plundering Champagne. She returned with her army to Soissons with much booty and spoil.

## 101. THE BATTLES OF THE ORVANNE AND ZÜLPICH, AND THE DEATH OF BRUNHILD (*LHF* 37-40)

*Cf. 58, Fredegar, cc. 16, 19, 20, 27, 37-42.*

37. At that time Childebert the king of Austrasia had two sons, the elder, called Theudebert, by a concubine, and the younger, called Theuderic, by his queen [Faileuba]. He sent Theuderic and his grandmother Brunhild to Burgundy, the kingdom of the great king Guntram.

At that time Queen Fredegund died, old and full of days, and was buried in the basilica of Saint Vincent the Martyr at Paris.

Theuderic, king of Burgundy, was handsome, energetic, and extremely rash. On the advice of his grandmother Brunhild he assembled an immense force from Burgundy and brought it against his cousin Chlothar [II]. When Chlothar heard, he mustered the army of the Franks and quickly advanced against Theuderic. The kings came together with their armies at the river Orvanne in the region of Sens and and attacked each other. Such a host fell in the battle that the river, filled with corpses, ceased to flow because of the congealed blood. In that battle an angel of the Lord was present above the host holding a drawn sword. King Chlothar, seeing his forces decimated, fled to the fortress of Melun on the Seine, and later reached Paris. As for Theuderic, plundering the region as far as the town of Essonne [near Corbeil], he retired laden with spoil.

38. Chlothar left Paris and entered the forest of La Brotonne.

Brunhild offered Theuderic worse and worse advice.

"Why do you fail to demand the treasure and kingdom of your father from Theudebert," she said. "You know he's not your brother but was born in adultery by your father's concubine."

Theuderic, as he was savage at heart, on hearing this mustered a huge army and brought it against his brother Theudebert. They came forth to fight at the fortress of Zülpich. The fighting was fierce, and Theudebert seeing his army decimated, fled to Cologne. And so Theuderic burned and plundered the land of the Ripuarians.

The people submitted to him, saying, "Spare us, lord king, and our land — we are already yours — stop destroying the people."

"Either bring me Theudebert alive," said Theuderic, "or cut off his head and bring me that, if you want me to spare you."

They entered the city, lying about one thing after another, and said to Theudebert, "This is your brother's demand: give up your father's treasure, which you have in your possession. Then, he says, he will withdraw his forces."

After they had told these lies, he took them into the treasury of the palace. When he had the store rooms opened to have treasure brought to him, one of them drew his sword and struck him in the neck. They took the head and held it up on the wall of Cologne. Seeing this Theuderic seized the town and took the rich treasury.

When the Frankish magnates were swearing oaths to him in the church of Saint Gereon the Martyr, it seemed to him as if he were stabbed treacherously in the side.

"See to the entrances," he said. "I don't know which of these perjuring Ripuarians has stabbed me."

When they rolled back his robes, they could find nothing but a small purple mark.

He left there with much spoil and, taking with him the sons and the beautiful daughter of his brother King Theudebert, went back to Metz where Queen Brunhild had arrived. The children were seized and Theudebert's sons killed. In fact, the younger of them, in his baptismal robes, was struck against a rock and his brains smashed in.

39. Theuderic saw that his niece, the daughter of Theudebert, was beautiful and wanted to marry her.

Brunhild said to him, "How can you take the daughter of your brother?"

"Have you not told me," he said, "that he was not my brother? Why have you caused me to commit this sin of killing my brother, you evil devil."

He drew his sword intending to kill her. But she was taken away by the nobles who were standing around her, and slipping into the chamber of the palace, barely escaped.

Hating him with a passion, she prepared a poisoned drink and gave him the deadly concoction by the hands of servants. Unaware, Theuderic drank. Growing weak and his wicked spirit failing him in his sins, he died. Brunhild killed his small sons.

40. When these kings were dead, the Burgundians and Austrasians made peace with the other Franks and raised Chlothar up to be sole ruler of all three kingdoms. Chlothar mustered an army and brought it into Burgundy. Feigning peace, he asked Brunhild to come to him, pretending that he was intending to take her as a wife. Arrayed in royal state, she came to him at the river and fortress of Tiroa.

When he saw her, he said, "Enemy of God, why have you committed such evil and dared to destroy such a great royal lineage."

Then he assembled together the army of the Franks and Burgundians. They all shouted out that Brunhild deserved the most shameful form of death. On Chlothar's orders she was placed on a camel, paraded around the whole army, and put to death by having her feet tied to untamed horses and her body torn to pieces. Fire was her final resting place, and her bones were burned.

The king returned home, having made peace all around. The noble Gundolandus, a diligent and distinguished man, was mayor of the palace in the court of the king.

## 102. CHLOTHAR AND DAGOBERT (*LHF* 41)

41. At that time there was a son of Clothar called Dagobert, a powerful energetic boy, clever in all things and most cunning. When he grew up, the king sent him to rule Austrasia with Duke Pippin. The Austrasian upper Franks assembled and set Dagobert over themselves as king.

Also in those days, the Saxons were very rebellious and brought an army made up of many peoples against King Dagobert and Chlothar. As for Dagobert, he assembled a large force, crossed the Rhine, and without hesitation went to fight them. The fighting was fierce and Dagobert was struck in the helmet. A small lock of hair was cut off which his swordbearer, standing behind him, collected from the ground.

Dagobert, seeing his forces taking losses, said to the retainer, "Go quickly now to my father with the lock of hair from my head and ask him to help us before the whole army perishes."

He sped away, crossed the Ardennes forest, and reached the river. Chlothar with a great army had arrived there. When the messenger quickly appeared bringing the king his son's shorn lock, the king was beset by severe anguish. To the blare of the trumpets, he set out at night, crossed the Rhine, and hastened to help his son. When they united they joyfully clapped hands. Setting up camp along the river Weser, they pitched their tents.

Bertoald, duke of the Saxons, was standing on his side of the river, ready to agree to a fight. Hearing the people shouting, he asked why this was so.

They answered, "Lord Chlothar the king comes, and for that reason the Franks are glad."

"Liars," he jeered, "you are frightened out of your wits when you say you have Chlothar with you, for we have heard he is dead."

The king was also standing there wearing his mail coat, a helmet on his head, his hair, streaked with grey, tumbling down. When he removed the helmet and the head of the king could be seen, Bertoald recognized that he was the king and said, "Are you here, you false mule."

The king heard this and became quite offended at the insult. He quickly entered the Weser river on horseback and swam across. As he was wild at heart, he pursued Bertoald. The army of the Franks swam after him and could barely get across because of the wide expanse of water.

And so King Chlothar pursued Bertoald, fighting fiercely with him.

Bertoald said, "Get away from me king before I kill you. For if you get the better of me, everyone will say that you struck down your slave, the pagan Bertoald; but if I kill you then a great story will be heard among all peoples how the boldest king of the Franks was killed by a slave."

But the king never acknowledged his words and pressed on after him.

A horseman of the king followed him at a distance shouting, "Be strong against your enemy, my lord king."

The king's arms grew heavy for he was clad in mail. Pressing on he killed Bertoald, raised his head up on a lance, and returned to the Franks. They were mourning, for they did not know if anything had happened to the king, but when they saw him, they were elated with joy.

The king wasted the whole land of the Saxons and killed the people. He did not leave a person alive that was taller than his sword, which is called a *spatha*. This was the mark the king made on that region and then returned victorious to his land.

# CHAPTER SEVENTEEN

# EPILOGUES AND POSTSCRIPTS: FROM CHARLES MARTEL TO THE END OF MEROVINGIAN KINGSHIP

*The faint tracks of the last Merovingian kings can be traced in their diplomas, but, in the historiography of the rule of Charles Martel and his sons, the monarchy virtually recedes from view. In November 751, Charles's son Pippin III assumed the title of king of the Franks. Charles's descendants, the Carolingians, reigned until the tenth century.*

## A. THE VICTORIES OF CHARLES MARTEL

### 103. THE FIRST CONTINUATOR OF FREDEGAR, a. 724-35

*Count Childebrand, Pippin III's uncle, was responsible for compiling a revised version of Fredegar's chronicle containing continuations from the year 640 to 751. Thereafter, Childebrand's son, Count Nibelung, took over patronage of the project, bringing the continuations down to the death of the first Carolingian king, Pippin, and the accession of the young Charlemagne in 768. The excerpts below are from a section of the chronicle known as the First Continuation.*

*The so-called First Continuation is based on an Austrasian version of the Neustrian History of the Franks (LHF) with an addition based on a source that ended in 735; the First Continuation is thus also a continuation of the LHF. Only the additional chapters (11-17), carrying on from where the LHF stopped, are translated below. These chapters recount Charles's efforts to exercise his authority south of the Loire in Aquitaine and Burgundy, and east of the Rhine as far as Bavaria. Troubles in these areas were not settled by the events described below. Chapter 13 refers to the famous battle of Poitiers (now dated to 733) against the Arabs from Spain. Sunnichild, mentioned in c. 12, became Charles's consort and mother of his son Grifo.*

*With the continuators of Fredegar we pass in sensibility and viewpoint into the realm of Carolingian historiography.*

Source: Three editions have been consulted: (1) *Fredegarii et aliorum chronica*, ed. Bruno Krusch, MGH SRM 2 (1888), pp. 168-93; (2) J. M. Wallace-Harill, ed. and trans., *The Fourth Book of the Chronicle of Fredegar* (London, 1960), pp. 80-121; (3) *Continuationes*, ed. and trans. Andreas Kusternig, in *Quellen zur Geschichte des 7. und 8. Jahrhunderts,* ed. Herwig Wolfram (Darmstadt, 1982), pp. 272-325. Translation by A.C. Murray

[11] After these events [see **59**, c. 53], Prince Charles followed Ragamfred and invested the city of Angers. When Charles had laid the region waste, he returned with a great deal of spoil. In the same period, the Saxons rose in rebellion [a. 724], but Charles arrived among them anticipating the rebellion, put an end to it, and returned home the victor.

[12] Later, after a year had passed [a. 725], he gathered together a large expedition, crossed the Rhine, marched through the Alamanni and Suevi and reached the Danube. He crossed the river and took possession of Bavarian territory. When he had subjugated the region, he withdrew with much treasure and a certain matron by the name of Beletrude and her niece Sunnichild.

[13] During the same period, Duke Eudo withdrew from the terms of the treaty [cf. **59**, c. 53]. When Prince Charles learned of this through messengers, he marshaled an army and crossed the Loire. Eudo was put to flight and Charles returned home with a large quantity of loot taken from his enemies for the second time in one year.

Since Duke Eudo saw that he had been overthrown and made a laughing stock, he roused the faithless Saracens to help him against Prince Charles and the Franks. The Saracens came forth under their king, who was called 'Abd ar-Rahman, crossed the Garonne, and reached Bordeaux. Burning churches and killing people, they advanced to Poitiers. They burnt the church of Saint Hilary, which is distressing to report, and intended to destroy the house of the blessed Martin. Prince Charles boldly deployed his forces against them and, warrior that he is, fell upon them. With Christ's help, he pulled down their tents, rushing to battle to grind them to pieces. And when he had laid low and killed their king 'Abd ar-Rahman, he trampled their forces. Fighting and winning the day, Charles triumphed, a victor over his enemies.

[14] The next year, moreover, the distinguished warrior Prince Charles quickly entered the kingdom of Burgundy and turned over the territories of that kingdom to diligent men, the most tried and true members of his *leudes,* to oppose rebellious and faithless peoples. Peace achieved, he handed over Lyonnaise Gaul to his followers. He authorized judicial agreements and, confidently exercising his authority, returned home.

[15] In those days, Duke Eudo died [a. 735]. When he heard this, the aforesaid Prince Charles took the counsel of his chief officials and again crossed the Loire river. He came to the Garonne taking possession of the city of Bordeaux and the fortress of Blaye; he seized that region and subjugated it,

with its cities and fortresses in the suburban districts. He returned in peace victorious with the help of Christ, King of kings and Lord of lords. Amen.

[16] The course of the years to the present can be calculated like this: from Adam and the beginning of the world to the flood, 2242 years; from the flood to Abraham, 942 years; from Abraham to Moses, 505 years; from Moses to Soloman, 479 years; from Solomon to the rebuilding of the temple in the times of Darius, king of the Persians, 512 years; from the restoration of the temple to the advent of our Jesus Christ, 548 years. Therefore, from the beginning of the world to the passion of our lord, Jesus Christ, are 5228 years, and from the passion of the Lord to the present year, which is year 177 in the cycle of Victorius, Sunday, the Kalends of January [1 Jan.], are 735 years. To complete this millennium, there are 63 years left [that is, 5937 years have been completed since the creation of the world].

[17] Furthermore (I omitted this earlier), that fearful seagoing people the Frisians broke out in a bloody rebellion. Prince Charles boldly made preparations for a naval expedition. Assembling a fleet of ships, he eagerly took to the high seas, reached Westergo and Ostergo, islands of the Frisians, and set up camp on the banks of the river Boorn. He killed Bubo, the pagan leader of those counseling treachery, and defeated the Frisian forces, smashing and burning the sanctuaries of their idols. Laden with loot and spoils, Charles returned victorious to the kingdom of the Franks.

## 104. THE BATTLE OF POITIERS IN THE MOZARABIC CHRONICLE OF 754

*The* Mozarabic Chronicle, *which begins in 611 and ends in 754, was written by a Latin Christian of Arab Spain and was likely conceived as a continuation of the historical work of Isidore of Seville. The excerpt below is its account of the events leading to Charles Martel's victory over the Arabs near Poitiers. It diverges in important points from the Frankish version.*

Source: Jose Eduardo Lopez Pereira, *Cronica Mozarabe de 754: edicion critica y traduccion* (Zaragoza, 1980), cc. 79–80. Translation, A.C. Murray.

79. In era 769 [A. D. 731], in year 12 ½ of the emperor Leo, 113 of the Arabs and 9 of [Caliph] Hisham, 'Abd ar-Rahman, a warlike man, was overjoyed to come to power suddenly and excelled everyone for a period of three years.

A moor called Munnuza, who was well endowed with courage and fame, on hearing that his people were crushed by the wanton cruelty of judges throughout Libya, quickly concluded a peace with the Franks and made preparations to seize power in Spain from the Saracens there. And since he was well-prepared for battle, the affairs of the palace were thrown into confusion when all learned of this. But not many days later, 'Abd ar-Rahman mounted an expedition against the rebel, mercilessly pursuing him in a fury. Munnuza was attacked when found in the town of Cerdanya, and overcome by the siege and walled in for some time, he suddenly burst out, giving in to flight by the judgment of God and losing his reputation. Now he was already completely damned because, thoroughly intoxicated with shedding the blood of innocent Christians there, he had ended the life of the illustrious bishop Anambadus in the bloom of manhood by burning him. Having been overcome by thirst due to the scarcity of water in the city, though it once flowed there in abundance, and on the point of imminent death with the army in pursuit, Munnuza remained on the loose, changing his whereabouts, since he could find nowhere to run. A duke of the Franks called Eudo, as part of a treaty to hold back Arab attack, had once given his daughter to him to be his wife and to yield to his pleasures. Although Munnuza made no haste to free her from the band of pursuers, he made ready his own soul to pay the debt it owed death. And so as the royal forces closed in, already wounded, he threw himself from a high peak onto sharp rocks to mock them and so he would not be taken alive, and breathed his last. They cut off his head immediately when they found him lying there and delivered it to the king along with the daughter of Eudo, the aforementioned duke. The king arranged to have her transported by sea in an honorable fashion to the exalted prince [the Caliph].

80. At that point, 'Abd ar-Rahman, seeing the land full of a large number of his troops, cut through the mountains of the Basques, and treading the rocky passes underfoot like they were the plains, invaded the lands of the Franks. Advancing deep he so chastised the land by the sword that only God knows the numbers of those dying or perishing; for Eudo fled after offering battle beyond the rivers Garonne and Dordogne.

It was then that 'Abd ar-Rahman, pursuing Duke Eudo, had the urge to despoil Tours by destroying the palaces and burning the churches, and when he came head to head with the consul of Austrasia, Charles, a warlike man from an early age and skilled in the military art, who had been warned by Eudo.

There the two sides tormented one another in small clashes for almost seven days until, finally, there was a general engagement. Though the fighting was fierce, the northern peoples, standing unmoved like a wall, kept their ranks together as if contracted by the chill of northern climes, and slew the Arabs by the sword in the flash of an eye. The people of Austrasia, imposing because of the size of their bodies and quite hard to deal with because of their use of armor, found the king and struck him in the chest, killing him. But then, with nightfall, they immediately broke off the battle, contemptibly holding up their swords, and, at the sight of the huge camp of the Arabs, withdrew to fight another day.

And rising from their own quarters at daybreak the Europeans looked out over the tents and canopies of the Arabs, laid out as a camp just as earlier. Not knowing that the whole place was quite empty, and thinking that inside the forces of the Saracens had readied themselves to fight, they sent scouts who found that all the columns of the Ishmaelites had been put to flight. They had all passed the night in silence, dispersing in close order to return home. When the Europeans had made sure that covered trenches had not been concealed along the paths as a trap, they looked in astonishment everywhere around the camp to no avail. And since they were by no means concerned with pursuing the Arab peoples, they returned home happy, having only divided the plunder and booty in a suitable fashion.

*The next entry is dated to era 772, i.e. A.D. 734.*

# B. FROM THE CORRESPONDENCE OF SAINT BONIFACE

*The English mission to Frisia that started with Wilfrid (cf. **61**) continued from the 690s onward under Willibrord, who was consecrated archbishop of the Frisians by Pope Sergius in 695; Willibrord established his see at Utrecht under the protection of the mayor Pippin II. In 719 the Papacy commissioned another Englishman, the West Saxon Wynfrith, to preach in Frisia and Thuringia. Wynfrith was given a new name, Boniface, and in 722 was consecrated bishop, but with no fixed see; in 732 the Pope appointed him archbishop. Boniface's activities spread from Frisia, Hesse, and Thuringia, eventually, to Bavaria, where he undertook a reorganization of the church. In 739, he was appointed papal legate, which gave him considerable authority within the Frankish church, provided the mayor was sympathetic to his reform aims. In 746 his see was established at Mainz. He returned to the Frisian mission field in the last year of his life and was martyred at Dokkum in 754.*

*Boniface's enterprise has left a rich body of sources in* vitae *and, especially, letters. The preponderance of English sources on missionary activity and, in particular, the large number of letters between Boniface and his correspondents, and the perspectives they espouse, can be misleading. The following points may help establish a context for reading the following brief excerpts from Boniface's correspondence.*

*First, by no means all of the territories in which Boniface was active were pagan. In regions like Bavaria episcopal organization was already established, even if in some disarray. Lapsed Christians, poorly instructed clerics and laity, as well as wilfully corrupt and powerful bishops, figure more prominently among Boniface's preoccupations than paganism.*

*Second, Christianity was no stranger to the areas Boniface evangelized (he had con-*

*tinental and insular precursors in the missionary enterprise), nor was Frankish power, which in its heyday in the seventh century and earlier cut deep into trans-Rhenine territories.*

*Finally, Boniface's efforts to evangelize pagans and improve the standards of Christian laity and clergy had a political background: namely the expansion of Frankish rule into trans-Rhenine territories by the mayors of the palace, with the support of powerful members of the Frankish episcopacy.*

Source: *The Letters of Saint Boniface*, trans. Ephraim Emerton (New York, 1940); with a few, minor, revisions. Roman numerals in brackets in the document headings are Emerton's numeration; Arabic numerals refer to the Latin edition by Michael Tangl (MGH Epistolae selectae 1 [1916]).

## 105. CHARLES MARTEL COMMENDS BONIFACE TO ALL FRANKISH OFFICIALS, a. 723 [XIV, 22]

To the holy and apostolic bishops, our fathers in Christ, and to the dukes, counts, vicars, *domestici*, and all our lesser officials and itinerant representatives (*missi*) and all who are our friends, the illustrious Charles, mayor of the palace, your well-wisher, sends greeting.

Be it known to you that the apostolic man in Christ, Father Boniface, a man of apostolic character and a bishop, came to us with the request that we should take him under our guardianship and protection. Know that we have acquiesced with pleasure and, hence, have granted his petition before witnesses and commanded that this written order signed by our own hand be given him, that wheresoever he may choose to go, he is to be left in peace and protected as a man under our guardianship and protection to the end that he may render and receive justice. If he shall be in any need or distress which cannot be remedied according to law, let him and those dependent upon him come in peace and safety before our presence, so that no person may hinder or do him injury, but that he may rest at all times in peace and safety under our guardianship and protection.

And that this may the more surely be given credit, I have signed it with my own hand and sealed it with our ring.

## 106. BISHOP DANIEL OF WINCHESTER ADVISES BONIFACE ON THE METHOD OF CONVERSION, a. 723-24 [XV, 23]

*This letter is one of the few early medieval sources that sheds any light on the possible forms of intellectual exchange between missionaries and northern pagans.*

To the venerable and beloved prelate Boniface, Daniel, servant of the people of God.

I rejoice, beloved brother and fellow priest, that you are deserving of the highest prize of virtue. You have approached the hitherto stony and barren hearts of the pagans, trusting in the plenitude of your faith, and have labored untiringly with the plowshare of Gospel preaching, striving by your daily toil to change them into fertile fields. To you may well be applied the Gospel saying: "The voice of one crying in the wilderness," etc. Yet a part of the second prize shall be given, not unfittingly, to those who support so pious and useful a work with what help they can give and supplement the poverty of those laborers with means sufficient to carry on zealously the work of preaching which has already been begun and to raise up new sons to Christ.

And so I have with affectionate good will taken pains to suggest to Your Prudence a few things that may show you how, according to my ideas, you may most readily overcome the resistance of those uncivilized people. Do not begin by arguing with them about the origin of their gods, false as those are, but let them affirm that some of them were begotten by others through the intercourse of male with female, so that you may at least prove that gods and goddesses born after the manner of men are men and not gods and, since they did not exist before, must have had a beginning.

Then, when they have been compelled to learn that their gods had a beginning since some were begotten by others, they must be asked in the same way whether they believe that the world had a beginning or was always in existence without beginning. If it had a beginning, who created it? Certainly they can find no place where begotten gods could dwell before the universe was made. I mean by "universe" not merely this visible earth and sky, but the whole vast extent of space, and this the heathen too can imagine in their thoughts. But if they argue that the world always existed without beginning, you should strive to refute this and to convince them by many documents and arguments. Ask your opponents who governed the world before the gods were born, who was the ruler? How could they bring under their dominion or subject to their law a universe that had always existed before them? And whence, or from whom or when, was the first god or goddess set up or begotten? Now, do they imagine that gods and goddesses still go on begetting others? Or, if they are no longer begetting, when or why did they cease from intercourse and births? And if they are still producing offspring, then the number of gods must already be infinite. Among so many and different gods, mortal men cannot know which is the most powerful, and one should be extremely careful not to offend that most powerful one.

Do they think the gods are to be worshipped for the sake of temporal and immediate good or for future eternal blessedness? If for temporal things, let them tell in what respect the heathen are better off than Christians. What gain do the heathen suppose accrues to their gods from their sacrifices, since the gods already possess everything? Or why do the gods leave it in the power of their subjects to say what kind of tribute shall be paid? If they are lacking in such things, why do they not themselves choose more valuable ones? If they have plenty, then there is no need to suppose that the gods can be pleased with such offerings of victims.

These and many similar things which it would take long to enumerate you ought to put before them, not offensively or so as to anger them, but calmly and with great moderation. At intervals you should compare their superstitions with our Christian doctrines, touching upon them from the flank, as it were, so that the pagans, thrown into confusion rather than angered, may be ashamed of their absurd ideas and may understand that their infamous ceremonies and fables are well known to us.

This point is able to be made: if the gods are all-powerful, beneficent, and just, they not only reward their worshippers but punish those who reject them. If, then, they do this in temporal matters, how is it that they spare us Christians who are turning almost the whole earth away from their worship and overthrowing their idols? And while these, that is, the Christians, possess lands rich in oil and wine and abounding in other resources, they have left to those, that is, the pagans, lands stiff with cold where their gods, driven out of the world, are falsely supposed to rule. They are also frequently to be reminded of the supremacy of the Christian world, in comparison with which they themselves, very few in number, are still involved in their ancient errors.

If they boast that the rule of the gods over those peoples has been, as it were, lawful from the beginning, show them that the whole world was once given over to idol-worship, until by the grace of Christ and through the knowledge of one God, its Almighty Founder and Ruler, it was enlightened, brought to life, and reconciled to God. For what is the daily baptism of the children of believing Christians but purification of each one from the uncleanness and guilt in which the whole world was once involved?

I have been glad to call these matters to your attention, my brother, out of my affection for you, though I suffer from bodily infirmities so that I may well say with the Psalmist: "I know, O Lord, that thy judgments are right and that thou in faithfulness hast afflicted me." Wherefore I earnestly pray Your Reverence and all those who serve Christ in spirit to make supplication for me that the Lord who gave me to drink of the wine of remorse, may be swift in mercy, that He who was just in condemnation may graciously pardon, and by His mercy enable me to sing in gratitude the words of the Prophet: "In the multitude of my thoughts within me thy comforts delight my soul."

I pray for your welfare in Christ, my very dear colleague, and beg you to bear me in mind.

## 107. REPLIES OF POPE GREGORY II TO QUESTIONS OF BONIFACE, 22 NOVEMBER 726 [XVIII, 26]

*It was common practice for Boniface to write letters asking for doctrinal advice on tricky matters encountered in his ministry. This is one of the replies.*

Gregory, servant of the servants of God, to his most reverend and holy brother and fellow bishop Boniface.

Your messenger, the pious priest Denuald, has brought us the welcome news that you are well and prospering, with the help of God, in the service for which you were sent. He also brought a letter from you showing that the field of the Lord which had been lying fallow, bristling with the thorns of unbelief, has received the plowshare of your instruction, plowing in the seed of the word, and is bringing forth an abundant harvest of true belief.

In this same letter you inserted several paragraphs of inquiries as to the faith and teaching of this Holy and Apostolic Roman Church. And this was well done; for the blessed apostle Peter stands as the fountainhead of the apostolate and the episcopate. And to you who consult us about ecclesiastical matters we show what decision you have to take according to the teaching of apostolic tradition, and we do this not as if by our own personal authority, but by the grace of Him who opens the mouth of the dumb and makes eloquent the tongues of infants.

You ask first within what degrees of relationship marriage may take place. We reply: strictly speaking, in so far as the parties know themselves to be related they ought not to be joined together. But since moderation is better than strictness of discipline, especially toward so uncivilized a people, they may contract marriage after the fourth degree.

As to your question, what a man is to do if his wife is unable on account of disease, to fulfill her wifely duty: it would be well if he could remain in a state of continence. But, since this is a matter of great difficulty, it is better for him who cannot refrain to take a wife. He may not, however, withdraw his support from the one who was prevented by disease, provided she be not involved in any grievous fault.

In regard to a priest or any cleric accused by the people: unless the evidence of the witnesses to the charge against him is positive, let him take oath before the assembly, calling as witness of his innocence Him to whom all things are plain and open; and so let him keep his proper standing.

In the case of one confirmed by a bishop, a repetition of this rite is prohibited.

In the celebration of the Mass, the form is to be observed which our Lord Jesus Christ used with his disciples. He took the cup and gave it to them, saying: "this cup is the new testament in my blood; this do ye as oft as ye take it." Wherefore it is not fitting that two or three cups should be placed on the altar when the ceremony of the Mass is performed.

As to sacrificial foods: You ask whether, if a believer makes the life-giving sign of the cross above them, it is permitted to eat them or not. A sufficient answer is given in the words of the blessed apostle Paul: "If any man say unto you, This is offered in sacrifice unto idols, eat not for his sake that shewed it, and for conscience sake."

You ask further, if a father or mother shall have placed a young son or daughter in a cloister under the discipline of a rule, whether it is lawful for the child after reaching the years of discretion to leave the cloister and enter into marriage. This we absolutely forbid, since it is an impious thing that the restraints of desire should be relaxed for children offered to God by their parents.

You mention also that some have been baptized by adulterous and unworthy priests without being questioned whether they believe, as it is in the ritual. In such cases you are to follow the ancient custom of the Church. He who has been baptized in the name of the Father, Son, and Holy Spirit may on no account be baptized again; for he has received the gift of His grace not in the name of the one who baptizes, but in the name of the Trinity. Let the word of the Apostle be observed: "One God, one faith, one baptism." We require you to convey spiritual instruction to such persons with especial zeal.

As to young children taken from their parents and not knowing whether they have been baptized or not, reason requires you to baptize them, unless there be someone who can give evidence in the case.

Lepers, if they are believing Christians, may receive the body and blood of the Lord, but they may not take food together with persons in health.

You ask whether, in the case of a contagious disease or plague in a church or monastery, those who are not yet attacked may escape danger by flight. We declare this to be the height of folly; for no one can escape from the hand of God.

Finally, your letter states that certain priests and bishops are so involved in vices of many sorts that their lives are a blot upon the priesthood and you ask whether it is lawful for you to eat with or to speak with them, supposing them not to be heretics. We answer, that you by apostolic authority are to admonish and persuade them and so bring them back to the purity of church discipline. If they obey, you will save their souls and win reward for yourself. You are not to avoid conversation or eating at the same table with them. It often happens that those who are slow in coming to a perception of the truth under strict discipline may be led into the paths of righteousness by the influence of their table companions and by gentle admonition. You ought also to follow this same rule in dealing with those chieftains who are helpful to you.

This, my dear brother, is all that need be said with the authority of the Apostolic See. For the rest we implore the mercy of God, that He who has sent you into that region in our stead and with apostolic authority and has caused the light of truth to shine into that dark forest by means of your words may mercifully grant the increase, so that you may reap the reward of your labors and we may find remission for our sins.

God keep you in safety, most reverend brother.

Given on the tenth day before the Kalends of December, in the tenth year of our most pious and august lord Leo, by God crowned emperor, in the tenth year of his consulship and the seventh of the emperor Constantine his son, in the tenth indiction.

## 108. POPE GREGORY III PROMOTES BONIFACE TO THE RANK OF MISSIONARY ARCHBISHOP AND SENDS HIM THE PALLIUM, ca. 732 [XX, 28]

*Gregory III was Gregory II's successor.*

To our very reverend and holy brother and fellow bishop, Boniface, sent by this Apostolic Church of God to enlighten the people of Germany and those in the surrounding countries who are still lingering in the shadow of death and involved in error, Gregory, servant of the servants of God, sends greeting.

It was with great satisfaction that we learned from a repeated reading of the letter from Your Sacred Fraternity that by the grace of Jesus Christ multitudes have been converted by you from paganism and error to a knowledge of the true faith. We, together with the whole Church, applaud such an increase, as we are taught in the parable of him to whom five talents were given and who gained also another five. For this we have ordered the gift of a sacred pallium to be sent to you to be received and worn by the authority of the Holy Apostle Peter, and we direct you to be recognized as an arch-bishop by divine appointment. How you are to use it you will learn by apos-tolic instructions; namely, you are to wear it solely when you are celebrating a solemn mass or when you may have occasion to consecrate a bishop.

But, since you declare yourself unable to impart the means of salvation to all who are converted to the true faith in those parts, since the faith has already been carried far and wide, we command you, in accordance with the sacred canons and by authority of the Apostolic See to ordain bishops wher-ever the multitude of the faithful has become very great. Do this, however, after prayerful reflection, lest the dignity of the episcopate be impaired.

As to that priest who, you say, came to us a year ago and received from us absolution for his crimes, be advised that he made no confession to us, nor did he receive from us any absolution that he might return to his evil lusts. If you find him given over to error, we order you, by the power of the Apos-tolic See, to discipline him according to the sacred canons, him and any oth-ers like him, if perchance you find such. When he came hither he said, "I am a priest," and he asked us for a letter of recommendation to our son Charles [Martel], and that was the only favor we granted him. If he conducts himself badly, we desire you to put him under a ban, him and all the rest of them.

Those who, you say, were baptized by pagans we order you to baptize again in the name of the Trinity, if the fact is proved.

You say, among other things, that some have the habit of eating wild horses and very many eat tame horses. This, holy brother, you are in no wise to permit in future, but are to suppress it in every possible way, with the help of Christ, and impose suitable penance upon the offenders. It is a filthy and abominable practice.

You inquire whether offerings for the dead are permitted. The teaching of Holy Church is that anyone may make offerings for his truly Christian dead, and that the priest may remember them in his prayers. And, although we are all subject to sin, it is fitting for the priest to remember the faithful dead and he should make intercession for them; not, however, for the ungodly, even if they were Christians, shall such service be allowed.

We direct that those who are uncertain whether they have been baptized or not and those who were baptized by a priest who also sacrificed to Jupiter and who ate of sacrificial food are to be baptized [again].

We decree, that [in contracting marriage] every one shall observe the rules of relationship even to the seventh degree.

In so far as you are able, prevent a man who has lost his wife from marry-ing again in the future more than once.

One who has murdered his father, mother, brother, or sister may not receive the body of the Lord so long as he shall live, excepting at the moment of death as a viaticum. Let him also abstain from eating flesh or drinking wine during his natural life. Let him fast on the second, fourth, and sixth day of the week, and thus with lamentation wash away the offense he has committed.

You say that among other evil practices in those parts, some Christians are in the habit of selling slaves to the heathen for sacrifice. This, my brother, you are especially to forbid and prevent in the future. It is an impious crime, and you are to impose upon the guilty person penance similar to that for homicide.

Whenever you ordain a bishop let two or three other bishops be with you, that your action may be acceptable to God and that you may perform the consecration with their approval and in their presence.

These things, beloved brother, we desire you diligently to observe. Carry on with earnest devotion the work of salvation already begun, so that you may receive for the riches that you have contributed a reward of eternal blessedness from the Lord our God.

We have had made out the privilege you request. We send it with this letter, praying that you may receive the fullest and most complete reward under the protection of the Lord our God, for the conversion of the erring to Christ our God.

My God preserve you in safety, most reverend brother.

## 109. BONIFACE TO POPE ZACHARIAS ON THE LATTER'S ACCESSION TO THE PAPACY, EARLY IN 742 [XL, 50]

*By the time the following letter was written, Boniface had been made papal legate (a. 739), Charles Martel had died (a. 741), and his sons Pippin III and Carloman had succeeded to his authority.*

To our best beloved Lord Zacharias, the apostolic man wearing the insignia of the supreme pontificate, Boniface, a servant of the servants of God.

We must confess, our father and lord, that after we learned from messengers that your predecessor in the apostolate, Gregory of reverend memory, pontiff of the Apostolic See, had been set free from the prison of the body and had passed on to God, nothing gave us greater joy or happiness than the knowledge that the Supreme Arbiter had appointed your fatherly clemency to administer the canon law and to govern the Apostolic See. We gave thanks to God with uplifted hands. And so, just as if we were kneeling at your feet, we most earnestly pray that, as we have been devoted servants and willing disciples of your predecessors under the authority of Saint Peter, so also we may be worthy to be the obedient servants of Your Holiness under the canon law. It is our earnest desire to maintain the Catholic faith and the unity of the Roman Church. As many hearers or learners as God shall grant me in my missionary work, I will not cease to summon and urge them to render obedience to the Apostolic See.

We have also to inform Your Paternity that by the grace of God we have appointed three bishops over those peoples in Germany who have been to a certain extent won over and converted and we have divided the province into three dioceses. The bishoprics of these three towns or cities where they were ordained we beg you to confirm and establish by your authority in writing. We have appointed one episcopal see in the fortress called Würzburg, another in the town of Buraburg, and a third in a place called Erfurt, which was formerly a city of heathen rustics. The choice of these three places we earnestly pray you to strengthen and confirm by your own charter and by authority of your apostolic office, so that, God willing, there may be in Germany three episcopal sees founded and established by apostolic order and under the authority and direction of Saint Peter. And may neither the present nor any future generation presume to break up these dioceses or to defy the orders of the Apostolic See.

Be it known also to Your Paternity that Carloman, duke of the Franks, summoned me to him and requested me to bring together a council on the part of the Frankish kingdom which is under his rule. He promised that he would do something toward reforming and reestablishing the ecclesiastical discipline, which for a long time, not less than sixty or seventy years, has been despoiled and trampled upon. If, therefore, he is really willing, under divine inspiration, to carry out this purpose, I should have the advice and direction of your authority — that is, the authority of the Apostolic See. The Franks, according to their elders, have not held a council for more than eighty years, nor have they had an archbishop or established or restored anywhere the canon law of the Church. For the most part the episcopal sees in cities are in the hands of greedy laymen or are exploited by adulterous and vicious clergymen and publicans for secular uses. If, then, I am to undertake this business by your orders and at the instance of the aforesaid duke, I desire to have at once the command and the suggestions of the Apostolic See, together with the Church canons.

If I find among these men certain so-called deacons who have spent their lives since boyhood in debauchery, adultery, and every kind of filthiness, who entered the diaconate with this reputation, and who now, while they have four or five concubines in their beds, still read the Gospel and are not ashamed or afraid to call themselves deacons — nay rather, entering upon the priesthood, they continue in the same vices, add sin to sin, declare that they have a right to make intercession for the people in the priestly office and to celebrate Mass, and, still worse, with such reputations advancing from step to step to nomination and appointment as bishops — may I have the formal prescription of your authority as to your procedure in such cases so that they may be convicted by an apostolic judgment and dealt with as sinners? And certain bishops are to be found among them who, although they deny that they are fornicators or adulterers, are drunkards and shiftless men, given to hunting and to fighting in the army like soldiers and by their own hands shedding blood, whether of heathens or Christians. Since I am the recognized servant and legate of the Apostolic See, my word here and your word there ought to agree, in case I should send messengers, as I have done in the past, to learn the decision of your authority.

In another matter, also, I have to ask your advice and permission. Your predecessor of reverend memory directed me in your presence to name, God willing, a [certain] priest as my heir and successor in the service of the Church in case of my death. If this be the will of God, it is agreeable to me. But now I am in doubt and do not know whether it can be done, because since then a brother of that priest has killed an uncle of the duke of the Franks and up to the present time we do not know how and when that quarrel will be settled. I pray you, therefore, to give me your authority to act in this choice, with the approval of the servants of God, as may seem best to us all for God and for the advantage and spiritual profit of the Church and the protection of religion. May I have your consent to act in this matter as God shall deign to inspire me, since it does not seem possible to accomplish it against the wishes of the prince?

I have further to seek the advice of Your Paternity in regard to a certain perplexing and scandalous report which has come to us recently and has greatly disturbed us, filling with confusion the priests of our churches. A certain layman of high station came to us and said that Gregory of sainted memory, pontiff of the Apostolic See, had granted him permission to marry the widow of his uncle. She had formerly been the wife of her own cousin but had left him during his lifetime. She is known to be related in the third degree to the man who now desires her and who declares that permission was granted him. She formerly made a vow of chastity before God and took the veil but laid it aside and was married.

The aforesaid man declares that he has a license from the Apostolic See for such a marriage as this! But we do not believe this to be true; for a synod of the church of the Saxons beyond the sea, in which I was born and reared, namely the synod of London, convoked and directed by disciples of Saint

Gregory, the archbishops — Augustine, Laurentius, Justus, and Miletus — declared such a marriage union, on the authority of Holy Scripture, to be a heinous crime, an incestuous and horrible offense, and a damnable sin. Wherefore, I beg Your Paternity to deign to enlighten us as to the true doctrine in this case, that scandals and schisms or new errors may not arise and increase therefrom among the clergy and the Christian people.

Some of the ignorant common people, Alamannians, Bavarians, and Franks, hearing that many of the offenses prohibited by us are practiced in the city of Rome imagine that they are allowed by the priests there and reproach us for causing them to incur blame in their own lives. They say that on the first day of January year after year, in the city of Rome and in the neighborhood of Saint Peter's Church by day or night, they have seen bands of singers parading the streets in pagan fashion, shouting and chanting sacrilegious songs and loading tables with food day and night, while no one in his own house is willing to lend his neighbor fire or tools or any other convenience. They say also that they have seen there women with amulets and bracelets of heathen fashion on their arms and legs, offering them for sale to willing buyers. All these things, seen by evil-minded and ignorant people, are a cause of reproach to us and a hindrance to our preaching and teaching. It is of such things that the Apostle says reprovingly: "Ye observe days and times; I fear I have labored with you in vain." And Saint Augustine said:

He who believes in such evil things, as incantations or diviners or soothsayers, or amulets, or any kind of prophesies, even though he fast, or pray, or run to church continually, and though he give alms generously, or torment his body with all kinds of tortures, it shall profit him nothing so long as he does not abandon these sacrilegious rites.

If Your Paternity would prohibit these heathen practices at Rome, it would bring rewards to you and the greatest advantage to us in our teaching.

Some bishops and priests of the Frankish nation who were adulterers and fornicators of the worst kind, whose children born during their episcopate or priesthood bear witness against them, now declare, on returning from the Apostolic See, that the Roman Pontiff has given them permission to carry on their episcopal service in the Church. Against this we maintain that we have never heard that the Apostolic See had ever given a decision contrary to canonical decrees.

All these things, beloved master, we make known to you that we may give an answer to these people upon your authority and that under guidance of your instruction the sheep of the church may not be led astray and that the ravening wolves may be overcome and destroyed.

We are sending you some trifling gifts, not as being worthy of Your Paternity, but as a token of our affection and our devoted obedience, a warm rug
and a little silver and gold...

## 110. A DECREE OF CARLOMAN, MAYOR OF THE EASTERN FRANKS, BASED ON DELIBERATIONS OF SYNODS IN 742 AND 743 [XLIV (56)]

*Boniface, who had already used a council to reorganize the Bavarian church, finally got
the councils he wanted from the Frankish mayors. Carloman summoned two, generally
dated to 742 and 743; Pippin held one a year later. The following decree of Carloman
concerning the deliberations of the two councils in his realm were included in collections
of Boniface's correspondence. The council of 742 is known as the* Concilium Ger-
manicum, *that of 743 as the* Synod of Estinnes.

### The First Synod, a. 742

In the name of our Lord Jesus Christ, I, Carloman, duke and prince of the
Franks, in the seven hundred and forty-second year of the Incarnation of
Christ and the twenty-first day of April, with the advice of the servants of
God and my chief men, have brought together out of fear of Christ the bishops of my realm with their priests into a council or synod — namely, Archbishop Boniface, Burchard [of Würzburg], Reginfried [of Cologne], Wintan
[of Buraburg], Willibald [of Eichstädt or Erfurt], Dadanus [of Utrecht or
Erfurt], and Eddanus [of Strasbourg], together with their priests — that they
might give me their advice how the law of God and the service of religion,
fallen into decay under former princes, might be reestablished, and how the
Christian people might attain salvation for their souls and not perish through
the deceit of false priests.

And, by the advice of my priests and nobles, we have appointed bishops
for the several cities and have set over them as archbishop Boniface, the delegate of St. Peter.

We have ordered that a synod shall be held every year, so that in our presence the canonical decrees and the laws of the church may be reestablished
and the Christian religion purified.

Properties, of which churches were defrauded, we have restored and given
back to them. We have deprived false priests and adulterous or lustful deacons
of their church incomes, have degraded them, and forced them to do
penance.

We have absolutely forbidden all servants of God to carry arms or fight, to enter the army or march against an enemy, except only so many as are especially selected for divine service, such as celebrating mass or carrying relics — that is to say, the prince may have one or two bishops along with chaplains, and each prefect one priest to hear confessions and prescribe penance. We have also forbidden the servants of God to hunt or wander about the woods with dogs or to keep hawks and falcons.

We have also ordered, according to the sacred canons, that every priest living within a diocese shall be subject to the bishop of that diocese. Annually during Lent he shall render to the bishop an account of his ministry, in regard to baptism in the catholic faith, to prayers, and the order of the mass. Whenever, according to canon law, the bishop shall make the rounds of his diocese for the purpose of confirmation, the priest is to be ready to receive him with the assembly and assistance of the people who are going to be confirmed. On Holy Thursday let him ask the bishop for fresh consecrated oil and bear witness before the bishop of his chastity, his way of life, and his belief.

We have ordered, according to canonical warning, that unknown bishops and priests, wherever they may come from, shall not be admitted into the service of the church without approval by a synod.

We have decreed, according to the canons, that every bishop within his own diocese and with the help of the count, who is the defender of the church, shall see to it that the people of God perform no pagan rites but reject and cast out all the foulness of the heathen, such as sacrifices to the dead, casting of lots, divinations, amulets and auguries, incantations, or offerings of animals, which foolish folk perform in the churches, according to pagan custom, in the name of holy martyrs or confessors, thereby calling down the wrath of God and his saints, and also those sacrilegious fires which they call "niedfeor," and whatever other pagan practices there may be.

We have further ordered that after this synod held on April the twenty-first, any of the servants of God or the maids of Christ falling into carnal sin shall do penance in prison on bread and water. If it be an ordained priest he shall be imprisoned for two years, first flogged to bleeding and afterward further disciplined at the bishop's discretion. But if a clerk or monk fall into this sin, after a third flogging he shall be imprisoned for a year and there do penance. Likewise a veiled nun shall be bound to do the same penance, and all her hair shall be shaved.

We have decreed also that priests and deacons shall not wear cloaks after the fashion of laymen, but cassocks according to the usage of the servants of God. Let no priest or deacon permit a woman to live in the same house with him. Let cloistered monks and maids of God live after the Rule of St. Benedict and govern their lives accordingly.

## The Second Synod [a. 743]

And now, in this synodal assembly, called for the first day of March in the place called Estinnes, all the venerable priests of God, the counts and prefects have accepted and confirmed the decrees of the former synod and have promised to carry them out and observe them.

The whole order of the clergy — bishops, priests, deacons, and clerics — accepting the canons of the ancient fathers, have promised to restore the laws of the church as to morals and doctrine and form of service. Abbots and monks have accepted the rule of the holy father, Benedict, for the reformation of the regular life.

We order that corrupt and adulterous clerics who have defiled the holy places and monasteries by occupying them until now shall be expelled and made to do penance, and if, after this declaration, they fall into the crime of fornication or adultery they shall suffer the penalties prescribed at the former synod. The same with monks and nuns.

We order also, by the advice of the servants of God and of the Christian people and in view of imminent wars and attacks by the foreign populations which surround us, that for some time longer, with God's indulgence, we shall hold back for the benefit of our army a portion of the properties of the church as *precaria* owing *census*. Annually, from each *casata* [of these ecclesiastical properties] one solidus, that is twelve denarii, shall be paid to the church or monastery; in event of the death of the person to whom the property was entrusted as a *precarium*, the property shall revert to the church. And, if conditions again are such as to compel the prince to so order it, let the *precarium* be renewed and a new contract be written. But let extreme care be taken that churches and monasteries whose property is granted in *precarium* are not reduced to poverty and suffer want; and, if their poverty is compelling, let full possession be restored to the church and the house of God.

We likewise command that, in accordance with the canonical decrees, adultery and incestuous marriages contrary to law are forbidden and are to be punished at the discretion of the bishop; Christian slaves are not to be conveyed to pagans.

We have also decreed, as my father [Charles Martel] did before me that those who engage in pagan practices of any sort are to be condemned to pay a fine of fifteen solidi.

# C. FROM MAYORALTY TO KINGSHIP

## III. FROM THE SECOND AND THIRD CONTINUATION OF FREDEGAR

*The so-called Second Continuation of Fredegar written under the direction of Count Childebrand (see* **103**, *above) ends in 751. I accept the old emendation, followed by Krusch, of* consulato *for* consulto.

*The Third Continuation was written under the direction of Childebrand's son, 'the illustrious Count Nibelung'; it ends with the death of Pippin and the succession of Charlemagne and Carloman in 768. The meeting of the king and pope took place in January 754. The young Charles is Charlemagne, aged twelve.*

Source and translation as above, **103**.

### The Second Continuation

[22] At this time [a. 739] the blessed Pope Gregory [III, a. 731-41] twice sent to Prince Charles an embassy from Rome, the seat of holy Peter the apostle, bearing the keys of the revered tomb, a link of the chains of Saint Peter, and innumerable fine presents, an event never seen or heard of before; the pope was seeking an agreement whereby he would leave the imperial side and confer the Roman consulship upon the aforesaid prince. Charles welcomed the embassy with grand and lavish honors and gave costly presents, sending them and extra gifts to the threshold of Saints Peter and Paul by means of his own men Grimo, the abbot of the monastery of Corbie, and Sigibert, a monk of the basilica of Saint Dionysius the martyr.

*Charles died soon after this (a. 741). The kingdom fell to two of his sons: Carloman, who ruled Austrasia, Alamannia, and Thuringia, and Pippin, who ruled Neustria, Burgundy, and Provence. (A third son, Grifo, was excluded from power.)*

*The Continuation gives an account of Pippin's and Carloman's wars against the Gascons, Alamanni, Bavarians, and Saxons. Carloman retired to a monastery in Rome in 747.*

*The pope in the next excerpt is Zacharias, a. 741-52.*

[33] At this time [a. 751], having, with the advice and consent of all the Franks, sent a message to the apostolic see and having received the papacy's authorization, his Highness Pippin was raised to the throne of the kingdom with his queen Bertrada by the election of all the Franks, consecrated by the bishops, and acknowledged by the princes in the fashion that antiquity demands.

## The Third Continuation

[36] King Pippin crossed the Ardennes and took up residence at the royal villa of Diedenhofen on the Moselle [a. 753]. A message arrived that pope Stephen [II, a. 752-757] was hurrying from Rome to meet him with a large escort and many gifts and had already crossed the Great Saint Bernard Pass. On this news, the king gave orders for the pope to receive a most warm welcome and joyful celebrations. His son Charles was instructed to go to meet the pope and bring him before the king at the royal villa of Ponthion. There the Roman pope met the king and conferred many gifts upon him and the Franks. The pope asked for help against the Lombards and their king Aistulf, whereby he could free himself from Lombard intimidation and double dealing and put a stop to the tribute and contributions the Lombards were illegally demanding of the Romans. At this point Pippin had elaborate arrangements made for Pope Stephen to stay the winter at Paris in the monastery of Saint Dionysius.

King Pippin sent an embassy to Aistulf, king of the Lombards, asking him to pay proper respect to the blessed Peter and Paul and not enter the regions of Rome in a hostile fashion and to stop making wicked and unholy demands that were illegal and had never been accepted by the Romans.

[37] King Pippin failed to get what he asked for and Aistulf rejected his request. The next year the king ordered all Franks to meet him, as was their custom, on the Kalends of March [1 March 754] at the royal villa of Berny. He took counsel with his leading men and, in the season when kings go forth to war [cf. 2 Sam. 11:1], set out for Lombardy with Pope Stephen, accompanied by the nations of his kingdom and columns of Franks. The army went by way of Lyonnaise Gaul and Vienne and reached Saint-Jean-de-Maurienne.

At this news, Aistulf, king of the Lombards mobilized the entire army of the Lombards and came to the narrow pass called the valley of Susa. There with his all his forces he laid out a camp and wickedly attempted to defend himself with projectiles, machines of war, and an ample arsenal that he had basely prepared against the Roman empire (*res publica*) and the apostolic Roman see...

*Pippin was victorious in the battle that followed and Aistulf fled. The war against the Lombards took two campaigns and two years before its completion. Aistulf was forced to concede papal and imperial territory and to recognize the lordship of the Franks and promised to resume the tribute once paid by the Lombards to the Frankish kings (cf. 58, c. 45).*

## 112. FROM THE *ROYAL FRANKISH ANNALS*

*Another version of Pippin's assumption of kingship is given by the* Royal Frankish Annals, *which cover the period 741-829. The* Annals *were closely connected with the royal court and were composed by several authors; the excerpt is by the first author writing, ca. 787/93.*

Source: *Annales regni Francorum 741-829,* ed. Friedrich Kurze, MGH SRG in usum scholarum separatim editi 6 (1895). Translation by A.C. Murray.

a. 749. Bishop Burchard of Würzburg and the chaplain Fulrad were sent to Pope Zacharias to inquire whether it was good or not that kings in Francia at the time wielded no power. Pope Zacharias informed Pippin that it was better to call the man who had power king rather than the man who did not. To avoid upsetting the political order, the pope commanded by virtue of his apostolic authority that Pippin be made king.

a. 750. Pippin was elected king according to the custom of the Franks, anointed by the hand of Archbishop Boniface of holy memory, and raised to the kingship of the Franks in the city of Soissons.

Childeric [III, a. 743-51], who was wrongly called king, was tonsured and sent to a monastery.

a. 753. Pippin marched into Saxony and Bishop Hildegar was killed by the Saxons at the fortress called Iburg. Pippin emerged the victor nevertheless and came as far as Rehme. On his return from this campaign, he got a message that his brother Grifo, who had fled to Gascony, had been killed.

In this year Pope Stephen came to Francia seeking aid and support for the rights of Saint Peter. Carloman, monk and brother of King Pippin, also came to Francia under orders from his abbot to try to overturn the pope's request.

a. 754. Pope Stephen confirmed Pippin as king by holy anointing and anointed as kings with him the king's two sons, the lords Charles and Carloman.

The lord Archbishop Boniface, who was bringing the word of God to Frisia, was made a martyr of Christ while preaching.

# D. EINHARD ON THE LAST MEROVINGIANS

*Einhard was born about 775 and served in the courts of both Charlemagne and his son Louis the Pious. Einhard's famous biography of the king and emperor Charlemagne was written ca. 820s. Its opening retrospective glance at the Merovingians created an abiding image of the feebleness of the dynasty's last kings — the* rois fainéants *of French historiography.*

Source: *Einhardi vita Karoli Magni*, ed. Oswald Holder-Egger, MGH SRG in usum scholarum separatim editi 25 (1911), c. 1. Translation by A.C. Murray.

## 113. FROM THE *LIFE OF CHARLEMAGNE*

The Merovingian line, from which the Franks were accustomed to choose their kings, is thought to have lasted until the time of Childeric, who was deposed, tonsured, and shoved into a monastery at the command of the Roman pontiff Stephen. But although the line appeared to end with Childeric, it had long since been devoid of strength and was renowned for nothing but the empty name of king. The wealth and power of the kingdom was held by the palace prefects, called mayors of the palace, to whom ultimate authority belonged. Nothing was left to the king but to sit on the throne, with his flowing hair and long beard, and pretend to rule, satisfied only with the royal name: he would receive ambassadors who came from all over and, when they departed, provide them as if on his own authority with replies that he had been directed or even commanded to give. And except for the empty title of king and the precarious living-allowance that the prefect of the palace at his discretion provided for him, he possessed nothing of his own but one estate — and even that produced a very small income. He obtained lodging there along with a small number of servants to tend to his needs and to provide him with service. Wherever he had to travel, he went by wagon, drawn by yoked oxen and driven by a teamster in country fashion. In this way he used to go to the palace, or to the public assembly of his people that convened every year for the sake of the well-being of the kingdom, and in this way he used to return home. The prefect of the palace took care of the administration of the kingdom and provided for the execution and planning of everything that had to be done inside the palace or out.

# GENEALOGIES

## Note

Not all offspring, wives, or consorts are included in the following genealogies.

The abbreviation m. stands for a recognised sexual union between a king and his consort, whether or not it entailed marriage in a formal sense or the queenship. Descent lines are connected where possible to m. or the appropriate consort, but in many cases such pecision is beyond our knowledge.

The names of kings are capitalized in genealogies 1-4, but only those who ruled in their own right. King's sons entitled to bear the royal title are in lower case.

Sequences of siblings, from left to right, do not necessarily correspond to the birth order, which is not always known; the sequence has sometimes been determined by graphical requirements.

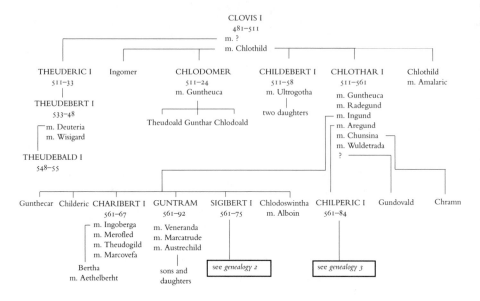

Genealogy 1. The Early Merovingians: Clovis, his Sons, and Grandsons

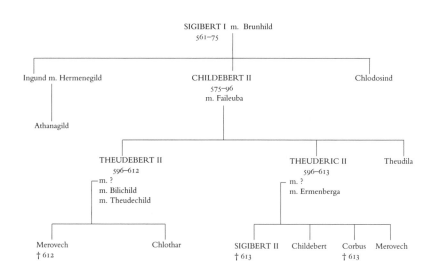

Genealogy 2. The Early Merovingians: Sigibert I, Brunhild, and their Descendants

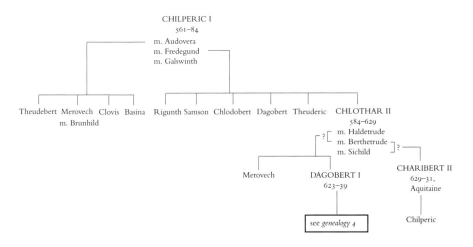

Genealogy 3. *The Early Merovingians: Chilperic I, Fredegund, and their Descendants*

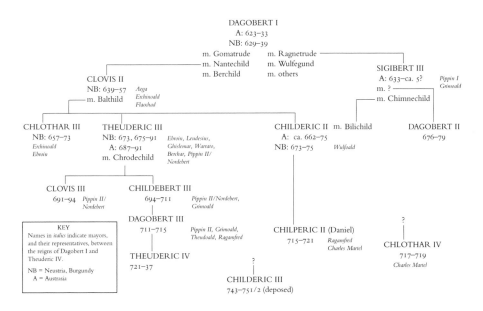

Genealogy 4. *The Later Merovingians: Dagobert I and his Descendants*

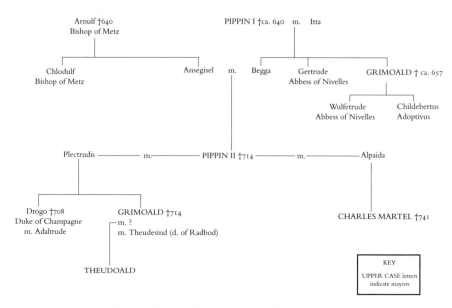

Arnulf †640
Bishop of Metz

Chlodulf
Bishop of Metz

Ansegisel   m.   Begga

PIPPIN I †ca. 640   m.   Itta

Gertrude
Abbess of Nivelles

GRIMOALD † ca. 657

Wulfetrude
Abbess of Nivelles

Childebertus
Adoptivus

Plectrudis ———— m.———— PIPPIN II †714 ———— m.———— Alpaida

Drogo †708
Duke of Champagne
m. Adaltrude

GRIMOALD †714
m. ?
m. Theudesind (d. of Radbod)

CHARLES MARTEL †741

THEUDOALD

KEY

UPPER CASE letters
indicate mayors

*Genealogy 5. The Arnulfings or Pippinids (Early Carolingians)*

# MAPS

Based on Auguste Longnon, *La Géographie de la Gaule au VI*ᵉ *siècle* (Paris, 1878), and Eugen Ewig, "Die fränkischen Teilungen und Teilreiche (511–613)," in his *Spätantikes und fränkisches Gallien, Gesammelte Schriften*, ed. Hartmut Atsma, Beihefte de Francia 3/1, 1: 114–171.

The sources do not make us privy to all the details of the division of 561 (and even less, those of 511), and so this map is an approximation of what that division would have looked like; most of its details are quite sound, some less so.

# WESTERN PROVINCES OF THE ROMAN EMPIRE ca. 400

This map, and the list that accompanies it, is based mainly on the *Notitia Dignitatum* and *Notitia Galliarum* (ed. Otto Seeck [1876; reprt. Frankfurt am Main, 1962], and cf. A.H.M. Jones, *Later Roman Empire* [Oxford, 1973], 1069–70, 1451–1461).

Upper case letters designate dioceses, the boundaries of which are marked by heavy lines; provinces are marked by thin lines and Arabic numerals. The dioceses of Dacia and Macedonia belonged to the eastern parts of the Empire.

## Prefecture of Gaul

### BRITAIN
1, 2. Britannia I, II
3. Maxima Caesariensis
4. Flavia Caesariensis
5. Valentia

### SPAIN
1. Tarraconensis
2. Carthaginiensis
3. Baetica  4. Tingitania
5. Lusitania  6. Callaecia
7. Insulae Balearum

### GAUL
1, 2. Germania I, II
3, 4. Belgica I, II
5. Maxima Sequanorum
6, 7, 8. Lugdunensis I, II, III
9. Lugdunensis Senonia
10. Alpes Poeninae et Graiae

### SEVEN PROVINCES
1. Viennensis
2. Alpes Maritimae
3, 4. Narbonensis I, II
5, 6. Aquitania I, II
7. Novempopulana

## Prefecture of Italy

### ITALY
1. Alpes Cottiae  2. Liguria
3, 4. Raetia I, II  5. Aemilia
6. Venetia et Istria  7. Flaminia et Picenum Annonarium

### ROME AND SUBURBICARIA
1. Rome  2. Tuscia et Umbria
3. Picenum Suburbicarium
4. Samnium  5. Campania
6. Apulia et Calabria
7. Bruttii et Lucania  8. Sicilia
9. Sardina  10. Corsica

### DIOCESE OF AFRICA
1. Mauretania Caesariensis
2. Mauretania Stifensis
3. Numidia  4. Africa  5. Byzacena
6. Tripolitania

### DIOCESE OF ILLYRICUM
1. Noricum Ripense
2. Noricum Mediterraneum
3, 4. Pannonia I, II  5. Valeria
6. Savia  7. Dalmatia

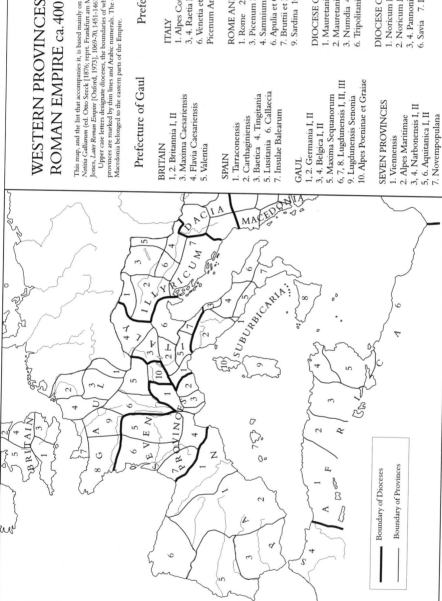

Map 1  Western Provinces of the Roman Empire ca. 400

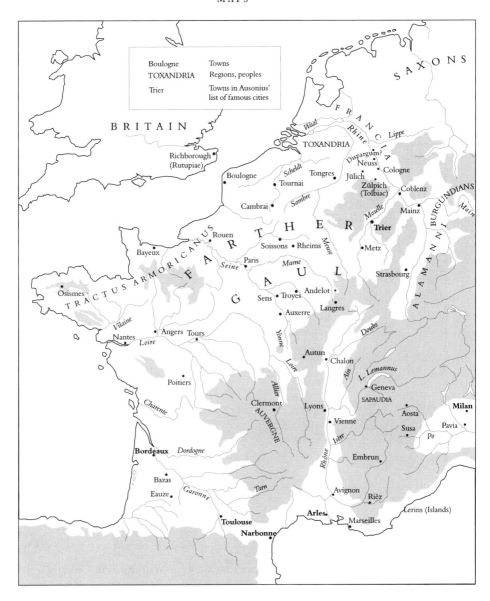

Map 2. Gaul in the Early Fifth Century

Map 3. Spain and the Western Mediterranean in the Fifth Century

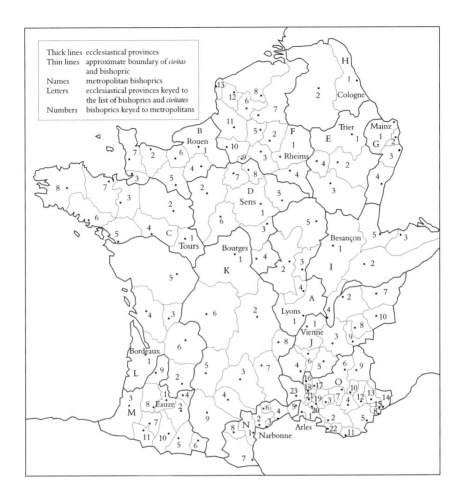

Map 4. Bishoprics, Late Fifth to Late Seventh Centuries

## BISHOPRICS AND *CIVITATES* OF GAUL
## FROM THE LATE FIFTH TO THE LATE SEVENTH CENTURIES

The Roman-period *civitates* were in large measure the basis for the secular and ecclesiastical divisions of the Merovingian kingdom. As a result, the Merovingian ecclesiastical province and its bishoprics reflected the provincial groupings of the late Empire. The seats of most, but not all, Merovingian bishoprics were located in the old *civitas* capitals; the seats of most metropolitans were located in old provincial capitals.

The following list of Merovingian-period bishoprics (column 1) has been keyed to the *Notitia Galliarum,* a fifth century list of Gallic cities grouped by provinces and (secular) dioceses (column 2). Note that while the the list of ecclesiastical metropolitans and suffragans of the Merovingian period follows in its main outlines the *Notitia,* some reorganization has had to be made to the *Notitia* to bring it into line with the episcopal list.

In the list each bishopric has been given its modern name (column 1), followed by the name of the *civitas* according to the *Notitia* (column 2). The see of the metropolitan in column 1 has been placed in capital letters as has the name of the Roman province and diocese, which has also been put in boldface, in column 2. The few Roman period *civitates* unattested as bishoprics have been left out. Bishoprics whose towns are not mentioned in the *Notitia* as *civitates* or *castra* have been placed in italics. Brackets in column 2 identify the original placement of a *civitas* in the *Notitia*, if that differs from the order of metropolitan and suffragan bishops in column 1. Parentheses in column 1 mark alternate, or fuller, forms of a name, and occasionally the name of the region; in column 2 they mark alternate, and later, names added to the *Notitia Galliarum*. A slash separating names in column 1 indicates the movement of a bishop's seat from one town to another.

In the *Notitia* the term *civitas* (meaning not just 'city,' as an urban area, but also the dependent countryside) is usually followed by the name of the people in the genitive plural. Thus the *civitas Parisiorum*, is the 'city of the Parisi.' The term for a Roman provincial capital was *metropolis civitas*.

## THE GALLIC PROVINCES

### A. LUGDUNENSIS PRIMA

| | |
|---|---|
| 1. LYONS | Metropolis civitas Lugdunensium |
| 2. Autun | Civitas Aeduorum or Augustodunum |
| 3. Chalon(-sur-Sâone) | Castrum Cabillonense |
| 4. Mâcon | Castrum Matisconense |
| 5. Langres | Civitas Lingonum |

### B. LUGDUNENSIS SECUNDA

| | |
|---|---|
| 1. ROUEN | Metropolis civitas Rotomagensium |
| 2. Bayeux | Civitas Baiocassium |
| 3. Avranches | Civitas Abrincatum |
| 4. Evreux | Civitas Ebroicorum |
| 5. Sées | Civitas Saiorum |
| 6. Lisieux | Civitas Lexoviorum |
| 7. Coutances | Civitas Constantia |

### C. LUGDUNENSIS TERTIA

| | |
|---|---|
| 1. TOURS | Metropolis Turonorum |
| 2. Le Mans | Civitas Cenomannorum |
| 3. Rennes | Civitas Redonum |
| 4. Angers | Civitas Andecavorum |
| 5. Nantes | Civitas Namnetum |
| 6. Vannes | Civitas Venetum |
| 7. Corseul | Civitas Coriosolitum |
| 8. Osismes (Carhaix) | Civitas Ossismorum |

**D. LUGDUNENSIS SENONIA**

| | |
|---|---|
| 1. SENS | Metropolis civitas Senonum |
| 2. Chartres | Civitas Carnotum |
| 3. Auxerre | Civitas Autisioderum |
| 4. *Nevers* | *Civitas Nivernensium* |
| 5. Troyes | Civitas Tricassium |
| 6. Orleans | Civitas Aurelianorum |
| 7. Paris | Civitas Parisiorum |
| 8. Meaux | Civitas Melduorum |

**E. BELGICA PRIMA**

| | |
|---|---|
| 1. TRIER | Metropolis civitas Treverorum |
| 2. Metz | Civitas Mediomatricum (Mettis) |
| 3. Toul | Civitas Leucorum (Tullo) |
| 4. Verdun | Civitas Verodunensium |

**F. BELGICA SECUNDA**

| | |
|---|---|
| 1. RHEIMS | Metropolis civitas Remorum |
| 2. *Laon* | *Civitas Lugduni Clavati* |
| 3. Soissons | Civitas Suessionum |
| 4. Châlons(-sur-Marne) | Civitas Catalaunorum |
| 5. Vermand/Noyon | Civitas Veromandorum |
| 6. Arras | Civitas Atrabatum |
| 7. Cambrai | Civitas Camaracensium |
| 8. Tournai | Civitas Turnacensium |
| 9. Senlis | Civitas Silvanectum |
| 10. Beauvais | Civitas Bellovacorum |
| 11. Amiens | Civitas Ambianensium |
| 12. Thérouanne | Civitas Morinum |
| 13. Boulogne | Civitas Bononiensium |

**G. GERMANIA PRIMA**

| | |
|---|---|
| 1. MAINZ | Metropolis civitas Magontiacensium |
| 2. Worms | Civitas Vangionum (Vuarmacia) |
| 3. Speyer | Civitas Nemetum (Spira) |
| 4. Strasbourg | Civitas Argentoratensium (Stratoburgum) |

**H. GERMANIA SECUNDA**

| | |
|---|---|
| 1. COLOGNE | Metropolis civitas Agrippinensium (Colonia) |
| 2. Tongres/Maastricht | Civitas Tungrorum |

**I. MAXIMA SEQUANORUM**

| | |
|---|---|
| 1. BESANÇON | Metropolis civitas Vesontiensium |
| 2. Avenches | Civitas (H)Elvitiorum, Aventicus |

| | |
|---|---|
| 3. Windisch/Constance | Castrum Vindonissense |
| 4. Belley | Civitas Belisensium |
| 5. Basel | Civitas Basiliensium |

## THE SEVEN PROVINCES

### J. VIENNENSIS

| | |
|---|---|
| 1. VIENNE | Metropolis civitas Viennensium |
| 2. Geneva | Civitas Genavensium |
| 3. Grenoble | Civitas Gratianopolitana |
| 4. Alba/Viviers (Vivarium) | Civitas Albensium |
| 5. Die | Civitas Deensium |
| 6. Valence | Civitas Valentinorum |
| 7. Martigny (Valais) /Sion | Civitas Valensium, Octodurum |
| | [Alpes Graiae et Poenninae] |
| 8. Tarentaise | Metropolis civitas Centronium, Darentasia |
| | [Alpes Graiae et Poenninae] |
| *9. Maurienne* | *Civitas Mauriennensis* |
| *10. Aosta* | *Civitas Augusta* |

### K. AQUITANICA PRIMA

| | |
|---|---|
| 1. BOURGES | Metropolis civitas Biturgium |
| 2. Clermont(-Ferrand) | Civitas Arvernorum |
| 3. Rodez | Civitas Rutenorum |
| 4. Albi | Civitas Albigensium |
| 5. Cahors | Civitas Cadurcorum |
| 6. Limoges | Civitas Lemovicum |
| 7. Javols | Civitas Gabalum |
| 8. Velay | Civitas Vellavorum |
| 9. Toulouse | Civitas Tolosatium [Narbonensis prima] |

### L. AQUITANICA SECUNDA

| | |
|---|---|
| 1. BORDEAUX | Metropolis civitas Burdigalensium |
| 2. Agen | Civitas Agennensium |
| 3. Angoulême | Civitas Ecolisnensium |
| 4. Saintes | Civitas Santonum |
| 5. Poitiers | Civitas Pictavorum |
| 6. Périgueux | Civitas Petrocoriorum |

### M. NOVEMPOPULANA

| | |
|---|---|
| 1. EAUZE | Civitas Elusatium |
| 2. Auch | Metropolis Civitas Ausciorum |
| 3. Dax | Civitas Aquenesium |
| 4. Lectoure | Civitas Lactoratium |

5. St-Bertrand-de-Comminges — Civitas Convenarum
6. Couserans (St-Lizier) — Civitas Consorannorum
7. Lescar — Civitas Bernarnensium
8. Aire — Civitas Aturensium
9. Bazas — Civitas Vasatica
10. Tarbes — Civitas Turba ubi castrum Bigorra
11. Oloron — Civitas Illoronensium

## N. NARBONENSIS PRIMA

1. NARBONNE — Metropolis civitas Narbonensium
2. Béziers — Civitas Beterrensium
3. *Agde* — *Civitas Agatensium*
4. *Maguelonne* — *Civitas Magalonensium*
5. Nîmes — Civitas Nemausensium
6. Lodève — Civitas Lutevensium
7. Elne — Civitas Elnensium
8. Carcassonne — Civitas Carcassonensium

## O. NARBONENSIS SECUNDA, ALPES MARITIMARUM, PARTS OF VIENNENSIS

1. ARLES — Civitas Arelatensium [Viennensis]
2. Aix-en-Provence — Civitas Aquensium
3. Apt — Civitas Aptensium
4. Riez — Civitas Reiensium
5. Fréjus — Civitas Foroiuliensis
6. Gap — Civitas Vappencensium
7. Sisteron — Civitas Segestericorum
8. Antibes — Civitas Antipolitana
9. Embrun — Metropolis Civitas Ebrodunensium
10. Digne — Civitas Diniensium
11. *Toulon* — *Civitas Telonensium*
12. Senez — Civitas Sanisiensium
13. Glandève — Civitas Glannatena
14. Cimiez/Nice — Civitas Cemelensium
15. Vence — Civitas Vintiensium
16. St-Paul-Trois-Châteaux — Civitas Tricastinorum [Viennensis]
17. Vaison — Civitas Vasiensium [Viennensis]
18. Orange — Civitas Arausicorum [Viennensis]
19. Carpentras — Civitas Carpentoratensium [Viennensis]
20. Cavaillon — Civitas Cabellicorum [Viennensis]
21. Avignon — Civitas Avennicorum [Viennensis]
22. Marseilles — Civitas Massiliensium [Viennensis]
23. Uzès — Castrum Uceciense (Civitas Ucetecensium, Eucetica) [Narbonensis prima]

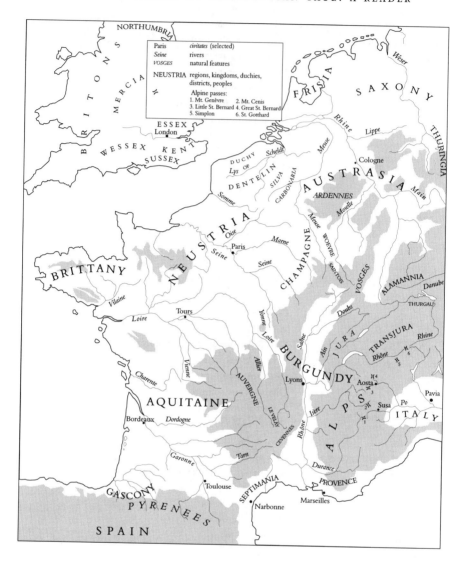

Map 5. Regions of Gaul and Its Neighbours in the Merovingian Period

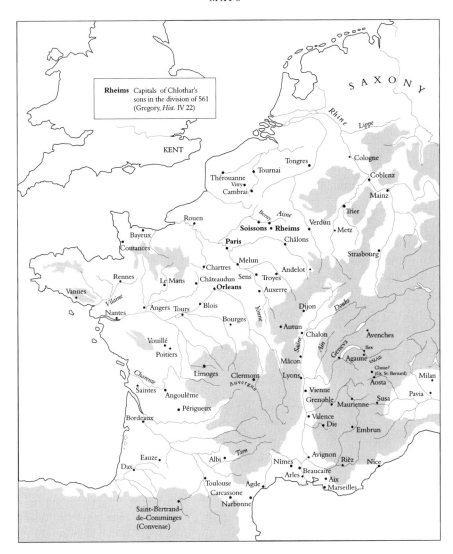

Map 6. Gaul in the Sixth Century

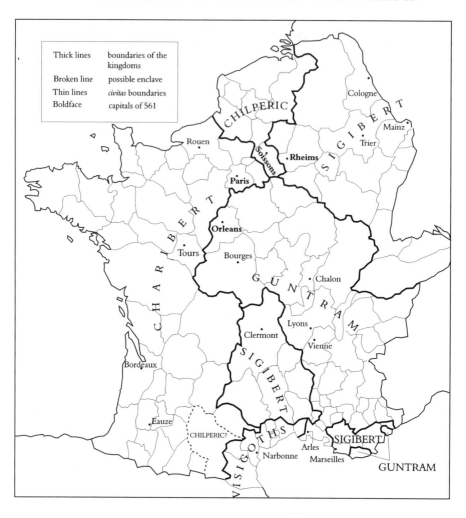

Map 7. The Division of 561 (cf. Gregory, *Hist.* IV 22)

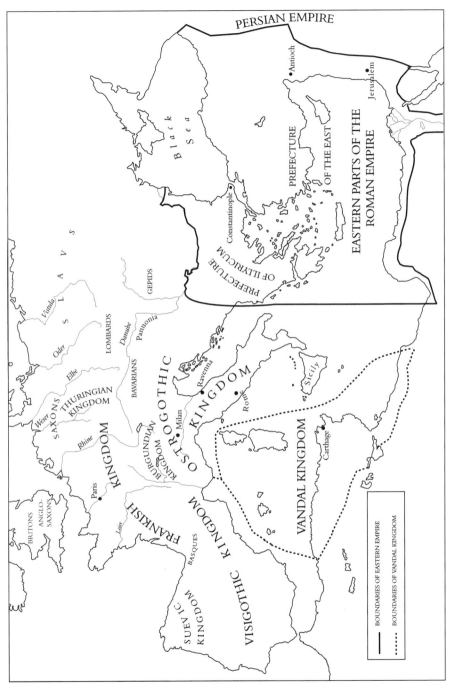

Map 8. West and East on the Death of Theodoric the Great, a. 526

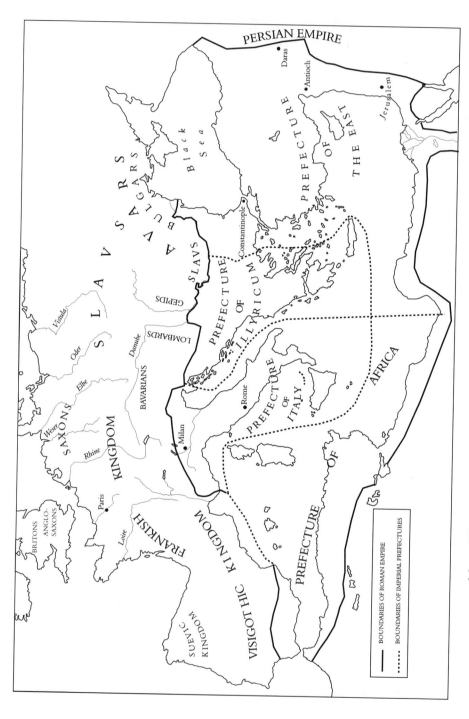

Map 9. West and East around the Death of Chlothar I (a. 561) and Justinian (a. 565)

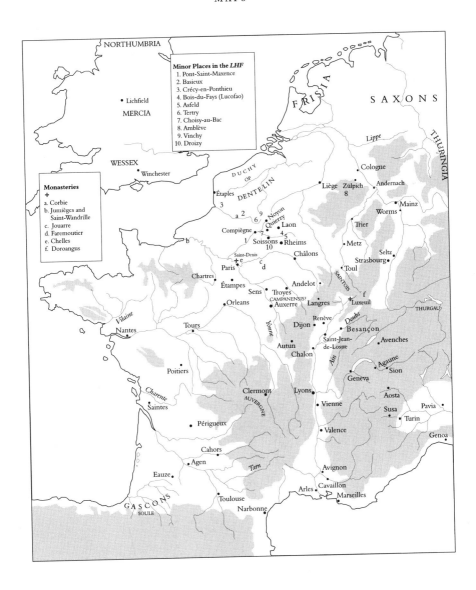

**Minor Places in the *LHF***
1. Pont-Saint-Maxence
2. Basieux
3. Crécy-en-Ponthieu
4. Bois-du-Fays (Lucofao)
5. Asfeld
6. Tertry
7. Choisy-au-Bac
8. Amblève
9. Vinchy
10. Droizy

**Monasteries**
+
a. Corbie
b. Jumièges and
   Saint-Wandrille
c. Jouarre
d. Faremoutier
e. Chelles
f. Doroangus

NORTHUMBRIA

• Lichfield

MERCIA

WESSEX
• Winchester

SAXONS

FRISIA

THURINGIA

Lippe

Cologne

DUCHY OF DENTELIN

• Étaples
3
a 2
6 9 • Noyon
7 • Quierzy
Compiègne • 1 4
Soissons • Rheims
10

Liège  Zülpich  Andernach
8
• Mainz
Worms •
• Trier
• Metz
Seltz •
Strasbourg •
• Toul

Saint-Denis
+ c c
Paris • d

Chartres

Étampes
Sens
Orleans
Troyes
CAMPANENSIS?
Auxerre

Andelot •

Langres

SANTOIS

f
+ Luxeuil
THURGAU

Nantes

Vilaine

Tours

Yonne

Dijon
Renève
Doubs
Besançon •
Saint-Jean-
de-Losne
Ain

• Avenches

Autun
Chalon

Agaune
• Sion

Poitiers

Charente

Saintes

Clermont
AUVERGNE

Lyons •

Geneva •

Aosta •

Vienne •
Susa •
Pavia •
• Turin

• Périgueux

• Valence

Genoa •

Cahors
• Agen

Eauze •

Tam

Avignon •

GASCONS
SOULE

• Toulouse
Narbonne

Arles •
Cavaillon
Marseilles

Map 10. Gaul in the Seventh Century

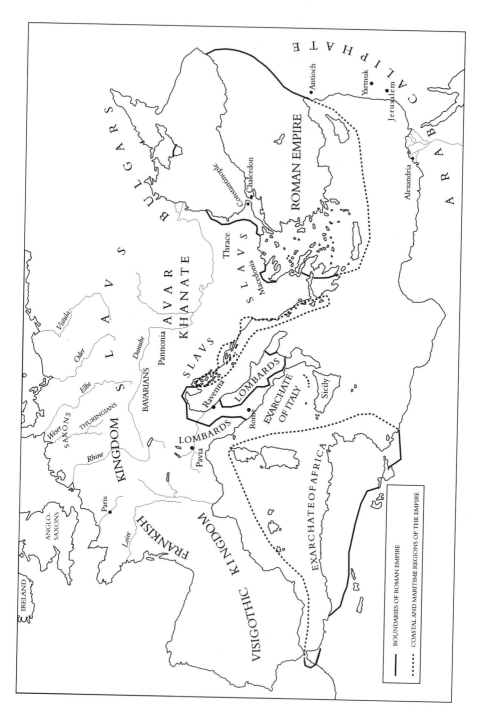

Map 11. West, East, and the Caliphate ca. 660

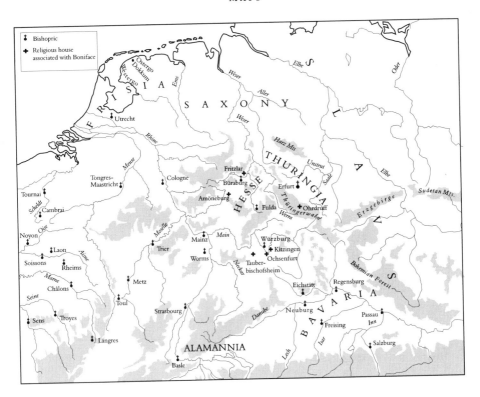

Map 12. East of the Rhine in the Early Eighth Century

# INDEX

Numbers refer to documents